NEW OXFORD HISTORY OF MUSIC

VOLUME II

THE VOLUMES OF THE
NEW OXFORD HISTORY OF MUSIC

THE EARLY
MIDDLE AGES
TO 1300

EDITED BY
RICHARD CROCKER
AND
DAVID HILEY

OXFORD NEW YORK
OXFORD UNIVERSITY PRESS
1990

Oxford University Press, Walton Street, Oxford OX2 6DP

Oxford New York Toronto
Delhi Bombay Calcutta Madras Karachi
Petaling Jaya Singapore Hong Kong Tokyo
Nairobi Dar es Salaam Cape Town
Melbourne Auckland

and associated companies in
Berlin Ibadan

Oxford is a trade mark of Oxford University Press

Published in the United States
by Oxford University Press, New York

© Oxford University Press 1990

British Library Cataloguing in Publication Data
The New Oxford history of music.—2nd
ed.
vol. 2: The early Middle Ages to 1300
1. Music, to 1960
I. Crocker, Richard L.   II. Hiley, David
III. Early medieval music up to 1300
780'.9
ISBN 0–19–316329–2

Library of Congress Cataloguing in Publication Data
The Early Middle Ages to 1300.
(New Oxford history of music; v. 2)
Rev. ed. of: Early medieval music, up
to 1300. 967
Bibliography: p.   Includes index.
1. Music—500-1400—History and criticism.
I. Crocker, Richard L.   II. Hiley, David.
III. Early medieval music, up to 1300.
IV. Series: New Oxford history of music (2nd
ed.) ; v. 2.
ML160.N440 1989 vol. 2   780'.902   88–22469
ISBN 0–19–316329–2

Printed in Great Britain by
Richard Clay Ltd, Bungay, Suffolk

ACKNOWLEDGEMENTS

The present volume was conceived in 1977 at the instigation of the late Editor, Gerald Abraham. Various chapters were drafted in the years immediately following, and the work of editing was begun. Additional editorial assistance was provided by Prof. David Hiley, who reviewed the materials—by now extensive—for the entire volume. Prof. Ernest Sanders reviewed the concluding two chapters on polyphony. I want to express my thanks to these scholars and to the contributors, as well as to the staff of the Oxford University Press for making this volume possible.

Richard L. Crocker

University of California, Berkeley

CONTENTS

PART IV: Medieval Polyphony in Western Europe

ILLUSTRATIONS

ABBREVIATIONS

The following abbreviations are used in the notes and bibliography:

AcM   *Acta Musicologica*
AMw   *Archiv für Musikwissenschaft*
Eg   *Études grégoriennes*
JAMS   *Journal of the American Musicological Society*
MGG   *Die Musik in Geschichte und Gegenwart*
ML   *Music and Letters*
MQ   *The Musical Quarterly*
MT   *The Musical Times*
New Grove *The New Grove Dictionary of Music and Musicians*
NOHM   *New Oxford History of Music*
PRMA   *Proceedings of the Royal Musical Association*

PITCH REFERENCES

References in text or tables to notated pitch follow the medieval convention, not Helmholtz' system, but with modern upper and lower strokes in extreme cases, as follows:

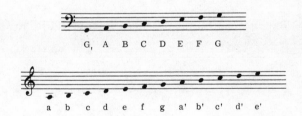

INTRODUCTION

RESEARCHES of the last thirty years have provided an abundance of material and new insights for this new volume on *Early Medieval Music*, and have also raised problems of organization that seem insoluble within the framework available. The problems mostly concern where to begin, and what to do with all the material that might be involved with the several possible beginnings.

The solution inherited from Volume I, *Ancient and Oriental Music*, was of a philosophical nature: that volume dealt with 'the music of the Non-Christian world' (which the editors described as a 'world in which music is regarded as a power creating a magic effect upon the listener'). Volume II, perforce, is to deal with music in the Christian world, in which 'Music could now be used primarily as *laus Dei . . .*'. The effect of this solution was not unlike that of some traditional Church historians, who recounted, under the rubric 'history of music', the legends of Judeo-Christian church music (Jubal, David, Christ, Gregory, Guido) with only sideways glances outside the Church. The same result seemed virtually forced upon us by the nature of the sources, the music of the Christian world being in evidence only in sources from *c.* 900 on. Since this is cult music, one naturally assumed that it had already existed for a long time more or less as it was in 900; its prior history could presumably be traced back through the cult— and only there.

In this way, to study the history of Christian music, scholars had to study the history of the Church and its cult, even though on one hand this history had to be traced through almost a millennium until actual music appeared in the sources around 900, and on the other hand this history had to be traced more or less without reference to music of the wider world, the 'non-Christian world'. By extension of the same argument, if antecedents to Christian music were to be sought, then it should be in the antecedent to the Christian Church, namely Judaism. This argument was the more persuasive since alternatives were not very encouraging: attempts made to connect Christian music to what we knew of Greek classical music (namely, its theory) did not convince. Only gradually, with the model of syncretism as studied in other historical disciplines before us, have we come to see past the categories of 'Greek, classical', 'Roman, classical', 'Christianity', 'Judaism', 'Middle Ages', to find the historical continuum in which the study of early Christian music could more realistically be placed.

Since 1950, the growth of studies in Byzantine chant alone makes it now difficult to include Byzantine chant as a preliminary chapter in this volume—which at its conclusion is concerned exclusively with Western European music. Nevertheless, Byzantine chant, different from the Western chant repertories in so many essential ways, is one of the few great repertories preserved in a written record that dates from the early Middle Ages, and in that respect can be dealt with in a manner at least parallel to that habitually used for Gregorian chant.

The repertories of the other Eastern churches, however, pose problems of entirely different order and magnitude. These other repertories—Syrian, Armenian, Coptic, Ethiopian—are now represented by a vigorous and growing scholarly literature; and rightly so, for if Gregorian and Byzantine chant are to be pursued back to their origins long before their written records through a study of cult, then there is every reason to include in that study all the other cultic repertories that together made up the rich totality of early Christianity. But since those other repertories do not have written records—at least, none as accessible as those of Gregorian or Byzantine chant—their inclusion brings with it several consequences. First, the study of cult, as complementary or actually supplementary to the study of music, becomes ever more comprehensive and important; but this entails a comparative study of cult (not just Christian) across the whole spectrum of Mediterranean civilization in the centuries around the time of Christ—in other words, under the Roman Empire. Second, the study of these repertories, preserved only through non-written practice continuous down to the present, suggests if not requires the application of ethnomusicological techniques and materials for effective evaluation as evidence for ancient practice. And third, by reflex, the non-written phases of Gregorian and Byzantine chant come under increasingly close and imaginative scrutiny in their own right, rather than being simply presumed as prior existence of the written states.

Indeed, once seriously included in the account of early Christian music, all these 'other' repertories strongly suggest multiple rather than simple development in early Christian music. (And this was already the inescapable implication of Byzantine chant for the Gregorian.) Exploration of the non-written phase of Gregorian chant could no longer consist simply of finding, among the remains of the history of the Church in Rome, traces of the musical forms preserved after 900. In his remarkable work *De cantu et musica sacra* (1774), Martin Gerbert assembled a rich collection of references to music and cult from patristic literature; this work was the immediate source of such references for succeeding generations of scholars, who used it, however, more and more selectively, until by 1958 a standard work could say that 'very little' of this was 'of actual importance from our point of view', meaning that very little of the documented references from the early period could be matched up with the presumed projection back into that period from later written practice. More recently these early references are being given more serious consideration at face value, even if that means revising our ideas about what musical practice in the early period must have been like.

But now, taking into account all these materials along with the approaches they suggest, it becomes clear that the history of early Christian music is not to be dealt with merely by tracing accounts (in part legendary) of the development of the forms appearing in the written record from 900 on; rather, the task is entitled 'Ritual Song in the Roman Empire', and needs to begin with the fully developed music of the ancient Near East, then continue on through ritual song for all kinds from Syria to Spain. Such song is represented, unfortunately, only in texts not melodies; but these texts, studied in as broad a context (ethnomusicological as well as musicological), will yield a more realistic picture of early Christian music. The problem is not that such a study cannot be surveyed in a volume the size of this one— it could be, but only in one whose period was given as, say, 500 BC to AD 600, rather than 600 to 1300.

The basic study by Johannes Quasten, *Musik und Gesang in den Kulten der heidnischen Antike und der Christlichen Frühzeit* (Münster, 1930), pointed the way towards establishing the context needed for an account of ritual song in the ancient world, specifically of ritual song in the time of the early Christian Church. And the equally important point of view of Solange Corbin, in *L'Église à la conquête de sa musique* (Paris, 1960), suggests that the early Church used music in a more restricted way than has been traditionally and piously assumed. We have always known of the hostility of the Fathers towards instrumental music (including thereby a broad range of musical activity in the Roman culture); but it now appears that the early Church, before the fourth century, may not have sung its liturgy as much as we once thought, or may not have sung the kinds of texts and melodies we once assumed. The survey by Carl Kraeling and Lucetta Mowry in Volume I[1] indicates the kinds of texts the early Church did sing.

It becomes more and more clear that the events of the fourth

---

[1] Pp. 303 ff.

century—long acknowledged to be of profound importance for the development of the Church in general—were so for her music as well. Indeed, the idea of Christian music as we have it (even if not yet in the forms in which we have it) can be said to begin only in the fourth century. That fascinating time would require a book of its own, so manifold and complex are the factors coming to bear upon Christian music. On the one hand the fourth century brought the development of public Christian ritual, with what Dom Gregory Dix called the 'Sanctification of Time'—the development of the liturgical calendar, the historicization of liturgy in terms of local martyrs as well as of the life of Jesus in the Holy Land. On the other hand there was the development of monasticism—anti-urban, anti-historical, anti-pathetic toward public ritual, and with incalculable effect upon ritual song in medieval music. It would be a major task simply to untangle, within the famous account of Egeria (the abbess who made a pilgrimage from Spain to Jerusalem around 385 and reported on liturgy and chant there in detail), the cult practices associated with historicization of the Holy Places from the activities of the monastics who participated along with the urban clergy. Egeria's account is only part of the wealth of fourth-century material on ritual song; but to realize the wealth we must take it on its own terms.

From the fourth century to the sixth—say, 350 to 600—there was intense development resulting in a broad spectrum of ritual song that was used variously in various places. Between 600 and 800 emerged the repertories of Byzantine and Roman chant, and towards 800 (speaking very roughly on this broad time scale) both these repertories began to be standardized. Simultaneously they started to become dominant over other liturgies and repertories in their respective spheres of influence, Eastern and Western; and both began the process of being written down. This process was long and complex—and interacted in complex ways with both the standardization and the dominance over other repertories. Indeed, many details may not be accessible to us until the notations reach stages (towards 1200) where we can be reasonably certain of reliable transcription.

Of all the things that need to be done in the study of early Christian music, and that previous accounts attempted to do, this volume restricts itself primarily to surveys of the repertories of Byzantine and Roman chant as preserved, with brief accounts of the state of our knowledge concerning other repertories from the early period. Summary accounts of Syrian and Armenian, Coptic and Ethiopian chant will be presented, not as a history of early Christian chant but rather as introductions to medieval repertories persisting alongside Byzantine chant. It is important to note that each of these repertories existed before and independently of the Byzantine repertory, but at a certain moment each underwent strong Byzantine influence that profoundly affected subsequent development. It was impractical to divide each account into a pre-Byzantine and post-Byzantine section; and on the other hand it made no sense to place Byzantine chant before Syrian and the others. As a result the discussion of Syrian chant and the others will anticipate, in some terms and concepts, the subsequent exposition of Byzantine chant, to which the reader will have to refer.

Similarly, the chant of the Western churches will begin with introductions to Old Beneventan, Ravennate, Milanese, Celtic, Gallican, and Hispanic chant, as preserved in fragmentary forms, then go on to the Roman chant in its two written records, 'Gregorian' (or Frankish-Roman) and 'Old-Roman' (or Urban-Roman). Again, technical terms and concepts will be treated only in connection with Roman Chant, and will be anticipated without full discussion in the sections on Old Beneventan and the others that come before.

Once past the Gregorian repertory, as counterpart of the 'Old Rome' in the West to the Byzantine repertory of the 'New Rome' in the East, this book will deal exclusively with medieval music of Western Europe. This, beginning with the discussion of 'New Frankish forms', would be a logical place to start a book, once the preceding material had been placed in a volume of its own, as 'Music under the Roman Empire'. Yet even that solution would not be completely adequate, since in the West the phases of development that can be placed 'under the Empire' (that is, before 600) are distinctly different from the phase in which Roman chant assumes the forms recorded for us (that is, after 600); historiography, unfortunately, does not provide us with a standard period centred on the years 600–800, except as the 'Dark Ages', a concept less and less useful to us today. (For the East historians have created, out of necessity, a period especially for the Byzantine Empire.) Furthermore, while we can now easily separate Frankish and subsequent Western medieval chant from the Gregorian, which we believe to be established (at least in principle) by the time of its first written record around 900, still it remains to be seen how much subsequent change can be demonstrated to have occurred between 900 and the completely unambiguous notation of the later Middle Ages. (A similar problem separates the relatively secure Middle Byzantine notation from the early notation of the tenth century.) The changes could conceivably be large enough to make us conclude that the formative period of Gregorian chant extended to 1200 in at least some respects, and that therefore the discussion of

Gregorian chant should not be separated too far from that of Frankish and medieval chant, on the grounds that even though these are two distinct styles and repertories they coexisted in time for at least parts of their respective developments, with possible interaction.

One more problem is posed by Chapter X, on 'Instrumental Music'. This account begins with musical instruments at the close of antiquity, and ends only in 1300 at the close of the period covered by the volume, straddling the division between Medieval Monophony (Part III) and Polyphony (Part IV). It is placed at the start of Part IV.

So the problems of periodization—along with the problems of planning books in accord with such periodization—remain essentially unsolved for early medieval music.

R.C.

University of California at Berkeley,
October 1989

PART I
Christian Chant of the Eastern Churches

I

CHRISTIAN CHANT IN SYRIA, ARMENIA, EGYPT, AND ETHIOPIA

By Miloš Velimirović

SYRIAN CHANT

THE first Christian communities outside Jerusalem and Palestine were formed in the city of Antioch, and thus the territory of present-day Syria was one of the first areas in which Christianity gained sizeable followings.[1] The first significant translations of Christian writings were made in Syria. It was also from Syria that missions started in the direction of Armenia and Greece, while Alexandria appears to have received its Christian message directly from Jerusalem.

By the early fourth century the need for a formulation of the basic beliefs precipitated the crisis that forced the new church to define its Creed at the first two ecumenical councils (AD 325 and 381). The next century, however, witnessed more than one schism in the Eastern Mediterranean, and first in Syria. At the Third Ecumenical Council of 431, the so-called Nestorians refused to accept the definitions voted by the majority; being already in positions of power in the dioceses of Eastern Syria, the Nestorians seceded and have remained steadfast in their beliefs to this day. The Nestorian Church was active with missionaries who reached India and China at one point; but at the present it is restricted primarily to the territories of Iraq and Iran. While the Third Ecumenical Council had dealt with the proper term for the Virgin Mary (whether she gave birth to a 'god' or a 'man') the Fourth Council became involved in an even more explosive issue—the presence of one or two natures in Jesus. The West Syrians, accepting the belief that there was but a single nature (i.e. they were 'monophysites') parted ways with the other churches at that time. Although it is common to call the West Syrian Monophysites by another name,

---

[1] For the spread of Christianity in the first centuries, see standard encyclopaedias such as *New Catholic Encyclopedia*; *Religion in Geschichte und Gegenwart*; *Lexikon für Theologie und Kirche*; *Dictionnaire du Spiritualité*; *Catholicisme, Hier, Aujourd'hui, Demain*.

'Jacobite', they prefer to be known as the 'Syrian Orthodox Church'. The East Syrian Nestorians call themselves the 'Assyrian Church of the East'.

Another group, the Maronites, stood by the side in these early centuries; at the time of the Crusades the Maronites came into contact with Rome, and ever since have accepted Roman authority. In each of these three groups there were smaller subgroups that remained faithful to the basic Greek rite and dogma, and since they were, politically speaking, 'faithful to the Emperor' (i.e. of Byzantium), the adherents of such subgroups were known by the common term 'Melkite' (from *malke*, a term for emperor). While details of liturgy and dogma differ among these groups, the religious services have much in common and, especially within a particular territorial denomination, the 'orthodox' and 'catholic' groups may be using each other's service books.

As Christian groups grew in size and in significance, there were some that came to be viewed as heretical by the majority of others. One such group adopted the poems of Bardesanes (c.154–222), who was active in Edessa (now Urfa, in Turkey, close to the Syrian border).[2] Bardesanes is credited with writing a psalter that emulated the Hebrew Psalter. This new poetry acquired great popularity, owing considerably to the fact that it was sung to popular melodies which were composed (it is said) by Bardesanes' son Harmonios. The explanation of subsequent centuries (not an easy one to accept) is that the melodies were 'catchy', the populace became enamoured of them, and as people hummed them they repeated the heretical texts of Bardesanes—and so adopted the meaning of these texts as their own beliefs. It was this that the orthodox church had to combat.

The counter-attack was a simple one. Ephrem the Syrian (306?–73), a native of Nisibis, who later in life moved to Edessa, wrote poems as *contrafacta* to Harmonios's tunes, containing orthodox teachings instead of the heretical ones of Bardesanes.[3] By means of Ephrem's texts the threat of heresies seems to have been eliminated. A prolific writer, Ephrem used three basic poetic forms: *memra* (which was recited without music), *madrasha*, and *sogitha*.[4] *Madrasha* means

---

[2] The basic study of Syrian literature is still Anton Baumstark, *Geschichte der syrischen Literatur* (Bonn, 1922). See also his contribution to the *Handbuch der Orientalistik*, iii, *Semitistik* (Leiden, 1954), 169.

[3] See the detailed study of these authors and their period in Arthur Vööbus, *History of the School of Nisibis, Corpus Scriptorum Christianorum Orientalium*, 266 [= Subsidia, 26] (Louvain, 1965).

[4] Baumstark, *Geschichte der syrischen Literatur*, p. 39; see also Vööbus, *Handschriftliche Überlieferung der Memre-Dichtung des Ja'qob von Serug, Corpus Scriptorum Christianorum Orientalium*, 344 [= Subsidia 39] (Louvain, 1973), 17.

'instruction', and was used for didactic purposes. Ephrem is credited with writing more than three hundred poems of this type, but his authorship cannot be assumed for all of these. In the *madrasha* a soloist sang a long stanza, followed by the choir responding with a relatively short refrain. The soloist's stanza consisted of four to ten half-verses, most often in a pattern of $7+7$ syllables. The choral refrain (*onita*) was repeated after each stanza; it could be a single line of text, or could consist of several verses making up a short stanza. The *sogitha* (plural *sogjatha*) had several stanzas (usually five to six), often in dialogue form. Each stanza had four lines of text, and the whole was connected by an acrostic, which was often alphabetical, but at times contained the author's name hidden in the initial letters of the verses. There are examples of extremely lengthy *sogjatha* with more than fifty stanzas in dialogue form; some scholars believe that a few segments of these could have been acted in dialogue during the long vigils of such feasts as Christmas and Epiphany, thus containing the roots of the later liturgical drama.[5] Most of the early examples are anonymous; the most significant ones are from a somewhat later period. Among the most important poets of this genre are Narsai (*c.* 410–503), who received the nickname 'harp of the Spirit',[6] and Jacob of Sarug (*c.* 450–521). Narsai is also believed to have introduced the custom of indicating the name of the 'model stanza' to which the new texts were to be chanted.

There is a long-standing tradition that contemporary with Ephrem the Syrian still another manner of chanting came into existence, namely 'antiphonal' singing. It is interesting that all accounts involving the origin of antiphonal psalmody refer to Syria. While it is entirely possible that by the mid-fourth century a certain degree of prominence was given to antiphonal performances in addition to the responsorial manner of singing, the chances are that the actual practice is much older and may have originated even further to the East. Yet regardless of the question of origin there are sufficient references to indicate that by the end of the fourth century antiphonal singing did spread to the West, to Constantinople and Milan as well.[7] From then on it became one of the standard forms of chanting in all Christian services.

Much of the poetry used in the Syrian services was written in Syriac, but some of it was still being written in Greek. Among those who wrote in Greek was Severus of Sozopolis, who was Patriarch of

[5] François Graffin, SJ, 'La soghita du cherubim et du Larron', *L'Orient Syrien*, 12 (1967), 481 ff.

[6] See Vööbus, *History of the School of Nisibis*.

[7] See the summary of views in 'Christian Church, music of the early', *New Grove*, iv. 367.

Antioch from 512 to 518 (he lived 460–538?).[8] His poems, preserved only in Syrian translation, have been thought to be the first examples of a collection containing references to the ecclesiastical modes, the Byzantine *echoi*. While in the critical edition of Severus's hymns the modal numbers are included, the editor E. W. Brooks states in his preface, '. . . they are no doubt recensions made for liturgical purposes, which also appears from the fact that the hymns are arranged according to the 8 tones to which they were set; whence the collection is often known as the Octoechos, *though in the two chief MSS, the tones are not mentioned except in a few places, where they seem to be later additions*'.[9] Both Egon Wellesz and Eric Werner made references to this edition but both seem to have overlooked the italicized segment of the sentence. In short, the arangement as *octoechos* does not date from the period of the composition of poems but relates to their editing in sources from later periods.[10]

Other liturgical poetry in Syria from the period of Severus (the sixth century) includes the work of Romanos, who departed from Syria for Constantinople to become the best known poet of *kontakia*. Furthermore Syria developed in this century the form of *qala* (or *qolo*), a word which means 'tone' and 'tune'. The creation of this form is attributed to Simeon the Potter, deacon of Ghezir.[11] One of its traits appears to have been an alternation of long and short verses often linked with the chanting of short doxologies.

Alongside its own forms, Christian services in Syria accepted some Greek forms, specifically the *kanon* from Byzantium (called in Syria *qanune iaonaie*, 'Ionian kanons'). The term *enjane*, which has been interpreted for a long time as a Syrian equivalent of the Byzantine *kanon*, actually should be used as a term for responsorial verses for psalms, while *kanon* seems to be a term for verses for the biblical canticles.[12]

For comparison with other Eastern Christian groups, it is of interest to note that Syrians divided the Psalter into twenty segments, each called a *hullala*, and each in turn subdivided into *marmiata* (singular *marmita*), consisting of varying numbers of psalms. A

---

[8] The reference to 'Sozopolis' is to distinguish this Severus from others of the same name; see his *vita* in *Patrologia Orientalis*, ii.

[9] *Patrologia Orientalis* vi. 6.

[10] See 'Severus' and 'Oktoechos', *New Grove*, xvii. 204 and xiii. 524. See also the new study by Aelred Cody, OSB, 'The Early History of the Octoechos in Syria', *East of Byzantium: Syria and Armenia in the Formative Period* (Washington, DC, Dumbarton Oaks, 1982), 89, which suggests that before the system of eight modes there was a peculiarly Syriac system of seven modes (*heptaechos*).

[11] Baumstark, *Geschichte der syrischen Literatur*, pp. 47, 158 f.

[12] Heinrich Husmann, 'Eine alte orientalische christliche Liturgie: altsyrisch-melkitisch', *Orientalia Christiana Periodica*, 42 (1976), 168.

twenty-first *hullala* contained the biblical Canticles, but only four of them instead of the larger number in the Greek tradition. The Psalter seems to be the most significant book to be used in the Night Office, which starts with the evening service (*ramsham*), the nocturnal service (*lelya*, also *liljo*) as an equivalent of Matins, and the morning hours service (*sapra*) that corresponds to Lauds in western practice.[13]

One point common to all Syrians appears to be that no group has ever developed a rational system of musical notation that could be adopted by all. Owing to the absence of a stable notation, there are now no examples of medieval melodies from Syria: all melodies used for the purpose of demonstrating Syrian tradition are modern ones, which in part may reflect a tradition based on oral transmission, but also contain later accretions. Much study is still needed before we can discern the original strains of an indigenous creative musical tradition.

The process of collecting melodies and writing them down was started in the second half of the nineteenth century by French Benedictines.[14] After *c*.1960 a tremendous breakthrough was made by Heinrich Husmann, who has become involved in a systematic collection as well as analytic study of musical aspects of Syrian services, supplementing the work on liturgical aspects being done by the Benedictine monk Juan Mateos.[15] Among recent discoveries, not yet fully grasped and evaluated, is the presence of Byzantine neumatic notation in Syriac manuscripts, which represents the impressive feat of combining the right-to-left Syrian script with Byzantine neumatic notation of the Coislin type. The so-called 'dot notation' (or 'point notation'), though attested in Syrian as well as in Greek sources, does not seem to offer specifically musical features and may have been intended as a supplement for *ekphonesis* (intoned liturgical reading).[16]

A transcription of modern chanting (as recorded by Husmann in Chicago) of a traditional *madrasha*, is shown in Ex. 1.[17] As one might

---

[13] Husmann, 'Syrian Church Music', *New Grove*, xviii. 472.

[14] The most important and voluminous was the work of J. Jeannin.

[15] Besides Husmann's article on 'Syrian Church Music', see his contribution to K. G. Fellerer, ed., *Geschichte der katholischen Kirchenmusik*, i (Kassel, 1972), 57. The basic study by Juan Mateos, dealing with the Morning Office, is *Lelya-Sapra: Essai d'interprétation des matines chaldéennes*, *Orientalia Christiana Analecta*, 166 (Rome, 1959). The German periodical *Ostkirchliche Studien* publishes valuable bibliographical surveys.

[16] Most recently the dot notation was studied by Denise Jourdan-Hemmerdinger, *Studies in Eastern Chant*, 4 (1979), 81. On the use of Byzantine notation with Syrian texts see Husmann, 'Syrian Church Music', and the edition in facsimile of MS Sinai, Syr. 261, *Göttinger Orientforschungen*, ix/1-2 (Wiesbaden, 1975-6). See also J. Raasted, *Musical Notation and Quasi Notation in Syro-Melkite Liturgical Manuscripts*, *Cahiers de l'Institut du moyen âge grec et latin*, 31 (University of Copenhagen, 1979), 11-37, 53-77.

[17] From Husmann, 'Die Gesänge der melkitischen Liturgie', in K. G. Fellerer, ed., *Geschichte der katholischen Kirchenmusik*, i (Kassel, 1972), 160. In this scale the note below f is a quartertone below e; the g is relatively high between f and a flat; the b flat is relatively low.

Ex. 1

expect in the Near East, the intervals of the chants require a completely different approach to listening on the part of a western listener. Even if there are segments that sound diatonic using well-tempered intervals, the nuances are much greater than in the present western musical tradition. This point is valid not only for Syria but for the whole Near East.

ARMENIAN CHANT

The term 'Armenian' was first used by the Greeks for a people which called itself Haikh and its land Haiastan.[18] Armenians lived in a vast area from the eastern third of Asia Minor to the Caspian Sea and Persia to the east, and from the southern slopes of the Caucasus to Syria in the south-west. At one time that was a part of the cultural sphere known as Urartu, which, it seems, became assimilated by Armenians. The territory of the western basin of the rivers Tigris and Euphrates was a pawn in the rivalries between the Roman Empire and the Parthians in the period of early Christianity. This precarious territorial position prevented Armenians from enjoying free growth in a unified state. Christianity played a significant role in the unification process by contributing to the growth of literature in the Armenian language as well as rallying Armenians around their own Christian church.

The legendary beginnings of Armenian Christianity are linked to the names of the Apostle Bartholomew and of Thaddeus (one of the 'seventy'), who are said to have come to the Armenian lands as early as AD 34 to begin their missionary activities. A few names of Armenian Christian martyrs from the second and third centuries have been seen as proof of the existence of Christian groups in that period, in an essentially heathen land with a large number of deities. The official conversion to Christianity of Armenia, as a land, took place under King Tiridat III, and the traditional date is usually given as 301, although recent research suggests a somewhat later one. Tiridat became a convert under the influence of Gregory ('son of Anak'), now called the 'Illuminator'. Through the activities of Gregory and Tiridat Armenia became the first state to accept Christianity as its official religion. In the fifth century the Armenians came to be viewed as monophysites.

Gregory was educated in Caesarea in Asia Minor and brought with

[18] The best introduction to Armenia in English, as a land, its history and culture, is by Sirarpie Der Nersessian, *The Armenians* (New York, 1970). Extremely useful is the survey of church history in a textbook for Armenian parishes in California, by Krikor Sarafian, *The Armenian Apostolic Church: Her Ceremonies, Sacraments, Main Feasts and Prominent Saints* (Fresno, California, 1959).

him Greek influence and missionaries. In the late fourth century, however, the Persians held sway over Armenia, and forbade the use of the Greek language in 385. This decree may have forced the Armenians to create their own alphabet (since in the fourth century Greek and Syrian appear to have been the only literary languages in this area). The invention of the Armenian alphabet of thirty-six letters is attributed to Mesrop Mashtots, a learned cleric who sought several solutions until finding the right one by combining a large number of Greek letters with some Syrian to obtain the new alphabet about AD 405. Once this new alphabet was accepted, it contributed to an outburst of literary activities starting with the translation of the Scriptures.

There is a deeply ingrained tradition that in the process of translation the Psalter was separated from the books of the Old Testament, and that this was due to the activities of Mesrop Mashtots and his great contemporary Sahak Partev (i.e. Isaac the Parthian, son of Nerses the Great and the great-great-grandson of Gregory the Illuminator) who was the *katholikos* (patriarch and spiritual head) of the Armenian Church for over half a century, from 387 to 439. Tradition furthermore has it that to these two men can be attributed a division of the Psalter into eight '*kanons*', thus creating the first Armenian *octoechos*—a claim that belongs more to legend than to fact.

The earliest Armenian hymnody appears to have originated in a manner similar to that in the Greek-speaking areas of the Near East, namely, by paraphrases of psalm verses.[19] Such hymns were known as *k'tzurd*. Literary historians view *k'tzurd* as the Armenian counterpart of the Byzantine *troparion* and the Syrian *madrashe*. The word *k'tzurd* literally means 'additional' or 'added'. The term was used not only for original hymns but also for fragments of psalms, selected verses standing alone as a separate hymn in some instances.

Scholars in Soviet Armenia see a close relationship between Armenian folk-songs and folk-singers on one hand and the growth of religious hymnody on the other. The singers known as *goossan(s)* and *vypassan(s)* appear as Armenian equivalents of bards and travelling musicians known in other cultures.[20] Through the activities of these musicians—it is presumed—Armenian folk-song elements penetrated the melodies used in churches.

---

[19] The most comprehensive history of Armenian literature is by Manuk Abeghian; 2nd rev. edn. in Russian trans. *Istoriya drevnearmyanskoi literatury* (Erevan, 1975), 273.

[20] Brief description (in Russian) in *Muzykalnaya entsiklopediya*, ii (Moscow, 1974), 114.

LITURGICAL BOOKS

Among the nearly dozen liturgical books necessary for the celebrant and assistants in the performance of the daily ritual services only three appear to pertain to music, and these are known to have had musical notation even in the Middle Ages. Of these only one, the collection of hymns called *sharakan*, has been studied by scholars so far.[21] It has tentatively been compared to the Byzantine *Heirmologion* and *Sticherarion*. The other two, *gandzaran* and *manrussum*, are said to contain melismatic chants with more complex notation; and their repertory is similar to that of Byzantine *kondakaria*, and to chants contained in the Byzantine *Psaltikon* and *Asmatikon*.[22]

These collections apparently came into being under Byzantine influence, which was considerable both politically as well as culturally. By the eighth century the poetic genre of *kanon* makes its appearance in Armenia and, as in Byzantium, contributes to the growth of poetry paraphrasing the Canticles of the Old and New Testaments. The Byzantine term *kanon* received its Armenian equivalent in the term *karg*, yet it must be noted that the Armenian sequence of model Canticles differs from the order of these models in the Byzantine tradition.

The word *kanon* in the Armenian tradition acquired two different meanings: on the one hand it designated the sequence of hymns to be used in the course of one day; on the other it designated one of the eight divisions of the Psalter (with its appended Canticles), and each of these divisions appears to be performed in one of the eight modes of the *octoechos*. While the Byzantine *kanon* is a structure based (in theory at least) on the nine Canticles within a single *kanon*, the Armenian *karg* was always a sequence of eight odes, each ode being known as a *sharakan*. (The term *sharaknots* was introduced later in the eleventh century, as a name for a collection of *sharakans*.) The beginnings of the organization of *kanons* into a book appears to have been the work of Stepanos Syunetsi the Second (d. 735), a contemporary of John of Damascus. The division of the Psalter into eight *kanons* is much more justified when attributed to him. Stepanos has also been credited with the invention of the neumatic notation known as *khazy*, the authorship of a number of *k'tzurds*, as well as the sequence of eight *kanons* for consecutive Sundays. It is presently believed that while the

[21] The pioneering work was that by N. Enim, republished in 1914 in Moscow as *Sharakan, bogosluzhebnye kanony i piesni armyanskoi vostochnoi tserkvi*. More recent results in Abeghian's *Istoriya*.

[22] N. K. T'ahmizyan, 'Les Anciens Manuscrits musicaux arméniens et les questions rélatives à leur déchiffrement', *Revue des études arméniennes*, NS 7 (1970), 267, with 8 plates.

invention of the notation may be a legend, the other attributions are probably correct.[23]

According to the leading Soviet Armenian musicologist T'ahmizyan, the Armenian *octoechos* passed through two different stages in its evolution. T'ahmizyan identified an 'early' *octoechos* of the fifth century, which he associated with the chanting of psalms and biblical Canticles; and a second stage, which he associated with the *kanon* poetry of the eighth century. Since by this time the texts were no longer exerpts from the Bible but new poetic creations, he concluded that this activity created a 'new' *octoechos*. (T'ahmizyan further claimed that there was a third 'mini-*octoechos*' coexisting from the outset for use with original texts, i.e. *k'tzurds*, and containing meiodic formulas of Armenian church music.) In the Armenian terminology for modes the presence of some terms suggests the actual existence of more than eight modes.[24]

The activity of St Gregory Narekatsi (i.e. of Narek) falls in the period between 950 and 1011. In addition to being one of the most important Armenian medieval mystics he was a poet who distinguished himself by writing a new genre of poetry called *tagh*, which dealt with both spiritual and secular aspects of life.[25] The most significant of all poets who contributed to the *sharaknots* seems to have been Nerses 'the Graceful' (Shnorhali), who was *katholikos* of the Armenian Church from 1166 to 1173 (he was born in 1102). No less than a fifth of the whole content of the *sharakan* collection of close to 1200 hymns is attributed to Shnorhali. The latest dated additions to the collection seem to date from about the mid-fourteenth century.

NOTATION

Like almost all their neighbours, Armenians notated their chants (when in due course they came to do so) only in monophonic ways. In practice a number of instruments were used in addition to the voice, and continue to be used to this day, but were limited to the percussive quality of cymbals and bells.

As for the *khazy* neumatic notation, the earliest document with signs viewed as the initial forms of the *khazy* dates from about the

[23] For various Armenian uses of the term *kanon* see T'ahmizyan, *Teoriya muzyki v drevnei Armenii* (Erevan, 1977), 47 f. For Stepanos Syunetsi, ibid., 165, and Abeghian, *Istoriya*. See also Husmann, 'Die Gesänge der armenischen Liturgie', in K. G. Fellerer, ed., *Geschichte der katholischen Kirchenmusik*, i (Kassel, 1972), 99.

[24] T'ahmizyan, *Teoriya*, pp. 160 ff. The term for a mode in Armenian is *tsain* ('voice'), analogous to Russian *glas* as a translation of Greek *echos*.

[25] See Robert Atajan, 'The "tagh" as the Bearer of Humane Principles in 10–12th Century Armenian Monodic Music', *II. International Symposium on Armenian Art* (Erevan, 1978; 16 pp., separate).

ninth century with only eight signs. By the twelfth century their number grew to about twenty-four and remained there, although it appears that some signs were discontinued while some others were introduced in their stead. Unfortunately, however, the exact meaning of this neumatic notation remains enigmatic, as no key to its interpretation has yet been discovered. The best guess at this time is that the signs performed a mnemotechnical function as a reminder to singers how to perform a melody learned by oral transmission.

Even if the knowledge of the neumatic notation was a part of a well-known system in the Middle Ages, by the eighteenth century its meaning was lost. Thus at the beginning of the nineteenth century a Constantinopolitan Armenian Hampartzum Limondzhian (also known as Baba Hampartzum, 1768–1839) invented a new musical notation which was widely used in the course of the nineteenth century by Armenians.[26]

ARMENIAN CENTRES IN EUROPE

An important role in the preservation as well as in the propagation of the Armenian musical traditions has been maintained by the monastic order of Mechitarists, who since the early eighteenth century have had a monastery in Venice, and from Napoleonic times another in Vienna. Both of these centres have cultivated Armenian traditions by publishing a variety of documents related to Armenian chant and their transcriptions in modern Western European musical notation. Since Armenians use a non-tempered pitch system for their chanting, the modern transcriptions leave something to be desired with regard to the actual sound of the melodies, but an approximate idea may be obtained from the following musical examples. Ex. 2(i) shows the Magnificat as chanted in the traditional manner in the second

Ex. 2

(i)

[26] See Atajan, 'Ambartsum Limondzhian i ego notopis', *Musica Antiqua*, v (Bydgoszcz, 1978), 493. For the earlier, medieval notation see his 'Armenische Chazen', in *Beiträge zur Musikwissenschaft*, 10 (1968), 65; there are other studies by Atajan and T'ahmizyan in Russian and Armenian. Earlier descriptions of Armenian notation by previous scholars, including Peter Wagner, Johannes Wolf, and Egon Wellesz, have all been superseded by the new writings in Armenia.

(ii)

authentic mode.[27] For the Magnificat there are traditional recitative-like melodies in each of the modes. Ex. 2(ii) shows the same melodic formula expanded in its *dartsvatsk* aspect, in a variety of both rhythmic and melodic complexities, including oversized intervals only incompletely rendered in the Western notation.

A few short examples are by no means a sufficient documentation for an extremely rich body of chants.[28] Since 1954 a steady stream of volumes has been published in Venice in a series initiated by Fr. L. Dayan, containing hundreds of melodies in the interpretation of the Mechitarists. Except for the work going on in Armenia, in the USSR, and in the Venetian centre, very little work is being done on this body of chants. A separate Viennese tradition of the Mechitarists has been studied to some extent by Husmann.

COPTIC CHANT

It is generally accepted that the term *copt* (or *Kopt*, and its derivative, *coptic*) represents the Europeanized version of the Arabic term *qibṭ* which, in turn, was the Arabic pronunciation of the Greek term οἱ Ἀιγύπτιοι (*hoi Aigyptioi*) which Greeks used to designate the population of the Nile valley in pharaonic times. The term may also have been a Greek designation for the city of Memphis on the Nile. From a place-name and an ethnic designation, the term Copt came to

[27] T'ahmizyan, *Teoriya*, pp. 171, 176.

[28] The Society for Study of Armenian Music (founded in Los Angeles in 1980) considers documentation as one of its principal projects. No discussion of the Armenian musical traditions is complete without a reference to the first modern student of melodies and notation, Sogomon Sogomonian, better known as Komitas (1869–1935); see *New Grove*, x. 166.

designate the monophysite Christians of Egypt.[29] While they were populous in the early centuries of Christianity, their numbers diminished considerably after the Arab conquest of Northern Africa (c. 639–40). No more than ten per cent of the present population of Egypt remains known as Copts, and the term now designates religious affiliation in a predominantly Moslem land.

The term Coptic is also applied to a vast body of art and literature which appears to represent the last stage of the language of pharaonic Egypt. The linguists distinguish several dialects, two of which were used for a substantial number of works of Christian literature. These two dialects are the 'sahidic' dialect of Upper (i.e. southern) Egypt and the 'bohairic' dialect of Lower Egypt (the northern part around the delta of the Nile).[30]

The head of the Coptic Church has a title that designates him both as 'Pope' and as 'Patriarch of the see of St. Mark'. The latter term reflects a tradition that it was the Evangelist Mark who founded the first Christian community in Alexandria, as early as AD 44. There are at present no reliable documents supporting this claim; more significant traces of Christianity are found only in the second half of the second century, with such personalities as Clement of Alexandria.

Having reached the important trade centre of Alexandria, Christianity spread at first among the Jews and in other big cities. Thus it was only in the latter part of the third and the fourth century that Christianity penetrated other areas of Egypt. The persecution under the Roman Empire did not stop the growth of Christianity, and in the peaceful interludes Christians built their shrines as a minority religion. It is reported, for example, that in the city of Oxyrhyncus at about the year 300 there were one Jewish synagogue, a dozen heathen temples, and only two Christian churches. A century later the number of Christian churches increased to about a dozen, and by AD 500 to more than thirty.[31] Oxyrhyncus is important as the source of the oldest document of what is believed to be a sample of Christian chant (with Greek text) from the late third century.[32]

Since Alexandria was one of the most significant centres of Hellenistic culture in the Eastern Mediterranean, competing with Antioch for pre-eminence, it comes as no surprise that in Coptic documents and literature there is a strong admixture of Greek words. To this day within the Christian services there are a number of chants containing

[29] This designation is valid only for the period after the fifth-century religious controversies.
[30] See Fr. Menard's statements about the difficulties of separating Coptic from Arabic traditions, *Encyclopédie des musiques sacrées*, ii (1969), 229 ff.
[31] See *Dictionnaire du spiritualité*, iv (1960), col. 535.
[32] Cf. *New Grove*, iv. 367; also *MGG*, iv (1955), cols. 1051–6.

Greek texts (e.g. *Trisagion* and Kyrie eleison). Under Arab domination and especially after the move of the Greek patriarchate from Alexandria to Cairo in the eleventh century, a substantial penetration of Arabic vocabulary can be observed in Coptic texts.

ORIGINS OF COPTIC CHANT

As the Christian population of Egypt is descended from the inhabitants of pharaonic Egypt, the question of the origins of the Coptic chant and its traditions is often raised. Do they reflect in any way the traditions of music in Ancient Egypt? Can one, by studying the music of the Copts, learn something of its antecedents? While the current knowledge of musical practices of Ancient Egypt is limited, nevertheless it does appear that some of the details of ancient practice have their counterparts in contemporary musical practices of the Copts. Thus Hickmann believed he had demonstrated satisfactorily the presence of 'cheironomy' in both Ancient Egypt and in present-day practice, by comparing Ancient Egyptian paintings and modern singers.[33] Another point: blind singers occupied a distinguished place in the ritual of the Coptic Church, and also in Ancient Egypt. While not all Coptic singers are blind, their presence points to another Coptic tradition, the total absence of musical notation, with reliance on oral transmission. While oral transmission does preserve the basic melodic skeletons of traditional chants, each singer embellishes these melodies. Melismata are particularly copious on some vowels. Around 1900 a considerable amount of literature was written about presumed associations of some chants with magic, and references were made to 'gnostic chants'.[34] In the light of the thorough-going revision of views concerning gnosticism after the discoveries at Nag-Hammadi (a revision that is still in progress), we cannot yet try to draw new conclusions about the role of such chants.

One influence that cannot be ignored, however, is that of the Jewish settlements in Egypt, since Christians were in the very beginning viewed as a sect—one of the many Jewish sects then active. The Coptic manner of singing psalms appears to be related to the practice of the Eastern Mediterranean Jewish communities. As seems to be the practice in almost all Near Eastern countries from the Mediterranean to India, Coptic singers indulge in extended improvisations and variations of basic melodic formulas. Large numbers of such formulas

---

[33] Hickmann, 'Observations sur les survivances de la chironomie égyptienne dans le chant liturgique copte', *Annales du Service des antiquités de l'Égypte*, 49 (1949), 417.

[34] For instance, C. E. Ruelle, 'Le Chant gnostico-magique des sept voyelles grecques', *Documents du Congrès international d'histoire de la musique* (Paris, 1901), 15.

comprise the body of *maqāmat*, which is still so little understood by western scholars.[35]

It is curious if not ironic that there is no notation in evidence among the Copts, whose one important centre is Alexandria. The traditional view of scholars for decades has been that Byzantine neumatic notation (and by extension Western notation as well) had its roots in the system of accentual markings of the Alexandrian grammarians. Yet there is not a trace of any early Coptic notation that could be used for transmission and preservation of melodies.

THE COPTIC SERVICES

The services of the Coptic Church are described as being highly elaborate and extensive, requiring great amounts of time. Beside the celebrant and assisting deacons, the congregation is also expected to participate in the chanting of hymns, while professional singers enjoy special eminence for certain chants and certain feasts. As a functional chant, the Coptic is part of a cycle of services organized in a calendar similar to that in use in the Ethiopian Church; both churches use a calendar related to the Julian calendar (also known as 'old style'), consisting of twelve months of thirty days each, with an added set of five days (six in a leap year), making a thirteenth 'short' month.

It appears that Coptic chanters use a staggeringly large set of church books for all needs of the religious services, amounting to some twenty-five different types of books, not all of which are of interest for music.[36] Among the hymns the most numerous appear to be hymns to the Virgin (called by a Greek term, *theotokia*), used particularly during the month of Kiakh (which corresponds to Advent in preparation for the celebration of the Nativity).[37] Another type of hymn is *psali*, chanted at evening and midnight prayers and during communion. The same term, *psali*, can also designate a paraphrase of a psalm or a Canticle.

There is a sizeable book designed as an 'antiphonary', called *Difnar*, which contains hymns to the saints and doxologies known as *turuhat*. A substantial part of Coptic hymnography is of Byzantine origin, and the actual Coptic creations have not yet been studied in depth. While the Copts use the term *echos*, the Byzantine term for 'mode', they seem to use it to designate specific melodies associated with certain texts. *Theotokia* for Sundays, Mondays, and Tuesdays are sung to a

[35] The term *maqám* appears to designate at various times various concepts, and is often translated to mean either 'scale' or 'mode' or even 'melody', perhaps similar to the Indian *râga*.
[36] See H. Malak, in *Mélanges Eugène Tisserant*, iii (Vatican City, 1964), 1.
[37] See Ilona Borsai, 'Un Type mélodique particular des hymnes coptes du mois de Kiahk', *Studia musicologica*, 13 (1971), 73.

single melody designated in the *Difnar* as 'echos Adam', since the word 'Adam' begins the text of the *theotokion* for those days. The remaining days of the week use the melody 'echos Batos' for the singing of the *theotokia*, since the text of these hymns begins with the word 'Batos', which is the opening word of the canticle describing the burning bush Moses saw.[38] There is a fourteenth-century theoretcial treatise attributed to Abu'l Barakat that contains references to eight modes and arranges them in a pattern not unlike that of the Byzantine system. It is notable, however, that the first mode in Barakat's listing is called 'Adam' and the second 'Batos', while the third is 'sanghari' and the fourth 'kiahk' (or the tone for the month of December). This listing suggests the possibility of a confusion of concepts of Byzantine origin with those indigenous to the Copts.

METHODS OF PERFORMANCE

On the basis of recordings and or observations made by witnesses of the religious services in Coptic churches, it appears that all the basic patterns of performance (soloistic, choral, responsorial, and antiphonal) are present in Coptic traditions. Besides chanting, singers also use musical instruments—specifically a sistrum-like rattle, drums, and cymbals. The most pronounced aspect of this tradition, however, seems to be the special stress on improvisation and embellishments introduced by each singer. In a surrounding in which oral transmission plays such an important role, each singer is expected not only to demonstrate his performance skills but to assert himself as the true carrier of the venerable tradition of the church and its chants.

Students of Coptic musical traditions, able to recognize specific features of the chant, note differences between these and the Arabic chanting traditions. According to these experts, the Coptic chant is much closer to diatonicism than to the Arabic musical style and tradition. As the following musical examples demonstrate, however, it is a system considerably removed from the well-tempered system of Western music, and requires a different approach.

An interesting example of chanting as transcribed by Hickmann, the first modern researcher of this chant, contains a set of fourteen melodies, all of which can be reduced to a relatively simple formula. The elaborate chanting in Ex. 3(i) is that of the doxology;[39] its

---

[38] Borsai, 'Y a-t-il un "octoechos" dans le système du chante copte?', *Studia Aegyptiaca*, i (=*Festschrift V. Wessetzky*), (Budapest, 1974), 39; see also *New Grove*, iv. 730–3.

[39] From Hickmann, 'Koptische Musik', *Koptische Kunst: Ausstellungskatalog Villa Hügel* (Essen, 1963), 116.

Ex. 3

(i)

(ii)

al - le - lu - ia

reduction to a simple unadorned shape, according to Hickmann, would appear as in Ex. 3(ii).

The presence of innumerable minor 'shakes' in the tone-production has been demonstrated in the highly refined transcriptions of Ilona Borsai, based on her own recordings made in Egypt. Ex. 4 shows the simple announcement of a Psalm of David as recorded in two variants.[40]

ETHIOPIAN CHANT

The Greek term *Aἰθίωψ* (*aithiops*) appears to have been applied originally to the southern neighbours of Egypt, primarily Nubians; it literally means 'burnt faces' or 'dark complexions'. In time it came to be applied to the present-day land of Ethiopia, also known as Abyssinia—a name of Arabic origin, *al-Habash*, for the territory which Arabs not only visited but even colonized to some extent before the Christian era.[41] There has been a considerable mixture of populations and cultures in this area, so that what is now called Ethiopian literature, for instance, is a legacy of writings in a language called *ge'ez*; this language is for practical purposes extinct, although it was used down to this century for ecclesiastical literature. *Ge'ez* seems to be of Semitic origin, brought to the territory of Ethiopia from

---

[40] From Borsai, 'Deux chants caractéristiques de la Semaine Sainte copte', *Studies in Eastern Chant*, 4 (1979), 5.

[41] E. Littman, 'Äthiopien', in *Religion in Geschichte und Gegenwart*, i (3rd edn. (1957), cols. 137 f.

Ex. 4

southern Arabia in the first millennium BC. The present-day language is Amharic.[42]

In almost all discussions of Christianity in Ethiopia, it is viewed as an extension of the Coptic Church—which it was until 1959, when the Ethiopian Church obtained its independence. The fourth-century beginnings of Christianity in Ethiopia are recounted in legends, preserved in writing by Rufinus (d. 410).[43] But it was only with the arrival of the so-called 'nine saints' (probably Greek monophysite monks from Syria) at the end of the fifth and the beginning of the sixth century, that literary activities began with the translation of the Scriptures, Coptic hymnody, and the establishment of liturgical services.[44] The evolution of religious history in Ethiopia represents a fascinating mixture of Hellenistic traditions of Alexandria, of Byzantine and Syrian missionary activities, and of some deeply rooted Hebraic practices as well.[45]

ST YARED AND THE *DABTARA*

The period of the sixth century is also the time of the presumed

[42] E. Littmann, *Semitistik*, Handbuch der Orientalistik, Abteilung 1: Der Nahe und der Mittlere Osten, Bd. III (Leiden/Cologne, 1964), 375 ff.

[43] Edward Ullendorff, *Ethiopia and the Bible* (London, 1968); Friedrich Heyer, *Die Kirche Äthiopiens* (Berlin and New York, 1971).

[44] See above, n. 41; see also Bernard Velat, 'Éthiopie', *Dictionnaire du spiritualité*, iv (1961), cols. 1453–77.

[45] See Kay K. Shelemay, 'The Liturgical Music of the Falasha in Ethiopia' (Ph.D. Diss., University of Michigan, 1977) (University Microfilms 77-20, 539).

activity of the greatest Ethiopian religious poet, St Yared (a counterpart of Romanos and John of Damascus in the Byzantine tradition,
and St Gregory in Rome), who was credited with miraculous gifts and
deeds that consolidated the services and chants in the Ethiopian
traditions. St Yared's influence appears to have been of crucial
significance for Ethiopian liturgical practices, although it is nearly
impossible at present to discern how much of what is attributed to him
is truly datable from the early centuries of Christianity. From the
seventh century onward the picture changes rapidly with the Moslem
conquest of Egypt, yet in spite of that the links with Alexandria
remain unbroken, and in practice the Ethiopian Church remained an
offshoot of the Alexandrian patriarchate of the Copts until the
twentieth century.

St Yared is credited with establishing the three basic 'modes' of
Ethiopian chanting. These modes are *ge'ez* (to be distinguished as a
technical term from the designation of the language), *'ezl* and *araraye*,
which to this day are the only modes in use by the professional singers.
These singers, called *dabtara*, represent a paraliturgical order of
substitute priests. Even though never ordained formally as priests,
their presence is essential to services in the Ethiopian Church, and
they can perform services in the absence of ordained priests.[46] *Dabtara*
are trained in special schools and study with teachers renowned for
their knowledge of the musical repertory and for the quality of their
performances. Their education is devoted to the development of
memory as the basic method of transmission, although each *dabtara*
does learn a musical notation, which seems to have been introduced
only in the sixteenth century. Each *dabtara* is expected to collect a
book of all chants ever to be used in any of the religious services of the
Ethiopian Church. The process of training lasts up to fifteen years.

In addition to chanting, the *dabtara* had to learn a sacral dance
called *aquaquam*, as well as the use of musical instruments which
enrich the services with a sizeable volume of sound. (In the Amharic
language the word for secular music, *zafan*, is also applied to the
dance,[47] suggesting that the concept of dancing is inseparable from
music, so it is not surprising that religious services include not only
chanting but also dancing, in addition to instrumental music.) It has
been reported that for special feasts in some large churches the
number of *dabtara* singers and musicians performing at one time can

[46] See Velat, 'Les Dabtara éthiopiens', *Les Cahiers Coptes*, 5 (1954), 21; Velat's introductions
and commentaries to *Patrologia Orientalis*, vols. 32 and 33 (which sum up his life work),
represent the most authoritative statements on chanting in Ethiopia. See also Michael Powne,
Ethiopian Music: An Introduction (London, 1968), 105.

[47] M. Mondon-Vidailhet, 'La Musique éthiopienne', in A. Lavignac and M. de la Laurencie,
eds., *Encyclopédie de la musique*, pt. i, vol. v (1922), col. 3180.

be as high as three hundred. Although a number of musical instruments are known to be used, three are prominent and most frequently encountered: the *kebero* (or *kabaro*), a large drum hanging from the neck of the player; *sanasel* (or *tsenatsel*), a rattle-like set of small bells similar to the Egyptian sistrum; and *meqomia* (*maqwamia*), a long stick which, it seems, serves at times like the baton of a twirler and as a conducting stick—and also as a support to lean against during the interminably long services.

Besides transmitting chants from the earliest periods of Christianity in Ethiopia (undoubtedly with re-composition in oral transmission), the *dabtara* are also expected to create new poetry and hymns. Theirs is a special form known as *qene*, consisting of single stanza of two to twelve lines of text with a single rhyme. There is no official collection of the *qene*, since each one is viewed as the personal property of the individual *dabtara*-singer.

SERVICES AND SERVICE-BOOKS

Religious services in Ethiopia are organized in a calendar peculiar to the Copts and Ethiopians; both follow the Julian calendar with a year of twelve months of thirty days each, with the added intercalary days making a thirteenth month. The church year starts on 29 August of the Gregorian reckoning. Whereas the Copts in Egypt use the 'era of the martyrs', starting their calendar from AD 284 (that is, the beginning of Diocletian's persecution of Christians), the Ethiopians use the 'era of the Incarnation', which is seven to eight years behind the Gregorian (so that the year 1980 is the year 1972–3 in the era of the Incarnation). Beginning in the last decade, however, a number of changes are taking place in Ethiopia,.

After some casual comments about Ethiopian practices, the first serious western attempts at learning and understanding Ethiopian chant began with Villoteau's work in Egypt. His results were restated by Fétis and Mondon-Vidailhet. Significant work in this area was also done by Egon Wellesz. The first truly scientific studies of Ethiopian chant, however, started in the 1950s when a number of scholars made recordings of the chanting by the *dabtara* and of folk-songs as well. Not all the materials already assembled have found their way into print, so that in spite of tremendous progress in the collecting of chants, analytical studies still lag behind. Yet we have now gained a better understanding of the contents and arrangement of music books used by the *dabtara*. Schools offering instruction in chanting teach what is known as *zema* or music for the religious services.[48] There are

[48] See Velat, 'Les Dabtara éthiopiens', p. 27, and Powne, *Ethiopian Music*, pp. 105 ff.

six types of books, each of which is a collection of chants that a capable *dabtara* must learn. Two of these books are used for the eucharistic service (for which Ethiopians have no fewer than sixteen different anaphoras, more than any other Christian church). The six books are as follows.[49]

Qeddāsè: the equivalent of the Western Missal, containing the Ordinary of the Mass and texts of anaphoras.

Zemmarè: a collection of psalmody used mostly at the ending of the Mass, honouring the Communion and the saints for each day of the year.

Me'eraf: the Common of the Office, namely chants for the celebrant, which are at times chanted in a dialogue with the congregation, chants listed as melody-types, studied in schools and used in the Office with texts that vary from day to day, and also hymns in honour of the Virgin. This book cannot be used alone but only in conjunction with the next two.

Deggua: a kind of antiphonary for the year, excluding Lent; it appears to be the most sizeable volume in use in services and contains proper hymns for each day of the year—thus an equivalent of the Proper of the Time.

Soma Deggua: an antiphonary for Lent; this is the first book to be studied and memorized by a *dabtara*.

Mawāše'et: another antiphonary of more restricted use, primarily for funeral services, and specific hours for about fifty feasts; it contains proper hymns with their psalmody.

When a *dabtara* prepares a set of these books with texts of the chants, he usually provides these also with a musical notation known as *meleket*, which can be traced only in manuscripts since the sixteenth century. The main purpose of this notation is mnemotechnical, a reminder to an already trained singer. The notation gives clues to groups of melodic formulas referred to as *serayou*. Each of the three modes mentioned earlier has a number of these *serayous*, some of which are interchangeable and migrate from one mode to another. The most extensive study of this notation so far was undertaken by Wellesz, but he did not offer specific transcriptions of melodies from

[49] In addition to Velat's introductions in *Patrologia Orientalis*, vols. 32 and 33, see his 'Hymnes eucharistiques éthiopiennes', *Rhythmes du Monde*, 27ᵉ année (1953), [NS vol. I], 26; and 'Le Mawāšè'et et les livres de chant liturgique éthiopiens', in *Mémorial du cinquantenaire de l'école des langues orientales de l'institut catholique de Paris 1914–1964*, Travaux de l'institut catholique de Paris, 10 (Paris, 1965), 159.

Ex. 5

∧	light accent
–	heavy accent
⩜	trill

↗ ↘	slides up or down
⩜⩜	vibrato
↑ ↓	higher or lower in pitch

the notation.[50] In the 1960s Bernard Velat published the most extensive collection of transcriptions of melodic formulas and fragments from the very large number of hymns he edited. A detailed analytical study of the hymns and of their structure, as well as of the role of the individual melodic formulas, still remains to be done. Some of the melodic formulas from Velat's collection are shown in Ex. 5.[51]

---

[50] Wellesz, 'Studien zur äthiopischen Kirchenmusik', *Oriens Christianus*, NS 9 (1920), 74; see also the addendum by S. Euringer, ibid., 10–11 (1923), 151–4.

[51] Although there are isolated 'complete' examples of transcriptions of Ethiopian chant in studies by Mondon-Vidailhet, Wellesz, and Powne, none of them matches the thoroughness of Velat, who was assisted by Denise Jourdan-Hemmerdinger in painstaking transcription into Western notation. Extensive appendices of melodic formulas are published in *Patrologia Orientalis*, vols. 32 and 33. The examples given here come from Velat's 'Musique liturgiques d'Éthiopie', in J. Porte, ed., *Encyclopédie des musiques sacrées*, ii (Paris, 1969), 235, 237. There is a recording of Ethiopian chants by Jean Jenkins (UNESCO).

II

BYZANTINE CHANT

By MILOŠ VELIMIROVIĆ

THE term 'Byzantine chant' is applied to the monophonic settings of melodies, vocally performed, in use in the Greek Orthodox Church in the Middle Ages, contemporary with the Eastern Roman Empire, better known as the Byzantine Empire. As with all other musical traditions of the Eastern Mediterranean, the earliest stages of the melodies and their evolution are unknown; all assumptions are made on the basis of later practice, with inferences of logical development of the liturgical as well as complementary musical actions.

Two conflicting theories, still embattled, are being advanced about the basic steps in the formation of Byzantine chant. On the one hand it is assumed that since the majority of the population at least understood if they did not actually speak Greek (which was the language most commonly used for commerce and communications throughout the Eastern Mediterranean), and since the substantial majority of early Christian documents had been transmitted in Greek, therefore the actual practice of chanting in the emerging Greek Orthodox Church may have evolved from the pre-Christian Greek traditions, which, in turn, may have been heavily influenced by the folk-song patterns of the Greek-speaking population. Any attempts at establishing such a link, however—especially with Ancient Greece—have so far remained extremely tenuous and undocumented. On the other hand, since Christianity emerged in Jerusalem and spread at first through the Jewish communities from Antioch in the east to Rome in the west, it has been assumed that Jewish religious, as well as musical, practices were the dominant element in the development of several Christian regional practices, including Byzantine chant.

It cannot be stressed strongly enough that the melodies used by Christians—with the single exception of the Oxyrhyncus papyrus[1]

---

[1] See *New Grove*, iv. 367; *MGG*, iv (1955), cols. 1051–6.

with its hymn—were not committed to writing for several centuries: the earliest written documentation of music in use in the Eastern Orthodox churches dates from about the tenth century. Thus it is impossible to reconstruct the actual sound of music as it was sung in Greek-speaking ecclesiastical gatherings before the tenth century. And even these earliest notated examples remain problematic, involving a considerable amount of guesswork as to their actual meaning; it is another two centuries before musical notation reaches a stage of development with some degree of certainty for deciphering melodies and transcribing them into modern notation.

While the beginnings of Byzantine chant emerge from the mist of centuries past, the term continues to be used down to the present in Greece as a designation of *any* chanting which finds acceptance in the performance of the daily ritual of the Greek Orthodox Church. Thus two terminologies are involved: Greeks use 'Byzantine chant' as a designation for the chant of the Greek Orthodox Church from its very beginnings to the present; while non-Greek western scholarship uses the term for the chant of the Greek Orthodox Church of the Middle Ages, only down to the fifteenth century (when Constantinople fell to the Turks on 29 May 1453). Western scholars call the chant used from the fifteenth to the eighteenth centuries 'Neo-Byzantine', since it did undergo some stylistic changes in that period. The reform initiated by Archbishop Chrysanthos in the early nineteenth century affected musical notation through the homogenization of tradition by fixing the melodies in print; after this reform there emerged a body of 'neo-Greek' chants, or simply a 'Chrysanthine tradition', which is being further modified at present by individual attempts at polyphonic settings—not accepted by the majority of Greeks.

It should be added, however, that there is no clear-cut break between the medieval and the 'Neo-Byzantine' tradition, only a process of evolution from oral transmission with some help from the written documents, to written transmission in which individual cantors deem it a duty to contribute to the evolution of melodies by recording their own variants and additions.[2] The period of the seventeenth and eighteenth centuries produced a plethora of highly melismatic melodic ornamentation in the traditional chants.

[2] Western scholars have so far investigated the sources of Byzantine chant up to the late fifteenth century. The most significant stylistic changes of later periods seem to have occurred in the seventeenth century by gradual elimination of certain additional signs in red ink. It is presumed that these signs in red supplied notes for a 'full' performance of the melodies, and that the black notation only sketched them. The resolution of the red signs has acquired the name of 'exegesis' or 'analytic method'. This process has so far been studied only by Greek scholars. If they are correct, there might be a parallel between this procedure and the notation of operatic arias during the baroque era, when performances departed from the written score and each

Still another point to be kept in mind when discussing Byzantine chant is that this term should be used exclusively for Greek traditions and not for any other ethnic tradition, even if initiated by Greek missionaries. Christianity was transmitted by Greeks to many of its neighbours. Contrary to the practice of Roman missionaries, who insisted on the use of Latin in the spread of Christianity in Western Europe, Greeks from the outset favoured the translation of the Scriptures into the vernacular of the ethnic group which was being converted. Thus, although some basic concepts and even melodies of Byzantine origin may have penetrated into a new ethnic group, the subsequent evolution of such texts and singing progressed in the native language of that group (e.g. Russian), and should be studied and examined separately rather than as a presumed branch of Byzantine chant.

The historians of the Byzantine Empire have for a long time been aware of the extremely close relationship between the Imperial Court and the Christian Church, with the centre of power shifting from one to the other at various periods in the tortured history of the Empire. The immediate consequence of this relationship for the study of the chant is to realize that the imperial pomp and circumstance have penetrated the manner of chanting in some services, and on the other hand liturgical chants became an inseparable part of some imperial ceremonies and processions. Any attempt to separate these ceremonies and single out secular from liturgical aspects misses the point of this deep interrelationship of church and state in the Byzantine tradition. The present-day knowledge of these chants and processions involving singers at the Imperial Palace is still too scanty to give us a clear picture of the role of music in these surroundings—differing as they do from purely liturgical services.[3]

There is a strong tendency among present-day Greeks to claim a deep relationship between Byzantine chant and Greek folk-song, and it is important to stress that the earliest recorded examples of Greek folk-song date from the late sixteenth if not the seventeenth century, thus outside the chronological limit of the Byzantine Empire.[4] While it

---

singer added his own embellishments. Greek scholars claim that their exegeses demonstrate a fixed pattern of embellishment, not mere improvisation. The only study in English dealing with some aspects of this riddle is by Grigorios Stathis, 'An Analysis of the Sticheron Τον ηλιον κρυψαντα by Germanos, Bishop of New Patras [The Old 'Synoptic' and the New 'Analytical' Method of Byzantine Notation]', *Studies in Eastern Chant*, 4 (1979), 177. See below, p. 51.

[3] The role of music in the imperial ceremonies needs to be investigated; the only study so far is Jacques Handschin, *Das Zeremonienwerk Kaiser Konstantins und die sangbare Dichtung* (Basle, 1942).

[4] The most recent and only reliable discussion of this subject is by Dimitri E. Conomos, 'The Iviron Folk Songs: a Re-examination', in *Studies in Eastern Chant*, 4 (1979), 28–53.

is entirely possible that there may have been a steady intercourse between the melodies in use for folk festivities and those used for the liturgical services of the Church, this relationship requires a much more thorough study than has hitherto been conducted before such a link can be documented and accepted by modern scholarship.

In sum, Byzantine chant is a liturgical, functional chant sung in Greek during the religious services of the Greek Orthodox Church in the later Middle Ages. It is entirely vocal, as the canons of that church have never permitted the use of musical instruments in its services. It is monophonic, as not one source of the medieval musical traditions contains any trace of polyphonic setting. Byzantine chant is modal in the sense that its pitch structure is dependent on a type of organization different from that of the present-day Western scales. The Byzantine tonal system has eight basic modes constituting the so-called *octoechos*. Byzantine music is written in a very peculiar system of neumatic notation which evolved from a primitive state into a highly elaborate one of individual notational signs for pitch relationships, durations, and signs for the 'quality' of sound and for melodic ornamentation. This system, considerably modified and modernized in the nineteenth century, remains in use to this day in Greece, although outside Greece religious communities are switching to the five-line staff and Western European notation.

In order to understand fully what is going on in any melody of Byzantine chant, one should try to understand the meaning of its text. A grasp of the text will reveal varying degrees of interrelationship between text and music, including even instances of modest 'tone-painting'.

THE HISTORY OF BYZANTINE CHANT

The official title of the so-called Byzantine Empire included a reference to Rome, for Byzantine Emperors considered themselves successors of Roman Emperors. There was no city of Constantinople before its formal dedication in AD 330, and only from that date can one begin to follow the history of the Eastern Roman Empire. Earlier references to Greek chanting are classified as documents of the Early Christian tradition; thus, properly speaking, only developments and events after the middle of the fourth century and in Greek-speaking transmission should be considered as of Byzantine origin. By that time, it appears, both choral and soloistic singing were fairly well established in Christian religious services.

The fourth century is an extremely interesting period in which lived and worked a great many Fathers of the Church, some of whom were

to play an increasingly important role in the formulation of the ritual
as it evolved in subsequent centuries. Thus, one encounters, more or
less side by side, Basil the Great and John Chrysostom, the authors of
the two basic types of Byzantine liturgies in use down to the present.
Among their contemporaries in the West were St Ambrose of Milan,
followed by St Augustine; also St Jerome, the translator of the Latin
Bible, whose travels made him a familiar figure in both East and West;
and St Hilary of Poitiers, who was exiled for a while in Asia Minor,
where he might have had some first-hand experience with Eastern
Christian practices before returning to Gaul.

Whether the liturgical services attributed to Basil and John Chrysostom are as old as the period of their authors' lives and activities is
not relevant, and it can be left to the historians of liturgies to pursue
the exact dating of these services.[5] The crucial point is that the services
attributed to these authors became widespread within a few centuries,
and their basic outlines fixed by the time the written documentation
with musical notation (signifying that specific melodies were to be
used with specific texts) began to appear.

Although some texts for liturgical services can thus be dated to the
earliest centuries of Christianity, any assumption that the melody as
preserved in later documents may date back to the time of an 'old' text
is probably unwarranted. And yet indirect references to musical
practices provide data sufficient to infer the types of chanting and to
obtain, if not an authentic, then at least a probable idea of the sounds
that may have echoed through the early assemblies of Christians.
Thus, besides the singing by a soloist (which can be traced to some
Jewish precedents in the Temple services), we also encounter in the
fourth century the chanting in alternation between two choirs (antiphonal singing), which is solidly documented for that period; the actual
practice might be older and have originated further east than Antioch,
whence the practice appears to have spread to the West.[6]

While individual singers and groups of trained singers undoubtedly
played a very significant role in the important churches and cathedrals, as for instance in the Hagia Sophia in Constantinople (which
was dedicated in the sixth century as the largest Christian temple of
that period), it remains unknown to what extent and at what point the
congregation itself became involved in some aspects of the services.
Whether it was a simple recitation of prayers or a more solemn
reading—which hardly qualifies as 'music' except for its use of a
limited tonal range—the congregation undoubtedly contributed some

---

[5] See H. G. Beck, *Kirche und theologische Literatur im byzantinischen Reich* (Munich, 1959).
[6] See pp. 5 and 83.

form of musical enrichment. From simple nodding in consent of the meaning of the texts of prayers and in glorification of the unfathomable, expressed in the simple Amen (So be it!), congregational responses grew in significance and in form. And even if they had been restricted to the Amen alone, such a word was later to become musically elaborated.

One of the reasons for the growing length of the music was that the liturgical action itself required more time. To give a single example, as the congregation expanded, the celebrant needed more and more time to prepare bread and wine for Communion. In addition to being an expression of the awe and devotion of the assembled Christians, chants for Communion acquired the function of filling up the time. In the Byzantine tradition there came into existence the chanting of the Cherubic Hymn ('We who mystically represent the Cherubim') during the preparation of the host; there were also other Communion hymns, in use in the fourth to sixth centuries.

In these instances we often encounter texts for which more than one author is listed; claims and counter-claims of authorship are then advanced by historians of literature as well as by liturgists. Much as we would like to know for each text who the actual author was, this is not a subject for musicologists to ponder. What we want to know is whether the melodies for these early texts can be retrieved. The absence of any meaningful musical notation before the tenth century makes it highly unlikely that these melodies can ever be documented, which is not to say that tentative suggestions and reconstructions of such melodies are impossible. Whether such reconstructions will be accepted or rejected depends, in part, on the degree of trust in an oral tradition. It is a very difficult question how faithfully an oral tradition can transmit a melody over several centuries. Even if a melody is inseparably linked to a specific text, even if the fixation has some magical qualities with deviation from the original bringing curses upon a performer, still it is hard to accept the theory of unchangeability in music (one of the most volatile of arts) when transmitted orally, so easily is music influenced by the changing taste of performing musicians from one generation to the next. The basic lines of tradition can be, and unquestionably are, maintained in an oral transmission; but melodic details are susceptible to change.

Besides filling the time for actions at the altar or during the procession, music had additional functions as announcements preceding reading from Scriptures, to which the congregation was expected to pay very special attention. Music could and did help generate the feeling of enthusiasm propounded in some texts, by introducing expressive if not emotional (at times even martial) sounds in melodies.

With Christianity spreading to every village in the realm, it is reasonable to believe that there must have co-existed a great variety of manners of performance of the liturgical services, depending on the resources available in each church. Small parish churches had limited resources, and relied on the participation of the congregation with only a bare minimum of trained singers for the musical highpoints of the liturgy. Large urban cathedrals undoubtedly indulged in growing numbers of professional singers, and tolerated virtuoso excesses— which are bound to proliferate when several singers are competing for attention and rank in the hierarchy of Greek Orthodoxy, a counter-part to the imperial layers of importance at the Court and in the state itself.[7]

An examination of the basic heritage of texts, and of the relation-ship of the number of settings of texts, points to a curious dialectic between the two. The more texts were written by poets for the celebration of specific feasts, the fewer melodies for such texts seem to have been composed, and the more the method of *contrafactum* seems to have dominated their composition. The fewer the texts for some services (here referring specifically to the established liturgies, but in some cases to certain fixed parts of the Offices as well), the more numerous become the melodies composed and transmitted. Thus liturgists see an ossification of services when the texts stop proliferat-ing, while musical documents frequently contain more and more settings of the same texts, indicating the possibility of choice to singers as to which melody to sing—perhaps in order to provide some variety, precisely because the text remained unchanged for centuries.[8] The growth of the number of melodies and of individual settings of texts already fixed began in earnest in the fourteenth century (according to the existing musical manuscripts), and went into a wild weed-like

---

[7] While there seem to be no lists naming singers and members of various choirs, we surmise that the rank of ecclesiastical hierarchy was enhanced by more festive and more elaborate performances than in small parish churches. Singers in the 'Royal Chapel' of the Emperors bore titles of 'protopsaltes', 'domestikos' etc. See especially Beck, *Kirche und theologische Literatur*, pp. 113 f. and n. 9 below. An amusing story of singers competing and creating problems out of professional jealousy may be found in Velimirović, 'Two Composers of Byzantine Music: John Vatatzes and John Laskaris', *Aspects of Medieval and Renaissance Music: A Birthday Offering to Gustave Reese* (New York, 1966), 818.

[8] The proliferation of compositions using fixed text is particularly prominent in the last centuries of Byzantium. See e.g. the large number of Cherubic Hymn melodies and of those for the Trisagion, discussed by Conomos, *Byzantine Trisagia and Cheroubika of the Fourteenth and Fifteenth Centuries* (Thessaloniki, 1974), analysing 18 melodies for the Trisagion and more than 15 of Cherubic Hymns. See also the chart demonstrating the growing number of settings of single verses in a single psalm-text, in Miloš Velimirović, 'The Prooemiac Psalm of Byzantine Vespers', *Words and Music: The Scholar's View. A Medley of Problems and Solutions Compiled in Honor of A. Tillman Merritt* (Harvard University, 1972), 317.

growth under the Turkish domination, after the fall of the Byzantine Empire in 1453.

In the study of musical practices in Byzantium there are a number of unsolved problems which do not necessarily have to do with the melodies but with problems of actual performance. One puzzling problem has been the rather small number of singers designated for the cavernous space of the Hagia Sophia in Constantinople. In Justinian's instructions and listing of categories of types of people serving in this cathedral, he provided for a very small number of singers and yet a large number of 'readers' to read psalms and other texts during the Offices (which had begun to assume larger proportions).[9] Hagia Sophia is unique among Byzantine churches, and one might raise questions about its acoustical properties, whether they were well enough suited to singers so that a small number could provide the volume of sound needed to fill the space. Some documentation in smaller Balkan monastic churches seems to suggest that their architects were fully aware of the need for musical resonance, and that they provided some sort of resonance chamber to enhance the voices of the singers. Thus jugs and other earthenware were built into the area just beneath the cupola, in the pendentives, to provide echoing space.[10] It remains unknown whether this is an isolated phenomenon or one that may have been spread all over the Near East.

BYZANTINE LITURGICAL SERVICES

The daily cycle of services in the Byzantine practice is similar to that of most other Christian traditions. There is one basic service which includes the Eucharist and is known as the 'Liturgy' (in the West this is the Mass). Other services are the Offices, of which the most important are Vespers (*Esperinos*), Matins and Lauds (*Orthros*). In addition there are shorter Offices associated with specific hours of the ecclesiastical day. In present-day practice the full cycle of daily Offices is observed only in monastic communities, and even there in reduced form compared with the medieval traditions. The Divine Liturgy and the Offices are based primarily on a daily and weekly cycle continued

[9] Justinian, upon the completion of the building of the Hagia Sophia, is said to have assigned 25 singers and 110 'anagnostes' (readers) to assist the clergy in the services; cf. Egon Wellesz, *A History of Byzantine Music and Hymnography* (Oxford, 2nd edn. 1961), 113, citing Pseudo-Codinus. Extremely important new findings on singers are listed by C. Patrinelis in his study: 'Protopsaltae, Lampadarii, and Domestikoi of the Great Church during the post-Byzantine Period (1453–1821)', *Studies in Eastern Chant*, 3 (1973), 141.

[10] Data from no fewer than eighteen churches are assembled by Slobodan Nenadovic, 'Rezonatori u crkvama srednjevekovne Srbije' [Resonators in Medieval Serbian Churches], *Recueil des travaux de la faculté d'architecture Université de Belgrade*, V, 5 (Belgrade, 1960), 3. For a similar practice elsewhere cf. Kenneth Harrison, 'Vitruvius and Acoustic Jars in England during the Middle Ages', *Transactions of the Ancient Monuments Society*, NS xv (1967–8).

throughout the year. Additional 'proper' texts are provided in accordance with an annual cycle of feasts and events associated with the life of Jesus and with the saints, with specific chants for each occasion.[11]

Shown below are outlines of the sung portions of Esperinos, Orthros, and the Divine Liturgy (according to the basic version, that of John Chrysostom). Varying requirements for individual days, particularly for saints' days, may involve a larger number of *stichera* and *troparia*. (In parish churches the sung parts are considerably shortened, and many texts are simply recited.)

Chants for Esperinos (Vespers)

Prooemiac Psalm (Psalm 103, selected verses only)
First Stasis of the First Kathisma (selected verses from Psalms 1–3)
'Kyrie ekekraxa' [Κύριε ἐκέκραξα] ('Lord, I cried unto Thee'—selected
　　verses from Psalms 140–2 with proper *stichera*)
'Phos hilaron' [Φῶς ἱλαρόν] ('O gladsome light'—hymn)
Prokeimen (hymn, proper to the day of the week)
(at Vigils a procession with proper *stichera* could take place here)
Aposticha *troparia* (proper to the day)
Apolytikion (dismissal hymn, proper to the day)

Chants for Orthros (Matins and Lauds)

Hexapsalmos (Psalms 3, 37, 62, 87, 102, 142)
'Theos Kyrios' [Θεὸς Κύριος] ('God is Lord who has shown us light'—
　　hymn)
Psalms of the day, with three 'sessional' hymns
Eulogetaria ('Praises of Resurrection', concluded by triple Alleluia)
Anabathmoi ('Gradual' Psalms 119–33)
Prokeimen (introduction to the reading of the Gospel for the day)
Psalm 50 with *troparion* (proper to the day)
Kanon, consisting of:
　　Odes 1–3
　　Hypakoe (hymn)
　　Odes 4–6
　　Kontakion (*prooemium* and first stanza only)
　　Life of the Saint of the day (lesson)
　　Odes 7–9
　　Exaposteilarion (hymn; in Lent another kind of hymn, Phota-
　　　　gogikon)
Lauds (Psalms 148–50)
Pasa pnoe [Πασα πνοή] ('Let every breath'—Psalm 150, v. 6)

[11] There is an extremely useful survey of the daily and annual cycles by Mother Mary and Archimandrit Kallistos Ware, *The Festal Menaion* (London, 1969).

Great Doxology [Δόξα ἐν ὑψιστις] ('Gloria in excelsis' = 'Doxa en ypsistis')

'Trisagion' ('Thrice holy', i.e. 'Holy God, Holy Mighty, Holy Immortal')

Troparion (proper to the day)

Dismissal

Chants for the Divine Liturgy (Eucharistic service)

Antiphon I (Psalm verse proper for the day; on Sundays from Psalm 102)

Antiphon II (Psalm verse proper for the day; on Sundays from Psalm 145).

O monogenis ('Only begotten Son' = flO μονογενὴς Υἱὸς; hymn often attributed to Justinian, sixth century)

Antiphon III (Psalm verse with the *troparion* of the feast; on Sundays 'Beatitudes' with proper *troparia*)

(At the 'Little Entrance' Procession:)

    Deute proskinisomen [Δεῦτε προσκυνήσωμεν] ('Come, let us worship'—Psalm 94, v. 6)

    Troparion (sometimes *Kontakion*, proper for the day)

    'Trisagion' ('Thrice holy')

Prokeimen (before the Epistle, proper to the day)

Alleluia with verses (before the Gospel, proper to the day)

(Dismissal of the Catechumens; from here on, 'Mass of the Faithful')

(at the 'Great Entrance' Procession:)

    Cheroubikon [Οἱ τὰ Χερουβὶμ = We who mystically represented the cherubim.] ('Cherubic Hymn')

Creed

Anaphora, or Eucharistic prayer, with some responses by choir, and three hymns:

    It is meet and just to worship the Father, Son and Holy Spirit ...

    Holy, Holy, Holy, Lord of Sabbaoth

    We praise Thee, we bless Thee, we give thanks unto Thee ...

also:

    It is meet and right to bless Thee ... Mother of God ...

Lord's Prayer

Communion verse (proper to the day)

    (as the doors to the altar open, choir sings:

        Blessed is he that comes in the name of the Lord)

    (upon communion:

        'Let our mouth be filled'—hymn Πληρωθήτω τὸ στόμα ἡμῶν)

Dismissal

THE DEVELOPMENT OF BYZANTINE MUSIC

A history of the development of Byzantine music has yet to be written. One of the problems is that some of the earliest poets—who may also have been the *melodes* or composers of music for their own texts— lived in a period before the use of musical notation, and the melodies recorded at a later period may or may not represent the composer to whom the melody may be ascribed. Only from about the thirteenth century is there anything like close approximation of the dates or lives of composers and of the written record of their work. By the fourteenth and fifteenth centuries there is every reason to believe that the compositions of contemporary composers are faithfully recorded and seldom mixed up or represented as someone else's work. Among a number of objectives in Byzantine musicology, one (which certainly might be accomplished within a relatively short time) is a catalogue of works attributed to composers from the seventh to the twelfth century. So far, only some works have been attributed with any degree of reliability, while for a number of composers there is at present no way to gauge their total output. Attributions vary from manuscript to manuscript, some of the texts are transmitted in more than one version, and questions of authenticity and even veracity may at times be raised.

THE *KONTAKION*

Of all Byzantine poetry used with music in religious services, two types stand out—*kontakion* and *kanon*.[12] The first of these, *kontakion*, is definitely older, being documented in the Byzantine practice in the sixth century.[13] Its origins are undoubtedly Syriac. The name of Romanos the Melodos, who was apparently a Jew converted to Christianity, from Berytos (Beyrut), is mentioned as having brought this form to Constantinople, where he wrote one poem after another in the early years of the sixth century.[14] Thus he not only introduced this poetic form into the Byzantine practice but also wrote the largest number of examples. Although probably a sizeable number of other poets also cultivated this form, at present these others are evaluated through the prism of Romanos's achievements in the *kontakion*. We

---

[12] H. Husmann, 'Hymnus und Troparion', *Jahrbuch des Staatlichen Instituts für Musikforschung, Preussischer Kulturbesitz* (Berlin, 1971), 7.

[13] See C. Floros, 'Das Kontakion', *Deutsche Vierteljahrsschrift für Literatur- und Geistesgeschichte*, 34 (1960), 84 ff.

[14] The most recent study, superseding previous works and with as complete a bibliography as possible, is by José Grosdidier de Matons, *Romanos le Mélode et les origines de la poésie réligieuse à Byzance* (Paris, 1977).

have eighty-five to eighty-eight authenticated examples representing his legacy.

The basic function of the *kontakion*, as it was used in the course of the sixth and seventh centuries, appears to have been to serve as a poetic paraphrase of the sermon for the day, usually on the occasion of a feast celebrated on a special day in the church calendar in a very elaborate fashion. The Syriac *sogitha* is usually mentioned as the principal model from which the Byzantine *kontakion* evolved,[15] and there are substantial resemblances in poetic pattern as well as in rendition between these two types of poetry. For a very long time Romanos has also been viewed as the author of the most famous example of the *kontakion*, the one known as the *Akathistos* hymn. This hymn, dedicated to the Virgin and chanted both at the feast of the Annunciation and during the Saturday of the Fifth Week of Lent, consists of twenty-four stanzas with an extensive *prooemium*. Within the last century there has been a pendulum-like swing of opinions concerning the authorship of the *Akathistos*, attributions being made to Romanos as well as to Sergius, Patriarch of Constantinople, a century later than Romanos.[16]

The performance of a *kontakion*, including the *Akathistos*, suggests a prominent role for a soloist, who sings highly elaborate melismatic melodies for the main stanzas while the chorus rounds off these with the relatively less complex refrains. While the *prooemium* has a different melody, the basic body of the *kontakion* was apparently chanted to the same melodies (two, one for odd-numbered, one for even-numbered stanzas) with only minor variants for the twelve to eighteen stanzas. The *kontakion* appeared suddenly in the Christian services of the sixth century, and held sway over the Morning Office for almost two centuries; its significance diminished rapidly when a new type of poetic structure with somewhat greater variety of melodies made its appearance, and supplanted the *kontakion* in popularity and in its role in the Morning Office. The new form was that of a *kanon* consisting of nine odes.[17] As the *kanon* gained in prominence the *kontakion* was reduced to a single stanza with its introductory *prooemium*; this remnant of the *kontakion* was inserted between the sixth and seventh odes of the *kanon* as a diversion.

---

[15] See also A. Baumstark, *Geschichte der syrischen Literatur* (Bonn, 1922), 39 f. and 303.

[16] The most recent critical discussion of this question is in C. A. Trypanis, *Fourteen Early Byzantine Cantica* (= *Wiener Byzantinische Studien*, v, 1968), 17.

[17] See Velimirović, 'The Byzantine Heirmos and Heirmologion', in Wulf Arlt *et al.*, eds., *Gattungen der Musik in Einzeldarstellungen: Gedenkschrift Leo Schrade*, i (Berne, 1973), 192.

THE *KANON*

The poet instrumental in launching the new genre of the *kanon* appears to have been Andrew of Crete (*c.* 660–*c.* 740); but there are good reasons to believe that Germanos I, Patriarch of Constantinople from 715 to 730 (he died in 734) may have also been involved.[18] In the course of the eighth and subsequent centuries a large number of poets wrote *kanons*; the two best known are John of Damascus and Cosma of Jerusalem (also known as Cosma of Mayuma).

The *kanon* is based on the principle of paraphrase of the biblical Canticles. The Codex Alexandrinus, of the fourth century, has no fewer than fourteen of these 'Psalms outside the Psalter'; in the course of centuries their number was reduced to nine, and as such became the 'rule' (which is what *kanon* means) for subsequent poetic paraphrase. The nine biblical Canticles are:

1 Exodus (xv, 1–9): Song of Thanksgiving after the crossing of the Red Sea.
2 Deuteronomy (xxxii, 1–43): Moses admonishes the Hebrews.
3 I Samuel (ii, 110): prayer of Hannah, mother of Samuel.
4 Habbakuk (iii, 2–19): prayer of Habbakuk.
5 Isaiah (xxvi, 9–19): prayer of Isaiah.
6 Jonah (ii, 29): prayer of Jonah.
7 Daniel (iii, 26–45 and 52–56): prayer of Azaria and the first hymn of the Three Children in the Fiery Furnace.
8 Daniel (iii, 57–88): second hymn of the Three Children in the Fiery Furnace.
9 Luke (i, 46–55 and 68–79): the Magnificat as the song of the Theotokos, and the Benedictus as the song of Zacharias.

While these biblical Canticles may have at first been sung in their entirety and without additions, by the sixth century it had become customary to expand them with paraphrases. By the eighth century the singing of the original Canticles had become restricted, probably to no more than the opening line or two of the original text, while the paraphrases had become more and more extensive. In the new pattern that emerged, the *kanon* now consisted of nine odes, each of which was to emulate in content the respective biblical Canticle. Thus if the topic presented in an ode dealt with Jonah, the ode was understood immediately to be the sixth ode of the *kanon*, since the sixth Canticle was that of Jonah. As far as the structure of each individual ode is concerned, the following conventions were observed: each ode consisted of one model stanza and three to four additional stanzas. The

[18] Ibid. 198.

first was soon designated as *heirmos* ('model stanza'), while the stanzas following, modelled on the *heirmos* in sentence structure, disposition of stresses, and of course in melody, came to be known as *troparia*. Thus a poet-composer composed a *heirmos* which served as a model for the three to four *troparia*. A *heirmos* and its *troparia* made up an ode. Nine such odes made up a *kanon*, which was performed after Psalm 50 in the Orthros.

It is presumed that in an actual service the *kanon* was sung in full during the Middle Ages (at present it is seldom sung except for high holidays). After the third ode there was a brief intercalation of another type of hymn (*hypakoe*) and a collect; after the sixth ode a *kontakion* (actually, as we saw, only the *prooemium* and first *oikos* or stanza) was inserted, together with the reading about the saint of the day. Depending on the festivity and the type of church there could have been additional elaboration after the seventh and eighth odes, when singers would make a small procession in the centre of the church and sing jointly (rather than antiphonally, as they had performed the individual stanzas). In subsequent centuries additional hymns were appended to the *kanon* making its performance even more elaborate.

Kanon poetry, and therefore the musical composition of the *kanon*, enjoyed great popularity from the eighth century until well into the twelfth; and even in later periods, if only in isolated instances, *kanons* were still being written. Compared to the *kontakion*, the *kanon* as a whole presented a musical enrichment of the services with its nine melodies, one for each ode, even though stylistically these melodies were far less melismatic than the *kontakion* (at times even syllabic). In a full performance of a *kanon*, the congregation was confronted with nine melodies instead of the single—albeit melismatic—melody of the *kontakion*; and the danger of stylistic sameness was avoided by the insertion of the *hypakoe* after the third ode and the *kontakion* after the sixth. What *kanon* and *kontakion* have in common is the principle of the model stanza—used in other types of chants as well.

STICHERA

Besides *kanon* and *kontakion*, there were numerous hymns, frequently consisting of a single stanza. These short poems, dedicated to an individual saint's memory, were chanted in the course of the proper services—either the Divine Liturgy or Esperinos, or Orthros. Most of these short hymns are known as *stichera* (singular, *sticheron*). This term, which seems to refer essentially to the fact that 'verses' are involved, is probably derived from an expression meaning 'short paraphrase in verse', something akin to *syntomon sticheron*. In subsequent centuries *stichera* came to be designated with additional terms reflecting their derivation; thus *sticheron idiomelon* (or simply *idiomelon*) had a melody of its own and was not related to other *stichera*. On the other hand, an *automelon* had a tune that could have been used for paraphrases with different texts; finally *prosomoion* meant that the *sticheron* in question was modelled on a pre-existing *sticheron*, in melody if not in text. As happened with the *kanon*, *stichera* continued to be composed throughout subsequent periods. New ones might be composed even today, as hymns to newly canonized saints, but the chances are that most of the recent productions are based on old models, and there are no truly new *idiomela* in current practice.

HYMNOGRAPHY UNDER THE RESTORED EMPIRE

In the turbulent history of the Byzantine Empire, the thirteenth century brought troubles that disrupted the continuous development of Byzantine hymnography. In 1204, at the behest of the Venetian mercantile interests, the western European knights assembled for the Fourth Crusade, besieged and conquered Constantinople, and established what came to be known as the 'Latin Empire', which lasted until 1261. Then the Greeks managed to reconquer their capital and re-establish the Byzantine Empire for another two centuries until its final collapse under the Turkish onslaught. So far as music is concerned, it appears that this was a period of stabilization of traditional melodies, and of the firm establishment of a new stage in musical notation that had just been accepted by most of the scribes in the last decades of the twelfth century—what is now called the Middle Byzantine neumatic notation. Beginning with the late thirteenth century the number of names of musicians and composers recorded as authors of chants increased substantially. Yet in the area of poetry no new forms appeared, at least not of the type of poetry that would have been chanted.

It is believed that in the earlier stages of the development of Byzantine music poet and composer were almost invariably the same person. For this latest stage of the history of the Byzantine Empire there are indications that poets no longer wrote the music; at the same time the musicians seemed to be content to use pre-existing texts, seldom creating their own texts to go with their new melodies. There are, of course, exceptions to this trend, and some poets did write texts to pre-existing melodies.

Liturgical studies are needed to confirm the impression, gained from purely musical manuscripts of this later period, that the services, especially Esperinos and Orthros, were becoming more and more elaborate (presumably more so in monastic communities than in parish churches). There was a concomitant growth of musical compositions which, as far as can be ascertained, had no further significance than to serve as 'time-fillers', often using nonsense syllables. What could have prompted the extension in time of the services for which these dozens, if not hundreds, of so-called *kratemata* were being composed? Most of their 'text' consisted of nonsense syllables such as 'te-re-re', 'ti-ti-ti', or 'to-to-to', and their musical features seem curious in the few examples so far explored. There seems to be a hint of some higher level of musical organization, yet at the present time no systematic study of these works is available to confirm such a hypothesis. It seems clear that their function was to extend existing chants in order to make them last longer. *Kratemata* were assembled in a *kratematarion*; they were also called *teretismata* or *anagrammatismata*.

In the increasing variety of styles of music represented in musical manuscripts of the last two centuries of the Empire, there is an increasing number of musical compositions requiring a virtuoso manner of singing, as well as much more intricate types of melodic settings—even of hymns, which were at first intended to be performed in a stately, more dignified fashion. This process of embellishment, commonly designated *kalophonia*, gave rise to 'embellished *stichera*' or 'embellished *heirmoi*' as well by the sixteenth century, when special manuscripts with this type of repertory began to appear. One is tempted to say that a baroque style had come to Byzantium before it manifested itself in the West.

LITURGICAL BOOKS AND THEIR USE

There were relatively few types of strictly musical manuscripts in use in the Greek Orthodox Church; they were supplemented by a larger number of types of non-musical manuscripts that regulated the liturgy, and some basic knowledge of these is necessary in order to understand the application of the chant.

Basic for most churches is the *Typikon* (τυπικόν), which determines the solution of all potential conflicts in case of the simultaneous occurrence of more than one feast (for example, if the Annunciation falls on Good Friday). We say 'for most churches', since there is a great deal of variation in instances of some monasteries founded by either members of imperial houses or feudal lords; also, there are variances which are accepted and approved either by the founder or by the fact of a church being dedicated to a particular saint, in which case the celebration of the patron saint has precedence over a number of lesser feasts, as ruled by the *Typikon*. In addition to solving problems of this nature, the *Typikon* also deals with some details of the daily ritual. Although the profusion of *Typika* for various churches founded by donors throughout the centuries may suggest a bewildering array of rules, it is nevertheless possible to state that these differences, on the whole, are less significant than the similarities. In effect, one basic *Typikon* has been in use since approximately the twelfth century; it is of Palestinian origin (from the Lavra of St Sabas), and was adopted by the Constantinopolitan Church.[19] Its predecessor as a basic rule in some of the Constantinopolitan churches was the so-called 'Rule of the Studios Monastery', which had considerable influence on the beginnings of ecclesiastical practices among the Slavs.

The *Menaion* (μηναῖον) is a book for one month containing in the ideal case all the services for that month. A set of twelve *Menaia* comprises all the feasts and full services for each day of the church year, except for the movable feasts and their dependent and related days. In a full *Menaion* are listed the texts of all prayers and hymns, with or without musical notation; in addition the texts of the proper prayers, and also of the lives of saints are given. The *Menologion* (μηνολόγιον) is another collection of the lives of the saints, arranged in the order of the church year—which, incidentally, in Byzantine practice starts on 1 September. An abridged collection of the lives of the saints is known as the *Synaxarion*, which is used daily at Orthros since at least one saint is commemorated every day of the year.

The *Euchologion* (εὐχολόγιον), the name of which is derived from the Greek word for 'prayer', is not only a collection of prayers but in its fullest form contains the complete ritual for the priest and deacon with instructions for their performance of the ritual services; in addition it contains the full text of the three basic liturgies in use in the Greek Church.

The *Prophetologion* (προφητολόγιον) contains lessons from the Old Testament; in a sense it can be called a lectionary, and contained at one time a set of signs which, although having no real musical significance, did give the reader some idea of voice inflections for the solemn readings.

The *Apostolos* (ἀπόστολος) contains the readings from the Acts of the Apostles and from Epistles, mostly those of St Paul.

The *Evangelion* (εὐαγγέλιον) is the text of the Gospels from the New

---

[19] An edition of a *typikon* with commentary and glossary by J. Mateos, *Le Typicon de la grande église, Orientalia Christiana Analecta*, 165/166 (Rome, 1962).

Testament. There are two types of *Evangelion*: one is the full sequence of the four Gospels, and is known as the *Tetraevangelion*; the other is that of the readings from the Gospels in order of the church calendar in the course of a year, and is referred to as the *Evangelistarion*.

The Psalter (ψαλτήριον) contains the 150 'Psalms of David' divided into twenty *kathismata*. Each *kathisma* is in turn subdivided into three *staseis* containing from one to five psalms. At the end of the Psalter, according to an old tradition, are attached the so-called 'Psalms outside the Psalter', namely the fourteen biblical Canticles.

The *Parakletike* (παρακλητική) is an important book for the study of hymnography as it contains the proper hymns for Offices as well as for the Divine Liturgy in the course of the church year. It is usually divided into eight segments, each of which is chanted in one particular mode (or *echos*, as it was called in the Byzantine tradition); thus the whole set contains the hymns of the *octoechos*, that is, of the system of the eight modes. There are other hymns proper to the day of the week; thus a specific hymn would be sung each Monday. Such hymns would be sung in a different mode each week depending on which mode was required in the sequence of the *octoechos*. Understanding these complex musico-calendric systems is one of the cantor's difficult tasks.

The *Horologion* (ὡρολόγιον) is basically a 'book of the hours', with some later additions.

The *Triodion* (τριώδιον) contains the Offices for Lent. Its name is derived from the fact that most *kanons* in that season contain only three odes in *daily* services except for Saturdays and Sundays. This manuscript can be musically notated.

The *Pentekostarion* (πεντηκοστάριον) represents the continuation of the *Triodion* for the rest of the movable part of the church calendar, covering the period from Easter Sunday to the first Sunday after Pentecost. This book very seldom contains musical notation.

While only some of the preceding books contain musical notation (e.g. *Menaia*, *Triodia*), the others are nevertheless necessary to a cantor in the Byzantine tradition since the musical books do not necessarily contain the full texts of hymns, and it is for these that one has to have recourse to volumes without musical notation. More books that usually contain musical notation are listed below.

The *Heirmologion* (εἱρμολόγιον) contains the *heirmoi* (the model stanzas for odes in a *kanon*). In many *kanons*, the second ode is missing, for it was a long-standing tradition to omit it. The reasons for this remain obscure; not one of the explanations offered so far has proved satisfactory. The number of medieval manuscripts of the *Heirmologion* preserved with musical notation is relatively small—

barely forty in all. One possible explanation for this rather small number is that manuscripts of this type were used daily, hence became worn out and fell apart, leaving only a few to be preserved for posterity.

The *Sticherarion* (στιχηράριον) is a bulky volume when preserved in its entirety. It may best be described as a musical equivalent of the *Menaion*, as it contains the proper hymns for every day of the church year arranged in the order of the calendar starting with 1 September. An examination of the *Sticherarion* also reveals the fine point that each day in the Byzantine tradition started with Esperinos and ended in the afternoon on the next day. In addition to the cycle of the twelve months, a full *Sticherarion* also contained proper hymns for Lent and the period beyond Easter to the feast of Pentecost (the equivalent of *Triodion* and *Pentekostarion*). Furthermore, a *Sticherarion* also contained some hymns from the *octoechos* and other special groups of hymns. The number of medieval *Sticheraria* still in existence goes into hundreds (probably more than 600); no systematic study with an overview of all existing manuscripts has yet been attempted. In later centuries some segments of the *Sticherarion* became separate books, yet even these have not been investigated by modern scholarship. Strunk refers to the 'standard abridged *Sticherarion*', stating that the abridgement became effective in the mid-eleventh century; at present there is no available study dealing with the non-abridged version of this type of manuscript nor of the repertory that became eliminated in the process.

Both types of musical manuscripts, *Heirmologion* and *Sticherarion*, contain melodies which are essentially syllabic or mildly melismatic. In the case of later sources, especially from the fifteenth century onward, there are copies of each of these types containing 'embellished melodies' of highly melismatic character. This process of embellishment, or *kalophonia*, seems to represent in some of its manifestations a process of de-composition of the original melodic style, and the growth of a style of professional singing whose aim appears to have been to impress the audience with vocal artistry and virtuosity rather than to convey the message of the text, which had been the main function of chanting in the earlier periods of Byzantine chant.

The two following types of musical manuscripts are from an earlier period, the twelfth to fourteenth centuries. They contain highly melismatic melodies for the Divine Liturgy. One of them was intended for the soloist(s), the other for the highly trained choir of accompanying singers used in the larger churches.

The first of these, the *Psaltikon* (ψαλτικόν), was a book for the *protopsaltes*, the soloist, and is preserved in only eight copies. The second, the *Asmatikon* (ἀσματικόν), was a book for the professional choir, containing significant parts of the liturgical chants; it is preserved in only six copies. These small numbers in no way represent the true significance of these manuscripts; if anything, their significance is in inverse proportion to the number of copies preserved. The *Psaltika* contain sizeable portions of the soloistic repertory including *kontakia* and the responsories for the liturgies. Among the types of chants copied in the *Asmatikon*, the most profusely represented are the Communion chants, *koinonika*—besides the refrains for some of the soloistic chants represented in the *Psaltikon*.

At about the beginning of the fourteenth century still another type of musical manuscript came into existence. Known as *Akolouthiai* (ἀκολουθίαι), it contained the Ordinary chants for Esperinos and Orthros as well as for the three basic liturgies, including the Cherubic hymns and Communion chants. It appears, perhaps deceptively so, that the *Akolouthiai* type of manuscript came into existence as a substitute for the missing *Asmatika*. Much more work is necessary to provide a clear picture of the orderly succession of the various types of musical manuscript in the Byzantine tradition.

THE CONCEPT OF MODE IN BYZANTINE CHANT

The Byzantine term that is the equivalent of 'mode' is *echos* (ἦχος). This term may be found in some of the oldest manuscripts containing texts of hymns, dating perhaps as early as the seventh century (these hymns are to be sung, even though the manuscripts contain no musical notation).[20] It seems clear that at this stage the term *echos* meant 'melodic pattern' or 'formula', rather than 'scale'. Within the body of Byzantine chant there are eight *echoi* that constitute a system called *octoechos*. Contrary to earlier opinions that the *octoechos* may have been documented as early as the beginning of the sixth century, it now appears that the earliest reference to it dates from the seventh century if not the eighth.[21]

Some of the earliest information about the *octoechos* comes indirectly from the adaptation of this system in the Latin West. In the

[20] The earliest reliable document containing a reference to a 'mode' appears to be Papyrus Rylands 466, believed to date from the seventh century. Cf. Colin H. Roberts, ed., *Catalogue of the Greek and Latin Papyri in the John Rylands Library*, iii (Manchester, 1938), 28–35.

[21] The origin of the eight modes as a system in Byzantine and other Mediterranean traditions is an unsolved problem. It was mistakenly believed, by Wellesz and others, that the earliest reference to the *octoechos* was to be found in the writings of Severus of Antioch. It is now generally agreed by scholars that the formation of a system is of later date, and is probably of Byzantine origin. See p. 6 and Husmann, 'Oktoechos', *New Grove*, xiii. 524.

eighth or ninth century, Latin chant was classified according to a
system of eight modes; chants which had the same melodic endings
were regarded as being in the same mode. The character of the eight
modes was illustrated by a set of eight *echemata*, each *echema* being a
phrase of melody. According to the earliest witness, the theorist
Aurelian of Réomé (*c.* 850), the eight modes were grouped in pairs,
each pair including an 'authentic' (higher) and 'plagal' (lower) mode.
The four pairs were designated by Greek terms, *protus*, *deuterus*,
tritus, *tetrardus* ('first', 'second', 'third', 'fourth'). In the western
system, these four terms designated the final note, and these became
located on the scale as D, E, F, and G. Eventually the pitch content of
each mode was expressed as a scale, and the term 'mode' was
transferred to these scales. (These scales were given the names from
Greek antiquity 'dorian', phrygian', 'lydian', 'mixolydian', but there
was no correspondence of pitch content between the two systems.)
The usual way of referring to the modes of the West is by number,
from one to eight. A conspectus of different terminologies and
numberings is given in Table 1.

TABLE 1 Terminology and Numbering of Modes

Early definition	Western numbering	Later name	Final tone	Byzantine	Slavic
Protus authentus	Tonus 1	Dorian	D	Echos I	Glas I
Protus plagalis	2	Hypodorian	D	I pl.	V
Deuterus authentus	3	Phrygian	E	II	II
Deuterus plagalis	4	Hypophrygian	E	II pl.	VI
Tritus authentus	5	Lydian	F	III	III
Tritus plagalis	6	Hypolydian	F	III pl. (barys)	VII
Tetrardus authentus	7	Mixolydian	G	IV	IV
Tetrardus plagalis	8	Hypomixolydian	G	IV pl.	VIII

With the advent of Byzantine musical notation in the tenth century,
some of the notational signs began to be used to designate the specific
modes. It seems that the numeral alone was insufficient to indicate
the tonal framework of the mode, and so neumes were added to the
number to indicate the endings of the melodic formulas specific to the
mode; these endings, apparently, were sung as intonations before
the piece of chant itself was begun. These intonational neumes along
with the modal number are called—in modern times—*martyriae*, but
this term has not been found in medieval sources.[22]

[22] For some examples of shapes and combinations of the *martyriae* see Wellesz, *A History of
Byzantine Music and Hymnography*, p. 302.

In the Byzantine tradition the *echoi* were not regarded as scales until the end of the fifteenth or sixteenth century. And even then the range of any given melody is not restricted to the octave-segment specific to its *echos*. Furthermore, there is usually more than one final per *echos*. These variable uses confirm the impression that in the earlier stages the *echos* was not a scale but rather a set of melodic formulas. It has been the experience of scholars studying Byzantine chant in the manuscripts that the use of melodic formulas is one of the most basic features of the chant, and one of great assistance in transcribing from neumed sources.[23]

Discussion of what we regard in modern times as problems of music theory are strangely absent from the surviving treatises written during the Byzantine Empire. There are some treatises available, but they do not deal with contemporary musical practice; rather they are relatively long compendia of Ancient Greek theory. They do not in any way reflect music as it was practised in the lifetimes of their authors, but instead discuss music as one of the liberal arts and mainly in terms of mathematical proportions.[24]

Much closer to the practice of the Byzantine cantors are the relatively short *papadike*, which contain lists of neumes and basic indications for their chanting and basic meaning. In some manuscripts, one may find a song appended with a text consisting of a simple catalogue of names of neumes. This 'learning song' has been attributed to John Koukouzeles,[25] and if this attribution is correct, it again shows an attempt, more than 120 years after the majority of the notational signs had been introduced, at making the meaning of the neumatic notation more understandable.

Finally, as regards solmization syllables, Byzantine medieval music knew of no such device; the syllables *pa*, *vou*, *ga*, etc. are all nineteenth-century inventions. The presence of terms like *ananes* suggests their use as intonational devices; but all attempts to discover their meaning remain fruitless. One of the curious features added to Byzantine chant in its later periods (still some time before 1500) is the set of signs called *phthorai*, interpreted as 'modulation signs'.[26] They

[23] See Nanna Schiødt, 'A Computer-Aided Analysis of Thirty-five Byzantine Hymns', *Studies in Eastern Chant*, 2 (1971), 129.

[24] Lukas Richter, 'Antike Überlieferungen in der byzantinischen Musiktheorie', *Deutsches Jahrbuch der Musikwissenschaft*, 6 (1961), 75; see also his 'Fragen der spätgriechische-byzantinischen Musiktheorie', *Byzantinische Beiträge* (Berlin, 1964).

[25] See Gabor Devai, 'The Musical Study of Cucuzeles in a Manuscript of Debrecen', *Acta antiqua Academiae scientiarum hungariae*, 3 (1955), 151; see also his review of other sources, 'The Musical Study of Koukouzeles in a 14th-Century Manuscript', ibid., 6 (1958), 213.

[26] Conomos, 'The Treatise of Manuel Chrysaphes', *Proceedings of the XI. International Musicological Society Congress, Copenhagen 1972* (1974), ii. 748.

are most often encountered in longer compositions and seldom appear in shorter chants. The *phthorai* indicate a departure from one *echos* and a 'modulation' to another. While in recent years considerable progress has been made in our understanding of the use of the *phthorai*, it seems that additional studies are still required for a full grasp of their implications.

NEUMATIC NOTATION

During the last few decades it has been customary to say that the origins of the Byzantine musical notation are to be sought in the prosodic (that is, accentual) signs of the Greek grammarians of the Hellenistic age, presumably in Alexandria. Yet this assumption runs into far too many obstacles. For one thing, in the tradition most closely associated with Alexandria, the Coptic, the prosodic marks do not appear in any of the manuscripts believed to contain traces of texts to be chanted. Thus any reference to the Alexandrian grammarians must remain an unconfirmed hypothesis.

The earliest reference to signs which may have had some implied musical meaning appear in texts intended for solemn readings, dating from about the fifth century. By the eighth century such signs became systematized, though there was still no way of writing down the 'flow' of a melody or detailed indication of the change of pitch in an individual syllable of text. What this so-called ekphonetic notation did indicate was the use of stresses in some specific segments of text, sentences to be brought out in reading, and an occasional cadential stop. Some of the signs of the ekphonetic notation show some graphic resemblance to signs which were to appear later in a purely musical type of neumatic notation. It is worth noting that recent research has pointed out the resemblance of some of the ekphonetic signs to those in use in the Masoretic versions of the Hebrew Old Testament. Egon Wellesz also believed he had detected links between the ekphonetic signs and the Syriac accents.[27]

The ekphonetic notation was copied consistently down to the seventeenth century, when the meaning of the signs may have already been forgotten. The most important listings of these signs appear in two manuscripts of the eleventh and twelfth centuries: Sinai 8 and Leimonos 38, both of which have been studied by Carsten Hoeg. Intended as an aid for the solemn readings, this was not a real musical notation.[28]

---

[27] A more recent study, incorporating previous findings on the relations of Masoretic signs and Byzantine neumes, by E. J. Revell, 'Hebrew Accents and Greek Ekphonetic Neumes', *Studies in Eastern Chant*, 4 (1979), 140.

[28] See Gudrun Engberg, 'Ekphonesis', *New Grove*, vi. 99–103.

A system of neumes with musical meaning emerges in Byzantine manuscripts only around 950, although it may have existed at an earlier date, since the earliest known manuscript already shows a fairly elaborate system of signs. This stage, called 'Early Byzantine notation', was in use from the mid-tenth century until approximately the last quarter of the twelfth. It is by no means a unified system of neumes, and underwent steady evolution leading to increasing con-sistency in the use of specific signs. In this period there were actually two systems of neumes in use. These systems are now named after the French collections of manuscripts in which the representative samples were first observed and studied in the course of the present century: the 'Chartres' notation and the 'Coislin' notation. These co-existed for some two hundred years, then the Coislin eventually prevailed and evolved by the 1170s into the more specific, elaborate system called 'Middle Byzantine notation'. The Chartres type receded, except for a few signs which continued in modified form beyond the twelfth century.

Early Byzantine notation still presents problems for scholars. In the first place it is not an easily and immediately readable notation; in fact it can be read reliably only with the help of later sources that support the shapes and sequence of neumes observable in sources of the 'Early' notation. At the outset, neumes were used sparingly and not even above each syllable of text. By the middle of the eleventh century, however, the melodic intention becomes much clearer as each syllable of text is given a single neume of its own.

Even at this early stage it is possible to observe what was to become the fundamental rule of Middle Byzantine notation, namely that the signs designate melodic movement in terms of direction and size of intervals. It is not a pitch notation in terms of specific pitches with specific names. It cannot be stressed strongly enough that *no medieval manuscript contains a single indication about absolute pitch*. The basic principle of Byzantine notation is intervallic. Yet one of the crucial features missing in this Middle Byzantine notation is indication of the exact sizes of intervals: there is nowhere an indication of the difference between major and minor intervals of the same type (for instance, thirds). The neumes simply designate the intervals of a second, or a third, and that is all. It is in such instances that knowledge of the melodic formulas and of the *echoi* comes to the rescue. In oral transmission, of course, the singer knows when to use the various sizes of intervals he is to sing; the majority of cantors in most churches of the Greek-speaking world were professionals who had learned the basic repertory from their teachers and knew most of the melodies by heart. Manuscripts were used sparingly, mostly as reminders for the proper hymns chanted once a year. Chants that were required to be performed much more frequently were memorized and were repeated without recourse to a musical manuscript. Continued dependence upon oral transmission meant the continuing possibility of variants in any given melody, so that even with neumatic notation there is no way of knowing the one and only version of any of the chants. Manuscripts do reveal a great number of variants even in copies from the same scriptorium or even in identical types of manuscripts copied by a single scribe.

In addition to the signs for intervals, the Coislin system also had some semblance of signs for rhythmic values (longer and shorter), as well as suggestions for agogic principles. These signs were presented in an ingenious as well as economical system that could be memorized with a minimum of effort. The problem of determining the starting pitch from which the subsequent intervals would be chanted was solved by the intonation formulas, which appear in elaborate as well as abridged forms. As these formulas were memorized, the modal framework of any given *echos* was instantly available to the singer, and the chanting could then proceed, as already mentioned, at the pitch level that was most agreeable to a singer's own range.

MIDDLE BYZANTINE NEUMES

The neumes of the Middle Byzantine notation, in use from the late twelfth to the fifteenth century, can be described briefly as follows. First of all, the signs for the melodic movement are divided into two basic groups, one containing the so-called 'bodies', the other the 'spirits'. The first of these, the 'bodies', move stepwise only, which for practical purposes means that they indicate the interval of a second either upward or downward. 'Spirits', on the other hand, indicate movement by leap; only two intervals are spelled out in the listing of neumes, a third and a fifth, again with special neumes for upward and downward motion. By skilfully combining 'spirits' and 'bodies' one can obtain any other needed interval. There are no fewer than six different signs for the ascending second, indicating a variety of agogic nuance.

In the Middle Byzantine notation a curious principle was applied with regard to the 'bodies' and 'spirits'. The basic rule required that no 'spirit' could stand alone without its 'body': while 'bodies' can stand alone and have a clear meaning of their own, no 'spirit' should be presented without its own 'body' to hold it and present it, as it were. When notated alongside each other—that is, a grouping of two

neumes in which the left one is a 'body' and the right one a 'spirit'[29] —
the body does *not* count as an interval, but lends its support to the
'spirit' for its own intervallic value. Thus a *kentema* (movement up a
third) preceded by an *oligon* (movement up a step) represents merely
movement up a third. When, however, the 'spirit' is placed on top of
the 'body', the intervallic values of the signs are added: thus a *kentema*
on top of an *oligon* indicates a movement up a fourth. In this way the
intervals of the fourth and sixth were obtained and the direction
(ascending or descending) was determined by the use of the appropriate neumes.

Besides these signs there are others which do not belong to either of
the two groups. One, of tremendous importance, is the *ison*, which
designates the repetition of a tone on the same pitch as that of the
preceding tone. With the appearance of this sign in the mid-eleventh
century a giant step was made toward the perfecting of Middle
Byzantine notation. Other signs indicated either the lengthening of the
rhythmic values or slight nuances in the tempo.[30]

The agogic signs started to proliferate from the thirteenth century
onward. A much later tradition credits the fourteenth-century musician Koukouzeles with the invention of these signs, and the Greeks
call them to this day as 'kukuzelian notation'. There is, however, no
basic difference in the use of neumes from the late twelfth and
thirteenth centuries and those from the fifteenth and even later
centuries. What does become noticeable, according to Stathis (who is
the only serious scholar of sources from the post-Byzantine period) is
the 'resolution' of these signs into ordinary neumatic notation revealing a highly melismatic style which remained 'hidden' in previous
centuries.[31] In other words, there is no proof that Koukouzeles
invented these signs though such a possibility cannot be excluded.

As already mentioned, Koukouzeles is also the presumed author of
the 'learning song' or 'school song' in which, as the cantor enunciates
the name of a neume in the text, he also executes its melodic motion
and in that way demonstrates the melodic meaning of each neume.
Some of the names of agogic neumes still leave something to be
desired so far as clarity is concerned. These *megalai hypostaseis* ('great
hypostaseis' or 'substances') may have been instrumental in introducing refinements into the singing, yet at times their presence poses

---

[29] The medieval scribes did not always observe this sensible rule, and there are innumerable
examples of 'spirits' standing alone without their respective 'bodies'; yet their absence does not
prevent proper interpretation and transcription.

[30] A reliable survey of notations is by Max Haas, 'Byzantinische und slavische Notationen', in
Wulf Arlt, ed., *Paleographie der Musik*, I/2 (Cologne, 1973).

[31] See Stathis, 'An Analysis of the Sticheron *Tov*', p. 182, No. 20, and pp. 187–9.

TABLE 2 Basic Neumes in Middle Byzantine Notation

Neume	Name	Result
	Ison	Repetition of a pitch
	The 'bodies'	Movement by step, up or down
	Apostrophos	Movement a step down
	Oligon	Movement a step up

Additional signs for stepwise upward movement with stress

	Name	Result
	Oxeia	Some stress
	Petaste	More stress
	Pelaston	More stress
	Kouphisma	With a shake
	Dyo Kentemata	
	The 'spirits'	Movement by leap
	Elaphron	Movement a 3rd down
	Chamele	Movement a 5th down
	Kentema	Movement a 3rd up
	Hypsele	Movement a 5th up

These are normally combined with bodies, either the simple unstressed ones:

	Name	Result
	Apostrophos + Elaphron	3rd down
	Apostrophos + Chamele	5th down
	Oligon + Kentema	3rd up
	Oligon + Hypsele	5th up

or with the stressed ones:

	Name	Result
	Oxeia + Kentema	3rd up with stress
	Oxeia + Hypsele	5th up with stress

Other skips are shown by combinations of spirits placed *on top* of bodies:

	Name	Result
	Elaphron + Apostrophos	4th down
	Chamele + Apostrophos	6th down
	Kentema + Oligon	4th up
	Hypsele + Oligon	6th up
	Hypsele + (Oligon + Kentema)	7th up
	Hypsele + Kentema + Oligon	8ve up

Signs indicating length

	Name	Result
	Diple	Double length
	Dyo Apostrophoi	Double length (downward only)
	Kratema	Longer, with slight stress
	Tzakisma	Longer by half
	Apoderma	'Fermata'

Some of the signs for stress or length can be combined with Ison to indicate repetition of pitch with stress or length.

	Name	Result
	Ison + Oxeia	Repetition with stress
	Ison + Petaste	Repetition with more stress
	Ison + Tzakisma	Repetition, longer by half
	Ison + Diple	Repetition, double length
	Ison + Kratema	Repetition, double length with stress

problems of accuracy in transcription and their investigation requires considerably more work before the meaning of each can be precisely ascertained.

The basic notational principles of Middle Byzantine notation, as found in the musical manuscripts written from a little before 1200 until around 1500, remained essentially the same in later centuries as well, in the period of the so-called Late Byzantine notation—from mid-fifteenth century until the beginning of the nineteenth. At that time a radical reform of neumatic notation did indeed take place, eliminating many of the neumes and aiming at the creation of uniformity by using, for the first time, printed books and neumes in movable type rather than handwriting.

A listing of basic neumes appears in Table 2 above, and a chant from a relatively simple manuscript in Ex. 6.[32] A comparison of the neumes in the chant and the procedure used in the example will illustrate the basic principles of this notation and of its transcription.

Ex. 6

The chant in Ex. 6, in the fourth plagal mode, is the first ode in a new *Akolouthia* (early term for *kanon*), paraphrasing the song of Miriam, 'Let us sing to the Lord'. The *martyria* indicates the starting pitch as C, from which one counts for the chanting of the melody. The first neume above the first syllable is a *petaste*, which means a second upward with a stress, followed by an *apostrophos*, indicating a descending second; thereafter an *ison* on top of a *petaste* cancels the upward movement, hence the pitch is repeated but with the added

---

[32] Grottaferrata Heirmologion, Epsilon Gamma II, fo. 250ʳ.

stress of the *petaste*. The fourth neume is an *apostrophos* with an appended *tzakisma* extending its length. A simple *apostrophos* follows, lowering the pitch one step; an *oxeia* with a *tzakisma* points to an upward second with some extended duration and stress, and the last syllable of the word 'Ky-ri-o' has an *apostrophos* and *dyo apostrophoi*, which means there are two tones on that syllable, first one descending second and then another, the second one with extended duration. This brings us to the end of the first line of the transcription. By observing the meanings of the neumes in Table 2 and comparing them with the remainder of the transcription, the principles of the process will become clear.

EXAMPLES OF BYZANTINE CHANT

The best known chants are those for the Trisagion and the Cherubic Hymn, both from the Liturgy; examples have been published by Dimitri Conomos and Kenneth Levy.[33] In addition, Communion hymns often give singers as well as communicants opportunities to enjoy extended displays of musicianship.

The difference in musical effect from one mode to another can be conveniently illustrated by an ordinary chant from the Esperinos service, Psalm 140.[34] Ex. 7 shows only the opening exclamation, 'O Lord, I call to thee', as sung in each of the eight modes. The reason an ordinary chant such as this may be sung in any one of the eight modes is that beginning with Easter certain parts of the Office are governed by the *octoechos*, the cycle of the eight modes, each mode 'ruling' for a week. An ordinary chant such as Psalm 140 would be sung in the ruling mode from Esperinos at one Saturday until the next Saturday. (Certain chants proper to saints' days, however, are always sung in the mode in which they were composed; hence there may be a variety of modes present in any particular service.)

As transmitted in the manuscripts, chants show numerous variants due either to regional traditions or to changes in taste and style over the centuries. Both kinds of variants can be easily demonstrated. Ex. 8 gives the chant 'Theos Kyrios' ('God is the Lord'), which is sung at the Orthros after the hexapsalmos, from a fifteenth-century manuscript.[35] Ex. 9 shows the first two words of the 'Theos Kyrios' in five different versions: (i) the traditional version that appears in the majority of manuscripts in a stable form; (ii) a version from manuscripts representing practice in Constantinople; (iii) a version from the monastic

---

[33] See Conomos, *Byzantine Trisagia*; Kenneth Levy, 'A Hymn for Thursday in Holy Week', *JAMS*, 16 (1963), 127.
[34] Athens National Library, MS 2458, fo. 36ʳ.
[35] Athens National Library, MS 2406, fo. 56ʳ.

Ex. 7

Ex. 8

Ex. 9

tradition (without reference to a specific monastery); (iv) a local variant from Thessaloniki, which became a significant centre of musical practice in the course of the fourteenth and fifteenth centuries, and (v) a version from the monastery Vatopedi on Mount Athos. As can be seen, these versions have a considerable amount of melodic movement in common, yet each has an individuality of its own.

Ex. 10 shows two versions of the same chant, 'Theos Kyrios', in the fourth plagal mode, from two manuscripts, one copied in 1336, the other more than a century later in 1453.[36] The example demonstrates on one hand the endurance of the tradition, and on the other the changes in taste embodied in the slight variants. The melodic skeleton remains the same in the two versions, and the variants may represent the idiosyncrasies of a singer or copyist.

All these examples illustrate the basic types of chanting as practised in Byzantine musical tradition: the syllabic, neumatic, and melismatic. According to the traditional division of the repertory, syllabic chants include primarily the *heirmoi*; but in addition a sizeable number of *stichera* are also chanted in syllabic style, as are most of the psalm verses. Ex. 6 showed a *heirmos*; Ex. 11 shows a *sticheron*, in this case for the feast of Prophet Daniel (December 17), found in most *Sticheraria*; there is minimal use of more than one note per syllable of text (the example is less than a fourth of the whole piece).[37]

---

[36] Athens National Library, MS 2458, fo. 75ᵛ and MS 2406, fo. 48ʳ.
[37] Composite transcription on the basis of several *Sticheraria* from the thirteenth century.

Ex. 10

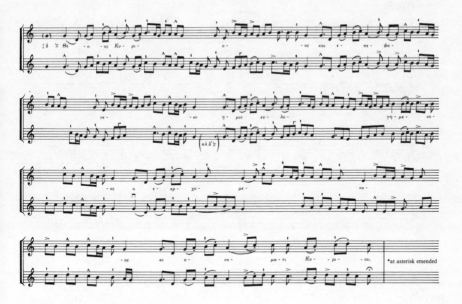

Ex. 12 contains several different stylistic elements. It shows settings by three composers of verse 33 of Psalm 103, the Prooemiac Psalm from the beginning of Esperinos.[38] The first six syllables are set in identical fashion by the three composers, in the manner of simple psalmodic recitation, using the recitation tone of mode IV plagal, with the whole step above for accented syllables. Since melodic formulas for the recitation of psalms are generally not noted in manuscripts, we have to infer them from the kind of recitation included in composed settings such as those of the example, which come from the fourteenth century. Studies on Byzantine psalmody have shown the close relationship of textual and musical stress; while Byzantine psalmody has many similarities with western psalmody, they are by no means identical.[39]

In all known settings of this verse from the Prooemiac Psalm for Esperinos, the last few syllables of the hemistich are set melismatically

[38] Athens National Library, MS 2406, fos. 24ᵛ–25ʳ.

[39] See especially Oliver Strunk, 'The Antiphons of the Oktoechos', *JAMS*, 13 (1960), 50; Velimirović, 'The Prooemiac Psalm', p. 317. See also Edward V. Williams, 'John Koukouzeles' Reform of Byzantine Chanting for Great Vespers in the Fourteenth Century' Ph.D. diss., Yale University 1968), 195–6 and 436–7, for a discussion of borrowings from composer to composer.

Ex. 11

MODE II

ύ" πνευ - μα - τι - κως η - μας πι - στοι συ - νη - γα - γε ση - με - ρον

ο προ - φη - της Δα - νι - ηλ και τρα - πε - ζαν προ - τι - θη - σιν

α - ρε - των δα - ψι - λως· πλου - σι - οις και πε - νη - σι και ξε - νοις

και αυ - το - χθο - σι· και κρα - τη - ρα νο - η - τον·

προ - ε - χον - τα να - μα ευ - σε - βει - ας. Και ευ - φραι - νον - τα

καρ - δι - ας πι - στων· Και πνευ - μα - τος

Α - γι - ου χα - ριν πα - ρε - χον - τα

(*en te zoi mou*, 'as long as I shall live'). Here the three different settings vary substantially. Then follows the preparation for the doxology (*lege*, in parentheses, sung by the cantor); then the doxology, beginning *doxa soi* ('Glory be to thee'), a kind of line that in this particular tradition follows each hemistich of the psalm. These added texts vary in wording but especially in melodic setting: in II, by Agathonos Koronis (mid-fourteenth century) the long repeated high notes on the word *doxa* are unusual if not unique. Few examples more directly

Ex. 12

Ex. 13

reflect the enthusiastic exclamation glorifying the deity—at the top of the range and with an obvious feeling of rejoicing.

Similar and yet peculiar in its own way is Ex. 13 which, in the manuscript, carries an indication that it is composed in 'the Latin manner' (*kata latinon*).[40] The text is half-verse 24a of Psalm 103, 'Countless are the things thou hast made, O Lord'. It includes, after the syllabic opening and the melismatic last three syllables of the psalm verse, the doxology, which begins with a glorification of the Holy Spirit and ends with the Trinity.

Perhaps the most typical for the Near East in general and for the Byzantine practice in particular are the highly melismatic chants, as opposed to the mild melismata that intrude into the syllabic state-

---

[40] Athens National Library, MS 2406, fos. 24ᵛ–25ʳ.

ments of many other chants. The most typical example of the Byzantine melismatic tradition is the *kontakion*. Although studied by a number of scholars, the number of *kontakia* at present available in print is relatively small.[41] The inclusion here as Ex. 14 of a transcription of a *prooemium* to a *kontakion* for the feast of St Thecla will serve as an additional example of the style.[42] As in so many other examples, the principle of melodic formulas is basic to the composition of melodies in use in the Byzantine tradition, as may be clearly observed in one *kontakion* after another. The formulaic structure of the chants is especially obvious when one observes the cadential formulas, and, of course, the openings of the individual pieces. In the transcription of the *prooemium* of the *kontakion*, of St Thecla, similar melodic segments have been copied one beneath the other to show the melodic relationships of individual verses and lines. The interweaving of the various melodic segments presents an extremely intricate pattern; a general survey of these patchwork structures is still a desideratum for future studies in Byzantine chant.

Since the use of texts, whether biblical or not, may be considered the norm for music in the liturgical services of the Greek—or Latin—Church, the presence of the *kratemata* presents an extremely curious challenge in their meaningless syllables, such as 'te-re-re'.[43] Up to the present there has been no systematic study of these chants; occasional samples, usually brief, have been included in some published transcriptions. One of the curious features of the *kratemata* is the fact that they are often labelled with unusual names, such as *viola*, *polemikon*, or *semantron*, etc. A piece with a particularly unusual title, *tatarikon*, 'in the manner of the Tatars', is shown in Ex. 15.[44] Examples of so-called 'Persian' music have already been published,[45] and these examples 'after the Latins', and 'after the Tatars', provide material for further study.

---

[41] For some examples, see Wellesz, *Trésor de musique byzantine* (Paris, 1934), and *Die Musik der byzantinischen Kirche, Das Musikwerk*, 15 (Cologne, 1959).

[42] Florence Bibl. Laurenziana, Cod. Ashburnham. 64, fo. 51ʳ.

[43] See Conomos, *Byzantine Trisagia*, pp. 261–86.

[44] Vatopedi MS 1495, fo. 338ʳ.

[45] Velimirović, 'Persian Music in Byzantium?', *Studies in Eastern Chant*, iii (1973), 179 ff.

Ex. 14

Ex. 15

'ποίημα τοῦ μαΐστορος λέγεται ταταρικόν'

Byzantine chant offers numerous challenges to the student through the variety of problems it presents. A separate problem, untouched here, is the relationship of the Byzantine melodies and their principles of musical organization to the traditions of Western Europe, as well as to closer neighbours—not only the Slavs, but perhaps more significantly the eastern and southern neighbours, something that has never yet been subjected to scholarly scrutiny. And last, but by no means least significant, is the problem of the aesthetics of Byzantine music, which must eventually be raised.

RUSSIAN CHANT

As is the case with most Near Eastern traditions of chants, there are no authentic medieval melodies of Russian chant in existence. There are numerous traditions, and a belief that the tunes currently in use are derived from ancient times or, as some singers claim, have been passed on from generation to generation in 'unchanged forms'—an assertion that modern scholarships can no longer accept without some nagging doubts.

The term 'Russian' chant is applied to the Eastern Slavs in general and their traditions of chanting in the services of the Russian Orthodox church.[46] Christianity penetrated what is now the territory of Russia perhaps as early as the ninth century. (There is a tradition that attempts to link the land with the Apostolic period as well, but the Slavs did not inhabit these areas in those earliest times.) The official date of the conversion of the Slavs is 988, when Prince Vladimir of Kiev accepted Christianity and ordered his subjects to follow his example. Since his conversion was politically motivated (he received a Byzantine princess as a bride), the spread of Christianity took some time to become fully accepted; the first missionaries were Greeks who also occupied prominent positions in the church hierarchy. The acceptance of Christianity was facilitated by the availability of basic texts of the Scriptures and of service books, which had been already translated into the so-called 'Old Slavonic' language in the third quarter of the ninth century by the 'apostolic brothers', Constantine (as a monk, Cyril) and Methodius, whose activities were centred among the Western Slavs in Moravia. Nevertheless, with the support of the Russian ruler Yaroslav 'the Wise' (reigned 1019–54), according to the 'Russian Primary Chronicle', an extremely intensive activity was organized in Kiev and many more books needed for the maintenance and spread of the new religion among the Slavs were translated.

The references in chronicles are fully supported by documentary evidence, though not of that early date. The earliest preserved musical manuscripts, in Old Slavonic and with musical notation, prove without any doubt that these sources, although dating from as early as the end of the eleventh century (but mostly from the twelfth and later centuries), retain the shapes of the Byzantine neumatic notation, which was in its developmental stage of about the middle of the eleventh century (Early Byzantine notation).[47] Accepting not only the texts for the religious services but the melodies as well, the Russians copied them unchanged into their books with the new language. While it is natural to expect that some changes would take place (as they did), it is still amazing to encounter instance after instance of

---

[46] See 'Russian and Slavonic Church Music', *New Grove*, xvi. 337.

[47] One of the basic works is Velimirović, *Byzantine Elements in Early Slavic Chant: The Hirmologion, Monumenta musicae byzantinae*, Subsidia, 4 (1960).

extremely clever and skilful adaptations of the texts to fit the structure of the melodies, with the result that stresses appear in both languages at basically the same places in a given hymn.

On the basis of comparative studies of the neumatic notation in Byzantine and Slavic musical manuscripts, it can be stated without the slightest doubt that all notational principles in use in Byzantium were transferred to Russia at first with the same meaning as among the Greeks. Since, however, this stage of the 'Coislin' notation is not readable alone (though individual examples may be worked out), the melodies in Russian transmission remain for all practical purposes unknown, and involve much guesswork as to their outlines as well as their details. The curious point in the transmission of this notation in Slavic sources is that, being on the periphery of the intellectual life of the period from the tenth to the fourteenth centuries, Slavic manuscripts preserved (or at least tried to preserve) the notation unchanged as if it were a matter of religious dogma. Yet there is no doubt that in the course of time melodies underwent transformation, and in Byzantium the neumatic notation itself was showing more precision than the earlier stages could offer. One of the indirect proofs that the notation began to require special explanation by the fifteenth century is the proliferation at that time of special *azbuky* ('alphabets') containing catalogues of neumes and explaining their meanings. Thus it is clear that the original interpretations must have become uncertain, and new meanings must have created doubts among the singers as to the actual correctness of the chanting.

Besides the mainstream of musical manuscripts of Russian provenance there is a small group of five manuscripts and a fragment of a sixth known as *kondakaria*, containing *kontakia* and an unusual notation which in some of its signs resembles the Early Byzantine 'Chartres' notation. In spite of recent claims that a clue for a transcription has been found, it remains enigmatic, as the examples studied are ambiguous, and attempts to transcribe other *kontakia* by the same method have not produced convincing results.[48]

In short, prior to the sixteenth century, when new trends make possible more successful interpretations and transcriptions, the only aspect of Russian chant that can be studied is the notation, though one is not necessarily able to obtain reliable transcriptions.

The investigation of remaining sources is made more difficult by the vagaries of Russian history. While there is a sizeable number of

---

[48] While Constantin Floros has presented some interesting examples in 'Die Entzifferung der Kondakarien-Notation', *Musik des Ostens*, 3 (1965), 7–71 and 4 (1967), 12–44, a testing of his method, currently in progress, has not yet confirmed all of his results.

manuscripts from the twelfth century, and a few from the thirteenth, the number diminishes to practically nothing of great value by the end of the thirteenth century and the beginning of the fourteenth, when Russia was invaded by the Tatars. Manuscripts start proliferating again in the fifteenth century, and increase to almost astronomical numbers in the sixteenth, when Russia began to become a power to be reckoned with in the political and military history of Eastern Europe. Thus the link between the early sources and the later ones is a very tenuous one.

Russian scholars have stated insistently that the melodies in use in the Russian church were very strongly influenced by folk-song. While this is unquestionably easy to observe in the present-day tradition (which presents a blend of trends and influences of the last few centuries), there is at present no documentary evidence of the melodic shapes of folk-songs in the Middle Ages, though ethnomusicological studies may offer some clues, as well as suggestions for future investigation of this problem. In addition, Russian churchmen (akin to some modern Greek counterparts) have tried to link the 'immutability' of the religious services with the 'unchangeability' of melodies that accompany the religious ritual. While there is no doubt that in some aspects the melodies of the fixed services may be transmitted faithfully, there is also no doubt that in any living religion there are always changes and variations. What passes as 'Russian chant' in the twentieth century is a conglomerate of influences, most of which are of a later date than the Middle Ages.

PART II

Christian Chant of the Western Churches

III

LATIN CHANT OUTSIDE THE ROMAN TRADITION

By KENNETH LEVY

DURING the centuries before the Carolingian Emperors imposed a single, ostensibly Roman, liturgical and musical usage throughout their domains, the various regions of Western Europe were served by distinctive local plainchant repertories. Four such repertories have come down to us essentially complete: (1) the Frankish-Roman, so-called 'Gregorian' chant that was spread during the sixth to eighth centuries from Rome, then during the eighth and ninth centuries from the Frankish centres of liturgical diffusion to become the universal plainchant dialect of the Latin Church; (2) the Urban-Roman or 'old Roman' chant, the chant used at Rome itself up to the late twelfth century; (3) the Milanese or 'Ambrosian' chant, used in the dioceses of Milanese Lombardy; and (4) the Hispanic, Old Spanish, Visigothic, or 'Mozarabic' chant of the Iberian peninsula. Vestiges of some other chant dialects have survived from the Beneventan and Campanian zones of southern Italy as well as from the Abruzzi, Ravenna, and other regions of the Italian centre and north. From outside Italy there are traces of the 'Gallican' chant that was native to the West Frankish kingdom until the later eighth century, and of the 'Celtic' chant that made its way to the Continent with the early Irish missions. If the unifying ideal of the Carolingians had been rigorously carried out, there would be none of the earlier dialects remaining other than the Frankish-Roman. But liturgical traditions die hard, and the European regions held on to certain local usages even after they were nominally expunged.

It was the neume-notation that preserved the vestiges of local chant even while it spread the Frankish-Roman music. The notation arose, perhaps during the late eighth century, certainly by the early ninth, and at some place 'between the rivers Seine and Rhine'.[1] The neumes

[1] E. Cardine, 'A propos des formes possible d'une figure neumatique', *Festschrift Ferdinand Haberl zum 70. Geburtstag* (Regensburg, 1977), 68.

of the ninth to early eleventh century remained staffless and clefless, essentially unheighted, transmitting only the outlines of the melodies as a memory-aid for singers who already knew how they went. With the more careful heighting and the lines and clefs that were introduced during the eleventh and twelfth centuries it became possible to transmit the full melodic substance of the chants. Three of the four complete repertories that have reached us—the Frankish-Roman, Urban-Roman, and Milanese—are transmitted in unambiguous heighted notations. The fourth, the Old Spanish repertory, survived until the later eleventh century, only long enough to be enshrined in the early imprecise stages of notation, so that for the Spanish chants there are just melodic skeletons without the flesh of pitches. The relics of Old Beneventan chant survived until the borderline of notational precision was reached in the eleventh–twelfth century. For the other dialects there are stray bits, sometimes transcribable as melodies, sometimes not.

To judge from what is preserved, the remote pre-history of the Latin plainchant dialects saw a certain common fund of musical materials spread among various local tradition. How much material there was in common is hard to determine since the rule of plainchant dialects is that each local usage imposes its own stylization on received melodic materials, leaving only a meagre trace of what went before. There are, for example, palpable Old Italian archetypes behind certain corresponding chants of the Frankish-Roman, Urban-Roman, and Milanese dialects, but the actual melodies have undergone so much local retouching that none of the detail of the 'original' may be preserved.

What the various Latin chant dialects have in common above all else is an agreement on broad principles of musical behaviour that are bound up with the shape and function of the liturgy the music embellishes. There is a common order for the chants of the Proper of the Mass, and to some extent also a common nomenclature (see Table 1). Corresponding liturgical functions tend to have the same kinds of music in the parallel liturgies. This can involve the same kinds of text (psalmodic, hymnodic, prose); in some cases the same specific text; the same choice of style (syllabic, moderately florid, florid); the same practice of performance (antiphonal, responsorial); in some cases the same choice of musical mode.

BENEVENTAN CHANT

The Beneventan zone of south Italy, centred in the once-powerful Lombard Duchy of Benevento, encompassed most of the southern

TABLE 1: Proper of the Mass

	Gregorian and Urban-Roman	Beneventan	Ambrosian	Mozarabic	Gallican
Entrance Chants	Introitus	Ingressa	Ingressa	Prae-legendum	Prae-legendum?
With the Lections	Graduale Tractus Alleluia, Verse	Graduale Tractus Alleluia, Verse	Psalmellus Cantus (Lent) Alleluia, Verse Ante-Evangelium Post-Evangelium	Psalmo (or Psalmellus) Clamor Threnos Alleluia, Verse ('Laudes')	'Respon-sorium' (?) Ante-Evangelium
Offertory	Offertorium	Offerenda	Offerenda	Sacrificium ad Pacem	Sonus, with 'Laudes'
Communion	Communio	Communio	Con-fractorium Transit-orium	ad Con-fractorium ad Acce-dentes	ad Con-fractorium Trecanum (?)

third of the Italian peninsula during the seventh to ninth centuries. On the South, only the tip of the Apulian heel and Calabrian toe were excluded. At the northern extremity the Beneventan zone reached almost to Rome. The chief ecclesiastical and cultural centres in the southeast were Brindisi and Bari; the line along the Adriatic coast ran from Trani and the Gargano to Chieti; on the Tyrhennian coast, northwards from Salerno through Naples, and as far as Gaeta and Terracina. Benevento itself lies to the east of Naples, while some hundred kilometres to the north, perched on a noble ridge of the Abruzzi, is the monastery of Monte Cassino, the mother house of the Benedictine Order. Founded in 529, Monte Cassino continued to dominate south-Italian spirituality, particularly during the eleventh century. In the year 788 a military victory by the Franks united the Beneventan zone to the Carolingian monarchy and set the stage for the suppression of the local musical rite and the importation of the Frankish-Roman musical usage. However the bond with the Germanic north remained a shaky one in the face of a continuing Saracen threat, and the Beneventans continued to be as closely allied with the Byzantine Emperor as they were with the Franks. The zone remained a cohesive artistic and cultural entity through the twelfth century. For a while its influence extended as far as the Dalmatian coast.

There is no more striking evidence of the refinement of Beneventan art than the distinctive script adopted for the writing of manuscripts and official documents. This so-called 'Beneventan script', beginning in the eighth century, represented an elegant stylization of the pre-Caroline minuscule book hand. The hundreds of manuscripts and fragments using this script were inventoried by the paleographer E. A. Lowe. They include a large number of liturgical books and fragments, which unfortunately begin only with the tenth–eleventh century so that their musical content represents almost exclusively the Frankish-Roman practice. There is no complete Sacramentary preserved with the prayers of the Old Beneventan rite, nor is there any complete manuscript of the Old Beneventan Gradual or Antiphoner. A single folio survives of what was apparently a full Old Beneventan Gradual, containing the end of the Christmas music and the beginning for St Stephen's day. Otherwise, Old Beneventan music is found in mixed documents that are basically Frankish-Roman, though with vestiges of the local rite holding on at certain points in the liturgical year. The most substantial sources of Old Beneventan Mass music are the manuscripts VI.38 and VI.40 of the Biblioteca Capitolare at Benevento; they transmit the music in a carefully heighted notation that is, however, without clefs or consistent lines so that the specific pitches often remain uncertain.

Altogether, there is old music for some two dozen feasts of the Beneventan calendar—Christmas, St Stephen, certain days in Lent, Palm Sunday, Maundy Thursday, Good Friday, Holy Saturday, Easter, the Archangel Michael (8 May), Ascension, Pentecost, John the Baptist, Peter and Paul, Lawrence, the Assumption, the feast of the Twelve Brothers, Martyrs (1 September), the Holy Cross, All Saints, Martin, and Andrew. Thus nearly all the major Beneventan feasts have preserved Mass music. Also found in manuscripts of the region are certain pieces of local origin, chiefly Alleluia verses, that are not in the typical Old Beneventan style but rather are compositions of the tenth to twelfth centuries in a regional 'New Beneventan' style that is distinguishable from the standard Frankish-Roman.

The rapid decline in vigour of the Old Beneventan practice can be traced in the liturgical provisions for three occasions. (1) In the year 760 the relics of the Twelve Brothers, Martyrs, reached Benevento and a feast was instituted in their honour. By that date some of the vitality had obviously gone out of the local musical tradition since the music assigned to the feast was not newly composed but simply arranged from existing Old Beneventan music for older, established feasts. (2) The latest addition to the Beneventan calendar that still receives Old

Beneventan music is the feast of All Saints, whose universal observance on 1 November seems to date from the time of Gregory IV (827–
44). As with the feast of the Twelve Brothers, the Beneventan music
for All Saints is arranged from existing pieces, not newly composed.
(3) In about 838, under Prince Sicard of Benevento (832–9), the relics
of St Bartholomew were translated from their temporary location in
the Lipari Islands to Benevento itself, where a church to house them
was begun and a new Mass was instituted.[2] The music supplied in this
case was no longer Old Beneventan at all, but Frankish-Roman. The
transition to the new rite was complete, then, during the early ninth
century. But some of the old practices hung on. When Stephen X was
the Abbot of Monte Cassino before being elected Pope in 1057, he still
felt obliged to forbid the use of non-Roman styles of music at the
monastery. He was successful there, for practically no traces of Old
Beneventan music remain among the Monte Cassino manuscripts.
What is preserved comes from elsewhere.

The Old Beneventan music has a generally Italianate character and
a specific stylization of its own. The feeling for the local musical syle
was strong enough that when a chant was inherited from some older
melodic tradition or borrowed from elsewhere the local style was
generally overlaid upon it. The Old Beneventan dialect is closest
musically to the Roman dialect, its neighbour to the North. But in
liturgical peculiarities and with regard to the choice of specific texts,
Benevento has closer ties with Milan than with Rome. It shares with
most Italian dialects the preference for gently sloped rather than
angular melodic lines, with stepwise motion predominating. The
generalities of Old Beneventan musical style have been ably summarized in works by Dom Bonifacio Baroffio.[3] The chants are mainly
centonate.[4] Their melodic fabric is made up of small units whose
primary attachment is to specific levels of pitch in the tonal system. A
good many of the melodic units reappear and are recombined in all
classes of Beneventan chant. There are a small handful of cadence
formulas, applied in both medial and final positions. A distinctive
feature of the Beneventan musical dialect is the use of repeated
podatus figures (two notes, ascending by a step) in recitation passages.

---

[2] The date of 808 given for this translation in *Paléographie musicale*, 14, pp. 450 f., is evidently
incorrect; the translation took place under Sicard, Prince of Benevento from 832–9: cf. *JAMS*,
23 (1970), 221, n. 100.

[3] B. Baroffio, in K. G. Fellerer, ed., *Geschichte der katholischen Kirchenmusik*, i (Kassel, 1972),
204–8. A comprehensive analytic edition of the corpus of chants in preparation by Thomas F.
Kelly, will provide the basis for future study.

[4] This term, derived from *cento* (patch), was originally applied to verbal texts put together
from various sources; it has come to be applied to chant melodies constructed in an analogous
fashion.

The repeated *podatus* fills the same function in the Beneventan repertory that the repeated *torculus* (three-note turns) fills in the Urban-Roman repertory. Beneventan chants are generally limited in their melismatic thrust to a moderately florid style. Long melismata are uncommon. There is nothing approaching the lengths of plainchant melismata north of the Alps, in Spain, at Milan, or even at Rome. Oddly, the longest Beneventan melisma comes from a Communion (for the feast of John the Baptist). And the 'antiphonal' Communions and Introits (Ingressae) tend to be more prolix than the 'responsorial' Alleluias and Offertories—just the opposite of what happens in the other liturgies.

The Beneventan system of modality can be determined only approximately because of the clefless notation and unsure pitch-heighting. It seems that the Old Beneventan rite used a smaller number of modes than eight for its Mass music. (The psalmody of the Office is unfortunately unknown.) There may have been just two large families of modal formulas, corresponding to the paired plagal and authentic forms of the Gregorian modes on G and D. The apparent narrowness of Beneventan modal usage makes the repertory seem archaic, but it is clear that a variety of liturgical and musical impulses went into its formation.

The Old Beneventan Ingressa for Maundy Thursday (Ex. 16[5]) begins with a typical recitation on a repeated *podatus*. The music goes on to a melisma (A) on [Domi-]*nus*, then to one of the standard

Ex. 16

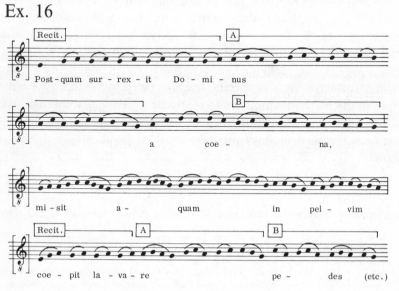

[5] *Paléographie musicale*, 14, p. 276.

Beneventan cadences (B). This series of elements (recitation, melisma, cadence) is repeated five times in the course of the long piece, which ends with an elaborate free passage. The Old Beneventan Ingressa for Pentecost (Ex. 17[6]) begins with the leap of the rising fifth, G to D, which is typical of the high G mode in all plainchant dialects. The chant is built out of common Beneventan centonate formulas and ends with an extensive Alleluia that it shares with the Ingressa for Easter Sunday. The Ingressae for Maundy Thursday (Ex. 16) and Pentecost (Ex. 17) have not only their texts but something also of their basic musical material in common with parallel chants of the Milanese repertory (see Exx. 26 and 30 below), but in each case overlaid with the characteristic local stylization.

Ex. 17

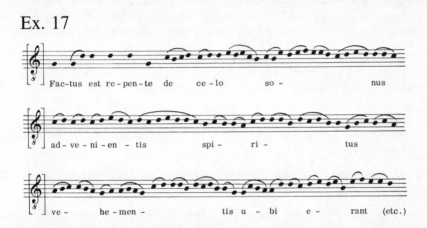

Fac-tus est re-pen-te de ce-lo so- nus ad-ve-ni-en-tis spi-ri- tus ve- he-men- tis u-bi e- rant (etc.)

Only half a dozen Old Beneventan Graduals are preserved, in diverse melodic styles. The two Graduals for Lent are long and florid.[7] The nine Old Beneventan Alleluias for which full music is preserved are all adaptations of the same basic melody, in both their refrain and verse. That melodic model is carefully accommodated to the different lengths of text and different accentuations, using the same techniques employed with such 'typical models' in other repertories. The Alleluia 'In conspectu angelorum' (Ex. 18[8]) is designed for the feast of St Michael on 8 May, a celebration particularly prized in South Italy

---

[6] MS Benevento, VI. 40, fo. 79[v]. Cf. below, p. 85.

[7] *Paléographie musicale*, 14, pp. 265, 282.

[8] Alleluia refrain: MS Benevento, VI. 38, fo. 53. Alleluia verse, *In conspectu*, MS Benevento, VI. 38, fo. 83; facs.: Bruno Stäblein, *Schriftbild der einstimmigen Musik, Musikgeschichte in Bildern*, iii/4 (Leipzig, 1975), 143.

Ex. 18

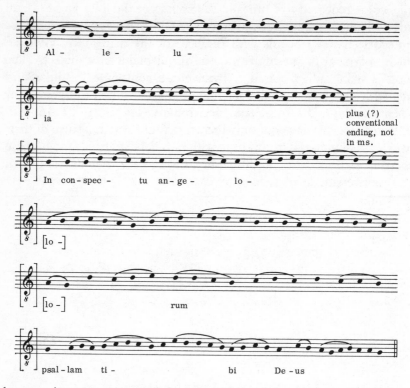

because it commemorated the apparition of the Archangel on Monte Gargano in the year 492 or 494.

The Old Beneventan Offertories number about twenty, and are melodically quite modest and short. Only the Offertory for St Lawrence has a verse. The text of the Easter Offertory, 'Angelus Domini', is the only one that is used as an Offertory in other rites (Ex. 19[9]). Here again is the typical *podatus* recitation at the start, followed by the repetition of chosen passages later on. The melodic elements are again shared in centonate fashion with other chants.

More than two dozen Old Beneventan Communions are preserved, in a variety of styles. The Communion for the Easter Vigil, 'Hymnum canite agni mundi' (Ex. 20), is a relic of an archaic Italian Mass for the newly baptized, whose musical provisions have practically disappeared at Rome although they persist in scattered fashion among the Central Italian, Ravennate, and Milanese traditions as well as at Benevento.[10] This Communion draws on the same fund of centonate

---

[9] MS Benevento, VI. 38, fo. 53.
[10] *Paléographie musicale*, 14, p. 446; cf. *JAMS*, 23 (1970), 183 ff.

Ex. 19

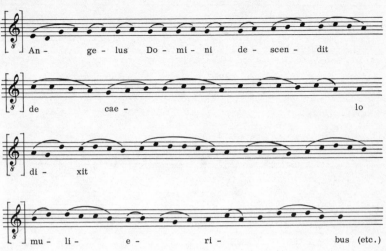

Ex. 20

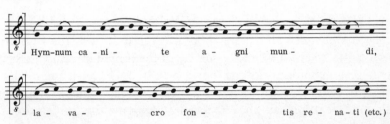

formulas as the more elaborate Communion for Easter Sunday, 'Qui manducaverit'[11] (Ex. 21), which is unique among the Beneventan Communions in having extra verses.

Apart from the Mass music, there are a small number of Beneventan ordinary chants, processional antiphons, responsories, and antiphons. The Office chants are poorly represented outside Holy Week. One of the most striking Beneventan traditions is the florid chant of the 'Exultet', accompanying the lightening of the Paschal Candle at the Easter Vigil. The Beneventan 'Exultet' music has a spectacular mode of transmission—in richly illuminated *rotuli* or 'Exultet Rolls', whose pictures are spread out for the congregation to view while the chant is being performed.

---

[11] MS Benevento, VI. 38, fo. 52ʳ⁻ᵛ; MS Benevento, VI. 40, fo. 28.

Ex. 21

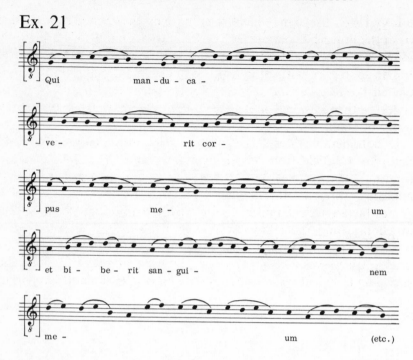

Qui man - du - ca - ve - rit cor - pus me - um et bi - be - rit san - gui - nem me - um (etc.)

CENTRAL ITALY, RAVENNA, AQUILEIA

Beneventan chant's closest neighbour to the south was the Byzantine chant cultivated in the Greek enclaves of the Ionian littoral and Sicily. Its closest neighbour to the north was the Urban-Roman chant, whose developed centonate stylization reveals some of the same Italianate features as the Beneventan chant—the preference for rounded melody, stepwise motion, and the repetitive *torculus* figures for recitations. Apart from Rome, little is preserved of local chant dialects from the central Italian regions of Lazio, the Abruzzi, Umbria, Tuscany, the Marches, Emilia, and Romagna. What remains seems largely to be a spill over from Milan-dominated Lombardy or from the Gallican rite farther north. A repertory of about three dozen antiphons *ante evangelium* are widely but unevenly diffused in central Italy. They were evidently sung between the Alleluia or Sequence and the Gospel. Most of the surviving *ante evangelia* are preserved in manuscripts such as Verona, Bibl. Capitolare, CVII (eleventh century), whose neumes do not permit staff transcription. Fortunately, there are some in later sources such as the tropers of Nonantola.[12] A small handful of *ante evangelium* chants appear in the Milanese

---

[12] G. Vecchi, *Troparium sequentiarium nonantulanum, Monumenta lyrica medii aevi italica, Ser. 1, Latina*, 1/1 (Modena, 1955). [Rome, Bibl. Casanatense MS 1741.]

liturgy. Their usage may have been more extensive in Gaul, to judge from the liturgical commentary of Pseudo-Germanus of Paris (to be discussed later). Another widely diffused group of chants in central Italian sources consists of upwards of a dozen antiphons that accompanied the *fractio panis* at great feasts. They show a miscellany of styles, with occasional archaic features that may again reflect the usage of Gaul.

Of considerable interest is an archaic responsorial tone for the Holy Saturday Canticle from Isaiah, 'Cantabo nunc' (Ex. 22), found in central Italian sources. On liturgical as well as musical grounds it appears to pre-date the familiar Gregorian Tract of the 8th mode, 'Vinea facta est'. The music is preserved in manuscripts from Norcia in Umbria and the region of Pistoia.[13] There is a chance that it represents an old Roman usage for the Canticle. Whatever local practice there was at Rome has already been suppressed among the surviving Urban-Roman sources in favour of the standard Gregorian Tract.

Ex. 22

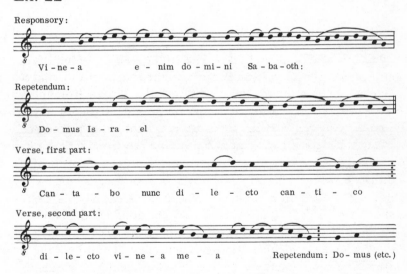

Nine verses follow, set to the verse-tone. The Repetendum 'Domus' completes each verse.

From the environs of Ravenna there are traces of a distinctive local dialect in two chants for the Easter Vigil: (1) an Alleluia with verses of the 135th Psalm, 'Confitemini Domino quoniam' (Ex. 23(i)[14]), and (2)

[13] MS Pistoia, C. 119, fo. 72ᵛ; *MGG*, x (1962), col. 1689.
[14] MS Modena, Bibl. Capit., O.I.7, fo. 101; MS Padova, Bibl. Capit., A.47, fo. 128ᵛ.

Ex. 23

an Offertory (?), 'Qui in Christo baptizati estis' (Ex. 23(ii)), whose cadences and Alleluia refrain share some musical material with the 'Alleluia, Confitemini'. Ravenna was one of the three major ecclesiastical centres of northern Italy during the last years of the Western Empire. It ranked in importance with Milan and Aquileia. The city gained prominence as the Imperial capital under Honorius (402), then fell successively to the Goths (493), Byzantines (540), Lombards (751), Franks (755), and the Papacy (757). The height of Ravenna's political and artistic eminence was reached during the fifth and sixth centuries, but its liturgical autonomy extended through the middle of the eighth century. There may have been a corresponding musical autonomy, but the only likely survivors of a Ravennate Mass formulary from the period before the Frankish conquest are the two chants given in Ex. 23. These chants, along with the Beneventan Communion for Holy Saturday (Ex. 20), are amongst the apparent relics of an early Italian formulary for the neophytes at the Easter Vigil. The Ravennate chants show a distinctive musical stylization, carefully worked, as are the parallel stylizations at Benevento, Rome, and Milan.

An eleventh-century movement of liturgical renewal at Ravenna was centred in the activity of St Peter Damian (1007–72). In an early manuscript collection of his hymns (Vatican lat. 3797) there are some unique musical entries: (1) a noted Mass formulary for St Apollinaris, patron of Ravenna; and (2) a noted Office for St Silvester. These chants may in fact be archaic, but they may also represent the fruit of a latter-day archaizing. Only one other chant is likely to represent a Ravennate practice of the eighth century or earlier. This is the hymn or versus 'Lux de luce Deus tenebris illuxit' (Ex. 24), which was sung at the lighting of the new fire at the Easter Vigil. The Ravennate version of this chant runs to ten hexameters, set to ten repetitions of the same musical pattern.[15] There is also a Beneventan version of the same chant, but with alterations that were made to accommodate it to the sequence-melisma of the Frankish-Roman 'Alleluia, Confitemini Domino'. The Ravenna hexameter version is evidently the older, while the Beneventan provides a unique example of pre-existent hymnodic material being refashioned into an early sequence.

The north-east Italian region of Aquileia and Grado has left indications of a significant liturgical usage, but nothing of musical consequence has turned up there to match the survivals of local chants at Benevento and Ravenna. Aquileia and Grado in early times were patriarchates with metropolitan churches. The earliest preserved musical manuscripts of the region, however, are no older than the

---

[15] MS Modena, O.I.7, fo. 102; MS Padova, A.47, fo. 129; *MQ*, 57 (1971), 48.

Ex. 24

(1) Lux de   lu‐ce De‐us te‐ne‐bris il‐lu‐xit A‐ver‐ni

(2) Ves‐pe‐re   quae pri‐   ma re‐ful‐gens lu‐ce di‐e‐i

(3) Vi‐ctor ab in‐fer‐   ni re‐me‐a‐vit ne‐xi‐bus a‐tris

(4) Sus‐tu‐lit in‐de su‐   os de‐vic‐to prin‐ci‐pe mor‐tis

(etc.)

eleventh century, and they reflect purely Frankish traditions that were carried across the Alps from Austria. The creation of a metropolitan see at Salzburg in the late eighth century doubtless helped to extinguish the liturgical patrimony at Aquileia.

MILANESE OR AMBROSIAN CHANT

Apart from Rome, only Milan and Spain have preserved their complete musical repertories, and only Milan transmits its music in wholly intelligible neumes. The name 'Ambrosian chant' which is generally applied to the Milanese repertory is a misnomer, since the bulk of the music is evidently of later date than that city's great bishop, who reigned from 374 to 397, and since a variety of sources— Roman, Gallican, and Byzantine—have evidently gone into the formation of the repertory. Yet Ambrose, along with his contemporaries Sts Jerome and Augustine, was a Doctor of the Church, and his authority naturally attached itself to the Milanese chant, much as the authority of Gregory the Great was attached to the Frankish-Roman chant. Ambrose was in fact the author of certain Latin hymn-texts that slowly spread among the other Latin liturgies. More than a dozen hymns are now considered to be his, but only four seem securely attributed: 'Aeterne rerum conditor', 'Deus creator omnium', 'Jam surgit hora tertia', and 'Intende qui regis Israel'. The typical Ambrosian hymn-stanza consists of four lines, each running to eight syllables which are generally composed as four iambs, though metric substitutions occur. Such hymns were confined mainly to the Office and were

not officially adopted at Rome until the eleventh century. Furthermore, the melodies transmitted for them are generally late in origin.
Most of the hymns circulate with a number of alternative melodies. As
many as fifteen are known for a single Ambrosian hymn-text,
compounding the problems of authenticity. The melodies thought
most likely to be ancient are those actually sung at Milan itself. In the
case of Ambrose's hymn 'Iam surgit hora' (for the Lesser Hour of
Terce) only one medieval melody is known. It is given in Ex. 25 after
an Ambrosian manuscript of relatively late date (fourteenth century)
now in the Biblioteca Trivulziana at Milan.[16]

Ex. 25

St Ambrose's biographer Paulinus recounts that in the spring of
386, during a quarrel with the Empress Justina, Ambrose shut his
flock and himself in the Basilica Portiana, and 'at this time, antiphons,
hymns, and vigils first began to be used in the Church at Milan'.
According to St Augustine's parallel account, 'the faithful kept guard
in the church ... It was then begun to sing hymns and psalms in the
Eastern manner [Syriac? Byzantine?] so that people should not faint
through weary grief'. Ambrose is accordingly credited with giving the
congregation a larger part in the service, not only through the simple
hymns, but also by adding 'antiphonal' (split choir) singing to the
responsorial psalmody already in fashion. Responsorial chants, sung
mainly by soloists, had only short refrains for the congregation along
with the florid music for soloists. The simpler antiphonal chants
divided the music more equally. Whatever the truth of such accounts,
it is unlikely that much fourth-century music survives in the known
Milanese repertory. The city had a chequered political and ecclesiastical history during the fifth to eighth centuries. It underwent the
influence of the Eastern Church, a migration of its see to Genoa, and a

---

[16] Bruno Stäblein, *Monumenta monodica medii aevi, I (Hymnen)*, (Kassel, 1956), 4. On
Ambrosian hymns, see further 'Syrian chant', in Ch. I; see also Ch. VII.

long period of Lombard rule. In 774 Milan became part of the Carolingian Empire, just in time to be affected by the Frankish-Roman movement of liturgical unity. Still, the Milanese rite, alone among the old Latin rites, has retained its own music in the city and some neighbouring dioceses down to the present.

The complete corpus of Milanese liturgical melodies is preserved in a substantial number of manuscripts with fully diastematic notation, beginning with the twelfth century. The authority of their musical repertory is pushed back to the eleventh or tenth century by a handful of earlier pre-diastematic fragments. A large proportion of the Milanese chants has been edited in modern editions by Dom Gregorio Suñol—the *Antiphonale missarum ... mediolanensis* (1935) and *Liber vesperalis ... mediolanensis* (1939). But non-Milanese material is patched in so that they are comprehensive enough for modern church usage, but unreliable for historical study. As elsewhere in northern Italy, Milan divided its worship between summer and winter churches, and its liturgical books do the same. An excellent complete manuscript of the winter season Mass and Office, dating from the twelfth century, is published in the *Paléographie musicale*, v and vi. While some of the summer chants are reprinted in Suñol's editions, many others remain unavailable.

The musical dialect of Milan is related to the broad Italian family of plainchants, showing general features in common with Rome and Benevento along with some specific interrelationships and borrowings. Some 350 of the Milanese chants share both their texts and basic musical materials with counterpart chants at Rome. They are supposed to be of Roman origin, though given a Milanese musical stylization. There are also traces of Byzantine and Gallican music, more abundant at Milan than in the musical liturgies to the south. The Milanese chants do not conform to the eight-mode system. They allow classification among the four finals on D, E, F, and G, but are not so easily divided between authentic and plagal forms of the mode as found in Byzantine and Frankish-Roman chants. Some classes of Milanese chant do not use all four finals. For instance, the Milanese Mass Alleluias ignore the F modes, as do the Byzantine Mass Alleluias. The Milanese chants generally cover a wider vocal range than those of the southern dialects. They often stretch to a twelfth, and have a tendency to exploit the upper reaches of their register. As with the Beneventan and Urban-Roman chants, the Milanese have a limited repertory of cadences that are applied to various classes of chant. The simple Milanese psalmody, transmitted in relatively late sources, differs from the Roman in having no medial cadences in the middle of its verses. The chants that are freely composed run the usual gamut of melodic densities, from syllabic to moderately florid to melismatic. Milanese melismata at their most developed have an expansiveness that is unmatched elsewhere in the Christian West. Many Milanese chants are built up in centonate fashion from a repertory of small melodic elements that are not the property of the individual chant but of a class of chants or a mode. There is the use of model or 'typical' melodies, where the same music is adjusted to fit a number of different texts. In melodic details, there is much use of small melodic units in varied and sequential repetitions, and there is the Italian preference for stepwise motion. For example, the upward leap of a fifth from D to A, found typically in D mode openings in Frankish and Byzantine traditions, often appears as an F–G–A or E–F–G–A in Milanese and central Italian traditions.

Among the five to six dozen Milanese Ingressae, the majority are related melodically to a corresponding Introit text at Rome. Yet the Ingressa is not—as at Rome—a processional chant. It is sung without psalmody, as at Benevento. The Milanese Ingressa for Pentecost (Ex. 26[17]) shares its text and musical substance with both the Beneventan Ingressa and the Gregorian Communion for that feast.[18] Such conversions of liturgical function are not uncommon between chants such as Introits and Communions that have the same musical density.

Both the Milanese Psalmellus (corresponding to the Roman Gradual Responsory) and the Milanese Cantus (corresponding to the Roman Tract) are florid chants. Milan retained the early liturgical custom of having three scriptural lessons in the opening, didactic part of the Mass ('missa catechumenorum')—the Prophecy, Epistle, and

Ex. 26

Fac-tus est re-pen-te de cae-lo so-nus ad-ve-ni-en-tis spi-ri-tus ve-he-men-tis, u-bi e-rant
(etc.)

[17] *Antiphonale missarum ... mediolanensis*, ed. Gregory Suñol (Rome, 1935), p. 253; MS Milano, Trivulziana, A.14, fo. 54ᵛ.
[18] See Ex. 17 and Ex. 62 in Ch. VI.

Ex. 27

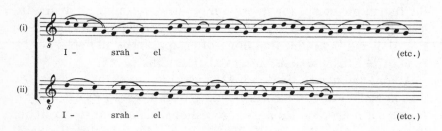

Gospel. Its Psalmellus and Cantus are likely to have found place originally before the Epistle, as is the case with the corresponding chant of the Byzantine liturgy, the Prokeimenon. There is a preference for the G mode among the Psalmelli, while there is no counterpart at Milan for the familiar centonate type of Frankish-Roman Graduals of the F mode. The opening of the Milanese Psalmellus 'Benedictus Dominus Deus Israhel' (Ex. 27(i)), compared with the corresponding Gregorian Gradual (Ex. 27(ii)), both for the season of Epiphany), shows the nature of the musical relationship.[19]

The Milanese Alleluia and Verse, sometimes identified as the *Post-Epistolam*, are melismatic chants that precede the Gospel as at Rome and Byzantium, and they also have various textual and modal-melodic parallels with those other two rites. There are only four common Milanese Alleluia refrains, serving the five to six dozen Alleluia verses. A small number of melodies is likewise used over and again for the verses. The Milanese chants begin as elsewhere with the melismatic refrain on Hallelujah, followed by the verse, then followed by an expanded repetition of the refrain. In some instances there are even two sets of elaborated repetitions, the first of them called the *melodiae primae*, the second set (still more expansive musically) called the *melodiae secundae*. The term *melodia*—in the singular—must

---

[19] Ex. 27(i) *Paléographie musicale*, 5–6; MS British Library, Add. 34209, p. 109; *Antiphonale missarum ... mediolanensis*, p. 66; Ex. 27(ii) *Graduale sacrosanctae romanae ecclesiae* (Rome-Tournai, 1908), 53.

signify the short individual thrusts of melisma that comprise the
elaborate musical organism of the *melodiae*. These progressively
unfolding, structured melismata are built up with ingenious inner
repetition and variation of phrases (see Ex. 28).[20] Similar melismata
are found in the Urban-Roman and Mozarabic sources. They are
most familiar in the repertory of Frankish melismata, added to the
Alleluia repetendum, that play a role in the emergence of the ninth-
century Sequence.

Ex. 28

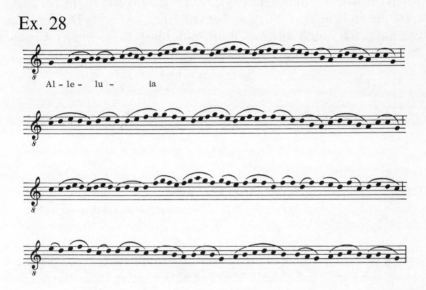

Al - le - lu - ia

The use of an antiphon *ante evangelium* following the Alleluia is
restricted at Milan to just a handful of important feasts: Christmas,
Epiphany, and Easter Week. Such chants are in a modest neumatic
style, and are more common among the central Italian and Nonanto-
lan sources than in Lombardy. The Milanese antiphons *post evangelium*, on the other hand, number about a hundred, and range in style
from the nearly syllabic, like 'Bene annunciavi' for the feast of 25
April, to others that are moderately florid. At least one of the *post-
evangelia*, 'Coenae tuae mirabili', for Maundy Thursday, is a textual
and musical borrowing from the Byzantine rite.

The Milanese Offerenda are related in their selection of texts and
musical style to the Offertory chants of the Roman, Beneventan, and
Hispanic rites. Like their Roman counterparts, the Offerenda are
florid chants with elaborately structured melismata of the same
progressively-unfolding type as found in the *melodiae* of the Alleluias.

[20] *Paléographie musicale*, 5–6, p. 269: [*Melodiae*] *de* [*Alleluia*] *Venite*.

Yet the total number of Milanese Offertories is smaller than at Rome, and extra verses are a rarity. Some Roman Offertories that run to two or more verses for a single feast at Rome are distributed at Milan to different feasts, one Roman verse to each Milanese feast. This is symptomatic of a makeshift nature in the Milanese Offertory provisions. The kind of musical relationship that exists between the Roman and Milanese Offertories can be seen in Ex. 29, which shows the beginning of the Offertory 'Erit [hic] vobis'.[21] This is assigned in the Frankish-Roman tradition to Friday in Easter Week, in the Milanese tradition to Pentecost. For another Offertory, 'Angelus Domini', the comparisons would involve four traditions: Beneventan, Urban-Roman, Milanese, and Frankish-Roman.

Ex. 29

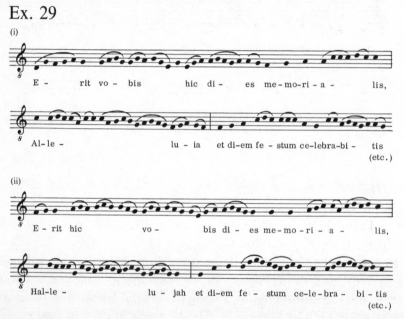

The Milanese *Confractoria* correspond in function with the Roman Agnus Dei. Their liturgical parallels are not with the Communion chants of Rome but with the Fraction chants of other liturgies. Nevertheless, textual and musical borrowings from the Roman Communions account for a number of the Milanese Confractoria, which tend to be in the same antiphon style.

The Communion chants at Milan, properly speaking, are the *Transitoria*, which have diverse origins. Their music is generally simple and many of the texts must be quite old. The Transitorium for

---

[21] Ex. 29(i) *Graduale sacrosanctae romanae ecclesiae*, p. 237; Ex. 29(ii) *Antiphonale missarum ... mediolanensis*, p. 256; MS Milano, Trivulziana, A.14, fo. 55ᵛ.

Easter, 'Venite populi', is likely to be a relic of the Gallican liturgy. The Christmas Transitorium, 'Gaude et laetare', involves a translation of a Byzantine hymn. Another of the Transitoria, 'Qui manducaverit', shares its text with the Beneventan Communion for Easter (Ex. 21). The Transitorium 'Postquam surrexit' (Ex. 30)[22], which is assigned at Milan to Saturday in Easter week, shares its text and a certain foundation of its music with the Beneventan Ingressa for Maundy Thursday (Ex. 16). Both chants may reach back to some early melodic provision for the *pedilavium* at Rome.

Ex. 30

Post-quam sur-re-xit Do-mi-nus   a   cae -   na,

mi - sit   a -quam in pel-vem, cae - pit la - va- re pe -des

(etc.)

CELTIC CHANT

Apart from the Italian peninsula, there are early musical traces of only three Latin rites—the Celtic, Gallican, and Old Spanish. There are none at all of the once-flourishing rites of North Africa, Braga, or Dacia. Even the Celtic rite that was known to St Patrick (d. 461) and St Columbanus (d. 615) has all but disappeared among musical sources. This happened despite the widespread missionary activity of Irish monks like Sts Gall and Columbanus, who during the seventh and ninth centuries spread their native liturgy to England, Brittany, Luxeuil, Switzerland, even Bobbio in north Italy. The original Celtic rite came essentially from Gaul when Ireland was Christianized during the fifth century., But by the later eighth to ninth century Ireland was already substantially dependent upon Roman usage, and after the conquest by Henry II in 1172 the prevailing Roman-English rite was officially imposed.

The early Irish liturgy is known best for the stupendous series of illuminated text manuscripts such as the seventh-century Book of Durrow and early eighth-century Book of Kells (both Gospel-books).

---

[22] *Antiphonale missarum ... mediolanensis*, p. 228; Milano, Trivulziana, A.14, fo. 17ᵛ.

The so-called Antiphoner of Bangor (between 680 and 691) is a service book mainly for the Office, containing the texts of prayers, hymns, and antiphons, but without any music. Among the texts are the Fraction or Communion antiphons, 'Sancti venite', 'Christi corpus sumite', and 'Corpus Christi accepimus'. The latter antiphon, whose origins can be traced to the Greek rite, is preserved in musical traditions at both Milan and Nonantola. The Stowe Missal (after 792) is as elegantly illuminated as the fine Irish Gospel-books. It is the oldest substantial relic of an Irish sacramentary or prayer-book. Its Celtic-Gallican liturgical basis is still apparent, but has been palpably Romanized. Physically it is a small book, designed for the personal devotions of its owner, and it contains only a handful of Mass formularies. Its Litany of Saints preceding the Roman Mass is prefaced by the unnoted antiphon 'Peccavimus Domine'.

Ex. 31

```
I - bunt  san - cti    de    vir - tu - te    in    vir - tu - tem
Al - le - lu - ia,    Al - le - lu - ia,    Al - le - lu - ia
[Vi - de - bi - tur   de - us   de - o - rum   in   Sy - on]
```

All musical traces of the Celtic rite were until recently thought to have disappeared, but two antiphons have been proposed as Celtic relics.[23] One of them, 'Ibunt sancti de virtute in virtutem' (Ex. 31), is an unicum, preserved with music only in Paris, Arsenal MS 279, a thirteenth-century *breviarium plenum* of Norman provenance. The piece has an impressive pedigree. According to the seventh-century *Vita Columbani* this antiphon was sung at Bobbio on 23 November 615 at the Saint's deathbed. After hearing it sung, the soul of Columbanus departed.[24] The other antiphon is 'Crucem sanctam subiit' (Ex. 32), which is found in many medieval Antiphonales, generally assigned to the feast of the *Inventio sanctae crucis*. In the Norman breviary of the Arsenal it appears directly before St Columbanus's 'Ibunt sancti'.[25] Both these 'Celtic' pieces are built on alliterative texts, and they have musical structures that progress, not by the usual process of continuous melodic thrust, but rather they are built up of the repetitions of sections, a procedure uncommon among

    [23] Stäblein, 'Zwei Melodien der altirischen Liturgie', in Heinrich Hüschen, ed., *Musicae Scientiae Collectanea: Festschrift Karl Gustav Fellerer zum Siebzigsten Geburtstag* (Cologne, 1973), 590.
    [24] Ibid. 593.
    [25] Idem.

Ex. 32

Cru - cem san - ctam sub - i - it, qui in - fer - num con - fre - git,

ac - cin - ctus est po - ten - ti - a, sur - re - xit di - e ter - ti - a,

Al - le - lu - ia

Roman antiphons. 'Crucem sanctam' also has a suggestion of rhyme, which is a feature of early Irish hymn texts.

ANGLO-SAXON CHANT

Anglo-Saxon England felt the influence of the Roman rite earlier than most of the rest of northern Europe, and it has accordingly preserved little or nothing of its ancient local usage. In 596 Gregory the Great sent Augustine, the prior of the monastery of St Andrew at Rome, to re-found the Church in England. Before he died in 604–5, Augustine became the first Archbishop of Canterbury. During the seventh century there were heated liturgical debates between England and Rome, but by the time of Bede (d. 735) and Egbert of York (d. 766) these had been ironed out and the English liturgy was thoroughly Romanized. Even the celebrated Lindisfarne Gospels, copied in England around 700, depend for their liturgical tradition on a Neapolitan or Campanian Gospel text that journeyed to England probably during the last third of the seventh century. Thus no certifiable traces of Anglo-Saxon musical usage are known. But one relic of the early Roman chant in Britain is worthy of comment. In the *Vita* of Augustine of Canterbury, and also in the *Historia* of Bede, it is recorded that as Augustine, despatched on his papal mission, was approaching Canterbury, there was sung sweetly the 'letanaliam antiphonam' 'Deprecamur te, Domine, in omni misericordia tua'. The text of this processional antiphon appears in the ninth-century Antiphonales of Compiègne and Senlis, and its musical tradition in a tenth-century manuscript of Noyon. The complete text, as cited by the English histories, evidently existed at the time of Gregory the Great. Two early melodies circulate for it. The one found in England (Worcester) is the earlier attested and the more widely circulated,

appearing also throughout France and northern Italy. Its opening
Ex. 33(i)[26] is in the D Authentic mode, but its modality thereafter is
less conclusive. The other melody, Ex. 33(ii),[27] is in the D Plagal mode
and has a narrower circulation, being found at Klosterneuberg in
Austria and in southern Italy at Benevento and at Sora, north of
Monte Cassino. The same melody is also found with stylistic retouch-
ings in the Urban-Roman tradition. Despite surface differences, it
appears that the two or three melodies may be branches of the same
musical tree. They illustrate the tendency of chants that at first
circulated orally and then in staffless neumes to be transcribed at
different levels in the tonal system—different 'transpositions'—when
they were converted to the staff notation. As to which melodic form
was sung in Britain in 596, it is simplest to suppose that it was the
melody actually found there in the thirteenth century, Ex. 33(i). Yet it
was doubtless a Roman, or perhaps a Campanian, melodic version
that Augustine and his party brought with them to Canterbury. Then
the sixth-century melody may have been like Ex. 33(ii). Or it may be
that the melody sung in the sixth century has since been so thoroughly
modified by later stylization that none of the known versions preserves the original melodic particulars.

Ex. 33

[26] Ex. 33(i) *Paléographie musicale*, 12, p. 227.
[27] Ex. 33(ii) *Paléographie musicale*, 15, fo. 157; MS Vat. reg. lat. 334, fo. 68ᵛ; publ. after MS
Graz 807 in *MGG*, i (1949–61), col. 542.

GALLICAN CHANT

The music of the 'Gallican' liturgy that was sung in France between the fifth and eighth centuries remains the great unknown among the early plainchant repertories. This Merovingian music was cultivated at what became eventually the centre of the Frankish Empire, and so was less resistant than other musical dialects to the Carolingian suppressions and homogenizations of the eighth and ninth centuries. In 753 the Bishop of Metz, Chrodegang, began to impose the Roman practice, and it would appear that only a small handful of Gallican chants, tucked in among the Frankish-Roman chants in later French manuscripts, survived the reforms begun then. Some other chants that still circulated later on in the Milanese and Old Spanish repertories may also reflect Gallican usage. But the total amount of music that can reasonably be considered Gallican remains quite small. Even the liturgical provisions of the Gallican rite of the sixth to eighth centuries can be reconstructed only approximately. There was none of the unity of practice that later was typical of Rome. The chief sources of the early rite in Gaul are the works of St Caesarius of Arles (d. 576) and St Gregory of Tours (d. 594), along with two anonymous writings, formerly attributed to St Germanus of Paris (d. 576), which represent the local rite of a Burgundian church during the seventh or early eighth century, perhaps that of Autun. These sources furnish no more than an approximate idea of the Gallican Mass ordo, and they are quite inadequate for the Office.

The music of the Gallican Mass began with an *Antiphona ad praelegendum* and its accompanying psalmody. What may be a survival of that usage has been singled out in one of the principal Frankish-Roman repositories of Gallican materials, a Gradual from the region of Albi (Paris lat. 776). The chant 'Prosperum iter faciat' (Ex. 34) appears there among other chants that are Carolingian and Roman. It is an alternative entrance chant for the Mass 'pro iter agentibus'.[28] As an element of a votive Mass it was perhaps under less pressure than the Masses of the Temporale and Sanctorale to give way to the newer Frankish-Roman provisions.

A deacon's monition to silence and attention was followed by the series of chants related to the three biblical lections. (As at Milan, there was a Prophetic Lection before the Epistle and Gospel.) The first of these chants was the *Trisagion*. In the Gallican rite as in the Milanese, the Gloria in excelsis appears, not at Mass but at Lauds,

---

[28] Stäblein, 'Gallikanische Liturgie', *MGG*, iv (1955), col. 1302 (after MS Paris lat. 776, fo. 135ʳ).

Ex. 34

Pro - spe - rum i - ter fa - ci - at no - bis - cum de - us no - ster

an - ge - lus do - mi - ni bo - nus co - mi - te - tur no - bis - cum

et be - ne di - spo - nat i - ti - ne - re no - stro

ut i - te - rum cum gau - di - o re - ver - ta - mur ad pro-pri-a

and its approximate place in the Mass is taken by the Trisagion, which is sung both in Greek and Latin: 'Sanctus Deus, Sanctus fortis, Sanctus et immortalis, miserere nobis'; *Agios o Theos, Agios ischyros, Agios athanatos, eleison imas.* Pseudo-Germanus calls this the 'Aius', thus rendering accurately the pronunciation in Byzantine Greek. The Trisagion served as an ordinary chant at just this point in the Byzantine Mass—the Divine Liturgy. It was one of a number of Greek or perhaps originally Syriac features that went into the Gallican liturgy at an early date. No ostensibly Gallican music is preserved for the Trisagion, but it is widely supposed that the Trisagion chant that appears in the Roman Good Friday service of the Adoration of the Cross made its way there from Gaul. The chant is shown in Ex. 35(i).[29] An authoritative Byzantine tradition for the Trisagion melody is shown in (ii). This thirteenth–fourteenth century version was sung at the *Epitaphios*, the ceremony of the cloth icon on Holy Saturday morning. The Roman and Byzantine musical traditions agree tolerably well on what appears to be an embellished modal recitative. The Gallican chant may have reflected this same tradition.

The Trisagion was followed in the Gallican Mass by the Kyrie eleison, recited or sung in a modest musical style by three boys. Next came the Canticle of Zachary (Benedictus; Luke i, 68–79), or in its place during Lent, the chant 'Sanctus deus archangelorum'. No

---

[29] Ex. 35(i) *Paléographie musicale*, 15, fo. 117ᵛ. Ex. 35(ii) MS Milano, Ambros. grec. 476, fo. 238ᵛ; cf. Kenneth Levy, 'The Trisagion in Byzantium and the West', *Report of the Eleventh Congress of the International Musicological Society* (Copenhagen, 1972) ii. 761.

Ex. 35

(i)

(1) A - gi - os   o The - os   (3) A - gi - os   a - tha - na - tos
(2) A - gi - os   y - schy - ros

(4) E - ley -   son   i - mas

(ii)

(1) Ἄ - γι - ος   ὁ Θε - ός,   (3) Ἄ -   γι - ος Ἀ - θά - να - τος
(2) Ἄ - γι - ος   Ἰ - σχυ - ρός

(4) ἐ - λέ -   η - σον   ἡ - μᾶς

Gallican music is known for these chants. The Prophetic Lection was sung by two choirs in alternation. Then there were two chants connected with the reading of the Epistle. One was the Canticle of the Three Children (the Benedicite from the book of Daniel). The other was a 'responsorium quod a parvulis canitur', most likely an elaborate composition of the sort found in the Gradual and Psalmellus chants of the other rites. The Gallican sources are ambiguous about the position of these chants in relation to the Epistle.

Accompanying the Gospel-book to the ambo there was a procession, and then another procession to take it away. The Trisagion was sung at both those processions, in Greek and Latin on the way in, in Latin only on the return. There is no solid evidence that an Alleluia with verse(s) was sung in connection with the Gospel reading. This is curious since nearly every other rite of the East and West has such a provision. The Burgundian practice described by Pseudo-Germanus mentions an antiphon *ante-evangelium*, which would parallel the handful of such pieces that are found in the Frankish and Milanese books. A likely survival of a Gallican *ante-evangelium* was identified by Gastoué in the chant 'Salvator omnium' (Ex. 36) for the feast of King Dagobert (d. 639), who was the founder of the monastery of St Denis. It is preserved in a thirteenth-century manuscript of St Denis.[30] As it has come down, this chant exhibits a distinctive modality in its

---

[30] Stäblein, 'Gallikanische Liturgie', col. 1308 (facs. of MS Paris lat. 1107), col. 1311 (transcription).

Ex. 36

Sal - va - tor   om - ni - um De - us   pec - ca -   to -   rum

re - gi   no -   stro   par -   ce ....

.... qua - pro - pter   le - to   o - re   di - ca -   mus

om -   nes mi -   se -   re - re

melodic skips and turns of phrase, one that is close to the D Authentic mode of Frankish-Roman chants, and certainly closer to the Gregorian D Authentic than what corresponds to D Authentic among the archaic Italian traditions. This raises an interesting speculation. It may be that this 'Gallican' chant has simply been 'Gregorianized' to suit a prevailing later taste. Or it may be that certain modal-melodic features that are generally recognized as 'Gregorian' should be acknowledged as Gallican. With so little certifiably Gallican chant preserved, there is no way to decide.

Following the Gospel of the Gallican Mass there was a homily. Then came the Preces, and as a conclusion of the 'missa catechumenorum', the formal dismissal of those who were not baptized. For the Preces, a form of litany, there arose a repertory of substantial musical refrains whose traces survive among southern French and Spanish sources. The Preces-refrain 'Dicamus omnes, Domine miserere' (Ex. 37)[31] translates the opening words of the 'Deacon's Litany', which comes at the corresponding point in the Byzantine Divine Liturgy. Perhaps noteworthy is the melodic similarity pointed out by Gastoué[32] between the words 'Dicamus omnes' opening this Preces and the melody given to those same words at the conclusion of the *ante-evangelium* 'Salvator omnium' in Ex. 36.

The Gallican Offertory, called the 'Sonus', may have been an elaborate chant of the kind found in the Roman, Milanese, Hispanic, and Beneventan Offertories. Pseudo-Germanus remarks that it was

[31] MS Paris, lat. 903, fo. 135ᵛ–136; cf. *MGG*, iv (1955), col. 1313.
[32] Amédée Gastoué, *Le Chant gallican* (Grenoble, 1939), 27.

Ex. 37

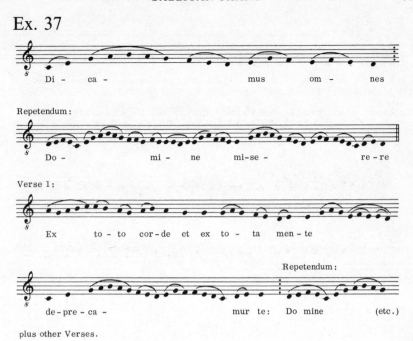

plus other Verses.

sung 'dulci melodia', and comments on its three-fold concluding Alleluia, called the 'Laudes', which was sung as the elements were deposited on the altar: 'that this Alleluia has a first, second, and third repetition signifies the three ages before the law, under the law, and under Grace'. A similar melodic authority attaches to the concluding Alleluias of the Cherubic Hymns—the Offertories of the Byzantine Divine Liturgy, which share the same melodies in certain of their Alleluias even though their main texts are different.[33] All direct traces of the Gallican Soni and their concluding Laudes-Alleluia have disappeared, but there are indications that some of their music survives among the Offertories of the Hispanic, Milanese, and Frankish-Roman traditions. At least one Frankish-Roman Offertory, 'Elegerunt' (Ex. 38), for feasts of St Stephen Protomartyr, represents a manifestly non-Roman and perhaps Gallican tradition.[34] Italian musical sources that are related to Rome generally prescribe the Gregorian Offertory 'In virtute tua' for St Stephen. The notation of 'Elegerunt' in early sources shows the distinctive neume, *pes stratus*, whose use according to Dom Cardine is limited to chants of 'Western' (that is, Spanish, Aquitanian, Gallican, or English) origin.[35] The *pes*

[33] Levy, 'A Hymn for Thursday in Holy Week', *JAMS*, 16 (1963), 166.
[34] MS Padova, Bibl. Capit. A.47, fo. 27; cf. C. Ott, *Offertoriale* (Paris, 1935), 161.
[35] E. Cardine, 'Sémiologie grégorienne', *Eg*, 11 (1970), 131.

Ex. 38

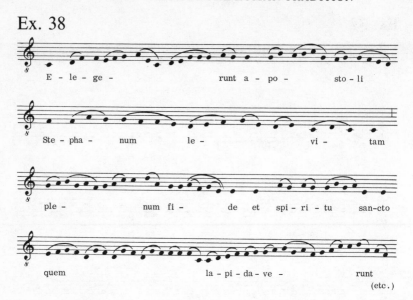

E - le - ge - runt a - po - sto - li

Ste - pha - num le - vi - tam

ple - num fi - de et spi - ri - tu san-cto

quem la - pi - da - ve - runt

(etc.)

stratus (a podatus or pes—two notes ascending—with an ornamental oriscus attached at the end) appears in the Offertory 'Elegerunt' on '-gerunt', 'plenum', and the concluding Alleluia.

The Gallican rite had provisions for a Fraction Antiphon at the division of the Host. Pseudo-Germanus says that 'as the Priest divides, the clergy in a suppliant manner sing the antiphon'. Upwards of a dozen musical relics of this musical practice are found among Gregorian manuscripts from Frankish to south-Italian regions. They are best represented in northern Italy. These Fraction Antiphons in Frankish-Roman sources constitute a likely block of Gallican remains. Some of their texts are of Eastern origin. Their concluding Alleluias are in a number of cases musically interrelated, thus perhaps reflecting the same kind of authority ascribed by pseudo-Germanus to the concluding Alleluias of the Gallican Soni. The most widely circulated of the Fraction Antiphons was the 'Venite populi' for Easter, whose text is already found in a seventh–eighth century palimpsest. The chant is given in Ex. 39[36] after a Ravennate manuscript of the twelfth century. At Easter in Benevento the Fraction Antiphon 'Emitte angelum' was sung during the eleventh century, while 'Venite populi' was put before the Offertory and sung as an antiphon 'ad procedendum sacrificium', evidently a makeshift calculated to preserve this venerable chant.

Between the Fraction and the Communion of the Gallican Mass

[36] MS Padova, A.47, fo. 135ᵛ; cf. Gastoué, *Le Chant gallican*, pp. 35–7; *Variae preces* (5th ed., Solesmes, 1901), 14.

Ex. 39

there was an Episcopal Benediction of which musical traces have survived. During the Communion itself a chant called the *trecanum* was sung. This probably had psalmody attached since a doxology is mentioned, but the description by Pseudo-Germanus is ambiguous, and no music can be identified with it. The Celtic Antiphoner of Bangor (later seventh century) transmits, as already mentioned, the Communion text, 'Corpus Christi accepimus' (Ex. 40), which reappears as a Transitorium at Milan, and in other north Italian rites as a Fraction Antiphon. The chant is variously assigned to Easter (at

Ex. 40

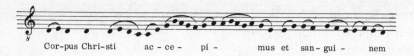

Cor-pus Chri-sti   ac - ce - pi -   mus et san-gui -   nem

e - ius   po - ta - ti su - mus ab o -   mni ma - lo

non ti - me - bi -   mus qui-a do - mi - nus

no - bi -   scum est ad -   iu - tor sit

et de - fen-sor in   se - cu - la se -   cu-lo - rum

Al - le -   lu -   ia

Nonantola), Christmas (Vercelli), and Pentecost (Ravenna).[37] The Ambrosian and north-Italian musical traditions represent variants of the same underlying musical material. In the light of the Celtic antecedents of the text, the music may be Gallican.

Apart from the Gallican Mass, there are possible survivals of

[37] MS Padova, A.47, fo. 183; cf. *Antiphonale missarum ... mediolanensis*, p. 320; Michel Huglo, *et al.*, *Fonti e paleografia del canto ambrosiano* (Milan, 1956), Tav. VI.

Gallican music in the chant for the 'Te Deum laudamus' that is widely adopted in Frankish-Roman sources, as well as in the standard melodic tradition for the 'Exultet'. A hoard of Gallican material may exist among the hundred-odd processional antiphons found among Roman Graduales and Antiphonales, which also have a manuscript collection for themselves, the Processionale. Unlike the simpler antiphons of the Office, the processional antiphons and those for other special occasions are often moderately florid in style, and without accompanying psalmody. They represent various origins. An antiphon like 'Deprecamur te' (Ex. 33 above) appears to be Roman. Some others are Gallican relics that survived locally, and in some instances even made their way to Rome. A mark of Gallican or Frankish origin, the *pes stratus*, is found in the neumatic notations of a number of processional antiphons. Melodic expansions on the second syllable of 'Al-le-luia' are another such mark. In a twelfth-century Gradual from the region of Pistoia (Pistoia, Bibl. Capitolare, C. 119) the series of antiphons for the Palm Sunday procession bears the heading, A[nti-phonas] Gallicanas. The antiphons that follow are found everywhere.

HISPANIC, OLD SPANISH, OR 'MOZARABIC' CHANT

The music of the Spanish 'Visigothic' church was given its definitive shape and ordering during the seventh century. Liturgical indications that correspond to the provisions of the later musical sources are found already in the *Etymologiae* and the *De ecclesiasticis officiis* of Isidore of Seville (d. 636). The Fourth Council of Toledo in 633 decreed 'a single order of prayer and chanting for all of Spain and Gaul', and this was followed by a period of intense liturgical activity sparked by three Toledan Bishops, Eugene (d. 657), Idelfons (d. c. 680), and Julian (d. 690), to all of whom musical activity can be ascribed. In the year 711 the old Visigothic kingdom, dating back to 466, fell victim to the Arab invasion, but already by that time the Old Spanish musical liturgy was essentially complete. The earliest surviving liturgy book from Spain, the so-called Orationale of Verona, was copied during the first years of the eighth century. Later in that same century the manuscript found its way to safety at Verona as a refugee from the Arab invasion. The Orationale is a prayer book having no primary musical provisions, but the copyist entered into its margins the unnoted text-incipits of some 800 musical items—responsories, antiphons, 'alleluiatic antiphons', and verses for the Office. From the correspondence between those text-incipits and the fully noted musical repertories of the tenth and eleventh centuries it is supposed that substantially all of the Old Spanish liturgical music was in existence before the Moslem conquest.[38]

The word 'Mozarabic', which is generally applied to the Old Spanish rite and its music, seems to come from *musta'rib*, signifying a Christian living under Moorish domination. So far as the date of the Spanish rite is concerned, this name is not at all accurate because the rite was formed earlier. Nor is the name accurate even for the surviving documents of the rite, most of which were copied in regions that were already reclaimed from the Moslems. Thus the north-eastern region of Tarragona returned to Christian rule during the eighth-ninth century. The recapture of Toledo in the centre of the peninsula, the chief ecclesiastical see of the Old Spanish rite, came about in 1085–6, putting a nominal end to the 'Mozarabic' period. But the regions to the south were not fully restored to Christianity until 1492 and the recapture of Granada. The word 'Mozarabic' nevertheless continues to be used for the old musical liturgy, and not without reason, since the majority of the sources date from the eighth to the later eleventh century, the general period of Moslem rule. As Christianity made an official return during the eleventh century, the local rite tended to be replaced by the Gregorian. Pope Alexander II in 1065 still sanctioned the use of the Mozarabic liturgical books. But after 1073 and the election of Gregory VII, that most energetic promoter of papal power, the old rite was doomed. The kingdom of Leon and Castile adopted the Gregorian rite in 1077. Toledo did likewise in 1086. It was the Roman rite in the monastic tradition of Cluny that generally came in at the time. Among the cities to the south that were still under Moslem rule, the Mozarabic rite probably held on longer. Since the sixteenth century, a few parishes of Toledo have continued to employ the Old Spanish texts of the liturgy, but the music that goes with it is of doubtful pedigree.

Unlike the music of the Gallican liturgy, of which only meagre traces have survived, the Old Spanish musical liturgy survives essentially complete. There are almost two dozen full manuscripts and about as many fragments, dating from the eighth to the twelfth or thirteenth centuries. They transmit the whole musical liturgy. Unfortunately it is not in a state that can be wholly reconstituted. The Roman suppression of the Spanish rite came about during the 1070s and '80s, just before the emergence of fully heighted neumes. Thus for the bulk of Mozarabic chants there are only the visual outlines of the music, the neumed skeletons without the substance of pitch. Even

---

[38] Louis Brou, 'L'antiphonaire visigothique et l'antiphonaire grégorien au début du VIII siècle', *Anuario musical*, 5 (1950), 3.

some of the first Spanish manuscripts introducing the Cluniac-Roman rite were written in imprecisely heighted neumes. In a single manuscript, the *Liber ordinum* of San Millan de la Cogolla, and there for only a handful of chants, the original Mozarabic neumes of the eleventh century were replaced by palimpsest Aquitanian neumes of the eleventh-twelfth century. Those neumes were heighted, and they allow the approximate transcriptions on modern staff of 21 chants of the Holy Thursday and Requiem Offices. But the great store of the Mozarabic repertory—some 3000 antiphons, 500 responsories, and 2000 other chants covering practically every liturgical requirement of the Hispanic Mass and Office—remain beyond melodic reclamation. Of the known manuscripts, about a third are from the central region of Toledo. The remainder represent scriptoria further to the north— San Domingo de Silos, San Millan de la Cogolla, San Juan de la Peña, Leon, etc. From the southernmost regions, where the Mozarabic rite probably endured under the prolonged Moslem hegemony, nothing seems to be preserved. This is particularly unfortunate, since manuscripts of the twelfth to fifteenth centuries from those regions might transmit Mozarabic chants in staff notation. Nothing of the sort is likely to be found. Even at Toledo, the adiastematic notation held on long after it might have been suppressed or modernized, perhaps into the thirteenth century. When Archbishop Cisneros around 1500 launched a revival of the old rite, he used the old manuscripts for the liturgy, but his music no longer corresponds to that of the early neume-notations. He would doubtless have used the old music if he had had it, but it was evidently not to be found. Outside Spain, there are traces of Mozarabic music in some of the same eleventh–twelfth century manuscripts of the Narbonais and Aquitaine that contain relics of Gallican chant. Some of the Preces transmitted in such manuscripts may represent a mixed Spanish-Gallican practice.

The two Spanish regions of the centre and the north from which all of the surviving Mozarabic musical manuscripts come show two distinctive styles of neumatic notation. Toledo in the centre has neumes with a pronounced horizontal thrust, while in the northern provinces from Leon through Aragon and Catalonia the thrust of the neumes is vertical. The Mozarabic melodies enshrined by the different neumes in the different regions are nevertheless often the same. There is no doubt that the two styles of notation belong to the main ninth-century family of European neumatic notations. Yet speculations continue to circulate about their origins. One theory is that the Mozarabic notation was already in existence before the Moslem invasion of 711. The Orationale of Verona has among its marginalia certain neumes that are tenuously ascribed to the manuscript's main hand, thus placing them in the early eighth century. There is a related theory that explains the striking differences in notational style between the Toledan and northern neumes as representing two branches of a common pre-Moslem source that would of necessity have developed independently on the two isolated sides of a blood-stained Moslem-Christian border. If this were so it would upset the generally held notions about the origin of European neumes in some Frankish region around 800. On balance, there seems to be no good reason to abandon the notion of Carolingian origin. The marginal neumes in the Verona Orationale are not securely dated. And the two varieties of Spanish neumes are better understood as outgrowths of Carolingian neume-scripts that reached Spain during the ninth or tenth centuries. The 'horizontal' (Toledan) and 'vertical' (northern) Spanish notations are not substantially farther apart than the Paleo-frankish and Aquitanian notations of ninth–tenth century France. Although the horizontal ductus of the Toledan notation has been fancifully interpreted as an imitation of Arabic script,[39] what it reflects may be nothing more than the look of neumes that in the first instance were squeezed into the narrow interlinear space of text manuscripts that were not designed to receive them. Thus the chant manuscript Toledo 35.4 (tenth century?; dated by Mundò c.1192–1208) still has chant texts that are written continuously, without horizontal space left for melismata. Where Toledo was content to perpetuate this situation, the Northern manuscripts with their vertical notation would represent a more developed state where adequate interlinear space was provided for the incipiently heighted neumes to be spread. The Toledan notation, then, may have remained close to some early stage of Carolingian notation while the northern Spanish notation may reflect some more modern practice, perhaps one that flourished in France or north Italy during the later ninth or tenth century.

Although the Old Spanish neumes are useless as to specific pitch, a good deal has been learned about their music from patient study of their neumatic outlines. The Mozarabic Trisagion, Alleluias, *Threni*, and *Clamores* of the Mass have been illuminated in studies by Dom Louis Brou, and the responsories and antiphons of the Office have been similarly illuminated by Don M. Randel. A great deal more will be learned as the other categories of Mozarabic chant undergo similar scrutiny. It is already clear that the Spanish plainchant melodies belong to the same general family of Western chants and operate

---

[39] Stäblein, *Schriftbild der einstimmigen Musik*, p. 34.

under the same broad principles as the Italian and Frankish melodies. The Spanish melodies are suited in style to their liturgical function and the solemnity of the calendar assignment. They exhibit the usual three densities of melodic style—syllabic, neumatic, and melismatic. They use both antiphonal and responsorial procedures and have both simple and florid psalmody. The reciting tones on simple psalmody inflect with the text-accent. Among the psalmodic intonations and cadences there are syllable-count formulas, including the archaic cadence-type of four elements applied mechanically and without regard for text-accent to the last four syllables of the verse, a type found in Byzantine chant.[40] There are indications of melodic accommodation between the beginnings or endings of the Spanish psalm tones and the beginnings or endings of their attached refrains. A number of different musical modes are represented, and though the exact number is uncertain, it appears that the Spaniards, like the Milanese and the Beneventans, did not subscribe to the eight-mode system to which the Frankish-Roman musicians began bringing their repertory into conformity shortly before the year 800. As in other chant repertories, each class of Mozarabic chant seems to have had its own preferences with regard to modal usage. Among the small number of Mozarabic antiphons and responsories that are transmitted in heighted Aquitanian notation in the *Liber ordinum* of San Millan, some are modally comparable to the Gregorian D Plagal, E Plagal, and perhaps G Plagal modes. Others present no obvious Gregorian analogies. The Old Spanish chants, like others of the Christian East and West, use the techniques of model melodies, where a melodic framework is accommodated to the phrase- and accentual-patterns of a number of diverse texts. The Spanish repertory also relies on the techniques of centonization, drawing on a common fund of musical elements and putting them into combinations where it is clear that no single one of the resultant melodies has served as the model for the others. As in other centonate repertories, the musical elements are subjected to accommodations at their beginnings and endings so that they connect properly with what comes before or after. There are examples of the identifications found in all centonate repertories between particular melodic elements and particular words of text, even when they occur in quite unrelated contexts. Whether the Spanish musical elements also attach themselves to specific pitches or levels in the tonal system, as they do in the Byzantine and other Western chants, cannot be answered, but there is every reason to suppose that they do.

[40] Oliver Strunk, *Essays on Musik in the Byzantine World* (New York, 1977), 155.

Ex. 41

Di - es   me -   i

tran - si -   e -   runt   co - gi - ta -   ti -   o - nes

me -   ae   dis - si -   pa - tae   sunt ....

Repetendum:

Li - be - ra   me   Do - mi -   ne, et   po -   ne

me   jux - ta   te

plus Verse.

An example of the Old Spanish melodic dialect is given in Ex. 41.[41] This is the responsory, 'Dies mei transie[r]unt', from the Mozarabic Burial Office, as transcribed in the palimpsest Aquitanian neumes of the San Millan manuscript. The same responsory with the same music appears in Northern-style Mozarabic neumes in the tenth–eleventh century Antiphoner of Leon. The melancholy text is a patchwork drawn from the Book of Job, a favourite source for Spanish plain-chant, though not for Roman. The Aquitanian neumes at San Millan are well heighted, but their notation lacks a clef so that the transcription, published originally by Padres Rojo and Prado, was offered by them with due reserve.

The Proper chants of the Mozarabic Mass begin with a *Praelegen-dum* whose function corresponds to that of the Gregorian Introit. It was sung antiphonally, with a verse and doxology. Its psalm-tones were the same as those for the antiphons of the Office. The Gloria in excelsis is found in a handful of Old Spanish musical versions, and at Mass, though at Milan and Gaul it was generally reserved for the Office. The Trisagion was regularly sung at the Spanish Mass with

---

[41] C. Rojo and G. Prado, *El canto mozárabe* (Madrid, 1929), 73.

both Greek and Latin texts, and elaborate musical provisions are preserved. There survive various settings for the *Benedictiones* that follow—the Canticle of the Three Children ('Benedictus es Domine Deus patrum nostrorum') from the Book of Daniel.

The *psalmi pulpitales* or *psalmi* or *psallenda* which come next in the Mozarabic Mass Proper correspond in function and style to the responsorial Graduals and Psalmelli of the Italian liturgies, and perhaps also to the 'Responsorium' of the Gallican Mass. About twenty Mozarabic feasts are provided with Clamores that extend the text of the Psallendum. They contain the acclamation, 'Deo gratias, Kyrie eleison'. The Threnos replaces the Psallendum on certain weekdays in Lent. Fewer than a dozen Threni are known, some texts being drawn from Job and Jeremiah, but most, as their name suggests, are from the Lamentations or Threnody of Jeremiah. They generally begin with the refrain, 'Quis dabit capiti meo' (Jeremiah ix, 1), which is followed by a handful of verses. The Threni all use the same elaborate music. On penitential days there are Preces sung at Mass following the Psallendum. There are also Preces in the Office. These litany-related chants have sometimes grown, as in the Gallican usage, into longer poetic stanzas that are set to music in semi-florid styles. In other cases the Preces are just short petitions with a refrain.

The Mozarabic chant called the 'Laudes' is the counterpart of the Alleluia with verse in the Roman, Milanese, Beneventan, and Byzantine Mass. A curiosity of the Spanish Laudes, however, is that they are sung, not before the Gospel, as is the universal practice, but afterwards. With respect to their responsorial performance, the expansiveness of their Alleluia refrains, and the further melismatic expansivenes of those refrains when they are resumed after the verse, the Spanish practice is like the others. A number of the Laudes share their texts with the Alleluia verses in Italian and Frankish liturgies, but their music is not visibly related. The name 'Laudes' was also applied to certain Mozarabic verses that were sung without an Alleluia during Lenten Masses. They are somewhat different in musical style.

The Mozarabic Offertory chant is called the 'Sacrificium'. It opens with a substantial musical section in florid style, followed by one or two verses in the same style (they are usually numbered II, III). Each verse returns to the final portion of the opening section as a repetendum. The arrangement can be seen in Ex. 42(i)[42] which shows the Sacrificium 'Erit hic vobis' for Friday in Easter Week as it appears in the Antiphoner of Leon. 'Erit hic vobis' is typical of the Mozarabic

---

[42] Ex. 42(i) *Antifonario visigótico mozárabe de la catedral de León, edicion facsimil*, ed. Brou and Vives (Madrid, 1953), fo. 178; Ex. 42(ii) MS Oxford, Bodleian Douce 222, fo. 143.

Ex. 42

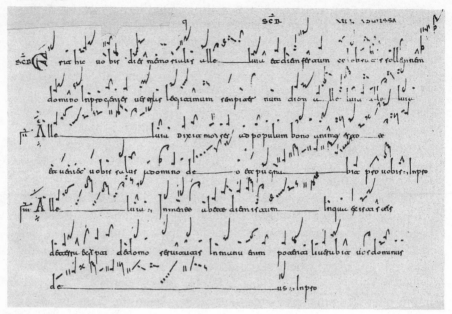

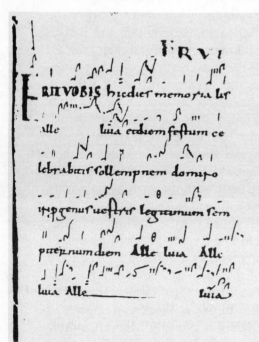

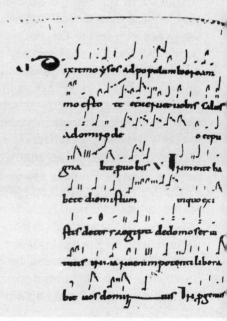

Sacrificia in employing a biblical text that is not drawn from the Psalter. It is not a continuous biblical excerpt at all, but rather a selection or *cento*, and essentially a *paraphrase*, amounting to freely-treated reminiscences and rephrasings from the books of Exodus and Leviticus. The texts of the Mozarabic Sacrificia are almost all distinctive compositions like this one, not traceable anywhere in the patristic or exegetic literature. They show every sign of having been compiled specifically for florid musical use as Offertories. What gives the Sacrificia particular interest among Mozarabic chants is that their distinctive texts, and in some cases their music, show links with the Offertory chants in other Latin liturgies. Thus the text of the Mozarabic Sacrificium 'Erit hic vobis' for Easter Friday, Ex. 42(i), also appears as the Offertory text for Easter Friday in the Frankish-Roman and Urban-Roman rites, and at Milan the same text appears as the Offertory for Pentecost. In connection with Ex. 29 above it has already been shown that the Gregorian and Milanese melodies for this Offertory text represent local versions of what amounts to the same underlying musical material. The staffless state of the Spanish neumes makes it impossible to say whether that underlying substance is also shared by the Mozarabic melody. But there is something even more singular about the music transmitted by the Mozarabic neumes. What they suggest are relationships of specific melodic details between the Mozarabic Sacrificium, Ex. 42(i), and the Gregorian Offertory, Ex. 29(ii)—apparent correspondences in the apportionment of melismatic densities and in the directions of melodic lines. The comparison can be made directly between the Spanish neumes in Ex. 42(i) and those of the Gregorian Offertory as noted in a north Italian manuscript of the eleventh century, Ex. 42(ii). In all, fewer than half a dozen of the preserved Mozarabic Sacrificia show the possibilty of such musical relationships with a corresponding Gregorian or Milanese Offertory. A satisfactory explanation has yet to appear; perhaps the most plausible one sees such Offertories as originating, not at Spain, Rome, or Milan, but in the lost tradition of the Gallican Offertories, whence they spread to the other rites during the seventh to ninth centuries.[43]

Rounding out the musical provisions of the Mozarabic Mass are the antiphons 'ad pacem', of which some half-dozen are preserved for major feasts. The Kiss of Peacc in the Mozarabic rite as in the Gallican was given in connection with the Offertory ceremonial. The so-called 'ad Sanctus' chants are a small handful of proper Mozarabic

---

[43] Further on these Offertories in the Roman repertory in Ch. VI.

pieces that served as amplifications or perhaps substitutes for the Sanctus at major feasts. Finally, there is a repertory of some three dozen Hispanic Fraction Antiphons ('ad confractionem panis'), and some two dozen Communion Antiphons ('ad accedentes'). The verses of the latter, like those of the Praelegenda, are sung to the same tones as the Office psalmody.

IV

LITURGICAL MATERIALS OF ROMAN CHANT

By RICHARD CROCKER

AROUND 1900 there was an intense controversy involving F. A. Gevaert, Amadée Gastoué, Peter Wagner, and others, concerning the role of Pope Gregory I (590–604) in the development of the repertory of chant that bears his name. Since 1950 the controversy has shifted to a somewhat different issue; but the persistent reality behind the Gregorian issue is that the time—if not the reign—of Pope Gregory represents a barrier. Since his time we can imagine the development of the repertory as it is preserved in sources after 750; before his time, that is, before 600, the development of Roman chant is hidden from us, for lack of data that can be fitted into a continuum. After 600, to be sure, we still have no agreed version of the development; we have enough information to imagine several possible developments, but not enough to decide among them.[1]

Gregory is not the first nor the last pope to be credited with contributing to a *cantus anni circuli*, a yearly cycle of chants; he is also credited with a *cento antiphonarius*, a 'patchwork antiphonary'. On the one hand, both accreditations have to be treated with circumspection on several counts; on the other, their import is so general as to tell us little—unless we read them assuming much to be true in Gregory's time that is evident only later. The term *cento antiphonarius* as a matter of fact exactly describes both the Antiphonale of the Mass and

---

[1] F. A. Gevaert, *La Melopée antique dans le chant de l'église latine* (Ghent, 1895–6); Amadée Gastoué, *Les Origines du chant romain; l'Antiphonaire grégorien* (Paris, 1907); Peter Wagner, *Einführung in die gregorianischen Melodien*, i *Ursprung und Entwicklung der liturgischen Gesangsformen bis zum Ausgange des Mittelalters* (3rd edn., Leipzig, 1911); Willi Apel, *Gregorian Chant* (Bloomington, 1958), especially pp. 47–50, 77–83, 507–15; Bruno Stäblein, introduction to *Die Gesänge des altrömischen Graduale Vat.lat. 5319*, by Stäblein and Margareta Landwehr-Melnicki, *Monumenta monodica medii aevi*, 2 (1968), 50*–61*; Andrew Hughes, *Medieval Music: The Sixth Liberal Art* (Toronto, 1974), Nos. 467–95.

that of the Office as we have them. But the same term could just as well apply to texts of entirely different substance, no longer preserved.

Gregory himself mentions more specific items (Alleluia, Kyrie eleison) that will concern us in due course. We should note that in spite of his protestations this pope (one of several with a Greek name) was accused of importing Byzantine liturgical customs.[2] Sergius I (687–701) is the pope usually mentioned in this context; but we could imagine Roman liturgy and chant throughout the seventh century as open to enrichment from the vigorous development in Constantinople and the Eastern Empire. At the same time, however, we hear also of the activities of three Roman abbots, Catolenus, Maurianus, Virbonus, from 657 on, a reference that seems to reflect more concretely musical activity in the Church and city of Rome.[3] That, surely, represents the period in which the selections of texts and the ways of singing them were institutionalized, and sent north and documented there, beginning right after 750. For in 752 Pepin, King of the Franks, decided that the Roman chant should be used in the Carolingian kingdom, and he sent Chrodegang, Archbishop of Metz, to Rome to initiate this operation of unparalleled significance for the history of Latin chant, and of Western music.[4]

The special qualities of Roman chant were primarily due to the unique position of Rome in the Latin West. Rome had always been first of all a city, then it had emerged as the head of an empire, and now it was emerging as the head of a church. It retained a very local— one might almost say, parochial—quality, simultaneously with a universal one. The administrators of Rome spoke both to the inhabitants of the city, and at the same time to those of the civilized world: *urbi et orbi* became a formula to describe the official proclamations of the pope, who in his own person combined the dual functions of Bishop of Rome and leader of the Western Church. As a picture of Rome's liturgical development and relationship with the Latin West has gradually emerged, it has become clear that the rite of the city of Rome was a local distillation, subject to local pressures, local needs, and local decisions, of ritual practices of the world at large.

Having learned to discriminate between chant of the Roman rite and chants of the Hispanic, Gallic, Milanese, and Beneventan rites, we have had more recently to distinguish between two repertories of chant for the same rite—the repertory of 'Gregorian' chant and that

---

[2] Egon Wellesz, 'Gregory the Great's Letter on the Alleluia', *Annales musicologiques*, 2 (1954), 7.
[3] Stäblein, *Die Gesänge des altrömischen Graduale Vat.lat. 5319*, pp. 54*–6*.
[4] Ibid. 62*–83*; G. Ellard, *Master Alcuin, Liturgist* (Chicago, 1956).

sometimes called 'Old Roman'.[5] These are both in some sense 'Roman', and the discriminations necessary in dealing more precisely with that word and concept now become relatively difficult. One necessary discrimination is between chant for the Mass and chant for the Office. Upon close examination in historical context the differences between these kinds of chant become sufficiently great to require separate treatment.

For the proper chants of the Mass, there is a single set of texts to be sung (with variation of detail to be mentioned later). As far as the eighth century or before is concerned, we would have no way of judging whether they were always sung the same way, or if differently, how differently, since the melodies were not written down. Subsequently we have two distinct written records of the melodies to be sung for these texts. The earlier of these two records was made primarily under Frankish supervision beginning around 800; a great deal of work went into the preparation of the written record (which eventually involved hundreds of manuscripts), and the relationship of this record to the Roman chant it was intended to record has been and will continue to be the subject of extremely difficult study. In any case, it is the earliest and best record we have of whatever was sung in the city of Rome. It is the record that has always been called 'Gregorian', more recently and more accurately termed 'Frankish-Roman'.

In speaking of this Gregorian, that is Frankish-Roman, written record, the Benedictine scholars use the term 'archetype of diffusion' to refer to an hypothetical text-state—a presumed manuscript, in effect—that would have represented the standard text approved by the Carolingian authorities, from which the Carolingian chant books were copied.[6] The time of this presumed archetype would be around, or shortly after, 800; its locale would be the Carolingian homeland in north-east France. Such a manuscript is not known to exist. Those who believe it did exist believe its contents can be reconstructed by working back, with standard text-critical methods, from the hundreds of subsequent Frankish chant books. It can be argued that such an archetype never existed, that the standard was never agreed upon, or at least never recorded; and that the high degree of correlation (which always includes some discrepancies) among the subsequent Frankish

---

[5] Stäblein, *Die Gësange des altromischen Graduale Vat.lat. 5319*, is the most comprehensive statement of the position. For a survey of opinions, see Hughes, *Medieval Music*, Nos. 605–63.

[6] René-Jean Hesbert, *Corpus Antiphonalium Officii. Rerum Ecclesiasticarum Documenta*, Series maior. Fontes, VII–IX, 6 vols. (Rome, 1963–79); see vol. V, pp. 22–3, 259, 270. Jean Claire, 'Les Répertoires liturgiques latins avant l'octoechos. L'office férial Romano-Franc', *Eg* 15 (1975), 85. Jacques Froger, 'The critical edition of the Roman Gradual by the monks of Solesmes', *Journal of the Plainsong & Mediæval Music Society*, 1 (1978), 81–97.

chant books is the result of common origins and informal concordance rather than actual filiation from a manuscript archetype. Scholars will continue to argue the point; in the meantime the expression 'archetype (of diffusion)' is a convenient way to refer to the result of the extraordinary efforts of the Carolingians to absorb and standardize for their own use the Roman rite and its chant.

The second record of the Roman chant was made over the period 1050 and 1300, and consists, for the Mass, of three manuscripts, all from Rome itself.[7] These contain the texts for proper chants at Mass, in a state that suggests an earlier stage of liturgical development than that indicated for the Gregorian record—that is to say, an eighth-century state; and a set of melodies that bears an extremely complex relationship to those of the Gregorian record, ranging from very similar to very different. This record has been labelled 'Old Roman', and while that term might be appropriate for the state of the texts, it is not so for the state of the melodies, which are not all old. The relationship of this record to whatever was sung in Rome in the eighth century is at least as difficult to determine as the relationship in the case of the Gregorian. The only proper way to refer to this repertory of chant is to speak of 'Urban-Roman' chant, and we shall do so here.

As for the chants of the Office, monastic scholars, speaking out of a lifetime of devotion to the faith and to the *opus Dei* (the daily work of psalmody) often speak of 'the Roman Office' as a given fact. Speaking in a more historical vein, these same scholars are apt to posit 'the Roman Office' as an archetype of practice, a single, original source. There is, however, no written record of the Roman Office in this sense. Monastics can express their allegiance of faith to the Roman Office in its purity, while scholars can observe the drastic changes in the outward form of this Office over the centuries, and inquire into who— in Rome or elsewhere—was doing it and in what ways. Around 530 St Benedict included in his Rule on the monastic life a number of directions about the Office.[8] It is generally believed that Benedict's version of the Office is a modification of Roman practice. That practice itself, however, can be established prior to 850 only with the greatest difficulty. In general we could divide the history of the Roman Office into the following periods: before St Gregory (600); from St Gregory to about 800, for which time a Frankish-Roman archetype analogous to but distinct from the one for Mass is assumed; the

---

[7] 'St. Cecilia Gradual 1071', Bodmer Philipps collection; Rome, Vat.lat.MS 5319; Rome, San Pietro MS F 22 (also San Pietro MS F. 11).

[8] Benedict, *Regula*, cap.VIII–XVIII; *The Rule of Saint Benedict, in Latin and English*, ed. and trans. Justin McCann (London, 1963).

Frankish-Roman, or medieval Office, basically dependent upon the archetype but with very extensive additions, lasting until the reforms of the Counter-Reformation at the end of the sixteenth century; and the Office, so reformed, up until further reforms after 1900. There are Urban-Roman sources for the Office (two manuscripts from the thirteenth century[9]), parallel to the Urban-Roman sources for the Mass; the relationship of these sources to each other and to the Frankish-Roman sources has not yet been thoroughly explored.

TOOLS AND MATERIALS

During the past decades scholars have gradually started sorting out the historical layers of Gregorian chants for the Mass. There are important differences of opinion, because the issues are very subtle, and on many basic points there is no agreement (perhaps no possibility of agreement). Side by side with the greatest sophistication in dealing with the musical sources after 900, we can observe naïvety in the reconstruction of presumed development before that date, or persistent postulation of over simple models. The main thing that has been gained is the idea that there was a historical development, as well as some idea of what kinds of issues would have to be resolved to determine what that development was.

Studies of the proper chants for the Mass begin with manuscripts containing only the texts. The most important tool we have for the study of the Gregorian repertory is the publication by Dom René-Jean Hesbert, *Antiphonale missarum sextuplex*, containing the texts of six of the earliest Antiphonales of the Mass in parallel columns for comparison.[10] The six manuscripts are from the ninth century. Although none of the six can be taken as the 'archetype of diffusion', or even as an immediate copy, the consensus of the six is as close to the presumed archetype as can be imagined at this time. If the text of a given piece of chant does not appear in one of these manuscripts, then there is no immediate justification for allowing this chant status in the Gregorian repertory (that is, in the Frankish-Roman archetype of diffusion), with the reservation that its melody might be in the repertory with a different text. There is a much broader reservation, however, that these six manuscripts are not the only ones there were, and that chants known from later manuscripts (but not these six early ones) might have existed earlier in manuscripts now lost, or even more generally, might have existed in a non-written state. The basic principle of research has to be, however, that lack of early represen-

[9] Rome, San Pietro MS B 79; London, Brit.Lib. Mus.Add.29,988.
[10] Hesbert, *Antiphonale missarum sextuplex* (Brussels, 1935).

tation can be counter-indicated only on good evidence—better evidence, that is, than the manuscript representation itself.

After the Sextuplex, the next valuable tool is the publication by Walther Lipphardt, *Der Karolingische Tonar von Metz*, an edition and study of one of the earliest tonaries.[11] A tonary is essentially a list of antiphons, for the Mass and for the Office, according to tone or mode. The actual melodies for these texts are first found in the three earliest notated Antiphonales, St. Gall 359, Laon 239, and Chartres 47, all accessible in photofacsimile editions in the *Paléographie musicale*.[12] These are followed closely by one of the most important early sources (from shortly after 1000), Montpellier H 159[13]—important to us because it contains alphabetic notation giving positive information about pitch. These manuscripts are indexed separately, but not yet in a published collation with the Sextuplex. Item-by-item comparison reveals additions made to the Gregorian repertory between the establishment of the archetype and 900, a most notable case being the replacement of the old Offertory for St Stephen (26 December) with what must be a Frankish piece, 'Elegerunt'.[14] This is the type of information that can be gained from comparison, which is essential in determining exactly which melodies belong to the Gregorian archetype.

From these earliest sources we can proceed directly to the editions of melodies in modern chant books dependent upon the Vatican edition of the *Graduale romanum*,[15] which, thanks to the labours of the Benedictine scholars over the last century, brings us as close to the

---

[11] Walther Lipphardt, *Der karolingische Tonar von Metz, Liturgiewissenschaftliche Quellen und Forschungen*, xliii (Münster, 1965).

[12] *Paléographie musicale, Les principaux manuscrits de chant grégorien, ambrosien, mozarabe, gallican, publiés en facsimiles phototypiques* (Société de Saint Jean l'Evangeliste): 10. *Antiphonale missarum Sancti Gregorii (IXe–Xe siècle)*: (*codex 239 de la Bibliothèque de Laon*, ed. A. Mocquereau (Tournai, 1909), 11. *Antiphonale missarum Sancti Gregorii (Xe siècle)*: Codex 47 de la Bibliothèque de Chartres, ed. *idem* (Tournai, 1912); Series 2:2. *Cantatorium (IXe siècle): No. 359 de la Bibliothèque de Saint-Gall*, ed. *idem* (Tournai, 1922). Michel Huglo, 'Gradual (ii)', *New Grove*, vii. 601–9. On chant manuscripts in general, see John Emerson, 'Sources, MS., II. Western Plainchant', ibid. xvii. 609–34.

[13] Finn E. Hansen, *H 159 Montpellier: Tonary of St. Bénigne of Dijon* (Copenhagen, 1974).

[14] Cf. above, p. 97.

[15] *Graduale sacrosanctae romanae ecclesiae de tempore et de sanctis*, SS.D.N.Pii X. Pontificis Maximi jussu restitutum et editum (Rome, 1908). (Or, with the same title, Editio altera Ratisbonensis juxta Vaticanam. Ratisbon, 1911.) *Graduale sacrosanctae romanae ecclesiae de tempore et de sanctis*, SS.D.N.Pii X. Pontificis Maximi jussu restitutum et editum, ad exemplar editionis typicae concinnatum et rhythmicis signis a Solesmensibus monachis diligenter ornatum (Desclee, 1945). Some, but not all, of the Proper chants for the Mass are in the *Liber usualis*, with introduction and rubrics in English, ed. Benedictines of Solesmes (Tournai, several editions). *Graduale Triplex, seu Graduale Romanum Pauli PP.VI cura recognitum et rhythmicis signis a Solesmensibus monachis ornatum, Neumis Laudenensibus (Cod.239) et Sangallensibus (Codicum San Gallensis 359 et Einsidlensis 121) nunc auctum* (Solesmes, 1979). *Le Graduel Romain*, ed. Solesmes, in preparation; see vol. II, *Les Sources* (Solesmes, 1957).

readings presumed for the archetype as we can come, without detailed collation of manuscripts.[16] An eventual 'critical edition' of the *Graduale* will undoubtedly refine many points of detail, and new perspectives on the problems of edition might conceivably bring a few substantial changes. Since the materials for Urban-Roman chant are few, the tools are easy to ennumerate: they include the transcription of manuscript Vat.lat. 5319 by Landwehr-Melnicki, and an inventory of the Mass books by Paul Cutter.[17]

Materials for the Office are roughly parallel to those for the Mass in nature, but less systematic and more fragmentary owing to the greater extent of the materials and of the problems, and the lesser extent of work devoted to the task. Dom Hesbert, again, has provided the indispensable foundation with a parallel edition of representative sources—not six of the earliest ones this time, and not merely six, but rather six for 'Roman cursus' and another six for 'Monastic cursus'.[18] These volumes provide basic access to the texts and repertory of antiphons and responsories as they were actually used in the period 850–1100. In the case of the Night Office there is no modern edition of the music that takes us anywhere close to the archetype, and the most convenient access is still through facsimile editions of medieval manuscripts—the Antiphonales from Lucca, Worcester and Sarum, whose published indices are very useful.[19] In modern edition, the *Antiphonale romanum* provides music for the Day Office (from Lauds to Compline), but as reformed early in the twentieth century under Pope Pius X. The *Antiphonale monasticum* contains the Day Office according to the Monastic cursus, incorporating some of the results of Benedictine research. Portions of the Night Office can be found in the *Liber responsorialis, Processionale monasticum,* and *Liber usualis.*[20]

---

[16] e.g. Hendrik van der Werf, *The Emergence of Gregorian Chant: A Comparative Study of Ambrosian, Roman, and Gregorian Chant* (Rochester, NY, 1983).

[17] P. F. Cutter, *Musical Sources of the Old-Roman Mass, Musicological Studies and Documents,* 36 (American Institute of Musicology, 1979). Max Lütolf, ed., *Das Graduale von Santa Cecilia in Trastevere (1071), Bibliotheca Bodmeriana, Reihe Texte, II* (Cologny–Genève, 1987).

[18] Cf. above, p. 115.

[19] See *Paléographie musicale,* 9. *Antiphonaire monastique (XIIe siècle): codex 601 de la Bibliothèque capitulaire de Lucques,* ed. A. Mocquereau (Tournai, 1906); 12. *Antiphonaire monastique (XIIIe siècle): codex F.160 de la Bibliothèque de la Cathédrale de Worcester,* ed. idem (Tournai, 1922); Series 2:1. *Antiphonaire de l'office monastique transcrit par Hartker: MSS. Saint-Gall 390–391 (980–1011)* 2nd edn., J. Froger (Berne, 1970); *Antiphonale Sarisburiense,* ed. W. H. Frere (Plainsong & Mediaeval Music Society), Introduction, Part I (1923); Part II (1925). See also Huglo, 'Antiphoner', *New Grove,* i. 482–90, and Emerson, 'Sources'.

[20] *Antiphonale sacrosanctae romanae ecclesiae pro diurnis horis* a Pio Papa X restitutum et editum ... (Rome, 1919); *Antiphonale monasticum pro diurnis horis* ... ordinis sancti Benedicti a Solesmensibus monachis restitutum (Desclée, 1934); *Liber responsorialis* pro Festis I. Classis et communi sanctorum juxta ritum monasticum (Solesmes, 1895); *Processionale monasticum ad usum congregationis Gallicae ordinis sancti Benedicti* (Solesmes, 1893).

CALENDAR

The Gregorian repertory is the first in the West to be preserved complete; in attempting to deal with it as a whole we need to be aware of the grouping of chants according to their functions in the Mass and Office, and in the various layers of the calendar. In order to deal with the melodic characteristic of chants, we need to know, for example, that a particular antiphon is for the Introit (function) for Christmas (calendar), which is part of the 'festal' as opposed to 'dominical' layer of Mass chants. In some respects the Office provides a more complete picture of structure and development than the Mass, and so both here and in connection with the texts and melodies it is convenient to begin with the Office, and then compare the Mass to it.

The Office is based upon a daily and weekly cycle, dependent upon the recurrence of the Lord's Day, the *dominica*, counted as the first day of the week; the others are called 'ferias' and numbered from two to seven (here, ii . . . vii). The Night Office is on a weekly cycle: it has specific materials for each feria, and an expanded form on Sunday; the whole pattern repeats each week. In the Day Office, Lauds and Vespers are on a similar weekly cycle, while the 'Little Hours', Prime, Terce, Sext, None, and Compline, are best thought of as on a daily cycle (see Table 1).

This ferial and dominical form of the Office was eventually supplemented, if not supplanted, by a festal form keyed into a complex annual calendar, to be discussed later. The larger part of music for the Office varies with this calendar, but rests upon the foundation of this daily and weekly cycle.

Mass originally recurred once a week on the *dominica*; there may

TABLE 1 Roman Office

Ferial	Dominical
Night Office (Matins)	
Nocturn	Nocturn I
	Nocturn II
	Nocturn III
Day Office	
Lauds	Lauds
Prime	Prime
Terce	Terce
Sext	Sext
None	None
Vespers	Vespers
Compline	Compline

have been no particular variation from one week to the next. From (at the latest) the fourth century on the Mass also became keyed into a complex calendar, so much so that little comparable to the ferial form of the Office remains visible (save the invariable Canon of the Mass). All the parts of the structure that involve Gregorian chant vary with the calendar.

The earliest elements of calendar in both Mass and Office were the readings from Scripture. These were first laid out on some yearly basis, although this, too, soon became overlaid with a system of festal observances. As the calendar developed by 800 these festal observances were grouped into two cycles, the 'Proper of the Time' or *Temporale*, and 'Proper of the Saints' or *Sanctorale*. The Sanctorale is easier to understand, consisting as it does of all the observances for individual martyrs and saints, singly or in small groups. Each observance is assigned a date, and we must note that 'date' here means the Roman secular calendar, with months and numbered days (sometimes using the specifically Roman system of *kalends* and *ides*). Slightly under one hundred observances are provided for in the archetype, most falling in summer (June, July, August, September), with a lesser concentration in January, and fewest in early spring.

Medieval and modern chant books are set out in sections corresponding to the Temporale and Sanctorale, but in addition there is a section called the 'Common of Saints' (*Commune sanctorum*). The historical development of this is complex and subject to much discussion. The Mass books of the Sextuplex have very little Common, almost all proper chants being assigned to specific saints' formularies. Later, chants used for classes of saints (apostles, martyrs, etc.) were grouped together in the Common. There were originally very few complete Offices, however, for individual saints, and much use was made of Common Offices; individual Offices multiplied throughout the Middle Ages.

The other main component, the Temporale, has to be understood in several layers. Presumably the oldest is that of the major feasts: these are five—Christmas, Epiphany; Easter, Ascension, Pentecost—and they fall into two groups as indicated. Christmas (Nativity of the Lord, *Nativitas domini*) and Epiphany are historically two different manifestations of the same midwinter festivity, on two different dates (25 December, 6 January) reflecting two different secular calendars (Western and Eastern).

The other group of feasts is based on Easter, the Resurrection of the Lord, which is linked to the Jewish Pesach (*Pascha*). This date has no connection with the Pagan-Roman calendar, indeed varies over a period of a Roman month. But the date of Easter, as Pesach, does not vary in the Jewish calendar; what varies is the relationship with the Pagan-Roman calendar, and consequently with the Christmas (and Sanctorale) cycle of feasts.

Around and between these two polar feasts—Christmas and Easter—the year was filled in by special weekly observances forming the 'dominical' layer. These vary greatly in their dates of institution, but as a layer are probably later than the major feasts. The six Sundays before Easter were organized (in a long, complex development) into the preparatory season of Lent, and the three Sundays before that into a 'Pre-Lent'. These, together with the six Sundays between Easter and Pentecost (Paschaltide), constitute a complete cycle oriented around

TABLE 2: The calendar of the Church

Temporale	Sanctorale
	Saints' days, designated by month and date
Advent (season) Sundays 1, 2, 3, 4	(December)
	Christmas: 25 December Epiphany: 6 January
Sundays after Epiphany 1, 2, 3* Pre-Lent (season)†	
Sundays: Septuagesima Sexagesima Quinquagesima	(February)
Lent (season) Sundays 1, 2, 3, 4, 5 Palm Sunday Holy Week	(March)
Easter Sunday Paschaltide (season) Sundays 1, 2, 3, 4, 5, 6 Ascension (Thursday after 5th Sunday)	(April)
Pentecost Sunday	(May)
Sundays after Pentecost 1–23*	(June)
	(July–November)

* In any given year one of these places will have more Sundays, and the other fewer, than indicated; the excess from one place is used to fill out the other.

† The dates of the Sundays from Pre-Lent right up to the last Sunday after Pentecost vary according to the date of Easter.

Easter. Equally dependent upon the date of Easter, but distinct from that cycle in character (and so long as to be a separate unit), are the twenty-three Sundays after Pentecost. The four Sundays before Christmas were organized into the season of Advent; the Sundays after Christmas, and the three Sundays after Epiphany, without being given much character as a season, constitute a post-Christmas part of the cycle. In considering the relationship of the calendar to the chronological development of the chant we must beware of assuming undue connection between the melodies, texts, and feasts; the traditional idea that the oldest feasts had the oldest melodies does not seem reliable.

PSALMODY

The Ferial Office has two main elements. One is the weekly recitation of the 150 Psalms of the Psalter; the other is the yearly cycle of lessons. In order to understand the use of these elements we have to appreciate the original thrust of monasticism in the fourth century, when to the alarm of established society (Christian as well as pagan), thousands of men and women of all ages and stations fled into the desert to renounce urban life and to meditate on ultimate things. A central aspect of ascetic discipline was the vigil—staying awake at night. As aids to wakefulness and meditation, readings and recitations were used, eventually regularized; the Bible became the most used (but not the only) resource for readings, and in particular the Psalter became the most used resource for recitation. The most characteristic use of Scripture for this ascetic purpose was to read or recite it straight through from beginning to end, then start at the beginning again, for the point was to avoid distraction by the lower appetites, occupy the middle levels of consciousness with edifying materials, hence freeing the upper levels of consciousness for mystic perception.

The purest use of the Psalter, then, would be to recite it straight through over and over, stopping only for expediency. The Psalter was in fact sometimes used in this continuous way. St Benedict, writing around 530, tells us that 'the fathers' recited the whole Psalter (150 Psalms) every night, and he apologizes for the laxity of his own Rule, which provides for a minimum of twelve Psalms a night.[21] His Rule in general represents the most successful Latin compromise between ascetic extremes and a rational communal life; and here a polarity must be kept in mind throughout the study of early medieval monasticism—a polarity between individual meditation and com-

---

[21] Benedict, *Regula*. Cap. XVIII.

munal worship. The purest model of early monasticism is the holy man in his cave, meditating. The forms of western Latin monasticism that generate music and worship services, however, are communal; the Night Office is the result of providing an orderly communal framework for individual meditation.

As the use of the Psalter became institutionalized, the Psalms were distributed throughout a weekly cycle in various ways—in the West, more or less according to Benedict's formula in his 'Rule', but in two slightly different versions, the 'Roman cursus' and the 'monastic cursus' (this last is a traditional, technical use of the term 'monastic' and does not imply that the 'Roman' cursus was excluded from monasteries).[22] These two versions are shown side by side in Table 3; included also is the scheme of lessons, which are an essential feature of the cursus.

In addition to recitation of psalms, the nightly meditative exercises included readings from the other books of the Bible, and other

TABLE 3 Outline of Psalms and Lessons of the Office

Roman cursus		Monastic cursus	
	ferial		
Night Office			
Nocturn:	12 psalms†	Nocturn I:	6 psalms
	3 lessons		3 lessons
		Nocturn II:	6 psalms
			1 lesson
	dominical		
Nocturn I:	12 psalms†	Nocturn I:	6 psalms
	3 lessons		4 lessons
Nocturn II:	3 psalms	Nocturn II:	6 psalms
	3 lessons		4 lessons
Nocturn III:	3 psalms	Nocturn III:	3 canticles
	3 lessons		4 lessons
Lauds: 5 psalms*		Lauds: 5 psalms*	
Canticle (Benedictus)		Canticle (Benedictus)	
Prime* ⎫		⎛ Prime*	
Terce ⎬ Psalm 118		⎜ Terce	
Sext ⎪ distributed in		⎨ Sext	
None ⎭ various ways		⎝ None	
Vespers: 5 psalms		Vespers: 4 psalms	
Canticle (Magnificat)		Canticle (Magnificat)	
Compline: 3 psalms		Compline: 3 psalms	

* Number of psalms subject to occasional difference or complexity.
† Subsequently reduced to three psalms.

[22] Ibid., cap.X, XVIII; Claire. 'Les repertoires liturgiques'; Andrew Hughes, *Medieval Manuscripts for Mass and Office* (Toronto, 1982).

materials as well—mostly patristic commentaries and saints' lives. The primary purpose was to edify and occupy middle levels of consciousness, similar to psalmody except that it involved listening rather than singing. The primary implementation (parallel, again, to the use of the Psalter) was to read through the Bible from beginning to end, and in a selected and distributed form this can still be perceived in the yearly cycle of the lectionary.

In the Ferial Office twelve psalms were sung every night, as specified by Benedict. In the Roman cursus these were sung in one 'Nocturn'; in the monastic cursus, in two Nocturns. The Roman Nocturn continued with three lessons. The monastic cursus also had three lessons in its first Nocturn; then, after the six psalms of the second Nocturn, it had only a short lesson.

For Sundays, both versions had a more elaborate arrangement. The Roman cursus had its usual first Nocturn, with twelve psalms and three lessons; then followed another Nocturn, with only three psalms, and three more lessons; finally a third Nocturn, with three psalms and three lessons. The monastic dominical Office had its usual first and second Nocturns each with six psalms, but each with four lessons; then a third Nocturn with no psalms (instead, three Old Testament Canticles), and four more lessons.

The dominical form of Roman as well as monastic cursus became the model for the festal Office used for feasts of the Lord and of the saints. In the Roman cursus the numerous psalms of the ferial Nocturn were reduced to three in the first festal Nocturn, making it symmetrical with the second and third Nocturns. The difference between Roman and monastic festal forms can be summarized as nine psalms, nine lessons for the Roman, as opposed to twelve psalms, twelve lessons in the monastic.

The rule of twelve psalms each night was a basic aspect of the recitation of the whole Psalter each week. Psalms 1–108 (with certain isolated omissions and other complexities) were sung at the rate of twelve each night beginning with Sunday and running through the week. Most of the remaining psalms, 109–147, were sung at Vespers, five each evening (four, in the monastic cursus). Psalms not included in these arrangements were sung at Lauds and at the Day Hours as either fixed or variable items. The complex arrangement of fixed and variable psalms at Lauds is such as to suggest that it pre-dates the rational plan of the Night Office and Vespers.

STICHIC TEXTS OF THE OFFICE

From a scrutiny of fragmentary evidence (much of it preserved in the complex history of the Office itself), it is possible to perceive a tension between monastic and non-monastic or parochial use of texts. The ordinary world of urban Christians worshipped once a week, or at most once a day (unless they were devout and attempted to follow a quasi-monastic discipline). In this ordinary ambience the Psalter was not said in a cursus (such as the Roman cursus), but instead individual psalms were selected for special festal purposes. Even those selected psalms might not be said complete, rigorously following the written text of Holy Scripture; rather, single lines might be excerpted and repeated, or other lines could be added; new poetic structures could be created and performed in a variety of combinations of solo and choral voices. All of this can be seen as normal for the wider world of ritual song, and the presence of these procedures in the Night Office represents a compromise between monastic discipline and the ways of parochial celebration.

The practice of excerpting single lines (in this case, from Scripture) and recombining them can be termed 'stichic', from 'stich' (Greek 'stichos', 'line' or 'verse'; compare 'hemistich', or 'distich'). Thus 'stichic' use of a psalm text can be set in opposition to 'cursive' use in which the psalm was sung complete as part of a cursus. Most of the texts of the Gregorian chant repertory are stichic in nature.

One of the most familiar stichic additions is this text:

> Gloria Patri et Filio et Spiritui sancto,
> Sicut erat in principio, et nunc et semper,
> et in saecula saeculorum. Amen.

This Trinitarian acclamation was added to most psalms sung in the Office. Since this one contains two lines (*Gloria . . . Sicut . . .*) it can be called a *distich*. It combines with psalms as a suffix (rather than as a prefix, or infix). The specific name for this particular suffix stich is 'the doxology' (the Greek text begins *doxa*) or 'the little doxology' (the larger one begins 'Gloria in excelsis'). As a suffix to psalms this distich is always treated as if it were the last two verses of the psalm; in other contexts it is treated differently. Sometimes the two stichs are separated; sometimes only the first is used.

At some point in the development of the Office, the lessons of each night came to be relieved by the singing of one or more chants that we now call 'responsories' or 'great responsories'.[23] The early history of

---

[23] Wagner, *Einführung in die gregorianischen Melodien* i, pp.16–21, 132–40; Apel, *Gregorian Chant,* pp. 180–85. See especially Helmut Hucke, 'Das Responsorium', *Gattungen der Musik in Einzeldarstellungen* (Bern, 1973), p.144, and 'Responsorium', *MGG*, xi, (1965) col.313. See also E.T.Moneta-Caglio, *Lo jubilus e le origine della salmodia responsorial* (Venice, 1976–7); H.Leeb, 'Die psalmodie bei Ambrosius', *Weiner Beiträge zur Theologie*, xvii (Vienna, 1967).

responsories is obscure. It can be said that while the form of the responsory works on principles clearly related to the call-and-response principle that is universal in ritual song and referred to in fourth-century patristic sources, it is just as clear that the great responsories that we have are far removed from that or any simple call-and-response form. Furthermore, the great variety in the selection, composition, and distribution of responsory texts during at least the eighth and ninth centuries indicates that such variety was a basic feature of responsories in the Office.

One use of responsories (it has been proposed as the original one) was to relieve the lessons with the singing of a psalm—not by the whole community, but rather by a soloist with a choral refrain.[24] The psalm would be selected (according to the reconstruction) from one of the psalms assigned for that night in the cursus. In this case, obviously, the 'psalmic' responsory would have no necessary relationship to the lessons it interrupted, and only an arbitrary numerical relationship to the next psalmic responsory that night, selected from the same cursus. Whether psalmic responsories are the original type or not, responsories in general frequently have no direct connection to the lessons they follow, or have a closer connection among themselves from one responsory to the next than to the intervening lessons.

In another, different use of responsories, their texts are taken from the very lessons they interrupt. In this case the relationship between lessons and responsories is as close as it can be: usually the responsory text is some prominent thought or image from the biblical narrative, not necessarily sung in its proper place in the narrative but functioning as a motif, a highlight, referring forwards or backwards to poeticize the narrative. Here the responsory can be described as a stich, a verse selected from Scripture and combined with other materials in a loose aggregate. The theory that sees psalmic responsories as the original ones sees other types of responsories as secondary phenomena that depart from the original purpose. It needs to be observed that the oldest state of psalmic responsories preserved consists of only a few verses from each of only a very few of the psalms of a given night of the week; hence even these psalmic responsories reflect a choice of materials that is 'stichic' rather than strictly 'cursive'. A great many responsories have non-scriptural texts, most often connected with proper Offices for saints' days and taken from the accounts of the life or passion of the saint. But a prominent and

---

[24] See R. LeRoux, 'Etude de l'Office dominical et férial. Les répons 'de psalmis' pour les matines de l'Epiphanie à la Septuagésime selon les cursus romain et monastique'.*Eg* vi (1963), p.39 plus tables.

especially interesting set of non-scriptural responsories is found in Christmas Matins.

Concerning responsories we have a specific report from Amalarius of Metz, writing around 830;[25] Amalarius describes the way the 'Roman cantors' sang responsories as opposed to the way the Frankish cantors sang them. When Amalarius speaks in this way he is one of our few direct witnesses for truly 'Old Roman' chant, that is, chant as sung in Rome around 800. No matter how unreliable or personal Amalarius' observations may turn out to be, we need to listen to them carefully.

Responsories are stichic combinations consisting of two elements— a respond and a verse. The verse is usually a bi-hemistich; the respond may have several phrases. The verse is always sung by the cantor(s). Amalarius tells us that the Roman cantors sang responsories in this way.

1.	Respond	cantors
2.	Respond	subcantors (i.e. the schola)
3.	Verse	cantors
4.	Respond	subcantors
5.	*Gloria Patri*	cantors
6.	Respond (second half)	subcantors
7.	Respond	cantors
8.	Respond	subcantors

The Franks did not have the whole respond repeated by the subcantors after the verse, only the second half (as the Romans did after the *Gloria Patri*). Amalarius goes on to speculate that the use of *Gloria Patri* is not original, and cites the custom in Passiontide, when *Gloria Patri* is not sung at responsories, and the procedure is:

1.	Respond	cantors
2.	Respond	subcantors
3.	Verse	cantors
4.	Respond	cantors
5.	Respond	subcantors

Amalarius' purpose in bringing up this point is that if only the second half of the respond is to be sung after the verse, in the Frankish manner, then the verse must be chosen so that its verbal sense leads on well to this second half. If the Roman manner is followed, then the verse is followed by the beginning of the respond, and the whole

---

[25] *Prologus antiphonarii a se compositi*, and *Liber de ordine antiphonarii*, XVIII, 6–8, ed. J.M.Hanssens (Città del Vaticano, 1950), i, pp.362, 31–6; iii, pp. 55, 18–38; see also LeRoux, 'Les repons "de psalmis"', *Eg* vi (1963), p.130ff.

structure need be less rigorously connected for, as he says, it is two things—respond and verse—not one.

This technical detail prompts several fundamental observations. First, Amalarius is referring to what is apparently an established custom of following the verse with only the second half of the respond. He says this is our custom, and by contrast he is reporting to his readers what is presumably unfamiliar to them, that the Romans do it differently. Furthermore, he shows no sign of urging a change in this Frankish custom, which because of its established nature we should probably call 'Gallican'. He does, however, urge a change, and a very interesting one: the verse should be selected so that good sense is maintained in the continuation into the second half of the respond. He refers to the good work done by Elisagarus in selecting verse texts (to replace the Roman ones) so that this will happen. So verses are at the cantor's choice, which is confirmed by the use of a tone at that point, as well as by the subsequent manuscript tradition, which offers a multiplicity of verses. But this problem has only arisen in the importation of Roman practice into Frankishland: in the Roman use itself there was no problem (there was no consecution needed from *Gloria Patri* to the second half of the respond, which functioned as echo); and presumably there was no problem in the established Gallican practice, for the texts would have been laid out to suit it. Only when Roman texts (and chants) are sung in Gallican procedure does the problem arise, and this was exactly the situation in Amalarius' day. We should note that his remedy is not necessarily to do it all the Roman way, but instead to alter Roman selection of verses to facilitate Gallican procedure. The view that sees the Roman practice as the original one and the Frankish as a recent, decadent one fails to take this into account. A choral response using the second half of an element is an ancient alternative in stichic combinations: the Gallican way is just another (old) way of doing it, one that has been acknowledged in other types of ancient 'Roman' practice.

Another important feature of stichic combinations attested by Amalarius' report is the immediate complete repeat by the subcantors of the respond sung first by the cantors. Given the length of these texts and the elaborate nature of the melodies, we should perhaps not have believed that so many repetitions would have been made if he had not told us; but the fact that they were tells us something definitive about why it is called a respond—*not* because the schola 'responds' to the verse (although they do that too), but because they repeat what the cantors sang. This is a call-and-response procedure in which the response is a literal repeat. The phenomenon is a familiar one, and so is the way of varying its uniformity by use of a subsequent contrasting solo element (here, the verse); but notice that it is followed in Roman practice by the whole call-and-response procedure, cantors repeated by schola. The predominant feature of the whole Roman form is the manifold repetition of the respond, for the verse is short, and comes only once; the *Gloria Patri*, here also short, is just another element of relief.

Responsories (eight or nine in the 'Roman' use, but the number can vary in the sources) are provided for feasts and for a relatively restricted number of saints' days, although the Common can be used for a much larger number. Then, responsories are provided for Sundays of Advent, Pre-Lent, Lent; that is, for Sundays from December to Easter, except for the few Sundays after Epiphany. Finally, sets of responsories are provided to go with the lessons read from August to November, taken from Old Testament history and the Prophets; these are laid out by months. All of this represents the systematic filling out of the year, week by week, with proper responsories, and accounts for a large part of the repertory.

Another kind of stich, regularly added to psalms in the Office, is called an 'antiphon', a term used in confusing ways in the sources.[26] In general the term is used in two different but related contexts: it can refer to a kind of piece (or combination of pieces), and it can refer to a manner of performance. There is reported a practice in Syrian monasteries of singing psalms and hymns in alternation between two halves of the community; around 350 this practice was introduced to devout lay communities, and subsequently spread to the West.[27] The generic Greek name for this practice of singing in alternation was 'antiphony'. This practice became associated with the much broader practice of combining stichs with each other and with psalms or hymns.

A variety of manners of performance using solos, half-choirs, and full choirs have been proposed for the combination of stichs and antiphony, and the best one can conclude is that each of these manners was almost certainly used at some time and place. As a result

[26] See the basic article 'Antiphone' in *Dictionnaire d'archéologie chrétienne et de liturgie*, ed. F. Cabrol, i, 2 (1907), col. 2461; also the study by J. Hourlier, 'Notes sur l'antiphonie', in Wulf Arlt, *et al.*, eds., *Gattungen der Musik in Einzeldarstellungen* (Berne, 1973), 116. For Greek practice see Oliver Strunk, 'The Byzantine Office at Hagia Sophia', and 'Antiphons of the Oktoechos', *Essays on Music in the Byzantine World* (New York, 1977), 112–50 and 165–90. As an example of new ideas in performance practice, see Corbinian Gindele, 'Doppelchor und Psalmenvortrag im Frühmittelalter', *Die Musikforschung*, 6 (1953), 296; standard discussions in Wagner, *Einführung in die gregorianischen Melodien*, i, pp. 21–30, 141–159; Apel, *Gregorian Chant*, pp. 45 f., 185 ff.; Stäblein, 'Antiphon', *MGG*, i (1949–51) col. 523; Michel Huglo, 'Antiphon', *New Grove*, i, 471.

[27] Cf. above, pp. 5, 83.

of the association of such stichs with antiphony, they were habitually called 'antiphons' in the Latin West, although not in the East where a number of more specific terms may possibly have identified various functions more closely. Also, in keeping with the long-run tendency of the Roman rite towards a simple, sober, restricted, uniform practice, the manifold stichic arrangements of the Eastern rites tended to be reduced to a simple stich framing a psalm (sung in antiphony) and so it was easy to call this stich an antiphon.

Antiphons were provided for the psalms and canticles of the Office in a bewildering variety of ways. Evidence from the sources as well as from Amalarius suggests that in the eighth and ninth centuries the use of antiphons in the Office was expanding. The Roman Ferial Office has six antiphons for its twelve psalms, the monastic cursus six or more. For the dominical or festal form, the Roman cursus eventually had an antiphon for each psalm—nine in all. For the festal form the monastic cursus eventually had thirteen (including one for the Old Testament Canticles of the third Nocturn). Special antiphons were provided for the New Testament Canticles of Lauds and Vespers, and many of these may be due to Frankish cantors.

Antiphons of the Office can be considered in three classes.

(1) Antiphons of the Psalter; these are sung in direct connection with psalms sung in the cursus, according to the distribution of the Psalter throughout the week. Not every psalm sung during the week had an antiphon, but many did, according to the arrangement. The text of each antiphon was taken from the psalm it accompanied, often from the first or second verse of the psalm; hence these are called 'psalmic' antiphons. Each antiphon was sung only with its psalm, and that psalm was always accompanied by its antiphon (except when a special feast or saint's day occurred, which will lead us to another class of antiphon). These psalmic antiphons are called 'ferial' because they are sung regularly in connection with their psalms on each weekday (feria) in order according to the distributed Psalter. They are called 'antiphons of the Psalter' for the same reason; and more particularly because when they came to be written down after *c.* 900 they were often entered in a book called a (liturgical) Psalter, which contained the 150 Psalms as they were sung in the Office (rather than as in the regular Bible), distributed according to weekly use and provided with antiphons (and often other material) needed in the Ferial Office. In singing the Office, then, the monastic community had only to refer to its liturgical Psalter, singing every psalm with its antiphon at the appointed hour, day after day throughout the week, week after week in perpetuity. These antiphons form a distinct class,

and it is essential to keep them clearly separate from the other classes.

(2) Antiphons of the Temporale and Sanctorale: (a) for psalms and Old Testament Canticles, (b) for Gospel Canticles. This class is really several classes, representing a very much larger number of anti-phons—ten or twenty times the number of class (1). What dis-tinguishes this as a class from (1) is that all these antiphons are appointed for a specific day of the year (rather than of the week), in connection with the special theme of that day. These antiphons may have texts taken from the psalms they accompany, or they may not; their texts may be taken from other psalms, or from combinations of psalm texts ('centonized' or 'patched-together' texts); or from other books of the Bible, or from non-biblical sources. These antiphons may be associated with only one psalm or Canticle, or they may not; they can move around to other psalms or Canticles.

One of the most interesting kinds of antiphons is psalmic in a sense, even though not used for psalms in a cursus. Some of the best examples occur in Christmas Matins.[28]

1.	Psalm 2	Ant. 'Dominus dixit' (Ps. 2, v. 7)
2.	Psalm 18	Ant. 'Tamquam' (Ps. 18, v. 6)
3.	Psalm 44	Ant. 'Diffusa est' (Ps. 44, v. 3)
4.	Psalm 47	Ant. 'Suscepimus' (Ps. 47, v. 10)
5.	Psalm 71	Ant. 'Orietur' (Ps. 71, v. 7)
6.	Psalm 84	Ant. 'Veritas' (Ps. 84, v. 12)
7.	Psalm 88	Ant. 'Ipse invocabit' (Ps. 88, v. 27)
8.	Psalm 95	Ant. 'Laetentur caeli' (Ps. 95, v. 11)
9.	Psalm 97	Ant. 'Notum fecit' (Ps. 97, v. 2)

Here the psalms are in an ascending numerical series, but at widely and irregularly spaced intervals. Obviously the psalms have been selected as appropriate in some way to the occasion. Each antiphon is psalmic. It can be argued that a series of Christmas psalms was selected, and then from each psalm an especially appropriate verse was used as its antiphon. It can also be argued, on the other hand, that *first* came a series of antiphons, consisting of favourite Christmas stichs, and then each antiphon brought with it a psalm. 'This is my Son, this day have I begotten thee' is a natural stich for Christmas; used as antiphon it would naturally bring with it Psalm 2, even though other thoughts and images in Psalm 2 might be more appropriate for some other feast.

The antiphons for Gospel Canticles are those for the Benedictus

[28] LeRoux, 'Aux origines de l'office festif. Les antiennes et les psaumes de matines et de laudes pour Noël et le 1er Janvier selon les cursus romain et monastique', *Eg*, 6 (1963), 65, especially the table after p. 170.

(Canticle of Zacharias) at Lauds, and for the Magnificat (Canticle of the Virgin Mary) at Vespers. These antiphons have to be classed separately because they tend to have special characteristics (among other things, they can get very long), and because they are so numerous—about as many as all those for psalms and Old Testament Canticles.

Gospel-Canticle antiphons can be taken from psalms just like many of the psalm antiphons of the Temporale and Sanctorale. The most frequent and characteristic source of Gospel-Canticle antiphons, however, is one of the four Gospels—not from the passages containing the Canticles themselves, but frequently from the Gospel reading at Mass for the Sunday. This reading is called a 'pericope' (a section 'cut out' from the continuing narrative and assigned to a day) and such antiphons are called 'pericope antiphons'. The pericope for Sexagesima, for example, is the Parable of the Sower (Luke viii) and the Gospel-Canticle antiphons provided for Lauds and Vespers are mostly taken from that text. These are very important examples of stichic combinations in that they combine texts and themes that have no intrinsic connection. The two ends of the continuum—ferial psalmic antiphons on one hand, proper Gospel-Canticle antiphons on the other—are so far apart as to suggest that the Latin use of the single term 'antiphona' subsumes several really different types of stichs.

Antiphons do not represent the purest monastic practice. They tend to call attention to themselves, and to their intrinsic meaning, hence away from the incessant cycle of psalmody as a meditative exercise. The Abbot Pambo inveighed passionately against stichs of all kinds when two of his novices returned from Alexandria reporting with enthusiasm about stichic arrangements in use there.[29] Western monasticism absorbed the stich as an alien, secular element, and turned it to meditative use—so much so that it often seems that of all types of antiphons the psalmic antiphons are the most appropriate, especially those associated with the weekly recitation of the Psalter. It would be an easy step to believe that the psalmic antiphons of the weekly Psalter are the oldest—indeed, the original—type of stichic arrangement in (Latin) Christian chant. That may even be true as far as the development of monastic chant goes; what needs always to be added is consideration of chant in other sectors of Christian culture, cathedral and parish. From those sectors may have come stichic arrangements in which the antiphons were not psalmic, not simple, not intimately

[29] The account of Abbot Pambo, much discussed in research on the Office, in Martin Gerbert, *Scriptores ecclesiastici de musica* (San Blasien, 1784), i. 2–4.

related to the psalm, but instead elaborate, disparate, essentially distracting from the psalmody, or not even used with psalmody.

The effect of proper antiphons, then, is to inflect a series of psalms to the particular meanings of a given occasion. One of the things (perhaps the main thing) that gives the Office its very great richness, is the interplay between the cycle of psalmody and the particular thoughts and images highlighted by proper antiphons. A given antiphon may point to Christmas; but another verse of the same psalm may suggest Easter. The antiphon without the psalm would be uni-dimensional (and was sometimes used in this way to make an unambiguous reference to an idea or event).

But the antiphon *with* the psalm is multi-dimensional; through the medium of continuous psalmody, resonances can be felt back and forth across the whole liturgical year, across the whole epic of salvation. The Psalter is peculiarly suited to this stichic inflection. Whether specifically Christian implications and allusions are present in the Psalter is, of course, a matter of Christian faith; such allusions are not there for a Jewish observer. The Christian had to regard them—as the Fathers did—as veiled allusions, prefigurations, 'through a glass darkly'. Precisely that quality lends itself to multiple cross-allusions, to an extensive, ever-deepening web of associations. The best visual analogue of the Office with its continuous psalmody and hundreds of antiphons (and other stichic elements) is a rich mosaic, or near-Eastern carpet, with detail so manifold that recurring patterns show up always in slightly different lights, while differing motifs can have unexpected similarity and resonance.

In its institutionalized form, then, the Office consisted not just of psalmody and lessons (its constituent cursive elements) but of complex combinations of these with stichic elements, of which antiphons and responsories were the most prominent. The psalms of the Night Office were provided with antiphons, in varying ways. Responsories were provided in general to follow each lesson. Both Lauds and Vespers had antiphons for each of their psalms. The Day Offices included other stichic items, among them a sentence from Scripture called a 'Chapter' (*capitulum*); a 'versicle and response'; and a 'short responsory'. The Canticles at Lauds and Vespers had their own special antiphons. In addition, a variety of devotional material, usually of a stichic nature and sometimes involving important musical items, could be added on at the ends of these Offices. The stichic materials, being variable, play an important part in the larger cycle that results from the whole Office.

Although the stichic materials do not weigh heavily in terms of bulk, when compared to the cursus of psalmody, they tend to make a much stronger impression, for several reasons. Their melodic settings are of course distinct from their surroundings, and not just because of the elaborate melodic style of the great responsories. Stichs in general are set to compact, self-contained melodic forms. They tend by their very morphology to be associated with each other, and as we perceive that, we perceive that their typical arrangements are non-linear and repetitive. They do not necessarily have a continuous relationship even with each other; and they often repeat the same thought or the same text. The repetition is the more striking as it can take place through different functions: a specific sentence can recur as versicle, later as response, as Chapter, as antiphon. The thoughts and images for a feast, a week, or a season acquire tremendous depth and richness through varying repetition in different functions and contexts—and are immensely enhanced by contrast with the wealth of relatively undifferentiated material flowing by in the psalms and lessons. The combinations allow half a dozen different themes to be set out and developed simultaneously, receiving unexpected resonance from the accompanying cursive material, which serves as an inexhaustible pool of associations as well as a medium through which the most abstruse correspondences can travel.

FORMULARIES FOR MASS

The medieval Latin Mass was a complex event whose historical development was very obscure and impossible to summarize here.[30] It consisted essentially of the Eucharist, or institutionalized re-enactment of the Lord's Supper, preceded by readings from Scripture, usually lessons from an Epistle and a Gospel. These primary elements were surrounded by a wealth of prayers and stichic materials. The Gregorian repertory includes relatively elaborate melodic settings of several stichic items—Introit, Gradual, Alleluia, Tract, Offertory and Communion (throughout the following discussion Alleluia will be omitted, and taken up later). Proper texts, each with its own melody, are provided for feast days and Sundays of the Temporale and Sanctorale. A set of proper texts for a particular occasion is called a Mass formulary. But we have to remember that by themselves these items form a relatively small part of what goes on at Mass; in particular the complete formulary for a given occasion includes two other more essential kinds of items, the lessons from Scripture (Epistle and Gospel, sometimes a Prophecy), and the prayers (Collect of the day, Secret and Post-communion). An outline of the Mass in its

[30] The standard work is J. A. Jungmann, *Missarum solemnia*, 2 vols. (5th edn., Vienna, 1962).

Frankish-Roman form is shown in Table 4. The Gregorian chant repertory, strictly speaking, includes only the items in the left hand column; other items were also sung, in various ways at various times. (The items in the second column will be taken up in Chapter VII.)

The proper texts of the Mass can be compared to the categories of antiphons and responsories, as already studied in the Office, and the comparison is a useful one; but the point of it is as much to show differences as similarities. The underlying difference is that the Mass is essentially a ritual act, while the Office is a collection of texts to be said or sung. The Mass, of course, includes many texts to be said or sung, but these function as accompaniment or explanation of the action, whereas in the Office there is no action other than the texts themselves. In the Mass, only the lessons, the Epistle and Gospel, are similar to the Office in this respect; and the Gradual responsory of the Mass is a post-lesson responsory of the same type as found in the Office. This sequence of lesson and responsory is the point of closest similarity in function between Mass and Office.

The materials of the Mass show no consistently cursive organiza-

TABLE 4 Proper chants and other items of the Frankish–Roman Mass

	Cantor & Choir	People	Reader	Celebrant
1.	Introit			
2.		Kyrie eleison		
3.		Gloria in excelsis		
4.				Collect
5.			Epistle	
6.	Gradual responsory (or Alleluia with Verse)			
7.	Alleluia with Verse (or Tract)			
8.			Gospel	
9.		Credo		
10.	Offertory			
11.				Offertory prayers (including Secret)
12.				Preface
13.		Sanctus		
14.				Canon
15.				*Pater noster*
16.				*Pax Domini*
17.		Agnus Dei		Fraction
18.	Communion	—Administration of Communion—		
19.				Post-communion collect
20.				Dismissal

tion similar to that of the Office. There are some fragmentary traces of cursive organization in the Mass propers, and much has been made of them; but comparison to the cursus of the Office helps place these cursive fragments into an appropriate context. The Epistles and Gospels for the major feasts are always chosen in accord with the theme of the feast—indeed, the choice of Gospel defines the theme of the feast. Sometimes a few Epistles or Gospels will be taken in series from the same book for several Sundays, but this happens in the dominical, not the festal layer, and in any case is nothing like the systematic reading from Scripture in the Night Office. Since what little psalmody there is at Mass is sung not in fulfilment of a cursus but as accompaniment to liturgical action (as at Introit and Communion), it could be and was shortened or omitted as expedient.

So the materials at Mass are essentially stichic not cursive, and must be compared to the proper stichic materials of the Office. The stichic Mass texts for major feasts and many other occasions represent the themes of those feasts. Some proper chants can be regarded as programmatic for a particular season, in particular Advent or Lent. Many of the other proper chants—especially for formularies in the dominical layer (and for the weekdays in Lent)—are not specifically thematic or programmatic, and seem to form a large pool of stichic texts that are merely appropriate to worship, and are assigned to various Sundays arbitrarily. Since these texts are usually from the psalms, they could be and sometimes were assigned to successive Sundays in ascending numerical order of the Psalter, producing a cursive effect. The model for this, however, is not the cursive psalmody of the Ferial Office, but rather the festal Office (such as Christmas Matins), where psalms selected for thematic reasons are arranged in a sporadic, intermittent numerical order. In the case of Mass texts this seems usually to be the result not of the genesis of the items in question but of a later, perhaps much later, ordering.

The formularies of the dominical layer have this special problem. On the one hand the dominical Mass was for the apostolic and sub-apostolic age the weekly recurrence of Easter, and as such it was theologically and historically prior to any other feast. On the other hand the pool of dominical proper texts as preserved may well be later than the festal propers, and may represent the desire to fill out 'the circle of the year' with propers similar to those instituted for feasts. The history of individual texts and formularies will be sorted out only with the greatest difficulty.

GRADUAL RESPONSORIES

Among the proper Mass texts, Gradual responsories have what may be the longest history—and certainly the most obscure. The choice of texts is shrouded by an almost exclusive use of psalter texts, which tend to reveal their thematic or programmatic rationale only obscurely. The function of the Gradual is that of a post-lesson responsory; that much, at least, is clear, especially when the Office responsories are taken as the immediate model. The case of the Gradual, however, has been complicated by Wagner's insistence that this 'responsorial psalm between the lessons' was an inheritance from the synagogue, that the melodies (especially that of mode 2) were among the oldest of the Gregorian repertory, and that many details of Graduals were connected with, or explained by, their presumed antiquity.[31] This had the immediate consequence of placing these most ornate melodies at a very early stage of Gregorian development, which raised many difficult musical questions. Subsequently Eric Werner made the very important point that there was in fact no synagogue model that could be presumed for a 'chant between the lessons' (responsorial or otherwise); Werner concluded that the Gradual might be a Christian invention.[32] This places the texts back in the neighbourhood of the Office responsories, and the ornate melodies in the later stages of Gregorian development (where Gevaert always thought they belonged),[33] which tends to be supported by more recent thinking in general about the formation of the Gregorian repertory.

There is still the persistent problem that what the Sextuplex consistently labels a R[esponsorium] G[raduale] many scholars take to be a directly descended later form of *psalmus responsorius,* a form presumed for the patristic period of the fourth and fifth centuries—at least, as far as the texts are concerned.[34] The implication is that the single verse provided for most Graduals in the Sextuplex is the remnant of a whole psalm, just as for the Introit. It needs to be observed that the case of the Introit is really very different, since the model there is the form psalm-plus-antiphon of Office psalmody. Responsories of the Office have one (variable) verse, and in the case of the very large proportion of responsory texts that are taken from sources other than psalms it is obvious that a complete psalm was never in the prehistory. There are the psalmic responsories, however, and one reason these have been made so important in the history of the Office is their possible relationship to the Gradual responsories at Mass. We have seen that it is very difficult to make a close connection

[31] Wagner, *Einführung in die gregorianischen Melodien,* i, pp. 81–92.
[32] Eric Werner, *The Sacred Bridge* (New York, 1959), 131 f.
[33] Gevaert, *La Melopée antique;* see the Introduction, especially pp. xxvii–xxxii.
[34] See *Dictionnaire d'archéologie chretienne et de liturgie,* i, 1 (1907), cols. 638 f. for Augustine's quotations of psalm responses; also Jean Claire, op. cit., p. 179.

between a psalmic Office responsory and a 'responsorial psalm', especially when the melodies are taken into account, and this difficulty will be even greater for the Gradual responsories at Mass.

The argument for the *psalmus responsorius* has always relied most on the unique case of 'Haec dies' for Easter.[35] This respond is verse 24 of Psalm 117. It is used on Easter Sunday with the verse 'Confitemini', which is verse 1 of the same psalm; then it is used on every feria of the following week, each day with a different verse taken from the same psalm. This is assumed to be the sole survivor of the original responsorial practice, in which, presumably, one verse of a psalm was selected as a festal stich to connect the psalm to a particular occasion, and used as a refrain after each verse of the psalm as it was sung straight through. All of that would be believable stichic practice, not unlike the inflection of psalms with antiphons at Matins. The reasons that 'Haec dies' still seems very far from a genuine *psalmus responsorius* are that (1) the whole psalm is not used (not even a large part); (2) there are anomalies in the succession of verses that are used; (3) it is spread out over a week, not sung on one occasion (unless we take seriously the one manuscript of the Sextuplex that indicates it for the Sunday); (4) the melody is very elaborate, making such a performance hard to believe in context; (5) this is a unique case for the special festivities of Easter, for which Psalm 117 has unique associations. What this example can show us in a more immediate and credible way is that (1) psalms can be excerpted in this and various other ways according to need; (2) thematically related materials—melodic as well as textural—can be traced over shorter or longer stretches of the calendar; and (3), 'responsorial form' is a matter of the way the materials are performed, not intrinsic to the materials themselves. All of these things will be valuable when we consider the problem of the Tracts.

The Graduals of the Christmas cycle have strong festal connections. The Graduals for Advent reflect the very consistent programme of that season, and this is true also of the Graduals for Ember Week, Wednesday, Friday and Saturday after the Third Sunday of Advent. Gradual texts for the Sanctorale, as might be expected, are strongly thematic: 'Vindica, Domine, sanguinem sanctorum tuorum'. So are the Graduals for much of the dominical layer, including the three Sundays of Epiphany, and especially those of Pre-Lent and Lent. The remaining part of the repertory—Sundays after Pentecost—is less thematic simply because it is more heterogeneous, and because the

[35] Wagner, *Einführung in die gregorianischen Melodien*, i, pp. 81–92; Apel, *Gregorian Chant*, pp. 182 f., Stäblein, 'Graduale', *MGG*, v (1956) cols. 632–59.

occasions themselves have little or no thematic definition. Here one is tempted most strongly to look for a psalmic cursus (as the Rheinau manuscript does). The texts continue to have a clear devotional character, however, and can still be so interpreted. There is a supplicatory group, with frequent expressions through the first-person psalmist, and passionate outcry characterized by the word 'clamor': 'Ad Dominum dum tribularer clamavi' (Second Sunday after Pentecost). These are concentrated in the first ten or twelve Sundays after Pentecost, and probably reflect the fact that these materials are shared with the Lenten weekday formularies. The remainder of the Pentecost Graduals show a much greater variety of theme (these formularies, including the melodies, are heterogenous in many respects). 'Favourite sentiment from the Psalter', however, continue to be an adequate and generally applicable explanation for all these texts.

There are a few Graduals with several verses. Three of these ('Domine audivi,' 'Domine exaudi,' 'De necessitatibus') are used on days in Lent that have three lessons instead of two; these Graduals come after the second lesson. The Sextuplex labels them as Gradual responsories, indicating a responsorial performance—a repeat of the respond after the verses. These Graduals use a special formulaic system (in mode 2), which was also used for three more longer pieces in the Sextuplex. Dom Hesbert reconstructed the use of these longer pieces as follows:[36] 'Qui habitat', originally for Good Friday, was moved to the First Sunday in Lent; 'Deus, deus meus' was provided for Palm Sunday; and close to the time of the archetype 'Eripe me' was provided for Good Friday. These last three were apparently to be sung without responsorial repeats, and were called Tracts; eventually the first three were also called 'Tracts', and in modern discussions all six, along with later adaptations, are treated as 'the Tracts in mode 2'.

Another larger group of texts, each with several verses, was sung in Lent to another special formulaic system in mode 8. These texts were used mostly on Sundays, with two lessons, and came after the Gradual responsory (that is, not directly after a lesson). They were sung without responsorial repeat, and were labelled 'Tracts'. In style and structure, that is, ignoring the performance of the repeat, they are very similar to the Lenten 'Graduals with several verses' in mode 2.

Three more such pieces in mode 8, for the Holy Saturday Vigil, are post-lesson chants of a particular type: they are lyric episodes that

---

[36] Hesbert, *Antiphonale missarum sextuplex*, pp. l–lx; Wagner, *Einführung in die gregorianischen Melodien*, i, pp. 98–101; Paolo Ferretti, *Esthétique grégorienne*, trans. A Agaësse (Paris, 1938), pp. 147–55; Apel, *Gregorian Chant*, p. 84.

occur at the end of a narrative lesson, as is most clearly shown in the story of how Moses led the Children of Israel across the Red Sea, while the Pharaoh drowned: 'Then Moses sang this song: "Let us sing ..."'. It has been argued that in such cases the lyric episode was originally sung by the lector in some way, and only later was the episode set as a separate song for the cantor.[37] The same construction appears at Ember Saturday in Advent (and at the other seasons) where the fifth lesson, from Daniel, describes the three men in the fiery furnace, followed by the song variously marked *hymnus* or *Benedictiones*—'Benedictus es Domine Deus'. At some later stage, then, these lesson-songs would have been set to the melody used for Tracts in Lent, for the Vigil of Holy Saturday. In the Sextuplex these chants are called *Cantica*; they have three or four verses. In all these matters the important factors would seem to be not the psalm from which the texts were drawn, but rather the way the texts are constituted in the sources before us, the way they are labelled, used in the liturgy, and set to music.

INTROITS

The Introit can be thought of as a psalm with an antiphon. No source assures us, however, that a complete psalm was ever sung at the Introit, and it can only be inferred from the way the reduced psalmody appears in the Sextuplex. Here the term 'introitus' hardly ever appears—just often enough to confirm that the first chant of the formulary was intended to serve in that function. This first chant of the formulary is regularly marked *ant[iphona]*; it is followed by the *psal[mus]*, a verse—usually the first verse—of a psalm. Then certain manuscripts of the Sextuplex further supply, after the superscription *ad r[epetendum]*, another verse usually from the same psalm. The intended procedure has to be reconstructed with the help of the *Ordines romani*, documents that are Frankish reports of Roman practice, beginning in the eighth century.[38] The practice at the Introit varies slightly, but can be imagined to include the singing of the antiphon, and as much of the psalm as desired by the celebrant (while he readies himself before the altar), then the *Gloria Patri*, then the repetition of the antiphon. (We should note, however, that *Ordo I* refers to this repetition as *versus*, presumably in the sense of 'stich', unless there is some confusion with the *versus ad repetendum*, still to be accounted for.)

The *versus ad repetendum* provided by two manuscripts of the

---

[37] Hesbert, *Antiphonale missarum sextuplex*, p. lxii, n. 1.

[38] Michel Andrieu, *Les Ordines romani du haut moyen age*, ii (1948), 81–4, sections 44–52.

Sextuplex has been thought to be a later compensation for the reduction of a whole psalm to the single verse regularly written down in the Sextuplex.[39] This is a credible interpretation. Another more elaborate interpretation is provided by an Eastern practice of following the performance of a complete psalm with the repetition of one or two verses selected from it.[40] This practice is actually much closer to that of the ferial antiphons of the Office than is the usual antiphon at the Introit, which may not be related to the psalm at all. In any case, the use of the *versus ad repetendum*, involving as it does another repeat of the antiphon (and, if the whole psalm were sung, of that verse, too), produces a combination very characteristic of stichic practice.

Introit antiphons are drawn largely—but not exclusively—from psalms; and they are often drawn in the centonized manner of festal stichs, not in the manner of Ferial Office antiphons. These distinctions are especially striking in the case of festal as opposed to dominical layers in the occasions for which the Introits are destined. Of the seven Introits for major feasts (including the three Introits for Christmas) only two are from psalms. Those two are 'Dominus dixit' for the First Mass of Christmas, and 'Resurrexi' for Easter; and of those two, 'Resurrexi' is centonized for the express purpose of getting a text that begins with the word, 'I have risen'. The other, 'Dominus dixit', is a most favoured text for Christmas. All of this seems entirely characteristic for the selection of festal Introits. The Introits for the Sanctorale are consistently thematic for their occasion, those of the dominical layer occasionally so. Many of the dominical layer, however, especially those for Sundays after Pentecost, can only be described as carefully selected, favourite pious sentiments from the Psalter; they are often of a supplicatory nature.

Introit antiphons never have only one phrase like ferial antiphons of the Office; their phrase structure is always compound or complex in keeping with their nature as festal stichs. This larger type of antiphon, like the larger antiphons of the Office, might represent a type quite different from the kind of refrain evident in the ferial antiphons. Here, again, the single term 'antiphon' as used at Rome may mask differences more evident elsewhere. We remember that at Milan the Ingressa was what in Roman terms is described as 'an antiphon-like chant with no psalm'.[41] It might be just as fair to describe these longer

---

[39] Hesbert, *Antiphonale missarum sextuplex*; see the listings for the MSS 'C' and 'S', *passim*; Apel, *Gregorian Chant*, pp. 190 f.

[40] See Miloš Velimirović, 'The Prooemiac Psalm of Byzantine Vespers', *Words and Music: The Scholar's View. A Medley of Problems and Solutions Compiled in Honor of A. Tillman Merritt* (Harvard University, 1972), 317.

[41] Cf. above p. 85.

Roman Introits as 'Ingressa-chants to which a psalm verse, a *Gloria Patri*, and in some cases a *versus ad repetendum*, have been added'. And if that were true, we could imagine that the addition took the form of either a whole psalm, or just a few verses, or just the one verse preserved in the earliest sources.

COMMUNIONS

The Communion antiphons are perhaps the most programmatic of all. While (as we shall see) the Graduals are almost entirely from psalms, and the Introits largely so, Communions for festal and seasonal occasions are largely not from the psalms, and this is an important consideration when evaluating the cursive elements that appear in Communions that *are* from psalms; these cursive elements occur most markedly in the weekdays of Lent. Communions for Advent are often from Isaiah, which is an important source for materials of all kinds for Advent. Communions for the Sanctorale are most often from one of the four Gospels. The Gospels are also used, in a selective way, for different parts of the festal layer: the Christmas cycle draws on Matthew, the Easter cycle on John. Often a Communion will be drawn from the Gospel for the day, hence will provide an echo at the end of Mass of an idea introduced earlier. In a more general way, Communions often repeat or echo texts used previously in the same formulary, especially in the Introit.

It is with all this in mind that we must approach the interesting problem of the Communions of weekdays in Lent. Much discussed, these are cursive in the limited sense that, beginning with Ash Wednesday, each is drawn from the next psalm in order, starting at Psalm 1 and getting as far as Psalm 26 by Palm Sunday.[42] The series includes every day except Sundays and Thursdays; these exclusions reflect, first, the very clear distinction between the dominical and weekday Masses (Mass formularies for weekdays in Lent were instituted at a particular time, long after those for the Sundays); and second, a long-standing distinction between feria v (Thursday) and the other ferias; Mass formularies for feria v were added last, perhaps under Pope Gregory II (715–31). So the Communions for Thursdays are not part of the cursus; four come from psalms (50, 70, 118) and two from John vi. Among the Communions from psalms, five have been replaced by texts drawn from the Gospel for the day.

What are we to conclude from this interesting complex of stichic and cursive elements? First, that the cursive factor is secondary, not

---

[42] Hesbert, *Antiphonale missarum sextuplex,* pp. xlvi f.; Apel, *Gregorian Chant,* p. 64.

primary; this is apparent from the fact that it has been applied to ferias not Sundays (also there is a problem in starting with Ash Wednesday, which is part of a later addition preceding the First Sunday in Lent). It is secondary in another sense, in that the cursus runs through the Communions only and reflects no correlation with the rest of the formulary, and certainly does not produce one. Second, this particular cursus is interrupted for good cause, the use of stichs from the Gospel for the day. Third, while this cursus does not reflect any initial stage of formation, neither does it reflect a final stage, since it is followed by the formularies for Thursdays, which are non-cursive. Fourth, we can observe that the choice of stichs is programmatic at the same time that it is cursive, in much the same way as antiphons for festal Matins.

We can regard the Communions of Lent, then, as a particular solution to filling out the 'circle of the year'. The propriety of a text for a particular occasion or function remains the primary determinate, and as a matter of fact this sense of propriety emerges more and more clearly the more one studies the whole repertory of chants at Mass. Often the language of the psalms, removed as it is from the immediate occasions commemorated in the Christian calendar, obscures the relationship between a text from a psalm and the occasion to which it is assigned. Here it is useful to remember that a text need not be firmly programmatic; it need only be appropriate, compatible with an occasion. And the power of far-reaching allusion must have been keenly felt by the seventh- and eighth-century liturgists at work on the formularies.

Large portions of the dominical layer have no clearly defined themes or programmes such as Christmas or Easter, Advent or Lent. In particular the Sundays after Pentecost are without such programmes, and here, coincidentally, we find more cursive arrangements comparable to those of the Lenten weekdays.[43] These two groups of formularies have much in common, and share many specific items—not whole formularies, but individual chants used in different formularies. There is an unresolved problem as to whether items, individually or in groups, were borrowed from Sundays after Pentecost for the Lenten cycle, or the reverse. Not only the Communions, but also the Introits and the Offertories show some organization (by ascending numbers of psalm texts) through the Sundays after Pentecost. The organization is not of the consecutive type of the Lenten Communions, however, but rather the intermittent type of Christmas

---

[43] Hesbert, *Antiphonale missarum sextuplex*, pp. lxxiv–lxxix.

Matins. It is not synchronized among the three series (Introits, Offertories, Communions), and in all three cases suffers interruptions and progressive deterioration towards the end of the cycle. Throughout this part of the repertory the sense of propriety in the selection of stichs remains strong, sometimes with reference to the function at Mass (Introit, Offertory, Communion) rather than to the occasion. This produces some striking results in the case of the Offertories, which we shall soon consider. In general one could imagine that, far from these texts being generated out of a cursus of psalmody, they first existed as a pool of appropriate items that for convenience were arranged in ascending numerical order according to their psalm of origin, then assigned in that order to the Sundays after Pentecost. Precisely this process can be seen operating in one manuscript of the Sextuplex (Rheinau) for the Graduals: these are not arranged in a cursus normally, but Rheinau so arranges them and reassigns them to the Sundays, thus reconstituting the formularies. The whole aspect of quasi-cursive psalmody in the Mass formularies strongly suggests that the Roman liturgists of the seventh and eighth centuries were placing great value on the cursus of the Office, and sought to arrange the stichic materials at Mass (materials that must have seemed to them to some degree idiosyncratic and arbitrary) into some more rational order, at a time when relatively large quantities of these materials were being generated or adapted to fill out the year-long calendar.

OFFERTORIES

The Offertories vary greatly in dimensions: they can be short, or very long. They have no 'psalm' (and no *versus ad repetendum*); but they do have a verse, like a responsory, usually two or even three verses, each followed by the repetition of a portion of the initial section.[44] What to call this initial section is a problem, and scholars hesitate between calling it an antiphon (with the implication that the verses are the remains of a reduced psalm, as presumed for Introit and Communion), and thinking of it as a respond, in which case the verses reflect normal responsory usage, in a more abundant state than that represented by the Gradual responsory which usually has only one verse (but the melodies of the Offertory verses cannot be very old).[45]

---

[44] Rupert Fischer, *Offertoires neumés avec leurs versets* (Solesmes, 1978); Ruth Steiner, 'Some Questions about the Gregorian Offertories and Their Verses', *JAMS*, 19 (1966), 162; Wagner, *Einführung in die gregorianischen Melodien*, i, pp. 106–13; Apel, *Gregorian Chant*, pp. 192–6; Hucke, 'Die Texte der Offertorien', in H. Becker and R. Gerlach, eds., *Speculum musicae artis: Festgabe für Heinrich Husmann zum 70. Geburtstage* (Munich, 1970), 193; Joseph Dyer, 'The Offertory Chant of the Roman Liturgy and its Musical Form', *Studi musicali*, 11 (1982), 3.

[45] Apel, *Gregorian Chant*, pp. 192–6.

Actually, the Sextuplex says nothing about 'antiphona' (not even elliptically, 'ad offertorium' as it does 'ad communionem'), but merely *Of[fertorium]*. Not all manuscripts provide the verses. We can be perplexed as to why the Offertory fails to conform to the standard categories; or we can acknowledge that these categories represent merely the normalizing predilections of certain sources, and recognize that ritual song, even at Rome, could include simply a stich with an (optional) verse or two.

The liturgical problem with Offertories is that their function has been presumed to be to accompany the bringing forward of the people's offerings;[46] but of this there seems to be no trace of a mention in the texts themselves. Given a similar lack of indication in Introits, that might not mean anything; but Offertory texts of the dominical layer do reflect a function—another one—and a few special Offertories make this explicit.

To mention the festal Offertories first and briefly, they can be naïvely programmatic, as for the First Mass of Christmas, 'Laetentur caeli' ('... of the Lord, who comes'); or sophisticated in their allusion to the theme, as for the Second and Third Masses, 'Deus enim firmavit' and 'Tui sunt caeli' (psalm texts concerning the Creation of the universe, with the allusion that this was the preparation of a place—specifically, the manger—where He might come). Other festal Offertories are similarly programmatic. Offertories of the dominical layer, however, often seem to speak the words of a prayer, a direct address to God; there are admittedly enough such texts in the psalms that almost any selection from the Psalter is going to produce a good proportion of them; none the less it seems characteristic of Offertories. Two cases provide Old Testament figures of such prayer: 'Precatus est Moyses in conspectu Domini' (12th Sunday after Pentecost), and 'Oravi Deum meum ego Daniel dicens' (17th Sunday after Pentecost). Then again the Offertories for the 7th and 8th Sundays after Pentecost (both may be non-Roman additions) refer specifically to the preparing of the altar for the sacrifice—an entirely distinct yet very appropriate function, but one that would involve a discussion of what was considered to go on at Mass in those centuries. Finally, there is the clear case of a Frankish addition, 'Stetit autem angelus', for St Michael's Day ('An angel stood before the altar of God with a golden thurible...'), referring to yet another ritual function. Indeed, while the Offertory is being sung, the celebrant is standing at the altar praying; and eventually the altar is censed. What is obvious in the case

---

[46] Jungmann, *Missarum Solemnia*, ii, pp. 34–40; Dyer, 'The Offertory Chant', p. 3.

of these striking texts is true in a general, if more subdued, way, throughout the repertory of chants for Mass: allusion to theme or programme, whether of occasion or function, is a primary determinant, even—or especially—in the selection of psalm texts.

V

CHANTS OF THE ROMAN OFFICE

By RICHARD CROCKER

CHANT for the Roman Office consists mostly of antiphons and responsories, in roughly equal proportions.[1] Of these two types, antiphons are the simpler in musical structure, and can well be considered first; they are not, however, necessarily older than responsories. Around the middle of the ninth century, close to the time of the archetype, Gregorian antiphons seem to number around 1,600. It has yet to be determined how many of these came from Rome, and how many are due to Frankish cantors, either as new melodies or as adaptations of Roman ones—or of pre-Carolingian Gallican melodies.

Just as the words of antiphons can properly be understood only in the context of the Office psalmody which they adorn and articulate, so the melodies of antiphons can be understood only together with the psalm tones used to chant the psalms. The psalms of the Office were sung in what comes down to us as a system of eight psalm tones, set out (in slightly purified form) in modern chant books more or less as used since the later Middle Ages.[2] Manuscript sources for earlier in the Middle Ages seem to show more variety, or inconsistency, in the use of these tones, but we do not yet have a full critical report to tell us how the earlier versions might have gone. The later versions, however, are sufficient for present purposes.

In general, psalm tones involve a pitch on which the psalm as a whole is intoned; this pitch is the *tenor* or *tuba*, in modern terms, the 'reciting tone'. In any one of the eight psalm tones it is surrounded by a certain configuration of whole and half steps. Each of the eight

---

[1] Cf. above, p. 117, for sources for Office chants.

[2] *Liber usualis*, ed. Benedictines of Solesmes (Tournai, various editions), 113–17; *Antiphonale monasticum pro diurnis horis* ... ordinis sancti Benedicti a Solesmensibus monachis restitutum (Desclee, 1934), 1210–19; Willi Apel, *Gregorian Chant* (Bloomington, 1958), 217–26; Terence Bailey, 'Accented and Cursive Cadences in Gregorian Psalmody', *JAMS*, 29 (1976), 463. Thomas Connolly, 'Psalm II. Latin monophonic Psalmody', *New Grove* xv. 322–32.

psalm tones has an 'intonation', which rises by step or leap through two or three notes to the reciting tone (see Ex. 43 below). Then each of the eight tones has a 'mediant' inflection, involving auxiliary-note motion around the reciting tone. And finally, after a resumption of the reciting tone, each of the eight tones has one or several alternative closing inflections, which usually fall through several notes.

Ex. 43

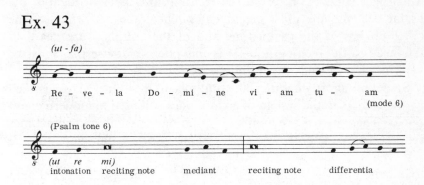

These melodic features of psalm tones accommodate the usual structure of psalm verses. These in general are each a syntactic unit, which in the Hebrew original were also a rhythmic or metric unit of some kind. In the Latin versions they are still syntactic units, but because of the literal nature of the translations, no longer have any regular rhythmic or metric structure, being, in effect, prose. A majority of verses are divided into two parts (some are not so divided, however, and many have three or more parts). The inflections of the psalm tones accommodate the usual division into two parts, with the first part being terminated with the mediant inflection.

Psalm tones are formulas that can be adapted to many different texts: any psalm can be sung to any one of the eight regular psalm tones. Each antiphon text, however, has its own melody, even though two or more antiphons may be very similar (indeed, antiphon melodies tend to come in families, as we will see). None the less, psalm tones and antiphons are essentially different in this respect. At present we do not know how the system of antiphon melodies and psalm tones came about, but in the practice as documented since the ninth century the procedure is this: the melody of the antiphon assigned for a particular occasion determines the choice of the psalm tone. The psalm tone to be selected is to match the configuration of whole and half steps in the antiphon melody; and from the several alternate endings provided for most of the eight tones, one is to be selected which facilitates the repetition of the antiphon, whether at the end of each verse or only at the end of the psalm. There is an element of choice in the selection of an ending, and sources vary in this choice. Each alternate ending of a psalm tone is usually called a *differentia* or 'difference'.

An antiphon is usually very much shorter than the psalm with which it is sung. As a result, the reciting note used throughout the psalm becomes the most prominent pitch of the performance; the other pitches of the psalm tone and of the antiphon are heard in reference to the reciting note. It is this pitch reference that must be kept in mind in studying antiphons.

Sometime shortly before 800, antiphons of the Office were classified by the Franks in the system of eight modes still used in modern chant books. These modes are numbered from one to eight, and sometimes referred to by the borrowed Greek names, dorian, phrygian, and the rest.[3] These modes were co-ordinated with the system of eight psalm tones, and this was the means of determining which psalm tone should be used to sing the psalm to go with any antiphon.

It has been acknowledged for some time that the Western system of eight modes followed rather than preceded the formation of the Roman repertory, and that it was probably contemporaneous with the diffusion of this repertory to the Frankish kingdom.[4] It is important for us to try to understand the antiphons of the Office, with their psalmody, as they might have been before the development of the modal system. A way to do this has been set forth by Dom Jean Claire in connection with the antiphons of the Ferial Office.[5] These particular antiphons are interesting because their pitch structures are sometimes not those most typical of the modal system; the context of the Ferial Office suggests that their idiosyncrasies represent practice of the eighth century or earlier.

The modal system, as used from 800 on, classified antiphons by their 'final' or last notes. Dom Claire shows that it is more useful to observe the note or notes on which the antiphon dwells rather than the note on which it ends. He draws attention to the fact that this final note is often not a good index to the pitch structure of the antiphon, and often not closely related to the reciting note. As we will see, the classification by final was made for a good and practical reason; but that reason was not the analysis of the melodies, and classification is

[3] Cf. above, p. 46.

[4] Cf. below, pp. 165–9.

[5] 'Les Répertoires liturgiques latins avant l'octoéchos. L'office férial Romano-Franc', *Eg*, 15 (1975), 85.

not particularly appropriate for analysis. Furthermore, the eight modes as classified by finals were placed upon the diatonic scale (the Greater Perfect System in diatonic genus as inherited from antiquity[6]) so that the final of modes 1 and 2 was D, of modes 3 and 4 E, of modes 5 and 6 F, and of modes 7 and 8 G; this location of the modes has been in use ever since. It is not clear, however, that these locations of the finals represent the relationship among the melodies in earlier practice.

In any case, finals are not good guides to melodic structure of earlier chant (specifically of eighth-century Roman chant), and letter-locations on the diatonic scale make comparison between modes difficult. For an unprejudicial understanding of the earlier stages of the repertory we need a way to compare patterns of internal structure directly. The best way is to use solmization, which gives precise designation of interval structure involving tones and semitones without reference to letter names. Solmization according to the hexachord—*ut, re, mi, fa, sol, la* (as in modern movable-*do* practice, with *ut* instead of *do*)—was developed soon after the year 1000, seemingly just for this purpose.[7] This medieval solmization is the most appropriate for description of chant.

It can be observed in general that the traditional psalm tones move within the pitch set represented by *ut–re–mi–fa*. Thus psalm tones 4 and 7 recite on *re*, psalm tones 1 and 6 on *mi*, psalm tones 2, 3, 5, and 8 on *fa* (in their received forms; before 1000 there seems to have been some use of *mi* instead of *fa* in tones 3 and 8).

Many of the alternate endings (differentiae) for these psalm tones are also contained with the set *ut–re–mi–fa*; but some of the differentiae, and most of the antiphons associated with the psalm tones, need more pitches, usually those lying below this set. Within the diatonic system the pitches below *ut* will either descend from *ut* through a tone, a semitone, and a tone; or will descend through a semitone, then a tone, and another tone. In the first case the pitches below the *ut* will be solmized (in descending order) *fa mi re*; considered in relationship to these, the original *ut* will be *sol*, and can be referred to as *ut–sol*.

```
                        ut  re mi  fa sol la
                ut re mi fa sol
for example:    C  D  E  F  G   a  b   c  d   e
or:             F  G  a  bᵇ c   d  e   f  g   a
```

In the second case, the pitches below the *ut* will be (in descending

[6] See R. P. Winnington-Ingram, 'Greece I. Ancient', *New Grove*, vii. 664.
[7] Crocker, 'Hermann's Major Sixth', *JAMS*, 25 (1972), 19.

order) *mi re ut*, and in relation to them the original *ut* will be *fa*, or *ut–fa*.

```
                    ut re   mi fa   sol la
            ut re mi fa
for example: G a b c d    e f    g a
or:          C D E F G    a bᵇ   c d
```

Using this nomenclature, all psalm tones and antiphons can be referred to the set *ut, re, mi, fa* in one of these two combinations, and hence more easily compared. In addition to making possible that comparison, solmization also calls attention to the prominent position of the set *ut, re, mi, fa* throughout the repertory, and provides a means of differentiating melodies and groups of melodies on the basis of their interior substance rather than just their final (or final and range) as in the modal classification.

ANTIPHONS OF THE FERIAL OFFICE

Ex. 43 shows the first of eight psalmic antiphons from the Ferial Office, in melodic versions established by Dom Claire on the basis of Urban-Roman manuscripts and a selection of Frankish-Roman ones.[8] 'Revela Domino' is sung on Monday (feria ii) in the Night Office with Psalm 36, 'Noli aemulari', of which it is verse 5 (first half). This text is one short, indivisible syntactic unit. It is easy to imagine such an antiphon being used in any of the performance arrangements that have been suggested: it could easily be repeated by the whole community after each verse had been sung antiphonally by the two halves of the community, or after each pair of verses, if that was the unit of alternation. Or it could be sung alternately by each half after the leader of each half had sung a verse. In text as well as melody it can be used in a variety of ways as desired, and that is the main conclusion we should draw.

The antiphon 'Revela Domino'[9] moves within a pitch set that can be solmized *ut re mi* (notated here F, G, a), ending on *ut*. It descends below the final *ut*, which is *ut–fa*, through *mi, re, ut*. The antiphon was classified as mode 6, and calls for psalm tone 6, which recites on *mi* (a), using the pitch set *ut re mi*. This shared use of the *ut re mi* (F, G, a) is what makes the psalm tone go with the antiphon, which, however, has the lower pitches not used in the psalm tone. As we will see, it is

---

[8] 'Les Répertoires liturgiques'; the transcriptions, appearing between pp. 20–50, are cited by number. For Urban-Roman psalm tones see also Helmut Hucke, 'Karolingische Renaissance und Gregorianischer Gesang', *Die Musikforschung*, 28 (1975), 4.

[9] Claire, 'Les Répertoires liturgiques', No. 6 (source 'Rom 1').

important to think of the shared pitches as a set, not just as the single pitch that is the reciting tone. In the performance of the psalm with antiphon, the reciting note and the other shared pitches will be extremely prominent, providing the basic continuum, and this will profoundly affect our perception of the whole antiphon. This does not mean that the antiphon melody is merely another statement of the psalm tone, for by contrast to the reiterated pitches of the psalm tone the lower pitches of the antiphon that are not included in the psalm tone will also be prominent, and the profile of the antiphon will emerge as distinct from the psalm tone.

Ex. 44

Cla - ma - vi   et   ex - au - di - vit   me   (an irregular psalm tone
                                                     reciting on *mi*)

The melody of 'Revela Domino' and its psalm tone are used for other ferial antiphons of the Night Office; Dom Claire identifies this as one of the basic melodies of the Roman Office. Another basic melody is used for 'Clamavi' (Ex. 44).[10] This melody occupies the pitch set *ut re mi fa* (notated here F, G, a, b flat). It is one of several ferial antiphons whose classification was not clear (because of its narrow range), and it was associated with one of the irregular psalm tones. The psalm tone recites on *mi*, however, and its pitch set is closely matched to the antiphon. Still another antiphon with irregular psalm tone is 'In tua justicia' (Ex. 45).[11] This one is based on the set *ut re mi fa* (G, a, b, c), ending on *mi*, and has a psalm tone that recites on *fa*. This is one of several melodies that Dom Claire believes is not part of the older Roman Ferial Office; for our purposes it is enough to see it as part of the standard Frankish-Roman repertory.

Ex. 45

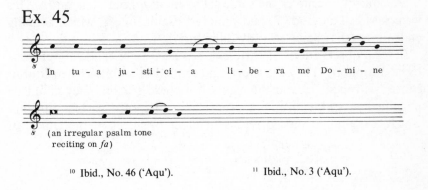

In   tu - a   ju - sti - ci - a   li - be - ra   me   Do - mi - ne

(an irregular psalm tone
reciting on *fa*)

[10] Ibid., No. 46 ('Aqu').   [11] Ibid., No. 3 ('Aqu').

The next group of antiphons are all based on the pitch set *ut re mi fa* (G, a, b, c) with final on *ut*; they were all classified as mode 8, and use psalm tone 8, which recites on *fa* (Ex. 46). The antiphon 'Deus deorum'[12] stays within this set. The other three antiphons, 'In veritate',[13] 'In ecclesiis',[14] and 'Avertit',[15] all include a note a whole step below the *ut*, and so this *ut* is *ut–sol*, and the note below is *fa*. There is a strong tendency, observable in 'Avertit', for this *fa* to be combined with the notes a third and a fifth above it (F, a, c) to form a group that contrast with the *ut* final. For 'Deus deorum' there is a differentia that ends on *re* (a), and in general psalm tones use many differentiae that do not end on the final of the antiphon.

Ex. 46

(i) (mode 8)

De - us de - o - rum Do - mi - nus lo - cu - tus est   (Psalm tone 8)

(ii)

In ve - ri - ta - te tu - a ex - au - di me Do - mi - ne   (Psalm tone 8)

(iii)

In ec - cle - si - is be - ne - di - ci - te Do - mi - no   (Psalm tone 8)

(iv)

A - ver - tit Do - mi - nus ca - pti - vi - ta - tem ple - bis su - ae   (Psalm tone 8)

'A timore'[16] occupies the same set *ut re mi fa*, but ends on *re*. This was classified as mode 2, and required psalm tone 2, which actually ends on *re* (that being its only differentia).

Several observations of various kinds need to be made about these ferial antiphons. They are short, and limited in ambitus; their liturgical use is repetitive and intensive. For these reasons they could be imagined as surviving intact over a long historical period. In other words, they might indeed represent older practices of the Office, of

[12] Ibid., No. 13 ('Aqu').   [15] Ibid., No. 15 ('Aqu').
[13] Ibid., No. 35*bis* ('Aqu').   [16] Ibid., No. 19*bis* ('Aqu').
[14] Ibid., No. 20*bis* ('Aqu').

Ex. 47

(mode 2)

A ti - mo-re i - ni - mi-ci e - ri -pe Do-mi- ne a - ni - mam me-am

(Psalm tone 2)

Roman or Gallican chant. For precisely the same reasons, however, they might also be subject to substantial change over a period, and indeed, the versions and sources presented by Dom Claire show just such change for the period 800–1200. Also, because of the limited ambitus, they do not tell us much about melodic style: the two whole tones of the major third *ut–re–mi* are not much more than simple inflections between two pitches a tone apart. Finally, even if these simple antiphons could be reliably placed in, say, the sixth century at the beginning of a process of development that led to much more varied and elaborate melodies, we should not conclude that these were the only melodies in existence in the sixth century, and that their subsequent development constitutes the general development of musical style in that time. These are the ferial antiphons of the Office, nothing more, a repertory of some thirty-six chants (Dom Claire adds another six from Lauds and thirty-five from Vespers for comparison).

The total antiphon repertory in the twelfth-century Urban-Roman manuscripts is more than 1,000, in the ninth-century Frankish sources over 1,600. There are fascinating developments within the ferial repertory, but these developments could just as well have been the result, rather than the cause, of developments in other repertories—or better, concomitant with other developments.

The versions of the antiphons shown here have been selected from the many versions studied by Dom Claire, whose purpose was to study the development of the repertory through the different versions. Ex. 48 shows Dom Claire's transcription of the ferial antiphon 'Fundamenta' in three versions;[17] the problem is to see that the substance of the antiphon is the same in spite of the different modal classifications and assignment of psalm tones. The first version (i) begins in an *ut re mi* set similar to 'Revela', and uses psalm tone 1, which, like psalm tone 6, recites on *mi*; but then 'Fundamenta' descends to end on the *re* (D) below the *ut*. Dom Claire argues that it

[17] Ibid., No. 32, (i) ('Aqu'), (ii) ('Rom 2'), (iii) ('Rom 1').

Ex. 48

(i)

Fun - da- men - ta   e - jus   in   mon - ti - bus   san - ctis   (Psalm tone 1
                                                                            reciting on *mi*)

(ii)

Fun - da- men - ta   e - jus   in   mon - ti - bus   san - ctis   (Psalm tone 8
                                                                            reciting on *fa*)

(iii)

Fun - da - men - ta   e - jus   in   mon - ti - bus   san - ctis   (Psalm tone 3
                                                                             reciting on *fa*)

is more fruitful to see this as a melody oriented around the *mi* reciting note and the *ut* beginning, with a 'terminal descent', rather than as a new class of melody based on the final *re* (D).

Continuing with the second version of 'Fundamenta' (ii), which uses psalm tone 8 reciting on *fa*, we can imagine this *fa* as standing a half step above the *mi* of the first version—as if psalm tone 8 were a slightly elevated version of psalm tone 1. This could also have been shown by notating the second version with two flats, a tone lower than it is notated; but the same can be accomplished by solmizing it with *ut* on G. It is based on the same *ut re mi* as 'Fundamenta' (i) (and also 'Revela') but without the terminal descent; and its *ut* is *ut–sol* rather than *ut–fa*. By hypothesis, both the first and second versions of 'Fundamenta' could have been derived from an imaginary prototype that resembled 'Revela'. The third version of 'Fundamenta' (iii) occupies the same set *ut re mi fa* as the second version (and here notated at the same place); its *ut* is *ut–sol*, and it has a terminal descent to *mi* (E); it uses psalm tone 3, reciting on *fa* (c). In other words, it has features of both the first and second versions. The point is not that transformations took place in this particular way, but rather that the treatment of variants in the Frankish-Roman sources (and especially in the Urban-Roman sources) will require a means of analysis more comprehensive than the modal classification by final.

ANTIPHONS OF THE TEMPORALE AND SANCTORALE

Antiphons of the Temporale and Sanctorale series are far more numerous (ten or twenty times, even within the ninth-century repertory) than the ferial group.[18] They are also more elaborate—longer, more extended in range, more complex in melodic inflection. They are not, however, more varied in overall stock of melodies, and in fact tend to concentrate on a relatively small group of melodies, much of it represented in Exx. 49–52 below.

Continuing for the moment the *ad hoc* nomenclature and classification of tonal structure used for ferial antiphons, we should first describe groups of antiphon melodies using *ut–re–mi* and ending on *ut–sol*, with a psalm tone that recites on *fa*. These groups include a multiplicity of melodies and families of melodies, as well as several overlapping pitch sets. It is possible—indeed, probable—that what we treat here as one very large group (because subsequently classified as mode 8) represents the confluence of a varied and disparate stock of melodies. As the classification proceeded, it may itself have forced modifications in the melodies to lessen the disparities and make the different types of melody seem less different than they previously were. In any case, the resulting class (mode 8) is one of the largest in the early tonaries.

All the melodies in Ex. 49 end on *ut–sol*, and extend below it.[19] At the least they include the *fa* below; that seems to be a distinctive feature of these melodies. This *fa* has an unstable relationship to the *mi* above, and this tension seems also to be a distinctive feature of these antiphons. The low *fa* (F) is often set in the ascending progression F–a–c, which tends to surround and bracket the final *ut* and the *mi* above it.

A real descent below this low *fa* occurs in some melodies of this class, not as a terminal but rather as a penultimate descent, as in 'Hoc est praeceptum' (Ex. 49(iv)); in 'Formans me ex utero' (Ex. 49(vi)) it occurs at the beginning as well. In some melodies of this class,

---

[18] See *Antiphonale Sarisburiense*, ed. Walter Howard Frere, Introduction (Plainsong & Mediæval Music Society, 1923–5), 64–76; François Auguste Gevaert, *La Melopée antique dans le chant de l'Eglise latine* (Ghent, 1895–6); Peter Wagner, *Einführung in die gregorianischen Melodien*, i, *Ursprung und Entwicklung der liturgischen Gesangsformen bis zum Ausgange des Mittelalters* (3rd edn., Leipzig, 1911); iii, *Gregorianische Formenlehre, Eine choralische Stilkunde* (Leipzig, 1921), 303–13; Apel, *Gregorian Chant*, pp. 392–404; Bruno Stäblein, 'Antiphon', *MGG*, i (1949–51), cols. 523–45; Walther Lipphardt, *Der karolingische Tonar von Metz, Liturgiewissenschaftliche Quellen und Forschungen*, xliii (Münster, 1965); Michel Huglo, 'Antiphon', *New Grove*, i. 471.

[19] (i) *Paléographie musicale*, 9: *Antiphonaire monastique (XIIe siècle): codex 601 de la Bibliothéque capitulaire de Lucques*, ed. A. Mocquereau (Tournai, 1906), 257; (ii) *Liber usualis*, p. 378; (iii) Frere, *Antiphonale Sarisburiense*, p. 75; (iv) *Antiphonale sacrosanctae romanae ecclesiae pro diurnis horis* a Pio Papa X restitutum et editum ... (Rome, 1919), p. [1]; (v) Frere, *Antiphonale Sarisburiense*, p. 74; (vi) ibid.

Ex. 49

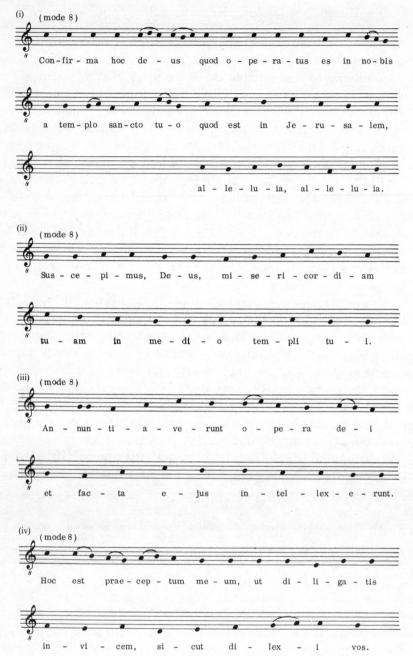

(i) (mode 8)

Con - fir - ma hoc de - us quod o - pe - ra - tus es in no - bis

a tem - plo san - cto tu - o quod est in Je - ru - sa - lem,

al - le - lu - ia, al - le - lu - ia.

(ii) (mode 8)

Sus - ce - pi - mus, De - us, mi - se - ri - cor - di - am

tu - am in me - di - o tem - pli tu - i.

(iii) (mode 8)

An - nun - ti - a - ve - runt o - pe - ra de - i

et fac - ta e - jus in - tel - lex - e - runt.

(iv) (mode 8)

Hoc est prae - cep - tum me - um, ut di - li - ga - tis

in - vi - cem, si - cut di - lex - i vos.

especially longer ones, this lower register is extensively developed, at the expense of the higher central locus.

None of these examples has the fully developed multi-phrase structure we shall find in larger antiphons; they show, at most, two phrases so closely linked as to be inseparable. This type of melodic construction is a characteristic setting of the classic stich, which may easily subsume a pair of hemistichs under a single integral structure.

In this class of antiphon, as in the others, there are frequent instances of a new text being set to the melody of an existing antiphon with minimal change; in such a case, where the original antiphon functions as a model melody, this may generate anything from one to a hundred new versions. Such a family of antiphons can be easily analysed and the results shown on a chart.[20] In many more cases, however, the degree of relationship among antiphons is much looser; two antiphons may share only an intonation or a cadence, or an interior turn of phrase. Or they may simply move in the same pitch set with very subtle similarities of motion.

Within the class of antiphons just mentioned, and more generally throughout the whole repertory of Latin chant, two complementary,

[20] See for example the chart of a mode 8 melody in Paolo Ferretti, *Esthétique grégorienne*, i, trans. A. Agaësse (Tournai, 1938), after p. 108.

if seemingly contradictory, processes were going on at once during the eighth and ninth centuries. Model melodies were generating increasingly broad, diffused groups of melodies through progressive individuation of detail, as well as by expansion or recombination of existing material; this process resulted in a greater and greater variety of melodies. And simultaneously a few model melodies were being used with increasing frequency, and increasing concentration on a few favourite turns of phrase; this process resulted in a greater and greater standardization of melody. The constitution of the repertory—the 'state of the art'—depended on the balance between these two processes at a given moment, and one or the other may well prevail, for very complex historical reasons. The antiphons of the Temporale and Sanctorale in general, and these antiphons in particular, are in the ninth century in a phase of great expansion, and we should allow for the possibility of both processes going on intensively. At present it is not possible to say to what degree these processes were carried on in Rome or in Frankishland, by Roman cantors or by Frankish.

Another large class of antiphons has a central pitch set *ut re mi* (F, G, a), and the reciting note of the psalm tone is *mi*. One relatively small group of this class of antiphon ends on the *ut*, and was classified mode 6 (as 'Revela'); it also has extension into the register below *ut*, but always in the body of the antiphon, never as a terminal descent. A much larger group—one of the largest groups of antiphons—has a terminal descent to *re*, and was classified as mode 1. Within this group there are several families of melodies. It is a general characteristic of the group that it has a well-developed set of intonation formulas that rise from the low *re*—usually from the *ut* below the *re* (C, D)—up to the reciting note *mi* (a). In conjunction with the terminal descent, the rising intonation gives the typical antiphon in this class an arch form, which has often been taken to be characteristic of all Gregorian chant. In many of the more developed or extended antiphons of this group, and even in some of the relatively simple ones, the terminal descent appears in non-terminal locations, or at interior cadences; and in general the lower register below the *ut–fa* is exploited. In antiphons of the Temporale and Sanctorale, however, the register above the reciting note is not much developed, leaving the reciting note itself near the top of the range for this group.

'Qui mihi ministrat' (Ex. 50(i)) is a melody much used in the Sanctorale, and also in the Temporale.[21] The intonation formula in particular is frequent, preserving its basic shape clearly throughout a number of logical modifications made to accommodate various

----

[21] (i), *Antiphonale Romanum*, pp. [14] f.; (ii) ibid. 306; (iii) ibid. 332.

Ex. 50

(i) (mode 1)

Qui mi – hi mi – ni – strat me se – qua – tur

et u – bi e – go sum, il – lic sit et mi – ni – ster me – us.

(ii) (mode 1)

Cor mun – dum cre – a in me De – us

spi – ri – tum rec – tum in – no – va in vi – sce – ri – bus me – is.

(iii) (mode 1)

Sol et lu – na lau – da – te De – um

qui – a ex – al – ta – tum est no – men e – jus so – li – us.

patterns of syllables and accents. The first phrase typically includes the *fa* above the upper *mi* (or sometimes a *sol* instead) near a principal accent, as an upper auxiliary. The second phrase typically begins on *re* (G), and sometimes as if reciting there (see 'Qui me confessus' from the same set of antiphons for Lauds). In such cases it is useful to keep in mind the pitch set (here, *ut re mi*, F, G, a) as a place where several different kinds of melodic activity, moving or static, can occur on any of the pitches of the set. The reciting note of the psalm tone is only one pitch of the set, one which has been stabilized for the sake of recitation of the body of the psalm text. The use of *re* (G) here as a temporary reciting note is only one of many such instances, and we should not place undue emphasis on the reciting tone, nor see great implications in shifts of reciting tone within a given chant.

Psalm tones 1 and 6 recite on *mi*, tones 2, 3, 5 and 8 on *fa*. From one point of view it is useful to see psalm tone 7 as reciting on *re*; this

shows its differences in terms of neighbouring intervals as compared
to the other reciting notes *mi* and *fa*. From another point of view it is
useful to see psalm tone 7's reciting tone as *sol*. Antiphons that require
this tone have their final on *ut*, coinciding with the final and pitch set
of antiphons in mode 8, whose reciting note is *fa*. Compared to that,
the reciting note for tone 7 can be seen as coming a whole step higher
than the one for tone 8, hence *sol*.

Ex. 51 shows three antiphons that use psalm tone 7, reciting on *re*
or *sol* (notated d).[22] Each of these three antiphons begins on and
around this *sol*, but soon drops to the *ut*. Each also gives some
emphasis to *fa* (c) in its second phrase, and in that respect shows
affinity with the central role of *fa* in antiphons classed as mode 8.

Ex. 51

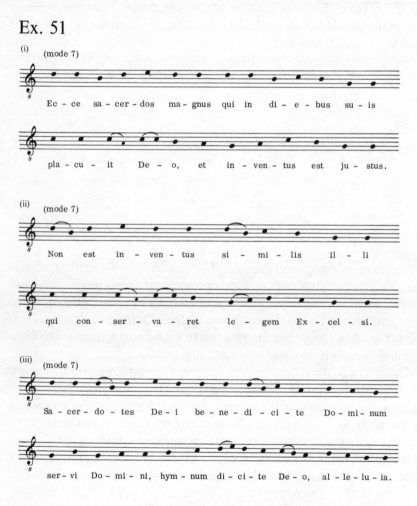

(i) (mode 7)

Ec - ce sa - cer - dos ma - gnus qui in di - e - bus su - is

pla - cu - it De - o, et in - ven - tus est ju - stus.

(ii) (mode 7)

Non est in - ven - tus si - mi - lis il - li

qui con - ser - va - ret le - gem Ex - cel - si.

(iii) (mode 7)

Sa - cer - do - tes De - i be - ne - di - ci - te Do - mi - num

ser - vi Do - mi - ni, hym - num di - ci - te De - o, al - le - lu - ia.

---

[22] (i), (ii), (iii), *Antiphonale Romanum*, pp. [39] f.

Ex. 52 shows one of the most striking instances of a model melody, one that has perhaps the largest number of adaptations.[23] This melody has two phrases, of which the first shows clear movement from *ut* up to *sol*, very reminiscent of the pitch set used in antiphons classed as mode 7 (and even sharing idioms with some of them). The second phrase circles around the *fa* (c), then drops to the *fa* below *ut* (F); this *fa* is then treated as *ut*, and the melody rises from this new *ut* to a new *sol* (c), to end on a new *mi*(a), The b flat, however, is in some instances avoided, in some made b natural, and hence there is ambiguity in the melody. This ambiguity is reflected in some uncertainty about the classification of the antiphon and the choice of psalm tone—occasionally tone 7, but generally tone 4, which has a reciting note on *re* like tone 7.[24] (In order to match the usual location of this antiphon on G-*ut*, psalm tone 4 has to be placed on d-*re* rather than the more usual a-*re*.) While many texts are set to this melody with skill and sensitivity to traditional Gregorian procedures, there is still something different about it. The melody is used extensively in both Temporale and Sanctorale, in some seasons, especially Advent. It is used as much for Gospel Canticles as for psalms; although here it may be significant that this melody is hardly ever used for Gospel Canticles on Sunday, while frequently on weekdays.

Ex. 52

The growth in the antiphon repertory may well have been greatest in the subclass of antiphons for the Gospel Canticles, Benedictus at Lauds, Magnificat at Vespers. In the Gregorian repertory of the Roman Office as we have it *c.* 870, these Gospel-Canticle antiphons are the single largest group—roughly half of the nominal total of 1,600 antiphons. Gospel-Canticle antiphons are provided for every

[23] *Antiphonale Romanum,* p. 238.

[24] Gevaert, *La Melopée antique,* thème 29, pp. 205–12, 322–30; Frere, *Antiphonale Sarisburiense,* p. 70; Wagner, *Einführung in die gregorianischen Melodien,* iii, pp. 309–13; *Paléographie musicale,* 15: *Le Codex VI.34 de la Bibliothèque capitulaire de Bénévent (XIe–XIIe siècle): graduel de Bénévent avec prosaire et tropaire* (Tournai, 1937), 40–6; Apel, *Gregorian Chant,* 339; Lipphardt, *Der karolingische Tonar von Metz,* 276–9.

feast and saint's day, every Sunday, and many ferias, primarily those of Advent and Lent. These two antiphons constitute the minimum provision of Proper chant for an occasion, the maximum being a complete set of antiphons (and responsories) for the Night Office, Lauds, Vespers, the Day Hours; the median provision is a set of five antiphons for Lauds with two for Gospel Canticles.

The repertory of Gospel-Canticle antiphons, with more than 800 in the early sources, is a rich one yet to be adequately described, analysed, and understood in a chronological (let alone developmental) context. It is full of variety in dimensions, from short and simple to extremely long and elaborate, and with many individual aspects. All the more striking is the concentration on the few classes of melody discussed above: perhaps three-quarters or more of the repertory was classed in modes 1, 7, 8, and 4-a; the antiphons for Sundays are restricted even more severely to modes 1 and 8, with the last class being the most used in the whole Temporale and Sanctorale for all kinds of antiphons.

THE INVITATORY

The Invitatory for Matins (Psalm 94 with an antiphon) presents a fascinating problem because of conflicting indications.[25] The item as a whole is absent from the three days preceding Easter, and since the liturgies of those days are usually taken to reflect an early stage, the implication is that the Invitatory was not part of the early Office. The Invitatory is widely used in the Monastic Office, and that, together with certain other indications (including the first one) could suggest that it is not specifically Roman. On the other hand, the wording of Psalm 94 preserved for this particular function (and only here) is not that of Jerome's text that became standard, but is usually taken to be the 'Old Latin' Bible text, which is thought to reflect early Roman use, and to have persisted in chant items down to around 600 (many Mass propers use wordings described as Old Latin). The idiosyncracies of the Invitatory Psalm include a division into five 'verses' instead of the eleven of Jerome's text; that is to say, the verses of the original are grouped into five groups, marked off by the return of the antiphon (all or part) in conjunction with a special terminal melodic formula in the tone used for the psalm. It has been argued that since the wording of the text (in details other than the grouping of verses) is 'old', this

---

[25] Frere, *Antiphonale Sarisburiense*, 62; Wagner, *Einführung in die gregorianischen Melodien*, iii, 176–87, 313–15; Hucke, 'Responsorium', *MGG*, xi (1863), cols. 313–25; Stäblein, 'Invitatorium', ibid., vi, cols. 1389–93; Ruth Steiner, 'Invitatory', *New Grove*, ix. 286–9. For an introduction to the problem of the Old Latin Bible, see Thomas Connolly, 'The Graduale of S. Cecilia in Trastevere and the Old Roman Tradition', *JAMS*, 28 (1975), 420.

grouping must also be 'old', hence the tone—or at least its plan—is 'old'. This is an attractive idea, but requires a very cautious approach.

The repertory of Invitatory antiphons includes a number that are psalmic (taken from Psalm 94 itself) and assigned in a manner comparable to that of the ferial psalmic antiphons. The melodies of the antiphons, along with the verse tones that go with them, appear in modes 2 to 7 only, not in modes 1 and 8. The distribution here is exactly opposite to that in other Office antiphons, especially Gospel-Canticle antiphons, where modes 1 and 8 are heavily used. Mode 4, in which appear not one but several Invitatory verse tones (more than in any other mode) has been taken to be 'Gallican' not Roman. Actually the only solid evidence for an 'old' or 'Roman' state of the Invitatory is the wording of the text; if that were shown to be not specifically an Old Roman usage, or to have been preserved as a pious antiquity for some extraneous reason, all the other features of the Invitatory would support the idea that it developed as part of the Monastic Office outside of Rome, with characteristic irregularity and profusion, extending far past the time of the archetype. But in spite of—or perhaps precisely because of—the extra-Roman monastic ambience, the grouping of the verses and the structure of the tones could be taken to represent wide-spread, long-standing traditions of ritual song.

The specific features of the Invitatory that seem important for the traditions of ritual song include the preservation of the return of the antiphon more often than just at the end; and also a melodic plan that is not a simple, regular bi-hemistich (as appears in the Office psalmody we know about), but rather a polystich that has several (approximate) repetitions of one element, followed by one statement of a second element (see Ex. 53).[26] Because of the emphasis on the bi-hemistich in the Psalter and in standardized Office psalm tones, we have been trained to think of these two elements as 'first half' and 'second half'; but the Invitatory is one of several pieces of evidence that suggests we should think of these things differently, and more generally, perhaps according to the model $a, a, a \ldots b$. We might be prepared to imagine that before the time of the archetype (when the Franks standardized Office psalm tones, and incidentally settled on Jerome's text, under the designation 'Gallican Psalter', for Office psalmody), psalms could have been sung in less regular, more elaborate arrangements.

In other details, the Invitatory verse tones present much material for thought, even allowing for the probability that at least some of

---

[26] *Liber usualis*, pp. 368 f.

Ex. 53

(v. 3) Quo - ni - am De - us ma - gnus Do - mi - nus

et Rex ma - gnus su - per om - nes de - os.

*quo- ni - am non re - pel - let Do - mi - nus ple - bem su - am

(v. 4) qui - a in ma - nu e - jus sunt om- ti - nes fi - nes ter- rae

et al - ti - tu - di - nes mon- ti - um i - pse con- spi -

cit.

* this hemistich lacking in Vulgate.

them were developed after the time of the archetype. They are highly inflected—more so than any of the psalm or Canticle tones, and almost as much as the responsory verse tones to be considered. This inflection is not so much ornamental as it is mobile; and instead of trying to account for all inflections as ornaments of a reciting tone, it would be better to say that these tones tend to make more and freer use of the central pitch set in recitation than do the simpler psalm tones; that is, they recite in the set, not on a single tone—and we can probably take this as a more basic, more universal phenomenon than the reciting tone. Treatment of cadence shows attention to the tonal plan of the whole rather than to a presumed notion of modal final. All the verses, 'earlier' as well as 'later' ones, seem to show a tendency for the terminal formula to lie lower than the other one, and this may reflect some very basic procedure of ritual song.

The basic difference in the use of ferial antiphons on one hand, and antiphons of the Temporale-Sanctorale on the other, is that the ferial antiphons were sung every week, while those of the Temporale and

Sanctorale were sung only once a year (except for antiphons in the Common of Saints that were used more frequently). This difference in use must have something to do with the non-regular, possibly older form of psalm tones for ferial antiphons (which are not regularly included in the standard collections of the Antiphonale), as compared to the high degree of regularity that was imposed on the antiphons of the Temporale and Sanctorale. These differences, in turn, must have something to do with the confluence of events around 800, in which— either by historical coincidence or by dynamic connections not yet made fully clear—the antiphon repertory was (1) greatly expanded and co-ordinated with an annual cycle, (2) imported from Rome to be imposed on the Frankish kingdom, (3) written down in standard collections derived from an archetype, or at least compared with each other. The concomitance of these events is a matter of historical record; the possible relationships and effects of one on another stagger the historical imagination. Straightening out our understanding of those relationships will continue to be the main problem of the specifically 'Gregorian', that is, Frankish-Roman chant repertory.

FRANKISH CLASSIFICATION OF ANTIPHONS

One of the most important things the Frankish cantors did was to try to bring the repertory under control by classifying it; and to do this they had to invent a classification system. We do not know how this happened, we have only the end result, the system—or systems— referred to as 'the four finals', or 'the eight modes', and the co-ordinate system of eight psalm tones. Since our understanding and identification of Gregorian melodies is so intimately tied to these systems, we need to understand as much as we can of their genesis at this point.[27]

The antiphon repertory as we have seen it at the time of the archetype was based on a relatively small number of model melodies, formulaic systems, and idioms, operating within a few well-defined pitch sets. The words of the antiphons of Temporale and Sanctorale were written down. The singer needed to know which pitch set to use for the antiphon, and which tone for the psalm. Actually, as we have seen, antiphon and psalm tone fit together so closely that a single clue will answer both questions; for instance, a notation for the differentia would be such a clue.

How are the pitch sets to be identified? We have used here a

---

[27] Crocker, 'Hermann's Major Sixth'; Harold S. Powers, 'Mode', *New Grove*, xii. 376–84; Charles Atkinson, 'Parapter', in Hans-Heinrich Eggebrecht, ed., *Handwörterbuch der musikalischen Terminologie* (1972).

somewhat cumbersome solmization, for the express purpose of high-lighting the problem now under discussion. The most distinctive step taken by the Frankish cantors was to choose the final of the antiphon as the determinant of the class. This is certainly the most distinctive step they took, but not the only one. In order to see its significance we need to consider the alternatives: (1) they could have used the first note, or the opening group of notes; (2) they could have used the reciting tone, or the central locus around the reciting tone; (3) they could have simply listed all the antiphons in groups, to be memorized without further rationale; (4) they could have invented a notation that would automatically render redundant all the other solutions. In actual fact, the Frankish cantors did all of these things; and if we keep in mind the magnitude of the practical problem facing them—immediate performance of a standardized repertory of more than 1,600 antiphons (along with all the other chant not yet mentioned)—we can understand that they had to leave no step untried.

With modern notation of unequivocal pitch content, the psalm tone can be notated next to the antiphon, and both can be performed with no reference to the indications of mode, which are none the less still included in modern books. The Franks had available (in the nomenclature of the Greater Perfect System) an unequivocal way of naming pitches; and they very soon developed not one but half a dozen notations of their own, largely alphabetical, to specify pitch location.[28] All of these notations remained ancillary to the neumatic notation, and the reason is important. The neumatic notation itself, of course, gradually acquired unequivocal pitch content, definitively by 1200. But why so slow? And why not at first? Hucbald (writing around 900) tells us that the neumatic notation records and communicates nuance of performance.[29] In a context where for centuries melodies had not been written but—as a matter of course—memorized, and where the basic pitch content was perhaps the easiest, most obvious parameter to memorize (ut-re-mi), it is clear why the earliest neumatic notations were the most specific and rich in nuance of inflection and ornamentations; precisely because these were the parameters hardest to remember, most ephemeral. Rather than wondering why they did not modify neumatic notation to solve the pitch-set problem, we should notice that their other solutions to this problem relieved the

---

[28] Crocker, 'Alphabet Notations for early Medieval Music', Saints, Scholars, and Heroes (Studies in Medieval Culture in Honor of Charles W. Jones, 1979), ii. 79.

[29] Hucbald, De institutione harmonica, ed. M. Gerbert, Scriptores ecclesiastici de musica (St Blasien, 1784), i. 117 f.; Hucbald, Guido and John on Music, trans. Warren Babb (New Haven, 1978); Rembert Weakland, 'Hucbald as Musician and Theorist', MQ, 42 (1956), 66, in particular pp. 81 f.

neumatic notation of that burden. In passing, we should also notice that the development of a specific melodic notation, using neumes, took place sometime during the period 750–900 in the North, but without a single comment recorded from that time concerning what we would regard as an event of unparalleled significance in the history of music. Suddenly there it is in the sources around 900—a highly developed, sophisticated notation. Obviously its development was less significant to them than it seems to us; and the reason must be that what we assume a notation would do (communicate pitch content) was accomplished by them through other, more or less reliable means such as memorization and approximate reproduction based on pitch sets and formulaic systems.

Keeping in mind this state of affairs, we can consider the solution to the problem of identifying pitch sets. The Franks did indeed use the final of an antiphon to classify it, and they did it this way. They observed the ascents and descents through whole and half steps around each final; for instance around the final we have called *ut*(*sol*) they would observe a descent of a whole tone, and ascent of two whole tones followed by a semitone. Subsequently they located all the finals on the Greater Perfect System, using for analogy a similar method and terminology worked out for Byzantine chant (although the first hard documentation for the Byzantine system comes from the Frankish sources under discussion). The classes we have studied could have been located on the Greater Perfect System in any one of several ways. Four finals are used because that is all there are in the system; locating one of these four on *lichanos hypaton* and calling it *protus*, with *deuterus, tritus, tetrardus* on *hypate meson, parhypate*, and *lichanos* respectively, may be due largely to the influence of the Byzantine model.[30] Further, the antiphons using the same final had to be divided into two groups, authentic and plagal, to distinguish those whose final was close to the central locus from those whose final was reached by a terminal descent. Thus the 'first' final on *re* included our class with descent to *re* as *protus authenticus*, as well as the (otherwise unrelated) class with reciting note *fa* and final *re*. All of this took place before 800, leaving no trace except the completed classification in these terms; also at an early date the same eight classes were referred to as *primus, secundus . . . octavus*, the numbering we commonly use now.

Whatever the genesis of the four finals and eight modes, the Franks also classified antiphons by their central locus, using the psalm tone. That is, they stabilized the psalm tone practice in the system of eight

---

[30] Cf. above p. 46.

tones, and co-ordinated this system with the eight-fold classification based on finals. It is sometimes hard to keep these two systems ('mode' and 'psalm tones') distinct, because in some cases they are by nature the same thing: in the natural course of development antiphon and psalm tone share the same locus, and are in fact two expressions of the same locus. So in the end, mode 6 and psalm tone 6 are for practical purposes almost indistinguishable. On the other hand, further development brought anomalies, some more severe than others. In the case of mode 4, it is hard to see what connection it really has to psalm tone 4, since either they move in different registers, or they use different pitches and intervals in the same area (because of the prevalence of b flat at the top of mode-4 antiphons, contrasting with b natural of the psalm tone). In general it seems that the same final subsumes different central loci and reciting tones, and this, rather than just range or register, must be the real need for the authentic-plagal subclassification. On the other hand the same locus sometimes wound up in different classes of finals, as with modes 1 and 6, 2 and 8, 3 and 8, eventually 7 and 4-a, either because of terminal descent or of alternative ending tone within the locus. Only modes 7 and 8 seem to preserve in their joint classification their presumed original relationship, whereby 7 uses an elevated reciting tone in the same locus as 8. The central locus and psalm tone could be indicated simply by the psalm tone intonation and 'seculorum amen' ending, and these, or just the latter, were often used to classify antiphons.

TONARIES

The Franks did list all the antiphons in classes, for study and memorization. Such a classified list is a tonary, and tonaries are among our earliest Frankish chant sources, starting around 800.[31] The important one from Metz, representing the Carolingian Antiphonale around 870, has provided the basis for much of our discussion of the repertory of that time. Tonaries could be constructed in several different ways, including some or all of the means of classification discussed. Like notation at the other extreme, a complete classified listing makes the other solutions redundant: 'Memorize all the melodies, and sing all antiphons in this group to this psalm tone', makes unnecessary any further analysis. This injunction probably best represents prior practice, and it is fascinating to watch the Franks— systematic, curious, resourceful—move quickly from received tradi-

[31] Michel Huglo, *Les Tonaires, inventaire, analyse, comparison, Publications de la Société française de musicologie*, Troisième série, ii (Paris, 1971), 25–9.

tion to rational organization in the understanding of the chant repertory.

Within a tonary the antiphons are listed by the eight classes, *protus authenticus, protus plagis.* ... Within each class, the listing is subclassified by differentia to accommodate the practice of varying the end of the psalm tone slightly to make a nice connection with the repeat of the antiphon. This was in effect a subclassification by antiphon intonation, as opposed to the primary classification by final. As it turns out, the finals give a better alignment of antiphon pitch set and psalm tone than the intonation does; that is, a primary classification by intonation (rather than by final) might have resulted in a system far more cumbersome than the actual one.

Early tonaries included one other piece of information, not well understood, that probably was yet another aid in antiphon classification and may well have been one of the oldest such aids. These are the *echemata*, brief melodies underlaid with nonsense Greek syllables—sometimes imagined to be solmization syllables.[32] One is provided for each of the eight modes; some sources provide an additional terminal melisma for each *echema*. In either its shorter or longer version, the *echema* typically appears at the head of each listing of the eight classes of antiphons; what appears are the syllables—NONNENOEANE (or something) for authentic classes, NOEAGIS for plagals, with or without neumes—and at this time the neumes are staffless. In recent studies these are called 'intonation formulas' and their function is imagined to be similar to that of analogous Byzantine formulas. However, the Latin melodies—known definitely from a theorist's notation of *c.* 900—are clearly not intonations but rather conclusions; the one for authentic *protus* is clearly the terminal descent that transforms antiphons of mode 6 locus to mode 1 final. The other *echemata* similarly serve to identify typical endings. It seems that the *echemata* could function as memorized typical endings, to help identify the class of memorized antiphons. Hence the appearance of the *echema* at the head of each list of antiphons with a given final. Such a procedure, particularly functional at a non-written stage, may have been the first way of dealing with antiphon classification; it is perhaps already dysfunctional by the time of the first tonaries we have.

RESPONSORIES

The responsories of the Roman Office are provided with ornamental

---

[32] Bailey, *The Intonation Formulas of Western Chant* (Toronto: Pontifical Institute of Medieval studies, 1974).

melodies containing many neumes and occasional melismata in the responds.[33] The verses make use of a set of eight tones analogous to the eight psalm tones but much more ornamented—almost as neumatic as the responds. The melodies of the responds tend to be formulaic, and have been analysed as such; but here the essential step in research, not yet completed, is to sort out the large repertory of perhaps 1,200 responds into those that can reasonably be regarded as eighth-century Roman and those that are due to successive generations of Frankish cantors during the ninth, tenth, eleventh, and twelfth centuries. The means of doing this is the provision of new Offices, and new material for older Offices, after 850.

One of the most distinctive features of responsory melodies is the movement of the line. It does not have the clear profile of many antiphon melodies, being more ornamental; on the other hand it is not heavily melismatic, and does not have the exuberant, profuse surge of melody cut loose from close relationship to syllables. Responsory melodies move in an animated flow, with many of the syllables given neumes of three, four, or five pitches; and these neumes tend to move in alternating fashion back and forth within a small set of pitches. Characteristic examples can be found in Ex. 54[34] below.

This particular kind of melodic flow is of course not unique in responsories, appearing throughout chant repertories; it is, however, especially concentrated and consistent in responsories, and is especially noticeable because it is here often combined with an overall shape that has relatively little orientation toward a goal—much motion with little overall progress, resulting in a static effect. It is as if the singer wished to heighten the presentation of the text by keeping his voice in constant motion, moving almost every syllable back and forth through the interval of a second or a third, and often shifting the locus slightly from one syllable to the next, so that each phrase of text occupied a tonal realm of perhaps a fifth. We could think of this style of singing as a highly articulated vibrato—intense tone distributed over several adjacent pitches.

Here we need to observe the melodies used for the responsory verses, and to make a distinction between them and the style for the responds as just described.[35] On the one hand the verse tones share the

---

[33] Frere, *Antiphonale Sarisburiense*, pp. 3–61; Wagner, *Einführung in die gregorianischen Melodien*, iii, pp. 327–51; Ferretti, *Esthétique grégorienne*, i, pp. 243–65; Apel, *Gregorian Chant*, pp. 330–44; Hucke, 'Das Responsorium', in Wulf Arlt, *et al.*, eds., *Gattungen der Musik in Einzeldarstellungen: Gedenkschrift Leo Schrade*, i (Berne, 1973), 144, and 'Responsorium', *MGG*, xi (1963), cols. 313–25; Paul F. Cutter, 'Die altrömischen und gregorianischen Responsorien im Zweiten Modus', *Kirchenmusikalisches Jahrbuch* (1970), 33.

[34] *Antiphonale Sarisburiense*, pl. 'O'.

[35] For the responsorial verse tones, see Frere, *Antiphonale Sarisburiense*, p. 4; Wagner, *Einführung in die gregorianischen Melodien*, iii, pp. 188–216; Ferretti, *Esthétique grégorienne*, i, pp. 250 f.; Apel, *Gregorian Chant*, pp. 234–41.

Ex. 54

(mode 7)

Ec - ce e - go mit - to vos si - cut o - ves

in me - di - o lu - po - rum,

di - cit Do - mi - nus:

[Repetendum]

E - sto - te er - go pru - den - tes

si - cut ser - pen - tes

et sim - pli - ces si - cut

co - lum - be.

℣ Dum lu - cem ha - be - tis, cre - di - te

in lu - cem, ut fi - li - i

lu - cis si - tis di - cit Do -

mi - nus:

same kind of back-and-forth ornamental neumes on certain syllables (and this distinguishes the responsory verse tones from the psalm tones used for Office psalmody). On the other hand the verse tones tend to be more stable in their loci than the responds. This stability shows in the concentration on certain notes as reciting notes, and closely related finals—all as in Office psalmody, but with greater variability. Sometimes reciting notes are ornamented by a succession of identical two-note neumes—often found throughout the Gregorian repertory, but in a much more single-minded way in Urban-Roman and Old Beneventan sources, where an unbroken succession of two-note or three-note figures (for example, D E C, D E C, D E C, D E C . . .) may produce an awkward, puzzling situation.[36] Indeed it is one of the distinctive features of Gregorian style to avoid such redundancy with more varied patterns of ornamentation. We can, however, understand the Beneventan example as a simple, stylized way of reciting in a vibrato-like manner, and from that gain insight into the Gregorian verse tones—and by extension, the respond melodies too.

Beyond observing that there are many formulas, arranged in pitch sets or modes (each with a verse tone), the description of responsory melodies becomes abruptly complex. There have been a few sustained attempts to make the description, most notably and usefully by Frere.[37] Within each of the eight modes Frere identifies one or more (up to ten) groups of typical melodies; each group consists of melodies that have the same opening formula and share a significant number of others. The grouping by opening formula, however, is arbitrary and not very useful: many of the resulting 'groups' (as Frere himself points out) contain only a few responsories, and those sometimes share only their openings; and after listing all the groups in a mode, Frere then has to add a list of other responds that share the same formulas but not the opening one. Frere identified numerous formulas; generally each of his formulas is a cadence—half a dozen syllables set to cadential neumes, preceded by a few more syllables set to neumes of intonation or recitation. In any given respond, two or three of these cadences will form a phrase, and two or three phrases will form the respond. Frere's analysis, however, does not show the phrase struc-ture, nor does it show where the partial repeat starts. Hence he shows, for each respond, only a series of some five to ten cadences.

Responds show a clear concern for overall organization, but several factors make that organization sometimes hard to perceive. The foremost factor is the animated character of the line. Then, within each phrase the line often dwells on one set of pitches but cadences on

---

[36] Cf. above, p. 73.   [37] Loc. cit.

another. In Ex. 54 the first phrase dwells on the G then moves up a fifth to d; the second dwells on d and c, then drops to F for a cadence. Furthermore, there tend to be more cadences than phrases, that is, a single large phrase may have several internal cadences (as at 'luporum' in Ex. 54). Since each successive cadence tends to seek out a pitch different from the preceding one, there may be no obvious grouping of cadences and phrases. Indeed, an interesting mannerism, apparently characteristic of Roman eighth-century responds, is to repeat a principal cadence at the first subphrase following; but the rest of this phrase then goes on to cadence elsewhere. In Ex. 54 a principal cadence occurs at 'dicit dominus' on G; there is another cadence on G immediately following on 'prudentes', but this phrase continues to cadence on c at 'serpentes'.

The basis of the phrase structure has to be sought in the text, and here there seems to be concern to keep the number of syllables between the extremes of seven and sixteen (more or less) with a mean of eleven to thirteen. In Ex. 54 the phrases are eleven syllables ('oves'), twelve ('dicit Dominus'), thirteen ('serpentes') and nine ('columbe'); in the verse they are twelve and thirteen. These phrases can be grouped into an opening antecedent and consequent, with 'oves' a half-cadence on d, followed by a full cadence on 'Dominus' (approached by the most standard responsory cadence formula) on G; then a phrase ending on c, and a final phrase that ends on G echoing the cadence formula used before. The verse typically avoids the final of the responsory, and shows more than one reciting tone, in this case c and d.

Along with the repertory of antiphons of the Office, that of responsories suggests much more historical development than do the Mass chants—and that part of the development that lies after the time of the archetype can in principle be documented. As we take up the repertories of Mass chants we need to keep in mind not only the existence and vast extent of antiphons and responsories of the Office but also the continuity and expansion of these repertories throughout the Middle Ages.

VI

CHANTS OF THE ROMAN MASS

By RICHARD CROCKER

The repertory of Gregorian proper chants for the Mass—Introits, Graduals, Offertories, and Communions—is as a whole more stable than that for the Office. A number of additions were made to the repertory over the centuries, including new formularies for newly established feasts; new texts (or newly selected texts) were set, usually to older melodies. The Frankish-Roman formularies, however, were left almost completely intact, and with appropriate controls can be read out of modern chant books. The melodies themselves may also turn out to be more stable than those for the Office; but variant apparatus for the Mass chants is still not available, and work on the manuscript traditions for the Office chants has scarcely begun.

To a large extent, Mass chants can profitably be understood in the same categories as Office chants, namely as antiphons or responsories. It is then immediately clear that the Mass chants are in general longer and more complex than their counterparts in the Office: a typical Introit antiphon is longer and more ornamental than any typical Office antiphon; and while Gradual responsories may not be longer than Office responsories, they include more complex melismata. Perhaps the most important aspect of the comparison, and of the style of the Mass chants generally, is the greater degree of elaboration, of melodic working-out that they show. This may be related to the greater stability they seem to possess. In any case it seems helpful, if not essential, to approach the Mass chants with a clear idea of the styles of antiphons and responsories discussed in chapter V.

INTROIT MELODIES

In style and technique the Introit melodies are festal, and are to be compared with the antiphons of the Temporale and Sanctorale of the

Office, not with the ferial antiphons.[1] The distinctive feature of Introit antiphons is the type of neumatic ornament, which is relatively heavy compared with Office antiphons. There is a persistent use of groups of three, four, and five notes in ornamental configurations; not all, but very many syllables carry such neumes. Introits may vary considerably in length, from two to four phrases; but the level of intensity in the ornamentation is remarkably consistent—much more so than in the Communions. In tonal design, however, Introit antiphons are close to what we have seen in Office antiphons; they go beyond these only in certain ways. In other words, Introit antiphons combine a relatively restricted set of tonal plans with relatively heavy ornamentation, and the result often has the effect of seeming pompous or obscure. We miss on the one hand the clear lyric profile of the simpler Office antiphons, on the other hand the soaring flamboyance of the Graduals. While Introits approximate to the neumatic style of the Office responsories, they use relatively few of those particular idioms, and do not seem to have the 'fluttery' quality we have noticed in responsories.

There are between 140 and 150 Introits—separate texts, each with its own melody—in the Gregorian repertory. An exact count for this and other categories would depend upon several questions of detail concerning which formularies were to be included in the archetype; and local variation may make such questions ultimately indeterminate (Items represented only once or twice in the Sextuplex present difficulties.) The distribution of these 140 melodies among the eight modal classes is more even than in the case of the Office antiphons, but still uneven, and the unevenness seems more striking and interesting when seen in connection with the various layers—festal, dominical, ferial, saints' days. Comparison of the distribution with that in Urban-Roman Introits is also very interesting. When using the modal classification this way we have to remember that the Frankish classification by final is to some degree arbitrary, and may result in the inclusion in a single class of widely disparate melodic materials; and yet it does correspond to some stylistic reality. Thus within *protus* (D final), for instance, there will be a group of chants that share central pitch set, plan, or idiom, or all three. There will also be, even within

---

[1] Peter Wagner, *Einführung in die gregorianischen Melodien*, i, *Ursprung und Entwicklung der liturgischen Gesangsformen bis zum Ausgange des Mittelalters* (3rd edn., Leipzig, 1911); iii, *Gregorianische Formenlehre, Eine Choralische Stilkunde* (Leipzig, 1921), 322–6; Paolo Ferretti, *Esthétique grégorienne*, i, trans. A. Agaësse (Tournai, 1938), 266–78; Willi Apel, *Gregorian Chant* (Bloomington, 1958), 305–11; Bruno Stäblein, 'Introitus', *MGG*, vi (1957), cols. 1375–82; Hendrik van der Werf, *The Emergence of Gregorian Chant* (Rochester, 1983); Ruth Steiner, 'Introit', *New Grove*, ix. 281–4.

protus authenticus (mode 1) other melodies, or even other groups, that do not share those elements; and within *protus* as a whole, that is, including *protus plagalis* (mode 2) there are two very distinct groups that share the D final only through the accidents of classification. It often seems that an ideal solution would be to identify these groups (within modal classes) by the incipit of the particular chant that seemed most typical, and that might even be the prototype of the group. If that were possible, it would indeed be desirable; but as a method of classification it already presumes a conclusion about the genesis of the repertory. In some cases, indeed, there may have been a prototype, a single chant that was favoured, used again, imitated, modified, developed into a model melody. Or there may only have been a formulaic system—a way of singing Introits for saints. Perhaps there was once a prototype that disappeared in some reshuffling of the repertory. All of that is lost to view, and it is not prudent to imagine that we have sufficient information to identify prototypes in the repertory as we have it. It is a good and useful exercise to imagine other mechanisms of development.

The modal distribution in Gregorian Introits overall shows roughly equal numbers for modes 1, 3, and 4 (slightly over twenty each), somewhat less for modes 2 and 7 (slightly under twenty each), and still less for modes 8, 6, and 5. The slight representation for modes 5 and 6 seems to be in line with the distribution in the Office, where mode 5 is almost unknown, and mode 6 is not heavily used. The slight representation of mode 8, however, runs counter to the heavy use of this mode in Office antiphons, especially the elaborate antiphons for Gospel Canticles, and is a fact that needs pondering. In the Introits mode 8 is well represented in the festal group, and in the dominical layer—except after Pentecost; there are only two out of almost forty for saints, one for twenty-three Sundays after Pentecost, and none for ferias in Lent. This distribution might be understood as one for Sundays and feasts in winter and spring. Introits for mode 1, on the other hand, appear not at all for feasts and rarely in the winter Sundays, but heavily for Lenten ferias, Sundays after Pentecost, and especially for saints, where it accounts for ten out of almost forty items.

The overall modal distribution of Gregorian Introits is roughly comparable with that of Urban-Roman Introits, or at any rate close enough that the differences emerge clearly.[2] Before seeing what those differences are, however, it must be said that the comparison is

---

[2] See Thomas Connolly, 'Introits and Archetypes: Some Archaisms of the Old Roman Chant', *JAMS*, 25 (1972), 157.

preliminary and subject to the following kind of problem. Some chants (such as 'Intret oratio mea',[3] Saturday Ember Day in Lent) have the same melody in Gregorian and Urban-Roman sources, but a differences in terminal descent makes it mode 8 in Urban-Roman and mode 3 in Gregorian. Other chants (such as 'Verba mea'[4] for Saturday in the Third Week of Lent) have the same ending, hence the same mode, but otherwise cannot be called the same melody—even within the very loose limits of sameness that we must learn to use in comparing Gregorian and Urban-Roman. As a preliminary observation it seems that the cases in which the two settings of the same text, Gregorian and Urban-Roman, have different melodies in the same mode roughly balance those in which they have the same melody assigned to different modes, and so the overall distribution can perhaps still be regarded as similar. Given the idiosyncrasies of modal distribution this similarity can only mean some basic identity in repertory, and this is the fact that must be worked through all the very confusing differences between the two repertories.

Apart from actual importations of Gregorian items into the Urban-Roman sources (such importation would have taken place between 850 and 1050), examples of versions that are 'the same' can be seen in the Introits 'Dominus dixit me'[5] (First Mass of Christmas) and 'Resurrexi'[6] (Easter Sunday). The identity may not be immediately convincing, and only when it is realized that there are a large number of cases that consistently and reliably show the same degree of vague relationship, does the identity become more believable. Marginal cases of identity include, for example 'Puer natus'[7] (Ex. 55) (Third Mass of Christmas): at first glance these are simply two different melodies, one in mode 1, the other in mode 7. Closer scrutiny, in the light of many other comparisons of similar pairs, will reveal certain similarities of contour and placement of ornament that suggests this to be one melody sung with two different finals and certain other alterations.

To return to the similarity in overall modal distribution between Gregorian and Urban-Roman Introits, the salient point is the much

---

[3] Throughout the following discussion, page references for all Mass chants are given for *Graduale sacrosanctae romanae ecclesiae de tempore et de sanctis*, SS.D.N.Pii X. Pontificis Maximi jussu restitutum et editum (Rome, 1908) (= *GR*); *Die Gesänge des altrömischen Graduale Vat.lat. 5319*, ed. Bruno Stäblein and Margareta Landwehr-Melnicki, *Monumenta monodica medii aevi*, 2 (1970) (= *MMMA* 2). 'Intret oratio', *GR* p. 88; *MMMA* 2, p. 77.

[4] *GR*, p. 116; *MMMA* 2, p. 55.

[5] *GR*, p. 25; *MMMA* 2, p. 16.

[6] *GR*, p. 202; *MMMA* 2, p. 44.

[7] *GR*, p. 30; *MMMA* 2, p. 9. See Stäblein, 'Introitus'; Van der Werf, *The Emergence of Gregorian Chant*, i, part 2, pp. 73–5.

Ex. 55

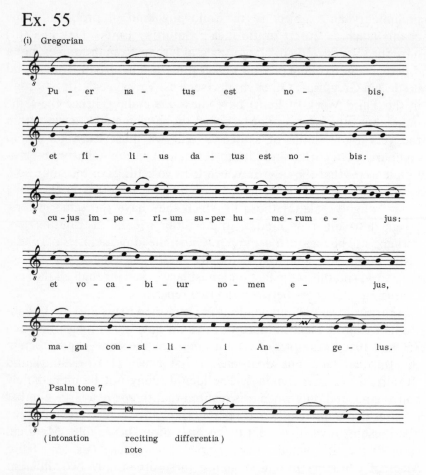

(i) Gregorian

Pu – er   na – tus   est   no – bis,

et   fi – li – us   da – tus   est   no – bis:

cu – jus im – pe – ri – um   su – per hu – me – rum e – jus:

et   vo – ca – bi – tur   no – men   e – jus,

ma – gni   con – si – li – i   An – ge – lus.

Psalm tone 7

(intonation   reciting   differentia)
                     note

higher number of Urban-Roman Introits in mode 4 (double the
Gregorian) and the much lower number in mode 7 (less than half).
Accounting for this difference will require thorough comparison of all
items, and—especially for the Urban-Roman—a reclassification
according to melodic structure rather than final, which is in some
cases handled whimsically in the Urban-Roman sources. There are
cases that show the underlying identity of modes 4 and 7 in terms of
central locus around a *sol* reciting note, as we observed for the Office
antiphons in mode 7 and 4-a. More generally, the Urban-Roman
source Vat.lat.5319 seems to interpret as mode 4 a number of pieces
classified differently in the Gregorian tradition. Also in general, the
level of agreement in modal classification between the two repertories
can be said to be highest for feasts and for Sundays in winter and early
spring, somewhat lower for saints' days; then it deteriorates towards

(ii)   Urban – Roman (Vat. lat. 5319)

Pu — er na – tus   est no –   bis,

et fi –   li – us da – tus est   no –   bis:

cu – jus im – pe – ri –   um   su – per

hu –   me – rum e –   jus:

et vo – ca –   bi – tur no – men e –   jus,

ma – gni con – si – li – i an –   ge – lus.

Psalm tone 1

(intonation reciting   differentia)
note

the end of the series of Sundays after Pentecost. It is at its lowest in
ferias in Lent, and especially after Easter.

The Gregorian Introits of the festal layer provide good illustration
of most of the kinds of tonal movement characteristic of Introits. For
purposes of comparison it will be helpful to imagine all of these seven
Introits oriented around the same *fa*, which involves thinking of those
in modes 2 and 4 at a level a fifth higher than they are notated in
modern chant books. 'Dominus dixit' (Ex. 56) (First Mass of Christmas) is a short, compact piece moving in a limited range; yet the
phraseology is remarkably sophisticated. There are three phrases of
text and music, with a stronger textual articulation for the first phrase,
and a stronger melodic articulation for the second (a half cadence on

Ex. 56

Do - mi - nus di - xit ad me:

Fi - li - us me - us es tu,

e - go ho - di - e ge - nu - i - te.

Psalm tone 2

(intonation   reciting   differentia)
note

the whole tone below the final). The third phrase, beginning like the first, touches again upon this whole tone below before closing. The central pitch is *fa* (notated F, read c, for comparison), and the central pitch set is *re–mi–fa*. One might argue from the word accents and type of neumatic ornament that the central pitch was really *re*, followed by an off-slide up to the *fa* in many cases; or, *contra*, that the *re* was simply an appoggiatura to the *fa*. We will observe the same situation in mode 1 Introits.

The same dimensions, range, tonal plan, and type of ornamentation (these are the kinds of factors that define a group of melodies) appear in the other festal Introit in mode 2, 'Ecce advenit'[8] for Epiphany. A relatively expanded tonal plan for mode 8 appears in the Introits for the Second Mass of Christmas, 'Lux fulgebit', and for Pentecost, 'Spiritus Domini', which has, in its second phrase, a very clear orientation around *fa* (notated c) and the central locus *ut–re–mi–fa*.[9] But it moves above that locus—if briefly—to *sol* and *la*; and in the introductory phrase, below to a distinct lower realm. Furthermore, this is one of the mode 8 melodies that presents another distinct realm overlapping the central one, outlined by the *fa* below the *ut*, together with the third and fifth above (F–a–c). This occurs near the beginning ('replevit'), and again in the alleluias at the end. This alternate realm is one of the things that distinguishes this melody from 'Ecce advenit' in

     [8] *GR*, p. 46; *MMMA* 2, p. 13.   [9] *GR*, p. 248; *MMMA* 2, p. 60.

mode 2; otherwise central pitch and locus are the same, and this is emphasized by the identity of the psalm tones used for these modes at the Introit, up to the differentia. The relationship of 'Spiritus Domini' to the Urban-Roman form is complex, having both clear similarities ('replevit') as well as differences; the Urban-Roman form is provided with psalm tone 6.

The other mode 8 Introit, 'Lux fulgebit'[10] for the Second Mass of Christmas, shows a much more intensive development of the F–a–c realm, with much use of b flat to support it. The Introit is long, with four phrases, the third of these being very long. The text is a highly centonized one from Isaiah ix, and it is probably this 'prophetic' style of prose (as opposed to the lyric forms in the psalms) that accounts for the phraseology.

The two mode 7 festal Introits, 'Puer natus' (Third Mass of Christmas) and 'Viri Galilei' (Ascension) both show vigorous assertion at their beginnings of the *sol* above *fa*; both, however, tend to lapse back to the *fa* as central pitch as they proceed. This brings with it an increased resemblance to the locus of mode 8, and indeed from that point of view there is little difference between the two groups. While we can specify plan and locus common to these (and other) mode 7 Introits, we would be hard put to identify a formulaic system out of which they were both made (aside from the opening formula).

The mode 4 Introit for Easter, 'Resurrexi' (Ex. 57), has a very strong concentration on *fa* in a locus *re–mi–fa*. The range is narrow, like the mode 2 Introit 'Dixit Dominus', and the motion similarly restricted. Only the cadence points, with very idiomatic cadence formulas, identify mode 4. This overall plan and final, however, are very characteristic of mode 4 antiphons (*ut–mi–sol*, with final on *mi*). The reciting tone for psalm tone 4, on the *la* above, seems unusually high compared to the positions of the other psalm tones in relation to their antiphons.

The festal layer contains no Introits in mode 1, and for an example we can well turn to the repertory of saints' day Introits, for which mode 1 is very characteristic. 'Sapientiam sanctorum'[11] (Ex. 58) (used for various saints in the Sextuplex) begins firmly on *mi*(a), and its first phrase confirms the *ut–re–mi* set. What is distinctive about the way this set is used in Mass antiphons (as opposed to those of the Office) is the extension upwards from the *mi*: with the b natural and c at the end of the first phrase, this *mi* is treated as if it were the seat of a cadence on *re*. The second phrase then establishes another whole realm in the upper register, based upon this new *re*. This happens frequently in

---

[10] *GR*, p. 28; *MMMA* 2, p. 77.   [11] *GR*, p. 23; *MMMA* 2, p. 10.

Ex. 57

mode 1 Introits; but perhaps even more frequent is a passing excursion into this upper register, as seen in the third phrase, with some ambiguity about whether the c is really part of another realm, or simply an intensified ornament of the a, which is the original *mi*. Successive stages in this upwards movement can be seen by comparing 'vivent', the least amount of upward movement and really nothing but a decorated *mi*, with '(e)orum', and that with the whole second phrase. In this particular antiphon there really is no low *re* until the terminal descent at the end of the last phrase. The upwards extension in mode 1 Introits has the immediate effect that the psalm tone is no longer at the very top of the range (as it is in mode 1 in the Office), and in this respect (as in others) the Mass chants are not a good guide to the

Ex. 58

simpler and perhaps more fundamental relationships of antiphons and psalms.

Throughout the modal classes of Introits discussed so far there is little evidence for formulaic systems. The one place where we might find such a system is in modes 3 and 4; this is suggested by the Urban-Roman repertory and its Introits for Lenten ferias. A Gregorian example is 'Confessio et pulchritudo'[12] (Ex. 59) (for St Laurence, also used at feria v of the First Week in Lent). Characteristic of this group is a series of more or less equivalent, or at least similarly shaped phrases that each rise from *ut* to *fa*, with or without a short descent at the end of the phrase.[13] The series of similar phrases is terminated by a contrasting phrase in a lower register—and this procedure can be observed often throughout the Gregorian repertory. In this particular Introit the high phrases start at 'Confessio', 'in conspectu', and 'sanctitas'; the final low phrase starts at 'in sanctificatione'. The melodic shapes are clearer in the Urban-Roman version (Ex. 60). This is simpler in its intonations, beginning with the *ut* (G), which is preceded in the Gregorian by something lower (by way of anticipating

---

[12] *GR*, p. 513; *MMMA* 2, p. 24.   [13] Cf. Connolly, 'Introits and Archetypes'.

Ex. 59

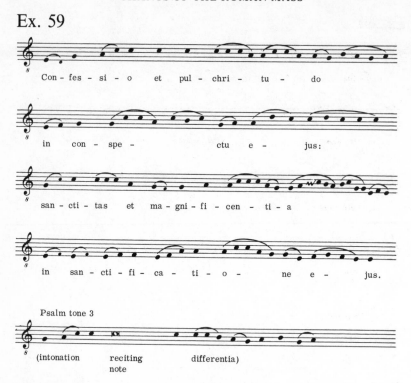

the terminal descent). And in the Urban-Roman, the final phrase is lower throughout, not just in its intonation—for the Gregorian cannot forgo a last upward surge on '(sanctificati-)o-(ne)'.

COMMUNION MELODIES

Communions are very similar to Introits in stichic plan and melodic style. Like Introits, they are often provided in the Sextuplex with a psalm (verse), and sometimes with a *versus ad repetendum* (also in the Urban-Roman sources), although both of these features disappear from the Frankish Mass Antiphonales soon after the time of the archetype.[14]

There are between 145 and 150 Communions in the archetype (and about the same number in the Urban-Roman sources)—that is, very close to the number of Introits. The modal distribution of Communions, however, is different, with more items in modes 6 and 8, and significantly less in mode 3. The Urban-Roman sources reflect the same differences in distribution (with the same reservations concern-

[14] Wagner, *Einführung in die gregorianischen Melodien*, iii, pp. 325 f.; Ferretti, *Esthétique grégorienne*, pp. 269–75; Apel, *Gregorian Chant*, pp. 311 f.; Helmut Hucke and Michel Huglo, 'Communio', *New Grove*, iv. 591–4.

Ex. 60

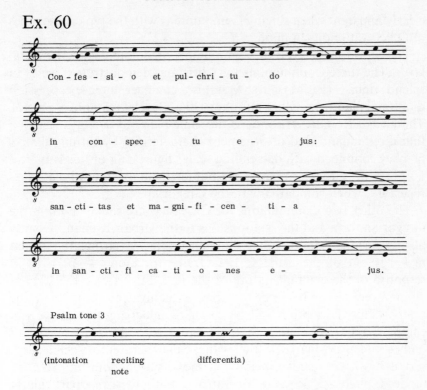

Con - fes - si - o   et   pul - chri - tu -   do

in   con - spec -   tu   e -   jus:

san - cti - tas   et   ma - gni - fi - cen -   ti - a

in   san - cti - fi - ca - ti - o - nes   e -   jus.

Psalm tone 3

(intonation   reciting   differentia)
note

ing this preliminary count). In comparing modal distribution between Gregorian and Urban-Roman there are the same kinds of problems as with Introits: the same melody may have a different ending (and psalm tone, if one is indicated), hence a different mode; or the melody may be really different, yet still be in the same mode. The modal distribution seems to correspond fairly well for feasts and Sundays, except for Sundays after Pentecost. The Lenten ferias again show many anomalies. There are again cases of exchange—implying some kind of equivalence—between modes 6 and 8, and between modes 4 and 7, as well as sundry other pairs.

Communions are similar to Introits, but not identical with them. One of the most distinctive types of Communion is that using a text from the Gospel pericope for the day; this type tends to bring with it a distinctive melodic style as well. The more usual (and allegedly the older) type has a stich from a psalm, of somewhat shorter dimensions than those of an Introit, and set to a roughly equivalent style of ornamentation. The ratio of length and ornamentation tends to give this type of Communion an even denser aspect than the Introits, and this often goes together with a curiously oblique leading of the melodic line—a subtle quality and one difficult to document, but clearly apparent when singing Communions with the typical melodies of Office antiphons in mind.

This more usual type of Communion predominates in the festal layer. The three Communions for Christmas demonstrate it well. 'In splendoribus'[15] (Ex. 61) (First Mass) is a compact, intense expression of a tonal plan from Office antiphons like 'Revela' (cf. above, p. 147). The Urban-Roman version uses the same plan but overlays it with a fuller, redundant kind of ornament characterized by turning figures (a–b–a) combined with descending scalar figures; all of this is typical not just of Urban-Roman Communions but of the whole Mass repertory, when compared with the Gregorian.

The other two Communions for Christmas are similar both in the Gregorian form and the relationships to the Urban-Roman. 'Exsulta filia'[16] (Second Mass), not a long piece, has a strong movement upwards out of the usual C–E–G frame for mode 4—perhaps in response to the exultant nature of the text. In this case the Urban-Roman version can better be described as 'equivalent' rather than 'the same'. (This description will be easier to understand when we can compare types of chants that are more formularized.) 'Viderunt omnes'[17] (Third Mass) is a stich with a single phrase; for such a short text it has a very active melody. It moves throughout an extended mode 1 pitch set as used for Introits, without using particularly idiomatic turns of phrase. This compact, highly profiled melody is considerably smoothed out in the Urban-Roman rendition. In 'Vidimus stellam'[18] (Epiphany) the Urban-Roman version is much more ornamental—or it might be that the Gregorian should be described as 'stripped down'. This, again, is a persistent difference between the two. In comparison to the very eloquent Gregorian version of 'Psallite Domino'[19] (Ascension), the Urban-Roman can be described as less effective.

The other two festal Communions have New Testament texts—'Pascha nostrum'[20] (Easter), and 'Factus est repente'[21] (Pentecost), and as often happens in that case the texts are longer, here two full phrases articulated with alleluias. 'Pascha nostrum' still uses the dense ornamentation of the melodies we have seen, producing a relatively large, heavy piece. 'Factus est repente' (Ex. 62) is much more syllabic, and represents a different type of Communion. In this case the difference is faithfully reflected in the Urban-Roman version as well,

[15] *GR*, p. 27; *MMMA* 2, p. 469.
[16] *GR*, p. 30; *MMMA* 2, p. 454.
[17] *GR*, p. 33; *MMMA* 2, p. 437.
[18] *GR*, p. 48; *MMMA* 2, p. 455.

[19] *GR*, p. 244; *MMMA* 2, p. 431.
[20] *GR*, p. 205; *MMMA* 2, p. 464.
[21] *GR*, p. 251; *MMMA* 2, p. 500.

Ex. 61

(i) Gregorian

In splen-do-ri-bus san-cto-rum, ex u- te-ro

an - te lu - ci - fe - rum ge - nu - i - te.

Psalm tone 6

(intonation reciting differentia)
note

(ii) Urban-Roman (Vat. lat. 5319)

In splen-do-ri-bus san - cto - rum

ex u - te - ro

an - te lu - ci - fe - rum ge - nu -

i - te.

Psalm tone 6

intonation reciting differentia
note

Ex. 62

Psalm tone 7

(intonation   reciting   differentia)
                      note

which, however, becomes more ornamented in its usual way toward
the end.

Both mode and melody correspond through these festal Communions in the two versions. More problematic comparisons are
encountered in the case of the five Lenten ferial Communions in which
psalmic items are replaced by texts from the Gospel pericopes; these
Communions give us a good look at other types. 'Oportet te'[22]
(Saturday of the Second Week of Lent) is an almost completely
syllabic setting of a speech quoted from the parable of the Prodigal
Son; the result is a very simple-looking melody, which on paper at
least seems to be typical of mode 8 Office antiphons; but somehow it

[22] *GR*, p. 104; *MMMA* 2, p. 498.

neither sings nor sounds that way, and on close inspection has clearly been shaped not in accord with a model melody or a formulaic system but rather with the text, following its inflections (compare 'fuerat .. perierat'). Most of this is lost in the more neumatic form of the Urban-Roman. 'Lutum fecit'[23] (Ex. 63) (Wednesday in Fourth Week) is another quotation of a speech from the Gospel, of the blind man cured by Jesus. 'Videns Dominus',[24] which is a real narrative, is very long for a stichic antiphon, resembling some of the antiphons for the Gospel Canticles.

Ex. 63

Lu - tum fe - cit ex spu - to Do - mi - nus,

et li - ni - vit o - cu - los me - os:

et a - bi - i, et la - vi, et vi - di,

et cre - di - di De - o.

Psalm tone 6

(intonation   reciting   differentia)
note

These chants are representative of a sector of the Gregorian repertory (data are not yet available concerning the extent of this sector) in which individual texts are provided with several different melodies, all within the Gregorian manuscript tradition.[25] It is presumed that in general such items are later additions to the repertory— that is, that none of the melodies is an early one; but that presumption cannot be imagined to hold without exception. Text-critical proced-

[23] GR, p. 125; MMMA 2, p. 448.
[24] GR, p. 127; MMMA 2, p. 449.
[25] Michel Huglo, Les tonaires, inventaire, analyse, comparison, Publications de la Société française de musicologie, Troisième série, ii (Paris, 1971), 152 ff.

ures for dealing with manuscript traditions will tell us which of the multiple versions was probably intended for the archetype of diffusion, but it may be very difficult to penetrate behind the archetype to sort out the multiple versions there. The relationship of the Urban-Roman record to multiple versions in the Gregorian is a topic for lively discussion and analysis.

OFFERTORY MELODIES

The melodic style of Offertories is more consistent than that of Communions; but Offertories vary greatly in length (not even taking into account the verses).[26] The consistency in style goes with an increased perceptibility of formulaic systems. While it is not possible yet to analyse and demonstrate the workings of formulaic systems in Offertories, still—when compared to Introits or Communions—there seems to be a greater family resemblance among members of a modal group.

Like every other type of Gregorian chant, Offertories have their own distinctive distribution among modal classes. What is peculiar about the Offertories is the preponderance of modes 2, 4, 6, and 8 compared with the others; the preponderance is especially strong in the case of mode 8, with over twenty items, compared with only two ('Confitebuntur', 'Eripe me .. Deus'), in mode 7. Nor is this simply hesitation in dealing with pieces of extended range (a frequent cause of changing classification between authentic and plagal subclasses); the Offertories in mode 8 have the very clear concentration on *fa* characteristic of that group (even when topped by a rise to *la*), and the two Offertories in mode 7 are clearly distinct in their orientation around the fifth *ut–sol*. The preponderance of the plagal classes might reflect a tendency of the Offertories to lie lower than their verses; that is, the verses lie relatively higher—as verse melodies (whether tones or not) typically do—and since the melodic style of Offertories is heavily ornate and active, the Offertories themselves tend to exploit the lower registers corresponding to the plagal classes, while the verses tend to push into the upper registers corresponding to the authentic classes. There is the persistently poor representation in mode 5. The net result is that Offertories in modes 4 and 8 account for almost half the repertory. It is difficult to perceive a rationale in the distribution;

---

[26] Wagner, *Einführung in die gregorianischen Melodien*, iii, pp. 418–34; Ferretti, *Esthétique grégorienne*, pp. 191–203; Apel, *Gregorian Chant*, pp. 363–75; Ruth Steiner, 'Some Questions about the Gregorian Offertories and the Verses', *JAMS*, 19 (1966), 162. Giacomo Baroffio and Ruth Steiner, 'Offertory', *New Grove*, xiii. 513–7. As noted above, p. 143, it is not clear whether the main part of the Offertory is an 'antiphon' or a 'respond'. It will be referred to here simply as 'Offertory', with the verse specified separately, as needed.

perhaps mode 3 is favoured in Lent (as it is for Introits for ferias), and perhaps mode 6 is favoured for saints' days. There are close to a hundred Offertories in the archetype, which means there is a good deal of multiple use in the Mass formularies, compared to the roughly 150 Introits.

The popularity of mode 4 for Offertories is apparent in the festal layer, where it is used in four of the seven formularies; the other modes are 1, 5, and 8. The four cases show the characteristic pitch set on *re–fa* (D–F); in the shorter 'Laetentur caeli'[27] (Ex. 64) (First Mass of Christmas) the set, with only two or three more pitches above, accounts for most of the piece, in spite of the relatively elaborate neumes of six or eight notes on some syllables, and relatively intense decoration of at least two or three notes on almost all syllables. 'Terra tremuit'[28] (Easter) is about the same length, except that an alleluia is appended; the pitch set is similar, except for some off-slides up to c. There is much to learn about these alleluias that are appended throughout Paschaltide; they are not treated regularly, and are formulaic without being standardized. Before its alleluia, 'Terra tremuit' ends on D, the *re* of the locus and a perfectly stable pitch in the set (this is a frequent situation in mode 4 chants). The alleluia, however, begins the same as the alleluia appended to the Offertory for Ascension, 'Ascendit Deus',[29] which is in mode 1; and the alleluia for 'Terra tremuit' is deflected to its ending on *mi*(E) only at the last moment. It is characteristic of the *mi* final for mode 4—and especially noticeable in the mode 4 Offertories—that it does not confirm the central locus in the same way that finals in mode 2, or 6, or 8 do.

'Confirma hoc'[30] (Pentecost) and 'Tui sunt coeli'[31] (Third Mass of Christmas) are longer, with three or four phrases instead of two. Idiom and type of ornamentation remain similar, as does also the pitch set. 'Tui sunt coeli' (Ex. 65) affords a close comparison with the Urban-Roman version: the two are virtually identical except that the Urban-Roman ends on D, simply because of the last neume—it could be oversight or scribal error, but it does result in the classification in *protus*. The Urban-Roman is slightly fuller in its style of ornamentation, as we observed in other cases; here, because the two are so close, we can notice some points of detail that tend to recur throughout the Mass chants. In the Urban-Roman the first three syllables are set to the repeated figure E–F–D; this is the figure often used in this fashion on a reciting tone. By comparison the Gregorian shows less simple

[27] *GR*, p. 27; *MMMA* 2, p. 305.
[28] *GR*, p. 205; *MMMA* 2, p. 320.
[29] *GR*, p. 243; *MMMA* 2, p. 322.
[30] *GR*, p. 251; *MMMA* 2, p. 301.
[31] *GR*, p. 32; *MMMA* 2, p. 288.

Ex. 64

Lae - ten - tur cae - li,

et ex - ul - tet ter - ra

An - te fa - ci - em Do - mi - ni:

quo - ni - am ve - nit.

Can - ta - te Do - mi - no can - ti - cum

no - vum, can - ta - te Do - mi - no

om - nis ter - ra

℣ Can - ta - te Do - mi - no: be - ne - di - ci - te

no - men e - jus:

be - ne nun - ti - a - te

de di - e in di - em

sa - lu - ta - re e - jus.

Ex. 65

(i) Gregorian

Tu – i   sunt   cae –   li   ...

et   ple – ni – tu –   di – nem e –   jus

tu   fun – da –   sti:

Ju – sti –   ti – a

et   ju – di –   ci –   um...

(ii) Urban – Roman (Vat. lat. 5319)

Tu – i   sunt   ce –   li   ...

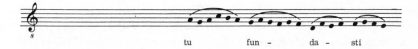

et   ple – ni – tu – di –   nem e –   jus

tu   fun –   da –   sti

ju – sti –   ti –   ae

et   ju – di –   ci –   um ...

repetition, and here again we can observe that the Gregorian seeks out a continuously varied succession of neumes or single notes for a recitation of this type in ornate chant. This can help us understand the oblique logic of many active but static passages in the Gregorian. Another example can be seen on 'et plenitudinem'. On 'ejus' immediately following, where the Urban-Roman has stepwise, flowing motion the Gregorian has repeated-note figures. The use of these figures is as characteristic of the Gregorian as the flowing stepwise motion is of the Urban-Roman. On 'Justitia' is one of those brief but frequent near-identities that may reassure us we are dealing with a single repertory of chant—a conviction easy to lose in the face of so much difference. On 'judicium' the flowing motion of the Urban-Roman obliterates the sharper, more telling profile of the Gregorian, just as it did on 'tu (fundasti)'.

Both the reiterative style and extremely active melodic movement are frequent in the verses for Offertories.[32] Their ornate style has suggested that they are not very old, that is, that they might date from the ninth century, not before. The profusion of ornament and the loose manner in which it is strung together might also suggest that in this case the recorded versions stand relatively close to a cantorial practice very much in the hands of soloists—possibly special ones; at any rate the verses do not show the artistic discipline apparent, say, in Gradual verses. Some such factors might account for their nature and relatively short history. Those of 'Laetentur caeli' (see Ex. 64)[33] are highly organized by re-use of material at verse endings. The verses of 'Tui sunt coeli',[34] more effusive, are none the less more restrained than many others. They also show the clear tendency to lie higher, and actually use mode 3 formulas instead of the mode 4 formulas of 'Tui sunt coeli' itself; we should note that this happens in the first verse, 'Magnus et metuendus', and the third, 'Tu humiliasti', but not in the second, 'Misericordia', which is back in mode 4—and this arrangement is not unique here. The third verse of 'Deus enim'[35] has a long melisma on its last word, 'in longitudinem die—rum', with repetition of motives, over a wide melodic range. This type of motivic repetition, encountered occasionally in the more elaborate types of Gregorian chant (especially in long melismata), fascinated the Franks and was to have much importance in their new kind of music. Like the verse tones of Office responsories, these free verses of Offertories often do not end

[32] Apel, *Gregorian Chant*, pp. 262, 368.
[33] Rupert Fischer, *Offertoires neumés avec leurs versets* (Solesmes, 1978), 15.
[34] Ibid. 18.
[35] Ibid. 16.

on the final of the Offertory itself, but on another note, often a neighbour, with attention paid to the retransition to the Offertory.

The usual practice seems to have been to repeat the last part of the Offertory after each verse—the same practice Amalarius indicated was normal for Frankish (we assume Gallican) performance of Office responsories. All that seems clear, as long as we do not try to work back from this typical stichic arrangement in a highly developed style to a presumed prototype of responsorial psalm. Related to this partial repeat may be at least some of the interesting structures peculiar to the Offertory repertory. In 'Domine in auxilium'[36] (Friday of Second Week of Lent, and elsewhere), after four phrases the first is exactly repeated in text and melody; this seems to be the phrase to be repeated after the verses. The same structure appears in 'De profundis'[37] (Twenty-third Sunday after Pentecost), and in a few Urban-Roman Offertories, but not necessarily the same ones. Another structure peculiar to Offertories, but seemingly not related to the partial repeat after the verse, is an immediate repetition of the opening phrase, with expanded ornamentation on a melisma. The most famous cases are in the two Offertories that begin 'Jubilate Deo'[38] (First and Second Sundays after Epiphany). In each case the repeat of the opening phrase replaces the neume on ('Jubi-)la-(te') with a very elaborate melisma (the second case also replaces the neume on 'ter-ra' with a shorter melisma). In other cases ('Benedictus es Domine, doce me ... in labis')[39] the rationale for writing out the phrase a second time is not so clear. Nor is it so clear what the repetition means for performance. Is this a solo, then choral, singing of a refrain, such as Amalarius describes for Office responsories? (And he does say, although without seeming to refer to this context, that it is appropriate for the chorus, with its stronger resources, to sing the melisma.) Or are the singers to choose between the first and second writing depending on whether they want to use the melisma? Or is there some other reason, possibly lost to us?

A few Offertories are strikingly different in length and conception from those of the festal layer, and from most of the dominical and ferial layers. Moderately long are 'Improperium'[40] (Palm Sunday); the Prayer of Daniel, 'Oravi Deum meum'[41] (17th Sunday after Pente-

[36] *GR*, p. 312; *MMMA* 2, p. 347.
[37] *GR*, p. 334; *MMMA* 2, p. 360.
[38] 'Jubilate ... omnis', *GR*, p. 50; *MMMA* 2, p. 363; 'Jubilate ... universa', *GR* p. 54; *MMMA* 2, p. 298. See also H. Wagenaar-Nothenius, 'Ein Münchener Mixtum: Gregorianische Melodien zu altrömischen Texten', *AcM*, 45 (1973), 249.
[39] *GR*, p. 67; *MMMA* 2, p. 329.
[40] *GR*, p. 158; *MMMA* 2, p. 377.
[41] *GR*, p. 315; *MMMA* 2, p. 288.

cost); the two Offertories referring explicitly to sacrifice, 'Sicut in holocausto'[42] (7th Sunday after Pentecost) and 'Sanctificavit Moyses altare Domino'[43] (18th Sunday after Pentecost). 'Vir erat'[44] (21st Sunday after Pentecost) is not only much longer than usual, but has an unusual text—the story of Job, with speeches in the verses—and some spectacular dramatic musical utterance, with repetitions of a purely rhetorical kind. The longest one is 'Precatus est Moyses'[45] (12th Sunday after Pentecost), a narrative and speech of Moses; the verses add very substantially to the length, continuing the story. In stature and continuity, as well as dramatic intent, such pieces have little to do with normal stichic texts for Mass. They are clearly special items; the liturgical question, and the question of repertory related to it, is why such special items do not appear in connection with feasts.

It has sometimes been thought that a distinctive feature of Gregorian chant is the sense of propriety in assigning the most elaborate chants to the most solemn parts of the liturgy and calendar, but here are these extraordinary Offertories mostly placed on Sundays at the bottom of the calendar, without much relationship to other proper elements. Perhaps in these cases purely musical or textual factors have been more determinative than liturgical ones; that is, perhaps—even within a ritual of Roman origin—the canons of propriety were not always as strict as modern commentators would have us believe. Or, for a different explanation, perhaps in these places we are looking at remainders from a previous stage of liturgical development whose logic and substance have otherwise completely disappeared.

GRADUAL AND TRACT MELODIES

The chants for Graduals and Tracts are in general distinct from those for Introits and Communions, with Offertories occupying a middle ground. As a stichic form Graduals are responsories, like Office responsories; hence there is a categorical difference with respect to Introits and Communions, which are closer to antiphons of the Office.[46]

The factors of modal distribution, assignment to calendar, use of formulaic systems, melismatic style, and verse construction are all closely related—perhaps more so in the case of Graduals and Tracts

[42] GR, p. 288.
[43] GR, p. 321; MMMA 2, p. 350.
[44] GR, p. 329; MMMA 2, p. 255.
[45] GR, p. 301; MMMA 2, p. 397.
[46] Wagner, Einführung in die gregorianschen Melodien, iii, pp. 369–96; Ferretti, Esthétique grégorienne, pp. 159–75; Apel, Gregorian Chant, pp. 344–63; Stäblein, 'Graduale', MGG, v (1956), cols. 632–59; Hucke, 'Das Responsorium', ed. Wulf Arlt, et al., Gattungen der Musik in Einzeldarstellungen: Gedenkschrift Leo Schrade, i (Berne, 1973), 172–9.

than with any other type of chant. Graduals and Tracts have been thought to make more consistent use of formulaic systems than other kinds of chant, although this observation needs to be qualified in certain ways. Graduals and Tracts have always been discussed in terms of the modal classification, and while this, too, needs careful qualification, it is a useful point of departure, for the real groupings based upon similarity of melodic substance tend to coincide to a high degree with the modal classifications. Yet in cases of anomalies the melodic substance must be the criterion for grouping rather than the final. Examples of anomalies are, on one hand, the fact that Graduals in mode 2 (the family traditionally identified as 'Justus ut palma'), make very consistent use of a melody that is completely distinct from the melody used with equal consistency in the Tracts in mode 2 that are more properly referred to as 'Graduals with several verses'. On the other hand there are formulas that are used in more than one modal class; traditionally called 'wandering melismas', these, too, require careful consideration for their implications for the whole repertory of Graduals and Tracts.

Graduals are classified as melismatic chant, and indeed their most distinctive feature is the use of melismata of ten or fifteen notes to one syllable, sometimes thirty or forty notes, in very expressive, intricately contoured melodic patterns. So the melisma is the most distinctive feature, but not the most useful in trying to understand many structural aspects of this kind of chant. One of the things a melisma does is interrupt the phrase structure of text and melody, extending the phrase and loosening the relationship to the text to the point of dissolution. As a result of this loosened relationship, there are two different ways of regarding the melodic structure of melismatic chant: it has been viewed as a syllabic psalm tone into which are interpolated melismata; or, alternatively, as a series of melismata into which the text has been interpolated in psalmodic recitation.[47] Neither approach yields completely satisfactory results. For while it is true that the melisma interrupts an underlying plan by prolonging a single syllable, what is being interrupted is neither a syllabic text nor a psalm tone, but rather a neumatic text moving through a relatively extended pitch set—exactly the conditions of Office responsories. If we remove from a Gradual the melismata (and there will usually be only a few of ten notes or longer) the remainder closely resembles an Office responsory, except that the ornamental style is slightly heavier; also the idiom is subtly different, that of the Graduals being a little more carefully

---

[47] Hucke, 'Gregorianischer Gesang in altrömischer und fränkischer Überlieferung', *AMw*, 12 (1955), 74.

worked, sharply profiled, idiosyncratic and less formulaic. This neumatic substance is as firmly tied to the phrase structure of the text in a Gradual as it is in an Office responsory; the phrase structure is only a little more difficult to perceive because of the slightly heavier quality of the ornamental overlay. It is this structure we need to understand in order to understand the melismata—which for their part are firmly rooted in the same pitch sets used for the neumatic substance, even if overrunning them in a characteristically ecstatic way.

There are approximately 116 Graduals in the archetype of diffusion (including the six 'Graduals with several verses', but counting 'Haec dies' only once—that is, not counting its repetition with separate verses during Easter Week). This is considerably less than the approximately 145 Introits. There is much multiple use of Graduals in Mass formularies, and this makes for a certain amount of confusion. The most frequent multiple use takes place between the Sundays after Pentecost and the ferias of Lent, and in the Sanctorale.

Almost half of the Graduals (about 47) are in mode 5, and granting much looseness in the formulaic system this modal class really does constitute one family of melodies. These Graduals in mode 5 are used for all kinds of occasions, including the Sanctorale (about half), the dominical layer (about half), and a few feasts and special occasions. The concentration in the Christmas cycle (Christmas—Second and Third Masses, the following saints' days on December 26, 27, 28, and Epiphany) is striking and certainly not coincidental. To complete the survey briefly at this point (we shall need to consider the liturgical assignments more closely in discussion of the several groups), Graduals in mode 1, numbering about 15 in the archetype, are divided about equally between the Sanctorale and the dominical-ferial layers; but the use is such as to suggest the Sanctorale as the most characteristic of this modal group. Graduals in mode 7, on the other hand, numbering about twelve, have only two for the Sanctorale, the rest being largely for Sundays. The dozen or so Graduals in mode 3 are very clearly concentrated in a Lenten cycle, with only two outside that season (and not very far outside). Another half-dozen items that are anomalous with respect to the modal classification are distributed in a similar fashion.

So far we have enumerated Graduals in modes 1, 3, 5, and 7, and that, indeed, accounts for almost all the Graduals except those in mode 2, to be discussed. The almost exclusive distribution to the authentic modes as opposed to the plagals is clear. In the Offertories we noticed an opposite tendency, and there it may have had something to do with the tendency of the Offertories themselves to lie in the lower part of the range, with their verses in the higher part; in other words, the classification there seemed to be according to the Offertories rather than the verses. The verses of the Graduals also tend to lie higher than their responds, and these often explore the lower registers. The Graduals, especially in their melismata, tend to move through a greater range, and more quickly, than do the Offertories, and this might be a reason why the responds were not classified in the plagal modes; for even though, for instance, a Gradual respond in mode 5 may start out in the lower register below the final, it soon moves definitely into the upper register. In any case the idioms and pitch sets of other types of chant in plagal modes are not completely absent from Graduals, in spite of the lop-sided classification.

As we saw in the Office, most responsories in the repertory of the archetype used the standardized tones for the verses. These verse tones are useful in a general way in helping us understand the behaviour of verses of the Graduals. It has long been observed that the Gradual verses make more consistent use of formulaic systems than do the responds, and in some cases it has been possible to speak of actual verse tones in the Graduals. In the Office responsories, even when the verses made regular use of tones, the responds did not (with the very interesting exception of a group of responds in mode 2); the use of formulaic systems in the responds hardly ever approaches the regularity of a tone—and here we should remind ourselves that what we call a tone can be regarded merely as an exceptionally rigorous use of a formulaic system. What comes together in a verse is (1) the cantor's choice of a stich complementing the stich of the respond, (2) sung to a rigorously controlled choice of formulas, (3) at the top of the central locus of the respond, (4) with a clear sense of being a contrasting episode within the aggregate. One of the aspects of contrast is that the verse of Office responsories is always a bi-hemistich; or at least, the tone is set up with that phrase structure in mind, whether or not the chosen text conforms. The bi-hemistich of the verse is usually not matched by a bi-hemistich in the respond; or at any rate the melody of the respond is more apt to proceed through a chain of single phrases having varied but not necessarily balancing cadences.

The verses of Graduals, too, can usually be construed as bi-hemistichs. 'Construe' is the important word here. Gradual verses vary in structure, are complex and obscure, and each one can be construed in different ways. The bi-hemistich normal for Office responsories is useful here as a model: in trying to construe a Gradual verse according to this model, we see either how it conforms, revealing a structural level not otherwise apparent; or we see that it does not conform, for specific cause; or—perhaps most frequent—we are made sensitive to structural ambiguities inherent in the kind of melody used for Gradual verses. With their heavily neumatic style occasionally interrupted by melisma, these melodies stretch out a few words (much less than a full syntactic phrase of text) over a full phrase of melody. Thus a bi-hemistich of text may extend through four or more melodic phrases. When this is combined with the persistent tendency of Gregorian art to cadence on a varied succession of tones, the result is a series of phrases that can be construed in more than one way. Furthermore, the complex style of Graduals seems to take advantage of this to reflect individual syntactic structures in the text. And here we are made aware of the great variety of such structures in the psalms: certainly many stichs selected for Gradual verses are not balanced bi-hemistichs. Some Gradual verse melodies cadence faithfully with textual subphrases, leaving the larger phrase-group as ambiguous in the melody as it is in the text. This is another situation suggesting that individualized treatment of textual phrases was the more traditional procedure, and that what we know as a tone (either the psalm tones or the more elaborate responsory verse tones) is cast as a bi-hemistich simply because if one has to choose a single standard form this is the one best adapted to all types of psalm verses or stichs. The bi-hemistich verse tone might be the norm that emerged, rather than the prototype out of which variety was generated.

The pitch set associated with an F final that we call mode 5 has not much concerned us so far, since it is represented hardly at all in antiphons of the Office, and only sparsely in Office responsories as well as Introits, Communions, and Offertories at Mass. The pitch set has the basic ambiguity that it seems to be built around a *re–mi–fa* (a–b–c) as a central locus—like mode 2, and coinciding largely with mode 8(G), but with a terminal descent below the *ut* of mode 8 to a *fa*(F). The ambiguity arises from the fact that this *fa*–below–*ut* (F) becomes associated with and supported by a b flat a fourth above it (as for example in the terminal melisma of the verse of 'Bonum est confidere', Ex. 66), and as this b flat becomes stable it forces a reinterpretation of the final from *fa–below–ut* into *ut*, and with it a reinterpretation of the central locus from *re–mi–fa* (a–b–c) to *mi–fa–sol* (a–b flat–c). Within the repertory of Graduals, the reciting tone c never gives the impression of having been elevated (as the *sol* of mode 7 does); on the other hand it frequently functions in context as a *sol* not a *fa*. Because of this persistent ambiguity it is easier to refer to letter-pitches than to solmization syllables in mode 5.

The Gradual 'Bonum est confidere' (Ex. 66) (14th Sunday after Pentecost), representing one of the most regular groups in mode 5 (Apel's Group I[48]), has clear parallelism in both respond and verse; and respond and verse are in parallel with each other.

R. Bonum est confidere in Domino
   quam confidere in homine
V. Bonum est sperare in Domino
   quam sperare in principibus

Ex. 66

This is faithfully reflected in the melody. The respond has a first phrase centred on F, with movement below to D and up to a and b flat; there is a brief cadence figure F–G–F. The second phrase is higher, centred on a; there is a modest melisma on the last syllable of 'confidere', returning to F. Then comes the penultimate descent, here to C—a feature found in many chants of all types; and a terminal melisma that moves first to a, then almost as an afterthought appends the standard final cadence on F. (This is the same figure used for final on G, but—in the versions we have—the highest note has been raised from b to c. Almost the same figure is used also on D.)

The verse has a cadence at the end of the first hemistich ('Domino') on a; the second hemistich also goes to a before appending the same final cadence as the respond. The verse is centred on C, with extravagant movement above and below for expressive decoration. This occurs in two large melismas, one on the third syllable ('est'), which can also be counted as the end of the first word-group ('Bonum est'); a lesser melisma occurs on the accented syllable in 'sperare'. There is a penultimate descent to F ('in') which is the bottom of the pitch set used in the verse, and a terminal melisma stressing first b flat, then c. The disposition of pitches is characteristic of mode 5 verses, that of cadences, phrases, and melismas is characteristic of Gradual verses in general. Apel's analysis shows these melodic formulas to be used exactly in this way in several Graduals, while reappearing in different contexts in several more.

The Gradual 'Christus factus est'[49] (Maundy Thursday), not a psalm text, has a long and a short phrase of text in the respond, set to three phrases of melody; and three phrases of text in the verse, also set to three phrases of melody. There is no clear bi-hemistich structure, and the relatively short phrases of melody seem to lend themselves perfectly to this construction.

The Gradual 'Constitues eos',[50] with a stock of idioms largely different from those seen so far, has in the respond three phrases of melody set to a clear bi-hemistich of text (two melodic phrases to the first hemistich). The verse has the same arrangement, only here we can notice the firm cadence on F ('filii'), which might be taken as the end of a pair of melody phrases. There is more to say about strong inner articulations such as this. The striking ascent on 'tuis' is one of many gracious turns of phrase that set the Gregorian art—especially as seen in the Gradual—apart from others.

'Misit Dominus'[51] (second Sunday after Epiphany) has a slightly

[49] GR, p. 169; MMMA 2, p. 134.   [51] GR, p. 52; MMMA 2, p. 138.
[50] GR, p. 339; MMMA 2, p. 130.

longer, more complex text. The respond is treated as a bi-hemistich with two textual subphrases set to three melodic suphrases in the first hemistich. In the verse the first hemistich is greatly extended by melismata, the first in what Apel calls 'reiterative style', the second a 'wandering' melisma, used in various contexts. Because of the extension this first hemistich appears as two complete phrases of melody. The second hemistich, treated more briefly, appears as a third phrase.

Some of the Graduals in mode 1 are more discursive than usual. 'Inveni David',[52] from the Sanctorale, is clearly tristichic in its respond, and each of the three larger phrases, cadencing on D, F, and D, has an interior cadence. The central locus is F–G–a, as usual, but introduced by the lower register and with several extensions up to c. The verse moves up to c (instead of a) for its accented syllables, with d and e for decoration; here the pitch set (even some of the figures) are indistinguishable from mode 5. 'Ecce quam bonum' (Sanctorale), with one textual phrase in the respond, has two melodic phrases. The verse seems specially constructed, with the first hemistich cadencing unusually on F. The text of the verse, 'Like the oil that ran down the beard, the beard of Aaron', is set so that the latter part follows a long melodic descent from high e to low A, forming the end of the penultimate descent. This grandiose low melisma appears also in the Gradual 'Timete' (Sanctorale).

Graduals in mode 7 are perhaps the most mobile in their melodies, with some very ecstatic melismata ('Clamaverunt' in the Sanctorale).[53] They also show the least systematic use of formulas in the verses, which are often bi-hemistichs, but also sometimes unclear. 'Jacta cogitatum'[54] (Lenten ferias and 3rd Sunday after Pentecost) has a clear bi-hemistich in the text of the respond, distorted by melismata in the second part; and two very uneven text phrases (short, then long) in the verse.

The Graduals in mode 2—the 'Justus ut palma' group (referred to here as '2-a' to distinguish them from other melodies on mode 2)—are split into three equal subgroups.[55] One subgroup is for Advent, and includes the four Graduals for Ember Saturday. Another subgroup is for the Sanctorale. The remainder are spread out over Christmas, Lent, and Easter, without a pattern. It has been customary to derive the formulaic system from a study of the most compact group of examples—in this case, the Graduals for Ember Saturday in Advent.

---

[52] *GR*, p. [3]; *MMMA* 2, p. 105; Apel, *Gregorian Chant*, pp. 350 ff.

[53] *GR*, p. [26]; *MMMA* 2, p. 161; Apel, *Gregorian Chant*, p. 356.

[54] *GR*, p. 278; *MMMA* 2, p. 165.

[55] Hucke, 'Das Responsorium', pp. 172 f.; 'Die gregorianische Gradualweise des 2. Tons und ihre ambrosianischen Parallelen', *AMw*, 13 (1956), 285.

The simplicity and regularity of this group, however, may be due to a late, routine adaptation; we should try first to understand the formulaic system as it appears in the other mode 2 Graduals, confusing as that may be. Here it is important to keep a subtle distinction in mind: an old melody can be used as a model at any time later in history (and 2-a was often used this way later in the Middle Ages, and even in modern times). Such use should have absolutely no influence upon our perception of this melody before the time of the archetype. Apart from the Advent Graduals, and especially in those for Christmas and Easter, there are important variations in the way the formulas are used.

Even so, it is a remarkably regular system, and especially in the verse, whose most frequent form can be understood as a bi-hemistich, as in the verse 'Dixit Dominus' (although here a fifth phrase, 'donec . . . tuos' has been interpolated (see Ex. 67).

Here we need our perception of extended phrase-groups. This verse melody is usually thought of as containing four phrases, and indeed in its usual form it does: the four normal phrases cadence on d ('meo') above the final, then on a ('meis'), then on the F below ('scabellum'), and finally on a ('tuorum'). The text, however, tells us that these four phrases should be grouped in twos. The cadences on the d above and the F below are half-cadences, and this is often shown by the way the line moves from these pitches back into the central locus. This locus is on *fa* and the *re*-final, that is c and a (these melodies are always notated on an a final in modern books, and medieval ones as well). The verse has the interesting feature that it begins with a strong move to the *sol* (d) above the locus, using it both for a reciting note and the half-cadence; the way this *sol* is expressed in the first melisma is perhaps hard to follow, and very characteristic of this group of Graduals. The rest of the first hemistich (that is, the second melodic phrase) eventually drops back to *fa* as a centre, and cadences on the *re*, with a curious drop of a fourth, found also in certain antiphons of similar pitch set. The regularity of this particular formulaic system makes clear the supplementary or alternative nature of another phrase of melody that can appear at this point for the sake of an extra phrase of text, as in 'Tecum principium',[56] or in lieu of the third phrase, as in 'Ne avertas'.[57] (This phrase cadences on *fa* with the same figure used in mode 5 for the phrase with analogous function.) The usual third phrase ('scabellum') makes the penultimate descent to the low F. This phrase initiates an approximate repeat of material from this end of the

[56] *GR*, p. 25; *MMMA* 2, p. 94.　　　[57] *GR*, p. 164; *MMMA* 2, p. 99.

Ex. 67

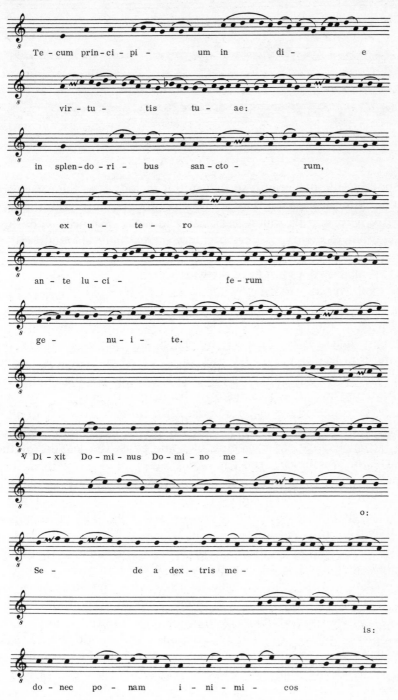

Te - cum prin - ci - pi - um in di - e

vir - tu - tis tu - ae:

in splen - do - ri - bus san - cto - rum,

ex u - te - ro

an - te lu - ci - fe - rum

ge - nu - i - te.

℣ Di - xit Do - mi - nus Do - mi - no me -

o:

Se - de a dex - tris me -

is:

do - nec po - nam i - ni - mi - cos

respond ('ante luciferum') so that in this melody type the verse ends
similarly to the respond. This rounding of the responsorial form, seen
clearly here, can be found less clearly in other instances within the
Gregorian repertory; it then becomes increasingly characteristic of
Frankish chant.

This melody does not have the wide-ranging habit of, say, mode 7,
and its moves above or below the locus are expressed in more subtle
ways. The first hemistich of the respond explores the lower register
much as in modes 5 and 1; this low-lying quality, admittedly not
strongly marked, is enhanced by the b flat that has entered the
manuscript tradition; how far back this lowered pitch goes is hard to
say. This whole opening phrase is peculiar to the respond and never
appears in verse, which has its own distinctive opening.

The Graduals in mode 3 are perhaps the most inaccessible of all.[58]
Buried, like the Tracts, in the Sundays and ferias of Lent, they tend to
be extremely long, approaching in some cases the lengths of the
Tracts, for which they furnish an important point of comparison. The
Graduals include striking melismata, marked by excessive stretches in
'reiterative' style; these alternate with melodic motions of great
fluidity, often of great expressiveness and beauty. The prevailing E
final tends to throw shadows over the whole, even though the central
locus is a clear *ut–re–mi–fa* (G–a–b–c). A passionate, rhapsodic
quality dominates. Even though many of the Graduals in mode 3
participate in a formulaic system, there is much variation in the use of
the system itself, and the modal group contains several anomalous
chants. A relatively straightforward example is 'Exsurge Domine, non
praevaleat homo'[59] (Ex. 68). (There are three mode 3 Graduals
beginning 'Exsurge', which is a theme-word in the Mass formularies
of Lent.) The verse has two text phrases (without being a strong bi-

[58] Apel, *Gregorian Chant*, pp. 352–5.   [59] *GR*, p. 105; *MMMA* 2, p. 117.

Ex. 68

Ex - sur - ge Do - mi - ne,

non prae - va - le - at ho -

mo:

ju - di - cen - tur gen - tes

in con - spe - ctu tu - o.

℣ In con-ver-ten - do i -ni - mi-cum me-um re - tror -

sum,

in - fir- ma-bun-tur, et per-i - bunt

a fa - ci - e

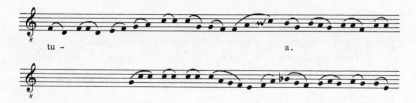

tu -   a.

hemistich), set to three phrases of melody, the second text phrase
having two melody phrases. The verse melody rises through a
common intonation up to the *fa* (c), which it uses briefly for a reciting
tone, then to a cadence on G. The second phrase has a re-intonation,
and another cadence on G, then continues with one of the standard
melismata ('facie'), which concludes with the penultimate descent and
the final melisma. The turning figure, used at the bottom of the
descent to form the return upwards, is almost the same in modes 3, 5,
and 2-a. The melisma on 'facie' has literal repetition of figure, that on
'tua' has a small melodic sequence. Most of this final melisma appears
at the end of the respond as a rounding. The respond itself has no
clear bi-hemistich; instead there are three phrases of melody, each
cadencing on the low D, followed by this final phrase. A bi-hemistich
could be construed if the cadence at the end of the second phrase
(coinciding with the colon in the textual bi-hemistich) were taken as a
full cadence on D borrowed from mode 1; the other two cadences on
D (first and third phrases) are standard half-cadences in mode 4. Such
oblique constructions are common in mode 3. The use of mode 4
cadences is entirely appropriate to the exploration of the lower
register in the first three phrases, as in Graduals in other modes.

Phrase plans in the verses tend to get longer and more complex as
Lent proceeds, and sometimes it seems as though two verses had been
strung together. As a contributing factor there is a tendency for the
verse to move through a series of similar phrases cadencing on the
same note, usually G; this is an important and perhaps seminal
construction that we noticed before in connection with the Introits in
mode 3. A simple example occurs in 'Exsurge Domine et intende'[60]
(Monday in Holy Week), with the cadences coming 'Effunde fra-
meam/et conclude/adversus eos/qui me persequuntur'. More complex
instances are found in 'Tibi Domine',[61] 'Eripe me Domine',[62] 'Exal-
tabo te Domine'.[63]

There are some other Graduals in the mode 3 class that use different
melodies, and show even more elaborate verse plans, for example,

[60] *GR*, p. 160; *MMMA* 2, p. 124.   [62] *GR*, p. 130; *MMMA* 2, p. 118.
[61] *GR*, p. 128; *MMMA* 2, p. 115.   [63] *GR*, p. 137; *MMMA* 2, p. 120.

'Exsurge Domine, fer opem'[64] and 'Ego autem.'[65] Taken all together, the Graduals in mode 3 are distributed in Pre-Lent and Lent in an interesting way, being assigned to every other Sunday.

'Tenuisti',[66] for Palm Sunday, is the longest of all Graduals (except for those more familiarly known as Tracts). Thought to be a late addition to the formulary, 'Tenuisti' is one of half a dozen Graduals not easily subsumed under the modal classifications discussed. It is nominally in mode 4, being one of two so classed in the tradition; the other is 'Domine praevenisti'[67] (Sanctorale), whose respond is clearly mode 4, and whose verse is just as clearly mode 1 (this can be understood according to the model of Offertories in mode 4 whose verses end on D below the final). The problem of the mode 4 Graduals would be eased if we acknowledge as similar those Graduals nominally classified as mode 3—or better, if we classified these chants of extended range simply according to final, in this case *deuterus* (E). The problem of identifying the melody group remains, and has to be dealt with item by item. 'Dilexisti'[68] (Sanctorale), classifed as mode 8, begins just like 'Tenuisti'; while moving in the pitch set for mode 8, it shows little of those idioms. 'Deus vitam' and 'Deus exaudi'[69] (Mondays in the Third Week and Fifth Week respectively), classed as mode 8, also show a fascinating variety of idioms and pitch sets. Up to the very last cadences in respond and verse they could be considered to be in any one of several melody groups—or in none. Perhaps they form their own group, a melody used only on these two occasions, then not again. And still another Monday Gradual, 'Adjutor meus'[70] (Second Week), is classed as mode 2 and shares no idioms with 2-a, although it has some points of contact with Tracts in mode 2. Filling out all those weekday formularies in the calendar for Lent entailed mustering up all the melodic material available; in some of these unusual chants we may be looking at very old, as well as very new material.

The six 'Graduals with several verses' (later called 'Tracts') make use of a special formulaic system classed as mode 2. They occur in close proximity to the Graduals in mode 3 and some of those anomalous Lenten Graduals, and can be regarded as yet another such group with even more elaborate verse stuctures. The complexity and

---

[64] *GR*, p. 122; *MMMA* 2, p. 113.
[65] *GR*, p. 162; *MMMA* 2, p. 101.
[66] *GR*, p. 154; *MMMA* 2, p. 102.
[67] *GR*, p. [42]; *MMMA* 2, p. 121.
[68] *GR*, p. [45]; *MMMA* 2, p. 158.
[69] 'Deus vitam', *GR*, p. 108; *MMMA* 2, p. 145. 'Deus exaudi', *GR*, p. 134; *MMMA* 2, p. 146.
[70] *GR*, p. 97; *MMMA* 2, p. 108.

irregularity of these structures makes the formulaic system a little hard to understand.[71]

After the first lesson on Good Friday is sung 'Domine audivi';[72] in modern times it is called 'Tract', but in the Sextuplex 'Resp. Grad'. The text is from the Prayer of Habakuk, but in a wording different from the Vulgate. There are five verses each cadencing with the same figure on D, and approached in one of two ways. The fourth of these phrases '(Deus a Libano', Ex. 69) is the simplest, in spite of the

Ex. 69

expressive melisma at the start. In text and melody this verse is a standard bi-hemistich, with a half cadence approached by formula on C below the final ('veniet'). This mediant cadence, and the final cadence at the end of the verse, are the two main signs of articulation in the system. There may be much extension before the mediant, often involving passing cadences on the D final; there may also be double statements of the mediant cadence, or of the whole first half, as needed for the text. In the first verse, the mediant cadence is sung twice in succession ('tuum', 'et timui'), which is unusual. In the second verse there is a modified cadence on C for the first text phrase ('innotesceris'), then the usual form for the second text phrase ('cognosceris'). It has often been observed that, while in the longer melodies of this

---

[71] Wagner, *Einführung in die gregorianischen Melodien*, iii, pp. 352–68; Ferretti, *Esthétique grégorienne*, pp. 139–50; Apel, *Gregorian Chant*, pp. 323–30; Hucke, 'Tractusstudien', in Martin Ruhnke, ed., *Festschrift Bruno Stäblein zum 70. Geburtstage* (Kassel, 1967), 116.

[72] *GR*, p. 177; *MMMA* 2, p. 228.

group certain formulas are reserved for the final verse, in the shorter ones some of these 'final' formulas (with the high b flat) appear in other verses too. But we need to note that when sung as a Gradual responsory, with the first 'verse' (or part of it) repeated as respond after each verse, or at least at the end, what looks like the final phrase of the chant as a tract is not the final phrase when sung as a responsory; these special formulas, then, would be best understood as special verse formulas.

After the second lesson on Wednesday of Holy Week is sung the Gradual 'Domine exaudi'.[73] There are six verses. The bi-hemistichs proceed very regularly, using a slightly different inflection for some of the mediant cadences on C. With these two Graduals clearly in mind, one can attempt 'De necessitatibus',[74] after the second lesson on Ember Wednesday. This is about the same length as the Gradual 'Tenuisti'. In structure it is a little more straightforward, in melodic style a little less flamboyant; apart from that it is hard to distinguish them. What we are dealing with, then, is a special formulaic system used for three Lenten Graduals that have two or more verses (plus the respond). The same system was also used for a particularly long text, 'Qui habitat'[75] formerly used as post-lesson responsory on Good Friday, then apparently transferred to the first Sunday of Lent. The system was used for another long text, 'Deus deus meus',[76] on Palm Sunday. Close to the time of the archetype it was used for a third long text, 'Eripe me',[77] to replace 'Qui habitat' on Good Friday.

The Sundays of Pre-Lent and Lent were each provided with Tracts in mode 8 (except for the First Sunday of Lent, and Palm Sunday— the 'Last Sunday').[78] This same formulaic system was also used for three Tracts in the Sanctorale, for the same season, and for three 'end-of-lesson' Canticles and a processional on Holy Saturday (also, exceptionally, for Ember Saturday in Advent). These texts are about as long as the 'Graduals with several verses', and differ structurally only in having no responsorial repeat.

What makes this (and similar phenomena) a system is an underlying way of implementing a bi-hemistich, perceptible through even a wide variety of alternate formulas. The pitch set here is the usual one on mode 8, *ut–re–mi–fa* (G–a–b–c), with *fa* used as a reciting tone,

---

[73] *GR*, p. 165; *MMMA* 2, p. 225.
[74] *GR*, p. 85; *MMMA* 2, p. 234.
[75] *GR*, p. 77; *MMMA* 2, p. 221.
[76] *GR*, p. 155; *MMMA* 2, p. 230.
[77] *GR*, p. 187.
[78] Wagner, *Einführung in die gregorianischen Melodien*, iii, pp. 312–22; Ferretti, *Esthétique grégorienne*, pp. 133–9; Apel, *Gregorian Chant*, pp. 213–32; Hucke, 'Tractusstudien'.

and *ut* as the final. The most important internal element is a mediant cadence on *fa* (F) below *ut*, in the same position and using very much the same figure as the mediant cadence in the 'Graduals with several verses' in mode 2. The F comes through an abrupt fall, not otherwise prepared. Quite apart from this cadence there is much exploration of a realm involving b flat as a relief to the extended use of c. The fall of the F for the mediant cadence is usually followed by a rise from the F back to the c, often through the figure F–a–c as intonation for the second hemistich. It may occur in slightly different ways, however, and that variety can be confusing.

This underlying bi-hemistich can be followed fairly easily through-out the four phrases of 'De profundis'[79] for Septuagesima (Ex. 70); and also through the four verses of 'Jubilate Deo'[80] for Quinquage-sima—except that here the second and third verses are short on text, so in the second verse the melody ends sooner than usual, and in the third verse presents only the second hemistich. In 'Commovisti',[81] Ad te levavi[82] (Psalm 122), 'Qui confidunt',[83] 'Saepe expugnaverunt',[84] the plan is perceptible despite a rich use of the available formulas. The Tracts in mode 8 are distinctive in their melodic inflections; actual identity of idiom with other types of chant in other modes is minimal.

Because of the Lenten ferias, and also because of the Tracts included in the Sunday formularies, the season contains an unusually high concentration of melismatic chant using formulaic systems. There has been a tendency in studying this material to focus on the standard formulas or the standard use of formulas, putting like melodies together and regarding the most frequent combination, the lowest common denominator, as the prototype. But in the original situation (including therein the tradition, the singer, and the listener) it might be that variant elements had a much higher value than mere variety. As we look at the whole Lenten array of the formulaic systems discussed, it seems clear that the systematic element in these systems is not any restricted succession of formulas, but rather the shape that includes them. The use of alternate formulas is frequent, and tends to get more so as the musical mood becomes more rhapsodic, passionate, or ecstatic. Under all these conditions a high value might have been placed on the use of an unusual variant, or even a 'wandering melisma', an alternative from another system, made unexpectedly and inexplicably appropriate by the cantor's art.

An account from Metz shortly after 750 (where Bishop Chrodegang

---

[79] *GR*, p. 59; *MMMA* 2, p. 250.
[80] *GR*, p. 66; *MMMA* 2, p. 249.
[81] *GR*, p. 63; *MMMA* 2, p. 252.

[82] *GR*, p. 105; *MMMA* 2, p. 237.
[83] *GR*, p. 119; *MMMA* 2, p. 240.
[84] *GR*, p. 131; *MMMA* 2, p. 238.

Ex. 70

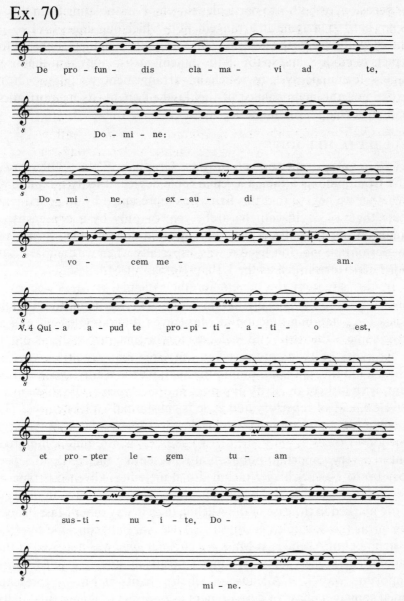

had instituted the most important schola north of the Alps for the propagation of Roman chant) tells us that certain singers were paid for singing Tracts on Holy Saturday in Latin and Greek.[85] Beyond the witness of bilingual performance (in itself of importance), this evidence suggests a practice of assigning particular chants—by category,

[85] Michel Andrieu, 'Règlement d'Angilramne de Metz (768–791) fixant les honoraires de quelques fonctions liturgiques', *Revue des Sciences religieuses*, 10 (1930), 349.

or occasion, or both—to particular singers. Extrapolating from this, it is not hard to imagine an arrangement in which one singer (or two, or three) would be responsible, say, for Graduals in mode 3, another for Tracts in mode 8, and so for all the difficult melismatic chant that used highly formulaic systems. Such an arrangement would go far in explaining the maintenance of this kind of chant, its memorization and performance in an annual cycle.

ALLELUIA MELODIES

The Gregorian repertory of Introits, Graduals, Tracts, Offertories, and Communions attained a remarkable degree of fixity around 850. Whether we believe that this fixity was represented by an actual text-state that we could call the archetype, or only by a consensus of tradition not formalized in any imaginable documentary form, is a matter of opinion. But fixed it was, especially when we compare it to other repertories such as the Urban-Roman or Milanese.

In this situation the chants for the Alleluia at Mass occupy a distinctive and perhaps pivotal position.[86] On one hand, the Alleluia has a long-standing function at Mass, even if a variable one; and at least some of the texts and melodies can be imagined to be as old as other types of chant preserved in the Gregorian tradition. On the other hand the representation in the Sextuplex is scanty and inconsistent, with little of the fixity apparent in other types, while subsequent development of repertory and style is substantial and extensive. The number of items represented in the Sextuplex (and a very large portion of them by only one or two sources) is not quite a hundred; but in a very important publication representing the medieval repertory up to 1100, Schlager included 410 melodies. Given this type of development, and also the fact that the tendency to draw on pools is more marked in the case of the Alleluia than in any other Mass Proper (as far as the Sextuplex is concerned), we can only conclude that the assignment of Alleluias at Mass *per circulum anni* was not fixed at the time of the archetype; or—to put it positively and in a much more important way—the Alleluia, of all the chants at Mass, represents ritual song in a phase of development as opposed to the unusual fixity imposed on the other types as a result of the Carolingian liturgical programme. We can imagine that what is observable in the develop-

---

[86] Karlheinz Schlager, *Thematischer Katalog der ältesten Alleluia Melodien aus Handschriften des 10. und 11. Jahrhunderts. Erlanger Arbeiten zur Musikwissenschaft*, ii (Munich, 1965) (= *ThK*); and *Alleluia-Melodien*, i (bis 1100), *Monumenta monodica medii aevi*, 7 (Kassel, 1968) (= *AMS*); 'Alleluia I. Latin rite', *New Grove*, i. 269–74; Wagner, *Einführung in die gregorianischen Melodien*, iii, pp. 397–417; Apel, *Gregorian Chant*, pp. 375–92; Stäblein, 'Alleluia', *MGG*, i (1949–51) cols. 331–50.

ment of the Alleluia repertory was also true—at an earlier time—of Introits, Graduals, and the rest. Only one very important factor is different: the use of notation to make a written record, which reveals the relative fixity of the other Propers, also reveals the relative fluidity of the Alleluia repertory in the same years. Perhaps this tells us that fixity was not a function of the written record—or fluidity of the lack of it.

The Alleluia at Mass is traditionally classified as a responsorial form, with the exclamation 'Alleluia' usually extended in a special melisma called the *jubilus*, serving as the respond; this respond frames a verse, usually a stich from the Psalter. In this case the repetition of the respond after the verse has survived more or less intact down to modern times. Furthermore the Alleluia includes a repetition at the beginning, where a cantor sings 'Alleluia', which is repeated by the choir; this is analogous to the procedure described by Amalarius for Office responsories, in which the respond is sung first by the cantor, then repeated by the choir. Such procedure has left no trace in the Gradual; in the Offertories, however, the repeat of the initial phrase 'Jubilate Deo' and other chants, written out in the earliest sources, might reflect such a procedure. In the Alleluia, the *jubilus* is not included in the cantor's first singing, so it might seem that all he does is intone the chant, with the choir repeating the intonation; but a repetition of an intonation is otherwise unknown in the West, and its sense is hard to imagine. The *jubilus*, on the other hand, is so much an appendage that it can be considered another section, another phrase, which the choir continues after making its structural repeat of the cantor's first phrase. As we shall see, the *jubilus* can be replaced later on in the piece by an even more elaborate melisma. And if Amalarius' prescription of the repeat is applicable here, so may be his remark that the melisma is appropriately sung by the choir with its stronger resources.

Perhaps the most important structural aspect of the Alleluia is the nature and genesis of the verse. Everyone agrees that the verse was added to the Alleluia at Mass as a verse, that is, as a stich designed to identify the singing of the Alleluia with a particular occasion. There never was a question of a presumed reduction from a complete psalm to a single vestigial verse, as is presumed in the case of the Gradual, and of the psalmic responsories in the Ferial Office. From the history of ritual song from the ninth century on, we know of the practice of adding verses in this manner; the Alleluia shows it happening at least in the eighth century and perhaps earlier. The question is, why cannot the addition of a verse be considered a perennial option in ritual song, to be presumed for other chants of a responsorial nature? The Alleluia with verse offers a perfectly good model for the development of the Gradual—just as good as that of a psalm with refrain, subsequently (and drastically) reduced to a single verse. And as in the case of the antiphon, the austere vocabulary inherited from Roman tradition may mask a multiplicity of models and intents.

It has long been observed that Alleluias can be located on a hypothetical line of development (running, presumably, through the seventh and eighth centuries), according to the absence or presence of a rounding of the end of the verse with the melody of the *jubilus*. The later practice, universally followed in Alleluias known to date from the ninth century, is to include the entire *jubilus* note-for-note (after initial modification to adapt the last words of the verse) at the end of the verse; this of course is followed by the responsorial repeat of the Alleluia and the *jubilus* again. The two melodies believed (on other grounds) to represent an earlier practice (Alleluia 'Dies sanctificatus' and Alleluia 'Dominus dixit') do not do this—in fact, make no reference in their verse melodies to their *jubili*. Some other cases can be located along a continuum between these two extremes, and hence presumably date from the intervening period. This rounding at the end of the verse is not peculiar to the Alleluia; we observed it already in the verse of the Gradual melody type 'Justus ut palma' (Mode 2-a). (See above, p. 203.)

Responsorial chants in Roman use are typically post-lesson chants. In this light the position of the Alleluia (like the Tract) immediately after the Gradual is anomalous. In the Milanese rite the equivalent of the Gradual came after the first lesson, the Prophecy; the Alleluia came after the second lesson, the Epistle. We have seen how the Lenten formularies with three lessons had Graduals after the first and second. When the Prophecy was dropped from the Roman Mass, the Gradual was shifted to after the Epistle, and the original 'post-Epistle' chant now followed the Gradual. In Lent this second chant was a Tract; that is, what had been the second gradual was now performed without responsorial repeat. In Advent, Christmas and Epiphany the second chant was an Alleluia. In Eastertide the first as well as the second chant was an Alleluia.

Generally speaking, the Alleluia verse is strongly thematic for feasts, seasons, and saints, less so for the dominical layers (ferias, save those in Easter Week, do not have Alleluias). The verses, at least those in the Sextuplex, draw to an unusually high degree on stichs already selected for Introits, Graduals, and so forth. Within the Sextuplex, the

Alleluias for the five feasts are firm and well represented. So, too, for the Sundays of Advent, and after Epiphany; not so, however, for the Sundays after Pentecost, and—what is perhaps surprising—for the Sundays after Easter, and especially the ferias of Easter Week. The Alleluia is imagined to be indigenous to the Easter season, and the season itself is certainly old. Why, then, do we not have a fixed series of ancient Alleluias? There may be many answers, but the simplest is that in the Mass formularies of the Sextuplex we are looking at the end product of arrangements long in the making. Also the melodic style of the Easter Alleluias does not suggest a very early date. The Sanctorale operates with a pool of Alleluias applied in various ways in the different sources.

It is difficult to get a clear idea of the repertory of Alleluia melodies at the time of the archetype because of the many cases in which the early notated sources provide alternate melodies for a given verse text. (When we refer here to an 'Alleluia' we shall mean an Alleluia with its verse, with melody.) There are between 90 and 100 Alleluias represented in the Sextuplex one way or another, that is, represented by from one to six sources. These are provided in manuscript sources up to 1100 each with from one to half a dozen melodies, including substantial variants as well as really distinct melodies. Some of these melodies are used many times as model melodies; others may be used once or twice as model melodies; still others are unique. There is the tendency observable throughout the Gregorian (and other) repertories to use a melody for many texts. This is not the same thing, however, as using several melodies for the same text, and this is not so frequently encountered in the case of Introits, Graduals, Tracts, Offertories, and Communions, important as it may be in the early notated sources, and in comparison with the Urban-Roman sources. Two factors seem to be at work: first, the multiple use of a given text for several occasions (as in the Sanctorale) may evoke—under the special conditions in the Alleluia repertory—different melodic settings; second, since the alternate melodies are provided in different manuscripts, the obvious conclusion is that they represent differing local usage, with each place getting its texts from some shared source but providing a melody of its own choosing. There is not yet a reliable way of telling from usage which of these melodies is the older, since we know from the much larger portion of the Alleluia repertory that came into existence after the time of the archetype that the development of new Alleluia melodies continued at an intense pace; and since all the alternate melodies for the texts of the Sextuplex are found in the same manuscripts that furnish the later repertory, many of the alternate melodies could also be from the time after the archetype, that is, from 850–1100.

Three melodies are used far more often than the others, and because of this and their liturgical placement have for a long time been regarded as the oldest Alleluia melodies. This conclusion might sometime be reviewed, since neither multiple use nor liturgical placement is a completely reliable index of age. In this case the conclusion is supported by the fact that these three melodies account for some thirty-seven out of fifty-four items in the Urban-Roman sources; but that, too, is not a completely reliable indication. The three melodies were once given names derived from their first appearance in the Graduale, hence Alleluia 'Ostende'[87] (from First Sunday in Advent), Alleluia 'Excita'[88] (Third Sunday), and Alleluia 'Dies sanctificatus'[89] (Christmas). Naming of melodies is an excellent procedure, and the only problem is settling on the most appropriate names. In this case 'Ostende' has recently been changed to a more likely prototype, 'Dominus dixit'[90] (Christmas), while 'Excita' remains as a purely arbitrary selection without a completely convincing replacement.

These three melodies are used for almost half the 90 to 100 Alleluias from the Sextuplex, but many of those cases have alternates that may represent prior use. Alleluia 'Dies sanctificatus' is most used (nineteen times), Alleluia 'Dominus dixit' next (fifteen), and Alleluia 'Excita' least (eight). These three have many fascinating musical features (Ex. 71). They represent three distinct central pitch sets and give the impression of having been selected because of this variety. Alleluia 'Dominus dixit' ('Ostende') (i) moves in the locus *ut–re–mi–fa* with emphasis on *fa* and final on *ut* (classified as mode 8). Alleluia 'Dies sanctificatus' (ii) (here, too, there are little-used alternate melodies) moves in the locus *re–mi–fa*, with final on *re* (classified as mode 2) but with some emphasis on the *sol* above *fa*; compared to 'Dominus dixit' it can sound slightly elevated. Alleluia 'Excita' (iii) has the locus *fa–sol–la*, with final *mi* below *fa* (classified as mode 4) and frequent descent to the *re* below that; for comparison it can be located on the same *fa* as the other two, and then gives the impression of being still more elevated. This distinction among the three pitch sets is the more noticeable since the profiles of the Alleluia-settings themselves (excluding the *jubili*) are not so different.

[87] *AMS*, 368; *ThK*, see pp. 638 f.; *GR*, p. 2; *MMMA* 2, p. 212.
[88] *AMS*, 175; *ThK*, 205, see pp. 619 f.; *GR*, p. 8; *MMMA* 2, p. 178.
[89] *AMS*, 118; *ThK*, see p. 564; *GR*, p. 31; *MMMA* 2, p. 171.
[90] *AMS*, 137; *ThK*, 271, see pp. 638 f.; *GR*, p. 26; *MMMA* 2, p. 217.

Ex. 71

(i)

Al – le –   lu – ia   ij

(ii)

Al – le – lu – ia   ij

(iii)

Al – le –   lu – ia   ij

Alleluia 'Dominus dixit' used the *fa* below *ut* to achieve the tonal ambiguity characteristic of this pitch set; the F–a–c is prominent. The *jubilus* is short. The verse is a bi-hemistich, with a mid-cadence on *ut* ('tu'); the second hemistich has two large melismata ('ho-die', 'te'), the second terminal; they are unique in their tonal mobility—especially with the b flats provided in some readings—even if not as flamboyant as some to be encountered. There is no rounding. Alleluia 'Dies sanctificatus' is a centonized text, not from the Psalter; there are three text phrases, set to a bi-hemistich followed by a third melody phrase that seems to recapitulate the first two. While the melody is not isolated in locus or idiom, it has many distinctive features, and on the other hand relatively few similarities to either the Tracts in mode 2 or the Graduals in 2-a; it certainly is no psalm tone. There is no rounding, and the *jubilus* is again brief. Alleluia 'Excita' also has a brief *jubilus*, but with a sequential repeat of a figure; figural repetition is to become especially characteristic of the Alleluia repertory (while not absent from other types of chant, as we have seen). There is rounding in the form of a full repeat of the Alleluia and *jubilus* (with modified incipit) at the end of the verse ('ut salvos facias nos'). This, combined with a long melisma on 'veni' concluding with a cadence on the final *mi*, and the lack or clear articulation in the text, make the underlying bi-hemistich less than clear; other cases, however, suggest that the cadence on *re* at 'tuam' is indeed the half-cadence of the bi-hemistich. The presence of a 'verse-melisma'—usually just one— becomes more and more prominent as the repertory develops, and as the melisma itself becomes longer and more formalized.

The modal distribution for the remaining Alleluia melodies used for items in the Sextuplex is more uneven than that for the Graduals, and seems to depend upon that of the Graduals in one important respect. There are virtually no Alleluias in mode 5 (Alleluia 'Beatus vir qui timet',[91] well represented for St Vincent, and used in Senlis for numerous other saints, is the principal exception). Mode 5 is not much used in most categories, as we have seen; it is used, however, for almost half of the Graduals, and the extremely poor representation in Alleluias might have something to do with that. The distribution of the other modes in Alleluias—mostly modes 1 and 7, with some 3—is due partly to the heavy use of the three model melodies, which represent modes 2, 4, and 8; partly to the increased range of later Alleluia melodies, making distinction between authentic and plagal meaningless; and partly to the popularity of the styles and idioms found in the Alleluias in modes 1 and 7—idioms that are subtly different, or used in subtly different ways, from those in Graduals and Tracts. Mode 1, associated with the Sanctorale in the Graduals and elsewhere, is used for an important group of Alleluias whose keyword is 'Justus' in some form—'Justus germinabit', 'Justi epulentur'.[92] Mode 7 is especially popular, with several brilliant representatives, including 'Adorabo', 'Laetabitur justus', and 'Te decet hymnus'.[93] This last, for a Sunday after Pentecost, is one of a small group with two verses (from the Psalter); another important example is 'Cantate',[94] also for a Sunday after Pentecost, in mode 1; with its spectacular melismata it shows the full extent of what was attempted in this idiom, just as 'Te decet' does for mode 7.

For all their vigour and luxuriance these Alleluias are not strongly innovative; their differences with respect either to the Graduals or the three model melodies remain basically subtle. The distinctive idiom of the Alleluia melodies may be described as flowing more smoothly than some others in the Gregorian repertory. While they do show much reiteration on central pitches, the reiterative figures seem interwoven with more fluid motion. They cover wide ranges, and sometimes with dramatic leaping figures, yet the overall design seems dominated by long, graceful curves. There is much figural repetition, especially in the melismata; and this is an important, distinctive feature, at least in

[91] *AMS*, 46: *ThK*, 227, see p. 627; *GR*, p. [41]; *MMMA* 2, p. 184.

[92] Alleluia 'Justus ut palma', *AMS* 276; *ThK* 38, see p. 567; *GR*, p. [43]. Alleluia 'Justi epulentur', *AMS* 266; *ThK* 77, see p. 580; *GR*, p. [25]. Alleluia 'Justus germinabit', *AMS* 274; *ThK* 119, see p. 592; *Gr*, p. [36].

[93] Alleluia 'Adorabo', *AMS* 7; *ThK* 382, see p. 672; *GR*, p. [64]; *MMMA* 2, p. 210. Alleluia 'Laetabitur', *AMS* 277; *ThK*, 274, see p. 640. Alleluia 'Te decet', *AMS* 495; *ThK* 360, see p. 664; *GR*, p. 295; *MMMA* 2, p. 206.

[94] *AMS* 61, 63; *ThK* 120, 121; see pp. 592 f.

degree, of this group of melodies. Still, the repetitions occur in an improvisatory manner that makes them seem to spring naturally from a Gregorian environment. This improvisatory quality is especially noticeable in long verses, but seems sometimes to involve a lack of discipline—something unknown in the Gradual repertory; in this respect the Alleluias stand closest to the Offertory verses. Figural repetition is potentially a constructionist feature, and is to be used so in the hands of other musicians; in these Alleluias it still flows freely with a sense of abandon.

Taken together, the Frankish Alleluia repertory and the Urban-Roman repertories of Mass and Office chants provide us with a window on the development and maintenance of repertories of ritual song before and beside the Gregorian. For the Gregorian repertory was the result of a unique combination of Roman and Frankish tendencies: Roman tradition was characterized by an unusual rigour and severity in the assignment of texts, and the Franks demonstrated an extraordinary urge towards fixation of text *and* melody, ultimately in written form. It was the combination of these two tendencies that resulted in the unique status of the Gregorian repertory, seemingly disconnected from the ordinary historical processes of change and development.

The Frankish tendencies towards fixation, which we met in their construction of tonaries, extended far beyond that to include their attempts to resolve anomalies in the classification of chants, their systematic arrangements of psalm tones and verse tones, their development of neumatic notations, as well as other types of notation including alphabetic pitch notation and various number and letter codes for modes and tones. It extended, finally, to the development of tonal constructs to facilitate the conceptualization of chant in performance and pedagogy—in short, the foundations of Western music theory. All of these impressive accomplishments, of course, coexisted with the new forms and styles of chant the Franks themselves were developing, but there in a much looser, freer context; it was the Gregorian that was problematic. Hence it was the Gregorian that elicited the most rigorous theoretical solutions, and the Gregorian that was most set apart by these. The Frankish Alleluia repertory shows us how a historical repertory developed in the hands of the Franks, when they were not so closely tied to the Gregorian. The Roman tradition, on the other hand, was more concerned with control of texts than of melodies: the Urban-Roman repertory as preserved shows a casualness in melody strikingly different from Frankish sources, no matter how much these may disagree among themselves.

More importantly, the Urban-Roman repertory, by its behaviour during the period 800–1100, gives us an idea of how such repertories were maintained in a non-written state. We have to remember that the Frankish-Roman and Urban-Roman chant repertories set one and the same repertory of stichs (from one and the same liturgy), to melodies that—as recorded—differ in extremely complex and various ways, along the spectrum from very similar to very different. These and other features of the relationship suggest strongly that there was at one point a single tradition of singing (as there was of texts); yet there is much more to be said about the relationship. What concerns us here is that during the recorded period (800–1100) it seems to have been the Urban-Roman repertory that changed in response to the Frankish-Roman, at least to the extent of accepting Gregorian items, and probably in many other ways too. The fixation achieved by the Franks had its impact: in the case of Hispanic and Beneventan repertories, as we saw, the Gregorian simply replaced them. What is remarkable about the Urban-Roman is that it survived to the extent that it did. The Milanese repertory also survived, at least in the immediate locale of Milan; but in an important article, Hucke[95] suggested that some of the distinctive features of Milanese chant, including some of the florid lengthy melismata, might well be later developments, and that some of the materials shared with the Gregorian might be the result of Gregorian infiltration during the period 800–1100. In other words, non-written repertories did change in this period, and must have changed as well before 800, even at Rome. And Frankish music, even for the Alleluia at Mass, could flourish in changeable profusion when the texts were not controlled by Roman canon. Only the combination Frankish-Roman generated the impression of abstract immutability characteristic of the Gregorian.

[95] Hucke, 'Die gregorianische Gradualweise des 2. Tons'.

III

Medieval Monophony in
Western Europe

VII

MEDIEVAL CHANT

By RICHARD CROCKER

IN trying to understand the matrix of the new, specifically Frankish chant that appeared after 850, we have to consider the relationship to Gallican antecedents. With not much to go on, we can probably describe the relationship as one in which a relatively small number of Gallican items provided a point of departure for far-reaching Frankish developments that resulted in many new forms and much new music. The importance of the Gallican models would be that they represented, better than did the Roman chant, the broader traditions of ritual song.

'Gallican' is a regional, cultural term; 'Frankish' a tribal, national one. The Franks were everywhere in Gaul, as conquerors; they resided in and administered a layered society. In the seventh and early eighth centuries the ruling Frankish dynasty was the Merovingian, and we must allow in principle at least that there could have been Merovingian-Frankish musical activity as distinct from Gallican. The Merovingian Franks, however, were not as yet very far advanced in the acculturation of letters and music. The Gallican liturgy and chant that we encountered in chapter III is from southern Gaul, and survives mostly in Frankish sources from the region of Aquitania, which can be regarded as one of three broad areas in which Frankish musical activity was to take place in the Carolingian period, that is, under Pepin 'the short', and his offspring, who ruled the Franks during the century 750–850. The homeland of the Carolingians (the family and household) lay between Rhine and Seine. To the East was a broad area including a network of rich, important monasteries in the Rhineland and Switzerland, often with close ties to the Carolingian leadership. After 843, with the gradual deterioration of that leadership and the subsequent division of the middle kingdom, 'Lothringen' (with tragic and apparently permanent effects upon Western Europe), there remained West Francia, with Aquitania to the south, and East

Francia. That, however, was after the Partition of Verdun; before then the central area was the primary scene of musical activity in the north. Social fabric and historical process in all these areas were extremely complex.

We should probably acknowledge the possibility of distinctive Frankish musical activity in the north from 700 onwards. If there was such activity it was undoubtedly restricted to certain locales. Its relationship to old traditions (if there were any) is indeterminate. There might well have been contact with, and use of, Roman materials in the same way that the Roman sacramentary is said to exist in the north in a form called 'Gelasian of the eighth century'. Whatever activity there was received a tremendous stimulus from the political decisions after 750 to import the Roman liturgy and chant and impose them on the Frankish realm.[1] The effects of that stimulus cannot be overestimated, but at the same time we know that such a stimulus produces no response if there is no readiness for it. When the stimulus came, the Frankish energies seem to have been completely absorbed, for a time, in learning the new chant, setting it in order, expanding the repertory through the use of model melodies and perhaps through more drastic adaptations. Until 850 we can pick up no consistent signs of independent musical activity; when it comes, it brings an undeniably new style of music.

Charlemagne's principal adviser in liturgics was Alcuin (735–804), an English scholar from York. Alcuin brought not only expert knowledge and ability, but also familiarity with English traditions of chant going back to the mission sent by Gregory the Great to Canterbury in 597. Especially prominent in the English tradition were Benedict Biscop (628?–90) and his pupil the Venerable Bede (672–735) from Wearmouth and Jarrow. These English resources came to bear on the Frankish experience very specifically through Alcuin's revisions and expansions of the Roman liturgical books, and perhaps in other more general ways. Another important insular influence came through the Irish monastics who had been carrying out missions on the continent since the sixth century. Singly or in small numbers they continued to visit European monasteries during the eighth and ninth centuries as teachers. They brought with them not only a great store of Latin learning but also the peculiar Irish monastic tradition of Latin and devotional forms—including prayers and litanies—often obscure and extravagant. Their presence on the continent is well

---

[1] See G. Ellard, *Master Alcuin, Liturgist* (Chicago, 1956); Bruno Stäblein and Margareta Melnicki-Landwehr, *Die Gesänge des altrömischen Graduale Vat.lat. 5319, Monumenta monodica medii aevi*, 2 (1968).

documented and often discussed;[2] a comprehensive evaluation of their impact on chant forms has yet to be made.

As we have seen in the previous chapters, estimates of the Frankish involvement with Gregorian chant range from simply learning it as it was, to virtual creation of the whole repertory. The reality lies somewhere in between, and is yet to be determined; but in any case the musical experience gained from the involvement was very substantial, and all assessment of subsequent Frankish musical activity must start with the acknowledgement that by 850 the Frankish cantors sang, on a regular basis, a very sophisticated repertory. If they then developed something different in musical style, that was by choice, and a very well-informed choice.

The extent of the Frankish contribution to the Gregorian Office has only recently begun to be realized. What came north from Rome between 750 and 850 must have been the Ferial Office, including a corpus of responsories for the Proper of the Time (essentially for Christmas, Epiphany, Easter, Ascension, and Pentecost, plus seasons of Advent and Lent, and the summer Old Testament responsories); a half-dozen Offices for the Common of Saints, and perhaps two dozen Proper Offices for Saints. Subsequent Frankish additions, filling out the complement of antiphons for the Proper of the Time, certainly included many antiphons for the Gospel Canticles at Lauds and Vespers (and, according to Dom Claire, may have included antiphons for the variable psalm and Old Testament Canticle at Lauds[3]). Then the Franks began adding complete Offices, with sets of antiphons and responsories for Matins. These often presented two interesting features, neither thoroughly studied nor well understood. Frankish Offices increasingly emphasized versified texts for antiphons and responsories (a kind of text already present in the Christmas Office[4]). Beginning with Stephen of Liège around 900, who is credited with three Offices—for St Lambert, the Finding of St Stephen, and the Trinity—the Franks cultivated the 'numerical Office', in which either the antiphons, or the responsories, or both, were composed so that the first item was in the first mode, the second in the second mode, and so on.[5] There were many arrangements using this principle, and all involve considerations apparently not present in the eighth-century Roman Office. In the process of composing Offices according to the

[2] Joseph Smits van Waesberghe, *Musikerziehung: Lehre und Theorie der Musik im Mittelalter*, *Musikgeschichte in Bildern* iii/3 (Leipzig, 1969).

[3] Jean Claire, 'Les Répertoires liturgiques latins avant l'octoechos. L'Office férial Romano-Franc', *Eg*, 15 (1975), 135 ff.

[4] Ritva Jonsson, *Historia: Étude sur la genèse des offices versifiés* (Stockholm, 1968).

[5] Richard Crocker, 'Matins Antiphons at St. Denis', *JAMS*, 39 (1986), 441–90.

modes the Franks generated melodic models, especially for antiphons but to some extent also for responsories, that used the idioms of the Roman chant in new configurations. The amount of musical composition that eventually took place in the generation of new Offices must have been very great.

One of the most important aspects we saw in the Gregorian repertory, and one that can be ascribed to its Roman component, is the strong emphasis on the Psalter as a source of stichs. This can be ascribed hypothetically to a strong influence of monastic thinking on the Office and Mass formularies developed in Rome, at an early date—presumably the sixth century. Another feature of the Gregorian repertory that has affected our thinking, but is perhaps illusory in that it need not accurately reflect eighth-century Roman practice or even ninth-century Frankish practice, is a relatively severe, simple, and prescribed use of stichs in combinations, one that does not suggest much elaboration, repetition, or cantorial option. We do know (say, from Amalarius' account of responsories) that what was written down was only the bare materials, and the order of performance was either known by tradition or modified on local discretion, so we should not ascribe the simple form in which the texts appear in the Antiphonale to Roman practice. Still, simply because the writing-down became so important in the later history of the chant, and preserved it for us, the simple written form of the combinations has made it harder for us to take seriously their full forms as they have to be reconstructed. And even when we imagine an Introit, Gradual, or Offertory in its full form, this in Gregorian chant is still sober and rational compared to combinations suggested to us from other contexts—especially Byzantine ones. Furthermore, because of the emphasis the Franks placed on fixing *the* 'official' version of the chant, we have persisted in trying to reconstruct *the* form of an Introit, Gradual, or Offertory, instead of acknowledging that option and variation are essential aspects of stichic combinations.

SOME STICHIC COMBINATIONS BEFORE 800

Even within Roman practice and Frankish tradition, examples can be found that better represent the more universal aspects of ritual song; the fact that these examples were not included in the archetype may tell us as much about the archetype as it does about these examples. Items to be considered here are the Gloria in excelsis, the Te deum, and litanies.

So strong has been the emphasis on its written, official version that the Gloria in excelsis[6] is not so easily recognized as a true stichic combination. It exists in various text-states, and was used variously as a hymn at Lauds (Gallican rite, sixth century), and as an entrance hymn at Mass for Easter (Roman rite, into the eighth century?), before eventually being classed as 'Ordinary at Mass'. At this point we start to discuss items that in modern consciousness form part of 'the Ordinary', and awareness of the early medieval state of things is helpful. An *ordo* is a list detailing the order of events, for our purposes for Mass or Office;[7] and *ordinarium* is a collection of ordines, although this term came to mean (among other things) more or less the same as ordo. Hence 'the ordinary' of the Mass simply lists all the items by type, in succession, e.g. 'Here is sung the Introit for the Day', for which the singers consult the Antiphonale. But for items whose texts do not change, the text was eventually included right in the ordo. Hence for singers, 'the Ordinary of the Mass' came to mean those invariant texts that were written down in the ordo, along with other texts that did not directly concern them. For historical purposes we need to keep all ideas of 'ordinary' out of the way, reserved for reference in the context of thirteenth- or fourteenth-century music, and take the items in question one by one as we meet them in the sixth, seventh or eighth centuries.

The Gloria in excelsis, in its final text-state, consists of a stich from Luke ii ('Gloria in excelsis . . .') originally sung by the bishop; a set of acclamations, perhaps sung by all together ('Laudamus te . . .'); three petitions in call-and-response from ('Qui tollis . . . R. Miserere nobis . . .'); and a doxology ('Quoniam . . .'). Not all of this text is present in the earliest recorded versions; and further additions were made in the ninth and tenth centuries. If we think away the text-state which some Roman or Frankish authority wished to be considered official and invariant, we have an excellent example of a stichic combination in its natural state of change. We do not know how it was sung before the eighth century—presumably with congregational participation, hence with relatively simple melody, hence one not very distinct from other simple melodies used for such purposes. Our first documented melody, *Gloria* A (Ex. 72),[8] is called that because it was not included in the modern chant books, which identify Gloria settings by Roman numerals. *Gloria* A may well be one that could justifiably be called

---

[6] Stäblein, 'Gloria in excelsis', *MGG*, v (1956), cols. 302–20.

[7] Michel Andrieu, *Les Ordines romani du haut Moyen âge*, 4 vols. (Louvain, 1961–71).

[8] Transcribed by Paul Evans, *The Early Trope Repertory of Saint Martial de Limoges* (Princeton, 1970), 254 ff.; Klaus Rönnau, *Die Tropen zum Gloria in excelsis Deo* (Wiesbaden, 1967), 206; Ruth Steiner, 'Trope (i)', *New Grove*, xix. 178 f.

Ex. 72

Glo - ri - a   in   ex - cel - sis de -   o.

Et   in   ter - ra pax   ho - mi - ni -   bus bo - nae

vo - lun - ta -   tis.

Lau - da - mus   te.

Be - ne - di - ci - mus   te.

A - do - ra - mus   te.

Glo - ri - fi - ca - mus   te.

(etc.)

Gallican, that is, in use in Gaul (even northern Gaul) before the Carolingian Franks became interested in, and took charge of, chant reforms. It shows idioms related to but not identical with Gregorian ones, and cannot be aligned with any one category of Mass item. Because it is an extended piece it contains more text, in different format, than a typical Gregorian piece made out of Psalter stichs; hence the idioms and the musical form are different. Among other distinctive features is a complex reiteration of figural patterns. There are problems in associating the pitch sets with modal classification— but not with the pitch sets familiar from Gregorian practice.

Another very important and closely related instance is the Te deum laudamus, the hymn that came to be sung at the conclusion of every festal Matins in the Roman Office, after the ninth lesson, as well as on occasions of thanksgiving—which may well be its more characteristic use.[9] The Te deum begins, not with call-and-response stichs, but with antiphonal stichs. The story of its inspired improvisation by Ambrose and Augustine singing antiphonally has long been discredited, but if we ignore the names, the rest of the story may well correspond to the realities of cantorial improvisation, non-scriptural language in hymns, and even of time and place of Latin antiphonal hymnody. In any case, there is more than one text-state, and the end of the received text shows clearly the addition of at least one versicle-and-response in the form of stichs from a psalm ('Salvum fac . . . Et rege . . .', Psalm 27, v. 9). There is only one melody for the Te deum; that is, throughout the Middle Ages it was chanted to one formulaic system. This particular system has a central locus *ut–re–mi* (G–a–b), extending up to the *fa* (c) for primary accents, and including a low *mi* (E) for intonations and some cadences (see Ex. 73). There is a distinct lower element used for certain stichs, centred on the low (*mi*) (E) and moving either through *ut–re–fa* (C–D–F) or *ut–mi–sol* (C–E–G). This part of the system might represent the low-lying terminal phrase hinted at in various kinds of Gregorian chant, for instance the Venite and certain Introits.[10]

The items closest to a stichic tradition are the litanies—which are referred to in the plural because a litany is a single petition and always appears (in this context) in relatively long series, and because there is more than one series. Litanies are a classic call-and-response chant, the call consisting of a relatively elaborate invocation, acclamation, or petition, the response typically short and simple—'Ora pro nobis', 'Kyrie eleison', or some similar expression; but even in a non-written state the responses can vary in the course of a long series of petitions, and can also take more elaborate form, approximating to versicle-and-response as in other forms. Litanies remained subject to cantorial option in the number and choice of petitions well into the Middle Ages, indeed, in some contexts they have always been. The best-known series of litanies is the 'Litany of the Saints', used on Holy Saturday and also on Rogation Days; its history of use and documentation is complex, and Roman practice seems to have been in interaction with the Byzantine East on one hand and as far west as

---

[9] *Graduale sacrosanctae romanae ecclesiae de tempore et de sanctis*, SS.D.N.Pii X. Pontificis Maximi jussu restitutum et editum . . . (Rome, 1980) (= *GR*), 115*–18*.

[10] Cf. above, pp. 164, 183.

Ex. 73

Te de - um lau - da - mus: te Do - mi - num con - fi - te - mur.

Te ae - ter - num Pa - trem   o - mnis ter - ra ve - ne - ra - tur.

Tu ad li - be - ran - dum su - sce - ptu - rus ho -   mi -   nem,

non hor - ru - i - sti Vir - gi - nis u - te - rum.

Sal - vum fac po - pu - lum tu - um Do - mi - ne,

et be - ne - dic he - re - di - ta - ti tu -   ae.

Ireland on the other. The formulaic system used for this series has a
locus on *fa*, with gradual ascent of the locus as the series proceeds.
The idioms, while not drastically different from others in Frankish-
Roman use, are none the less distinctive. Later Frankish practice
produced some more elaborate tones.[11]

STROPHIC HYMNS

The Gloria in excelsis and the Te deum are hymns—and very
important ones—in the general sense of 'song of praise to God'.
'Hymn' has also a much more specific formal sense, referring to a text
cast in the form of strophes, each strophe having the same number of
lines and syllables, each strophe sung to the same melody, which
therefore is repeated as many times as there are strophes in the text.

---

[11] See Edmund Bishop, 'The Litany of the Saints in the Stowe Missal', *Liturgica Historica*
(Oxford, 1918), 137; Peter Wagner, *Einführung in die gregorianischen Melodien*, i *Ursprung und
Entwicklung der Liturgischen Gesangsformen bis zum Ausgänge des Mittelalters* (3rd edn.,
Leipzig, 1911); iii, *Gregorianische Formenlehre* (Leipzig, 1921), 260–4; Stäblein, 'Litanei', *MGG*,
viii (1960), cols. 989–1003; *GR*, p. 196.

This kind of hymn has a very interesting history, not entirely clear, but exceptionally important for Christian chant, and perhaps even more important for the subsequent history of Western music in general.[12] One of the striking things about strophic hymns in early Christian chant is that they were not used in Roman chant, which is why they have not been discussed so far. They were, however, specified by Benedict in his descriptions of the Monastic Office, and they were used regularly outside of Rome, and throughout the Office. We need to add them to our picture of Latin chant at this point in order to get a complete picture of that chant as it presented itself as the foundation for further Frankish developments.

Another striking thing about strophic hymns is that they appeared relatively early in Christian chant—in the third century in the East (Syria), and towards the end of the fourth century in the West, introduced (according to Augustine and Paulinus) by Ambrose, who wrote some models; but there are also some texts by Hilary of Poitiers that must date from around 350.[13] It might be possible to claim that these strophic hymns represented a new concept of people's participation in worship. This was before there was a Monastic Office, and just during the time when weekly or daily devotional services (as opposed to the weekly Eucharist) were becoming institutionalized and widespread. There may have been no systematic use of the Psalter yet for such services. Ambrose could well have intended, with his adaptation of congregational, antiphonal singing, to provide models for the basic substance of devotional services. The distinctive features of his solution were the exact repetitions of syllable count in each line, in each strophe; this is what makes possible the repetition of exactly the same melody—and this, in turn, would be an immediate, obvious solution to congregational singing, as an alternative to call-and-response.

Ambrose's models became extremely important, but not right away. The idea of new texts was hotly debated in councils in the fourth, fifth, and sixth centuries, with various results; Roman practice excluded them, coming down heavily in favour of strict limitation to scriptural texts, especially the Psalter. While Benedict provided for a hymn at each Office, he did not specify which ones. Subsequent

---

[12] Early Latin hymn texts are collected in two volumes of the *Analecta hymnica medii aevi*, 50, *Lateinische Hymnendichter des Mittelalters*, ed. Guido Maria Dreves (1907), and 51, *Die Hymnen des Thesaurus Hymnologicus H. A. Daniels ... I: Die Hymnen des 5.–11. Jahrhunderts, und die Irische-Keltische Hymnodie*, ed. Clemens Blume (1908). The handbook for hymns is by Josef Szövérffy, *Die Annalen der lateinischen Hymnendichtung* (Berlin, 1964–5). The historical edition of hymn melodies is by Stäblein, *Hymnen I; Die mittelalterlichen Hymnenmelodien des Abendlandes, Monumenta monodica medii aevi*, 1 (1956).

[13] Cf. above, p. 83. Hilary's texts are in *Analecta hymnica*, 50, pp. 4–9.

monastic practice followed his provision, but it has been very difficult
to determine exactly what the cursus of hymnody was from Benedict's
time up to the documentation in the ninth and tenth centuries.[14] The
issue of 'ferial versus festal' that impinges so heavily on the study of
antiphons and responsories in the Office impinges here, too: some
scholars argue for the priority of those hymns that were assigned to
the Ferial Office. Whatever the priority, and whatever the assignments, there was at least one hymn for each Office (Matins, Lauds,
Prime, Terce, Sext, None, Vespers, and Compline), which meant
seven each day and one each night. Those for the Day Hours seem to
have been assigned so as to repeat each day the same; those for
Matins, Lauds, and Vespers were different each day of the week,
repeating on a weekly basis. This meant a repertory of some thirty
hymns for the Ferial Office. The hymns occupy prominent positions in
the Offices. They are provided with two types of stich: first, each hymn
used at the Office has a doxology (just as psalms have the 'Gloria
Patri'), except that the hymn doxology has to be versified to conform
to the hymn strophe; second, to hymns for some Offices is appended a
versicle-and-response.

   The use of hymns at the Office represents a very important, but
relatively restricted development during the fourth to eighth centuries.
We have to distinguish in this period between a liturgical and a
'literary' tradition for hymnography, the latter consisting of a very
substantial body of hymn texts including those by poets of first rank
such as Prudentius (348–413) and Venantius Fortunatus (d. after 600).
Clemens Blume,[15] after laying out the materials of these traditions,
came to the unlikely conclusion that the hymn was born out of the
liturgy. The materials themselves demonstrate something very different, perhaps the opposite. Hymns were there before the liturgy as
we know it: hymns might have been the basic materials out of which at
least the Office could have been made; and when that did not happen,
hymn production continued alongside liturgy. It took forms that—to
Western eyes at least—seem unliturgical. The hymns of Prudentius
can be long (20, 30, or 40 strophes), complex in metre, and narrative—
sometimes luridly so—in content. The diction is elevated, full of
imagery, elaborate and sonorous. These form a striking contrast to
the hymns of Ambrose, which, while certainly elevated in diction, tend
to be simpler and more restrained in content, expressing congregational worship; they are all only eight strophes in length, and of course

[14] See Blume, *Analecta hymnica*, 51; Walter Howard Frere, *Hymns Ancient and Modern
(Historical Edition)* (London, 1909), pp. xii–xxv.
[15] Introduction to *Analecta hymnica*, 50; but see F. J. E. Raby, *A History of Christian-Latin
Poetry from the Beginning to the Close of the Middle Ages* (2nd edn. Oxford, 1953).

have the standard syllable count developed by Ambrose. These are
what the Latin West considered (considers) 'liturgical'. If we look to
the East, however, we find all the features mentioned for Prudentius in
the *kontakia* of Romanos two hundred years later (he called them
'odes', 'hymns', 'psalms') and there incorporated into the Office.[16]

What did Western poets and their audiences do or intend to do with
hymns of the 'literary' tradition? Presumably these hymns were read
by someone, alone or in company, silently or aloud. Here we must
remember that however 'liturgical' the Office may seem to us, it was
essentially an exercise in reading aloud in a devotional company. If we
allow a continuum between a rigorously prescribed Monastic Office
under a 'Rule' extending through less rigorous devotional exercises
down to private meditations, we can imagine that the distinction
between literary and liturgical traditions of hymnography may be
more apparent than real. Such a continuum allows room for (among
other things) the practice of paraphrasing psalms and other scriptural
items into elaborate classical metre and diction; early examples are by
Meropius (d. 431), and the practice became especially important in the
ninth century and later.[17]

The interaction between the literary and liturgical traditions as
Blume laid them out became fascinating in the case of the most
important Gallican poet, Venantius Fortunatus. He wrote extensively
in verse, and out of some of his long poems (preserved as such in the
'literary' tradition) the 'liturgical' tradition made excerpts that were
assigned to specific liturgical function.[18] This involved some stichic
procedures. The hymn 'Pange lingua gloriosi proelium certaminis'
was provided with a doxology, and when used as a processional on
Good Friday the strophe 'Crux fidelis' was used as a refrain after each
of the other strophes. Out of the long poem 'Tempora florigero' was
excerpted another processional hymn beginning with line 31, 'Ecce
renascentis', but with that line and others preceded and followed by
line 39 as refrain, 'Salve festa dies'. The selection of lines varies for
different liturgical use, which can also involve distribution over days
of a week, or Sundays in Paschaltide. The procedure is the same as
selecting verses from a psalm and using one of them for an antiphon.

The 'literary' tradition of hymnography provided basic models for
further Frankish composition. The most popular model was to be the
Ambrosian strophe; others are trochaic tetrameter ('Pange lingua')
and the classical elegiac distich ('Salve festa dies'). We need add only

---

[16] Cf. above, p. 36.
[17] *Analecta hymnica*, 50, pp. 47–52, 213–15.
[18] Ibid. 70–88.

the Sapphic strophe, much used for saints' hymns. If we wish to stress the strophic aspects of this repertory, contrasting them with the stichic aspects of antiphons and responsories, we can single out the regular syllable count as the crucial factor. It is this regularity of line and strophe that opens the door to structural possibilities of limitless variety and incalculable importance for the subsequent history of Western music. And of course the language and content of hymns newly composed, no matter how indebted to traditions of poetry, leads on in ways that Psalter texts do not. But while acknowledging the importance of strophic aspects, we need also to see them as, in a sense, rationalizations of familiar stichic procedures. Refrains operate just as well with strict syllable count as with a free one. Furthermore it is possible to see in Ambrosian hymnody a new psalmody, in the specific sense that a strophe consists of a bi-hemistich with each hemistich containing sixteen syllables disposed in two eight-syllable phrases; the whole construction is sung to a bi-hemistich of melody that can be compared to a psalm tone (also a bi-hemistich) repeated over and over as many times as needed.

Concerning the melodies used for hymns we are even more in the dark than with antiphons and responsories. We have a large repertory of melodies preserved in sources after 1000, and virtually no way to decide which of these is older or younger. The essential fact of Ambrosian hymnody, and of the tradition dependent upon it, is that every strophe is sung to the same melody; this has the corollary that any text can be sung to any tune (of the same structure), and with that, any connection that might be presumed between a tune and a text (the basic tool in research on antiphons and responsories) is rendered of no effect. Sorting out the hymn tune tradition can only be done on purely intrinsic evidence. This has not yet been done, perhaps never can be done. All we can do is inventory the melodic possibilities as they present themselves in the Frankish repertory. Here we encounter the profound neglect of the melodic tradition: hymnologists have devoted extensive research to the texts, while virtually ignoring the melodies, which until recently were available for the most part only in modern chant books—and these, while treating the versions of Gregorian antiphons and responsories with increasing care and attention to the manuscript traditions, tended to edit the hymn melodies in whatever form came to hand. Bruno Stäblein has provided the first substantial edition of hymn melodies in a form suitable for research.[19]

[19] The melodies in Stäblein, *Monumenta monodica*, 1, are each numbered twice: the first number, in the margin, identifies the melody in the repertory as a whole; the second shows its position in a particular manuscript. (The subscript to the first number indicates the appearance of that melody in the volume.) The first number is the principal one used in the following discussion; it is given first, followed by the manuscript collection and the second number.

The repertory edited by Stäblein includes over five hundred hymn melodies, representing a not yet complete collation of medieval sources down to the fourteenth century. It is based upon the contents of ten hymnaries, representing the most important types, locations, and traditions of hymnody; the ten items were selected for a number of different reasons. They do not represent the oldest hymnaries, hence the repertory is not to be compared with the Sextuplex, but rather to Hesbert's *Corpus Antiphonalium Officii*, which also selected sources for a variety of reasons, the sources themselves being distributed over the greater part of the Middle Ages. In addition, Stäblein included supplementary entries from other manuscripts related to one or another of the ten. Useful—indeed, essential—as it is, being the only such collection of hymn melodies in modern edition, it does not have the same kind of usefulness as the Sextuplex; in some ways it is difficult to know exactly what representation in the collection may involve, when we try to confront this collection with whatever the historical reality of the hymn tradition (or traditions) may have been. We can read directly (this is its most useful operation) a list of hymn melodies most widely distributed throughout Europe; with somewhat more searching we can determine which of these widely distributed melodies was also used heavily. Also with some searching we can determine for which texts each melody was sung—whether only one, or several. (Conversely, it is very easy to determine from the tables to which melody or melodies each text was sung.)

All that is repertorial; the historical aspects are more difficult. If melodies from before 800 are preserved at all, they are almost certainly included in this collection, at least in some form (and the 'if' is a big one). One assumption would be that survivals from before 800 would have been favourite tunes, and would therefore be likely to have very broad collations; we could look for them among the most widely used melodies, or those most heavily used. That group does indeed yield some very likely candidates, but still based upon an assumption; and a later tune can also gain very wide circulation. Another assumption is that when a text is always or almost always associated with a single melody, then that melody belonged to that text from the beginning. But does that mean from when the text was written or from when the melody was composed? These questions become crucial when we apply a corollary of this assumption, in the case of texts whose authorship and date of composition are known from the literary tradition. (Crucial here, too, are the relations between literary and liturgical traditions; if the liturgical use of a text, such as 'Salve festa dies', was not part of the author's intent, then no matter how firmly tied to the text a melody is, the melody itself cannot be dated by the facts about the original poem.) It is, of course, possible for an old text to be sung universally to a much newer melody.

Given all these indeterminancies, it is not possible to think of a development of hymn melodies before the ninth or tenth century. It has always been tempting to think that at Milan we should find preserved the hymn melodies used by Ambrose for his first hymns; but in view of what has been said it seems naïve to see them in the opening hymns of Stäblein's collection, edited from a fourteenth-century Milanese source—that is, a thousand years after the fact. The hymn melodies in question here, Nos. 1, 3, 6, 8, and 14, are mostly used for Ferial Office hymns and raise all the problems of style, function, and development encountered in ferial antiphons. These particular melodies, however, have a reassuring distribution and use, and their smoothly flowing style, together with idiosyncrasies of tonal construction, do not suggest late origins. They could indeed represent an earlier usage, but that has to remain a possibility only.

Pitch sets may often resemble those of common antiphon classes, and on that basis the hymn melodies can be subsumed under the modal classifications; but the melodies tend to be more mobile within the set, and often do not concentrate on the locus in the manner of antiphons. There is the same sense as in antiphons that successive cadences should be on different pitches, and sometimes that the cadence at the end of a phrase represents a departure from the motion or locus of that phrase; on the other hand there is sometimes a strong connection between a phrase and its cadence, especially in melodies we could presume to be later and specifically Frankish. Similarly with finals: there are many instances where the final of the hymn melody emerges in a seemingly arbitrary fashion simply as the last note, making sense only in retrospect; in this respect hymn tunes resemble psalm tones, which can end on a variety of pitches—and in both cases the manifold repetition of the tune or tone makes this indeterminacy of final not only acceptable but desirable. There are also many instances where the final acquires an increasingly stable, central location in the pitch set and in the course of the melody. One of the most interesting tonal configurations of hymn melodies is the use of a pitch set classified as mode 4 (much used in hymn melodies); it is a very firm set from C up to a (*ut* to *la*), with a final on E (*mi*) that on one hand floats as something indeterminate and unexpected, on the other emerges as the centre of the locus and as the most reasonable final.

Thus melody No. 143, Ex. 74(i), below, in the version from the

Ex. 74

(i) (Stäblein 143, Nevers 44)

Ae - ter - ne   re - rum con - di - tor   noc - tem di - em - que qui re - gis

et   tem - po - rum das tem - po - ra   ut   al - le - ves fa - sti - di - um.

(ii) (Stäblein 1, Milan 1)

Ae - ter - ne   re - rum con - di - tor   noc - tem di - em - que qui re - gis

et   tem - po - rum das tem - po - ra   ut   al - le - ves fa - sti - di - um.

(iii) (Stäblein 1, Klosterneuberg 3)

Ae - ter - ne   re - rum con - di - tor   noc - tem di - em - que qui re - gis

et   tem - po - rum das tem - po - ra   ut   al - le - ves fa - sti - di - um.

twelfth-century Nevers manuscript Paris 1235 No. 44, used there for
Ambrose's text 'Aeterne rerum conditor', at Matins, instead of No. 1,
used for that text at Milan, Ex. 74(ii), shows a very clear locus on F–
G–a, with only one ascent to the c above, and cadences on the three
notes of the locus—all as in an antiphon; there is a typical terminal
descent to D final (*re*). The first two phrases form a convincing first
hemistich, with half-cadence on G; the second two phrases have
similar beginnings, which nicely sets off their different endings, the last
being the terminal descent. All these details are characteristic of hymn
melodies at their best, and perhaps of the earliest forms in which they
come to us. No. 1 also has a D final (at Milan), which stands at the
centre of the locus (but the locus is not as well defined). The pitch set
extends below and above, with all four cadences on the D. The first
phrase descends below, the second and third lie above, focusing on G
a fourth above; only the last phrase moves around the D in clear

relationship to it. The melody could be classed as mode 2, but without any idiomatic similarity to antiphons in that class. Another reading of the same melody from a fourteenth-century German source (Kloster-neuberg, No. 3) has the final on G, and the readings are such as to make the melody not only easily classed as mode 8, but even show idiomatic similarity to mode 8 antiphons. The note which was an F at Milan, and would have been b flat relative to the G final, has been raised to c, creating a gapped scale (there is no b or b flat). This is a relatively simple example of the kind of variants and ambiguities, as well as of the multiple representation in the sources, normal for the hymn repertory. Here, as elsewhere in early chant repertories, we have to proceed by melodic substance rather than simply the final, by real pitch set rather than notated representation. This is one and the same melody at Milan and Klosterneuberg (but a different one at Nevers), with significant differences in detail reflecting local use.

There are other examples of melodies (all 'international' and mostly well-known) with fairly clear resemblances to modal classes and their idioms. Among the possibly early melodies mentioned at Milan, No. 3 seems to be clearly mode 2 up to its ending on C (*ut*); it is treated variously in other sources. Nos. 4 and 8 are closer, each in its own way, to antiphons on *re*. No. 6, on G final, and notwithstanding the b flat at the end of phrase 3, has clear similarities to mode 8 antiphons, including the penultimate descent to E below; what is distinctive about it as a hymn tune is that this balances a similar turn in phrase 1, instead of happening only once as it would in an antiphon. No. 55, closely associated with the text 'Audi benigne conditor', is a very convincing mode 2, even with its third-phrase cadence a fourth above. No. 62, closely associated with 'Aeterne Rex altissime', is an equally convincing mode 8, with an ascent and descent through phrases 2 and 3, and characteristic use of the *fa* below *ut* and the F–a–c realm in the last phrase. An example in mode 4 of the kind referred to is No. 114; another example, No. 2, is inflected upwards in one German source to an F final. No. 115, a much-used melody, has the intonation, locus (G–a–b–c), internal cadences (on G), and terminal descent to E characteristic for mode 3. Another much used melody, No. 127, has a final *ut* notated in three different ways, on C, F, and G; it is perfectly comprehensible as a mode 7 melody, with similarities to antiphons.

Another group of melodies, three of which are shown in Ex. 75 below, includes a few closely associated with some old and datable texts. Melody No. 32, for Venantius Fortunatus' Good Friday proces-sional 'Vexilla regis prodeunt', is not so clearly related to an antiphon group. Its final is *re*, and the third phrase has an intonation formula

Ex. 75

(i) (Stäblein 53, Heiligenkreuz 16)

A so -lis or - tus car - di - ne ad us - que ter - rae li - mi - tem

Chri - stum ca - na - mus prin - ci - pem na - tum Ma - ri - a Vir - gi - ne.

(ii) (Stäblein 126, Nevers 3)

Ver-bum su - per - num pro - di - ens, a pa-tre o - lim ex - i - ens

qui na - tus or - bi sub - ve - nis cur - su de - cli - vi tem - po - ris.

(iii) (Stäblein 71, Heiligenkreuz 63)

Chri - ste re - demp-tor o - mni - um ex pa - tre, pa -tris u - ni - ce

so - lus an - te prin-ci - pi - um na - tus in ef - fa - bi - li - ter.

typical for mode 1, but there is an insistence on the *fa* above the usual locus (that is, B flat over a D final) that is not so typical. It almost sounds closer to the melody traditionally associated with Venantius' other most famous hymn, 'Pange lingua', melody No. 56, which has a typical mode 3 intonation; while the rest of the melody moves in the pitch set usual for this mode, it retains its own identity, even in comparison to a number of less distinctive hymns in the same mode. It has been maintained that this is the original seventh-century melody for the text. Melody No. 53, Ex. 75(i), was the favourite melody in use for Caelius Sedulius' abecedary hymn 'A solis ortus cardine'. (An abecedary hymn has successive strophes beginning with successive letters of the alphabet, in order; it is a special form of acrostic hymn. There are typically many more strophes than eight, of course.) Melody No. 53 has an E final, and moves in the pitch set of mode 4, except for an extended ascent in phrases 2 and 3. The melody in phrase 1 is distinctive, however, and it is most characteristic of hymn structure that the reference in line 4 to line 1 establishes this distinctiveness and gives the melody identity. A much favoured melody associated with an old text, 'Verbum supernum prodiens', Ex. 75(ii), caused later medieval notators much difficulty because of its peculiar construction. It begins as if in mode 4 with C–E–G, but then a further ascent with a b natural, and a final on a makes this or any other modal assignment impractical. The melody has to be taken on its own terms, as do many hymn melodies. The two phrases of the first hemistich arrive at and confirm a as cadence point; the third phrase makes its own version of a penultimate descent to link up very artfully with a repetition of the first phrase as the fourth. Some further important melodies in Stäblein's edition are No. 17, associated with the ninth-century text 'Veni creator spiritus'; No. 22, associated with 'O lux beata Trinitas'; and No. 67, the one most often used with 'Ave maris stella', a ninth-century text and one of the earliest for the Blessed Virgin.

It would be difficult to overstate the importance of phrase structure in the hymn strophe. Implicit in hymnody up to 800, it became explicit thereafter in the hymnody of the Franks and other Westerners. The hymn strophe offered a framework within which melodic detail (like textual detail) could be precisely located and its effect maximized. Inflections, cadences, ascents and descents, figural repetitions and variations all could be given an emphasis within this framework that could not be achieved in the less regular phraseology of an antiphon or responsory. The Franks' enthusiasm for these possibilities became apparent in the endless varieties of structure that emerged out of their hymnody. It would be fruitless and irrelevant to try to classify the various ways in which repetitions of melody took place within the strophe; it is essential, however, to observe such repetitions wherever they occur, noting their effect within that particular melody. And if the Ambrosian strophe was by far the favourite, it was not the only one. Alongside the other plans inherited from the sixth and seventh centuries, Frankish hymnodists were to develop still more, expanding to larger and more sophisticated structures; and after them, secular and vernacular song writers were to expand further still.

Ambrosian hymns are sometimes thought to have been sung in alternating long and short rhythms corresponding to the quantitative iambic metre that philologists assure us Ambrose used. There are many missing links between the presumed manner of recitation of classical pagan quantitative poetry and Christian congregational hymn singing if this long-and-short performance is to be made credible; but whatever the result, it draws attention away from the much more important manifestation of rhythm in the hymn strophe.

The most basic fact, once again, is the regularity of syllable count in the phrase, of the phrase in the strophe. So prominent is the regularity of the phrasing that it remains the primary feature no matter how heavy the neumatic overlay; similarly, the phrase shape is more or less unaffected by the choice of long or short values for individual notes or syllables. Whether long-short, or short-long, or equal, these do not affect the relative length of the phrases and their construction into strophes, and these factors are the ones most operative until the twelfth century.

NEW FRANKISH FORMS

Great efforts have been made by scholars to discover or explain why and how the Franks sang things at Mass other than what was contained in the 'official' book.[20] The discussion so far should be sufficient to suggest that it was the Franks who had made the official book, and who had made it 'official'. They had already added much; they could and would add more. Who was to complain, after all, except themselves? Rome was far away, uninterested, and not often consulted; and in the end Rome accepted most of the Frankish innovations anyway, including hymns at the Office and the Credo at Mass. It is equally unnecessary to ask why the Franks made up new items and styles. With their energy and interest in music they could hardly be expected to sing only imported chant for very long. The only necessary questions concern the relationship of the new items to the old, and these relationships vary across a broad spectrum.

Efforts have also been made to discover or formulate a single principle that might account for or subsume the new Frankish forms.[21] But things do not begin like that. In the beginning was the energy, not the idea; then came the models, soon to be discarded or drastically modified; then the new forms—and not just a single dominant one, but a whole procession of forms, several abreast. Before 850 we do not yet find new musical forms; but during this period of prodigious absorption of the chant from Rome, there are several essentially unrelated phenomena that have to be noted and placed in perspective.

At some time before 795 the Carolingian Franks developed a set of *laudes* or acclamations for Charlemagne; these were used after he was crowned emperor in 800, and are the 'imperial *laudes*'.[22] They use traditional Roman and Byzantine Imperial acclamatory text for-

[20] On medieval chant in general, see Ewald Jammers, *Der mittelalterliche Choral* (Mainz, 1954); Smits van Waesberghe, *Musikerziehung*.

[21] Richard Crocker, 'The Troping Hypothesis', *MQ*, 52 (1966), 182.

[22] Ernest H. Kantorowicz, *Laudes regiae: A Study in Liturgical Acclamations and Medieval Ruler Worship* (Berkeley, 1946).

mulas, in series resembling the litanies, and in that respect representing a living stichic tradition. They are distinguished from the litanies
by the use of refrains, especially 'Christus vincit, Christus regnat,
Christus imperat', more elaborate than just the response 'Miserere
nobis', or 'ora pro nobis'. The melody is in the style of the litany tones,
using a pitch set E–G–A, which on one hand is shared with the Te
deum and what may be an old tone used for congregational acclamations such as Sanctus,[23] and on the other hand with many other
Frankish novelties. The *laudes* bear witness to the great value for the
new styles of syllabic acclamations—brief, energetic, syntactically
independent and capable of manifold combination.

Around 830 Amalarius of Metz gives us an early witness to the use
of melismata: he mentions a *neuma triplex* that the Roman cantors
used to sing for the responsory 'In medio' for St John (27 December),
which was transferred to the Christmas responsory 'Descendit de
caelis'.[24] This was really three melismata, each longer and more
ecstatic than the preceding, each one added in turn to the repetendum
of the respond when it was sung after the cantor sang the verse, then
the 'Gloria Patri', then the respond. This documentation shows first,
how one melisma could be replaced by another (or more generally,
how melismata could be inserted or removed from chants); second,
how more elaborate melismata could replace simpler ones, for more
festive effect; third, how one melisma could be moved around from
one chant to another. This last, of course, is well known from the
repertory of Graduals; but the overall relationship of the melisma
practice referred to by Amalarius and that of the Gregorian repertory
is as difficult to be clear about as the other aspects that involve the
history of Gregorian and Roman chant in the eighth century. We can
say that the use of melismata in Gregorian Graduals is a sophisticated
one in that the melismata are incorporated into the chants in complex
ways not easily categorized; to say that they appear at the beginning
of the verse, or on the last syllable, or on a specially important
syllable, is to oversimplify. Precisely this kind of generalization can,
however, be made about the way melismata came to be used in the
hands of the Franks. We can also say that the kind of melisma that
attracted their attention, and that they themselves were apt to
develop, contained the figural repetitions present sporadically in the
Gregorian repertory, more intensively in chants we believe to be later

[23] Kenneth Levy, 'The Byzantine Sanctus and its Modal Tradition in East and West', *Annales musicologiques*, 6 (1958–63), 7; in particular pp. 29 ff.

[24] See a recent analysis of this much discussed witness by Ruth Steiner, 'The Gregorian Chant Melismas of Christmas Matins', in J. C. Graue, ed., *Essays on Music for Charles Warren Fox* (Rochester, NY, 1979). Amalarius's report in his *Liber de ordine antiphonarii*, *Amalarii Episcopi opera liturgica omnia*, 3, ed. J. M. Hanssens (Vatican City, 1950), 54 ff.

rather than earlier. These factors taken together suggest that the detachable, formularized melisma referred to by Amalarius and subsequently favoured by the Frankish singers represented a late stage of development.

In addition to the neuma triplex and other melismata associated with Office responsories, melismata could appear in Offertories, either within the verses, or in the repetendum. One of the most highly developed practices of melisma was of course in the Mass Alleluia, which as we saw was a practice continuing throughout the eighth to eleventh centuries. These are the melismata that show most clearly the constructivist aspects of Frankish melisma practice. The *jubilus* tends to reappear exactly at the end of the verse, and often involved figural repetition. Furthermore, from Amalarius again we hear about replacement of the *jubilus* in the repeat *after* the verse (that is, the respond) with a more elaborate melisma, called a *sequentia*.[25] Six such *sequentiae* are rubricked in the Mont-Blandin Antiphonale (in the Sextuplex), and Notker of St Gall included eight in his *Liber hymnorum* (884). Similar replacement melismata, on a grander scale, appear in the Hispanic sources, and still others in Italian sources, as well as in Milanese.[26] The Hispanic ones may date from the ninth century, the others may well be later, and in general we should allow for this melisma practice continuing throughout the early Middle Ages in its own way, leading to longer and more repetitive forms. But no matter how much longer and more repetitive, the Hispanic and Milanese forms seem to have retained the sense of rhapsodic effusion in a single prolongation characteristic of the eighth-century practice; they did not develop the more rationalized forms we shall encounter under Frankish influence.

Still another practice that can be documented in the early ninth century is underlay of text. In an entry dating from 817–34 in Regensburg (East Frankish), the text 'Psalle modulamina' has been placed, a syllable for each note, under the Alleluia 'Christus resurgens', Alleluia, *jubilus*, and verse; the verse text has been incorporated in the new text, which has simply filled out all the neumes and melismata syllabically.[27] The characteristic features of this procedure

---

[25] René Jean Hesbert, *Antiphonale missarum sextuplex* (Brussels, 1935), No. 199a; Stäblein, 'Zur Frühgeschichte der Sequenz', *AMw*, 18 (1961), 4; Crocker, *The Early Medieval Sequence* (Berkeley, 1977), 393 ff.

[26] Louis Brou, 'Sequences et tropes dans la liturgie mozarabe', *Hispania sacra*, 4 (1951), 27; Stäblein, 'Frühgeschichte der Sequenz', pp. 2 f.; *Paléographie musicale*, 5, pp. 268 f., vol. 6, pp. 321 f.; Steiner, 'Some Melismas for Office Responsories', *JAMS*, 26 (1973), 108.

[27] See Smits van Waesberghe, 'Zur ursprünglichen Vortragsweise der Prosulen, Sequenzen, und Organa', *Bericht über den siebenten internationalen musikwissenschaftlichen Kongress, Köln 1958* (Kassel, 1959), 252 and facs.; Crocker, 'The Sequence', in Wulf Arlt, *et al.*, eds., *Gattungen der Musik in Einzeldarstellungen: Gedenkschrift Leo Schrade*, i (Berne, 1973), 272 f.

are that the melody is pre-existent, the added text is new, the setting is completely syllabic, the contours of the melody are reflected in the syntax of the new text, and the original text is either preserved or reflected in some way, usually by assonance—especially in the case of texting of a melisma, where the original vowel is apt to generate the assonance prevailing in the new text. Such texting of a melisma is usually called 'prosula'. In the case of this earliest documented case, the Alleluia is pre-existent but not by much; it is not in the Sextuplex, only in the first three notated Antiphonales c. 900, so that the Regensburg entry of the texting is actually the earliest witness for the Alleluia. As an Alleluia it shows a typically ninth-century form, with extended *jubilus*, which is paraphrased throughout the verse (except for the grandiose 'verse-melisma' on 'mors', with figural repetition), then repeated at the end of the verse. 'Psalle modulamina' refers to the Harrowing of Hell, a favourite Paschal topic for the Franks, and one that could be elaborated at length and repeatedly, being scarcely alluded to in the sombre Roman psalter stichs. The texting of the verse-melisma uses acclamatory wording to reflect the repetitive aspects of the melodic figuration. All these details are characteristic of the curious practice of text underlay, which in the past exercised a powerful fascination on scholars and was taken as the fount and origin of medieval music. Not so very many instances of this practice can be placed in the ninth century, hence it is insignificant compared merely to the number of antiphons, responsories, and hymns produced at that time, not to mention new items to be considered. It is not primarily a musical development, since no new music is created: the best examples show a high degree of skill and imagination in handling words and an awareness of melodic values, but no specifically musical skill.

TROPES AND THE GLORIA IN EXCELSIS

Scholars used to subsume text underlay (or 'prosula') under the term 'trope', which they took in a very broad sense, and believed to be the most distinctive, most important artistic phenomenon of the Middle Ages.[28] Recent research restricts the term 'trope' to one particular group of chants, and we no longer need to attribute primary importance to this group. Furthermore, while distinguishing tropes clearly from other kinds of chant, we can see that tropes are neither new nor peculiar to the early Middle Ages in the West.

[28] Stäblein, 'Die Unterlegung von Texten unter Melismen. Tropus, Sequenz und andere Formen', *Kongress-Bericht New York*, i (New York, 1961), 12; 'Tropus', *MGG*, xiii (1966), cols. 797–826; Crocker, 'The Troping Hypothesis'.

Tropes are verses; that is, each trope is a verse, in the sense of being a stich—a line of text, relatively self-contained in syntax, sung to its own melody with or without participation in a formulaic system. Being a stich, a trope rarely appears by itself, but always in combination with other tropes and other kinds of chant. As in other repertories, the combinations are variable and at cantor's option, at least in principle; as in other repertories, however, the combinations tend toward fixation. The word 'tropus' as used here is a Carolingian adoption into Latin from Greek, of a root with the same meaning and application as 'versus'. The Carolingians never succeeded in standardizing the term 'tropus', and it appears in various forms; it also alternates with other terms, most often 'versus'.[29] The Carolingian repertory of tropes is different in substance from any other stichic repertory, and it is convenient to reserve the term 'trope' to this repertory. In so far as tropes are stichs, they are not new, but are simply the title under which the Carolingians continued the stichic practice known to them in special form in Roman practice, and in more general form from the whole tradition of ritual song. Indeed, in a few cases where a trope consists of a verse from the Psalter or other Scripture, it is stylistically identical with an antiphon. If it were not for two important facts—the insistence of Roman practice on Psalter-stichs, and the Frankish fixation of Roman practice in an official Antiphonale—the Carolingian repertory of tropes would appear as a continuation of the Roman repertory of antiphons. Indeed, it is sometimes thought that the Carolingian repertory of tropes is in fact continuous with the *Gallican* repertory of antiphons, and if that is difficult to verify, one reason is that the Gallican repertory is preserved—if it *is* preserved—only in the Carolingian trope sources themselves. Carolingian tropes are generally distinct from Roman chant in making extensive use of non-scriptural texts, for the most part newly composed in a style markedly different from that of the Latin Psalter. The melodies for Carolingian tropes are also newly composed, varying in style from very close to that of Roman antiphons, to subtly different and eventually very different.

There seems to be a basic principle that stichs are attracted to stichs, so that new stichic repertories tend to form around those already in existence—especially those still in an active state (as opposed to older repertories long since fixed). Thus the earliest Frankish tropes seem to be those for the 'Gloria in excelsis'; if these Frankish tropes can be placed starting around 800, then they can almost be said to continue

---

[29] Eva Odelmann, 'Comment a-t-on appellé les tropes? Observations sur les rubriques des tropes des Xe et XIe siècles'. *Cahiers de civilisation médiévale*, 18 (1975), 15.

the stichic state of the Gloria itself. The next repertory of Frankish tropes is that provided for Introit and Communion (and occasionally Alleluia and Offertory), starting later in the ninth century. As shown by the *versus ad repetendum* in the Carolingian Antiphonales,[30] and also the assumed reduction of the Introit psalm to one verse, the combination at the Introit was not quite fixed at the moment when the Carolingians added more verses, that is, tropes.

The distribution of Gloria tropes in the sources, studied in detail by Rönnau,[31] shows them to originate in connection with Gloria A, and to come from the area between the Rhine and the Seine, beginning in the ninth century or possibly in the late eighth. The repertory was greatly expanded in the Aquitanian sources from around 900 on into the eleventh century, including—but by no means limited to—the famous sources associated with the Abbey of St Martial at Limoges. A more restricted development took place at the Abbey of St Gall in eastern Switzerland. As with many repertories of medieval chant, this one shows the characteristic split between eastern and western, which can be dated in the last half of the ninth century; items appearing in both traditions therefore probably antedate the split, and come from the middle of the ninth century or earlier. The eastern tradition is characterized by skill and cultivated taste in classical Latin; the western tradition represents a more vigorous, abundant idea of musical style, in full contact with the available traditions of stichic chant, and ready to use the disjointed, casual Latinity of those texts.

Of all trope repertories, those for Gloria best represent the stichic tradition, and this is true for all the 111 items catalogued by Rönnau. The unit is the single verse, added along with other verses to Gloria in excelsis at the discretion of the cantor; thus each performance could involve a different set of verses, and also one and the same verse could be used on a number of different occasions, in ever-changing contexts. This is in the nature of stichs. But stichic repertories tend towards fixation, and the Franks in particular tended towards fixation in this as in many other aspects of musical style; this process can be observed in the Gloria tropes, without ever going to completion.

A number of stichs representing the early stage of Gloria tropes have been assembled by Rönnau. They range from short acclamations, such as 'Deus fortis et immortalis', through middle-sized ones (the rhyming language is characteristic), as 'Caelestium terrestrium et infernorum rex', to relatively long verses that tend to break into bi-hemistichs, for example 'O bone rex et pie domine clementiam

---

[30] Cf. above, p. 139.   [31] Rönnau, *Die Tropen zum Gloria.*

ineffabilem tuam magnificantes devote'. All these move within the pitch set for Gloria A, and use compatible melodic idiom. The longer ones tend to use cadences and other elements of the formulaic system associated with the Gloria. The effect of adding verses of this type to the Gloria is simply to expand it to a more elaborate, more festal dimension. If the verses were sung by the cantor and the Gloria itself by the schola (probably no longer the congregation, the melodies being difficult), then there would be the added dimension of contrast between solo and chorus, relieving the purely choral performance of a long piece.

One of the perennial functions of stichs is to identify a general item with a specific occasion, and many Gloria tropes came to do that; thus the Gloria was made proper to Christmas or some other occasion by the use of tropes, at least at the beginning of the piece, that referred to the feast. This was one of the procedures that led to stable sets of tropes with an identity, as opposed to a repertory of tropes to be used at the cantor's choice. One of the earliest such sets (and one of the few to appear in both eastern and western repertories) is 'Laus tua deus' (Ex. 76). Only the first two lines are stable, and the rest shows widely differing versions not only from east to west but throughout the western repertory, characteristic of the early stage.[32] The reference to the Nativity is echoed in some, but by no means all, of the other verses that make up the set in one or the other version. As the repertory developed, the opening four or five verses, where the reference to the feast usually occurred, tended to stabilize, forming a core. These verses were associated with the very short acclamations of the Gloria text, 'Laudamus te/ Benedicimus te/ Adoramus te/ Glorificamus te', and since the verses themselves were often long, they far outweighed the Gloria text itself, which appeared as an intermittent articulation or emphatic summary of the verses. This type of trope often antici-pated the meaning of the Gloria text to follow, and is therefore a prefix trope. This substantial, quasi-independent block of verses would then be followed by others, perhaps shorter or less proper, perhaps from the pool of stichs, at less regular or more widely spaced intervals in the Gloria text. At the end there was often a longer verse, frequently 'Regnum tuum solidum permanebit in aeternum', just before 'Jesu Christe'. This verse (and some similar ones) often carried a large Frankish infix melisma on 'per', with figural repetition and the other characteristics of such melismata (Ex. 77). This melisma was often underlaid with a text in syllabic style, distinct from the prevail-

---

[32] Ibid. 140, 211 f.

Ex. 76

1. Laus tu - a de - us re - so - net co - ram te   rex
LAUDAMUS TE

2. Qui ve - ni - sti pro - pter nos

rex an - ge - lo - rum de - us   BENEDICIMUS TE

3. In se - de ma - je - sta - tis tu - ae

ADORAMUS TE

4. Glo - ri - o - sus es rex is - ra - hel in thro - no pa - tris

tu - i   GLORIFICAMUS TE

ing neumatic style of the tropes, and sometimes with an increase in rhyme and assonance.[33] This is a fascinating coming together of trope, melisma, and text underlay (prosula); but the fact that these phenomena can coexist, or that the Frankish singer can bring them together, should not be taken as a sign that they belong together or that their combination is the starting point of Western music, as has sometimes been imagined.

Another important way in which tropes were brought to a more fixed state was in the use of classical verse-forms such as dactylic hexameters or elegiac distichs (these were the two forms most favoured by classicizing Carolingian poets). When elegiac distichs

[33] Ibid. 179–87.

Ex. 77

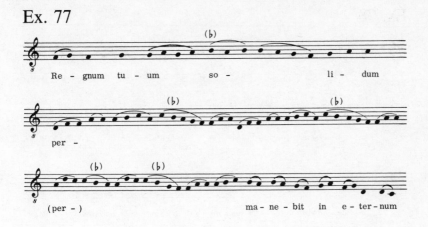

Re - gnum   tu - um   so -   li - dum

per -

(per -)   ma - ne - bit   in   e - ter - num

were applied to the opening four verses, the result was a massive block of very regular material that effectively dwarfed the Gloria text—even in the elaborate setting of Gloria A. This happens in the case of 'Laudat in excelsis' (Ex. 78), a West-Frankish set of tropes much used in Aquitania but less in East-Frankish sources. This might be from the end of the ninth century.[34] The East-Frankish version has only the opening verses; these are supplemented in an early West-Frankish source by a few verses from the pool; in other, later Aquitanian sources more distichs are added—up to a total of twelve. The melody for the distichs shows a very consistent application of cadences and formulas used more loosely in other long verses. The combination of melodic formulas with metric pattern gives the four opening verses a continuity and independence unique in degree—but not in kind— among Gloria tropes, and highlights the tendency throughout the trope repertory (as more generally in the stichic tradition) for two interlocking yet independent series to go on simultaneously.

Many of the hundred and more sets of Gloria tropes have distinctive features, if not artistic identity. What has not been carefully explored is the aesthetic quality of each set of tropes as an entity when taken together with the Gloria. In the early stages, of course, the overall result depended upon the cantor and was as ephemeral as the performance; we can study the overall result only as the sets of tropes stabilize. A precious remainder is the set 'Quem vere pia laus' (Ex. 79) attributed to Hucbald (*c.* 840–931), a leading and perhaps typical West-Frankish cantor at this most important time for medieval

[34] Ibid. 151–4, 232.

Ex. 78

1. Lau-dat in ex-cel-sis cae-lum ter-ram-que re-gen-tem

An-ge-li-cus coe-tus lau-dat et o-mnis ho-mo   LAUDAMUS TE

2. Te be-ne-di-cit o-vans an-ge-lo-rum cel-sa po-te-stas

Te mor-ta-lis ho-mo te be-ne-di-cit o-vans   BENEDICIMUS TE

3. Te ve-ne-ran-ter a-do-rant cun-cte ca-ter-ve po-lo-   rum

Te tel-lus pe-la-gus lau-dat a-do-rat a-mat   ADORAMUS TE

4. Glo-ri-fi-cant do-mi-num ru-ti-lan-ti-a si-de-ra cae-li

Glo-ri-fi-cant te rex cun-cta cre-a-ta tu-a   GLORIFICAMUS TE

chant.[35] This set consists of ten hexameters, in the pitch set for 'Gloria A' (but also used for Gloria IV) with internal cadences on *mi*, and *re*, and its last cadence (which is not the final of the piece) on *ut*. The melody is a sensitive, personal use of the idioms peculiar to this repertory. Each of the ten verses is set to its own melody, with careful use of figural repetition among verses. This set, representing a leading cantor's idea of how a set of Gloria tropes should go, shows a fixed and regular state.

[35] Ibid. 159, 240; Rembert Weakland, 'The Compositions of Hucbald', *Eg* 3 (1959), 152.

Ex. 79

1. Quem ve - re pi - a laus quem so - lum

con - de - cet hym - nus LAUDAMUS TE

2. Cun - cta su - per qui - a tu de - us es

be - ne - di - ctus in e - vum BENEDICIMUS TE

3. Qui do - mi - na - tor ad - es ce - li ter - re - que

ma - ris - que ADORAMUS TE

4. Glo - ri - a quem per - pes ma - net im - pe - ri - um

que per - hen - ne GLORIFICAMUS TE

5. De qua ple - na vi - gent abs - te - que

con - di - ta con - stant GRATIAS

6. Es qui - a tu cle - mens mi - tis pi - us

at - que be - ni - gnus QUI SEDES

7. Stat ti - bi nam pro - pri - um mi - se - re - ri vel - le

mi - sel - lis QUONIAM

8. San - cti - fi - cans om - nes tu - a quos ti - bi

gra - ti - a ne - ctit TU SOLUS

9. Tri - na ge - nu - flec - tit cu - i sub - di - ta

ma - chi - na re - rum TU SOLUS

10. Cun - cta vi - dens et cun - cta re - plens per

se - cu - la re - gnans
IHESU

The fact that the Frankish Gloria tropes follow closely the stichic state of the Gloria itself make it necessary to consider the melodic settings of the Gloria along with the tropes. New melodies for the Gloria were an important but not very large part of the Frankish repertory of chant for Mass.[36] As we saw, at some point in the eighth century elaborate settings start to appear; that is, one such setting appeared, 'Gloria A', and it is very elaborate; in documentation it antedates all the simple settings. Bosse's catalogue of Gloria melodies in the Middle Ages includes 56 items, probably representing most of what there were. Perhaps a third of these were known and used throughout Europe or a large part of it; the rest were known and used only locally. This is a characteristic medieval distribution, one that meets us here as we start to discuss repertories in their determinate historical setting rather than the relatively isolated (if not artificial) state in which the Gregorian repertory comes to us. The many melodies known and used locally attest to a broad-based musical activity—an active class of cantors with creative ambitions and skills, eager to develop their own musical repertory. The smaller group of melodies widely known and used are those local products that succeeded in artistry and favour.

After Gloria A the early important Frankish melodies are those known as Gloria IV, I, XIV, XI, and VI; of these, Gloria A and Gloria IV are the ones usually troped, especially Gloria A. We already saw that Gloria A was distinguished by a neumatic style, with a complex system of figural repetitions running throughout the whole piece. The style of Gloria IV is simpler, the use of formulas is more regular, with one succession of formulas being more or less repeated throughout. This shape appears in short form at 'Gratias ... gloriam tuam'. We should not confuse this with an Office psalm tone: it has no reciting tone, and no consistent bi-hemistich plan. If we compared it to anything in the Gregorian repertory it would be the verse tones of the responsories, or of the Invitatories, or the formulaic systems of Tracts; but the comparison is not very close. And even though it may be difficult at first to hear the identity of the idiom because of its simplicity, it is unlike anything we have encountered in the Gregorian or Urban-Roman repertories. The pitch set is that of Gloria A, but the locus is slightly different: Gloria A moved in *ut–re–mi*, with the main internal cadences (at verse ends) on *mi* or *re*, and with excursions both below the *ut* and above the *mi* to *sol* or higher; Gloria IV does not go

---

[36] Stäblein, 'Gloria in excelsis'; Detlev Bosse, *Untersuchung einstimmiger mittelalterlicher Melodien zum 'Gloria in excelsis'* (Erlangen, 1954). A selection of melodies is included in the Ordinaries in the *Graduale Romanum* and the *Liber usualis*, referred to by Roman numeral.

below the *ut*, has its main internal cadence on the *mi*, with much emphasis on the *sol* with frequent decoration above (the top note, printed c in modern sources, was in some early practices b or b flat). The common element between Gloria A and Gloria IV is the *mi* cadence in the centre of the pitch set *ut–la*, an arrangement that corresponds to what was classed as mode 4, but became so popular for hymns and Frankish forms such as these Gloria melodies (and their tropes), and treated with such freedom and novelty, that modal classification is neither very feasible nor useful. Other pitch sets used for Gloria melodies show the same similarities and differences relative to those of the Gregorian repertory.

One of the most striking aspects of Gloria melodies, to be found as well in many other manifestations of Frankish melody, is the way the figural repetitions achieve the effect of overall, independent musical system within a piece; indeed, this use of figural repetitions seems to be one of the principal ways in which the Franks directed their music towards the idea of a 'piece of music', a self-contained musical system, complete and unalterable. Stichic combinations tend to be irregular and rambling. In the Gloria melodies the Franks seem to have turned to a melodic system that would eventually be capable of creating its own form.

Gloria melodies and Gloria tropes come to us in a set of manuscript sources distinct from those of the Gregorian Mass Antiphonales. Actually we should say that it is the Mass Antiphonales that are distinct: whether or not they derive from a Frankish-Roman archetype, they often display a consistency and isolation unusual for documents of a tradition of ritual song. It is the 'other' manuscripts, not dealt with by Gregorian scholars (and hence for a long time hardly dealt with at all) that represent a living tradition, and so have resisted attempts at classification. These manuscripts are often called 'Tropers', and indeed that reflects one of the main items they contain; but there are many other items as well, and each manuscript is a problem in itself. These manuscripts extend from the tenth century up to the thirteenth, and are the basic sources for Frankish chant, or more generally medieval chant (as opposed to Gregorian or Frankish-Roman). A start has been made on a complete inventory by Heinrich Husmann's *Tropen- und Sequenzenhandschriften*.[37]

SEQUENCE AND PROSE

Around the middle of the ninth century there came out of the West-

---

[37] Répertoire Internationale des Sources Musicales B/V/1, 1964.

Frankish Kingdom a new form, the sequence or prose. This was the first of the distinctly new syntheses the Franks were to contribute to music.[38] The term 'sequence' is a translation of the Latin *sequentia*; but there is a reason for keeping the Latin term in another meaning, to which we will return in a moment. 'Sequence' refers primarily to the melody, 'prose' (Latin *prosa*) primarily to the text; melody and text are intimately linked, and either term can include both, that is, the whole piece. German scholars tend to use *Sequenz* as a categorical term, the French, *Prose*; in English, mostly from habit, we use 'sequence'.

A sequence, then, consists of a text set syllabically (for the most part) to a melody arranged in a series of couplets (for the most part)— that is, two successive lines of text sung to the same melody, then another two lines sung to another melody, and so forth. The first line, often the last line and occasionally one or more lines in between are 'singles', with only one line of text for the melody. Successive phrases of melody vary in length; two successive phrases are almost always of different length, varying from five or six notes (and syllables) to thirty or forty. Each line of text is usually a syntactic unit, but there are frequent cases of run-on from the first line of a couplet to the second, and less frequent but important cases of several phrases of melody (usually shorter ones) being run together in one large textual period. The concept of bi-hemistich is not easily applied to the couplets, for the lines of text, while of the same length (that is, syllable count) do not necessarily form a bi-hemistich in other respects; and the phrase of melody is repeated exactly without differentiation into first half and second half. This and all aspects of the sequence admit of exception: the form is flexible, and especially in the ninth century is in a state of active development that generates a variety of solutions. Early sequences frequently have unique arrangement of detail, and each has its identity.

The partnership of text and music is a remarkably even one, but one or the other may predominate in individual cases. In the hands of Notker of St Gall, an accomplished poet, the texts predominate; but with the exuberant musicality of the West-Frankish cantors the melodies become the most striking feature, and this is true for the greater part of the medieval sequence repertory. The melodies have a clarity and purpose as yet unheard on the medieval scene. They move with strength and grace, avoiding ornamentation on one hand and

---

[38] Wolfram von den Steinen, 'Die Anfänge der Sequenzendichtung' *Zeitschrift für Schweizerische Kirchengeschichte*, 40 (1946), 190, 241; 41 (1947), 19, 122; Stäblein, 'Sequenz', *MGG*, xii, cols. 522–49; Crocker, *The Early Medieval Sequence*; 'The Sequence'.

recitation on the other. They range through relatively broad pitch sets to clearly prepared goals at cadence points. Perhaps the most distinctive feature is a recurrent overall shape, in which relatively shorter phrases at the beginning are gradually extended as the melody ascends into a higher register, reaching a climax in a phrase near the end, followed by a descent for a suitable conclusion. The progress of this shape is explicit: it hides nothing of its operation, but is immediately comprehensible. As the repertory develops there is more and more use of figural repetition to provide subtle continuity and organization to the shape, and while that may not be apparent at first hearing it is readily susceptible of analysis. These melodies have their own style, their own values, different from those of the Gregorian repertory in important respects. They lack—perhaps consciously avoid—the sense of mystery, the cantorial rhapsody and effusion, even ecstasy, of the Gregorian Graduals, also the sense of deep sophistication, of suave urbanity that can be felt throughout the Gregorian repertory. Instead they have a sense of direction, of excitement and éclat on the one hand, of immediate familiarity and accessibility on the other, that is new.

So clear and direct is the end product that it has always seemed as though there must be some clear origin, some single prototype that would account for the relatively abrupt appearance on the Carolingian scene. No such origin or prototype has turned up, and we need rather to believe that the Frankish cantors put together their new synthesis in a short time, without a prototype but using a variety of materials lying close at hand, now used in a new way, with a mastery of musical form won from the strenuous encounter with Roman chant, and a generous allotment of native imagination and creative energy. The ingredients include the *sequentia* (it is convenient to retain the Latin term for this particular use) as described by Amalarius around 830—a replacement melisma for the repetition of the *jubilus* at the repeat of the Alleluia after its verse. We have samples of the *sequentia*, and it is plain that they are different in style, structure, and dimension from the early sequence; they are shorter, more rhapsodic, and not consistently organized into couplets. Some of them are underlaid with prosulae, thereby approaching the sequence with its text; but again, the textual organization is different, in much the same respects. At some early point in its development the Franks went so far as to incorporate the sequence into the Mass, placing it right after the Alleluia, resulting in the succession Gradual (Roman chant), Alleluia (Roman, but more and more Frankish-Roman, chant) sequence (Frankish chant). This liturgical position, combined with the tradition of calling it *sequentia*, and also the notational practice of writing down the sequence melodies without text, as melismata, each beginning with the text 'Alleluia', all projected the image of the sequence as a texted replacement *jubilus*; but there are too many discrepancies for the image to be believed. And there are some early and very typical sequences that do not conform to the image.

Trying to understand the sequence in terms of the stichic tradition is difficult, but perhaps rewarding. Here we have to consider the alternate name, *prosa*. Many of the lines of a sequence or prose could be considered stichs or verses, and then we could imagine the sequence as a whole to be a stichic combination; indeed this way of looking at it has valuable consequences. Sometimes individual lines echo materials from other sequences or other types of pieces; sometimes lines are substituted or replaced, added or subtracted, in a manner that suggests cantorial option. Yet the manuscript tradition yields the overall impression that sequence shape is determinate.

Furthermore, the frequent cases of run-on and extended period in the texts that cut across the repetitions of melodic phrases, as well as the complex and often irregular constructions in the melodies, raise a basic question concerning stichic construction. 'Verse' has the basic meaning of termination at the end of the line, and run-on over the end of a melodic phrase is not at all characteristic of verses in the sense of stichs; here is where the term *prosa*, the explicit opposite of *versus*, is applicable to show a basic feature of the new form. These texts are not prose in the sense of being without linear or stichic structure, but only in the sense of running over that structure often enough, and treating it irregularly enough, so as not to allow the term 'verse'. In Gloria tropes, again, we have observed the tendency towards regular length lines; these could even take on the form of verse in the extreme sense, that of a line measured according to one of the classical metres such as the hexameter. That does not happen in the prose (at least, not for a long time), neither in the case of an individual line nor in the succession of lines, which almost always differ at least enough not to be considered verse. In this respect especially, the sequence is unique: it occupies an unstable middle ground between stichic combinations such as Gloria tropes on one hand, and completely fixed, very regular strophic hymns on the other.

The features of the early sequence can be observed in 'Ecce vicit' (Ex. 80), a sequence for Easter.

Other examples from the early repertory are 'Laudes deo', 'Haec dies quam excelsus', 'Haec est sancta solemnitas', 'Clara gaudia'. Special attention should be paid to 'Nostra tuba', perhaps one of the

Ex. 80

1. Ec - ce vi - cit ra - dix Da - vid, le - o de tri - bu Ju - da.

Mors vi - cit mor - tem et mors no - stra est vi - ta.

2a. Mi - ra - bel - la et stu - pen - da   sa - tis in - ter om - nes vic - to - ri - a,
  b. Ut mo - ri - ens sic su - pe - ra - ret for - tem cum cal - li - da ver - su - ti - a.

3. Sus - ce - pe - rat mors in - dem - nem quem te - ne - re num - quam

po - tu - e - rat prop - ter cul - pam.

4a. Dum am - bi - it, il - li - ci - ta quae te - ne - bat ju - ste per -
  b. Am - bi - e - re vo - lu - e - rat in suc - ces - su et re - man -

(4a) di - dit ac - qui - si - ta
(4b) sit e - va - cu - a - ta.

5a. In se re - ful - sit de - fi - ci ex - tre - mi - tas
  b. Hic ve - rus est a - gnus le - ga - lis qui mul - tis

(5a) Ut qui - bus ad vi - tam fu - e - rat lar - gi - tur
(5b) Se ma - ni - fe - sta - vit fi - gu - ris; tan - dem se

(5a) in - gres - sum do - na - ret et re - gres - sum
(5b) pro mun - dum ho - sti - am de - dit pa - tri

(5a) ad per - ci - pi - en - dam ve - ni - am.
(5b) ut re - di - me - ret mem - bra su - a.

6. Re - gnum e - jus ma - gnum et po - te - stas e - jus pri - ma in se - cul - la.

earliest; and to 'Fortis atque amara' and 'Stans a longe', along with those listed, as representative of the first stage.[39] Three larger sequences, also early but perhaps dependent stylistically on those listed, are 'Nunc exultet', 'Christi hodierna', and 'Rex omnipotens'. None of those mentioned has a clear, confirmed relationship to an Alleluia of the Mass; that relationship can be observed in two sequences that use the Alleluia 'Justus ut palma' as an incipit, 'Praecursor Christi' and 'Haec dies est sancta', of which the first seems slightly earlier—or at any rate the second better represents the kind of melodic constructions that gradually emerged out of the early sequence. The sequences associated in West-Frankish sources with Advent Alleluias show the great complexities encountered in tracing the relationship with the Alleluia, and may occupy a middle ground between the larger, independent sequence with the full range of stylistic novelty, and the smaller traditional *sequentia*; but this middle ground might well have been occupied *after* the development of the large sequence, not before it, and as a *rapprochement* to the *sequentia*—it could have coincided with the establishment of a relationship to the Alleluia of the Mass, and with the incorporation of the sequence into the Mass.

Prominent in this group of early sequences is the use of the pitch set characteristic of *tetrardus* (modes 7 and 8); because of the exuberant melodies a pitch set larger than that of either mode 7 or 8 is required. These melodies are firmly seated on the *ut* of the *ut–re–mi–fa* (G–a–b–c) locus, using it almost exclusively for cadences at the ends of each line; the only other consistent cadence pitch is the *sol* above, used in very rational fashion for certain interior cadences in the contrasting higher register. The lower register, treating the central *ut* as *sol* and descending to the *ut* below, is also used in a clear, consistent fashion, usually restricted to certain phrases. The *fa* below the central *ut*—familiar from Gregorian practice, where we found it convenient to place the *ut* on G and refer to the F–a–c realm associated with this *fa*—is similarly used in a consistent fashion for certain phrases, usually as a penultimate departure before the final approach to the cadence. Sense of location is very strong in sequence melodies, both within the pitch set at any given moment, and in the piece as a whole, which regularly ascends through the set towards the climax near the end. Other early sequences use mostly the *re* final of mode 1 (to a much lesser extent, mode 2); there are a few isolated examples of a *mi* final (modes 3 and 4), and nothing that might be considered as modes 5 and 6, at least in the early repertory. Just as the early Gloria tropes

[39] Ibid. 279, 285 f.

seem to have exploited a single tonal realm, so too did the early sequences—though one distinctly different from the Gloria tropes.

While the main part of the sequence is syllabic in style, first and last phrases (which are usually singles) are often treated in a slightly neumatic style, acting as a frame to the whole piece. When there is a relationship to an Alleluia of the Mass, it occurs in the first phrase; and even when there is no relationship, there is often a general reference to Gregorian style in first and last phrases. This takes the specific form of stepwise descent to the final cadence, in contrast to a cadence that seems to have been specially developed for—or at least heavily used in—the early sequence: this cadence approaches the last note from one step below, either G–F–G (for *tetrardus*) or D–C–D (for *protus*). It has long been observed that this is no Gregorian cadence formula, even though the pitches may occur from time to time in the Gregorian. These formulas appear regularly at phrase endings throughout a typical sequence, recalling the somewhat more varied use of non-Gregorian cadences in Gloria tropes in similar positions. In both cases it is possible to understand these several cadences as half-cadences, and in the sequence this usage becomes so consistent as to make clear the sense of unified structure that extends over the whole piece.

The climax of some melodies exhibits a remarkable conjunction of movement into the upper register with the longest phrases of the piece, which are broken up into subphrases, often in the pattern *a a b* (recalling figural repetitions in typical Frankish replacement melismata). These subphrases tend to be especially lyric, introducing an element of special charm that in later development of the repertory tends to contribute to a loosened and more episodic sense of structure; in the earliest and best pieces, however, this merely provides point and definition to the climax. These subphrases also tend to avoid even the half-cadence formula, being left really 'open' in function. The structural effect is to open up the whole last period of the piece in a long melodic arc, articulated into smaller units but kept from closure; in its rational way it has something of the effusion of the Gregorian cantorial style. Morphologically this reproduces the shape of a *whole* respond that concludes with a large melisma in which figural repetition in the *a a b* pattern occurs. That is, the whole sequence resembles in plan the whole respond, only the sequence is more rational in its disposition of the materials. The same shape can be seen (with differences, of course) in a Gloria with its tropes, in particular the 'Regnum' stich added near the end; when its melisma is sung as such, the resemblance is to the respond; when the melisma has a prosula, the resemblance is more to the sequence. Again, the sequence is more rational, the Gloria showing a looser conjunction of disparate elements.

The development of the sequence repertory, as shown in sources of the tenth and eleventh centuries, is not without continuing references to stichic practice. Lines, or couplets, or whole blocks of material can be added to sequences, or (less often) subtracted; replacements of one set of phrases with another is common—and not arbitrarily, but with the sense of overall form clearly in view. Very common is the supplying of a second line of text to convert a single into a couplet—this by way of standardizing sequence form. More interesting is the appearance of a special kind of phrase group (called 'versus' in modern research) either by being composed into a new piece, or added to an already existent one, at certain point in the structure, most often at phrases 5 and 9.[40] These 'versus' have short, regular lines, sometimes rhyming and almost always with the acclamatory style of the *laudes*; they are set in lightly neumatic style, and otherwise stand out from their surroundings. As episodes in the structure they recall the verse of a responsory, an effect that is heightened when two or three of these sets recur alternately with more usual material. Whatever sense we make out of these, it is clear that large-scale design is a principal concern of the composer of a sequence.

Originating in the region between Rhine and Seine, around the mid-ninth century, the sequence was soon taken to St Gall, where new texts were provided, first to West-Frankish melodies, then to local East-Frankish ones, by Notker of St Gall. (It is Notker's preface to his sequences, the *Liber hymnorum*, that provides us with this information, the most explicit description of the development of early Frankish repertories.[41]) Here again is a core of repertory common to East and West, dating from mid-century, followed by two separate and largely unrelated repertories from the end of the ninth century and extending through the tenth. East-Frankish sequences after Notker are fewer in number, often impressive in their idiosyncrasy or thoughtfulness.[42] The West-Frankish repertory, more especially the Aquitanian repertory, developed profusely with a large number of sequences, showing much re-use and standardization of melodic and textual material but also much imagination, experimentation, and

[40] Stäblein, 'Zur Frühgeschichte der Sequenz', pp. 8–33; Heinrich Husmann, 'Sequenz und Prosa', *Annales musicologiques*, 2 (1954), 77; Crocker, *The Early Medieval Sequence*, pp. 385 ff.

[41] Text of Notker's Preface in von den Steinen, *Notker der Dichter*, ii (Berne, 1948), 8 ff.

[42] Some published in Nicholas de Goede, *The Utrecht Prosarium, Monumenta musica Neerlandica*, vi (1965), and Otto Drinkwelder, *Ein deutsches Sequentiar aus dem Ende des 12. Jahrhunderts* (Graz, 1914).

development towards new styles, to be discussed later. Both the East-Frankish repertory, grouped around Notker's *Liber hymnorum*, and the West-Frankish and Aquitanian repertories show the typical spectrum between very popular items and those of purely local significance. The West-Frankish repertory is also represented in English sources, especially the two manuscripts known as the 'Winchester Troper'.[43] The numerous Italian sources appearing after 1000 were dependent upon either the East- or West-Frankish repertories, separately or in some complex combination.

INTROIT TROPES

A whole class of tropes was associated with the Proper chants of the Mass—Introit, Alleluia, Offertory, and Communion.[44] By far the largest portion of these was associated with the Introit, so that Introit tropes can be taken as representative of the whole class; after them in frequency and importance are tropes for Communion, Offertory, and Alleluia. This class of tropes, headed by the Introit tropes, was the largest and most prominent group of all tropes: its presence in a manuscript is what makes that manuscript a Troper. The extent of the repertory is hard to determine (as is the case of other medieval repertories); Weiss, in his edition of 352 sets of Introit tropes (almost 1500 verses) from the Aquitanian sources, refers to some 1000 melodies for sets of tropes that can be found in medieval sources; some 400 texts were printed in the *Analecta hymnica*; Evans, editing a typical troper from the early eleventh century, included 214 sets of various kinds of tropes. Editions of the material are proceeding, but in various ways. *Corpus troporum*, the important modern critical edition of texts, edits according to the basic nature of tropes as verses, treating each trope or verse as a unit; it takes up the repertory by calendar. Weiss groups the tropes into sets associated with specific Introits (as the tropers themselves do, with much variation), and proceeds by region.

Introit tropes seem to be substantially more numerous than Gloria

---

[43] Alejandro Planchart, *The Repertory of Tropes at Winchester* (Princeton, 1977), and Andreas Holschneider, *Die Organa von Winchester* (Hildesheim, 1968).

[44] The old edition of texts in *Analecta hymnica*, 47 and 49 is being superseded by the *Corpus troporum* (*Studia Latina Stockholmiensia*, 21), 1, *Tropes du propre de la messe, 1, Cycle de Noël*, ed. Ritva Jonsson et al., 2, *Prosules de la messe, 1, Tropes de l'alleluia*, ed. Olof Marcusson; 3, *Tropes du propre de la messe, 2, Cycle de Pâques*, ed. Gunilla Björkvall, Gunilla Iversen, and Ritva Jonsson. Melodies of Introit tropes are edited by Günther Weiss, *Introitus-Tropen, Monumenta musica medii aevi*, 3 (1970); see also Evans, *The Early Trope Repertory*. For discussion, see Stäblein, 'Zum Verständnis des "klassischen" Tropus', *AcM*, 35 (1963), 84; Husmann, 'Sinn und Wesen der Tropen, veranschaulicht an den Introitustropen des Weihnachtsfestes', *AMw*, 16 (1959), 135; Planchart, *The Repertory of Tropes at Winchester*; Steiner, 'Trope'.

tropes, but to appear slightly later—at the end of the ninth century
rather than the beginning. Several conditions concerning their appearance and function need to be noted. The Introit (or other Proper
function at Mass) has a relatively official status as an element of the
archetype, and association with the Introit brought with it, of course,
inclusion at Mass. The repertory of Introits, as well as their texts and
music, was relatively fixed in the archetype. These aspects differentiated the Introit somewhat from the Gloria. Compared to the
Gradual, on the other hand, the Introit (with Offertory and Communion) represented a stichic tradition whose options were closer to
hand; with the psalm verses being reduced to only one, the *versus ad
repetendum* appearing in some sources but not others, and the number
of repetitions of the antiphon (called *versus* in *Ordo romanus* I![45])
varying in practice, it is easy to imagine this stichic tradition being
continued with tropes.

Introit tropes represent a wide variety of textual and melodic styles;
the various, often conflicting, descriptions of this repertory provided
by modern scholars seem due in part to the fact that different scholars
take into consideration different selections from the whole repertory.
It is indeed a varied repertory, and on the one hand includes items that
seem as close to a specific Introit as it is possible to get, while on the
other hand it seems to offer the eleventh-century monastic composer
an opportunity to develop melodic styles that lead directly to later
medieval music. All of that awaits a thorough stylistic study of the
repertory, as does the chronology and development of Introit tropes.

Here as elsewhere a trope is a verse, and an Introit trope is a verse
added to an Introit to expand the combination. The most usual
practice was to prefix a trope to a phrase of the Introit antiphon; and
usually several tropes were added to a given Introit antiphon, one
before each phrase of the antiphon. Thus there might be two, or three,
or four (infrequently more) tropes for a given antiphon, and these
taken together form a set of tropes (Ex. 81).[46] A trope could also be
prefixed to the psalm verse, to the *Gloria Patri*, to the repeat of the
antiphon and to the *versus ad repetendum* (if any), but all these were
much less frequent. Sets of tropes, however, vary for any given Introit
from one manuscript to the next; the constitution of the set reflects, in
other words, the kind of cantorial option basic to stichic practice. The
tropes themselves are often relatively stable in wording, if less so in
melody.

[45] Andrieu, *Les Ordines romani*, Ordo Rom. I, Introit.
[46] Paris B.N.lat.n.a. MS 1235, fo. 184v; ed. Ellen Reier, 'The Repertory of Introit Tropes at
Nevers' (Diss., University of California, Berkeley, 1981), iii, p. 9.

Ex. 81

1. Gau - de - a - mus ho - di - e qui - a de - us de - scen - dit

de ce - lis

et prop - ter nos in ter - ris PU - ER NA - TUS (etc.)

2. Quem pro - phe - te di - u va - ti - ci - na - ti sunt

ET FI - LI - US (etc.)

3. Hunc a pa - tre jam no - vi - mus ad - ve - nis - se in

mun - dum CU - IUS (etc.)

4. Am - mi - ra - bi - lis con - si - li - a - ri - us de - us

for - tis prin - ceps pa - cis MA - GNI

The texts of Introit tropes are very infrequently from Scripture;
typical instances occur in connection with the antiphon 'Puer natus'
for Christmas (Third Mass), where the antiphon text is centonized
from Isaiah ix, and a trope may provide additional stichs from the
same source. The overwhelming majority of Introit tropes are newly
made texts. Their language is often elaborate—occasionally elegant,

frequently pretentious, but almost always showing ambitions toward artistic elevation. The content ranges from very close connections with a specific antiphon, through expressions that are merely appropriate to a particular feast or saint's day (and can be added almost anywhere in that Mass formulary without loss of propriety) to general expressions of celebration or solemnity that could be used on any occasion.

The Romans used stichs from Scripture for festal occasions, and the result was frequently a tenuous or at least allusive relationship between stich and occasion, leaving much to be made explicit. Introit tropes very frequently have the specific function of making this relationship explicit, spelling out or at least suggesting the connection between Psalter-stich and feast or saint's day. If we believed in a tradition of Gallican stichs, mostly non-scriptural and often composed with close relationship to the occasion, we could imagine the Frankish tropes as a *rapprochement* between that Gallican tradition and the alien Roman practice—abstract, severe, and obscure—that abruptly replaced it. Even if we do not believe in such a Gallican tradition of any substantial extent, still it is easy to see that Roman practice carries out the idea of ritual song for festal occasions in only a very oblique way, and that a more specific way hardly needs much explanation. Even within, or adjacent to, Roman practice there are a few instances of more normal practice: the non-scriptural Introit antiphon for St Agatha ('Gaudeamus omnes diem festum celebrantes') and the non-scriptural responsories for Christmas Matins ('Hodie nobis rex caelorum') are among many indications of the broader stichic tradition.

In general the melodic settings of individual tropes employ fully shaped, complete phrases, often of ample dimensions. Besides being verses in the general sense of all stichs, tropes are sometimes verses in the more specific sense of, say, the verse of a responsory, that is, episodic; and in that sense, just like any such verse, a trope may cadence on some pitch other than the final of the antiphon (a typical Gregorian antiphon, as we saw, also has internal cadences on pitches other than the final). There is no reason to see in that variety of cadence pitch anything other than the need for variety and articulation among phrases as the combination becomes larger.

Introit tropes make classic use of the pitch sets associated with the modes—more so, often, than do the antiphons from which the modal classifications were developed. Perhaps it is not surprising that the cantors who struggled with the problem of classifying the Gregorian antiphons should then proceed to write at least some melodies that used the modes without anomalies and ambiguities. Sequences show anomalies, but mostly because of their exuberant overflow of range; the locus of each phrase is often solidly in a familiar modal framework. It does seem that since Introit tropes, by design, coexisted with antiphons, they should make a compatible use of pitch set; in any case, they do. What is striking, however, is that while Introit tropes also make use—abundant use—of idioms associated with these pitch sets, the idioms in question are for the most part not those distinctive of Introit antiphons but are drawn from a broader and less distinctive repertory; perhaps we hear references most often to one or another kind of Office antiphon. In trope melodies we find an idealized antiphon style, as the Gregorian might well be observed by a Frankish cantor standing at the distance of a generation or two from the formulation of the archetype. Now when a trope being composed to go with a particular antiphon uses the corresponding pitch set and the idioms that in general are associated with that set, then naturally there will be similarities between trope and antiphon melodies; and it would be perfectly easy for the composer of the trope to maximize the similarity by direct figural quotation of the antiphon. What is remarkable is that he does not do this so very often, and the similarities are apt to remain in the realm of general similarity. A more important result of close comparison of antiphon and trope melody is the greater strength and identity of the Gregorian antiphon: compared to this particular Frankish style, the Gregorian impresses us with how little sense of formula there really is in Introit antiphons, how individual each antiphon is. Precisely this individuality is hardly ever reflected in the trope melodies.

The effect of continuity among the tropes and separation of them from the phrases of the antiphon is especially marked when the tropes are cast in hexameters, which are frequent (about a quarter of the repertory as a whole, concentrated in tropes for saints, where they can account for half the existing tropes). The hexameter line is relatively long, compared to phrases of antiphons; and more important, the strong traditional form of the hexameter (even though not reflected in the detail of the melodic setting) establishes a recurrent phrase-rhythm that dominates the combination. In the much less frequent case of elegiac distichs, the discrepancy in bulk is so great that the piece is clearly a series of distichs punctuated by fragments of Introit.

The first trope of a set, prefixed to the first phrase of the antiphon (hence to the Introit as a whole), is often longer than those that follow; it may be one long phrase, or have two phrases. Any Introit trope, in any position, can be prefatory in its wording (ending, for example, with a hortatory 'psallamus dicentes'); but the first trope of a set is particularly apt to have this wording and this function. Sometimes it is several phrases long, forming a phrase group—and in such cases could apparently be used by itself, without any further tropes being added to the second and following phrases of the antiphon. Such an introductory polystich is indistinguishable in shape from a larger antiphon, for instance the Gospel Canticle antiphons of the Office, which of all the Gregorian items it most closely resembles; both types are longer than the morphological norm, and may be expansions in some sense. There are other hints, too, that the Frankish stichic practice of the ninth, tenth, and eleventh centuries began with relatively independent, self-contained stichs that could be used in a variety of unsystematic ways, and moved only gradually towards a systematic filling-out of all the appropriate or available moments.

Out of the 350-odd trope sets edited by Weiss, some 40 or 50 can be counted as introductory polystichs, and some of these are elaborate—occasionally narrative or in dialogue. The most famous example is 'Quem quaeritis', the dialogue of the three Marys and the angel at the empty sepulchre, for Easter.[47] There has been extensive discussion of the 'Quem quaeritis', as to whether it is a trope, and if so, what kind; whether it is a drama, and if so, what kind; what its 'original' function and position were; and the nature of its connection with later medieval drama.[48] It is labelled both 'tropus' and 'versus' in manuscripts, and since trope and verse are one and the same thing in these sources, 'Quem quaeritis' can be described by either or both terms. In nature it is an introductory polystich; its text contains dialogue drawn from Gospel narratives via stichs already in use for antiphons and responsories. The melody is in the idealized antiphon style used for Introit tropes. In nature and function it closely resembles 'Quem quaeritis' for Christmas, and 'Quem creditis' for Ascension, both of which were presumably modelled upon the Easter 'Quem quaeritis'. The melodic relationship to the Easter Introit, 'Resurrexi', is no closer or further away than other comparable introductory polystichs. It was also used at the end of Matins, just before the Te deum, and also at the formation of a procession that took place between Lauds and Mass on Easter morning. In true stichic tradition, it does not stand alone, but can be combined with a variety of other materials. In the tenth century, broadly speaking, this combination is one involving parts of the Mass or the Office; in the eleventh century other kinds of material, less directly associated with Mass or Office, become involved, and in

[47] Weiss, *Introitus-Tropen*, p. 246, No. 230.   [48] See Ch. VIII.

those contexts the dialogue's possibilities for representation and personification become more explicit.

On one hand the discussion of 'Quem quaeritis' as the 'origin of medieval drama' has been unnecessarily complicated by an over-refined idea of 'liturgical' as opposed to 'non-liturgical'. Consideration of the history and development of the chant used at Mass and Office, and especially appreciation of the role of the stichic tradition in generating that chant, reveals a broad margin of what is 'liturgical', whose content was determined to a considerable extent by cantor's choice. On the other hand, there has been an insufficient distinction between liturgy and drama, with an excessive emphasis on liturgy as drama. Liturgy—that is, the liturgy of the Mass—is not drama, it is ritual act; nothing in these acts is being dramatically represented or personified. Processions, too, are first of all ritual action. The Office, on the contrary, is not action of any kind; it is merely reading a lot of texts. The history of medieval liturgy shows many instances in which representation or personification is introduced into Mass and Office, and this coincides with the development of a category that can certainly be defined as play, and may involve aspects of drama. It seems significant that the position of the play in the Office is at the end of the long Night Office, and it has been observed that the function of a play in this position is to express and release dramatic tensions generated from the layers of meaning and multiple associations in the texts of Matins. The position of the play at Mass, on the other hand, is usually at the beginning; the ritual act follows the play as conceptual and emotional consequence—the celebration of Eucharist amidst the special circumstances that identify and enhance this particular feast.

Other examples of introductory polystichs include 'Petro ad hostium' for Sts Peter and Paul, and 'Quem cernitis' for St Stephen; there is also a straight narrative for St Stephen, 'Statuerunt apostoli'. We need to understand all of these, along with 'Quem quaeritis', as extended introductory polystichs, different in textual inflection from the others but similar in phrase structure and melodic style. They were generated out of the normal development of tenth-century Frankish chant, out of the antiphon style as used in Introit tropes, combined with the question-and-answer quotations from the Gospel narrative, already present in the Gregorian repertory. Analogues that should be kept in mind (even though there are no direct connections, and many dissimilarities) are the narratives, dialogues, and dramatic scenes in the *kontakia* of the sixth and seventh centuries, and *kanons* of the eighth and ninth centuries of Byzantine chant, appearing in a tradition where stichic development combined with strophic to produce very extended, completely independent compositions.[49]

Another famous introductory polystich is 'Hodie cantandus est', a Christmas trope from St Gall.[50] The repertory there was much smaller, and in part involved prosulae. Examples such as the 'Hodie', as well as the set ascribed to Tuotilo, who can be placed at St Gall around 900, show the careful use of Latin characteristic of East-Frankish products, while the repertory as a whole does not project the sense of melodic exuberance apparent in the West. Research of St Gall tropes is hampered by the lack of diastematic notation until the twelfth century, towards the close of the trope repertory.

KYRIE ELEISON

The singing of 'Kyrie eleison' at the Roman Mass in the seventh and eighth centuries (probably in Gaul as well), involved both a simple congregational response, perhaps only 'eleison', and for at least some occasions stichs sung by the cantor.[51] Our first documentary knowledge of specific Kyries, however, comes only from Frankish times and Frankish manuscripts, from the same Tropers that have given the materials studied so far. As far as documentary evidence goes, we have to conclude that these settings of Kyrie appeared on the Frankish scene later than Gloria tropes, sequences, or Introit tropes; that only a small number appeared in the ninth century (perhaps only one), after 850; and that the earliest (like the Gloria melodies) were the most elaborate. It has often been thought that the simplest of the Kyries preserved were the earliest, and were to be identified as the congregational melodies sung in the seventh or eighth centuries. This is the same hypothesis encountered with Gloria melodies, and has the same problem, namely that the sources do not support it. Equally tenuous is the idea that the elaborate Frankish melodies preserve in their intonations and conclusions the ancient formulas used for congregational response. We can imagine, however, that these Frankish melodies do involve stylized reminiscences (as opposed to exact preservation) of certain features of the congregational rendition. In any case the Frankish Kyrie contains several distinctive features strongly suggestive of stichic practice.

---

[49] Cf. above, p. 5, 37.

[50] See Corpus troporum, 1, 1, pp. 294–7.

[51] Stäblein, 'Kyrie eleison', MGG, vii, col. 1931–46. For the Deprecatio Gelasii, a stichic combination used earlier at Rome, see Joseph Jungmann, Missarum solemnia, 2 vols. (Vienna, 5th edn., 1962), i, pp. 433–6. See also Jonsson, 'Quel sont les rapports entre Amalaire de Metz et les tropes liturgiques?', Atti del XVIII Convegno di Studi Todi 1977 (Todi, 1979).

The terminology to be used for Kyrie eleison presents problems. To approach it in the simplest way, we can see in the Frankish Kyries the succession of stichs, each ending 'eleison', that we should assume from what we know of the previous history of Kyrie. With the fixation of the number of petitions at nine (thrice 'Kyrie', thrice 'Christe', thrice 'Kyrie'), presumably by the Franks around 800,[52] we can regard the Kyrie as consisting of nine stichs, more or less equal in length (with one important exception, the ninth, to be considered), and we can call each of the nine a 'verse', as some sources label them. Calling these nine Latin stichs 'Kyrie verses' has the advantage of distinguishing them from another kind of stich that functions as an introduction to the whole Kyrie or to a section of it, much like an Introit trope, and this kind is conveniently called a 'Kyrie trope'.[53] Often such a Kyrie trope is prefixed to each group of three Kyrie verses. (It is common practice, however, to refer to the nine stichs themselves as 'Kyrie tropes', and then care must be taken to distinguish them from the three introductory tropes.)

There is a further aspect to the problem, presented by the double notation of the melodies for the nine verses of any given Kyrie. As with the sequence, these melodies are often notated twice, once in syllabic fashion with the complete verse, and again in melismatic fashion with only the text 'Kyrie eleison'. As with the sequence, at least four possibilities present themselves. First, the melismatic and syllabic versions can be sung in some kind of alternation, most likely verse by verse (this would result in an 18-fold Kyrie, for which there is at least one piece of evidence).[54] Second, either the syllabic *or* the melismatic version could be used, as desired; in modern times only the melismatic version came to be used. Third, the melismatic and syllabic versions could be sung simultaneously (the melismatic by the choir, the syllabic by the cantor).[55] Fourth, the two versions could be simply the result of a desire to make the adiastematic notation as informative as possible: melismatic notation gives a better picture of the melody, but the syllabic version is necessary for the proper alignment of notes with syllables. The first, second, and third alternatives all involve cantorial option, and the whole matter is perhaps best regarded as an aspect of stichic practice. The various possibilities do not affect the

---

[52] Andrieu, *Les Ordines romani*, Ordo IV, ii, p. 159.

[53] Bjork, 'The Kyrie Trope', *JAMS*, 33 (1980), 1–41; 'Early Settings of the Kyrie eleison and the Problem of Genre Definition', *Journal of the Plainsong & Mediæval Music Society*, 3 (1980), 40–8.

[54] Andrieu, *Les Ordines romani*, Ordo XV, iii, p. 121.

[55] Smits van Waesberghe, 'Zur ursprunglichen Vortragsweise der Prosulen, Sequenzen, und Organa', p. 252.

important structural aspects of the Kyrie melodies. The possibility of simultaneous performance (not allowed by some scholars) has interesting implications for polyphony of the eleventh and twelfth centuries.

During the ninth century (and even into the tenth) there may have been only one festal Kyrie used by the Franks, with the text incipit 'Tibi Christe supplices' (or 'Te Christe rex', Ex. 82[56]). It is essential to know this melody as an example of the new Frankish style, and it is interesting to speculate on the ways it might refer to the earlier stichic practice. Verse 1 (and 3) has the intonation rising through *ut–re–mi* that has been thought to be reminiscent of an earlier Kyrie formula. The text of each verse typically includes an acclamation, epithet, or expression of praise or petition concluding with 'eleison'; each verse is self-contained—at least, in the sense of not running over to the next verse; the syntax is loose in the manner of acclamatory *laudes*, so that the syntax of a verse may not be grammatically complete. In verses 1 to 6 there are suggestions that 'eleison' might have been slightly melismatic in another version (replacing, for instance, 'ut nostri digneris'), as is sometimes the case in other early Kyrie verses. What is involved is the possibility that the response 'eleison', sung by the congregation, might have been in a slightly different style from the cantor's stich. In the same vein, we are still close enough to an earlier *ad libitum* practice to raise at least the possibility that verses 2 and 5 represent something different from verses 1 and 3, 4 and 6. The phrase plan of this melody as preserved in the sources is *a b a c d c e f e* (extended); this becomes a frequent plan, representing a principle of alternation basic to Kyrie composition in the later repertory. The other basic plan, equally well represented by composition in the later repertory, is *a a a b b b c c c*, but only by hypothesis could this plan be projected back to the earlier practice. The fact that verses 1 and 3 are the same melody could conceivably represent a form of this Kyrie that had only two verses in the first group, and two in the second; verses 2 and 5 could be later additions. Or, the interruption of simple repetition with contrasting phrases 2 and 5 might represent one of the basic cantorial options for Kyrie; these might even be stichs to which no response was made. Finally, the subphrase repetitions with which verse 9 is extended, as well as the intensification through melodic ascent, easily suggest the shape of a call-and-response series.

---

[56] Margareta Landwehr-Melnicki, *Das einstimmige Kyrie des Lateinischen Mittelalters, Forschungsbeiträge zur Musikwissenschaft*, 1 (Regensburg, 1968), melody No. 55; Stäblein, 'Kyrie eleison'; Evans, *The Early Trope Repertory*, pp. 266 ff.; *Graduale Romanum* (and *Liber usualis*), Kyrie ad. lib. VI. Ex. 82 is from Paris B.N.lat.MSS. 1084,1118.

Ex. 82

1. Ti - bi Chri - ste sup - pli - ces ex - o - ra - mus cun - cti - po - tens,

ut no - stri di - gne - ris e - lei - son.

2. Ti - bi laus de - cet cum tri - pu - di - o ju - gi - ter at - que ti - bi

pe - ti - mus do - na et e - lei - son.

3. O bo - ne Rex qui su - per a - stra se - des et Do - mi - ne

qui cun - cta gu - ber - nas e - lei - son.

4. Tu - a de - vo - ta plebs im - plo - rat ju - gi - ter

ut il - li di - gne - ris e - lei - son.

5. Qui ca - nunt an - te te pre - ci - bus ad - nu - e

et tu no - bis sem - per e - lei - son.

6. O the - os a - gi - e sal - va vi - vi - fi - ca

re - dem - ptor no - ster e - lei - son.

7. Cla-mat in-ces-san-ter nunc quo-que con-ci-o et di-cit e-lei-son.

8. Mi-se-re-re fi-li De-i vi-vi no-bis tu e-lei-son.

9. In ex-cel-sis De-o ma-gna sit glo-ri-a e-ter-no Pa-tri

Qui nos nu-mi-ne gu-ber-nat pro-pri-o re-si-dens

in ar-ce su-per-na

Di-ca-mus in-ces-san-ter om-nes u-na vo-ce e-lei-son.

Whatever may have been the cantorial antecedents, the basic shape as presented in Ex. 82 is important for the development of the repertory. What is striking about these verses is that they are not combined with Gregorian antiphons, and are not involved in any accommodation either to neumatic antiphonal idiom or to the corresponding pitch sets. They reflect only the freely unfolding series of cantorial practice, as formalized into a nine-fold shape. In being independent the Kyrie resembles the sequence; but it differs from the sequence in having the nine-fold shape. Furthermore the thrice-three-grouping suggests symmetries and repetitions in the phrase plan not indigenous to the sequence, but thoroughly exploited in the Kyrie—not only in terms of phrase plan but especially in terms of intricate figural returns that eventually bind up a Kyrie melody in remarkable ways. This control of figure is not yet present in 'Tibi Christe supplices'; as is often the case, the large shape appears first, to be filled in by figure later. This melody does have, however, the straightforward melodic flow, shared with the sequence, that permits and encourages the control and perception of figural similarities. The melody flows in stepwise syllabic motion so smoothly that we are hardly aware how long the lines are and how much range they eventually traverse. As with sequences, the locus at any given moment is perfectly clear, the overall motion strongly directed.

Melnicki's catalogue of 226 Kyrie melodies from a large list of manuscripts (but very few English ones) shows the familiar distribution of medieval chant repertories between a relatively small group of internationally known melodies and a much larger group of those known and used only locally. The repertory starts to accumulate only in the late tenth and eleventh centuries, hence does not have a component that dates from before the split into East and West Frankish, except for 'Tibi Christe supplices'. There are clear groupings by regions, but perhaps less clear than some of the other trope repertories. Widely used melodies could be used locally with different texts. Like sequences and hymns (but unlike Gloria and Introit tropes), production of new melodies continued on after the eleventh century—at least, for melodies. The small group of widely used melodies is well represented in the modern collections of the *Graduale romanum* (and the *Liber usualis*), especially when the *ad libitum* melodies are taken into consideration.

'Clemens rector' (Kyrie *ad lib.* I) is a very large piece on the scale of 'Tibi Christe supplices'. It has a D final, with a very clear sense of locus combined with an extended range. There is a well-developed system of figural repetitions. The *ad libitum Kyries* II, III, and V are good examples of the eleventh-century Western repertory (and by this time we can refer to this repertory as 'French'). These melodies all have relatively elaborate plans, but are less extended than 'Clemens rector'. Kyries III, IV, VI, VII, and XIV (of the first series, not *ad libitum*, in the *Graduale* or *Liber usualis*) can represent the tenth-century repertory. Two of these, Kyries II (E final) and VI (G final) have the alternating phrase plan *a b a* . . ., while Kyries IV, VII (G final), and XIV (G final) have the repetitive plan *a a a*. . . . The pitch sets are classic expressions of the modal classes associated with these finals. Yet Kyrie IV, 'Cunctipotens genitor' (a widely used melody but seemingly not one of the earliest) uses the pitch set for mode 1 but with strong use of a a fifth above the expected final D; this D is used as final for verses 1 to 6, but not for 7, 8, and 9, which all end on the a. This is not the only case of an unexpected (but not unprepared) final in medieval chant; these cases need to be dealt with not in terms of modal classifications but intrinsic structure. This and other cases were sometimes corrected to conform to expectations in the eleventh-century sources themselves. More important than modal classifications, even than pitch sets, are the ways the melodies move in new,

clear lyric shapes, and the way the phrase repetitions imprint these
shapes in the ear, giving them emphasis and significance. The directed-
ness of the melodic shapes is obvious in such simple examples as the
scalar passages in the G final Kyries VII, XIV, and XII, also in the D
final Kyrie XI. In the first two of these, the scalar passages are
repeated regularly at the end of each verse (at least up to verse 6),
which has the effect of throwing into relief the varied first halves of
each verse. The sense of purposiveness, of being this way rather than
that, is an all important distinction between the style of Kyries and
sequences on one hand and the rhapsodic effusion of Graduals and
even Alleluias on the other. Even where the Kyries achieve a rhapsodic, ecstatic effect comparable to that of a Gradual—in the ninth
verse—it is accomplished with the visible, rational means of climactic
ascent and exact melodic repetition.

As in the case of Kyrie and Gloria, there seems to be one principal
Sanctus melody in the Frankish ninth- and tenth-century repertory,
shown by manuscript representation and use with tropes to be the
most favoured for feasts;[57] this melody (Thannabaur No. 223) is
preserved in the *Graduale romanum* at Mass XV. While relatively
simple in style, it is solemn and eloquent. The five lines of text are set
each to a self-contained antiphon-like melody, with a clear overall
plan brought about by using similar music for 'Pleni sunt caeli' and
'Benedictus qui venit', and the same music for the two statements of
'Osanna'. A few comparable melodies show up in the Tropers from
around AD 1000. The collection in one of the two Winchester manuscripts (as listed by Planchart[58]) includes the melody preserved in the
Graduale romanum in Mass I, as well as others not so preserved, but
seeming to share similar idioms.

The Winchester collection includes eight trope sets that probably
date from before 1000, representing the North French repertory. One
of the most popular, for Sanctus XV, is 'Ante secula Deus pater'.[59]
The four verses of this set are placed after each 'Sanctus' and before
the 'Benedictus'—a typical arrangement. The first three verses seem to
be true infix tropes: that is, the melodies show traces of motivic
connections both with the preceding 'Sanctus' and the following one.
Another representative example is 'Pater lumen aeternum'.[60]

The verse structure of Agnus dei varies in the sources and presum-

[57] Peter Thannabaur, *Das einstimmige Sanctus der römischen Messe in der handschriftlichen
Überlieferung des 11. bis 16. Jahrhundert, Erlanger Arbeiten zur Musikwissenschaft* i (Munich,
1962).
[58] Planchart, *The Repertory of Tropes at Winchester*, i, pp. 277–83.
[59] Evans, *The Early Trope Repertory*, pp. 260 f.
[60] Planchart, *The Repertory of Tropes at Winchester*, i, p. 324.

ably varied in actual performance in the ninth and tenth centuries and even later. Eighth-century Roman use seems to have involved as many repetitions as needed of the verse 'Agnus dei, qui tollis peccata mundi: miserere nobis'. Eventually the Franks fixed the number of repetitions of this invocation at three, but this fixation occurred at various times in different places. (The substitution of 'dona nobis pacem' for the last 'miserere nobis' did not become standard until the eleventh century.) The different uses of the Agnus dei verse were associated with different configurations of tropes—and the association of tropes with original is here so intimate as to make separation sometimes difficult. Gunilla Iversen, who edited the tropes for the *Corpus troporum*,[61] identified two principal tenth-century models. In the East-Frankish model, the verse 'Agnus ... nobis' came three times, with an infix trope each time between 'mundi ... miserere'. In the West-Frankish model the verse 'Agnus ... nobis' came once, followed by several tropes each followed by 'miserere nobis'. Iversen concluded that the function of the trope in this case was to amplify and develop the single invocation 'Agnus ... nobis'.

Charles Atkinson showed that the melody for Agnus dei II—or rather, the first of the three phrases as given in the *Graduale romanum* (Schildbach No. 226)—was the oldest Agnus melody preserved.[62] Like Sanctus XV, it is solemn and eloquent; it was used as the principal festal Agnus, and was the one most used with early tropes. Iversen's edition of trope texts shows that a few sets were widely used in the tenth century, and used in a variety of configurations. Most favoured were the introductory tropes 'Quem Johannes' (No. 50) and the trope set beginning 'Qui sedes ad deteram patris, solus invisibilis rex' (No. 63). These could occur together, with Agnus dei II, as at Winchester.[63] These trope melodies tend to have less character than the Agnus melody itself, that is, the tropes are closer to the neutral antiphon style observed in Introit tropes; they do, however, resemble the verse-like style used for some early Gloria tropes.

FRANKISH MUSIC THEORY

The new Frankish chant discussed in this chapter, dating from the period 850–1000, comes after the time of most intense absorption of the Roman repertory, which took place in the hundred years from 750 to 850. But the process of absorption continued after 850, while the

[61] Corpus troporum, 4, *Tropes de l'Agnus Dei* (1980), pp. 217 ff. Martin Schildbach, *Das einstimmige Agnus Dei und seine handschriftliche Überlieferung vom 10. bus zum 16. Jahrhundert* (Erlangen, 1967).
[62] 'The Earliest Agnus Dei Melody and its Trope', *JAMS*, 30 (1977), 1.
[63] Planchart, *The Repertory of Tropes at Winchester*, pp. 325 ff.

new Frankish chant was being created; it took the form of 'theory' in the sense of rationalization of tonal constructs required to grasp the Gregorian melodies. This experience of trying to make sense out of the Roman chant was eventually expressed in the distinction made by leading Frankish cantors between 'musicus' and 'cantor', between the musician who understood what he was doing, and the singer who merely kept on singing from memory what he had learned by rote.[64] The urge to understand and organize seems to underly the whole development of Frankish music theory.

We have already encountered the question of how much the Frankish cantors might have modified the Roman chant the better to systematize it. We saw the first expression of Frankish theory in the purely practical form of the tonary, the classification of antiphons (and other types of chant) according to final, in order to rationalize the matching of antiphon with psalm tone. Subsequent essays on theory continued to address practical problems and to provide pragmatic solutions. Only very gradually did this theory become truly theoretical in the sense of being either abstract or speculative. This happened more or less in the degree to which the theoretical compendia of late antiquity (Boethius mainly, but also Martianus Capella) became applicable to the problems addressed by the Frankish cantor, and compatible with the type of solution he found useful. The Franks started from the problems of singing and teaching chant; they were aware of, and admired, the model of rational theory in Boethius, but at first found little use for it. Consequently they either ignored it, or adapted fragments of it, sometimes in arbitrary ways; sometimes they took only terminology, or abstract formulations, which they then applied as they wished to rational structures of their own making. While more faithful and thorough-going recapitulations of Boethian theory can be found during this period, they always seem to be in strange isolation from the practicum of the chant, and in the guise of antiquarian studies. The tension between the theoretical models of antiquity and the practicum of the chant continued for centuries; but it was the practicum that generated the rational tone structures which provided the thrust for Western theory.

The principal problem that concerned the Frankish cantors was the framing of appropriate tonal structures for understanding the chant they had to sing. The most pragmatic approach to this problem was to find the structures in the chant itself, and this approach is manifest in the tonaries, where the theoretical components are so minimal and so

---

[64] *Hucbald, Guido and John on Music*, trans. Warren Babb, ed. Claude Palisca (New Haven, 1978), 105.

close to the chant as to be isolated only with difficulty. Aurelian of Réomé, the first theorist known to us by name, would better be described as teacher or commentator;[65] he sticks very close to the chant itself, and his analytical tools tend to be those of grammar rather than the more abstract tools of antique scale-formations—let alone mathematics. Hucbald of St Amand (c. 840–931), whom we have met as leading cantor, wrote a very important treatise, De harmonica institutione.[66] Hucbald, too, stays close to the chant, taking all his examples from the daily repertory (including, however, a first-generation sequence, 'Stans a longe'); but Hucbald has the characteristic rational, constructive approach, apparent in the way he divides up the Greater Perfect System inherited from the Greeks into tetrachords that are made out of the four finals of chant— re, mi, fa, sol— even though this tetrachord, as tetrachord, has no such function or even status in antique theory. Hucbald was trying to make sense out of the abstract, unwieldy, and largely useless Greater Perfect System by means of pitch relationships immanent in the chant and manifest in the whole and half-steps around the finals as found in the classes in the tonary.

Other Frankish theorists were to try the same approach. In general it can be observed that the patterns of tones and semitones around each of the four finals can be located on the Greater Perfect System only with difficulty and inconsistency, and the Frankish cantors looked hard for a scalar formation that would systematically accommodate the scalar patterns really but separately existing in the classes of chant. A variety of solutions, making a determined use of Boethian interval calculus, appeared in a collection of writings (the work of several theorists) known to us as the Alia musica;[67] these writings date mostly from the end of the ninth century. While characteristic in their approach, and fascinating for the variety of interpretations of what we once thought naïvely was the modal system, the solutions in the Alia musica seem no more fruitful for us than they did for singers at that time.

The solutions represented in another set of treatises, the Musica Enchiriadis and the Scolica Enchiriadis (apparently the work of one author, writing around or shortly before 900[68]) seem to have enjoyed

[65] See Lawrence Gushee, 'Some Questions of Genre in Medieval Treatises on Music', in Wulf Arlt, et al., eds., Gat'ungen der Musik in Einzeldarstellungen: Gedenkschrift Leo Schrade, i (Berne, 1973), 365.

[66] Martin Gerbert, Scriptores ecclesiastici de musica (Sankt Blasian, 1784), i, pp. 152–212; Weakland, 'Hucbald as Musician and Theorist', MQ, 42 (1956), 66; Crocker, 'Hermann's Major Sixth', JAMS, 25 (1972), 19–37.

[67] Ed. Jacques Chailley (Paris, 1965).

[68] Ed. Hans Schmid, Musica et Scolica Enchiriadis una cum aliquibus tractatuli adjunctis, Bayerische Akademie der Wissenschaften, Veröffentlichungen der Musikhistorischen Kommission, iii (Munich, 1981).

greater popularity, even though they are more drastic in nature. The author began with the tetrachord of the finals—*re, mi, fa, sol*—as Hucbald had done; but instead of locating this tetrachord alternately conjunct and disjunct on the Greater Perfect System (in effect, A, B, C, D; D, E, F, G; a, b, c, d ...; although neither this nor any other alphabetic notation was in standard use until well after 1000), the author of *Musica Enchiriadis* built a new, unheard-of scale with all the tetrachords disjunct (in effect, G, A, B flat, C; D, E, F, G; a, b natural, c, d; e, f sharp, g, a ...). The author invented a special notation ('Daseian' notation) to express this scale. Its purpose was to provide a module, the tetrachord of the finals, made out of the most familiar chant material, to be used as a tool to understand whatever formations might be encountered in chant or in any more extended scales. (The author also applied it to polyphonic singing, as discussed in chapter XI; *Musica Enchiriadis* is our earliest source for Western polyphony.)

Judging from fragments of the Daseian notation found in a number of sources, and also from the strong criticism of this scale by certain theorists after 1000, it seems to have enjoyed at least limited use during the tenth century; and indeed, while unorthodox, it is not impractical. The main reason it seems so unorthodox is that we judge it in terms of the orthodox system that was definitively established by these same critics around 1050. Considered in terms of music theory of the ninth and tenth centuries, when there was not yet a standard scale or a standard alphabetic notation—or even a standard neumatic notation with definitive pitch content—*Musica Enchiriadis* appears not wayward but rather merely as one resourceful solution among several.

Around 1000 neumatic notations developed a much greater degree of definitive pitch content. Simultaneously there was increased activity in chant theory, particularly outside the area between the Rhine and the Seine, that is in Italy and East Francia, and other areas as well. The most important group of theoretical writings came from northern Italy, and began with the *Dialogus*[69] (long ascribed to Odo, but now considered anonymous), thought to be from Northern Italy shortly before 1000. In this seminal, but very pragmatic, treatise we meet for the first time the use of the monochord to teach the beginner and to help him practise his intervals; and the use of the alphabet A to G, with repetition in the upper octave. This type of alphabet notation (as opposed to several other types introduced in the tenth century) predicates a systematic use of octave duplication—in sharp distinction to the system of *Musica Enchiriadis* with its duplication at the fifth.

---

[69] Michel Huglo, 'L'Auteur du dialogue sur la musique', *Revue de musicologie*, 55 (1969), 119.

The scale and notation of the *Dialogus* did not immediately supersede all others, but eventually it provided the basis for the scale and nomenclature that found its way into modern times (as well as for the system used in this book).

$$A\ B\ C\ D\ E\ F\ G\ a\ \genfrac{}{}{0pt}{}{\text{b natural}}{\text{b flat}}\ c\ d\ e\ f\ g\ a'$$

The thought of the *Dialogus* was carried on by Guido of Arezzo (*c.* 990–1056[70]). Also very pragmatic in approach, Guido sought a variety of means to reconcile the scale of the *Dialogus*—the most convenient scale, but still abstract like the Greater Perfect System— with the advantages of the short scalar fragments surrounding the finals and represented by the tetrachord of the finals. In Guido's *Micrologus*, around 1030, this attempt resulted in several interesting observations, and by 1050 in a tonal structure of the greatest importance, the hexachord, which can be most easily conceived as the tetrachord of the finals with a whole tone added on to each end. Even though the complete hexachord system and nomenclature (including the term itself) did not appear until later, Guido provided the solmization that came into general use for this formation: *ut | re mi fa sol | la*. The same formation was arrived at almost at the same time by Hermannus Contractus (1013–54) in Reichenau in eastern Switzerland.[71] Hermannus was the pupil of Berno of Reichenau (but Berno had come from Prüm). Berno's treatise, *Prologus in tonarium*, adapted the system of species of fourths and fifths, as used by Boethius, to make it more useful for chant; it was a good way of thinking about scale segments, but a little cumbersome. Hermannus elaborated the system of species, then moved on from that to the formation of the hexachord as a pitch set that needed to be learned in only one species; it was used to understand extended scales.

With the development of the hexachord around 1050, the search of the early Frankish theorists for a simple, rational tonal construct reached its goal. Scalar constructs, at least as used in chant, became stabilized for a time, and the results were set down in a type of treatise that on one hand became relatively standardized, and on the other hand absorbed greater and greater amounts of abstract and mathematical analysis from Boethius. Simultaneously (beginning with *Musica Enchiriadis* and continuing through Guido) another type of material on polyphony began with severely practical precepts analogous to

[70] *Micrologus*, ed. Smits van Waesberghe, *Corpus scriptorum de musica*, 4 (1955); *Hucbald, Guido and John on Music*, trans. Babb; Crocker, 'Hermann's Major Sixth'.

[71] Leonard Ellinwood, *Musica Hermanni Contracti* (Rochester, NY, 1936); Hans Oesch, *Berno und Hermann von Reichenau als Musiktheoretiker* (Berne, 1961).

those of the tonaries. These polyphonic precepts will be discussed in chapter XI.

SACRED MEDIEVAL CHANT AFTER 1000

Latin chant from 1000 to 1150 and after has not been studied in any systematic or comprehensive way. The attention of Gregorian scholars has been on the materials of the archetype, and how these might be extracted from the manuscript sources (the bulk of which, admittedly, fall into the period 1000–1150 and the following two centuries). Research on Frankish chant of the period 850–1000 has been defined by the relatively clear categories of Sequence, Trope, Hymn, or items such as Kyrie and Gloria in excelsis. There are also important studies of individual localities and manuscripts, branching out to descriptions of the larger scene as far as the author's interests and abilities permitted. What has been missing—and still cannot be provided—is a broad understanding of medieval monophony that sees Latin sacred chant as the normal musical expression of its time, yet sees that chant in a context and tradition not limited by the idiosyncrasies of the strictly Gregorian repertory.

One of the most striking aspects of sacred Latin chant after 1000 is the increase in lyricism. Phrases tend to become very clear. At its best, this quality is song-like, nostalgically familiar; when less successful it tends towards the singsong. It results in shapes that are intensive rather than expansive. This lyricism has several components, all important. Pitch sets and finals are handled with an increased sense of short-range focus. Melodic profiles within the phrase tend to be curved and recurved with clear relationship to the pitch sets. Low-level rhythms come under greatly increased control and regularization—and this is true both of the words and of the melodies, considered either apart from their words or in melismata.

Among a large variety of shapes at the higher levels of organization, it is possible to single out as the most important aspect a new integration of strophic and stichic principles. The Ambrosian hymn (cultivated continuously throughout this period as in the preceding one) is the most extreme expression of strophic form. The sequence is one kind of shape generated out of stichic combinations; the Kyrie is another such kind; these can be viewed as fixation of the combinations that in Introit tropes still responded to cantor's choice. After 1000 there is a tendency towards strophic forms that exhibit within the strophe something of the freedom and irregularity of the stichic combination.

WORDS AND RHYTHMS

The increased control exerted over low-level rhythms after 1000 was expressed both in words and in melodies (both in syllabic and melismatic passages). Later, after 1150, musicians developed systems for low-level rhythms in purely musical terms, without any necessary connection to words, and while those systems can be discussed only with reference to the new music after 1150 (Notre-Dame polyphony), it is important for us here to keep in mind such development as an end-product, in order to see that in the period 1000–1150 (as well as in monophony for a while thereafter) the object of rhythmic control is not just words.

The most difficult aspect for us is keeping separate a number of parameters that we are accustomed to perceiving in close combination—syllables, stress, length, long and short musical values, rhythms, metres, phrases. Discussion of musical rhythms (even very sophisticated modern discussions) have habitually made use of terms and concepts drawn from poetry; and if that use has sometimes been uninformed or confused, so has the reverse use of musical concepts of rhythm by students of poetic structures. We need at this point to review the basic facts concerning words and rhythms in the relevant traditions, keeping all the elements as clear and distinct as possible. Subsequent discussion can of course deal with the materials in a more synthetic way.

The student of classical Latin, in Carolingian times and down to the present, learned that each form of each word had an accent or stress on a certain syllable: 'cá-no' (I sing). Since stress was indigenous to Western languages from then on, the student had an intuitive idea of accent, which he applied to his Latin (what *kind* of accent it was in classical times is a matter that does not concern us here). He also learned that vowels can be long or short: 'ca-nō', the 'o' is long because the first person singular ending is long 'o'. The relationship between accent and quantity in classical Latin is governed by rules he and we had to learn (and may have difficulty remembering); what concerns us here is that the relationship is not expressed by the statement, 'accented syllables are long', as in the case 'că-nō', where the 'a' is short and accented, the 'o' long and unaccented.

As long as he read Cicero's prose, the student had to worry about length only in order to distinguish grammatical forms. When he came to Virgil and epic verse, he had to learn a convention of organizing the verse with long and short syllables. He had to identify which syllables were long: some were long by position, as when followed by two consonants, which made the syllable long even though the vowel was short; and some were long because the poet treated them in that way, or because the reader had to treat them in that way to make sense— 'sense' meaning conformity with the patterns of dactylic hexameter, a verse of six units (feet), in which the first four feet could be either long-short-short (dactyl) or long-long (spondee), the fifth long-short-short, the last long-indeterminate. The student learned the first line of Virgil's *Aeneid*,

$$|- \quad \cup \quad \cup \quad |- \quad \cup \quad \cup \quad |- \quad // \quad -|- \quad -|- \quad \cup \quad \cup \quad |-\underline{\cup}$$

Ár- ma vir-/úm-que cá-/no   Tró-/jae qui /prí-mus ab /ó-ris

1   2   3   4   5   6 7   8   9   10   11 12   13   14 15

with the division into feet and the long and short syllables as indicated. Later he learned a great many more verses of Virgil, and possibly went on to compose hexameters himself, following the conventions he had learned. The Carolingians wrote thousands of hexameters, including many as Introit tropes. When they set hexameters to music, as in tropes, there seems to have been no consistent musical accommodation or even acknowledgement of the hexameter rhythm—apart from the very important one of the verse as a unit. Specific accommodation could have taken two forms. The musical notes over long syllables could have been written as long; or the neumatic ornamentation could have been arranged so that the short syllables had only one or two notes, with the long syllables carrying the groups of three or four notes. Some scholars have tried to identify either or both of these possibilities in individual cases, but no general practice has been demonstrated. A third possibility is that observance was made in performance; there is no way of being sure that happened, or if so what form it took.

When the cantor sang or set a hexameter, what he did take into account was the number of syllables in the line; and also the caesura (the break in the line quoted, after 'cano'), treating this relatively long type of verse as a bi-hemistich. This treatment reflects the extremely important stage in the development of medieval poetry between the quantitative forms (such as dactylic hexameter) learned from the models of classical antiquity, and the forms governed by accent that were developed in the Middle Ages—actually in the period 1000– 1150. The overall development can be expressed in three stages: (1) quantitative (classical antique), (2) syllable counting (early medieval), (3) accentual and usually rhyming (later medieval); a full discussion would involve much qualification of this simple schema. For example, hymns by Ambrose himself are usually understood to be quantitative, in the metre 'iambic dimeter' (four feet, each short-long, in each of four verses). Furthermore, quantitative practice permits many conventionalized exceptions, and iambic dimeter is understood to allow spondees in the first and third feet (at least in the first and third verses). The first strophe of Ambrose's hymn used for Matins is printed here in two long lines instead of four short ones, to show its nature as a distich.

$$- - \mid \cup - \mid - \quad - \mid \cup - \quad - \quad - \mid \cup - \mid \cup \quad - \mid (\cup) -$$

Ae-tér-/ne ré-/rum cón-/di-tor   nóc-tem /di-ém-/que qui /ré-gis

1   2   3   4 5   6 7 8   1   2   3   4   5   6   7   8

$$\underset{\cup}{} - \mid \cup - \quad - - \mid \cup - \quad \cup - \mid \cup - \mid - - \mid \cup -$$

Et tém-/po-rum /das tém-/po-ra   ut al-/lé-ves /fas-tí-/di-um

1   2   3   4   5   6   7   8   1   2   3   4   5   6   7   8

The accents are shown immediately over the syllables; the quantities over the accents (final syllables are indeterminate but nominally long). A complete perception of the rhythmic structure would include the number and arrangement of the verses in the strophe, the number of syllables in each verse, the disposition of long and short quantities, and the disposition of accents. Faced with this very elaborate complex of rhythms, the early medieval cantor seems to have adopted a characteristically simple, reductionist view: he ignored the quantities, and finding that the accents formed no regular pattern, he ignored those too, and took into account only the number of syllables. For him, this verse form consisted of eight syllables in each of four short lines; or of sixteen syllables with a caesura in the middle, in each of two long lines. He would, of course, be aware of the word accents, and might even observe one or another in his melodic setting; but they provided no regular basis for structure.

In a very sophisticated analysis, Dag Norberg[72] has shown that, as a result of another important parameter (the disposition of word shapes in classical quantitative verse), poets writing quantitative verse in antique conventions frequently ended up with certain patterns of word accents even though they had not used these as primary determinants of the verse in the first place. For instance, to quote another verse the Carolingian student might have memorized, the first line of an Ode by Horace:

[72] *Introduction à l'étude de la versification mediévale, Studia Latina Stockholmiensia*, 5 (1958).

$$— \; ∪ \; | — \; — \; | — \; ∪ \; ∪ \; | — \; ∪ \; | — \; ∪$$

Ín-te-/ger ví-/tae sce-le-/rús-que /pú-rus

1 2 3   4 5   6 7 8   9   10 11

This is one of the 'lyric' metres, typically irregular in rhythm and floating in quality; it is the first line of a Sapphic strophe, much used by Franks especially for saints' hymns. The process traced by Norberg (and extending over the centuries of transition from the first to the tenth) results in this accent pattern.

Ín-te-ger ví-tae scé-le-rús-que pú-rus

Norberg's fascinating analysis accounts for the generation of a number of medieval accentual structures. How far, and in what ways, it affects musical forms has yet to be shown.

The ways in which word accents came to affect musical forms seems rather to have been this. Within the context of regular syllable count in couplets or strophes, word accents were also regularized. This could happen, for instance, in sequence couplets, where there was a prior tendency to match word structures in the two lines of the couplet. It most characteristically happened when the persistent assonance at the ends of lines in a couplet included the last accented syllable and became rhyme. (The word 'rhyme' is spelled in this manner because it is another manifestation of 'rhythm', since two words cannot rhyme unless their accent patterns match, and rhythm in later medieval verse is primarily a matter of matching accent patterns.) The similarity in accent pattern at the end of the lines was extended backwards along the line, and at the same time tended towards regularity—of which the simplest forms were accents occurring every other syllable and accents occurring every third syllable. Lines could begin or end with an accented or unaccented syllable. The important aspect was not the pattern itself, but the fact that, being a pattern, it reflected regularity over a longer stretch of the piece—ultimately the whole piece.

The analytic vocabulary developed by late antique metricians and rhythmicists was elaborate and comprehensive enough to describe virtually any durational configuration. For complex historical reasons, modern scholars fell into the habit of using this terminology and analysis to handle accentual syllable count in medieval verse. The result has been endless confusion. Medieval theorists also use antique terminology, but on a much more restricted basis, and with simpler, more comprehensible results. The confusing factor in modern usage has been the assumption of a necessary connection between stress and length. There may in fact be a connection made by the composer of a specific piece; but there is no necessary, systematic connection—and the overwhelming weight of medieval as well as modern practice shows this. The main point is that we can deal with accent or stress in any text without any consideration for long or short duration. In actual performance, it would seem obvious that the way to project a stressed syllable is to stress it. The consideration of a long duration to project a stressed syllable (in cases where this is not expressly desired by the composer) seems to be due to a confusion of classical quantity with medieval accent, encouraged by the inappropriate transfer of terminology from one to the other; or by a naïve conception of the relationship of words and music. Similarly, long and short durations can be discussed (as in the development of polyphony) without any necessary, systematic connection with accent.

Influential for regularization of accent was the model provided by Venantius' hymn.[73]

> Pán-ge, lín-gua, glo-ri-ó-si   próe-li-um cer-tá-mi-nis   8 + 7
> 1   2   3   4   5   6 7 8   1   2 3   4   5 6 7

Only the odd-numbered syllables carry accents, the even-numbered regularly being unaccented; also the last syllable is unaccented. The line is divided, not exactly by caesura but more by rhythmic convention, after eight syllables. (The regularity of accent in this metre, as used by Venantius, has been thought to go back to Roman marching songs, reflecting a more popular form of poetry than that represented by Virgil's sophisticated quantitative techniques.) 'Pange lingua' presents a model of a bi-hemistich of about the length of a hexameter (and close to that of half an Ambrosian strophe), with the simplest kind of rhythm—alternating accented and unaccented syllables; the two hemistichs are identical except for the end of the second one. All these ingredients were combined and recombined to form great quantities of accentual verse after 1000. The pattern received rhyme in the final accented syllables and many other places as well.

TEXT AND MELODY IN THE LATER SEQUENCE

As with all categories of chant, the chronology of individual sequences in the eleventh century has yet to be determined, and until that is done, no very precise idea of development can be gained. The direction of the development can, however, probably be represented by 'Laudes crucis attollamus', a very popular text associated with the

[73] *Analecta hymnica*, 50, p. 71.

rapidly growing cult of the Cross; the text seems to date from the later eleventh century.[74] Its melody made use of idioms already widespread in the mature sequence repertory, and was itself used for other texts, most notably 'Lauda Sion slavatorem', the sequence for Corpus Christi that is one of the five retained in the modern *Graduale romanum*. The text shows extensive use of the 8 + 7 bi-hemistich, in the very characteristic expansion 8 + 8 + 7.

> 1   Láu-des crú-cis at-tol-lá-mus   8
>   nos, qui crú-cis ex-sul-tá-mus   8
>   spe-ci-ál-i glór-i-a   7

Accents fall only on odd-numbered syllables; all even-numbered syllables are unaccented—this being the complete expression of a regularized accentual rhythm. For the time being we should still regard the last syllable of the 7-syllable line as an exception: it is not accented—at least, not by *word* accent—any more than it is at the end of the 8-syllable lines of the Ambrosian strophe. So persistent is the binary alternation of accented and unaccented syllables in the rest of the lines that an accent is easily projected upon the last syllable, and eventually musicians treat it as if it were accented; but throughout the period we are dealing with, the last word of the 7-syllable line is regularly a polysyllable of three or more syllables, with the accent on the antepenultimate.

Furthermore, the combination of 8 + 8 + 7 has to be regarded as one long verse (not three verses), even though its length exceeds the norm for verses of the Western tradition—that is, roughly the 16 syllables of a dactylic hexameter. This is an expanded bi-hemistich. The reason we know it is one verse is that it appears (in subsequent verses of this and similar sequences) as one verse of a couplet. The reason it is so long is that long lines are characteristic of sequences. The reason it can be so long, and still have the effect of shorter verses without the unmeasured effect of prose, is that it is made up of a combination of strictly measured modules—and this is the basic, central fact of the new style of text set to music in the eleventh century.

The rhymes, then, in phrase 1 ('-lámus', '-támus') are internal rhymes, not end rhymes; this is not apparent in phrase 1, but is in the sequel.

> 2a Dúlce mélos tángat cáelos   2b Vóce víta non discórdet;
>   dúlce lígnum dulci dígnum   cum vox vítam non remórdet
>   crédimus melódia.   dúlcis est symphónia.

---

[74] Ibid., 54, p. 188; Carl Allan Moberg, *Über die schwedischen Sequenzen* (Uppsala, 1927), ii, No. 1; de Goede, *The Utrecht Prosarium*, p. 83; *GR*, p. 270.

The end rhymes are 'glória', '-ódia', '-phónia'. And yet in the broad
view we should say that the effect is so hierarchical, the articulations
into phrases and subphrases carried out so consistently at different
levels, that it becomes increasingly difficult to say that the verse exists
and is measured at only one level, in one certain length.

At the lower levels the rhymes are capable of playful variation, and
enter into a more general manipulation of sense and phoneme that
runs through this style of text. In phrase 1, 'crucis attollamus crucis
exsultamus'; in phrase 2, 'dulce melos . . . caelos, dulce lignum . . .
dignum'; in phrase 2b, 'non discordet . . . non remordet', preceded by
'voce vita . . . vox vitam'. Combined with the propulsion of the regular
accents, this manipulation of phonemes produces very strong rhythmic inflections, within the framework of the exactly regular phrase
lengths and configurations. Indeed, rhythm in these texts is completely manifested in, and expressed by, such combinations of phrase
structure, rhyme, and accent pattern. The rhythms are very strong and
unmistakable: they require no additional feature in performance, or
explanation in analysis. To say that such texts require, or demonstrate, a musical setting in long and short durations is to introduce a
gratuitous rhythmic dimension, and to misunderstand the nature of
rhythm manifest in the text as it stands. To be sure, the text *can* be
performed with odd-numbered syllables given a duration twice as
long as even-numbered syllables, and the result is a blatant reinforcement of the already obvious accentual pattern. Or it can be performed
with the odd-numbered syllables short and the even-numbered syllables long, with the result being equally insistent but oblique in
quality. Or it can be performed without difference of duration, in
which case the rhythms inherent in the words manifest themselves
directly. In the eleventh century notation the melodies are without
differentiation of long and short values, and there is no reason to
provide any such differentiation.

The relationship of the textual rhythms to the melodic shape has
several interesting and important aspects. At the highest level, each
phrase of melody is repeated to accommodate the couplets in the text
(2a, 2b, etc.) in traditional sequence fashion—only now, with many of
the phrases exactly the same length and structure (phrases 2, 4, 5, 6, 7,
8, 9) the disposition of the melodic phrases has an important function
in marking off the text phrases and in identifying this as a sequence
not a hymn (Ex. 83). Within the phrase, the melody has relatively little
articulation into subphrases: while it shapes itself smoothly enough to
the eight-syllable subphrases, it does not usually mark them off with
conventional cadences, nor does it usually dispose itself to reinforce

Ex. 83

1. Lau - des cru - cis at - to - la - mus nos qui cru - cis ex - u - la - mus

spe - ci - a - li glo - ri - a.

2a. Dul - ce me - los tan - gat cae - los dul - ce li - gnum dul - ci di - gnum

cre - di - mus me - lo - di - a.

3a. Ser - vi cru - cis cru - cem lau - dent qui per cru - cem si - bi gau - dent

vi - tae da - rent mu - ne - ra.

4a. Di - cant om - nes et di - cant sin - gu - li a - ve sa - lus to - ti - us sae - cu - li

ar - bor sa - lu - ti - fe - ra.

5a. Haec est sca - la pec - ca - to - rum per quam Chri - stus rex cae - lo - rum

ad se tra - xit om - ni - a.

(etc.)

the accent patterns. And the frequent groups of two or three notes for a syllable show no tendency to support accents. The co-ordination of melodic pattern and textual rhythm is almost completely concentrated in the use of melodic cadences, all on the same pitch (G–*sol–ut*), at the end of each phrase (1, 2a, 2b, 3a, 3b, etc.). In this way, combined with the repetitions for couplets, the melody underlines the larger rhythms.

The conduct of the melody line within the phrase is remarkably agile and far-ranging, even though graceful and smooth in its effect. It can, and frequently does, cover an octave within the phrase, a sixth within the subphrase. The motion is sometimes almost completely scalar, with very little inflection, and at other times involute, yet always subsumed under the very strong overall shape. Equal in importance to the rhythmic components of this shape are the tonal ones: the melody moves within a large but clearly defined and maintained pitch set framed by the fifth and octave G–d–g, with occasional use of a realm extending a fourth or fifth below the G. The pitch set seems to be potentially present at all times, so that the melody is capable of moving anywhere within the set at any time. Long-range melodic direction has much less function than in the earlier sequence; dwelling within a register still operates—we can still identify some phrases or subphrases as lying high or low—but the mobility of the line makes this a matter of emphasis rather than actual restriction to a register. All of these features of melodic organization seem characteristic of eleventh-century melody, which often produces an effect of great warmth and brilliance by continuously filling out an extended pitch set. The same general statement might be made about the Gregorian melismatic style; but by now (three centuries later) the style of melodic inflection—not to mention the rhythmic regularity— makes the difference obvious.

Almost by surprise, we note that the traditional features of the sequence are maintained, at least in principle. After 3a, a regular phrase $8 + 8 + 7$, there is an element $10 + 10 + 7$ that is either part of an overcouplet, or a single of the kind and at the place we would expect one in the older sequence (the sources, characteristically, hesitate about the treatment of this element). The regularity through phrases 4–9 is striking and novel; in phrases 10–12 a gesture towards a different phrase length is made, taking the form of adding eight-syllable modules—first $8 + 8 + 8 + 7$, then $8 + 8 + 8 + 8 + 7$. The appearance of exceptionally lyric subphrases (10: 'semper facit'; 11: 'mundi vera'; 12: 'atque servos') also maintains old traditions of the sequence.

'Laudes crucis' is one of the more regular eleventh-century sequences, and in that respect may well represent the most important tendencies of its time—as shown in its own popularity and in its indirect representation (through 'Lauda Sion') in the post-Tridentine repertory. Other sequences could be less regular, more like the older models. 'Congaudentes exultemus',[75] for the new St Nicholas Office— also very popular in the twelfth century—uses an 8 + 7 module both in combination with another 8 and in other more complex and indivi- dual combinations. 'Mane prima sabbati',[76] reflecting the cult of Maria Magdalena (similarly current in the twelfth century), begins with seven-syllable modules (7 + 7 + 7, 7 + 7 + 7 + 7), then shifts to eight syllables with such a remarkably forceful low-level rhythm that it is heard rather as fours: 'Quae dum plorat/ et mens orat/ facto clamat/ quod cor amat,/ Jesum super omnia' (Ex. 84). Other ex- amples, including 'Ave Maria gratia plena',[77] 'Stola jucunditatis',[78] 'Missus Gabriel',[79] and 'Rex Salomon',[80] all show various accommo- dations of the older sequence with the newer styles of text and melody.

ASPECTS OF MELODIC STYLE IN VARIOUS CHANTS

The textual elements we have been discussing—syllable count, rhyme and accent, verse and groups of verses—are among the most promi- nent shaping forces in music of the eleventh century; and these elements become more prominent as the elements are progressively abstracted from the traditional forms in which they came to the Franks, and reconstituted and recombined in new ways. In an important sense, medieval chant never did produce a refined melisma- tic style comparable to that of the Gregorian repertory. Frankish melismata appeared as large, highly structured events, relatively self- contained (often insertable and detachable) and not integrated into the whole piece. The other characteristic appearance of melismata was in the alternate notations for sequence and Kyrie melodies: if these notations represent actual melismatic performance, then of course there was a repertory of Frankish melismatic chant, but in that case it was just as isolated from text—more so, in fact—than were the detachable melismata. During the period 1000–1150 the primary

---

[75] *Analecta hymnica*, 54, p. 95; Moberg, *Sequenzen*, No. 22; de Goede, *The Utrecht Prosarium*, p. 111.
[76] *Analecta hymnica*, 54, p. 214; Moberg, *Sequenzen*, No. 8; de Goede, *The Utrecht Prosarium*, p. 34.
[77] *Analecta hymnica*, 54, p. 337; Moberg, *Sequenzen*, No. 34; de Goede, *The Utrecht Prosar- ium*, p. 63.
[78] *Analecta hymnica*, 54, p. 86; Moberg, *Sequenzen*, No. 63.
[79] *Analecta hymnica*, 54, p. 298; Moberg, *Sequenzen*, No. 54.
[80] *Analecta hymnica*, 55, p. 35; Moberg, *Sequenzen*, No. 60.

Ex. 84

1. Ma - ne pri - ma sab - ba - ti sur - gens de - i fi - li - us

no - stra spes et glo - ri - a

5a. Quae dum plo - rat et mens o - rat

fac - to cla - mat quod cor a - mat

Je - sum su - per om - ni - a

6a. O Ma - ri - a ma - ter pi - a stel - la ma - ris ap - pel-la - ris

o - pe - rum per me - ri - ta

(etc.)

determinant of musical form seems to have been the texts and the new shapes they took.

Primary, but not only: running parallel to the regularization of syllable count and accent in the text, that is, a regularization of rhythm, was a regularization of melody, operating in syllabic, neumatic, and melismatic passages alike. This regularization expressed itself in a finely crafted flow of figural (motivic) repetition and development. This had always been a distinctive feature of Frankish as opposed to Roman—even Frankish-Roman—chant, and was steadily refined and maximized. In some kinds of chant during the eleventh century this kind of figural control shows clearly. Sometimes it enters into dialogue with manipulation of textual element—and sometimes in ways so intricate that we cannot tell whether the procedure is basically musical or textual.

Ex. 85

A familiar example is provided by Kyrie IX[81] (Ex. 85); first documented in the twelfth century, and presumably dating from shortly after 1100, this melody was provided with Latin verses beginning 'Cum jubilo'. In its larger shape it faithfully reflects the practice of the tenth century, while the extent to which figural control is carried out shows how such shapes could be filled after 1000. The figures involved are from four to eight notes long. In the first verse we have to distinguish three figures—the first eight notes, the next four, and the last eight. Comparison of successive verses will show how some of these figures are retained, while new ones are introduced; how figures return from earlier verses, and are recombined. These figural recombinations overlap the arrangement of 'Kyrie' and 'Christe' in complex ways. The seventh verse transposes the figure from the second verse into the upper octave. The immediate repetition of figure in the last verse continues the basic practice of Frankish melismata; but within a piece in which so much control is exerted, this practice seems to have a new force. And the figural control is closely integrated with the tonal framework, so that D–a–d emerges as completely stable, informing us at all times of the location and progress of the line.

The period 1000–1150 and after provides us with by far the larger numbers of settings of Kyrie, Gloria, Sanctus and Agnus dei, for those that can be reliably dated before 1000 are not so numerous. The Gloria melodies present an interesting situation since their text does not reflect the new syllable count and accent. The new Gloria melodies tend to use the mobile wide-ranging melodies seen in the new sequence, in a looser and sometimes curious relationship to the text. Gloria ad lib. I[82] (Ex. 86) uses an elaborate figural system spread out over a strenuous range, in relatively close correlation with the stichic structure. As the piece continues, it becomes clear that a group of phrases set out in the ecstatic high register is rounded off by one in the low register, seemingly an old pattern. What is new is the effect of exact figural return in cases such as 'voluntatis . . . Jesu Christe . . . Jesu Christe . . . Dei', and the way the G or d can resonate like a bell when struck by the passing line. The penultimate descent on 'patris' seems a knowing modern reference to ancient practice, framed by the extension of the figural system into the 'Amen'. Gloria IX,[83] using the same pitch set on G sol–ut, shows the same exuberant movement

---

[81] Graduale Romanum, Mass IX; Melnicki, Das einstimmige Kyrie des lateinischen Mittelalters, Forschungsbeiträge zur Musikwissenschaft, i (Regensburg, 1968), No. 171; Analecta hymnica, 47, p. 160.

[82] Graduale Romanum, ad. lib. I; Bosse, Untersuchungen einstimmiger mittelalterlicher Melodien, No. 24.

[83] Graduale Romanum, Mass IX; Bosse, No. 23.

Ex. 86

Glo - ri - a   in   ex - cel -   sis De - o.

Et in ter - ra pax ho - mi - ni - bus bo - nae vo - lun - ta - tis.

Lau - da - mus te Be - ne - di -   ci - mus te

A - do - ra - mus te Glo - ri -   fi - ca - mus te.

Gra - ti - as a - gi - mus ti - bi prop - ter ma - gnam glo - ri - am tu - am.

Do - mi - ne de - us, Rex cae - le - stis, De - us pa - ter om - ni - po - tens.

Do - mi - ne Fi - li u - ni - ge - ni - te Je - su Chri - ste.

Do - mi - ne de - us A - gnus de - i Fi - li - us Pa - tris . . .

(etc.)

throughout the set with perhaps less economy of figural control.
Gloria II[84] has the same kind of movement based on D *re*; figural
control is less evident here, but a larger melodic grouping is more
evident: the stichs are arranged into paragraphs as the melody runs
through roughly the same cycle of phrases six times ('. . . voluntatis,
. . . gloriam tuam . . .'). Gloria V,[85] on G *sol–ut*, also cycles through a
set of phrases, and more strictly, but here the large melodic grouping
is shorter (it begins on 'Laudamus', again on 'Gratias').

[84] *Graduale Romanum*, Mass II; Bosse, No. 19.
[85] *Graduale Romanum*, Mass V; Bosse, No. 25.

Melodies for Sanctus proliferated after 1000. The catalogue by Peter Thannabaur lists 230 melodies, with many additional variants.[86] Production of new melodies was most intense during the eleventh and twelfth centuries in France, slightly later in Germany. As usual, the repertory includes a small number of very favoured, 'universal' items, along with a much larger number represented only in a few sources, reflecting local practice. The universal melodies are well represented in the *Graduale Romanum* and include Sanctus II (Thannabaur No. 203), IV (No. 49), VIII (No. 116), XI (No. 202), XII (No. 177), XVII (No. 32), XVIII (No. 41). Items with more restricted distribution include Sanctus I (No. 154), III (No. 56), VI (No. 17), VII (No. 54), IX (No. 33), XIV (No. 184). Some of these continue the practice of setting the Sanctus text as five distinct verses, usually with literal repetition of the melody of the first 'Osanna' for the second. The melodies themselves show increased concern for finely wrought design, with sometimes intricate and often very lyric contours. Occasionally a charmingly song-like quality appears, as in one of the most popular of all, Sanctus XVII. Somewhat more serious and elaborate are Sanctus XI and XII.

The explicit repetition of melody for the two 'Osanna' is sometimes carried through in a special and interesting manner in certain of the other most favoured melodies, such as Sanctus VIII, II, and especially IV. A relatively small number of motives is used throughout a melody, and while it is clear that motives are being repeated, the pattern of repetitions is sometimes not so clear. Sanctus IV (a very widely used melody) shows interesting dislocations in the series of motives, and of their alignment with the phrases of text; the effect is one of casual disordering, but the intent seems to be carefully conceived and worked out, perhaps for the sake of a mystical rendering of the text.

The Sanctus continued to be troped, most often with an infix verse after each 'Sanctus', often with an additional verse later, and sometimes with an introductory trope. (Thannabaur's interim list of tropes includes 239 items.) A special kind of trope was sometimes provided in the guise of a prosula for an 'Osanna' melisma.[87] These texts were sometimes cast in the new forms using syllable count, accent, and rhyme.

Melodies for Agnus dei also proliferated after 1000.[88] These melodies tended to emphasize the integrity of the individual phrase for

[86] *Das einstimmige Sanctus.*

[87] Thannabaur, 'Anmerkung zur Verbreitung und Struktur der Hosanna-Tropen in deutschsprachigen Raum und den Ostlandern', in Martin Ruhnke, ed., *Festschrift Bruno Stäblein zum 70. Geburtstag* (Kassel, 1967), p. 250.

[88] Schildbach, *Das einstimmige Agnus Dei.*

each invocation of the Agnus dei. While the most favoured melodic arrangement for the (gradually standardized) plan of three invocations was *a b a*, this arrangement seems to have been introduced as a way of varying the older use of the same melody for all invocations. At any rate, the use of a different melodic phrase for the middle invocation shows traces of an *ad libitum* practice. The first phrase, the main one, attains great lyricism and eloquence in the best examples, which show carefully sculptured designs, often with an arch form rising expressively to the mid-point. Relatively well-known melodies preserved in the *Graduale romanum* are Agnus dei I (Schildbach No. 236), IV (No. 136), VI (No. 89), XV (No. 209), XVI (No. 164), and XVII (No. 34), all dating possibly from the eleventh century. Slightly later examples are Agnus dei III (No. 161), IX (No. 114), XI (No. 220), XII (No. 267), XIV (No. 100), and ad lib. I (No. 95). Many of these—but by no means all—are troped in one or several sources. But while Schildbach's catalogue lists 267 Agnus dei melodies (and numerous variants), the edition of trope texts in the *Corpus troporum* includes only 78 sets of tropes.[89] In the large majority of Agnus dei melodies, each is represented in only one local repertory (one manuscript, or very few closely related). Perhaps we can see in this a gradual shift of interest from tropes to the Agnus dei itself; individualization was apparently achieved through a distinctive musical setting rather than by addition of tropes. The prevalence of local use shows the desire of cantors, choirs, and congregations to have their own melodies here even more than with Sanctus. And for both Sanctus and Agnus dei the production of new melodies in the eleventh, twelfth, and thirteenth centuries seems to dovetail with the production of polyphonic settings of these texts in the fourteenth and fifteenth centuries.[90]

The production of chants for those texts not set in the Gregorian repertory paralleled the production of new antiphons and responsories for the Office. Much more careful study of all these kinds of chant is needed to make clear the distinguishing factors of medieval chant styles. Somewhere in between these two groups lies the repertory of votive antiphons—as yet virtually unmapped. At some point in the development of the Monastic Office (just when has not been made clear) it became customary to commemorate saints or feasts other than the principal one being celebrated by singing merely an appropriate antiphon, followed by a versicle and response, and a collect, to

[89] Iversen, *Corpus troporum*, 4, *Tropes de l'Agnus Dei* (1980).

[90] See Julian Brown, Sonia Patterson, and David Hiley, 'Further Observations on W₁', *Journal of the Plainsong & Mediæval Music Society*, 4 (1981), 53.

form a typical combination. There was nothing to prevent a psalm from being included; but since the commemoration occurred in addition to the psalmodic cursus for the day, there was no particular reason to have one, and the proper antiphon was used by itself. One of the results of the growing cult of the Virgin Mary was the regular addition of a commemorative antiphon at the end of Compline, and of the many antiphons in honour of Mary composed during this period (and later), four eventually became fixed on a seasonal basis— 'Alma redemptoris Mater' (winter), 'Ave Regina caelorum' (spring), 'Regina caeli' (Easter to Pentecost), and 'Salve Regina' (season after Pentecost).[91] Two of these used to be ascribed to Hermannus Contractus but are now considered anonymous,[92] and thought to date from the twelfth century. The sources do not suggest the immediate popularity of, say, 'Laudes crucis', and the story of how they became installed as ordinary at Compline has yet to be told. Compared to such other examples of Marian antiphons as are available, they show excellent qualities; as is elsewhere the case, the selection that resulted in the repertory preserved in modern chant books was informed and discriminating. From an historical point of view, however, the position of these four antiphons will require some investigation. Like the chants for Gloria and Sanctus, beneath a seemingly conservative format they conceal modern features of twelfth-century chant: some are organized around couplets (freely interpreted in prose texts and only approximate melodic repetition); most move within a very strong octave framework; three are based on *ut* and the other on *re*. All show the closed, lyric phraseology of later medieval chant, only superficially deflected by neumatic style.

This kind of inner lyricism, operating without many of the outward mechanisms of regular accent, obvious rhyme, and exact correspondence of syllable count, appeared frequently in later medieval chant. Perhaps one of its most extreme manifestations, certainly an engaging one, is in the antiphons, responsories, hymns, and sequences of Hildegard of Bingen (1098–1179), Abbess of a Benedictine house in the Rhineland.[93] She experienced visions throughout her later years, from about 1150 onwards, and expressed these visions in a variety of literary and musical forms, including the kinds of chant named. Her poetic language was ecstatic, rich with fantastic imagery inspired by her inner vision of her subject, which was most often the Blessed

[91] *Antiphonale Romanum*, pp. 54–7; *Liber usualis*, Sunday at Compline.

[92] Oesch, *Berno und Hermann*, pp. 148–53.

[93] *Hildegard von Bingen: Lieder*, ed. Pudentia Barth, M. Immaculata Ritscher, and Joseph Schmidt-Görg (Salzburg, 1969).

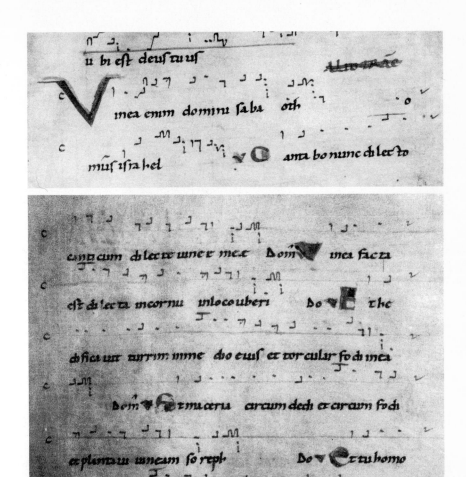

I. ROME, BIBLIOTECA VALLICELLIANA, C. 52, fo. 79r (*bottom*), fo. 79v (*top*)

Part of Holy Saturday tract *Vinea enim domini* (possibly Old-Roman)

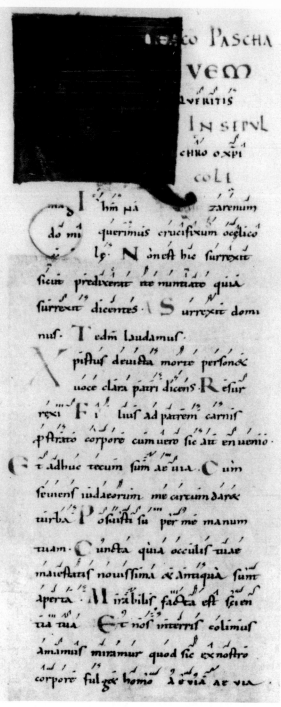

II. PARIS, BIBLIOTHÈQUE NATIONALE, FONDS LATIN, 9448, fo. 33v
Easter dialogue, introit *Resurrexi* with trope verses *Christus devicta morte*, etc.

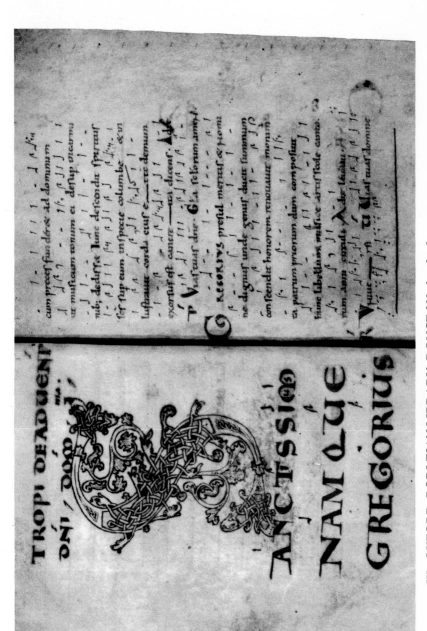

III. OXFORD, BODLEIAN LIBRARY, DOUCE 222, fos. 2v–3r

Tropes *Sanctissimus namque Gregorius* and *Gregorius presul meritis* for the introit *Ad te levavi*

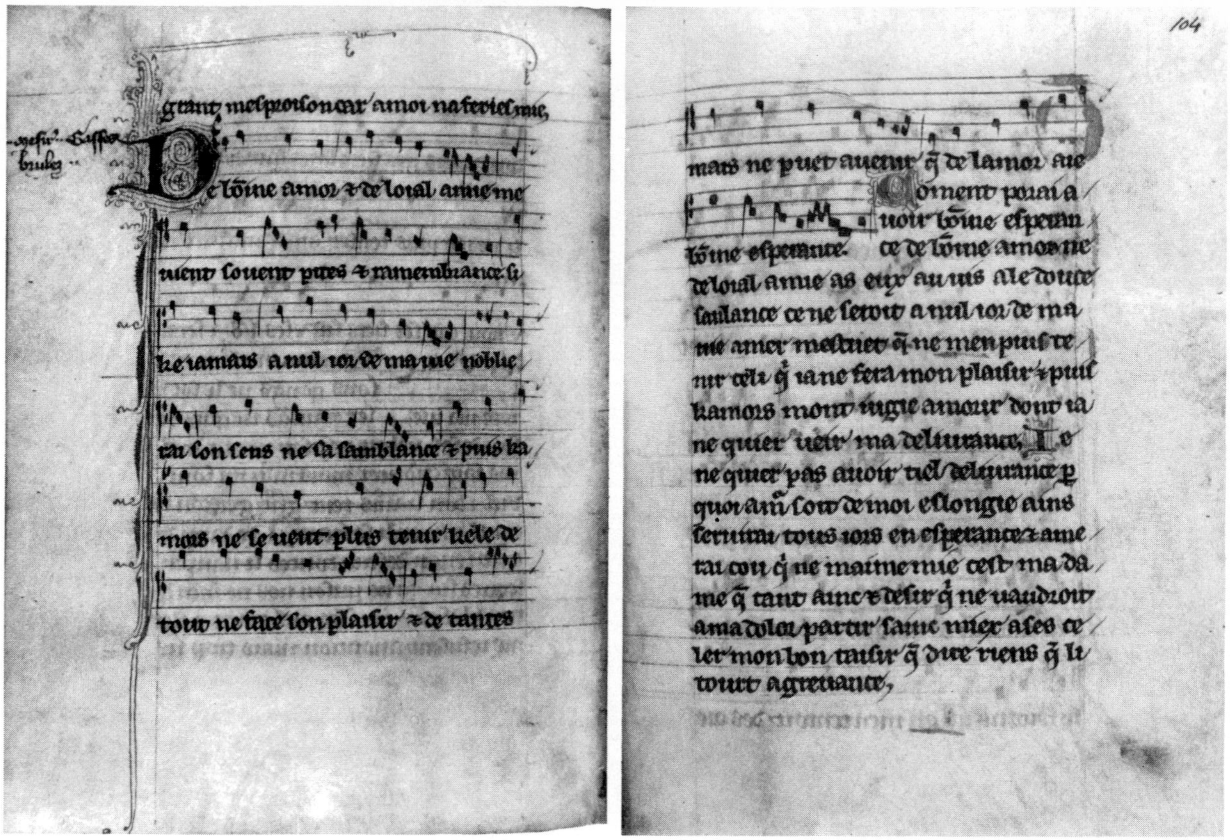

IV. LONDON, BRITISH LIBRARY, EGERTON 274, fos. 103v–104r

End of Jehans de Neufvill *Desoremais est raisons*, Gace Brulé *De boinne amor et de loial amie*

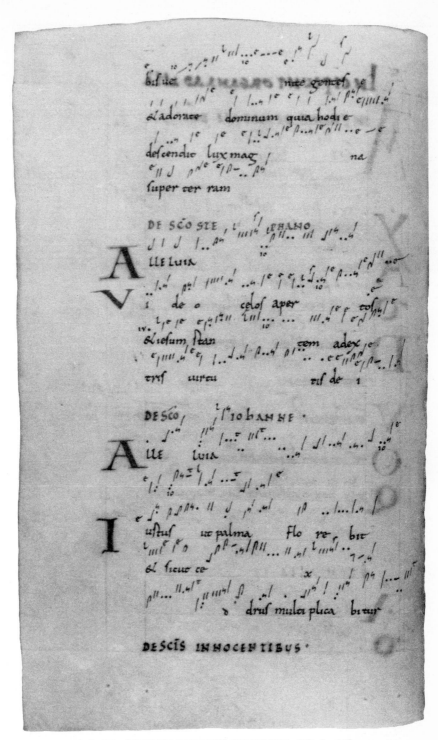

V. CAMBRIDGE, CORPUS CHRISTI COLLEGE, 473, fo. 163v

Organum for Alleluias *Dies sanctificatus* (end only), *Video celos* and *Iustus ut palma*

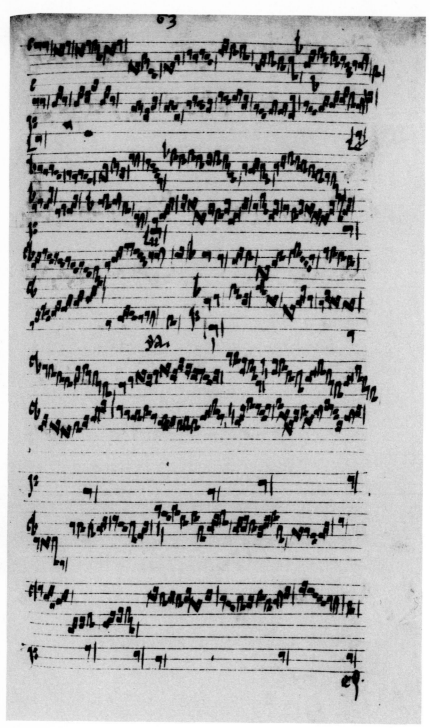

VI. WOLFENBÜTTEL, HERZOG-AUGUST-BIBLIOTHEK, HELMSTEDT
628, fo. 63r [55r]

Alleluia dies sanctificatus (a3)

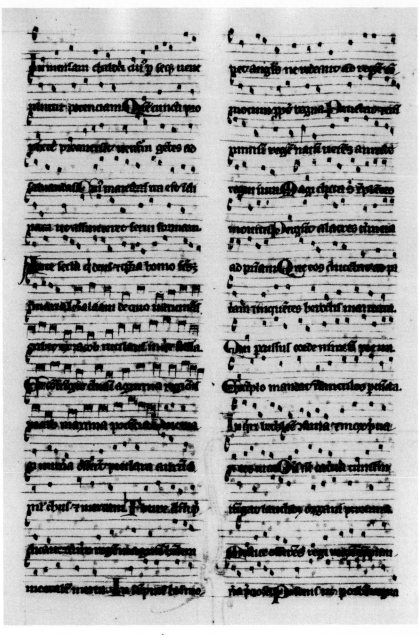

VII. PARIS, BIBLIOTHÈQUE DE L'ARSENAL, 135, fo. 240v

Part of sequence *Epiphaniam domino*, 'Balaam' verses notated with large note-heads

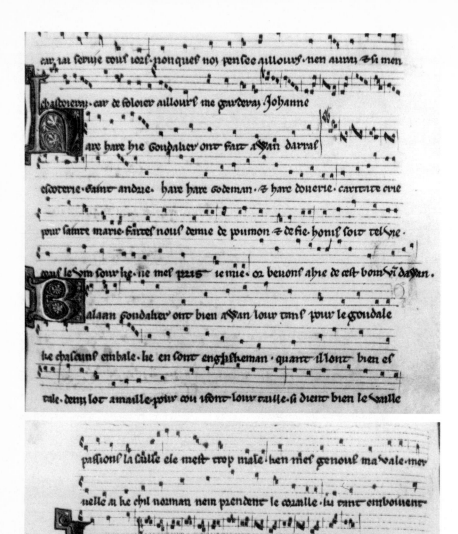

VIII. PARIS, BIBLIOTHÈQUE NATIONALE, FONDS FRANÇAIS 12615,
fo. 180r (*bottom*), fo. 180v (*top*)

Motet *Hare hare hie/Balaan Goudalier/Balaam*

Virgin Mary or Saint Ursula (martyred with her companions in antiquity at Cologne). The traditional forms of antiphon and responsory are maintained, although the pieces are sometimes long (as often happens in the later treatment of these forms). The sequences, however, depart from Frankish norms and instead have the free prose shapes of Psalter texts and either approximate melodic parallelism or none at all. Chant for Hildegard seems to have been a melodic response to her inner vision, a cantorial effusion that used the standard neumatic language but with an extraordinary intensity and individual inflection. The neumatic ornamentation is rich and heavy, the ranges great, the melodic motion active. The lyricism is often very persuasive.

AQUITANIAN *VERSUS*

Comparison of chant such as Hildegard's with Aquitanian novelties from around 1100 shows what a wide variety of things took place within the development of later medieval chant. These developments were local: we need to know the musical repertories at monastery after monastery, is possible over a period of a century or two at each place. As it is, we know of only a few places, one of them being St Martial of Limoges, where were preserved most of the Aquitanian repertories of tropes and sequences.[94] One of the most remarkable accidents of preservation is the manuscript Paris B.N.lat. 1139, from St Martial(?) *c.* 1100: it contains the most extensive cross-section of new forms and styles of Aquitanian chant of its time.

The items that concern us at the moment are a series of some forty chants with intensely rhyming texts, in content mostly associated with the cycle of Christmas festivities (including much acclamation of the Virgin), and perhaps intended for use in the Office during this season. Many are marked 'versus' in the manuscript, and this is the most convenient term for the category of chant; here we have to understand this term (overworked in the Middle Ages) specifically in the sense, also traditional, of 'organized line'—organized here with syllable count, regular accent, and rhyme. Some of the *versus* conclude with the words 'Benedicamus domino ... Deo gratias', which is a versicle and response used at the end of Matins, Lauds, and Vespers; the quotation, which is integrated into the rhyme and scansion of the *versus*, indicates their use at the conclusion of those Offices.

[94] Stäblein, 'St. Martial', *MGG*, xi (1963), cols. 1262–72; Chailley, *L'École musicale de St. Martial de Limoges* (Paris, 1960); Evans, *The Early Trope Repertory*. See also Nancy van Deusen, *Music at Nevers Cathedral: Principal Sources of Mediæval Chant*, Musicological Studies, *30/1–2* (Institute of Medieval Music, 1980).

The variety of forms is bewildering, but the common element is the intense use of rhyme and accentual scansion in the texts, which may operate in close conjunction with melodic organization or independently of it. The rhyme is notable for its own sake.[95]

Radix Jesse castitatis	li-li-um	11
stella novum nova profert	ra-di-um	11
rosa mitis et conculcans	li-li-um	11
exultatis, captivatis,		8
morti datis, mater natis		8
dedit gratis vite	bre-vi-um	9
Nova profert	ra-di-um	7
virgo dei	fi-li-um	7
qui est salus	om-ni-um	7
qui non habet in-	i-ti-um	8
in hoc venit ex-	i-li-um	8
dare nobis con-	si-il-um	8
Cujus in prae-	co-ni-a	7
intonet ar-	mo-ni-a	7
resonet sym-	pho-ni-a	7
a patri nato		5
athanato		4
athanato		4
de virgine	Ma-ri-a	7
Ergo per haec	gau-di-a	7
gaudet caeli	cu-ri-a	7
gaudeat ec-	cle-si-a	7
vociferans pro-	di-gi-a	8
per haec sacra sol-	lem-ni-a	8
patrem natum de	fi-li-a	8
per haec sacra sol-	lem-ni-a	8

All the end rhymes (except 'María') are proparoxytone ('lílium'). Most of the lines are either 11 syllables long or 7 or 8; those 11 or 7 have the end rhyme, those in 8 vary: if they have the end rhyme, an extra syllable is placed usually in the middle, interrupting the regular alternation of accent; or the 8-syllable lines appear in connection with internal paroxytone rhymes ('-átis'). In each of the four large sections of this text there seems to be a progression from regularity at the beginning through some kind of irregularity or at least change. The most intense internal rhymes seem to appear at the breakdown of the line pattern established at the beginning.

[95] Leo Treitler, *The Aquitanian Repertories of Sacred Monody in the Eleventh and Twelfth Centuries* (University Microfilms International, 1978), iii, No. 5, p. 28.

As with all chant, the structure of the text is intimately associated with the melodic structure in syllabic passages, less associated in neumatic or melismatic passages. In the large, heavily melismatic versus such as 'Ex Ade vitio',[96] 'Laetabundi jubilemus',[97] 'Senescente mundano filio',[98] 'Omnis curae homo',[99] or 'Novum festum celebremus',[100] the text structure does not directly affect the melismatic passages. They are, however, distinctly different from the Gregorian in style, even from previous Frankish melismatic style. These in the Aquitanian *versus* tend to fill out the pitch set with direct stepwise (that is, scalar) motion, relieved often by simple repetition or melodic sequence (Ex. 87).[101] These are not usually in the form of the grand replacement melisma, with repetitive figural pattern in the form *aab*, but more in the nature of extended neumatic overlay. Neither the intricate 'reiterative' style of the Gregorian melismatic chant, or the 'fluttery' style of the responsories is in evidence.

Ex. 87

Tra - xit   pri - mor -   di - a.

Melismatic *versus* of this type are often in sections, and the sections may contrast in style, some being almost completely syllabic—a kind of differentiation not found in traditional responsories. In 'Laetabundi jubilemus' the first section is largely syllabic; it frames middle sections that are heavily melismatic. The whole might be regarded as an analogue of a responsorial form such as Alleluia, with a very elaborate verse. In 'Ex Ade vitio' and 'Alto corde gaudeamus' the shift in style is associated with shifts in line structure, such as those in the text of 'Radix Jesse'. The varying line structures of many of these texts suggest stichic combinations—only here, as in the sequence, the texts we have are the result not of cantorial option but of composition, producing the effect of a *ad libitum* combination in a deliberate, self-conscious way.

Another sign of contact with the stichic tradition is the frequent use of refrains; some, as in 'Castitatis lilium'[102] or 'Plebs domini'[103] are relatively short; others, such as 'Lilium floruit',[104] seem to be long or complex. Much about the way the refrains were used needs further

[96] Idem, No. 1, p. 25.   [99] Idem, No. 22, p. 39.   [102] Idem, No. 16, p. 36.
[97] Idem, No. 8, p. 31.   [100] Idem, No. 29, p. 44.   [103] Idem, No. 12, p. 34.
[98] Idem, No. 19, p. 38.   [101] Idem, No. 11, p. 33.   [104] Idem, No. 14, p. 35.

clarification, and one of the striking things about the repertory of Aquitanian *versus* is the variety and fluidity of formal structures at the sectional level.

Patterns at the level of individual lines are most easily perceived at the beginning of *versus*. A few begin with the same melodic phrase repeated several times, as in 'Eva virum dedit'.[105] Some, like 'Noster cetus',[106] have clear bi-hemistichs (in this case 8 + 7), but continue on without melodic repetition. Still others, such as 'Virginis in gremio',[107] begin with the first two bi-hemistichs (7 + 7) grouped into a distich and set as a couplet (repetition of the melody) (Ex. 88). The couplet structure is typically not carried out after the opening; succeeding lines, even if the same length and pattern, are set to a dazzling succession of changing melodic phrases. These can occasionally resemble in grouping the sequence ('Sollemnia praesentia'), occasionally take on strophic repetition ('Resonemus hoc natali'), but more often are free extensions, carried forward by the momentum of the regularity of count and accent set in an easy syllabic style. This momentum makes the verses flow together and fuse, so that the length of the verse is no longer determinate—it might contain four syllables, or eight, or sixteen, or thirty-two. And something analogous happens to the melodic shapes. They can be miraculously clear and plastic, as in 'Plebs domini', with its refrain 'Mariam vox, Mariam cor' (Ex. 89), or 'Annus novus in gaudio';[108] or simply run together in true *melos*, unending flow, as in 'Virginis in gremio', with a rhapsodic effusion comparable to the Gregorian melisma but from a different world.

The units of text and melody we have been discussing are long and complex. They resemble traditional stichic combinations in containing verses of various lengths and patterns, and sometimes refrains. In another sense, and at another level, they are often strophic, in one of two ways. The whole melodic unit may be repeated with a second strophe of text; or only the structure of the text may be repeated, with new text and new melody. Typically there are two strophes (as when the first ends 'Benedicamus', the second 'Deo gratias'), or if more, then not many more. This requires us to take a broader view of strophic than we have heretofore. Our model of strophic composition so far has been the Ambrosian strophe—four lines of eight syllables each, which can be considered as two lines of sixteen, each line a bi-hemistich, together forming a distich (8 + 8, 8 + 8). The other common hymn strophes are the 'Pange lingua' type (8 + 7, 8 + 7, 8 + 7), and the Sapphic (5 + 6, 5 + 6, 5 + 6, 5). If we regard as strophic anything with a

---

[105] Idem, No. 18, p. 37.   [107] Idem, No. 24, p. 41.
[106] Idem, No. 9, p. 32.   [108] Idem, No. 2, p. 26.

Ex. 88

Vir - gi - nis in gre - mi - o   ma - net lux in - fi - ni - ta,

na - sci - tur in me - di - o   ter - re sa - lus et vi - ta,

cu - jus in ob - se - qui - o   vox pa - tris est au - di - ta.

Nam sub-di - tur in - fan - ci - ae   mi - rae gi - gas po - ten - ti - ae

et ge - mi - ne sub -stan-ti - ae   no-bi-li - tan-da, cla - ri-fi-can - da,

haec di-es est a-man - da,   haec di-es con lau-dan - da, haec di-es reci-tan-da

In qua no - bis pa - tent po - li pa - la - ti - a,

in qua Chri-sti cla-ret mi-se - ri - dor-di-a,   cle - men-ti - a, po-ten-ti - a

un - de no - van - tur et con - gau -dent om - ni - a.

Nec im - mer - i - to   ho - ste per - di - to,   plus gau-de -mus so - li - to

plau-sus lau-dis in - cli - to,

in - vin-ci - bi - lis trac-ta - tur, in pal-pa-bit pal-pa-tur

jam na - tu - re de - bi - tum con - fun - di - tur,

jam qui nos de - vi - ce - rat de - vin - ci - tur,

jam quod e - rat per - di - tum, re - di - mi - tur

Max - i - ma glo - ri - a mul - ta - que gra - ti - a

ce - le -sti- um, ter - re-stri-um et om-ni- um e-ter-no sit auc-to - ri,

qui pro-pri- um per fi - li-um et om-ni-um no-strae me-det lan-guo - ri.

sa - ne - tur et do - lo - ri, sa - ne - tur et do - lo - ri.

melody exactly repeated for successive textual units of similar structure, we should have to acknowledge that psalmody is a special
strophic form, in which the strophe was a bi-hemistich of variable
length, sung to a repeated melody. Generally we reserve 'strophic' for
an exactly maintained textual pattern, so that the melody can be
literally repeated. But when the 'strophe' becomes very long and
complex, and the number of repetitions few, then we may be dealing
with a different phenomenon. The term 'cursus' has sometimes ᴜᴄen

Ex. 89

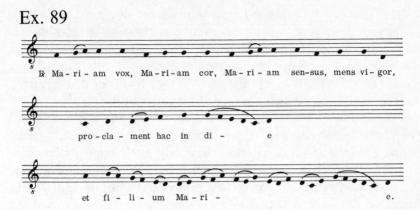

℞ Ma – ri – am vox, Ma – ri – am cor, Ma – ri – am sen-sus, mens vi – gor,

pro – cla – ment hac in di – e

et fi – li – um Ma – ri – e.

used to describe such structures in early medieval chant; 'Rex caeli', a ninth-century Frankish chant, has a 'double cursus', that is, two very long complex strophes.[109] Whatever term we use, we can see in the Aquitanian *versus* not an expansion of the Ambrosian strophe, but rather the coalescing into large-scale symmetries of the kind already fixed in the sequence and Kyrie, now rationalized and modularized by patterns of syllable count, accent, and rhyme.

OFFICES AND PLAYS

Always a combination of various kinds of texts said and sung in various melodic styles, the Office—that is, newly composed Offices— was increasingly dominated by the new rhyming, accentual songs. This took three special forms, popular after 1100: the rhymed Office, the farsed festal Office, and the chant play (also called 'liturgical drama', or 'medieval music drama'). These vary greatly in form and textual materials, but share many musical materials.

The Office contained versified elements at the time of the archetype, and these increased steadily during the composition of new Offices during the tenth and eleventh centuries.[110] At some point not yet determined, versification was applied systematically to sets of anti- phons, sets of responsories, eventually to sets of paraphrases of the psalms for a particular Office. (These versified psalm paraphrases formed one of the points of origin of the metrical Psalter, which in turn became the backbone of Reformation psalmody and congrega- tional singing.) After 1000, versified forms in the Office became subjected to accentual scansion and rhyme; the result is known as the

[109] Nancy Phillips and Michel Huglo, 'The Versus Rex caeli—Another Look at the so-called Archaic Sequence', *Journal of the Plainsong & Mediæval Music Society*, 5 (1982), 36–43.
[110] Jonsson, *Historia*.

rhymed Office.[111] One of the purposes in composing a rhymed Office would have been to provide a relatively homogenous set of materials for the night and day of special observance. We should not look so much for unity, perhaps, as uniformity and regularity; this at least would carry out the thrust of the early Frankish Offices that arranged antiphons and responsories in numerical order of modes.[112]

The number of rhymed Offices is very large, and the number of individual antiphons and responsories virtually uncounted; initial mapping of the musical repertory has only just begun. Preliminary reports indicate that extensive transfer of melodic material from one Office to another took place, so that many pieces can be described as formulaic. We should note, however, that the formulas involved are not necessarily those of the Gregorian style (except in the case of Offices in deliberately conservative style, such as the Corpus Christi Office[113]—and even there the Frankish treatment of Gregorian style is readily apparent). The use of melodic formulas in Offices of the twelfth century and later represents the maturity of *medieval* chant, and is comparable to the extensive formulaic composition in the melodies provided for the sequence texts attributed to Adam of St Victor in mid-twelfth century.[114] Composition by formula is not specifically or solely a property of 'archaic' music, but can occur naturally within the developmental cycle of any style of music—most characteristically in a later phase where many idioms have become set and can be combined in a variety of ways. The rhymed Office seems to represent the most large-scale application of the idioms of rhyming accentual chant in the later Middle Ages.

A somewhat different intent, perhaps, is perceivable in the special festal Offices that appeared in the twelfth and thirteenth centuries. These tended to consist of a much wider variety of materials, and combined in a single Office according to the discretion and imagination of the compiler. The two most famous such Offices are those of Sens and Beauvais (each with a very large new cathedral in the thirteenth century).[115] These Offices are for New Year's Day—an occasion with multiple associations. It was the Octave of Christmas, and eighth-century monastic practice provided a Night Office that was

[111] Henri Villetard, *Office de Pierre de Corbeil* (Paris, 1907); *Office de Saint Savinien et de Saint Potentien* (Paris, 1956); Weakland, 'The Compositions of Hucbald'; Andrew Hughes, 'Rhymed Office', *New Grove*, xv. 804.

[112] Cf. above, p. 148

[113] Thomas Mathiesen, 'The Office of the New Feast of Corpus Christi in the *Regimen Animarum* at Brigham Young University', *Journal of Musicology*, 2 (1982), 13.

[114] Margot Fassler, 'Who was Adam of St. Victor? The Evidence of the Sequence Manuscripts', *JAMS*, 37 (1984), 233–59.

[115] Wulf Arlt, *Ein Festoffizium des Mittelalters aus Beauvais* (Cologne, 1970).

closely related to the Christmas Night Office. A Mass in honour of the
Virgin was traditionally celebrated. As the historical dimension of the
Proper of the Time was developed, this day was taken to commemorate the Circumcision of the Christ-child a week after his birth. Finally,
of course, it was the beginning of the secular New Year, and
furthermore was part of the mid-winter festivity celebrated for
whatever reason. A great deal of musical material was interpolated
into the Office on this occasion, often in the form of *versus* to be sung
during processions, by way of ornamenting the ceremonial movement
within the Office from one item to the next. Here we meet the term
'conductus', a piece with which to conduct someone or something;
conductus are typically strophic *versus* in rhyming accentual chant.[116]
There are other, shorter kinds of chants that elaborate on or replace
antiphons and versicles of the Office. Materials may be adapted from
some other purpose. The variety of materials is great; the rationale for
their coexistence is provided by the Office and Mass for the day. The
sense of 'stuffing' (which is the meaning of the term 'farse') is very
much in evidence. These Offices are precious to us first because they
preserve chants we might not otherwise know (some of the materials
are also known from the Aquitanian repertory of *versus*, others are
not), second because they show us these individual items incorporated
into an actual event.

Liturgical drama (described in Chapter VIII) began with the trope
dialogue 'Quem queritis', and continued throughout the Middle Ages
to use the musical resources of medieval chant. After 1100, liturgical
dramas sometimes resemble rhymed or festal Offices in combining a
variety of musical items. The distinctive aspect of a play, of course, is
whatever dramatic quality the text has; the function of the melodies in
relationship to the drama will be taken up in Chapter VIII in
connection with individual plays. The general kinds of chant used in
plays are, first, trope style, that is, the idealized antiphon style
developed for Carolingian tropes; second, rhyming, accentual chant,
as in the *versus*; and third, adaptation, quotation, or paraphrase of
chants (mostly antiphons) already in the Mass or Office. By 1100 the
Office itself contained a substantial amount of Frankish additions in a
variety of styles, so that even a direct quotation of a liturgical item
may overlap in style with the first two types. When rhyming, accentual
chant in strophic forms predominates, the drama may resemble a
rhymed Office. With a generous mixture of quotations or antiphon
types, it resembles rather a festal farsed Office.

[116] Jacques Handschin, 'Conductus', *MGG*, ii (1952), cols. 1615–26; Wolfgang Osthoff, 'Die
Conductus des Codex Calixtinus', in Martin Ruhnke, ed., *Festschrift Bruno Stäblein zum 70.
Geburtstag* (Kassel, 1967), 178.

VIII

LITURGICAL DRAMA

By SUSAN RANKIN

The liturgical books of the medieval western church preserve a large repertory of dramatic representations intended for performance on the highest church festivals. Of widely varied form, these 'dramatic ceremonies' or 'plays' drew on the literary and musical as well as dramatic skills of their creators. Like the liturgical ritual itself, they were expressed in Latin words and were sung throughout. This musical dimension continued to distinguish the Latin liturgical plays from their secular and vernacular counterparts, even when interaction between liturgical and non-liturgical dramatic compositions led to the adoption of characteristics atypical in one or other repertory.

Liturgical plays first appear in the tenth century, initially the product of widespread interest in new liturgical composition of many kinds. The earliest examples are of two types, based on biblical stories relating to the Nativity and Resurrection of Christ. An Easter play represents the visit of women to Christ's tomb on Easter morning and their encounter with an angel (or angels); and a Christmas or Epiphany play represents the journey of three Magi from the east in search of the new-born child. The origins of such plays can be traced back not only to the chants and semi-representational ceremonies of the liturgy, but also to the traditions of classical drama fostered in court circles and schools. Indeed, in terms of what could be achieved in a liturgical context, this early period was clearly a time of experimentation, the content and manner of presentation (and by inference the function) of extant dramatic compositions varying a great deal. The various versions of Easter and Magi plays recorded during this early period (i.e. the tenth and eleventh centuries) form the subject of the first two sections of this chapter. Subsequent sections deal with the emergence of new subject types of liturgical drama after the late eleventh century, as well as new forms of the Easter play.

The texts of the plays are edited in two monumental works of scholarship. Published in 1933, Karl Young's *The Drama of the Medieval Church* provides a comprehensive survey of all types of Latin church plays.[1] Walther Lipphardt's *Lateinische Osterfeiern und Osterspiele* deals only with the Easter plays, but includes the texts of almost every known example.[2] For every play mentioned below, reference is made to one and where possible both of these editions.

In the past 150 years, much of the attention paid to liturgical dramas has been primarily directed to establishing their relation to later medieval vernacular plays (and hence their significance in the history of drama). Such work has tended to focus on theatrical qualities—how a story is presented, the sequence of events and degree of detail, the movement and presentation of characters. Several recent studies have helped to correct this unfortunate balance, exploring the qualities of the plays in relation to the liturgy, their composition from constituent parts of the liturgical chant, and their ritual function within the liturgical service. Thus, the two aspects of 'play' and 'ceremony' have to some extent been separately evoked, and even set in opposition to each other. Here, rather than confuse the issue by choosing the term 'ceremony' on some occasions and 'play' on others, I refer throughout to 'play'; this does not constitute a judgement of the nature of liturgical drama, but is merely intended as a neutral term.

THE *QUEM QUERITIS* DIALOGUE IN THE TENTH AND ELEVENTH CENTURIES

Prominent among the new chants composed in the wake of the Carolingian liturgical renaissance is the famous Easter dialogue *Quem queritis*. Created before 930, this short piece must have attracted wide attention from very early on; in contrast to the vast majority of tropes—with which liturgical repertory it tended to circulate—*Quem queritis* became known in eastern as well as western Frankish areas. By the end of the century it had been integrated into the liturgies of institutions in southern and central France, southern England, and along the Rhine in German-speaking countries, as far east as St Gall. There can be little doubt that its potency as a part of the Easter liturgy, combined with extreme succinctness of expression, lay behind this rapidly achieved popularity. The earliest extant version is recorded in an Aquitanian Troper dated in the first half of the tenth

---

[1] Karl Young, *The Drama of the Medieval Church*, 2 vols. (Oxford, 1933). Some of the manuscript citations are now out of date, the manuscripts being housed in different or renamed libraries.

[2] Walther Lipphardt, *Lateinische Osterfeiern und Osterspiele*, 6 vols. (Berlin, 1975–81). This provides extensive bibliographical references, and, in vol. 6, details of manuscript sources.

century (Paris, Bibliothèque nationale lat. 1240); although the melodies are notated in semi-diastematic neumes, they can be interpreted with reference to later precisely pitched concordances (Ex. 90).[3] No rubrics survive to elucidate the manner of performance of this dialogue, but its textual and musical construction tells much about its purpose.[4] The opening question 'Quem queritis' and its answer 'Ihesum nazarenum' establish a setting (beside Jesus' tomb), as well as the identities of the interlocutors: heavenly beings (*celicole*) and followers of Christ (*christicole*). Once the purpose of the followers' quest—to find Jesus' body—has been elicited, the heavenly creatures tell of Christ's resurrection, commanding his followers to tell the news abroad: 'ite nunciate'. The joyful announcement 'Alleluia resurrexit Dominus' and thanksgiving 'Deo gratias' round off the dialogue, leading to the singing of the Easter Mass Introit *Resurrexi*.

The parallel between this poetic composition and the Gospel accounts of a meeting between an angel (or angels) and women visiting the tomb early in the morning after the sabbath[5] is easily recognized; indeed it would be difficult to avoid. Yet *Quem queritis* cannot simply be regarded as a poetic (and potentially dramatic) realization of the Gospel story, however clear its relation to that narrative. Not only does it neither begin nor end like the biblical accounts, but it explicitly names no one, except Jesus. The music underlines this lack of character definition: far from attempting to contrast heavenly and earthly speakers, the melodies for the opening question and answer are similarly constructed, each divided into three segments with final D, and using the plagal range around D. The high points in the musical composition are in fact literally those where the melody moves away from its otherwise low tessitura: for the angel's words 'Non est hic surrexit' and for the womens' response 'Alleluia resurrexit Dominus'.

With both musical climaxes emphasizing announcements that Christ is risen, the object of the entire dialogue emerges as the communication of this news to the celebrating community. For the performer or listener, the phrase 'hodie resurrexit leo fortis' brings the song right into the present: the celebratory 'Alleluia' is not just that of Marys returning from the tomb (in any case the Gospels do not

[3] Fo. 30ᵛ, reproduced in Young, *Drama*, i, Plate VI; ed. Young, *Drama*, i, 210, and Lipphardt, *Osierfeiern*, i, No. 53.

[4] The relation between the function and liturgical placing of this specific version of *Quem queritis* is discussed by C. Clifford Flanigan, 'The Liturgical Context of the *Quem queritis* Trope', *Comparative Drama*, 8 (1974), 45–62.

[5] Matthew 28: 1–7; Mark 16: 1–8; Luke 24: 1–9.

Ex. 90

Quem que - ri - tis in se - pul - chro o chris - ti - co - le?

Ihe - sum na - za - re - num cru - ci - fi - xum o ce - li - co - le.

Non est hic sur - re - xit si - cut ip - se di - xit:

i - te nun - ci - a - te qui - a sur - re - xit.

Al - le - lu - ia re - sur - re - xit do - mi - nus ho - di - e

re - sur - re - xit le - o for - tis chris - tus fi - li - us de - i

De - o gra - ti - as di - ci - te ei - a.

mention their return), but of all those present in the church. Thus, despite its adoption of a biblical story as a backdrop, the liturgical function of this early form of *Quem queritis* appears more focused on celebration in the present than narration of past events.

Just as striking as *Quem queritis*' wide diffusion is the variability of its presentation in the early sources. Sung immediately before the Introit of Easter Mass in southern French and Italian monasteries, in northern French, English, and north German monasteries it was usually placed before the closing hymn of Matins, Te deum laudamus,

while at St Gall it was sung during the procession before Mass.[6]
Further, variation in liturgical placement generally went hand in hand
with textual modifications, as comparison of a version from Prüm[7]
with that of Paris 1240 shows:

> Quem queritis in sepulchro o christicole?
> Ihesum nazarenum querimus crucifixum o celicole.
> Non est hic surrexit sicut predixerat;
> ite nunciate quia surrexit dicentes:
>
> *Antiphona*:
>
> Surrexit Dominus [de sepulchro
> qui pro nobis pependit in ligno alleluia]
> Te Deum laudamus

Where the version in Paris 1240 had 'Alleluia resurrexit Dominus',
this has the Office antiphon *Surrexit Dominus de sepulchro*,[8] musically
unrelated to the rest (Ex. 91).[9] It is far from clear which, if indeed
either, of these two versions represents the form in which *Quem
queritis* was first conceived, with its original liturgical placing.[10]

Ex. 91

Sur - re - xit   do - mi - nus   de   se - pul - chro

qui   pro   no - bis   pe - pen - dit   in   lig - no

al - le - lu - ia

---

[6] The evidence supporting one or other of these three liturgical positions as the original is
discussed by Timothy J. McGee, 'The Liturgical Placements of the *Quem quaeritis* Dialogue',
JAMS, 29 (1976), 1–29, and David A. Bjork, 'On the Dissemination of *Quem quaeritis* and the
Visitatio Sepulchri and the Chronology of Their Early Sources', *Comparative Drama*, 14 (1980),
46–69.

[7] Paris, Bibliothèque nationale lat. 9448, fo. 33ᵛ; ed. Young, *Drama*, i, 579, and Lipphardt,
Osterfeiern, ii, no. 312.

[8] The text edited as No. 5079, in René-Jean Hesbert, *Corpus antiphonalium officii*, 6 vols.
(Rome, 1963–79), iii: *Invitatoria et Antiphonae* (henceforth *CAO*).

[9] From Paris, Bibliothèque nationale lat. 12044, fo. 106ʳ (St-Maur-des-Fossés), conforming to
the neumes of the Prüm incipit.

[10] See Helmut de Boor, *Die Textgeschichte der lateinische Osterfeiern* (Tübingen, 1967), 67–
80; Flanigan, 'Liturgical Context'; Johann Drumbl, 'Ursprung des liturgischen Spiels', *Italia
medioevale e umanistica*, 22 (1979), 45–96; Bjork, 'Dissemination'; Susan Rankin, 'Musical and
Ritual Aspects of *Quem queritis*', in Gabriel Silagi, ed., *Liturgische Tropen* (Munich, 1985), 181–
92.

However, in as much as the ritual function can be understood through the sung words and music, the two versions remain relatively close; even though the Prüm dialogue lacks a second musical climax, it still follows the fundamental pattern of announcement and celebration.

Both these versions of the dialogue appear in Tropers, a kind of liturgical book which often lacks detailed rubrics. With no more information about the place in either church where the dialogue was sung, nor anything of the manner of its performance, an assessment of the balance of ritual and representational elements, and of the relation between these and the different liturgical positions, cannot be made. But in those tenth- and eleventh-century sources which do include more detailed rubrics, a significant degree of variation in the manner of performance becomes apparent, only one factor—the singing of the dialogue as an exchange between individuals or groups of singers—remaining constant.

On the one hand, versions such as that from Novalesa in northern Italy involve no actions or movement during, or associated with, the singing of the dialogue:[11]

In die sancto Pasce, cum omnes simul convenerint in ecclesiam ad Missam celebrandum, stent parati duo diaconi induti dalmaticis retro altare dicentes: Quem queritis in sepulchro Christicole?
Respondeant duo cantores stantes in choro: Ihesum nazarenum ...
Item diaconi: Non est hic ...
Tunc cantor dicat excelsa voce: Alleluia resurrexit Dominus.
Tunc psallat scola: Resurrexi ...

These rubrics refer only to deacons and cantors as the singers; since deacons often wore dalmatics, none of the singers is dressed in an unusual way. On the other hand, a contemporary source connected with the Benedictine abbey at Melk[12] (west of Vienna) has rubrics explaining how two priests represent two angels sitting by the tomb, and how two deacons with covered heads, wearing dalmatics and carrying thuribles filled with incense, represent women bringing spices, seeking Christ's tomb. In this version, once the priests (angels) have sung 'Non est hic', the deacons (women) lift a cloth from the altar, as if it were the gravecloth mentioned in John 20: 7, so often depicted in medieval paintings of this scene. While both versions move towards the same conclusion—communal celebration of the resurrection—that from the Novalesa underplays the dimension of represen-

---

[11] Oxford, Bodleian Library Douce 222, fo. 18[r-v]; ed. Young, *Drama*, i, 215, and Lipphardt, *Osterfeiern*, i, No. 29.
[12] Melk, Stiftsbibliothek 109 (*olim* 1056); ed. Young, *Drama*, i, 241, and Lipphardt, *Osterfeiern*, ii, No. 264.

tation inherent in the dialogue, likening its performance to much
other liturgical ritual. In contrast, the Melk ceremony exploits the
parallels between *Quem queritis* and the Gospels, deliberately charac-
terizing the singers as angels and women, and, in the display of the
gravecloth, including an action which is not mentioned by the sung
text and can only be understood by returning to the Gospel story. By
organizing the ceremony in this way, the composers of the Melk
version show themselves more concerned with the acting out of a
narrative than those at Novalesa.

It is differences of this kind, between versions acted out and not
acted out, that have led some scholars to draw a distinction between
'liturgical items with dramatic tendencies' and 'true drama'; in particular, Karl Young used the criteria of impersonation and mimetic
action to determine whether a given text constituted an authentic play
or not.[13] With hindsight, such rigid categorization appears arbitrary
and anachronistic:[14] the very multiplicity of forms and ways in which
the dialogue was integrated into the liturgies of different churches in
the first two centuries of its existence is evidence of a great flexibility of
approach by those responsible for liturgical matters.[15] None the less,
even if Young's labels appear inappropriate and his interpretation
teleological, the fact remains that *Quem queritis* could be performed in
more or less representational forms during this period. And the
subsequent development of representational drama within the liturgy
lends historical significance to the attempt to differentiate between
these forms.

Evidence that the dialogue's narrative potential was exploited very
early on comes from two eleventh-century copies of the *Regularis
Concordia*, 'The Monastic Agreement of the Monks and Nuns of the
English Nation'.[16] The product of a council held at Winchester *c.* 973,
this code of monastic law was prepared principally under the guidance
of Bishop Ethelwold (d. 983).[17] Here *Quem queritis* is presented in a

[13] See especially Young, *Drama*, i, 79–80.

[14] The earliest and most detailed critique of this aspect of Young's work is that by O. B.
Hardison, Jr., *Christian Rite and Christian Drama in the Middle Ages* (Baltimore, 1965).

[15] For discussion of the ritual function of the dialogue in this earliest period see Hardison,
Christian Rite; C. Clifford Flanigan, 'The Roman Rite and the Origins of the Liturgical Drama',
University of Toronto Quarterly, 43 (1974), 263–84, and 'Liturgical Context'; Blandine-
Dominique Berger, *Le Drame liturgique de Pâques du xe au xiiie siècle: Liturgie et théâtre* (Paris,
1976); Johann Drumbl, 'Ursprung', and *Quem quaeritis: Teatro sacro dell'alto medioevo* (Rome,
1981); Rankin, 'Musical and Ritual Aspects'; Anselme Davril, 'Johann Drumbl and the Origin
of the *Quem Quaeritis*: A Review Article', *Comparative Drama*, 20 (1986), 65–75.

[16] London, British Library Cotton Faustina B.iii, fos. 159–198 with Tiberius A.iii, fos. 174–
177, and Cotton Tiberius A.iii, fos. 3–27; ed. and trans. Dom Thomas Symons, *Regularis
Concordia: The Monastic Agreement of the Monks and Nuns of the English Nation* (London,
1953).

[17] See Thomas Symons, '*Regularis Concordia*: History and Derivation', in David Parsons, ed.,
Tenth-Century Studies (London, 1975), 37–59.

setting strongly marked by the attempt to identify it with the Gospel stories, both in sung texts and in actions.[18] During the third (i.e. last) lesson of Easter Matins, four monks go out of the choir to vest: one returns wearing an alb (a white garment), and sits by 'the sepulchre', holding a palm branch (a symbol of the victory of Christ over death). While the third responsory is sung (*Dum transisset*:[19] 'And when the sabbath was past, Mary Magdalene, and Mary the mother of James, and Salome, had bought sweet spices, that they might come and anoint him') three others, wearing copes (highly decorated garments) and carrying thuribles, move towards the sepulchre 'step by step, as though searching for something'. The source even includes the explanation 'Now these things are done in imitation of the angel seated on the tomb and of the women coming with perfumes to anoint the body of Jesus'. The move towards literal re-enactment of the biblical story was accompanied by expansion of the sung text. This version not only combines the typically French five-sentence dialogue (as in Paris 1240) with the typically German closing text 'Surrexit Dominus de sepulchro' (as in Prüm),[20] but also introduces the words of Matthew 28: 6 'Venite et videte' ('Come and see the place where the Lord lay'), making it representationally feasible for the 'women' to find a gravecloth, which they then display.

Neither source of *Regularis Concordia* has musical notation, but two Winchester books of the later tenth and mid-eleventh centuries provide notation for a closely related *Quem queritis* ceremony.[21] Both Winchester Tropers have all the sung texts mentioned by incipit in the *Regularis Concordia*, as well as a further item 'Cito euntes' (Matthew 28: 7).[22] The musical notation confirms that both new texts, as well as the concluding 'Surrexit Dominus de sepulchro', are sung to their usual Office antiphon melodies,[23] probably already known in the Winchester chant repertory before the introduction of *Quem queritis* (Ex. 92).[24] This expanded ceremony effectively divides into two parts,

[18] Ed. Young, *Drama*, i, 249, 581, and Lipphardt, *Osterfeiern*, ii, Nos. 395–6.

[19] *CAO* 6565.

[20] Here Winchester has the same text as Prüm but a different melody; the Winchester setting is in the eighth mode with final G, that of Prüm in the fourth mode with final E. Both melodic versions of the Office antiphon are widely represented in medieval chant books, sometimes even copied side by side. Their history prior to the twelfth century remains confused. For a discussion of the relation of the two melodies to liturgical dramas see Clyde W. Brockett, 'The Role of the Office Antiphon in Tenth-Century Liturgical Drama', *Musica disciplina*, 34 (1980), 5–27.

[21] Cambridge, Corpus Christi College 473, fo. 26ᵛ and Oxford, Bodleian Library 775, fo. 17ʳ⁻ᵛ; ed. Young, *Drama*, i, 587, 254, and Lipphardt, *Osterfeiern*, ii, Nos. 424, 423.

[22] Since 'Cito euntes' follows 'Venite et videte' immediately, and both texts are sung by the angel, it is entirely possible that 'Cito euntes' was omitted from the *Regularis Concordia* version as a result of the policy of recording only the incipits of sung items.

[23] 'Venite et videte': *CAO* 5352. 'Cito euntes': *CAO* 1813. 'Surrexit Dominus de sepulchro': *CAO* 5079. On the melodic traditions for this last, see n. 20 above.

[24] Both Tropers are notated in semi-diastematic English neumes; this transcription uses later French and English sources to interpret the Winchester melodies.

Ex. 92

ANGELICA DE CHRISTI RESURRECTIONE

Quem que – ri – tis in se – pul – chro chris – ti – co – lae?

SANCTARUM MULIERUM RESPONSIO

Ihe – sum na – za – re – num cru – ci – fi – xum o ce – li – co – la.

ANGELICE VOCIS CONSOLATIO

Non est hic sur – re – xit si – cut pre – di – xe – rat;

i – te nun – ci – a – te qui – a sur – re – xit di – cen – tes:

SANCTARUM MULIERUM AD OMNEM CLERUM MODULATIO

Al – le – lu – ia re – sur – re – xit do – mi – nus ho – di – e

le – o for – tis chris – tus fi – li – us de – i.

De – o gra – ti – as di – ci – te ei – a.

DICAT ANGELUS

Ve – ni – te et vi – de – te lo – cum u – bi po – si – tus

e – rat do – mi – nus al – le – lu – ia al – le – lu – ia.

ITERUM DICAT ANGELUS

Ci - to e - un - tes di - ci - te dis - ci - pu - lis
qui - a sur - re - xit do - mi - nus al - le - lu - ia al - le - lu - ia.

MULIERES UNA VOCE CANANT IUBILANTES

Sur - re - xit do - mi - nus de se - pul - chro
qui pro no - bis pe - pen - dit in lig - no al - le - lu - ia.

the first (consisting of the dialogue sentences) presenting one episode in the encounter, the second (consisting of the three antiphons) presenting a second episode. The text goes through a similar ritual process in each of these:

Information	('Non est hic'; 'Venite et videte')
Command 'Go and tell'	('Ite nunciate'; 'Cito euntes')
Announcement	('Alleluia resurrexit'; 'Surrexit Dominus')

Nevertheless, the melodies of the dialogue sentences sound stylistically and modally distinct from the three antiphons. This new episodic design inevitably favours narrative qualities of the ceremony: not only is more of the 'story' told, but the whole performance is much less concise, causing the old ritual objective—announcement of the resurrection to the assembled community—to lose prominence.

The Winchester example illustrates just how easily and how far representational ceremony could develop within a liturgical framework in the late tenth century. This particular ceremony was not itself influential outside of the Anglo-Norman orbit, but the compositional procedures which it embodies—free alteration of available structures of text and music and development of explicit representational elements—are precisely those which were to allow and encourage a great flowering of dramatic composition for the liturgy during the next 400 years. However, in terms of text expansion or alteration, none of the tenth- and eleventh-century sources of *Quem queritis* transmits a version markedly different from those described above; the duration of any *Quem queritis* ceremony, whether more or less explicitly representational, remained short. After the initial diffusion of the dialogue, it was only in the late eleventh and early twelfth centuries and under the widespread influence of new poetic impulses, that Easter ceremonies including *Quem queritis* underwent major recomposition and expansion. These longer versions were generally performed before the Te deum laudamus of Easter Matins; although not in exact accord with medieval usage, it has become modern practice to refer to any *Quem queritis* ceremony performed at Matins, including that from Winchester, as the *Visitatio Sepulchri*.[25]

MAGI PLAYS

While the majority of tenth- and eleventh-century sources of *Quem queritis* are standard liturgical chant books (usually Tropers or Graduals), and come principally from Benedictine foundations, the early sources of the *Officium Stelle* or Magi play present a quite different picture. Of five sources (including fragments) securely datable before 1050, only one shows the Magi play copied in the context of other liturgical chants, as well as integrated into the liturgy of the institution for which the book was prepared (the Benedictine monastery of Münsterschwarzach).[26] The other pre-1050 sources— the flyleaf of an ornamental Psalter, empty pages in a book of Sermons, the end of a Treasury and book catalogue, and the last page of a bible—are far enough dissociated from liturgical singing to suggest that, unlike *Quem queritis*, the Magi play did not originate within the liturgy. Moreover, while the origin of two sources remains obscure,[27] the other two belonged to communities of canons (Ste Corneille de Compiègne and the Frankfurt Salvatorstift).[28] Whatever its meaning, this contrasted pattern of transmission is only one of many fundamental dissimilarities between the Magi plays and the Easter dialogue; in length, literary style, musical organization and dramatic *modus operandi*, the new plays are quite unlike any contemporary ceremonies involving *Quem queritis*.

The earliest non-fragmentary source of a Magi play is that from the

---

[25] The introductory rubric 'ad visitandum sepulchrum' is characteristic of several eleventh-century German sources; but the title *Visitatio Sepulchri* appears not to have been used before the beginning of the thirteenth century.

[26] Lambach, Stiftsarchiv, fragment of a *Liber Ordinarius*; ed. Drumbl, *Quem quaeritis*, 299.

[27] Paris, Bibliothèque nationale lat. 1152, fo. 173ᵛ; ed. Young, *Drama*, ii, 443; and Paris, Bibliothèque nationale lat. 8847, fo. 91ʳ; ed. Drumbl, *Quem queritis*, 307.

[28] Paris Bibliothèque nationale lat. 16819, fo. 49ʳ⁻ᵛ; ed. Young, *Drama*, ii, 53. Frankfurt-am-Main, Stadt- und Universitätsbibliothek Barth. 179; ed. Drumbl, *Quem queritis*, 294.

abbey of Ste Corneille de Compiègne, copied in the first half of the eleventh century. The play is based on the story from the Gospel of St Matthew of the wise men's journey from the east, their meeting with Herod and subsequent discovery of the child at Bethlehem, and finally Herod's order to slaughter the young children. According to the rubrics, the play involved a large number of characters, including three Magi, Herod, his ambassadors (*legati regis*), messenger, scribes, and soldier (*armiger*), two women at the crib in Bethlehem, and an angel—a minimum of thirteen in all. Clearly, all these characters acted out their parts and moved around where appropriate, the overall character of this movement being that of a liturgical procession visiting stations. The Magi move from the place at which they initially meet to Herod's court (most of the members of which remain stationary), then on to the crib, and finally away in another direction, following the angel's warning to return by another route.

From a literary point of view, the sung texts evince considerable sophistication and originality. Only two texts constitute direct biblical quotations: the scribes read the prophecy 'And thou Bethlehem in the land of Juda art not the least . . . ' (Matthew 2: 6), and the last line of the whole play 'Suffer the little children to come unto me . . . ' (Mark 10: 14) is sung by an angel. It is obviously intended that both be heard *as* exact quotations. With the bible, the liturgy, and an apocryphal book (the Protevangelium of James)[29] as background sources, all other texts represent new original composition, ranging from simple prose to an impressive series of hexameters. Far from being haphazardly positioned, these hexameters reveal the same appreciation of dramatic impact in performance as the biblical quotations, for they begin at the point where the Magi first meet a member of Herod's entourage, thus endowing his courtiers with formal and learned attributes.

The music is equally well-controlled and dramatically orientated, showing a clear concern to establish the distinction between individual characters, and sometimes even the relation between them.[30] The melodies for the Magi's opening lines illustrate this (Ex. 93).[31] All three phrases are in a D-mode, each giving prominence to the tones a and c, whether below or above the central D. The linking of final

---

[29] Ed. by E. Hennecke, in W. Schneemelcher, ed., *New Testament Apocrypha* (London, 1963), 370–88.

[30] Madeleine Bernard, 'L'Officium Stellae Nivernais', *Revue de musicologie*, 51 (1965), 52–65, describes the 'climat musicale' used for each different character (or group of characters).

[31] The Compiègne source has adiastematic neumes; the melodies of this and the following example are transcribed from a source with closely concordant melodic versions: Madrid, Biblioteca Nacional 289, fos. 107ᵛ–110ʳ.

Ex. 93

Primus:

Stel - la ful - go - re ni - mi - o ru - ti - lat

Secundus veniens a meridie:

Que re - gem re - gum na - tum mon - strat

Tertius ab australi parte:

Quem ven - tu - rum o - lim pro - phe - ti - a si - gna - ve - rat

cadences and opening intonations through the use of the same note, and continuation of melodic patterns established in each preceding phrase, gives the group of three phrases melodic coherence. At the same time, different intonations and tessituras ensure that each phrase is heard as a discrete part of a larger whole. In this uncomplicated way, the music reinforces the dramatic organization, introducing the Magi as three separate persons with a common purpose.

A more conspicuous example of the use of simple musical techniques to characterize situations or individuals comes in the Magi's encounter with Herod (Ex. 94). Each of Herod's questions has a melody in the plagal G-mode, while the Magi answer in the authentic D-mode. The contrast inherent in the juxtaposition of two different modes, used in different positions, is further intensified by the different intonation formulas of each melodic pair: a rise through a fourth in Herod's melodies is countered by the leap of a fifth in the Magi's. The resulting discontinuity between the four melodic elements of this exchange not only corresponds to the repeated question/ answer structure, but also interprets the dramatic situation, expressing conflict between the two parties, whose objectives are in stark opposition (both wish to discover the new-born king, Herod in order to destroy him, the Magi in order to worship him).

For one short episode—the dialogue between midwives and Magi beside the crib—the first Magi composer probably used the *Quem queritis* dialogue as a conceptual model. Otherwise, up to the mid-eleventh century, the Magi plays and *Quem queritis* ceremonies developed entirely separately, and, as far as can be judged from extant sources, in different institutions. It is not even clear that during this

Ex. 94

[Rex]

Re - gem quem que - ri - tis

na - tum es - se quo si - gno di - di - cis - tis?

Magi:

Il - lum na - tum es - se di - di - ci - mus

in o - ri - en - te stel - la mon - stran - te.

Rex:

Si il - lum reg - na - re cre - di - tis di - ci - te mic - hi.

Magi:

Hunc reg - na - re fa - ten - tes cum mis - ti - cis mu - ne - ri - bus

de ter - ra lon - gin - qua a - do - ra - re ve - ni - mus

tri - num de - um ve - ne - ran - tes tri - bus in mu - ne - ri - bus.

Primus: Secundus: Tertius:

Au - re re - gem   Tu - re sa - cer - do - tem   Mir - ra mor - ta - lem

period the Magi play was performed as part of a liturgical office. However, while the early Compiègne version gives no clue as to the intended time and place of its performance, it is certain that it belongs to a tradition of related texts, many of which were conceived for liturgical purposes, including those from Nevers, Rouen, and Strasbourg Cathedrals, the Norman Cappella Palatina in Palermo, Györ (Hungary), Münsterschwarzach, Bilsen and two plays in the Fleury Play-book.[32] But the process of liturgical integration was far from easy, and could entail the elimination of entire scenes, or even characters. The Rouen play gets rid of Herod altogether, substituting a descriptive responsory *Magi veniunt ab oriente*[33] for the Magi's dialogue with Herod. Two of the three Nevers versions omit Herod's discussion with his scribes, and several versions do not have the final Compiègne episode showing the enraged Herod ordering his soldiers to kill the young children. Still other versions go in quite the opposite direction, extending the earlier Magi play to include more circumstantial amplification of the biblical story. One of the most elaborate, copied towards the end of the eleventh century into a book belonging to Freising Cathedral,[34] opens with a processional song accompanying Herod's entrance, and includes long negotiations between Herod's officers and the Magi, followed by fairly aggressive questioning of the Magi by Herod. Another example, copied in the early twelfth century in a book of unknown origin,[35] has an inspired theatrical touch: arriving before Herod two of the Magi address him in completely unintelligible language:

Ase ai ase elo allo abadac crazai nubera satau loamedech amos ebraisim loasetiedet inbedo addoro otiso bedoranso i et i iomo bello o illa et cum marmoysen aharon et cum cizarene ravidete qui adonay moy

and

O some tholica lama he osome tholica lama ma chenapi ha thomena.

Small wonder then that the liturgical reformer Gerhoh of Reichersberg (1093–1196)—once a student in the Freising Cathedral school and later *magister scholae* at Augsburg, close to Freising—should single out plays representing Herod or the slaughter of the Innocents for especial condemnation.[36]

NEW COMPOSITIONS OF THE LATE ELEVENTH CENTURY AND AFTER

Starting in the late eleventh century, two new trends manifested

---

[32] The Györ source is Zagreb, University Library MR 165, fos. 28ᵛ–30ʳ; ed. Drumbl, *Quem queritis*, 303. For Münsterschwarzach, see above, n. 26. All the others are ed. in chs. 18, 19, and 20 of Young, *Drama*, ii.

[33] *CAO* 7112.

[34] Munich, Staatsbibliothek 6264a, fo. 1ʳ⁻ᵛ; ed. Young, *Drama*, ii, 93.

[35] Montpellier, Faculté de Médecine H.304, fos. 41ᵛ–42ᵛ, with no musical notation; ed. Young, *Drama*, ii, 68. For more details of this source see below, 000 and n. 83.

[36] See his *Tractatus in psalmos*, ed. J.-P. Migne, *Patrologia Latina*, 221 vols. (Paris, 1844–64), vol. 194, col. 890.

themselves in liturgical drama. The first was the unprecedented expansion in the range of dramatic compositions for the liturgy. Not only did new forms of the *Visitatio Sepulchri* incorporate more episodes, but also every other type of liturgical drama to appear in the Middle Ages was invented before the end of the twelfth century. These new types include the Easter Pilgrims' play (*Peregrinus*), several plays for the Christmas season (*Officium Pastorum, Ordo Rachelis, Ordo Prophetarum*), the Play of the Wise and Foolish Virgins (*Sponsus*), the Raising of Lazarus, miracles of St Nicholas, and the Play of Daniel (*Ludus Danielis*). One of the most interesting traits of this great blossoming of new composition is its plurality: in the overall pattern no individual institution dominates, only a few of the new types appearing in the liturgical books of several centres, and then generally within geographically restricted orbits. Meanwhile, both old and new forms of the *Visitatio Sepulchri* continued to grow in popularity, the numbers of extant sources far exceeding that of any other form of liturgical drama.

The second new trend in dramatic composition for the liturgy concerns not its subject matter, but the means of expression: the new verse style already apparent in other song repertories, liturgical and non-liturgical, infiltrated the drama also.[37] Characterized by regular rhyme and verse patterns and equally systematic melodic structures, these lyrics combined rhythmical poetry with melodies of a new tonal

Ex. 95

37 Verse forms in the Latin liturgical drama were the subject of Wilhelm Meyer's study *Fragmenta Burana* (Berlin, 1901).

quality. The Easter plays become full of these verse songs, a particularly favourite place to add them being before the dialogue, so that the women making their way to the sepulchre can sing of their grief and despair.[38] *Omnipotens pater altissime* (Ex. 95)[39] is one of a group of strophes shared by plays within the French orbit (including those from Vich, Tours, Origny, and Egmont);[40] each strophe has three 10-syllable lines followed by a refrain, sung to a simple F-final melody. A typically German series, appearing in plays from Einsiedeln, Engelberg, Rheinau, Hersfeld, Cividale, Barking, Wilton, and Origny (amongst others),[41] has three 15-syllable lines per strophe (Ex. 96).[42] One of several other sets of lamenting strophes has a curious transmission pattern, turning up in plays from Braunschweig and

Ex. 96

He - u no-bis in-ter-nas men-tes   quan-ti pul-sant ge - mi - tus

pro nos-tro con - so - la - to - re   quo pri-va - mur mi - se - re

quem cru-de - lis iu - de - o - rum   mor-ti de - dit po - pu - lus.

---

[38] The relationships between various versions of these introductory verses are discussed by De Boor, *Textgeschichte*, 346–62 (text), and Walther Lipphardt, *Die Weisen der lateinischen Osterspiele des 12. und 13. Jahrhunderts* (Kassel, 1948) (music).

[39] Tours, Bibliothèque municipale 927, fo. 1ᵛ (of unknown origin).

[40] Vich: Biblioteca Episcopal 105, fos. 58ᵛ–60ʳ; ed. Young, *Drama*, i, 678, and Lipphardt, *Osterfeiern*, v, No. 823. For Tours, see below, n. 61. Origny: St Quentin, Bibliothèque municipale 86, 609–25; ed. Young, *Drama*, i, 413, and Lipphardt, *Osterfeiern*, v, No. 825. Egmont: The Hague, Koninklijke Bibliotheek 71.J.70, fos. 162ᵛ–170ʳ; ed. Lipphardt, *Osterfeiern*, v, No. 827.

[41] Einsiedeln, Stiftsbibliothek 300, 93–4; ed. Young, *Drama*, i, 390, and Lipphardt, *Osterfeiern*, v, No. 783. Engelberg, Stiftsbibliothek 314, fos. 75ᵛ–78ᵛ; ed. Young, *Drama*, i, 375, and Lipphardt, *Osterfeiern*, v, No. 784. Rheinau: Zürich, Zentralbibliothek Rheinau 18, 282–3; ed. Young, *Drama*, i, 385, and Lipphardt, *Osterfeiern*, v, No. 797. Hersfeld: St Gall, Stiftsbibliothek 448, 105–6; ed. Young, *Drama*, i, 667, and Lipphardt, *Osterfeiern*, v, No. 788. Cividale, Museo Archeologica Nazionale 101, fos. 77ʳ–79ᵛ; ed. Young, *Drama*, i, 378, and Lipphardt, *Osterfeiern*, v, No. 781. Barking: Oxford, University College 169, 121–4; ed. Young, *Drama*, i, 381, and Lipphardt, *Osterfeiern*, v, No. 770. Wilton: Solesmes, Abbaye-St-Pierre 596, fos. 59ʳ–64ᵛ (nineteenth-century copy of a fourteenth-century manuscript); ed. Susan Rankin, 'A New English Source of the *Visitatio Sepulchri*', *Journal of the Plainsong & Mediæval Music Society*, 4 (1981), 1–11. Origny: see n. 40 above.

[42] This is the Engelberg version (see n. 41 above).

Ex. 97

He - u pi - us pas - tor oc - ci - dit

quem cul - pa nul - la in - fe - cit

O res plan - gen - da

He - u ne - quam gens iu - da - i - ca

quam di - ra fren - det ve - sa - ni - a

plebs e - xe - cran - da

Dublin, as well as in the Fleury Play-book;[43] the Fleury version has marvellously expressive refrains (Ex. 97).[44]

As a result of the expansion of subject matter and the adoption of a new style of versification, new dramatic compositions of this period often include an extraordinary mixture of 'old' and 'new' material, with varied stylistic qualities. Many old prose texts were rewritten in verse form, generally requiring new melodies. And, since the bible acted as common source for both dramatic texts and liturgical chant, texts appropriate to certain dramatic episodes were often already associated with familiar chant melodies, removing the necessity to compose new ones. Just as often, however, a chant setting of a

[43] Braunschweig: Wolfenbüttel, Landeshauptarchiv VII B 203, fos. 23ʳ–27ᵛ; ed. Lipphardt, *Osterfeiern*, v, No. 780. Dublin, Archbishop Marsh's Library Z.4.2.20, fos. 59ʳ–61ʳ, and Oxford, Bodleian Library Rawlinson liturg.d.4, fos. 130ʳ–132ʳ; ed. Young, *Drama*, i, 347, and Lipphardt, *Osterfeiern*, Nos. 772–3. Fleury: ed. Young, *Drama*, i, 393, and Lipphardt, *Osterfeiern*, v, No. 779; for further details of this source see 352–5 below.

[44] Orléans, Bibliothèque municipale 201, p. 220.

particular text might be rejected because of its complex style or modality. The resulting mosaics of unchanged old, recomposed, and newly-invented material did not always possess a high degree of musical integrity, but they rarely lacked melodic interest.

VISITATIO SEPULCHRI PLAYS

Sometime in the late eleventh century, in the region bounded by Augsburg, Passau, and Salzburg, someone rewrote the *Quem queritis* dialogue, retaining the incipits of the first three sentences of the older version, but discarding the rest.[45] For these longer texts, completely new melodies, all in the plagal E-mode, were provided. Since in those areas where the new dialogue was adopted staffless neumes remained the standard musical notation long after the eleventh century, a thirteenth-century source, from Marienberg near Helmstedt, has been used for this transcription (Ex. 98).[46] These melodies show none of the careful building up and breaking of patterns used so effectively in the

Ex. 98

ANGEL:

Quem que-ri-tis o tre-mu-le mu-li-e-res in hoc tu-mu-lo plo-ran-tes?

THREE WOMEN:

Ihe - sum na-za-re-num cru-ci-fi - xum que-ri-mus.

ANGEL:

Non est hic quem que-ri-tis sed ci-to e-un-tes

nun-ci-a-te dis-ci-pu-lis ei - us et pe-tro

qui-a sur-re - xit Ihe-sus.

[45] See especially De Boor, *Textgeschichte*, 131 ff., and Michael L. Norton, 'The Type II Visitatio Sepulchri: A Repertorial Study' (Unpub. Ph.D. Diss., The Ohio State University, 1983).

[46] Wolfenbüttel, Herzog-August-Bibliothek 309 Novi, fos. 68ʳ–69ᵛ; ed. Lipphardt, *Osterfeiern*, v, No. 791.

older dialogue, although the high intonation for 'Non est hic' may well imitate the older version; rather, in an idiom much closer to Gregorian antiphons than that of the original *Quem queritis*, they create a homogenous musical vehicle for the words.

The context in which the new dialogue first appears may help to explain the aims which inspired this recomposition. The new dialogue is rarely found on its own as part of a one-episode play, but almost always in conjunction with other texts which realize a second episode. The race of the two disciples, Simon Peter and John, to the sepulchre (John 20: 3–10) is triggered by the women's report 'Ad monumentum venimus', newly-composed for the play. As the disciples run to the sepulchre, the Office antiphon *Currebant duo simul* accompanies them;[47] finally, after finding a gravecloth in the tomb, the disciples sing another new composition, 'Cernitis o socii' (Ex. 99).[48] Another integral part of this new form of Easter play was the introductory 'Quis revolvet'; as in the dialogue an older text with the same incipit

Ex. 99

CHORUS:

Cur-re-bant du - o si -mul et il - le a - li - us dis-ci - pu - lis

pre - cu - cur - rit ci - ci - us pe - tro et ve - nit pri - or

ad mo - nu - men-tum al - le - lu - ia.

PETER and JOHN:

Cer-ni -tis o so - ci - i ec-ce lin- the-a -mi-na et su -da - ri - um

et cor - pus non est in se - pul - chro in - ven -tum.

[47] *CAO* 2081.
[48] From Prague, Knihovna Narodnia Universitni I.D.20, fo. 69ᵛ; ed. Young, *Drama*, i, 654, and Lipphardt, *Osterfeiern*, iv, No. 645.

was rewritten (Ex. 100).[49] A conspicuous characteristic of this new ensemble of texts is their interest in descriptive detail; the women, previously only referred to as *christicole*, are now addressed 'O tremule mulieres' (O fearful women), their weeping and lamenting evoked more than once. Aspects of the biblical story neglected in the old dialogue are now deliberately introduced: the women's concern about the stone, and who is to roll it away, their explicit report 'angelum domini sedentem vidimus', as well as the disciples' discovery of a gravecloth. This last is now truer to the biblical account than those earlier versions in which the women find the cloth. In all this, the new play shows itself as more than a formal recomposition; rather, it has an entirely new inner conception.[50]

Ex. 100

Quis re - vol - vet no - bis ab os - ti - o la - pi - dem

quem te - ge - re sanc - tum cer - ni - mus se - pul - chrum?

Versions of the Easter play which use the new dialogue and the disciples' race are typical of the whole German realm, found in sources from centres as far apart as Haarlem, Zürich, Prague, and Krakow.[51] In modern studies, plays with the disciples' race are usually distinguished as 'second stage', as opposed to those of the 'first stage', which have the visit to the sepulchre only.[52]

In France, further development of the Easter play took rather different paths, few as far-reaching as wholesale recomposition. With a great deal of local variation, many French plays preserved the old *Quem queritis* dialogue as the kernel of a series of texts which introduced no new characters (hence the common designation 'first stage'). One fairly extensive addition within this framework was the Easter sequence *Victime paschali laudes*. Although probably com-

[49] As Ex. 99.

[50] De Boor, *Textgeschichte*, 147.

[51] These are the versions edited by Lipphardt in the third and fourth volumes of his *Osterfeiern*.

[52] Various scholars divide these categories according to different criteria; for a full discussion see Michael L. Norton, 'Of "Stages" and "Types" in *Visitatione Sepulchri*', *Comparative Drama*, 21 (1987), 34–61 and 127–44.

posed by Wipo, chaplain to the Emperor Conrad II,[53] this sequence appears only rarely in German plays, but is very characteristic of those from the region around and including Paris (Le Mans, Bourges, Sens, Châlons-sur-Marne, Soissons, Laon).[54] In a typical setting, the sequence would be divided into three parts; the first, announcing the victory of life over death, sung by the women to the choir; the second, beginning 'Dic nobis Maria', sung in dialogue between the cantor and each of three women, and the third by the cantor and choir (Ex. 101).[55] The sequence's greater engagement with interpretation of the resurrection than with portrayal of what happened means that it acts not so much as narrative extension of the dialogue but as amplification of the older announcement and celebration structure.

Elsewhere, a group of plays broke new ground by introducing the individual figures of Christ and Mary Magdalene. A scene depicting their encounter after the resurrection appears in several sources of Norman and English origin, and was probably composed in the later eleventh century. The texts are taken directly from John: 11–17, beginning with the angels' question 'Mulier quid ploras' and Mary Magdalene's reply 'Quia tulerunt', proceeding to Jesus' query 'Mulier quid ploras? Quem queris?' (at which Mary mistakes him for the gardener), and ending with the warning 'Noli me tangere'. Showing no connection with available chant models, the melodies for this scene share an E final and several phrase shapes as well as short motifs, and were obviously composed expressly for use in the play. They achieve the same kind of homogenous effect as those of the German recomposed dialogue; there is absolutely no hint of those techniques of characterization and expression of a dramatic situation used to such good effect in the Magi play. Although the idea of incorporating this episode in the Easter play may have travelled from west to east, the concrete designs for its dramatic integration and musical presentations certainly did not: the dialogue of Mary Magdalene and Christ used in various plays from further east bears no relation to the

---

[53] A marginal note on p. 17 of Einsiedeln, Stiftsbibliothek 366 (a collection of hymns and sequences copied at Einsiedeln in the twelfth century) records Wipo's authorship. For further bibliography see Josef Szöverffy, *Die Annalen der lateinischen Hymnendichtung*, 2 vols. (Berlin, 1964–5), i, 372–4, and *Religious Lyrics of the Middle Ages* (Berlin, 1983), 484–6.

[54] Paris: 29 sources, most ed. Young, *Drama*, i, 275 ff., 286 ff., 605 ff., and Lipphardt, *Osterfeiern*, i, Nos. 122–49; also London, British Library Harley 2927, fos. 285ᵛ–286ʳ. Le Mans: 2 sources, ed. Young, *Drama*, i, 288, 613, and Lipphardt, *Osterfeiern*, i, Nos. 113–14. Bourges: 3 sources, ed. Young, *Drama*, i, 293, 616, and Lipphardt, *Osterfeiern*, i, Nos. 96–8. Sens: 2 sources, ed. Young, *Drama*, i, 554, 615, and Lipphardt, *Osterfeiern*, i, Nos. 164–5). Châlons-sur-Marne: 4 sources, ed. Young, *Drama*, i, 279, 579, 610, and Lipphardt, *Osterfeiern*, i, Nos. 99–102. Soissons: 1 source, ed. Young, *Drama*, i, 554, and Lipphardt, *Osterfeiern*, i, No. 166. Laon: 2 sources, ed. Young, *Drama*, i, 620, and Lipphardt, *Osterfeiern*, i, 111–12.

[55] From Paris, Bibliothèque nationale lat. 15613, fo. 239ʳ⁻ᵛ.

Ex. 101

Tunc vertant se mulieres ad chorum et veniant cantando simul:

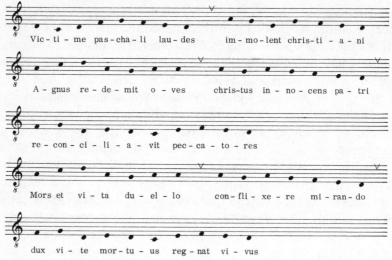

Vic - ti - me pas - cha - li lau - des im - mo - lent chris-ti - a - ni

A - gnus re - de - mit o - ves chris-tus in - no - cens pa - tri

re - con - ci - li - a - vit pec - ca - to - res

Mors et vi - ta du - el - lo con - fli - xe - re mi - ran - do

dux vi - te mor-tu - us reg - nat vi - vus

Tunc cantor stet in medio chori et dicat mulieribus:

Dic no - bis ma - ri - a quid vi - di - sti in vi - a?

Prima mulier sola:

Se - pul-chrum chris-ti vi - ven - tis et glo-ri-am vi - di re-sur-gen -tis

Secunda mulier sola:

An - ge - li - cos tes - tes su - da - ri - um et ves-tes

Tercia mulier sola:

Sur - re - xit chri-stus spes no - stra pre-ce - dit su -os in Ga - li -le - a

Cantor ad chorum:

Cre - den - dum est ma - gis so - li ma - ri - e ve - ra - ci

quam iu - de - o - rum tur - be fal - la - ci

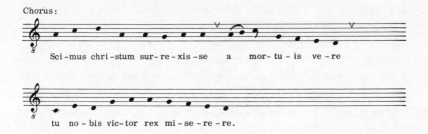

Chorus:

Sci-mus chri-stum sur-re-xis-se a mor-tu-is ve-re tu no-bis vic-tor rex mi-se-re-re.

Norman composition, and must have been conceived quite independently. At least two different sets of melodies appear to have been in circulation in the German realm, and there is much more variation between eastern forms of the play. The plays which include Mary Magdalene and Christ have the modern designation 'third stage'.[56]

These various new scenes and textual additions constitute the most widely-transmitted blocks of material added to, or substituted for, the *Quem queritis* dialogue in the *Visitatio Sepulchri* during the later Middle Ages. However, even when they had absorbed the same new ideas, no two versions of the play turned out the same, either in their dramatic structure or their sequence of sung texts. For no institution merely accepted another's version of the play without making alterations and improvements, in order to create an ensemble effective in a different architectural environment, or to conform to the requirements and potential of liturgical practice there, or just to suit local dramatic, textual, and musical taste. This interactive process encouraged the proliferation of short songs (often necessary to round off the corners of plays set in new environments), as well as more serious recomposition.

Under conditions so favourable to individual enterprise, plays of every possible size and quality were created, including some of great length, and many whose literary and dramatic design was worked out with considerable care. An Easter play recorded in an early twelfth-century Troper from Vich[57] has the earliest extant version of an encounter between the women and a merchant selling ointment, as they make their way to the sepulchre. With 86 lines arranged in 18 strophes preceding the *Quem queritis* dialogue, attention is drawn away from the dialogue to focus on the affective content and technical artifice of the preceding songs; the dialogue has become merely a suitable structure to which lyric composition could be attached (Ex. 102). Easter plays in two thirteenth-century sources, one from the

[56] All such versions are edited by Lipphardt in the fifth volume of his *Osterfeiern*.
[57] See above, n. 40.

Ex. 102

Li - cet so - ro - res plan - ge - re
plan - gen - do chri - stum que - re - re
que - ren - do cor - pus un - ge - re
un - guen - do men - te pas - ce - re
De fle - tu vi - so vul - ne - re
di - lec - to mag - no fe - de - re
cor mon - stra - tur in o - pe - re.

Benedictine monastery of Klosterneuburg (near Vienna),[58] the other in the *Carmina Burana* collection,[59] introduce the characters of Pilate, his soldiers, the high priests, a chorus of Jews, and the devil, expanding the narrative basis of the play considerably. That such plays retained a connection with the Office of Matins, without being incorporated in it, is suggested by the opening rubric of the *Carmina Burana* play:

Incipit ludus immo exemplum Dominice resurreccionis. Cantatis matutinis in die Pasche omnes persone ad ludum disposite sint parate in loco speciali secundum suum modum et procedant ad locum ubi sit sepulchrum.

---

[58] Klosterneuburg, Stiftsbibliothek 574, fos. 142ᵛ–144ᵛ; ed. Young, *Drama*, i, 421, and Lipphardt, *Osterfeiern*, v, No. 829.

[59] Munich, Staatsbibliothek lat. 4660a, fos. 5ʳ–6ᵛ; ed. Young, *Drama*, i, 432, and Lipphardt, *Osterfeiern*, v, No. 830. For further details of this source see below, pp. 355–6.

In fact, the term 'Ludus' was never used in a purely liturgical context; here it identifies a composition which stands on the borderline between liturgical and non-liturgical religious drama.[60] With over 300 lines, the Tours Easter play (preserved in a thirteenth-century manuscript of unknown origin) is the longest extant example belonging to this liturgically-based tradition.[61]

Ex. 103

Angels:

O vos chris - ti - co - le quem que -ri - tis es - se do - len - tes ?

Un - guen -tis - que sa - cri un - ge - re quem cu - pi - tis ?

Marys:

Que -ri - mus o su - pe - ri ci - ves ihe- sum cru - ci - fi - xum.

Di - ci - te quis no - bis sus- tu - lit hunc mi - se - ris.

Angels:

Non ia - cet hic qui - a sur- re - xit; ve - ni - te et vi - de - te.

A group of plays from the Benedictine convents at Poitiers, Troyes, Origny, and Wilton[62] share yet another recomposition of the *Quem queritis* dialogue (Ex. 103).[63] The Origny play is noteworthy not only for its length, including a negotiation with a merchant for ointment, the central dialogue at the sepulchre, the encounter of Mary Magdalene and Christ, and the race of the two disciples to the sepulchre, but also for its introduction of lyrics in the vernacular. These occur at two

---

[60] See below, pp. 352–6.
[61] Tours, Bibliothèque municipale 927, fos. 1ʳ–8ᵛ; ed. Young, *Drama*, i, 438, and Lipphardt, *Osterfeiern*, v, No. 824.
[62] Poitiers: Bibliothèque municipale 25, fo. 103ʳ⁻ᵛ; ed. Lipphardt, *Osterfeiern*, i, No. 153. Troyes: Bibliothèque municipale 792, fos. 301ᵛ–302ᵛ; ed. Young, *Drama*, i, 603, and Lipphardt, *Osterfeiern*, i, No. 170. For Origny see above, n. 40. For Wilton see above, n. 41.
[63] From St Quentin, Bibliothèque municipale 86, 616–17.

separate points, first in the dialogue between Marys and the merchant, and second in the dialogue between Mary Magdalene and an angel. Some of the strophes in the first of these episodes are no more than straight translations of their Latin counterparts, sung to essentially the same melody (Ex. 104).[64] These longer plays reveal an extremely complicated pattern of textual and musical interrelationships; even allowing that much information regarding paths of transmission is now lost, it seems hardly credible that the writers or composers of

Ex. 104

(Origny)

Di nous mar-chans tres bons vrais et loi - aus

cest un - gue - ment se tu ven - dre le veus

di tost du pris que tu a - voir en veus.

He - las ver - rons le nous ia - mais.

(Vich)

Dic tu no - bis mer - ca - tor iu - ve - nis

hoc un - guen - tum si tu ven - di - de - ris

dic pre - ci - um nam iam ha - bu - e - ris.

He - u quan - tus est nos - ter do - lor.

[64] From St Quentin, Bibliothèque municipale 86, 612–13, and Vich, Biblioteca Episcopal 105, fo. 58ᵛ.

some did not know at least two different versions of the *Visitatio Sepulchri* before they set about creating their own. An Easter play such as that in the Fleury Play-book could comprise material of Norman and German origin, as well as standard liturgical songs and new original composition. The unique and at the same time cosmopolitan nature of such plays was the result of extensive reworking of received material, a process motivated by original conceptions of how the narrative of the play should be disposed, and the expressive effects (lamenting, joy, astonishment) which the author wished to achieve.

PEREGRINUS PLAYS

There is no evidence to suggest that the story of Christ's appearance to Mary Magdalene after the resurrection was ever separately enacted, before its inclusion in the *Visitatio Sepulchri*. In contrast, three other appearances of the risen Christ reported by the Gospels of Luke and John formed the subject of the Peregrinus plays, performed at Vespers on Easter day, or on the first or second day following. The Peregrinus plays share with the Norman settings of Mary Magdalene's meeting with the risen Christ a close adherence to the Vulgate in the actual wording of the sung texts as well as the story, and this differentiates both from the *Quem queritis* dialogue. The story is that of an encounter on the road to Emmaus between two disciples and a stranger, whom they do not recognize as Jesus. The disciples invite this stranger to eat and rest with them for the night; sitting at table, he breaks bread and, in the moment of recognition, vanishes (Luke 24: 13–31). The second appearance (represented in all Peregrinus plays except those from the Cathedrals of Rouen and Padua) takes place in Jerusalem, where the two disciples have arrived, eager to tell the other disciples of their experience. Now Christ appears to the assembled company, displaying the flesh of his hands and feet as proof of his resurrection (Luke 24: 33–9). Some plays also add an episode from St John's Gospel, that of Christ's appearance before all the disciples, including the doubting Thomas (John 20: 24–9).

In the Emmaus story, as well as in John's account of Mary Magdalene's meeting with the risen Christ, the relevant biblical passages were in large part expressed in direct speech, and did not require any conversion for dramatic use. One of the rubrics in the Paduan play[65] indicates the Gospel as the sole source of sung texts:

Et ipse Christi dicit ad eos:
    Qui sunt hii sermones quos confertis ad invicem?
Et prosecuntur verba Evangelii ...

[65] Ed. Young, *Drama*, i, 482.

This opportunity to extract suitable texts from a commonly available source meant that composers working in separate institutions could independently produce Peregrinus plays with similar texts. Of the surviving versions, several which share material were, most probably, isolated creations. Several Peregrinus plays of French and Sicilian origin, however, share non-biblical, non-liturgical elements, indicating their common relation to at least one original Peregrinus composition. The earliest extant sources of Peregrinus plays are three Sicilian books copied in the early and mid-twelfth century.[66] Later sources which share original texts and music with these three comprise books from Beauvais,[67] Rouen,[68] and Saintes,[69] and the Fleury Play-book.[70] Three long Easter plays, in Tours 927[71] and in manuscripts from Maastricht and Egmont[72] include the *Quem queritis* dialogue, with preceding material, the Mary Magdalene's meeting with Christ, and some Peregrinus episodes textually and musically related to the autonomous Peregrinus plays. We might also add to this list references to the performance of Peregrinus plays at Bayeux, Lille, Malmesbury, and Lichfield; thus, a pattern of diffusion concentrated in northern France, England, and Sicily emerges.

Plays which show no specific relation to the French tradition include the *Versus de Pelegrinis* of Vich (early twelfth century),[73] a play recorded in the fragments attached to the *Carmina Burana* manuscript,[74] and a short ceremony described in a thirteenth-century Ordinale for the Cathedral of Padua. A striking detail of this Paduan ceremony is the throwing down of wafers from the roof of the church 'to be caught by all who are able', following Christ's breaking of bread

[66] Madrid, Biblioteca Nacional 288, fos. 172^v–173^v; 289, fos. 117^r–118^v; Vitrina 20–4, fos. 105^v–108^r; ed. Young, *Drama*, i, 459 (289), 477 (Vit. 20–4), and Lipphardt, *Osterfeiern*, v, Nos. 818–19, 811. The date and place of origin of the three manuscripts are discussed in David Hiley, 'The Norman Chant Traditions: Normandy, Britain, Sicily', *PRMA*, 107 (1980–1), 1–33, especially 17.

[67] Paris, Bibliothèque nationale lat.n.a. 1064, fos. 8^r–11^v; ed. Young: *Drama*, i, 467, and Lipphardt, *Osterfeiern*, v, No. 808.

[68] The play survives in four Rouen sources, only one of which has music: Rouen, Bibliothèque municipale 222, fos. 43^v–45^r; ed. with the other three versions Young, *Drama*, i, 461 (222), 692, and Lipphardt, *Osterfeiern*, v, Nos. 812–15.

[69] Paris, Bibliothèque nationale lat. 16309, fos. 604^r–605^r; ed. Young, *Drama*, i, 453, and Lipphardt, *Osterfeiern*, v, No. 816.

[70] Orléans, Bibliothèque municipale 201, pp. 225–30; ed. Young, *Drama*, i, 471, and Lipphardt, *Osterfeiern*, v, No. 817. For further details of this source see below, pp. 352–55.

[71] See above, n. 61.

[72] The Hague, Koninklijke. Bibliiotheek 76.F.3, fos. 3^r and 14^r; 71.J.70, fos. 162^v–170^r; ed. Lipphardt, *Osterfeiern*, v, Nos. 826–7. The melodies are ed. by Joseph Smits van Waesberghe, 'A Dutch Easter Play', *Musica disciplina*, 7 (1953), 15–37.

[73] Vich, Biblioteca Episcopal 105, fos. 60^r–62^v; ed. Young, *Drama*, i, 681, and Lipphardt, *Osterfeiern*, v, No. 823.

[74] Munich, Staatsbibliothek 4660a, fo. 7^{r-v}; ed. Young, *Drama*, i, 463, and Lipphardt, *Osterfeiern*, v, No. 820. For further details of this source see below, p. 355.

and disappearance; the falling wafers can be understood to be distributed by the risen Christ in heaven. In rendering the eucharistic parallel explicit, a transition from re-enacted story to ritual reality is effected, demonstrating once again just how close a play may come to standard liturgical ritual. It would have been impossible to provide a ritual conclusion of this nature for the French Peregrinus plays, since they usually went beyond this point in the narrative to include at least Christ's first appearance in Jerusalem.

Peregrinus plays used a much higher proportion of chant melodies than other liturgical plays, not because of an especial absence of creative impulse on the part of Peregrinus composers, but by virtue of the fact that for no other play was so much textual material already set as Gregorian chant. Unlike the *Exemplum apparicionis domini discipulis suis* in the *Carmina Burana* collection, however, the French and Sicilian Peregrinus plays are much more than mere collections of chants sung in an order corresponding to the Vulgate narrative: the common core of material shared by all versions in the group includes a significant number of non-Gregorian melodies, as well as some texts not derived from the bible or the liturgy. These new elements are integrated with the pre-existent material in a highly organized fashion,

Ex. 105

Disciples:

Ma‑ne no‑bis‑cum quo‑ni‑am ad ves‑pe‑ras‑cit

et in‑cli‑na‑ta est iam di‑es al‑le‑lu‑ia.

Sol ver‑gens ad oc‑ca‑sum su‑a‑det ut nos‑trum ve‑lis hos‑pi‑ci‑um

pla‑cent e‑nim no‑bis ser‑mo‑nes tu‑i quos re‑fers

de re‑sur‑rec‑ti‑o‑ne ma‑gi‑stri nos‑tri al‑le‑lu‑ia.

and can be identified at a whole series of different structural levels. In its most substantial form the new composition entailed the invention of speeches implied but not actually reported in the Vulgate, as well as melodies for these. Thus, for example, to emphasize the disciples' insistence that the stranger rest with them at Emmaus, the Vulgate speech 'Mane nobiscum' is followed by another beginning 'Sol vergens'. The new melody adopts the final (G) and range (G–g) of the Office antiphon melody for *Mane nobiscum*.[75] (See Ex. 105.[76]) Another example of a new text and melody is the lament 'Heu miseri', which opens with an expressive fall through a sixth. This follows the Vulgate speech 'Nonne cor', using the final (D) and range of the Office antiphon melody for these Vulgate words.[77] 'Nonne cor' itself exemplifies another, rather more hidden, procedure: that of composing extensions to chant melodies for sections of the Vulgate text not set in the chant, as here for the concluding phrase 'et aperiret nobis scripturas'. These words are set to melodic material heard again at the end of 'Heu miseri' (Ex. 106).[78] This linking of two distinct but

Ex. 106

Disciples:

Non - ne   cor nos - trum   ar - dens e - rat in no - bis de ihe - su

dum lo - que - re - tur   no - bis   in   vi - a

et   a - pe - ri - ret   no - bis scrip-tu - ras.

He - u   mi - se - ri u - bi   e - rat   sen - sus nos - ter

quo in - tel - lec-tus a - bi - e - rat   al - le - lu - ia.

[75] *CAO* 3690.
[76] From Madrid, Biblioteca Nacional 289, fos. 117ᵛ–118ʳ.
[77] *CAO* 3943.
[78] From Madrid, Biblioteca Nacional 289, fo. 118ʳ.

successively sung melodic units provides some insights into the ways in which old and new material could be integrated (i.e by the use of similar modal parameters), as well as the level of musical cohesion considered desirable by the Peregrinus composers. The *raison d'être* of a third category of new composition, melodies set to Vulgate texts for which a chant version was already available, may indeed be modal continuity between texts sung successively. In the case of the texts 'Pax vobis' and 'Videte manus' for example, neither has the usual chant melody; instead the three consecutive texts, 'Pax vobis', 'Videte manus', and 'Palpate' have new original melodies, all using similar modal patterns and motifs.

For some parts of the play, however, new composition was hardly required, as in the opening dialogue beginning 'Qui sunt hii'; all four parts of this exchange, including two speeches by the disciples and two by Christ, are taken from one long Office antiphon.[79]

All of this shows that those texts and melodies which form the core of the French and Sicilian Peregrinus plays were built up in an extremely careful way, using the liturgical chant as a major source of texts and melodies, but by no means depending on it entirely. The most important consideration seems to have been the faithful representation of Christ's various appearances to the disciples, following the Vulgate account; this determined the overall shape, many details of the texts, and not least the degree of 'realized' detail—each event, circumstance, and emotion described in the Vulgate being intentionally portrayed in what is sung. In fact, in the Sicilian plays, descriptive passages such as 'Cum autem' (Luke 24: 28: 'And they drew nigh unto the village, whither they went: and he made as though he would have gone further') are not only represented in actions and movement, but actually sung by a chorus. Rather than being organized to produce a specific ritual outcome (as in the *Quem queritis* dialogue) or concerned with the identities of individual characters (as in the Magi play), the three Sicilian and the Saintes Peregrinus plays simply present the Vulgate story, without dramatic adornment or manipulation. And, since there is no element of interpretation in their presentation of the story, they could almost be said to correspond closely to Gospel readings as liturgical acts.

The composer of the Beauvais Peregrinus play must have had access to the same model as that used by the Norman Sicilians; written down in the mid-twelfth century, this version has the same underlying narrative structure (including the Thomas scene), as well as many of the same texts and melodies which realize this structure. Only here, as

[79] *CAO* 4550.

in the Beauvais Circumcision Office and Play of Daniel,[80] the influence of the new song style is much in evidence, versified texts accounting for about one half of the whole play. In dressing up the old Peregrinus play the Beauvais composer mixed up prose and verse texts, forming his Peregrinus representation in three ways: first, he retained old prose texts and their associated melodies; second, he added new verse songs; and third, he rewrote some of the old prose texts in verse form. In the rewritten pieces the new text and melody often incorporate characteristic phrases of the old, rendering their derivation easily recognizable. A sequence of three texts from the end of the scene on the road to Emmaus illustrates all three procedures: *Declinante* is an entirely new song; *Mane nobiscum* is an Office antiphon; *Sol vergens* has been recomposed and versified (Ex. 107).[81]

Ex. 107

One disciple:

De-cli-nan-te ves-pe-ra　　noc-tis in-stant tem-po-ra

nec pa-tent i-ti-ne-ra　sub-sis-te　The other disciple: Ma-ne no-bis-cum...

Both disciples:

Iam sol ver-gens ad oc-ca-sum　su-a-det hos-pi-ci-um

nos-trum pa-ter ob-se-cra-mus　in-tres ha-bi-ta-cu-lum

pla-cent e-nim tu-i no-bis　ser-mo-nis col-lo-qui-a

que de nos-tri re-fe-re-bas　ma-gis-tri vic-to-ri-a.

---

[80] Both are preserved in one codex which retains its medieval binding: London, British Library Egerton 2615. The Circumcision Office is studied and edited by Wulf Arlt, *Ein Festoffizium des Mittelalters aus Beauvais in seiner liturgischen und musikalischen Bedeutung*, 2 vols. (Cologne, 1970). For the Daniel play see below, pp. 348–52.

[81] Paris, Bibliothèque nationale lat.n.a. 1064, fo. 9^{r-v}.

For that part of Christ's encounter with the disciples which immediately precedes these three texts the older model has been extensively expanded: three prose sentences are replaced by thirty-five lines of verse. This new rendition constitutes the only instance in a Peregrinus play of a realization of the verse 'And beginning at Moses and all the prophets he expounded unto them in all the scriptures the things concerning himself' (Luke 24: 27). Apart from this, the dimensions of the Beauvais play approximate closely to the longer of the Sicilian Peregrinus plays,[82] and both have the same liturgical position, as part of the procession to the font at Vespers.

The only Peregrinus play which attempts to go well beyond the details provided by the Vulgate narrative, adding new interpretative dimensions as well as many more texts, is that found in the Fleury Play-book. Here, the greater degree of complexity necessitated unusually detailed rubrics concerning dress and actions. In each successive appearance, Christ returns in ever more impressive garb: first he is dressed as a pilgrim, with bare feet, then in a white tunic, red cope, and embroidered cap, carrying a golden cross, later again in the white tunic and red cope, with a crown, and carrying both the golden cross and a book of Gospels (presumably richly decorated). Dressed thus, he is led out of the choir and shown 'to the people' (*ut videatur a populo*) at the end of the play. Despite its elaborate nature, this play must have been performed mainly out of the sight of the uninitiated. Not so the Peregrinus of Rouen Cathedral, which was performed in full view of all who chose to watch: the disciples entered by the right door in the west front and moved towards the font, followed by Christ, who entered by the left door in the west front. All three then proceeded towards a construction erected in the middle of the nave, described as 'in similitudinem castelli Emaus preparatum'. Like Rouen's version of the Magi play, however, its Peregrinus play represents a severely curtailed version of that performed elsewhere. None of Christ's appearances after the Emmaus meal are re-enacted. Instead the play concludes with part of the Easter sequence *Victime paschali laudes*, sung by the two disciples, two 'women', and chorus.

THE SHEPHERDS' PLAY

A Christmas play in which angels sing to shepherds is first described in the treatise *De Officiis Ecclesiasticis* of Jean, Bishop of Avranches (1060–7),[83] and later Archbishop of Rouen. Thus, like the Peregrinus

---

[82] In Madrid, Biblioteca Nacional Vitrina 20–4.

[83] Ed. by René Delamare, *Le De officiis ecclesiasticis de Jean d'Avranches, archevêque de Rouen (1067–79)* (Paris, 1923).

play, the *Officium Pastorum* or Shepherds' play first emerges at the end of the eleventh century, and in the Norman domain. But the diffusion of this Norman Christmas play is much more confined than that of the *Peregrinus*, and its liturgical position and ritual characteristics more akin to the *Visitatio Sepulchri*. In fact, it is built around another dialogue trope *Quem queritis in presepe*, itself modelled on *Quem queritis in sepulchro* (Ex. 108).[84]

This dialogue first appears in Aquitanian and southern French Tropers of the late tenth century as a trope of the Introit of the third Christmas Mass, *Puer natus est nobis*. It also turns up in some eleventh- and twelfth-century Tropers from northern France, Spain, and northern Italy.[85] *Quem queritis in presepe* was, without doubt, first conceived as an Introit trope; it must, therefore, have been in imitation of the widespread practice of placing *Quem queritis in sepulchro* in the Matins Office that its Christmas counterpart was transferred to a Matins position in some liturgical uses. At the Cathedral of Clermont-Ferrand, for example, the Christmas dialogue trope followed Te deum laudamus, joining the end of Matins to the beginning of the first Christmas Mass (Introit *Dominus dixit ad me*).[86] Sung by two boys (representing angels?) and two 'pastores' standing by the altar, its performance embraces the same mixture of ritual and understated representational elements as some of the simple *Quem queritis* ceremonies. At Padua, the trope gained a more explicit representational dimension by being performed around a crib, placed in the centre of the choir.[87]

The Paduan ceremony is recorded in a thirteenth-century book, that from Clermont-Ferrand in fourteenth- and fifteenth-century books. Clearly independent and established at a much earlier date, the Norman *Officium Pastorum* also adopted the *Quem queritis in presepe* trope, but added more texts around it, insisting more than these others on the biblical story of Christ's birth. Related versions include one preserved in a mid-twelfth-century manuscript, which also includes a treatise based on Jean d'Avranches' *De officiis ecclesiasticis* and a Magi play,[88] and those in liturgical books from Rouen and

---

[84] From Paris, Bibliothèque nationale lat. 1121, fo. 2ʳ⁻ᵛ.

[85] All trope versions of *Quem queritis in presepe* are ed. Ritva Jonsson: *Corpus Troporum*, 1, *Tropes du propre de la messe, 1, Cycle de Noël* (Stockholm, 1975).

[86] Paris, Bibliothèque nationale lat. 1274, fo. 28ᵛ, and three other sources ed. Young, *Drama*, ii, 11, and Victor Leroquais, *Les Bréviaires manuscrits des bibliothèques publiques de France*, 6 vols. (Paris, 1934), i, 341 and iii, 440; also Paris, Bibliothèque nationale lat.n.a. 116, fo. 407ʳ (unpublished).

[87] Padua, Biblioteca Capitolare ms. S, fos. 40ᵛ–41ᵛ; ed. Young, *Drama*, ii, 9.

[88] Montpellier, Faculté de Médecine H.304, fo. 41ʳ⁻ᵛ; ed. Young, *Drama*, ii, 12.

Ex. 108

Quem que - ri - tis in pre - se - pe   pas - to - res di - ci - te?

Sal - va - to - rem   chris - tum do - mi - num   in - fan - tem

pan - nis   in - vo - lu - tum   se - cun - dum ser - mo - nem an - ge - li - cum.

Ad - est hic   par - vu - lus cum ma - ri - a   ma - tre su - a

de qua du - dum va - ti - ci - nan - do i - sa - i - as di - xe - rat pro - phe - ta:

Ec - ce vir - go con - ci - pi - et et pa - ri - et fi - li - um

et nunc e - un - tes di - ci - te qui - a   na - tus est

Al - le - lu - ia al - le - lu - ia iam ve - re sci - mus christum na - tum   in terris

de   quo ca - ni - te om - nes   cum pro - phe - ta   di - cen - tes:

Pu - er na - tus est   no - bis...

Lisieux Cathedrals.[89] Outside of Normandy, some of the same material is found in the Fleury Play-book Magi play,[90] and also in the mainly vernacular Shrewsbury fragments from Lichfield Cathedral.[91]

This Norman play adds before the dialogue a scene in which angels sing to the shepherds, proclaiming the birth of Christ. This prompts the shepherds' movement to Bethlehem to find the new-born child, thus providing an appropriate narrative context for the *Quem queritis* dialogue. The first scene required no new text composition, for the Vulgate provided all the necessary speeches, expressed in the first person:

[Angel]. 'Nolite timere: ecce enim evangelizo vobis . . .'
       (Luke 2: 10–12: 'Fear not: for behold, I bring you good tidings')
[Angels]. 'Gloria in excelsis Deo et in terra pax . . .'
                              (Luke 2: 14)
[Shepherds]. 'Transeamus usque Bethlehem . . .'
       (Luke 2: 15–16: 'Let us now go even unto Bethlehem')

All three texts have new melodies in a fairly simple style, rather similar to those composed during the same period for the Norman Mary Magdalene scene added to the *Visitatio Sepulchri*.

The *Officium Pastorum* of Rouen Cathedral stands out as a more elaborate version of the Norman play than the others, with two short but delightful lyric songs. The first, sung by the shepherds as they process towards the crib, also appears in two contemporary collections of songs, and may therefore have been composed quite independently of the play.[92] It has two verses, with a repeated refrain (Ex. 109).[93] The second lyric addition, 'Salve virgo singularis', was sung before a statue of the Virgin and child, revealed from behind a curtain during the *Quem queritis in presepe* dialogue.

OTHER CHRISTMAS PLAYS

With the *Officium Pastorum* plays for Christmas Day, we reach a

[89] Rouen: Paris, Bibliothèque nationale lat. 904, fos. 11ᵛ–14ʳ; ed. Young, *Drama*, ii, 16. The whole manuscript is reproduced in facsimile in Henri Loriquet, Joseph Pothier, and Armand Collette, eds., *Le Graduel de l'église cathédrale de Rouen au xiii siècle*, 2 vols. (Rouen, 1907). Also three other sources, ed. Young, *Drama*, ii, 14, 428. Lisieux: Bayeux, Bibliothèque du Chapitre 662, fo. 591ᵛ; ed. Leroquais, *Bréviaires*, i, 115.

[90] Orléans, Bibliothèque municipale 201, pp. 205–6; ed. Young, *Drama*, ii, 84.

[91] Shrewsbury, Shrewsbury School VI, fos. 38ʳ–39ʳ; ed. Young, *Drama*, ii, 514; see also Susan Rankin, 'Shrewsbury School, Manuscript VI: A Medieval Part Book?', *PRMA*, 102 (1975–6), 129–44.

[92] Paris, Bibliothèque nationale lat. 4880, fo. 84ʳ, and Cambridge, University Library Ff.1.17(1), fo. 300ᵛ.

[93] Paris, Bibliothèque nationale lat. 904, fo. 12ʳ, with corrections based on the concordant version in CUL Ff.1.17(1).

Ex. 109

point beyond which no individual text tradition ever achieved wide acceptance. In fact, the relatively restricted diffusion of the Norman Shepherds' play, in comparison with that of the Peregrinus play (first composed during the same period), reflects a disparity between Easter and Christmas plays in general. The various types and single examples of extant plays for the Christmas season include, besides the Shepherds' and Magi plays, the *Ordo Rachelis* for the Feast of the Holy Innocents, *Ordo Prophetarum* for an unspecified day, *Ludus Danielis*, probably for the Feast of the Circumcision, and the large Christmas play in the *Carmina Burana* collection, again for an unspecified day; of these only the Magi play survives in more than a handful of sources.

THE *ORDO PROPHETARUM* AND *LUDUS DANIELIS*

As with most of the different kinds of play so far examined, the *Ordo Prophetarum* had its own unique origins: its text was derived from a sermon often read at Christmas and popularly attributed to St Augustine of Hippo (although probably not by him).[94] In this sermon, a series of witnesses including prophets, kings, and other Old and New Testament personages, along with Virgil and the Sibyl, are called on to speak concerning the coming of Christ and thereby testify against the Jews. This provided the basis for a dialogue structure, in which an ecclesiastical figure or figures (cantors, chorus, *appellatores*, *vocatores*) could interpolate celebratory songs, questions, and commentary between the testimonies of the witnesses (of whom at least thirteen appear in the plays). Two of the three extant sources, from Laon Cathedral (thirteenth century) and Rouen Cathedral (fourteenth century),[95] specify costumes for all characters, and, in the case of Rouen, movements and actions integrated into the general framework of a procession. The earliest source, in the oldest part of Paris Bibliothèque Nationale lat. 1139,[96] has no such rubrics, leaving some doubt as to the manner of its performance. However, its grouping in the manuscript with two other dramatic texts, an Easter play and the *Sponsus* (Play of the Wise and Foolish Virgins), implies that it was regarded as a similar kind of composition. This part of Paris 1139 was copied in the early twelfth century, not necessarily at St Martial-de-Limoges, although it was bound together with other material at the monastery in the early thirteenth century.[97] It is full of new poetic compositions of a religious nature, some with easily recognizable liturgical destinations, others more difficult to place. The new 'Procession of Prophets' dialogue appears no stranger in this context, being composed entirely in verse, although its metrical style is more old-fashioned than much that surrounds it.[98] In keeping with this entirely lyric expression, the music has the character of a lai, repeating or altering melodic structures according to the metrical pattern of the

---

[94] Migne, *Patrologia Latina*, vol 42, col. 1117; see also Young, *Drama*, ii, 125.

[95] Laon, Bibliothèque municipale 263, fos. 147ᵛ–149ʳ; ed. Young, *Drama*, ii, 145. Rouen, Bibliothèque municipale 384, fos. 33ʳ–35ʳ, and 382, fos. 31ᵛ–33ʳ; ed. Young, *Drama*, ii, 154.

[96] Fos. 55ᵛ–56ʳ; ed. Young, *Drama*, ii, 138.

[97] See Sarah Fuller, 'The Myth of "Saint Martial" Polyphony', *Musica disciplina*, 33 (1979), 5–26, and Hans Spanke, 'St. Martial-Studien: Ein Beitrag zur frühromanischen Metrik', in Ulrich Mölk, ed., *Studien zur lateinischen und romanischen Lyrik des Mittelalters* (Hildesheim, 1983), 1–103, especially 6 ff.

[98] Spanke, 'St. Martial-Studien', 46.

Ex. 110

Om - nes gen-tes con - gau -den - tes dent can - tum le - ti - ci - e

De - us ho - mo fit de do - mo Da - vid na - tus ho - di - e

and

Is - ra - el vir le - nis in - que de chris-to nos - ti fir - me

and

Da - ni - el in - di - ca vo-ce pro - pheti - ca fac-ta domi-ni-ca

text (see Ch. IX). Since all the melodic phrases move between C, F and c, and cadence on F, the overall effect is one of continuity, without the least hint of monotony (Ex. 110).[99] Unlike most other liturgical plays, the 'Procession of Prophets' has no developing narrative, but rather remains static, relating to one event, the birth of Christ. For a text structure lacking points of high tension and resolution, probably no more suitable musical expression than this changing but uniform interpretation could have been found.

One of the most interesting of twelfth-century liturgical plays is the *Ludus Danielis* of Beauvais.[100] Produced in a Cathedral school rather than a monastery, it opens with a clear announcement of the identity of its composers and their intentions (Ex. 111). The Play of Daniel

Ex. 111

INCIPIT DANIELIS LUDUS

Ad ho - no - rem tu - i chris-te Da - ni - e - lis lu - dus is - te

In Bel - va - co est in - ven - tus et in - ve - nit hunc iu - ven - tus.

[99] Paris, Bibliothèque nationale lat. 1139, fos. 55ᵛ–6ᵛ.

[100] London, British Library Egerton 2615, fos. 95ʳ–108ʳ; ed. Young, *Drama*, ii, 290; also ed. (with music) by W. L. Smoldon, *The Play of Daniel*, Plainsong & Mediæval Music Society (London, 1960).

combines material from the Old Testament book of Daniel and an apocryphal book, *Daniel and Susanna*, presenting the story of Daniel's interpretation of the writing on the wall for Belshazzar, and his glorification by that king, followed by the arrival of King Darius, who deposes Belshazzar, and later condemns Daniel to be eaten by lions. The prophet Habakkuk brings food to the distraught Daniel, who is then rescued by an angel. The play closes with Daniel's prophecy 'Ecce venit sanctus ille, sanctorum sanctissimus', followed by the hymns *Nuntium vobis fero de supernis* and Te deum laudamus. The rubrics evoke an unusually vivid *mise-en-scène*, including a pit equipped with lions into which Daniel is thrown; references in the rubrics to zither players who should accompany King Darius, and in a processional song to the dancers and musicians of his court, add to the impression of brilliant pageantry conveyed by the costume descriptions. The instruments mentioned by name are drums and *citharae*, but the song implies the use of a greater variety (Ex. 112).

Ex. 112

Si - mul om - nes gra - tu - le - mur   re - so - nent et tym - pa - na

Cy - tha - ris - te tan - gant cor - das   mu - si - co - rum or - ga - na

Re - so - nent ad ei - us pre - co - ni - a.

The Play of Daniel has much in common with the three Prophets' plays: all prophesy and celebrate the coming of Christ, are composed entirely in rhythmical verse, and show a corresponding absence of liturgical chants (except the hymns at the end of *Daniel*). But *Daniel* is a play of a quite different nature from the Prophets' play, drawing the listener into the story of a struggle between the spiritual and temporal worlds. One of several ironic dimensions of this dramatic composition is the use of a recurring refrain 'Rex in eternum vive', addressed to Belshazzar and Darius by all characters including Daniel—this despite his refusal to obey Darius' edict that 'for thirty days he [Darius] should be worshipped as the God of all, all other power of divinity being scorned'; the melody for 'Rex in eternum vive' underscores the irony by recalling that of the Carolingian *Laudes regiae* acclamations for 'Christus vincit, Christus regnat'.

Just as this opposition of the kings of heaven and earth has an obvious parallel in the Magi play, so too in the music of *Daniel* we are reminded of its Epiphany counterpart; composing without reliance on old material, the Beauvais students used music not only to interpret the dramatic situation according to ritual objectives, but also to explore the position of individual characters. They managed to do this in several ways, linking individuals with particular modal idioms (but not with any rigidity), altering the mode of successive texts sung by different characters, and contrasting simple with elaborate melodic styles, as well as wide and small ranges. For example, the three songs with the widest range in the play (a tenth) are associated with particularly impressive or dramatic moments: 'Iubilemus regi nostro',

Ex. 113

sung in praise of Belshazzar near the beginning of the play, 'Ecce rex', which accompanies the entrance of Darius, and 'Heu heu', Daniel's plea for pardon after Darius' order that he should be thrown to the lions (Ex. 113).

The other striking quality of the *Daniel* music—one which sets it apart from the Prophets' play—is the wealth of its melodic invention, matching each different poetic form (of which there are many) with a new group of melodic ideas. And the students of Beauvais displayed their delight in lyric composition of the newest kind, leaving aside the Gregorian-style melody so typical of many plays, especially those of Norman origin. Daniel's declamatory and lamenting 'Heu heu' shows eloquently how far from the idiom of Gregorian chant and how much closer to the world of the secular lyric the *Daniel* melodies can sound. Certainly, in their choice of mode and use of melisma, a small number of melodies imitate Gregorian idioms, while a majority of others adopt a simpler style associated with the sequence and conductus repertories. Still others lay emphasis on melodic ornamentation, although this remains controlled within a balanced formal design.

The closing rubric of *Daniel* specifies Te deum laudamus, thereby implying performance at Matins. And despite its non-liturgical manner of expression, *Daniel* is nevertheless thoroughly medieval and typically liturgical in relating its historical narrative to an event which happened much later (the birth of Christ). *Daniel* is obviously intended for the Christmas season; from the reference in the opening song to the young people or students of Beauvais we can infer an association with the day chosen for the subdeacons' feast, often January 1st (also the Feast of the Circumcision).[101] Support for this hypothesis is provided by the manuscript source, which also preserves an exceptionally detailed liturgy for the Circumcision Feast, written in the same scriptorium during the same period.[102]

THE FLEURY PLAY-BOOK AND THE *CARMINA BURANA*

First christened the 'Fleury Play-book' by Karl Young,[103] this group of four gatherings bound at the back of a manuscript now in the Bibliothèque municipale at Orléans is unique in its content, consisting of nothing else besides ten notated and rubricated plays (and a sequence added later).[104] These gatherings, written in the third quarter

---

[101] On the subdeacons' feast see Wulf Arlt, *Festoffizium*, ch. 3, 'Die Neujahrsfeier der Kirche und das "Narrenfest"'.

[102] Ibid. 23–6.

[103] Young, *Drama*, i, 665.

[104] Orléans, Bibliothèque municipale 201, pp. 176–243. Transcribed and reproduced in facsimile by Giampero Tintori and Raffaello Monterosso, *Sacre rappresentazioni nel manoscritti*

of the twelfth century by one hand, were bound together with a group of sermons at the abbey of St-Benoit-sur-Loire at Fleury before 1400.[105] The ten plays are arranged in groups, following the order of the liturgical year, except for the last two:

Miracle plays of St Nicholas   I *Tres filiae*
                                II *Tres clerici*
                                III *Iconia sancti Nicholai*
                                IV *Filius Getronis*

Magi play
Innocents' play
Visitatio Sepulchri
Peregrinus
Conversion of St Paul
Resurrection of Lazarus

The uniqueness of the collection lies not only in its size and exclusivity, but also in the association of these ten plays together: several with long-established liturgical traditions are mixed with others of more recent and less directly liturgical conception. Two extremes are represented by the *Conversion of St Paul*,[106] the only extant example of a Latin play on this subject (and probably created within the milieu to which the book belonged), and the *Visitatio Sepulchri*. In fact, with its assorted types of play and the variety of their textual and musical means of expression, the Fleury Play-book represents a compendium of church drama, liturgical and non-liturgical, derived from geographically diverse traditions. But the plays do not lack homogeneity, since the community which gathered these dramatic texts also imposed its own stamp—an emphasis on theatrical display and a love of rhymed verse in a myriad of patterns. Further, at least eight of the ten were probably intended for performance as part of a liturgical Office.

From a musical point of view, the plays fall into three groups. First, the two Christmas and two Easter plays, all of which are based on older models, have the usual mixture of old and new melodies. Second, the *Tres clerici* (in honour of St Nicholas),[107] and the

---

201 della Bibliothèque municipale di Orléans (Cremona, 1958). A much clearer facsimile is provided in Thomas P. Campbell and Clifford Davidson, eds., *The Fleury Playbook: Essays and Studies* (Kalamazoo, 1985).

[105] Michel Huglo, 'Analyse codicologique des drames liturgiques de Fleury', in Jacques Lemaire and Emile van Balberghe, eds., *Calames et Cahiers: Mélanges de codicologie et de paléographie offerts à Léon Gilissen* (Brussels, 1985), 61–78, studies codicological and repertorial aspects of the manuscript.

[106] Ed. Young, *Drama*, ii, 219.

[107] All four Nicholas plays are ed. Young, *Drama*, ii, ch. 26.

Ex. 114

(*Tres clerici*)

1st. cleric:

Nos quos cau - sa   dis - cen - di   li - te - ras

a - pud gen - tes   trans-mi - sit   ex - te - ras

dum sol ad - huc   ex - ten - dit   ra - di - um

per - qui - ra - mus   no - bis hos - pi - ci - um.

2nd. cleric:

Iam sol e - quos   te - net in   li - to - re

quos ad pre - sens   mer- get sub   e - quo - re.

Nec est no - ta   no - bis hec   pa - tri - a

er - go que - ri   de - bent hos - pi - ci - a.

Resurrection of Lazarus[108] both use repeated strophic melody, a procedure rendered possible by the repetition of one verse-pattern throughout the whole of each play (Ex. 114). Another St Nicholas play (*Tres filiae*) also belongs in this category: it has two melodies only, each associated with a particular verse-pattern. The third group includes the *Conversion of St Paul* and the other two Nicholas plays,

[108] Ed. Young, *Drama*, ii, 199.

Iconia sancti Nicolai and *Filius Getronis*. Like the Prophets' play, all three have a lai-like musical structure, such that with each new verse pattern a new melody is introduced. In fact, the melodic material is even more varied than this, since parts of the text which use the same pattern for a comparatively extended length of time may have two or even three different melodies.

Although the origins of the Play-book cannot be established with any certainty, something of the context in which it belonged can be surmised from the contents. The mixture of material, the interest in verse composition, and concern with the legends of St Nicholas all suggest that the plays were produced within a cosmopolitan student milieu. Palaeographical characteristics suggest that the book was written somewhere in the Île-de-France, by an individual who lacked access to a well-provided scriptorium. Probably, it was in the student circles of either Paris or Orléans, rather than in the confines of a Benedictine cloister, that this rich and varied collection of plays was enjoyed.[109]

The main part of the *Carmina Burana* codex, consisting of a collection of moral and satirical songs, love-lyrics, goliardic drinking songs, and religious plays, was compiled some fifty years after the Fleury Play-book (*c.* 1225–30).[110] Additions were made during the next century, including five more plays, making a total of seven in the whole codex:

	added
Christmas play	*c.* 1225–30
Play of the King of Egypt	*c.* 1225–30
Passion play	*c.* 1250
Peregrinus play	*c.* 1250
Assumption play (fragment)	*c.* 1250
Passion play (*Ludus breviter*)	middle or 2nd half of 13th cent.
Easter play	*c.* 2nd half or end of 13th cent.

Three of these—the Christmas and Easter plays, and the first Passion play—are much longer than anything so far encountered in the repertory of liturgical drama; the Christmas play actually amalgamates material from the Procession of Prophets, Magi, and Innocents

---

[109] The arguments presented by Solange Corbin in favour of an origin at the Abbey of St-Lhomer-de-Blois ('Le Manuscrit 201 d'Orléans: drames liturgiques dits de Fleury', *Romania*, 74 (1953), 1–43) have since been rejected by several scholars: see Huglo, 'Analyse'.

[110] Ed. in Bernhard Bischoff, *Carmina Burana: Faksimile-Ausgabe der Hs. Clm 4660 + Clm 4660a* (Brooklyn, New York, 1967). Complete edition of the text by Otto Schumann, Bernhard Bischoff, and Alfons Hilka, *Carmina Burana*, 3 vols. (Heidelberg, 1930, 1941, 1970); all the plays are in vol. iii. The most recent discussion of the place of origin of the manuscript is in Georg Steer, '"Carmina Burana" in Südtirol: Zur Herkunft des clm 4660', *Zeitschrift für deutsches Altertum und deutsche Literatur*, 112 (1983), 1–37.

plays into one discrete unit. Unfortunately, since the entire codex is notated in German staffless neumes, none of the music can be directly transcribed;[111] comparison with concordant sources allows the reconstruction of some parts, but much of the non-liturgical versified material has no pitched concordances.

The *Carmina Burana* plays and those of the Fleury Play-book have much in common: both collections draw textual and musical material from previous liturgical (including dramatic) traditions, at the same time manifesting a predilection for newly-composed rhythmical poetry and theatrical spectacle. Further, neither collection is recorded in a liturgical book intended for use in the choir. But the *Carmina Burana* plays have moved much further into the world of non-liturgical and vernacular drama than their earlier counterparts. None of the *Carmina Burana* plays has a decisive attachment to a liturgical office; but beyond that, features such as the introduction of the devil as a character, use of the title *Ludus*, comic elements, dancing, and elaborate theatrical effects (for example, Herod's demise 'gnawed to pieces by worms') neither grew within liturgical practices, nor at any stage typified widespread observances.

With plays such as these, we leave behind the period of widespread dramatic composition for the liturgy; surviving sources suggest that, apart from several plays composed in or for Benedictine convents, few new plays were actually created after the late thirteenth century. Nevertheless, liturgical plays long and short, simple and complex, continued to be performed in many centres until their almost universal suppression in the years following the Reformation.

---

[111] The music of the longer Passion play has been largely reconstructed by Thomas Binkley: see 'The Greater Passion Play from Carmina Burana: An Introduction', in Peter Reidemeister and Veronika Gutmann, eds., *Alte Musik, Praxis und Reflexion* (Winterthur, 1983), 144–57, and the recording by the Schola Cantorum of Basel *Das grosse Passionspiel*, Deutsche Harmonia Mundi (1984).

IX

MEDIEVAL SONG

By John Stevens

Medieval monophony sprang from abundant creative inspiration and took on a great variety of forms, techniques, and styles. Many of these have been described in the chapters on Roman, non-Roman, and medieval chant, associated more or less closely with the liturgy of Mass and Divine Office. Many more, those of secular song in particular, remain to be described here. But the distinction between 'liturgical' and 'non-liturgical' (a modern rather than a medieval distinction) cannot be made hard and fast; the inclusion or exclusion of repertories or single items in those chapters was to some extent arbitrary. The present chapter will gather in some of the materials not covered earlier because—for one reason or another—they were not sufficiently connected to Mass or Office.

While the distinction 'liturgical' is extremely problematic (witness the frequent use of the mediating category 'para-liturgical'), it is generally easier to distinguish 'sacred' from 'secular', and straightforward to distinguish 'Latin' from 'vernacular'. It is not possible, however, to align these distinctions with each other consistently—except for the fact that in the Middle Ages 'liturgical' chant is in Latin. Medieval monophony to be discussed in this chapter is sacred or secular, Latin or vernacular, in all possible combinations; they will all be called 'song'.

SOURCES

The closer to the liturgy of Mass or Office a repertory stood, the more likely it was to be preserved in written form by the monastic makers and keepers of records. Musical repertories and items less close to the liturgy are preserved less well—or not at all—from the earlier Middle Ages. Single items and smaller repertories are often preserved only in fragmentary form, or in books whose main contents are unrelated. During the thirteenth century, however, large repertories of song, mainly vernacular and secular, were collected in vast manuscript anthologies; these will provide our central materials.

The oldest surviving collection of clearly non-liturgical songs is in a well-known Paris MS (BN lat.1154); it includes primarily St Isidore's *Libri synonymorum*, as well as a litany, collects, and miscellany.[1] The songs vary greatly in theme and tone: penitential verses and prayers are found side by side with *planctus* (laments) for dead heroes (Charlemagne and his natural son Abbot Hugo), the Song of the Sibyl, narratives based on the Bible (Dives and Pauper), and a song by Gottschalk of Fulda written in exile to a young friend. Not all the songs are notated, and those that are use adiastematic (staffless) neumes. Similarly, in another early source, the so-called Cambridge Songs (Cambridge Univ.Lib. MS Gg.v.35) a few poetic texts are neumed, others not; the MS is a mid-eleventh century school reader.[2] Many of the poetic texts (such as *metra* from the *De consolatione philosophiae* of Boethius) were surely intended to be sung.

Another famous Aquitanian MS, Paris BN lat.1139, has already been mentioned (in Ch. VII) for its collection of Latin *versus* of the eleventh and twelfth centuries. In addition to further liturgical materials (Offices for the Virgin, and sequences), it contains some of the earliest Aquitanian polyphony (see Ch. XI), and liturgical dramas—the 'Procession of Prophets' and *Sponsus* (see Ch. VIII), which includes an early song in the Provençal vernacular. Latin songs include a Song of the Sibyl, and a lament of Rachel.

The thirteenth-century anthologies comprehend Latin as well as vernacular anthologies. The *Carmina burana* MS (Munich, Staatsbibl.MS clm 4660), compiled *c.* 1220–30 in Bavaria, is probably a song book rather than a strictly literary anthology, even though of over 250 lyrics and other items only ten have neumes;[3] this view is supported by the appearance of items in other MSS with indication of melodies—as in the mid-eleventh-century Evreux MS (Bibl.Mun.2) and the Later Cambridge Songs (Cambridge Univ.Lib. Ff.i.17).[4]

Another thirteenth-century collection of Latin songs is found at the end of the main source of Latin polyphony at Notre-Dame of Paris—

[1] Paris, Bibl. Nat. MS Lat. 1154; ninth to tenth centuries. For further details, see John Emerson, 'Sources, MS (II)', *New Grove*, xvii. 612, and Hans Spanke, 'Rhythmen- und Sequenzenstudien, *Studi Medievali*, NS 4 (1931), 286–320.

[2] John Stevens, *Words and Music in the Middle Ages: Song, Narrative, Dance and Drama, 1050–1350* (Cambridge, 1986), 114–19, with bibliographical references. Cited below as *Words and Music*.

[3] *Words and Music*, p. 517; the *Carmina Burana* MS includes some texts in German also.

[4] For the Evreux MS, see C. Hohler, 'Reflections on some Manuscripts containing 13th-century Polyphony', *Journal of the Plainsong & Mediæval Music Society*, 1 (1978), 11–12; for the Cambridge MS, see David Hiley, 'Sources, MS (IV)', *New Grove*, xvii. 652.

the Florence MS (Bibl.Med.Laur. Plut.29.1; see Ch. XII). The monophonic music is in two clearly defined sections: fascicle 10 contains *conductus* and *cantiones*; fascicle 11 contains *rondelli* (clerical dance songs).

The most famous of all English medieval songs, 'Sumer is icumen in', is found in a composite thirteenth-century MS (London, BL Harley, 978), which includes Latin monophonic pieces of the *lai* type, medical recipes, Goliardic verse, the Fables and *Lais* of Marie de France, a courtly poetess writing in England in the last decades of the twelfth century (see also Ch. XIV).[5]

Still another of the repositories of Latin medieval song—surely numerous at the end of the Middle Ages, even if not many are extant—is the Stuttgart Landesbibl. MS HB1 Ascet.95.[6] Possibly from Engelberg in the first half of the thirteenth century, the MS contains primarily medieval chant—sequences, *Benedicamus* verses, chants of the Ordinary (including tropes). Interspersed among these are Latin songs variously titled *conductus, carmen, planctus*. Some are best described as *cantiones*—'songs'—without particular liturgical connections. Among the known authors are Philip the Chancellor (of Paris, *fl.* 1218–36), and Walter of Châtillon.

Finally, it is not uncommon in the thirteenth (and early fourteenth) centuries to find songs embedded in narratives, such as *Renart le Nouvel*, the *Roman de Fauvel*, or Adam de la Bassée's *Ludus super Anticlaudianum*.

Composite manuscripts represent, perhaps, the normal ambience of medieval lyric. Almost by way of exception do we encounter in the latter part of the thirteenth century the 'standard' anthologies of secular song. These include four principal MSS for troubadour songs, and about twenty for trouvères. The troubadour and trouvère chansonniers are, for the most part, handsome if not grand manuscripts. That is to say, they are professionally written as to text, music, and illumination. The parchment copies which survive do not show the signs of wear and tear that they would if they had been used for day-to-day performance. On the other hand they are not fine enough for presentation copies. One may speculate that, coming late in the tradition they represent, some of them may owe their existence to the *puys*, especially the trouvère MSS of northern France; but as a group they are singularly devoid of identification marks.[7]

[5] Hohler, 'Reflections', pp. 2–38; E. J. Dobson and F. Ll. Harrison, eds., *Medieval English Songs* (London, 1979), 143, 246, 300.

[6] Wolfgang Irtenkauf, 'Zum Stuttgarter Cantionarium HB.1.95', *Codices Manuscripti*, 3 (1977), 22–30.

[7] The chansonniers and other major sources of vernacular monophonic song are succinctly and comprehensively described by Fallows, 'Sources, MS, (III)' *New Grove*, xvii, 634.

A striking feature of the MSS is their standardized presentation. This in itself suggests that they are the chance survivors of a widespread and well understood practice of chansonnier 'production'. It was usual to write the words first on a ruled page into which the staves (normally four-line, red) had been entered; double columning predominates. The music of the first stanza was then copied out above the notes and note-groups with careful regard for syllabization. The subsequent stanzas were written out as prose; the sole exception is the Milan chansonnier (Bibl. ambrosiana, R71 *superiore* G). Within the MSS the songs are generally arranged by author/composer, though the Vatican (Reg.lat.1490) and Lorraine (Oxford, Bodl. Douce 308) chansonniers prefer an arrangement by genre. In both cases a hierarchy is observed: kings (such as Thibaut IV, *roi de Navarre*) precede commoners; the *grand chant* precedes the *jeu-parti* and lesser forms. The *Chansonnier Cangé* (BN fr.846), however, arranges the authors alphabetically. Generally the pictorial illuminations are confined to the beginnings of sections; thereafter, a simpler floriation in red and blue alternates verse by verse.

There are additional MS collections for certain specialized repertories: two MSS preserve the melodies for the Italian sacred *lauda*; three preserve the melodies for the Spanish *Cantigas de Santa Maria*.

RHYTHMIC INTERPRETATION AND NOTATION

Even after the notation of pitch on a staff became standardized in the early thirteenth century, the notation of rhythm seems to modern scholars puzzling and in need of interpretation. We can be sure, however, that it was not puzzling to medieval scribes, performers, or composers: there is no failure here to make intentions clear. We should beware, moreover, of thinking that there is some abstruse problem to which we have not yet found the key. The varied, fluctuating, and continuously evolving sign-systems that constitute early medieval notation cannot be understood—any more than our everyday languages—without contexts. It is better that we should sometimes admit to being at a loss, rather than imagine there to be a single thread that links the whole.

Five prominent hypotheses for rhythmic interpretation have been put forward since La Borde's *Essai sur la Musique ancienne et moderne* of 1780.

1. The notations of the chansonniers, or at least some of them, are mensural (measured in specific ways); all should be so transcribed.

2. Each *note* has an equal duration (this is the 'equalist' theory), whether it occurs singly over a syllable, or in a group.
3. Each *syllable* has an equal duration (this is the 'isosyllabic' theory); thus a group of six notes over a syllable occupies approximately the same time as a syllable with only a single note.
4. The durations of the notes are determined by the theory of 'modal' rhythm, applied according to the metre of the poetic text.
5. The durations of the notes are determined by the rhythm of the text as recited or formally spoken (this is sometimes called 'declamatory' rhythm, but the term 'speech rhythm' is perhaps preferable).

Of these five, the one most favoured after 1900 was (4), that of modal rhythm.[8] This hypothesis was taken over by Jean Beck and Pierre Aubry from their teacher Friedrich Ludwig, who had discovered in thirteenth-century treatises the key to the rhythmic modes in the notation of polyphony of the school of Notre-Dame of Paris (1160–1240; see Ch. XII). Modal rhythm involves the regular alternation of long and short notes. Beck and Aubry (rivals rather than collaborators) both proposed that the key to rhythm in the songs of the troubadours and trouvères lay in an application of modal rhythm according to the metrical structure of the text, as expressed in the number of syllables in the line and the disposition of accents. In practical application many problems arose, and later 'modalists' made many modifications to increase the flexibility of the modal system, principally by mixing different patterns of long and short notes within one song. The fifth rhythmic mode, which in effect gives each syllable equal time, was a frequent refuge for editors troubled by the inconveniences of the other modes (Beck, Husmann, and others). A final stage was reached when the editor simply gave his own sense of what the rhythm might have been in the style of modal polyphony (see, for instance, Anderson's transcriptions of the *cantiones* from the Florence MS).[9]

Although the modal hypothesis enjoyed great popularity during the first half of the century, it has been increasingly questioned from

[8] The history of modal rhythm theory is the main subject of Burkhard Kippenberg, *Der Rhythmus im Minnesang* (Munich, 1962). A case for isoyllabic interpretation is presented in *Words and Music*, pp. 413–504, together with discussion of other hypotheses and the literature supporting them.

[9] Gordon A. Anderson, *Notre-Dame and related conductus: Opera omnia*, VI: *I pt. Conductus—Transmitted in facsimile X of the Florence Manuscript*, Institute of Medieval Music (1978).

several points of view; and it has subsequently begun to lose the confidence of performers, partly because of the stimulus of non-European styles of songs. There is still, however, no consensus as to the appropriate rhythmic transcription or performance. In this chapter the examples will be presented in a transcription that preserves the universal—and seemingly essential—feature of the sources, namely that the songs are *syllabic* artefacts: each syllable of text is given with its note or note-group (the traditional graphic groups called 'neumes' in chant and 'ligatures' in polyphonic notation). Analyses of rhythmic structure in this chapter are predicated upon a belief that the rhythm is 'isosyllabic' (hypothesis 3) in the chanson, and metric in the dance songs (possibly also in the *lai*). Between the extremes of chanson and dance song are other genres even harder to pin down, such as the *pastourelle*; but genre must always be seen as an important determinant. Two other factors may support an isosyllabic transcription: they are (1) medieval rhythmic theory and (2) the requirements of a balanced relationship between music and verse. 'Theoretical sources in the early Middle Ages oppose two main traditions of rhythm in song: one, known as *musica metrica*, describes sounds which are measured in longs and shorts and grouped in "feet"; the other, *musica ritmica*, specifically excludes durational values and deals with the organization of strictly counted syllables, unmeasured, into harmonious and balanced wholes.'[10] The *grands chants* of the troubadours and trouvères exemplify *musica ritmica*. A 'balanced relationship' (to take the second point) is not easy to define, but knowing as we do that the concept of 'number' with its insistence on *armonia*, balance, and proportion, is central to the medieval aesthetic of both music and poetry, it would seem natural that, when the two musics—of voice and of verse—are combined, then neither should predominate. The isosyllabic style is one way in which this 'double melody' can be realized.

In assessing this and other interpretations we need to remember that as the original notations developed from their earliest, most flexible forms towards the quadratic forms of the thirteenth century, they lost some of their suppleness and subtlety: in the need to specify pitches on a staff, they lost most of the ornamental neumes, preserving only in some sources some of the signs for liquescence (known and used also in the polyphonic repertories under the name *plica*). Nevertheless, the scribe still had at his disposal far more notational symbols than a modern editor. And whereas we tend to expect

[10] *Words and Music*, p. 415. See also Richard Crocker, 'Musica Rhythmica and Musica Metrica in Antique and Medieval Theory', *Journal of Music Theory*, 2 (1958) 2–23.

modern notations to give an exact indication of the music, the art of melody in these centuries is still close to oral tradition, subject to the whims of memory, the 'flowers' of melodic ornament, the creative vagaries of new singers. We are dealing with a living object.

GENRES, FORMS, AND STYLES

A typology of medieval monophonic song forms was a principal concern of many of the major scholars of the first half of the century—Friedrich Gennrich, Hans Spanke, Jacques Handschin, among others.[11] Their approach combined musicology with philology, as it was bound to do, since in some instances the form of a song (a refrain song, for example) cannot be determined on the basis of the music or of the words alone. Four basic formal categories were agreed upon: these were (1) the *laisse* type, which consists largely of the repetition of a single melody after the fashion of a litany, and like the litany allows variation as well as special phrases for rounding-off; (2) the refrain-song, such as the *rondeau*, associated with dance and characterized by contrast in a great variety of relations between verse (the changing element) and refrain (the static element); (3) the 'sequence type', including the *lai*, whose distinguishing feature is 'progressive repetition'—at its simplest *AA BB CC DD*, etc.; and (4) the strophic type, exemplified above all in chanson (*canso*), consisting of repeated stanzas identical in their metre and melody.

Rather than following these strictly formal categories I shall, while using them frequently, develop the concept of *genres*, which allows more flexibility and corresponds more naturally to the complex realities of the huge repertory of European song. Of these genres the dominant one in secular music is undoubtedly the chanson.

GRAND CHANT IN FRENCH AND PROVENÇAL

The northern French chanson of the trouvères is, at least in sheer bulk, the principal representative of a genre which also includes the troubadour *canso* with Provençal text, the Latin *cantio*, the Italian *canzone*, some of the Spanish *cantigas*. Over 2,100 trouvère poems survive and at least 1,400 melodies, the majority of which appear in several sources, in some cases as many as ten or so. It is hard to be precise since this huge repertory has not been fully transcribed and analyzed. A well-known song by Blondel de Nesle, one of the earliest

[11] See especially F. Gennrich, *Grundriss einer Formenlehre des mittelalterlichen Liedes als Grundlage einer musikalischen Formenlehre des Liedes*. (Halle (Saale), 1932). Summarized in part by Gustave Reese, *Music in the Middle Ages* (New York, 1940), 219–30. See also Pierre Bec, *La Lyrique française au moyen âge (xiiᵉ–xiiiᵉ siècles): Contribution à une typologie des genres poétiques médiévaux*, 2 vols. (Paris, 1977 and 1978).

trouvères (*fl. c.* 1180–1200), 'Bien doit chanter qui fine amours adrece' (R482)[12] will show how complex the problem may be (Ex. 115). Eleven versions of the melody are contained in ten manuscripts; they can be studied in the parallel transcription of Hendrik van der Werf, where the closely related group (trouvère MSS *KNPX*) is represented by a single line of melody.[13] Despite variations of pitch, disposition of ornament, use of plica, even choice of cadential notes, these are clearly versions of one melodic shape (but that is not to say that one original 'authentic' melody lies behind them all waiting to be reconstituted). MS *R*, however, is as usual widely divergent; and the two melodies in MS *V* are curiously discrepant in themselves.

The notion that the *grand chant* or 'high-style chanson' (here used as a generic term) was the principal courtly genre is not an invention of modern scholarship. It is explicit or implicit in many medieval treatises and song collections. The Lorraine Chansonnier, as already observed, makes it explicit in its division of material into *grands chants, estampies*, etc.; and the MS that contains the 'collected works' of Adam de la Halle gives the chanson a pride of place before *jeux-partis, rondets*, motets. Other MSS also have chanson sections, sometimes within a general arrangement of songs by composers. When vernacular song is discussed in treatises—not a common event—it is as a genre with rules of its own; this is the case with *Las Leys d'Amors* (after 1324).[14] Definitions will usually include references to the subject of the poem, its formal characteristics (rhyme, etc.), its style (ornamental or plain) and the type of melody appropriate to it. Such codifications are late in date and it cannot be taken for granted that the prescriptions of the academies and *puys* of the early fourteenth century necessarily accord in every respect with those of the earliest troubadours and trouvères. But the broad principles of chanson composition, in melody and verse, are beyond dispute. So also is, I think, the intent behind them.

The factors that define the *grand chant* can be grouped by subject, content, function, form, and style. The subject of the chanson is

[12] Throughout this chapter the letter 'R' followed by a number refers to the standard index, *G. Raynauds Bibliographie des altfranzösischen Liedes* [rev. edn. (enlarged by Hans Spanke), Leiden, 1955; repr. (with alphabetical index) 1980]. The entries can be complemented from R. W. Linker, *A Bibliography of Old French Lyrics, Romance Monographs*, 31 (University of Mississippi, 1979), and from U. Mölk and F. Wolfzettel, *Répertoire métrique de la poésie lyrique française des origines à 1350* (Munich, 1972).

[13] Hendrik van der Werf, ed., *Trouvères-Melodien I and II. Monumenta monodica medii aevi*, 11 and 12. (London, 1977, 1975) vol. I, p. 14. Ex. 115 in the present text reproduces the pious contrafact from London, BL Arundel 248 fo. 155.

[14] Adolphe F. Gatien-Arnoult, ed., *Las Flors del gay saber, estier dichas Las Leys d'amors*, 4 pts. *Monuments de la littérature romane*, i–iii (Toulouse, 1841–3).

Ex. 115

Bien deust chan - ter ky eust le - a - le a - mi - e;

2. ga - riz ser - roit ky bien la seust choi - sir.

3. A - mer co - vient mes coest la ma - ë - stri - e

4. de bien a - mer e fol a - mur guer - pir.

5. Car ki k'a - siet en fo - lur soen de - sir

6. de - ceuz en iert kant mieuz qui - de - ra jo - ir

7. ke fol a - mur fait alme e cors pe - rir.

8. Mes ky se prent a la dou - ce Ma - ri - e

9. de quoer ver - ray ne s'en poet re - pen - tir.

love—or better, Love, with a capital L, since what is described or represented is a generalized emotion. Thibaut de Champagne (1201–53)—'Le roi Thibaut'—opens one poem:

De bone amor vient seance et bonté
et amors vient de ces deus autresi.

(From true love come wisdom and goodness, and love comes from these two in its turn.)[15]

Another begins:

> Tuit mi desir et tuit mi grief torment
> viennent de la ou sont tuit mi pensé.

(All my desires and all my heavy torments come from the one place where all my thoughts reside.)[16]

The Lady is the source of all the Lover's experience, his pangs of desperation as well as his moral worth and imaginative ecstasies. And yet in all this we sense nothing individual. Thibaut is reading us 'lessons in Love's philosophy'. The case is different with many of the troubadours, who do indeed speak as particular Lovers—and in many other roles as well. But in the Provençal poets, too, we often have the sense that 'Love's philosophy' is also a social philosophy and the *preu* that is conferred is as much a matter of manners as of morals.[17]

For the twelfth and thirteenth centuries, unambiguous evidence about the nature of social life in the numerous courts and castles is virtually impossible to come by. Walter Map's intriguingly titled *Nugae Curialium* (Courtiers' Trifles) turns out to have nothing of the *chronique scandaleuse* about it at all.[18] There is no such thing, either, as a courtly 'Customary' or 'Consuetudinary'—books which enable the liturgical historian to follow quite literally step by step the great rituals and festivals of the Church. It is not until later in the Middle Ages that we can begin to feel the pulse of secular courtly life and to catch an unmistakable glimpse in chronicles and archives of a phenomenon which is often and appropriately referred to as the 'game of love'. For the earlier period of the troubadours and trouvères we are dependent on more slippery evidence—in particular, on the romances, which were the major genre of European literature from the mid-twelfth century onwards. But the songs themselves can help us too, if sensitively interpreted.

'Talking of love' was one important aspect of the game. In small, leisured societies which had to entertain themselves, 'clene courteous

---

[15] Text and translation from Frederick Goldin's anthology, *Lyrics of the Troubadours and Trouvères* (New York, 1973) 454; the scholarly editions from which the texts are taken are given in each case.

[16] Ibid. 456.

[17] Further on courtly ideals (*fin' amors*), the origins of 'courtly love', the genres, themes, motifs, etc. of troubadour and trouvère poems, see John Stevens and Theodore Karp, 'Troubadours, trouvères', *New Grove*, xix, sect. I. 3–6, pp. 190–3; sect. II. 2–4, pp. 195–6.

[18] Walter Map, *De Nugis Curialium*, ed. M. R. James, rev. C. N. L. Brooke and R. A. B. Mynors (Oxford, 1983).

carp', 'dous parler', was evidently much admired. It could take various forms, of which the *jeu-parti* (troubador *joc-partit*) was a favourite, consisting as it did of a stylized debate between two poets (or between one and a shadow-boxer) on a topic of love. Some *jeux-partis* survive with their melodies (cf. below).

One refined expression of Love with which we can make direct contact is that of song itself. Almost every troubadour or trouvère feels bound to proclaim—and some at very frequent intervals—that it is love and the joy which springs from love that cause him to burst forth into music and verse. 'Chanter m'estuet, quar joie ai recouvree' (I must sing for I have won joy again) writes Blondel de Nesle . . . 'Or chanterai de toi toute ma vie, / si te voudrai servir et honourer' (Now I shall sing of you my whole life long, / and serve you willingly and honour you).[19] Conversely, Le Chatelain de Coucy, lamenting lost happiness, says, 'quant joie me faut, bien est raisons / qu'avec ma joie faillent mes chançons' (since I have no joy, it is right / that with my joy my songs should cease).[20] None the less, the verbal art of the troubadours and trouvères is one of great sophistication; there is nothing casual or spontaneous about it.

The words and phrases which best sum up the technique of troubadour verse are images of forging (*il miglio fabbro*), of polishing (*trobar prim*), of interlacing (*entrebescar le motz*), of locking together (*motz serratz*), of carving, planing, filing (see Arnaut Daniel, *En cest sonet coind'e leri*).[21] It is an art of *maestria*, an art that 'masters' its materials. In addition to the *prim*, 'polished' style of writing, there are varieties of *trobar* labelled *clar*, *ric*, *braus*, *leu*, and *clus*. The use in itself of the word *trobar* is significant: the idea of 'finding out' (the *Inventio* of the Latin rhetoricians) is diametrically opposed to the 'wise passiveness' claimed as essential by the English Romantic poets.

There is no domain in which both troubadours and trouvères display greater inventiveness than in metre. They are master-metricians, and it is on this level that words and music most clearly engage. It has been calculated that in the troubadour repertory alone some 2,600 surviving poems display 1,575 different metrical schemes, and that 1,200 of these occur only once.[22] Such deliberately ambitious

[19] Goldin, *Lyrics*, p. 368.

[20] Ibid. 358.

[21] Ibid. 216. The intricacies of troubadour verse technique are studied by Linda M. Paterson, *Troubadours and Eloquence* (Oxford, 1974).

[22] See Hendrik van der Werf, *The Chansons of the Troubadors and Trouvères: A Study of the Melodies and their Relation to the Poems* (Utrecht, 1972), 63; Istvan Frank, *Repértoire metrique de la poésie des troubadours. Bibliothèque de l'Ecole des Hautes Etudes*, 303 and 308 (Paris, 1953, 1957).

ingenuity must have an over-riding *raison d'etre*. It is, to put it briefly, a delight in Number.[23]

In considering the music of *canso* and chanson we must keep three different but integrally related aspects of Number (*numerus*) in mind:

1. 'number' as the arithmetical procedure of counting stanzas, lines, syllables, and melodic units;

2. 'number' as synonymous with proportion, measure, balance, order, harmony (*armonia*). Dante observes that in a good *canzone* the 'number' of its constituent parts (*lo numero de le sue parti*) pertains to the musician: it is his skill to ensure a perfect harmoniousness—and here Dante is thinking surely of the words as having a 'music' of their own;[24]

3. 'number' as one way of expressing the nature of God, and the created structures of His universe.

The last of these aspects could seem altogether remote from practical considerations. But it is not, if it serves to remind us that there is a beauty in numbers which needs no justification; it exists to be contemplated, to be enjoyed. Such numbers, realized in the melody and verse of a chanson or other medieval song, do not have to symbolize anything; we are not entering the realm of numerology. Their sheer disposition is sufficient to give pleasure and convey truth.

One much admired, copied and imitated chanson by Blondel de Nesle, 'Quant je plus sui en paor de ma vie' (R1227), shows an unusual degree of numerical complexity (Ex. 116).[25] It consists of fourteen lines and uses seven different line-lengths—11 (or $10^\cup = 10$ plus a 'weak' unaccented syllable), 10 (ending accented), 8 (or $7^\cup$), 7, 6, 4, 3. The total number of syllables is 114 (118, if the weak endings are included). In 'Quant je plus', as in virtually every other *grand chant*, each syllable of the text has one note or small group of notes. The line-unit of the poem is also the phrase-unit of the melody. Except for the short lines, 9–10, 'qu'en doi je li / demander fors merci?' where the sense runs on (What should I ask of her but grace?), each line is a syntactic entity, or at least ends with a natural speech-pause (line 3). This gives a strong sense of stability to the form.

The basic structure is the one most commonly found in the chanson: A A B. Lines 1–4 form a couplet, the *frons*, which is divided into two *pedes* (A, A) with precise repetition of rhymes and melodies; lines 5–14 form the *cauda*, or 'tail' (B). In the *cauda*, except for the

---

[23] On 'number' in music and verse, see *Words and Music*, pt. 1, especially ch. 1, where further references are given.

[24] Dante, *Convivio* II. ix. 9.

[25] Ed. van der Werf, *Trouvères-Melodien*, *T*, p. 60 (MS I: Paris, BN fr. 12615, fo. 86ʳ).

Ex. 116

1. Quant je plus sui en pa - our de ma vi - e

2. et je mains doi par rai - son es - tre liez,

3. lors me se - mont ma vo - len - tez et pri - e

4. et fine a - mours, que je soie en - voi - siez.

5. S'e - le m'o - cit, siens en iert li pi - chiez;

6. trop a doc nom por fai - re vi - lo - ni - e.

7. Mais se je sui par mes ieus tra - veil - liez,

8. dont la vi,

9. qu'en doi je li

10. de - man - der fors mer - ci?

11. Puis - que par moi sui de joie es - lon - giez

12. je   ne   m'en doi   plain-dre mi -   e;

13. com - ment qu'aie es - té   i -   riez,

14. dou - ce - ment sui   en-gi -   gniez.

observance of the line-phrase unit, the melody and the verse go their
own ways—yet still with some repetition of melodic material: line 10,
syllables 4–6, recalls line 2 (= 4), syllables 7–10; and 12.5–8 recalls
5.6–10. When such a repetition occurs at the end of a line it forms a
musical 'rhyme' (and I shall refer to it as such). This musical rhyme,
however, has no evident relation either to the verse structure (line 10
'merci' does not rhyme with 2 'liez') or to the sense of the poem—and
this is typical.

Beyond the structural relation just mentioned—line-phrase equiva-
lance with syllable to note (or note-group) correspondence, set in
frons-cauda shape—the melodic unity of a *grand chant* is independent
of the text. It is here that the composer displays his mastery of
'number' in the wide sense of *armonia* (balance, proportion, measure).
The melody of 'Quant je plus' has many typical features. Its pitch
movement is conjunct. The stepwise movement by tone and semitone
is broken only occasionally within the line—and sometimes not even
between lines. The interval of a third between main notes (1.7–8; 2.1–
2, etc.) is often bridged by a liquescent (or *plica*). The precise pitch and
vocal style of the *plica* are a matter for conjecture. The movement by
thirds in 13.1–3 is less usual in the high chanson style, much more
common in *lai* and dance-song.

The temporal progression of the melody is varied by a mixture of
single notes and groups of varying length but rarely exceeding four
notes (see, however, 11.7 and 14.6). It may be observed here that they
are distributed, as in sacred medieval chant, without apparent regard
for accented or non-accented syllables in the text; and that they
congregate more in the second than in the first half of the line, and
more heavily again in the final lines than in the earlier.

The tonal plan of 'Quant je plus' is no less puzzling than that of
many other chansons, and since analytical study of the monophonic
repertories has not progressed very far, it is not easy to be sure what

terms to use. The factors chiefly involved are the structural tones and the cadences. The relationship of the final pitch to the rest of the melody varies as much in the secular repertory as it does in the sacred one, although in the simpler chansons the final does sometimes confirm the pitch-set and final of the *frons* (A–A). The analysis is further complicated by uncertainty (often, it seems, shared by the copyists themselves) about accidentals. Should the b at 9.1 be flatted to avoid the tritone (8.3 to 9.1)? In this song there appears to be an interplay between an orientation toward a D-final (1–4, picked up again in 8–9 and 11), in which a is a structural tone and F an 'open' cadence (1.3), and one toward a C-final (the cadence at 6.9–10 is almost gauche in its insistence), in which a is still strong but shares its importance with G (10, 12, and 13). The final cadence on G seems nevertheless to follow logically, after these indecisions, from the strong quasi-triadic force of 13 spanned by C and c, even though G has not previously occurred in this final position—except perhaps at the end of 7, where the plicated note leads into the F at the beginning of 8. Such baffling tonal indeterminacy is not the rule, but when it occurs in a large-scale chanson such as this it makes one wonder whether one should be looking for tonal unity at all.

Motivic repetition is one way in which a sense of unity can be achieved in the chanson style; it quite commonly links the *frons* with the *cauda*. 'Quant je plus' is not, in fact, as dependent as many other chansons on motivic repetition. Some of these repetitions have already been noted; another uses the 'pitch-set' G-a-a(G)-c to relate 7.1–4 to 13.3–7. Such motives are usually quite short, and may be transposed or inverted; 7.1–4, for instance, might be thought an inversion of 1.7–10. When they occur in several songs of the same repertory they may properly be called *formulae* of the style and not merely motives, which are the property of a particular song. In passing, we may note the unusual immediate repetition of the five-unit phrase 1.7–10 as 2.1–5 (and consequentially, 3.7–10 and 4.1–5). This is pattern, not play of motives. Other melodic echoes could be mentioned. But on the whole what is striking about the long ten-line *cauda* is its approximation to the *oda continua* style (see below), in which by a deliberate artifice no material at all is used twice.[26]

Finally, something must be said about what (for want of a better term) may be called dynamic shape. This is not the same as the formal structure; it is the quality of movement that informs the melody. In an intelligent musical performance this movement carries singer and

---

[26] This term can only properly be used of a complete chanson. See n. 28.

listener through from beginning to end with a sense of completeness. Clearly it depends on factors already mentioned, especially tonal structure and choice of cadence. But it also depends on the range and contour of the melody. Once again 'Quant je plus' is not easy to characterize. The typical chanson tends to reach a melodic climax marked by the highest pitches at about two-thirds of the way through (see 'Li plus se plaint', R1495 by Blondel) but in so far as 'Quant je plus' has this effect it is at the junction of the last two phrases (c / d c). The chanson opens at a high pitch, and with a repeated note; this is not at all uncommon. But lines 2 and 4 of the *frons* cadence at the bottom of the range on D. Then the *cauda* begins. Phrases 5–6 (with the thrice-repeated motive 5.1–4, 6.1–4, 6.5–8) settle with some insistence, even lower, on C, and appear to form an appendage to the sinking movement of the *frons*. Phrase 7 takes wing lightly, at a higher range, but the impetus soon fades, beginning with the short line (8) with its unexpected F and two further descents doubling the sense of closure (there is a reminiscence in 10 of the cadences to 2, 4, and 6). Phrases 11 and 12 form another 'movement', 11 picking up a motif from 5 and 6; the cadences are again low and the D is given an 'open' definition by the recurrent Cs. C now has a central organizing importance, and the high c leads strongly to the last line and the final G through a descending fifth confirmed by a near-melismatic cadence.

As this analysis suggests, one remarkable thing about the troubadour-trouvère repertory as a whole is the intricacy which is possible, and achieved, within the apparently narrow restraints of the genre— and this applies to all aspects of the chanson. The troubadours exercise greater freedoms in some directions; the trouvères in others. This 'unity in diversity', 'diversity in unity', we must now examine in more detail. But before doing so two caveats should be entered. The first is that we cannot be sure that the written material which survives does properly represent the complete state even of an aristocratic, 'courtly' music in the twelfth and thirteenth centuries. This is particularly the case in regard to the troubadours. It has sometimes been said that the troubadour repertory was much poorer than the trouvère in the lighter forms of chanson (pastourelle, dance-song, etc.). It is much more likely that such written records as there were have perished. Secondly, and related, we have to remember that our knowledge of these chansons depends on late evidence, consisting almost entirely of copies made long after the songs were first composed. Several of the chansonniers are only partially finished (the big troubadour MS *R* is startlingly defective) and others are palpably eccentric and unreliable (trouvère MSS *R* and *V*).[27] More than that, even the best manuscripts, separated as they are by as much as a century from the date of composition, may represent to some degree the tastes and predilections of a later generation. It seems hopelessly inappropriate to look for an *Ur*-text; but the modern view that all versions of a medieval melody are equally 'authentic' raises a further question: 'authentic' by what criteria—those of 1150 or 1225 or 1300?

FORM AND STRUCTURE

Few songs in the troubadour-trouvère repertory seem to depart fundamentally from two of the basic principles enounced—syllable-counting in syllabic style, and coincidence of verse-line with musical phrase. In regard to the third principle, the 'standard' structure A-A-B, the troubadours in particular show great diversity. We should not think of twelfth-century poet-composers as varying a standard form. Rather, they were experimenting with a variety of forms, one of which seemed eventually to meet their need to assert formality while allowing room for invention and diversity.

The form which on the face of it allows the greatest freedom is the *oda continua*,[28] in which each melodic phrase differs from all the others. The 'freedom' may turn out to be, in a long stanza, simply another kind of technical challenge—like the rhetorical practice of writing a long poem (*lai* or *complainte*) without repeating a rhyme-sound. Folquet de Marseilla, who seldom uses the strict A-A-B form, achieves, in 'Ja no.s cuich hom' (P-C 155, 11),[29] the full *oda continua*. No phrase is repeated and no regard is paid to the verse-form prescribed by the rhymes, which in stanza 1 are a a b a b b c c. (Ex. 117).[30] Though of an earlier generation, Bernart de Ventadorn favoured A-A-B form over the through-composed *oda*. But he also exercised much freedom. Sometimes, as in his 'Lai can vey la fuelha' (P-C 70, 25), the underlying structure is more like a series of repeated

---

[27] Troubadour MS *R* (BN fr. 22543) contains 1165 texts, 695 sets of staves but only 160 melodies. Trouvère MS *R* has been studied by Johann Schubert, *Die Handschrift Paris Bibl. Nat. fr. 1591* (Frankfurt, 1963).

[28] The term is Dante's (*De vulgari eloquentia*, II. x. 2).

[29] Throughout this chapter the letters 'P–C' in brackets refer to A. Pillet and H. Carstens, *Bibliographie der Troubadours, Schriften der Königsberger Gelehrten Gesellschaft, Sonderreihe*, iii (Halle, 1933).

[30] Ed. Hendrik van der Werf and G. A. Bond, *The Extant Troubadour Melodies: Transcriptions and Essays for Performers and Scholars* (Rochester NY, 1984), 90*. (All the songs in this edition are listed under their Pillet–Carstens numbers). The edition by Ismael F. de la Cuesta and R. Lafont, *Las cançons dels trobadors, Institut d'estudis occitans* (Toulouse, 1979), though less satisfactory in its presentation of the poetico-musical structures, gives the original notation of the MSS above the transcriptions in diplomatic form. Folquet's *canso* is on p. 202.

Ex. 117

1. Ja no.s cuich hom q'eu cam - ge mas can - cos

2. pois no.s cam - ja mos cors ni mas ra - ços:

3. car si.m jau - cis d'a - mors, eu m'en lau - ce - ra,

4. mas qe men - tis no.m se - ri - a nuls pros;

5. c'al - tre - si.m ten com se sol in ba - lan - ça

6. des - es - pe - rat ab al - qet d'es - pe - ran - ça,

7. pe - ro no.m vol del tot lai - sar mo - rir

8. per ço qe.m pos-ca plus so - vent au - cir.

quatrains—ABCD, ABCD, EF(? = B') CD'. The *frons/cauda* structure is virtually dissolved into this simpler idea. To hear all 7 stanzas and concluding *envoi* sung is perhaps more like the experience of strophic narrative. More striking still is the straightforward double-quatrain form of 'Conortz, aras say yeu ben' (P-C 70, 16), corresponding with the rhyme-scheme of the poem. 'La dossa votz' (P-C 70, 23) varies the standard scheme by introducing a repeat of the first-line melody in line 4 of the *frons*, (ABAA instead of ABAB). At least this is the case in the MS *R* version, though not in *X*,[31] where the same

---

[31] Troubadour MS *X* = trouvère MS *U* (the Chansonnier St Germain: BN fr. 20050, notated in Messine neumes).

basic melody is given as ABC?A'—which reminds us how extremely cautious one must be when generalizing about a melody when only a single source survives. Other structures used by Bernart include (in merely schematic terms) ABCADDEF; ABCDEFG(?B')D'; ABAB'C(cf.B)DB. A recurrent tendency is to link the last line of the *frons* to the last line of the *cauda*, whether by repetition, modification or short cadential 'rhyme'.

Later troubadours (especially Giraut Riquier, *c.* 1254–90) and trouvères such as Thibaut de Champagne (1201–53) and Adam de la Halle (*c.* 1245–?86) are more regular and predictable. The *frons* in Thibaut's numerous chansons is normally of four lines with musical repeat, ABAB; the *cauda*, of about equal length, is normally without formal repetition. The enormously popular chanson 'De bone amor vient seance et biauté' (R407) mentioned by Dante,[32] follows this 'standard' form; it also, incidentally, shows Thibaut's preference for equilinear forms, here the decasyllabic (Ex. 118).[33]

But Thibaut has ways of linking *frons* (1–4) and *cauda* (5–end). In 'Chanter m'estuet' (R1476)[34] he repeats the opening line of the song in an 'open' form as line 5; in 'Du tres douz non' (R1181) he does the same with the B-phrase of the *frons*, thus producing an embryonic form of the later *ballade*. And occasionally he unifies the *cauda* itself with a repeated phrase—never more strikingly than in the comparatively light chanson 'L'autre jour en mon dormant' (R339), where lines 5 and 6 are identical. With this can be compared lines 5 and 6 of Bernart de Ventadorn's 'Cant l'erba fresqu' e.l fuelha par' (P-C 70, 39).

Adam de la Halle, one of the last of the trouvères, exercises about the same degree of formal freedom as Thibaut. That is to say, he displays the standard form often enough to make any departure from it seem deliberate, not casual. His output of 36 chansons is stylistically homogeneous; the only real oddity is 'Amours m'ont si doucement' (R658), a *chanson de femme* with the musical form ABB'CD, repeated.[35] Among the formal variations are:

ABAB:CDB'E (Li jolis maus; R1186)
ABAB:CDEFGB' (Tant me plaist; R1273)

---

[32] Dante, *De vulgari eloquentia*, I. ix. 3; II. v. 4 (all references to Dante are to *Le opere di Dante*, ed. Michele Barbi and others: *Testo critico della Società Dantesca Italiana* (2nd edn., Florence, 1960).

[33] Ed. van der Werf, *Trouvères-Melodien*, II, p. 71 (MS *K*: Paris, Bibl. de l'Arsenal, 5189, fo. 49).

[34] Cited by Johannes de Grocheo as an example of *cantus versualis* in his *Theoria* (*c.* 1300) ed. E. Rohloff, *Die Quellenhandschriften zum Musiktraktat des Johannes de Grocheio* (Leipzig, 1972).

[35] Adam also wrote one *oda continua*, 'Dame, vos hon vous estrine' (R 1383).

Ex. 118

ABAC:DEFD′GH (Merveille est; R52)
ABCB:DBEFG (Ki a droit; R1458)

The most unusual is 'He! las, il n'est mais nus' (R149) with the scheme AA′AA′BA²CA′ (Ex. 119).[36] It is not easy to find reasons in features of the text for the repetitions of now this, now that, phrase of melody. The reasons are, rather, musical and have to do with the creation of a melody with euphony, balance, and proportion—'tanto più dolce armonia resulta, quanto più la relazione e bella' (Dante).[37]

[36] BN fr. 12615 (MS *T*) fo. 226ᵛ.   [37] *Convivio*, II. xiii. 23.

Ex. 119

He - las il n'est mais nus qui aint   A

2. ain - sint con de - e - roit a - mer;   A^1

3. chas - cuns a - mant or - en - droit faint   A

4. et veut go - ir sans en - du - rer,   A^1

5. et pour chou se doit bien gar - der   B

6. che - le con pri - e,   A^2

7. car tant est la fem - me proi - si - e   C

8. c'on ne li set que re - prou - ver.   A^1

Phrase plans tell us more than broad categories such as *oda continua* and 'ballade form', but are still crude instruments. We have to take a more microscopic view to see the real 'unity-in-diversity' of *le grand chant*. Thibaut's 'Feuille ne flor ne vaut riens' (R324) in the MS *D* version shows much detail of motive working within the phrase plan.

To some extent motivic analysis must rest on the rhythmic interpretation adopted, which in this chapter is the isosyllabic one (cf. above). In the ten-syllable line used throughout this song various groupings are possible. Thus, the syllables of line 1 (and 3) can be grouped 1.3...7...; line 2 (and 4) the same, or 1..4...8..; line 5 the same, or

Ex. 120

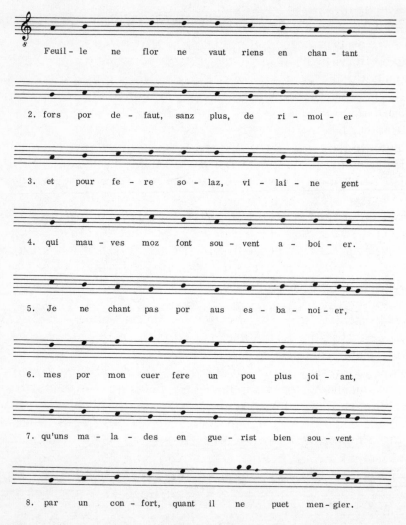

1..4..7...; line 6 the same, or 1...5.7... and so on. A melody such as
'Feuille ne flor', consisting entirely of single notes (except for three
finals), is obviously very malleable (Ex. 120).[38] It would be possible to
read the whole melody in triple metre (still retaining isosyllabism). Or,
one could interpret each line differently, without doing violence to the
apparently neutral implications of the music.

'Feuille ne flor' is evidently based on a series of recurrent rising and
falling conjunct thirds and fourths. They come so densely that it is
impossible to distinguish them in a hard and fast manner. The motif

---

[38] Paris, Bibl. de l'Arsenal (MS 5198) fo. 52.

abc (or its exact transposition def) appears in every phrase, either ascending or descending or both; similarly, the related G-a-b. Or, if one prefers to read the melody in 'fours' rather than 'threes', the motif G-a-b-c or its inversion can be found almost as frequently. Phrases 5 and 7 are virtually palindromic in structure; and the last phrase mounts the four-note version (8.4–6) on top of the three-note one (8.1–3) to achieve a climax (echoing 6.1–7) on the reduplicated g with *plica*.

Another factor which complicates the analysis of motives is their relation to the tonal plan of the piece. For instance, if one takes the opening motive (abc ascending) in conjunction with the cadences of 2 and 4 and 8, normally points of repose in A-A-B form, then a should presumably be felt as a 'clos' *final* (closed, resolved), or in modern terms a tonic; and G as 'ouvert' (open). In that case one might wish to weight the a's and c's of line 1 in order not to let the melody slip too glibly down to a settled G (1.10). But in 6 and 7 and 8.1–7 the G seems so strongly asserted as to be tonic. The final cba cadence comes then not as a fully expected conclusion but as a delightful, somewhat teasing surprise.

Movement by 'threes' seems to be a recurrent feature of Thibaut's chansons. His 'Chanter m'estuet' (R1476) (Ex. 121)[39] looks like a very close relation of 'Feuille ne flor'; indeed, line 1 of the former is virtually identical with line 2 of the latter (see Ex. 120). Such a motive as this qualifies also as a formula, i.e., a phrase, or procedure, from the common stock. Blondel frequently uses it as the initial motive of a chanson, and occasionally in the body of the melody (see the *cauda* of R1269, for instance). But it is not merely from trouvère stock; many troubadours use it, for example, Bernart de Ventadorn in 'Ar m'acosselhatz senhors', (PC 70, 6) (Ex. 122).[40] His song 'La dossa votz ay auzida' (PC 70, 23: MS *X* version) begins six out of eight lines with f-g-a.

Folquet de Marseilla, who in general has other favourite idioms and writes in a more melismatic style, sometimes uses simple stepwise ascent through a fifth, as in the *cauda* of his 'Tant mou de corteza razo' (PC 155, 23). Such simple rising motives can act as psalmodic intonations, and in some chansons they are followed by a recitation tone, as in Gace Brulé's 'Al quis touz le mauz' (R111).

One final example of motivic integration: Gace Brulé's 'Ire d'amors qui en mon cuer' (Ri/1) is a song commended by Dante as an

---

[39] Ibid., fo. 23.
[40] Van der Werf and Bond, *The Extant Troubadour Melodies*, p. 34*.

Ex. 121

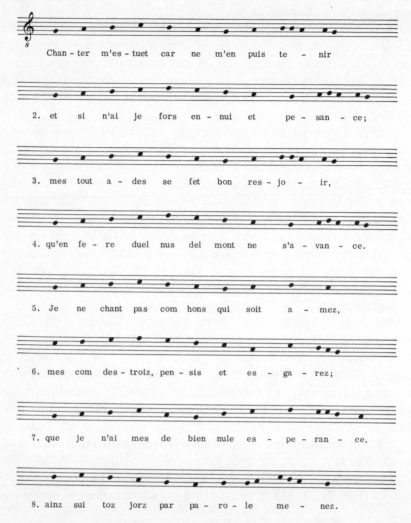

1. Chan - ter m'es - tuet car ne m'en puis te - nir

2. et si n'ai je fors en - nui et pe - san - ce;

3. mes tout a - des se fet bon res - jo - ir,

4. qu'en fe - re duel nus del mont ne s'a - van - ce.

5. Je ne chant pas com hons qui soit a - mez,

6. mes com des - troiz, pen - sis et es - ga - rez;

7. que je n'ai mes de bien nule es - pe - ran - ce,

8. ainz sui toz jorz par pa - ro - le me - nez.

example of *cantio illustris* (Ex. 123).[41] It is obvious that the stanza is rounded by the repetition of lines 2/4 as 8, but less obvious that the motif 2.8–10 recurs at the end of line 7 in a less ornamented, 'open' form. Further, A (line 1) differs from B (line 2) mainly in its cadential phrase (8–10) which is almost the same motive but a third higher. Between the initial phrases of 1/3 and 2/4 there is, in MS *K*, an even closer echo; this motive is used again in 6.1–4, and is modified in the cadence of the same line where it is a closed form of 5.7–10, and 'rhymes' briefly also with 1.10 and 3.10. A further echo is set up

---

[41] *De vulgari eloquentia*, II. vi. 6; Bibl. de l'Arsenal (MS 5198), fo. 62.

Ex. 122

Ar m'a - cos - se - lhatz se - nhors,

2. vos c'a - vetz va - lor e sen:

3. u - na do - na.m det s'a - mor

4. c'ay a - ma - da lon - ja - men;

5. mais e - ras say per ver - tat

6. que fay autr' a - mic pri - vat,

7. et anc de nulh com - pa - nho

8. com - pa - nha tan greu no·m fo.

between 5.1–4 and 7.1–4 a fourth higher. Finally, one may note the recurrence in mid-line (1, 2, 3, 4, 7, 8) of variants on the descending (G) F E D E C, and in 7.7–10 its inversion.

MINNESANG AND *GRAND CHANT*

Just as French was an international language, so the style of the *canso/chanson* was an international metrical-melodic style. The growth of the German *minneliet* (*Minnelied*, love-song) in the later twelfth and early thirteenth centuries seems to have been brought about by the adoption of the international style through the process of writing German contrafacts to Provençal and French melodies. German

Ex. 123

1. I - re d'a - mors qui en mon cuer re - pe - re

2. ne mi let tant que de chan-ter me tieg - ne.

3. Grant mer-veille est se j'en puis chan - con trai - re,

4. car je n'i voi l'a - chai - son dont el vieg - ne,

5. car li de - sirs et la grant vo - len - tez,

6. dont je sui si pen - sis et es - ga - rez,

7. m'a si me - né, ce vous puis je bien di - re

8. qu'a pai - nes sai co - noi - stre joi - e d'i - re.

poets did not borrow only melodies; they borrowed also concepts of love with which to mould and articulate their own experiences. Thus the German *hohiu minne* ('high love') corresponds roughly to the *fin' amors* of the romance languages; *vroide* (*Freude*) is the equivalent of *joi*, the state of spiritual exaltation induced by the imaginative experience of loving. Germany, moreover, produced two of the finest of all medieval romances, Gottfried's *Tristan* and Wolfram's *Parzival*.

The evidence for deriving early German courtly songs from troubadour and trouvère *grand chants* is, it must be stressed, entirely circumstantial. But, while individual cases could be disputed, the general truth cannot. The two almost conclusive types of evidence are the close paraphrase of a chanson in the same metre (i.e. following the syllabic structure and the rhyme scheme), and the close imitation of a complex metre, without paraphrase. Bernger von Horheim's 'Nu enbeiz ich doch des frankes nie' is modelled on stanza 4 of a chanson attributed to Chrètien de Troyes, 'D'amours qui m'a tolu a moi' (R1664); stanza 4 begins 'Onques del bevrage ne bui'.[42] Both poets claim to love more deeply than Tristan, even though they never drank the potion; it is the eyes that have led them into this state of deep captivity. Horheim must have had Chrètien in mind, even though the stanza form (octosyllabic, rhyming abab;baaba) is not so ingenious as to be conclusive in itself. On the other hand, Friedrich von Hausen (*c.* 1155–90) could surely not have stumbled by accident on the more complex pattern of his 'Ich denke underwilen'—abcabccbcc (Ex. 124).[43] It is identical with that of 'Ma joie premeraine' (R142) by Guiot de Provins (*fl. c.* 1185). The only metrical difference between the two is that the German poet gives all the six-syllable lines weak endings (i.e. 6 + 1); and at 7.4 he has a light hypermetric syllable (ma*n*ige). This latter feature is common in German as well as in English imitations of syllabic metres because of the greater importance of stressed syllables in the Germanic languages and the consequent tendency to care less about the lighter, unstressed syllables.

The chief difficulty in tracing and assessing German contrafacts arises from the extreme paucity of musical sources: there is no German equivalent to the rich group of major chansonniers which conserve the repertory of trouvère song. Our knowledge is scanty even of Walther von der Vogelweide, (*c.* 1170–*c.* 1250), the greatest lyric poet of the German Middle Ages, who wrote 86 Minnelieder, about 140 *Spruch*-poems and one *lai* (German *Leich*). The surviving music consists of two pieces in the so-called Münster Fragments (Münster, Staatsarchiv, MS. VII.51); two songs in untranscribable neumes (one from the *Carmina Burana* manuscript); and half-a-dozen or more melodies ascribed to Walther by name in later sources with texts written by other poets.[44] Melodies in this latter class are generally designated by the term *Ton* (plural *Töne*); they are in fact patterns of metre and melody, defined by syllable count, rhyme and pitch. Such patterns are available for general use; they are distinctive only on having titles and being sometimes of considerable length. Walther's

---

[42] The melody is printed with both texts by Ursula Aarburg, ed., *Singweisen zur Liebeslyrik der deutschen Frühe* (Düsseldorf, 1956), 27; see also Hugo Moser and Joseph Müller-Blattau, eds. *Deutsche Lieder des Mittelalters* (Stuttgart, 1968), 20–1 (German text only).

[43] Aarburg, *Singweisen zur Liebselyrik*, p. 20, No. 7.

[44] Full details are given by Burkhard Kippenberg, 'Walther von der Vogelweide', *New Grove*, xx. 193–5.

Ex. 124

Ma   joi – e   pre – me – rai – ne
Ich den – ke   un – der – wi – len,

2. m'est tor – neie en   pe – san – ce,
   ob   ich   ir   na – her wae – re,

3. las, je   ne   sai   por   coi
   waz ich ir   wol – te   sagen.

4. mais en – si   me   de – mai – ne
   daz kür – zet mir   die   mi – len,

5. la   foi   et   l'es – pe – ran – ce
   swenn ich ir   mi – ne swae – re

6. k'A – mors a   mis   en   moi.
   so   mit   ge – dan – ken   klage.

7. Se   je   par   bo – ne   foi
   Mich se – hent mani – ge   tage

8. doi   a – voir pe – ni – tan – ce,
   die liute in   der   ge – bae – re,

9. de   moi ne   sai   nul   roi,
   als   ich nicht sor – gen   habe,

10. fors que ma   mort i   voi.
    wan ichs al – so   ver – trage

poem 'Ich saz uf eime steine' was sung to *Der Reichston*, which must have had 24 lines arranged in alternating couplets of 6ᵁ and 8 syllables.[45] The so-called *Langer Ton* of Adam Puschman's manuscript *Singebuch* (1588) has the same dimensions, and may bear some resemblance to the melody Wolfram used three-and-a-half centuries earlier. We can only assume, even when the most stringent conditions are met and a German poet imitated a poem, that he did in fact take over its melody. There is no firm evidence; the doubt is unresolvable.

Similarly 'Mit saelden müeze ich hiute uf sten', fits *Der Wiener Hofton*, a melody from the Kolmarer Liederhandschrift of the mid-fifteenth century; but the same degree of uncertainty remains (Ex. 125).[46] Despite the lateness of this source, the song (the *Ton*) is demonstrably in the tradition of the *grand chant* running back for three centuries or more. The chanson structure A-A-B (called *Bar* form first by the German Meistersinger in the sixteenth century) is strictly observed, as is the coincidence of line and musical phrase. The pitch movement is perhaps slightly less conjunct than in many chansons, but only line 3 (= 6) could be described as 'angular'. The syllable-counting principle is still totally dominant and unquestioned, though we may expect slight accommodations to the needs of a Germanic language based on stress: elisions, of course, are an accepted part of the system, but the extra syllable at 'laz an' (4.4) is a modification of it. The temporal progression of the melody is not complicated by the frequent use of note-groups so characteristic of many of the high-style French chansons; some of the *Töne* are a little less austere, however, in this respect, for example *Der Reichston*.

It may not be wise to pursue the analysis much further, since, as Jammers observes, the Colmar melodies (and, even more, Puschman's) are surely simplifications, to be regarded as 'skeletons'—the biological metaphor seems apt.[47] But we may note that there are signs of a motivic pattern incorporating a rising 'gapped' fifth C E F G (phrase 8.1–4; transposed 9,10,15), rhyming cadence-figures (one on E, 2.6–8, 8.7–9, 14.8–10) another on C (F D C) 3.8–10; 9.5–7; 15.6–8;

---

[45] Moser and Müller-Blattau, *Deutsche Lieder des Mittelalters*, pp. 22–4; Ewald Jammers, *Ausgewählte Melodien des Minnesangs* (Tübingen, 1963), 164, No. 27a.

[46] Moser and Müller-Blattau, *Deutsche Lieder des Mittelalters*, pp. 24–5; see also Friedrich Maurer, ed., *Walther von der Vogelweide: Sämtliche Lieder* (Munich, 1972), opposite p. 25 (melody, measured version), p. 128 (text and German translation).

[47] Jammers, *Melodien*, p. 81. The Colmar MS (Munich, Staatsbibl. cod. germ. 4997, mid-fifteenth century), together with all the other manuscript sources of Minnesang, is described by Ronald J. Taylor, ed., *The Art of the Minnesinger*, 2 vols. (Cardiff, 1968), ii. 292; to his bibliography should be added Friedrich Gennrich, ed. *Die Colmarer Liederhandschrift: Faksimile-Ausgabe ihrer Melodien*, *Summa musicae medii aevi*, 17 (1967); and the succinct *New Grove* entry by Fallows, 'Sources, MS, (III).

Ex. 125

1. Mit   sael – den   müeze ich   hiute uf   sten
4. Krist her – re,   laz an mir   wer – den   schin

2. got   herre in   di – ner   huo – te   gen
5. die   gro – zen   kraft   der   güe – te   din,

3. und   ri – ten,   swar   ich   in   dem   lan – de   ke – re.
6. unt   pflic   min   wol   dur   di – ner   muo – ter   e – re.

7. als   ir   der   hei – lig   en – gel   phlae – ge,

8. unt   din,   do du in   der   krip – pen   lae – ge,

9. jun – ger   mensch unt   al – ter   got,

10. de – müe – tic   vor   dem e- sel   und   vor   dem   rin – de,

11. und   doch   mit   sael – den – ri – cher   huo – te

12. pflac   din   Ga – bri – el   der   guo – te

13. wol   mit   trui – wen   sun – der   spot,

14. als   pflic   ouch   min,   daz   an   mir   iht   er – win – de

15. daz din vil   gö – te – lich   ge – bot.

and a complete line repetition (cf. Ex. 124: 6–7) in the Abgesang, 11–12, in 'open' and 'closed' forms. There is, moreover, nothing unusual or anachronistic in the tonal plan. Contesting with the 'final', C, there is a main structural tone G (especially in the Abgesang) and a secondary structural tone, E (with suggestion of a pitch set E-G-b in the *Stollen*, and in phrases 13 and 14). The dynamic movements are: phrases 1–3, repeated 4–6; phrases 7–9; 10–13; 14–15. If a skeleton, it is certainly one with no bones missing.

Troubadour poems had not been exclusively concerned with 'courtly love': the *sirventes*, for example, treated moral or political subjects, often satirically; and many ostensible love-poems have (like the Elizabethan sonnet) the heart of their meaning in a philosophical or moral question. Similarly, Minnesang has a large number of songs on moral and religious themes. These are generally classified by Germanists as *Spruchdichtung*, with reference to their gnomic tendencies; but the term is used in a wide sense to denote not only didactic poetry but virtually everything that is not love-song. Some of these have already been mentioned. In melody and metre they are no less *grand chants* than the *Lieder*.

The Jena MS, the most important major near-contemporary source of Minnesang, contains a high proportion of *Spruch* songs.[48] The composers of the MS do not perhaps rival their contemporaries in the north of France in grace and elegance, but they have strongly individual styles, spread out on a spectrum between the robust, tonally stable, strictly syllabic style of 'Der kuninc rodolp minner got' by Der Unverzagte (Ex. 126)[49] and the elaborately melismatic 'Ich warne dich' by Wizlaw von Rügen (Ex. 127).[50]

GRAND CHANT IN ENGLAND

There is no doubt that the tradition of high style courtly song was known and practised in England. There is historical evidence that troubadours and trouvères visited England during the most creative period of the art; there is the known existence of the London *puy* a century or so later, at the end of the thirteenth century.[51] Most important of all is the survival of a small corpus of songs with Anglo-French texts in British sources. Some are versions of well-known

[48] Jena, Universitätsbibl., E1.f.101 (*c.* 1350): described by Taylor, *Minnesinger*, ii. 290; *New Grove*, loc. cit.

[49] Jena MS, fo. 40ᵛ; Jammers, *Melodien*, pp. 179–80. No. 39; Moser and Müller-Blattau, *Deutsche Lieder des Mittelalters*, p. 115–18 (with complete text).

[50] Jena MS, fo. 77; Jammers, *Melodien*, p. 182, No. 41.

[51] See Henry J. Chaytor, *The Troubadours and England* (Cambridge, 1923); the regulations of the *puy* are printed in *Munimenta Gildhalle Londoniensis*, ed. Henry T. Riley, Rolls Series, (London, 1860) vol. II, pt. I, pp. 216–28.

Ex. 126

Der ku - ninc Ro - dolp myn - net got un-de ist an

tru - wen   ste - te,

2. Der ku - ninc Ro - dolp hat sich ma-ni - gen   scan - den

wol vůr - sa - get.

3. Der ku - ninc Ro - dolp rich - tet   wol un-de haz - zet

val - sche   re - te,

4. Der ku - ninc Ro - dolp ist ein helt an   tugen - den

un - vůr - tza - get.

5. Der ku - ninc Ro - dolp e - ret got un-de al - le

wer - de vrou - wen.

6. Der ku - ninc Ro - dolp let sich dicke in ho - en

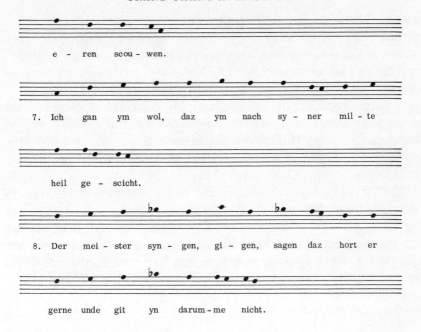

e - ren scou - wen.

7. Ich gan ym wol, daz ym nach sy - ner mil - te

heil ge - scicht.

8. Der mei - ster syn - gen, gi - gen, sagen daz hort er

gerne unde git yn darum - me nicht.

Ex. 127

1. Ich _____ war - ne dich, vil   jun - gher man ghe - tzar - te
3. Waz _____ dir da - von hey - les ghe - schicht, nu war - te

2. Halt mil - den _____ mŭt.
4. Daz du bist _____ gŭt.

5. Dem val - schen ra - te du ent - wi - che.

6. De hey - li - gen unt - phan ghe - li - che

7. Di - ne sco - ne sele in gho - - - - tes

ho - hez ri - - - che.

grand chants, such as 'S'onques nuls hom' (R1126); others are contrafacts such as 'Bien deust chanter' (R1120b); others are *unica* and probably indigenous compositions, such as 'Quant le russingnol se cesse', a *chanson pieuse* (R955a). The comparative absence of *grand chants* with English words, though disappointing, is nevertheless not surprising. French, not English, was the principal language of the court and courtly literature during the three centuries following the Norman Conquest. If there was any sense at this period of a linguistic nationalism, it did not take the form of competing with French as an international courtly language.

The surviving monophonic English songs of the thirteenth century are more frequently related, at least in form, to the sequence than to the chanson. 'Man mei longe him lives wene', however, is one of the exceptions (Ex. 128).[52] The moralizing text was a favourite—it was quoted by three separate preachers and is recorded in four manuscripts. The only extant version of the melody, in the Maidstone MS, may have been copied in Lincolnshire around the middle of the century; the hand is exceedingly informal and although the notes are carefully heighted in a prepared space, there are no staff lines. The song is in the standard A-A-B form, and has the expected features of *grand chant* melody—conjunct movement, single notes and note-groups related directly to the syllabic structure of the text, identity of musical phrase and text-unit. The tonal plan is stabilized, however, through a perhaps slightly unusual insistence on the opening pitch-set (c-e-g (cf. 5.1–3; 9.1–4) and on musical 'rhyme' (cf. 2,4,9,10).

GRAND CHANT IN LATIN: THE *CANTIO*

Modern scholars have used the term *conductus* to refer to two or three repertories that are largely separate from one another and are best considered separately. They are (1) songs associated with the liturgy and its extended 'secular' festivities, especially at Christmas and New Year as exemplified in the Offices of Sens and Beauvais; (2) the serious moral, political, religious, or amorous songs in high style exemplified in the Florence MS (Biblioteca Mediceo-Laurenziana, Plut. 29.1) fascicle 10, (and preceded in the MS by polyphonic settings in fascicles 8 and 9; see Ch. XII); (3) the Latin rondeaux (*rondelli*), dance-songs mostly on themes of religious celebration such as those collected in fascicle 11 of the Florence MS.

In this chapter, the term 'monophonic conductus' is limited to group (1). In Ch. XII, however, in referring to polyphonic music the

---

[52] Maidstone Museum, MS A.13, fo. 93ᵛ; see E. J. Dobson and F. Ll. Harrison, eds. *Medieval English Songs*, No. 6a for full information (their transcription is heavily edited).

Ex. 128

term 'conductus' will include all the kinds of texts found in the 8th and 9th fascicles of the Florence MS; the great majority of these texts are in the tradition of group (2).

In theme, and perhaps in function, the songs of group (3) are clearly linked with those of (1), but in style and form they are distinct. Group (3) will be treated later; here only group (2) will be considered.

It would be strange if there were no Latin songs in the *grand chant* tradition, the high secular style, since Latin was one of the principal languages of *entertainment* (as well as of much else), during the Middle Ages. Such songs I shall call *cantiones* to mark the community between them and the *cansos* and chansons discussed earlier. *Contrafacta* again form a good starting-point. 'Nitimur in vetitum' is a *contrafactum*, or vice versa (it is immaterial) of 'Quant li rossingols jolis' (R1559), variously attributed to Raoul de Ferrières and Le Châtelain de Coucy (d. 1205) (Ex. 129).[53] This well-known chanson (eight versions in seven MSS) is cited by the theorist Grocheo as a *cantus coronatus*,[54] and two other trouvère chansons are related to it.

The characteristics of this *cantio*/chanson are the expected ones: the units of melody have consistent numbers of syllables (7) and lines (10); the melodic progressions include nothing wider than a third except at line-ends; the line is stable within *ouvert* and *clos* cadential phrases. It is not in the standard AAB form but in a variant of it—ABACDE-FA'GC. The melody is subtly unified by initial motives (1 and 8; 2, 'diminished' in 4, 9, and 10; and 5, transposed in 7) as well as cadential motives (two can be distinguished, with variations).

One noteworthy difference between the Latin and the French songs concerns only the mood of the texts. The Latin opens in a starkly moral vein ('We strive for what is forbidden and desire what is denied to us') and ends with a macabre warning about the Day of Judgment—that day on which we shall look upon the wounds of the 'Easter victim' and find no hope. All our earthly lusts will be 'stink and fire and ice' (*fetor, ignis, glacies*). The French, on the other hand, tells of high summer: the poet will sing *con fins amis*; he has not yet attained his love but if he perserveres in her service, time and place will in the end bring him to this *grant joie*. Evidently no particular emotional character was felt to inhere in the melody itself.

There are not many love-songs in the Florence collection; most are

<hr/>

[53] 'Nitimur in vetitum' (Anderson K54) is on fo. 438 of the Florence MS; facsimile edn., L. Dittmer, *Faksimile-Ausgabe der Hs. Firenze, Biblioteca Mediceo-Laurenziana Pluteo 29.1*, Institute of Medieval Music. (Brooklyn, n.d. [1966–7]). References to 'Anderson' in the form given above are to G. A. Anderson, 'Notre-Dame and related conductus: A Catalogue raisonné', *Miscellanea Musicologica*, 6 (1972), 153–229; 7 (1975), 1–81.

[54] Grocheo (ed. Rohloff) p. 30.

Ex. 129

of a moral, contemplative or bitingly satirical nature. But it would be wrong to conclude from this that the collection has anything of the anti-courtly spirit, or didactic aim, that one finds in, say, the *Libre Vermell* or the *Red Book of Ossory*.[55] These latter are collections of *moralizations*—'gude and godlie ballatis', to use a sixteenth-century phrase—deliberately replacing 'lewd and worldly' songs. We learn from the Florence collections—and other Latin collections do not counter it—that the high style of melody was the appropriate vehicle for serious texts of a variety of kinds. It is characteristically used for 'In Rama sonat gemitus', a *cantio* lamenting the exile of Thomas Becket.[56]

The form and style of the *grand chant* were evidently appropriate for the formal lament (*planctus*) with Latin text, although the lament is often presented as a *lai*. 'Rex obiit et labitur', on the death of Alfonso VIII of Castile, is a single-stanza *cantio*, composed as an *oda continua* though with a good deal of motivic unity (phrase 8, echoing features of 1, sums up in part) (Ex. 130).[57] The tonal plan is not immediately obvious; the main tension seems to be between an 'open' a and a 'closed' G. Many Latin *cantiones* differ from their French counterparts in freer use of melodic ornaments. The longer note-groups (8.4, 9.4, and especially 5.1) are, however, neither so extensive nor so frequent as to upset the essentially syllabic movement of the melody; the melismata, if one may call them that, are 'contained' by the individual syllables.

Melisma properly so called is, however, found in some versions of *cantiones*, especially in an opening or concluding position. Ruth Steiner observes that of the 83 songs in the Florence MS fasc. 10, 38 'begin with fairly long melismas, and 27 end with them'.[58] In contrast to the melismatic ornaments just mentioned, these longer ones seem to be excrescent—they can be omitted (and are, in some sources) without damaging the song's integrity. In this respect they are similar to the melismatic *caude* of polyphonic *conductus* (see Ch. XII).

[55] *Libre Vermell*: Montserrat, Monasterio de S. Maria (no shelf-mark) contains 10 songs of which 5 are monophonic. *Red Book of Ossory*: Kilkenny, Republic of Ireland, Episcopal Palace (no shelf-mark) contains 60 Latin poems; marginal jottings in English and French appear to indicate tunes. No music given. For further details of these two MSS, see *Words and Music*, pp. 515, 517.

[56] Wolfenbüttel, Herzog-August-Bibliothek, Helmstedt 628 (W1) fo. 168ᵛ. See *Words and Music*, p. 69, Ex. 18.

[57] Burgos, Monasterio de Las Huelgas (no shelf-mark), fo. 161ᵛ: see Janthia Yearley, 'A bibliography of planctus', *Journal of the Plainsong & Mediæval Music Society*, 4 (1981), 12–52 (item No. L140). The standard edn. is by Higini Anglès, ed. *El Codex musical de Las Huelgas.* (*Musica a veus dels segles xiii–xiv*), 3 vols. (Barcelona, 1931 [facs.]).

[58] Ruth Steiner, 'Some Monophonic Latin Songs composed around 1200', *MQ*, 52 (1966), 56–70.

Ex. 130

Rex   ob - iit   et   la - bi - tur

2.   Cas - tel - le   glo - ri - a,

3.   Al - le - fon - sus   ra - pi - tur

4.   ad   ce - li   glo - ri - a[m].

5. Fons _____   a - ret   et   mo - ri - tur;

6.   do - nan - di   co - pi - a

7.   pe - tit   ce - les - ti - a,

8.   a   cu - ius   ma - ni - bus

9.   flu - xe - runt   om - ni - bus

10.   lar - gi - ta - tis   Ma - ri - a.

DANCE-SONG: *CAROLE, RONDEAU,* AND *REFRAIN*

The great central repertory of *grand chant* in various countries and languages was, so far as we can tell, an intellectual and imaginative experience addressed to the ear. In contrast to this is another repertory of song which is essentially bound up with physical movement. Dance-song is body-music. There is also a small surviving repertory of instrumental dances; it appears, however, to have little to do with the dance-songs now to be described. These may sometimes, of course, have been accompanied with instruments, but what is known of the social contexts does not invariably support that idea (see Ch. X).

Grand chant and dance-song contrast in another respect—that of rhythm. All the surviving dance-songs appear from their general context to be social, not solo, dances. Such dances are perhaps by nature metrical; they might be assumed to have the regular, recurrent beat for a company to keep step or sing together. In some instances dance-songs are mensurally notated, as in Adam de la Halle's dramatic *pastourelle, Robin et Marion*.[59] In the MS which contains Adam's 'complete works', (BN fr. 25566, trouvère MS W) there is a contrast between the mensural notation of *refrains* (a constituent of dance song to be described) and the traditional non-mensural notation of chansons and *jeux-partis*.

There are two repertories of dance-song. One is chiefly associated with courtly activity, and with *carole, rondeau,* and *refrain*. The other, the Latin *rondellus,* is apparently clerical. The two are closely connected in musical form and style, but there are very few direct links.[60]

The music of the French dance-song comes from many sources, few of which contain whole musical texts; and it survives mainly in the form of *refrains*. The term *refrain* has a particular and specialized meaning as applied to French songs *c.* 1150–*c.* 1350; this has to be distinguished from its usual meanings in musical and literary studies and in this chapter will be italicized. A *refrain* is a segment of melody, usually two or three phrases, with words. These segments are sometimes found on their own, sometimes as interpolations in other works where they may or may not be repeated as part of a strophic song.[61]

---

[59] The play is edited with music by Gennrich and by Varty, and translated by Axton and Stevens (see Bibliography). There are two MSS with music: BN fr. 25566 (trouvère MS *W*) and Aix-en-Provence, Bibl. Méjanes 572. The notation in these sources is not always free from ambiguities but is nevertheless basically mensural; see, however, the *chanson-de-geste* melody cited *Words and Music,* p. 224.

[60] One of the few is the concordance between the *rondellus* 'Veni, sancte spiritus' (BL Egerton MS 274, fo. 49) and the French *refrain* 'A ma dame ai mis mon cuer et mon pensé' (Montpellier Codex, fo. 231ᵛ and elsewhere).

[61] See Stevens, 'Refrain', *New Grove,* xv. 671–2.

From the literary point of view a *refrain* is a courtly saying. Sometimes it has the appearance of a proverb of Love, as in these examples.[62]

En ma dame ai mis	I have set my heart
mon cuer et mon panser	and my thought on my lady
De debounereté	It is from sweet behaviour
vient amours	that love comes

The sententious completeness of these *refrains*, parallelled in English by Chaucer's 'For pitee renneth sone in gentil herte', suggests that a *refrain* had an independent existence.[63] These two examples are both found, as it happens, in the same motet ('Trop sovent'/'Brunete'/*In seculum*) where they are sung at the same time. But the first, 'En ma dame', also occurs as a *rondeau*, in a trouvère chanson, in a *ballete*, and in two other motets. The second, 'De debounereté' appears in a *chanson-avec-des-refrains* and is quoted in two courtly poems.

Each *refrain* is a miniature but self-contained entity. The words have been described as 'emotionally direct, swift in thought and simple—even if they are at times hard to grasp analytically, it is never difficult to get the feel of them'.[64] This sense of completeness is characteristic of their music as well as of their words. The phrases of melody for a *refrain* are almost always clearly balanced; the melody itself is usually tuneful and this, with its clear orientation towards a final, makes it easier to memorize than most *grand chant* melodies.

The *refrain* is a combined literary, musical and—it seems certain—a social phenomenon. Its first appearances are in literary texts. Many of these sources do not have music, though the fictional context normally implies its existence; those that do may provide, for a given *refrain*, melodies that vary slightly or completely. The *refrain* 'Cui lairai ge mes amours, amie, s'a vos non' occurs in eight sources—two *rondeaux*, three *chansons-avec-des-refrains*, two motets, and in one French translation of Ovid's *Ars amandi*. Only five of these sources have music.[65] In Ex. 131, the melody is shown as it appears in the chanson 'Entre Godefroi et Robin'.[66] It is similar in the *chanson pieuse*, 'Ja pour yver' (R520) by Gautier de Coinci (Ex. 132(i)), but another source gives it with a lightly touched top c (Ex. 132(ii)) which

---

[62] See Nico H. J. van den Boogaard, *Rondeaux et refrains du XIIe au début du XIVe siécle* (Paris, 1969), refrains Nos. 662 and 468.

[63] For fuller discussion of the *refrain* and its disputed origins in relation to dance-song, *carole*, and *rondeau*, see *Words and Music*, pp. 171–8, 186–96.

[64] Peter Dronke, *Medieval Latin and the Rise of the European Love-Lyric*, 2 vols. (Oxford, 1965), i, pp. 32–3.

[65] Boogard, *Rondeaux et refrains*, refr. No. 387, gives details.

[66] BN MS fr. 12615, fo. 78 (Ernoul Caupains).

Ex. 131

A cui don - rai jou mes a - mors, a - mi - e, s'a vos non?

Ex. 132

(i)

Cui don - rai je mes a - mours, Me - re Dieu, s'a vous non?

(ii)

Cui lai - rai ge mes a - mours, A - mi - e s'a vos non?

softens the effect of the seventh.[67] The *refrain* 'Jamais amours n'oub-
lierai' has quite different melodies in three sources of the *Roman de
Renart*; yet all share the clear-cut, memorable quality.

The earliest known literary source into which *refrains* (and other
songs) are interpolated is the courtly romance *Guillaume de Dole*
(*c.* 1228) by Jean Renart.[68] The author says in the opening lines, 'This
romance is decorated with fine verses (*biaus vers*) such as an uncourtly
person (*vilains*) could not comprehend'. *Guillaume de Dole* seems to
have set a fashion, but it differs from some later texts in two respects:
it provides no music for any of the songs, and the *refrains* are always
incorporated into *rondeau*-type forms.

	Verbal Scheme	Presumed Musical Scheme
La gieus desoz la raime	a	A
—*einsi doit aler qui aime*—	A	A
clere i sourt la fontaine,	a	A
y a!	b	B
Einsi doit aler/qui bele aime a.[69]	AB	AB

[67] Ex. 132(i) is from Jacques Chailley, ed.: *Les Chansons à la vierge de Gautièr de Coinci* (Paris,
1959), No. 13 (pp. 143–6). Ex. 132(ii) is from the same, p. 66, based on Friedrich Gennrich,
Rondeaux, Virelais und Balladen, 3 vols., vol. i (Dresden, 1921), No. 127. The melodies are
transcribed by Gennrich, *Rondeaux*, from BN fr. 12615, fo. 122; BN fr. 372, fo. 12; and BN
fr. 1593, fo. 12. (The rhythmical interpretations supplied by Gennrich throughout this work do
not always have MS warrant.)

[68] Jean Renart, *Le Roman de la Rose ou de Guillaume de Dole*, ed. F. Lecoy, in *Les Classiques
français du moyen âge* (Paris, 1962). See further, *Words and Music*, pp. 168–9.

[69] Boogaard, *Rondeaux et refrains*, rondeau 1 (refr. 62).

or,

Main se leva bele Aeliz	a	A
—*dormez, jalous, ge vos en pri,—*	A	A
biau se para, miex se vesti,	a	A
desoz le raim.	b	A
Mignotement la voi venir	x	?C
cele que j'aim.[70]	B	?D

These are emphatically not to be seen as 'imperfect' *rondeaux* requiring emendation to bring them into line with the *forme fixe* so popular in the fourteenth century. In the fictionally idealized courtly scenes (festivities and ceremonies) which Renart gives as the social context of his songs, the term often used to introduce them is *carole*. No surviving medieval source, however, contains a collection, or section, of songs labelled *caroles*; it was not a precisely identifiable form. Rather, it was a set of constituents which might be fitted together in a number of ways to make a dance-song. The *rondeau*-type (with its defining 'half-refrain' in mid-verse) is one such way; terms such as *chanconetes, cançons de carolle, rondets, rondelets, conduiz* may have suggested others.

If *rondeaux* in this period followed a predictable form, it would in theory be possible to reconstruct the dance-songs of this type from the music (A-B) of the *refrain*, treating it as a 'refrain' in the normal sense. Fortunately some fully notated *rondeaux* survive in a Vatican chansonnier;[71] it contains ten by Guillaume d'Amiens (*fl.* late thirteenth century) (Ex. 133). The songs are in a non-mensural notation with undifferentiated longs but should almost certainly be transcribed metrically. It is significant that in the MS index *rondeaux* are not classed with *cançons* but with motets (*ce sont motet et roondel*).

Of the essentially courtly nature of the surviving dance-songs with French texts (almost all northern French, since Provençal has left few traces) the combined evidence of sources, literary and musical, leaves no doubt.

DANCE-SONG: *RONDELLUS*

The principal collection of *rondelli*, Latin dance-songs, is in the eleventh fascicle of the Florence MS (of which the tenth fascicle is the principal source of Latin *cantiones*, religious, moral, and political). These dance-songs, too, are best not called *conductus*. Even though most of them are certainly closer to liturgical occasion than the *cantiones* of fascicle 10, they appear to be unconnected, musically,

---

[70] Boogaard, *Rondeaux et refrains, rondeau* 2 (refr. 1335, 597).

[71] Rome, Vat. Reg. 1490 (? early fourteenth century), fo. 119ᵛ; see Boogaard, *Rondeaux et refrains, rondeau* 92 (refr. 338).

Ex. 133

with the repertory of paraliturgical conductus found in New Year ceremonies at Beauvais and elsewhere.[72]

It could be that in the realm of clerical festivity these twelfth-century *rondelli* do supply a gap left (in our knowledge if not in historical fact) by the dwindling recurrence of the earlier *conductus* repertory. On the other hand, they could be regarded as supplementing rather than as supplanting the *conductus*. A large group of Easter songs in the Florence MS were possibly for clerical entertainment and diversion after the long hours passed under the discipline and restraint of liturgical celebration. These Easter songs do not have their counterpart in the repertory of Sens and Beauvais, concentrated as it is on the festivities of Christmas and New Year. Moreover, the Florence songs are *rondelli*, i.e. in a form which does not occur in the festival *conductus* repertory.

Outside the Florence MS there are Latin dance-songs in a manu-

---

[72] See the two volume study (with transcription and full commentary) by Wulf Arlt, *Ein Festoffizium des Mittelalters aus Beauvais in seiner liturgischen und musikalischen Bedeutung* (Cologne, 1970).

script at Tours; in trouvère MS F; in Engelberg with German text incipits; in a manuscript associated with St Victor with French and Latin texts, without music.[73] Both the Engelberg and the St Victor MSS supply genuine pious contrafacts with a clear purifying motive behind them.

The great majority of these dance-songs, but not all, are in *rondeau*-type forms with some kind of shortened refrain in mid-verse. 'Processit in capite' was clearly popular, since it appears not only in Florence and Tours but also in a little group of three *rondelli* in an English source (Ex. 134).[74] To this source the Florence MS adds the last two lines of the example, which clarify the form. Subsequent stanzas (written as prose, without notation) make it clear that the first line must always be sung twice in this *rondellus*. Many small variations in the disposition of the text are displayed in the repertory; and sometimes, as in 'Culpe purgator',[75] the mid-verse refrain and the end-

Ex. 134

1. Pro - ces - sit in ca - pi - te -

2. om - nes gen - tes, plau - di - te -

3. pro - ces - sit in ca - pi - te

4. nos - tra re - sur - re - ci - o.

5. *Om - nes gen - tes, plau - di - te*

6. *ma - ni - bus pre gau - di - o.*

[73] Tours, Bibl. Mun. 927; BL Egerton 274; Engelberg, Stiftsbibl. 314; BN lat. 15131.
[74] Oxford, Bodl., MS Bodley 937 fo. 446ᵛ; and Florence MS fo. 466. See Anderson M21.
[75] Florence MS, fo. 466. See Anderson M22.

refrain have different words and different tunes. As scholars looking
for the genesis of a form, we may find this confusing. But it seems a
sensible, practical arrangement, since the *chorus* always sings the
melody which the *cantor* has just sung—a convenient feature if they
are singing in procession.

The Latin *rondelli* and the French *rondeaux* are similar in many
respects. They have the same freedom of form, balanced rhythms,
lucid tonality, 'open' and 'closed' phrases, syllabic movement, restricted range (a fifth or a sixth is normal). A study of their melodic
idioms (which are repetitive) would probably reveal more consanguity
with the *lai* than with the *grand chant*. Of the first twenty *rondelli* in
the Florence MS, over half have G-finals; several combine this with
some reference to the F below. In two respects at least they differ: the
Latin dance-songs are strophic; and they are not based on a pre-
existent corpus of *refrains*, in the special French sense.

TANZLIED

The dance-song in Germany for the twelfth and thirteenth centuries is
inseparably connected with the name of Neidhart von Reuental
(?1180/90–after 1236).[76] Despite the widespread imitation in Germany
of French romance (Hartmann von Aue, Wolfram von Eschenbach,
Gottfried von Strassburg, and others) there are no traces of romance
with intercalated lyric or *refrain*, as in the north of France. Neidhart's
songs are completely different from the *refrain*-based *rondeaux*; and
the principal reasons for regarding them as dance-songs have been,
first, the perpetual references to dance in the texts of the songs and
second, their presumed dance-like style. Neither of these reasons is
absolutely conclusive. The difficulty is compounded by the fact that
the Schratsche MS, the major source of Neidhart melodies and the
sole source of most of them, dates from the middle of the fifteenth
century, more than two centuries after Neidhart's death. The earliest
source of Neidhart's melodies is the early fourteenth-century manuscript fragment at Frankfurt; it contains four melodies to authentic
Neidhart texts, three of which are also in the Schratsche manuscript.[77]

A striking feature that tells against the hypothesis that the Neidhart
Lieder are actual dance-songs is their prevalent use of AAB form. The

[76] The authentic songs of Neidhart are ed. A. T. Hatto and R. J. Taylor, *The Songs of
Neidhart von Reuental* (Manchester, 1958); the unauthentic songs by Taylor, *Minnesinger* (see
n. 47 above), i, p. 120; ii, p. 184. Facsimiles of the whole corpus ed. Wolfgang Schmieder, *Lieder
von Neidhart (von Reuental)*, *Denkmäler der Tonkunst in Österreich*, lxxi (Jg. 37) (Vienna, 1930).
For further editions by Gennrich and by Rohloff, see Bibliography.

[77] The Schratsche MS (see Burkhard Kippenberg, 'Neidhart von Reuental', *New Grove*, xiii,
97–9), is Berlin MS germ. fo. 779; further described, Hatto and Taylor, *Songs of Neidhart*,
pp. 46–7. The MS fragment *O* is Frankfurt-am-Main, Staatsbibl., MS germ. oct.18.

two *Stollen* (the *pedes* of chanson terminology) may be of the normal two lines each as in 'Sumer diner suezen weter', or longer ('Owe, sumerzit' has six, with an *Abgesang* (*cauda*) of three, making a fifteen-line stanza).[78] Perhaps there is no reason why a dance should not have been devised to fit *Bar*-form. But the associations are all with the *grand chant* tradition.

Ex. 135

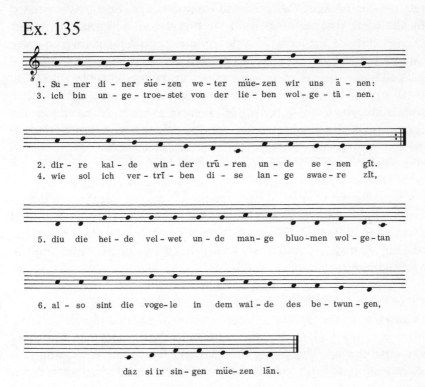

1. Su - mer di - ner süe - zen we - ter müe- zen wir uns ā - nen:
3. ich bin un - ge - troe- stet von der lie - ben wol - ge - tā - nen.

2. dir - re kal - de win - der trū - ren un - de se - nen gīt.
4. wie sol ich ver - trī - ben di - se lan - ge swae - re zīt,

5. diu die hei - de vel - wet un - de man - ge bluo -men wol - ge -tan

6. al - so sint die voge- le in dem wal - de des be - twun - gen,

daz si ir sin- gen müe- zen lān.

'Sumer diner süezen weter' (Ex. 135) exemplifies the special features of Neidhart's German chanson and shows how it may differ from the French (and Provençal) chansons discussed earlier.[79] The poet, in the conventional Winter-song opening, says goodbye to summer and equates 'dise langen swaeren zit' of winter with his own miserable state as an unrequited lover. The stanza-form is normal enough (rhyming ab ab c'xc) but the line-length is abnormal (*cauda* 15, 13ᵕ, 7). The phrase plan, ABAB CDE, where E forms a half-line musical

---

[78] See Moser and Müller-Blattau, *Deutsche Lieder des Mittelalters*, pp. 55–8 (with complete text); Hatto and Taylor, *Songs of Neidhart*, pp. 32–3 (text and translation of st. 1, with further paraphrase).

[79] See Moser and Müller-Blattau, *Deutsche Lieder des Mittelalters*, pp. 52–4 (complete text); Hatto and Taylor, *Songs of Neidhart*, pp. 30–1 (text and translation of st. 1, with further paraphrase) from the Vipiteno MS (Municipal Archives).

'rhyme' with B, is standard in the European chanson. Individual features, found in most of the songs in this small, late-transmitted repertory, include the tendency to make metrical groups by the repetition of single notes; see especially phrases 5 and 6.1–6, but also the beginning and end of the song. This must reflect the stress-structure of the German language and the much more direct physical relationship between the word and the notes. The effect is accentuated by the total absence of melisma or even two-note groups. Another individuality of the melodic style is the impression it gives that, even though the melody often moves by step, it is jumping up and down a gapped scale, instead of flowing smoothly as in a high-style chanson. In this particular *Lied* the scale is a pentatonic one ((C)DFGacd); only in phrases 2 (=4) and 7 does E carry any weight. Such melodic formation is said to be related to the *gesprungen* round-dance (*Reigen*) of the country folk whose festivities are depicted in the songs. And in consequence, the Neidhart melodies have been described as 'stamped with the rhythmic character of the dance and influenced by the instruments used for their performance'.[80] It seems, rather, as if they are much more what one might infer from the texts: they are examples of a 'courtly-popular' style—not genuine rusticity but a delightful playing with it, a popular art transformed by courtly needs, tastes, and techniques.

NARRATIVE MELODY

In addition to the high-style 'numbered' chanson and the dance-song, there is a third main melodic tradition—that associated with long narrative poems. Throughout the Middle Ages these were sung to a variety of melodies, sometimes with instrumental accompaniment, sometimes not. The reconstruction of these is not an easy task, but it can be a rewarding one.

Such epic-singing of a traditional kind as has survived into this century is a salutary reminder of the sheer variety of rhythm, 'mode' and style—not to mention the infinite shades of speech-melody that lie between song and the intonations of everyday conversation. Johannes de Grocheo writes in a well-known passage of his *Theoria* (c. 1300) that in the performance of *cantus gestualis* the number of lines is not fixed but variable and that each line should be sung to the same melody (*idem etiam cantus debet in omnibus versibus reiterari*).[81] But this prescription patently does not cover all the possibilities of

---

[80] Kippenberg, 'Neidhart von Reuental', p. 98.
[81] Ed. Rohloff, p. 130.

narrative melody in the early Middle Ages. The evidence suggests that there are at least four formal types which we need to have in mind.[82]

1. The lection tone, used in liturgical chant for the singing of lessons; it is essentially a reciting-tone with inflexions for commas, full stops, questions. The principal characteristics of this type of melody are its closeness to speech and its infinite extensibility.

2. The *laisse* type, associated with the performance of *chanson de geste* and the *gesta* (deeds) of saints. The *laisse* is a strophe of indeterminate length, in equal lines linked by rhyme or assonance. The melodies appear, on the scanty evidence available, to have more musical life than recitation, and to have such features as open and closed cadences and, perhaps, alternative options for the ends of *laisses*.

3. The *lai* type; similar to the sequence (AABBCC etc.) in form but much freer in the way it repeats versicles and melodic material in general. It is more melodious, again, and generally capable of standing on its own as melody.

4. The *strophic* type, familiar to us in folk-ballad. A single stanza-form with its melody is repeated without variation for as long as the narrative requires. It is especially common in medieval German narrative singing.

None of these four basic types, it should be said, is used exclusively as narrative melody.

The oldest surviving corpus of vernacular epic is British. The Old English epic poems date back, it is thought, to the seventh century (*Widsith*, *Genesis* and others), though the manuscripts which preserve them are later. *Widsith* itself is an idealized portrait of a *scop*, i.e. an epic poet/performer of superior social standing, as contrasted with the lower-class *gleoman*, predecessor of the *jongleur*.[83] There is no doubt that epic narratives were sung, and by nobles as well as *scops*: 'at times one bold in battle drew sweetness from the harp, the joywood; at times another wrought a measure true and sad; at times the large-hearted king [Hrothgar] told a wondrous story in fitting fashion' (*Beowulf*, 2105). Despite many passages associating harping and singing, not all scholars agree that Anglo-Saxon epic song was accompanied (see Ch. X).[84]

---

[82] See *Words and Music*, pp. 200–3 for musical examples, and ch. VI and VII for the more extended discussion of narrative melody upon which this section is based.

[83] See Peter Dronke, *The Medieval Lyric* (London, 1968), 'Introduction: performers and performance', for a wider context, especially pp. 17 ff.

[84] Jeff Opland, *Anglo-Saxon Oral Poetry: A Study of the Traditions* (New Haven, 1980), 256.

No music whatsoever survives for these Anglo-Saxon poems; and all theories (they have never been wanting) about their melodies and style of performance have been based on circumstantial evidence—on the text and its metrical principles, on the nature and capabilities of surviving instruments (i.e. reconstructions from archaeological research), on the close study of manuscript presentation (punctuation, accents, etc.). Various theories as to whether Old English narrative poems were spoken, recited, chanted, intoned or sung include the following.

(1) Recitation in heightened speech, either spoken or chanted on the analogy of psalm-singing; the half-line structure of Old English verse clearly lends itself to this.[85]

(2) Mensuration: each half-line is assumed to contain two bars of quadruple time; instrumental accompaniment provides the 'beat', and rests have to be inserted to fit the hemistichs into the musical frame.[86]

(3) Metrical stress, represented by differences in pitch. Five different contours are proposed using up to four distinct pitches. German sources may provide evidence for this by analogy.[87]

Of these hypotheses the second now appears totally anachronistic. The first commends itself to the imagination as a way of singing narrative, and has historical analogy in the liturgy, but is unsupported by any hard evidence. The third, at least for Britain, is entirely conjectural.

If Old English epic (and epic-related Scriptural) poems were sung, then it is possible that the only early Middle English vernacular epic in a related style, Lazamon's *Brut* (*c.* 1225), was also. But the verse-style was by that date archaic, and Lazamon's imitation of it is metrically diffuse, even disordered.

In the Old High German period narrative texts are scarce and musical hints almost non-existent. Between the *Hildebrandslied* (copied *c.* 810) and the *Nibelungenlied* (*c.* 1200–10) four centuries passed, leaving virtually no trace of epic music from what must have been a richly endowed period. Something has been made of one mid-ninth-century text, the *Evangelienbuch* of Otfried, a Benedictine monk.[88] But even if the accents in the text are neumes, and even if

[85] e.g. Eduard Sievers, *Altgermanische Metrik* (Halle, 1893); Max Kaluza, *A Short History of English Versification*, transl. Arthur C. Dunstan (New York, 1911). A similar case is argued on the basis of palaeographical evidence by Egon Werlich, *Der westgermanische Skop* (Münster, 1964).

[86] See especially John C. Pope, *The Rhythm of Beowulf* (New Haven, 1942), 93 ff.

[87] Thomas Cable, *The Meter and Melody of Beowulf* (Urbana, Illinois, 1974); see p. 96 for a conjectural 'musical score'.

[88] See Karl H. Bertau, 'Epenrezitation im deutschen Mittelalter', *Études germaniques*, 20 (1965), 1–17 for Otfried and for a general account of the medieval German *Epos* (i.e. epic and romance) and its music.

these neumes denote higher pitches on stressed syllables (cf. hypo-thesis (3)), Otfried's devout gloss on the Gospel in end-rhyming verse is about as far from the style of heroic epic as it could be.

German secular narrative in the centuries up to *c*. 1300 takes two forms—strophic (as in the *Nibelungenlied*) with a strophe of four lines (eight half-lines) rhyming aabb; and octosyllabic couplets (as in Gottfried's *Tristan*, from the early thirteenth century). The octosylla-bic couplets are derived, if somewhat roughly, from the standard, invariable metre of French romance, and consideration of them must be deferred. The strophic form, on the other hand, was not derived from French. The early fourteenth-century *Der jüngere Titurel* (and possibly also Wolfram von Eschenbach's *Titurel*) was sung to the 'Titurel-strophe'. The syllables are for the most part fitted with single notes, but there are a few groups, especially at line endings. The melody is conjunct, making use of the pitch-set CDFa, in the line-form ABCB. It has no obvious musical features that call for a measured rendering. These strophic narrative melodies are known as Töne (Ex. 136).[89]

There is no French epic poetry of the antiquity of the Old English and German poems. That is to say, it does not survive in written form. It was not until the twelfth century that the best-known *chanson de geste*, the *Chanson de Roland*, emerged from the shades in the written form which we have; but this event could only have been the culmination of long series of stories, legends, and songs about the heroic battle between Roland with 'the twelve peers' and the Saracens at Roncevalles in 778.

There is no shortage of literary evidence that the *chanson de geste* was sung. For instance, in the *Roman de la Violette* (early thirteenth century) the hero has to sing an excerpt from *Aliscans* (from the Charlemagne cycle) 'a clere vois et a douch son' (in a clear voice and to a sweet melody).[90] The *Roman* itself is in octosyllabic couplets, the epic insertion in monorhymed decasyllabics. The standard metrical form for the *chanson de geste* is the *laisse* with a variable number of equal lines. It needs therefore a melody suitable for continuous repetition and, presumably, slight variation also.

The direct musical evidence is very scanty indeed. Two short non-mensural melodies have often been printed. The first, from Adam de la Halle's pastoral entertainment, *Robin et Marion*, is clearly identified

---

[89] Bertau, 'Epenrezitation', p. 9, from Vienna, Nationalbibl. Ms 2675. The number of these fixed and traditional metrical-musical structures has been enlarged by Horst Brunner, 'Epen-melodien' in Otmar Werner, ed., *Formen mittelalterlicher Literatur* [Festschrift: Siegfried Beyschlag] (Göppingen, 1970), 149–78.

[90] Ed. Douglas L. Buffum, Société des Anciens Textes Français (Paris, 1928), lines 1403–8. For further details, see *Words and Music*, p. 223.

Ex. 136

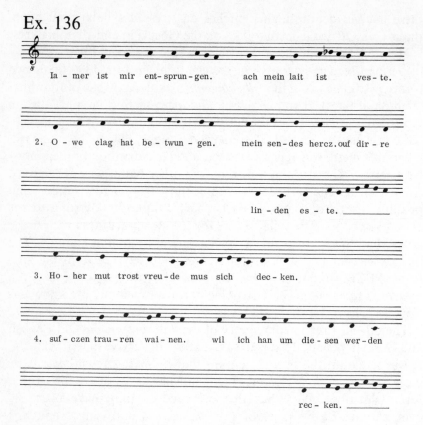

Ia - mer ist mir ent- sprun - gen.   ach mein lait ist   ves - te.

2. O - we clag hat be - twun - gen.   mein sen - des hercz. ouf dir - re

lin - den es - te. _____

3. Ho - her mut trost vreu - de mus sich   dec - ken.

4. suf - czen trau - ren wai - nen.   wil ich han um die - sen wer - den

rec - ken. _____

as a narrative melody: 'Je sai trop bien canter de geste' says the
character who sings it.[91] The second melody, associated with an epic
poem on the battle of Annezin consists of seven note-groups each with
the single syllable 'in' underlaid.[92] How it might fit the twelve-syllable
line of the *chanson de geste* is baffling.

A third well-known melody (again non-mensural) may perhaps
prove a more instructive narrative model; it occurs in *Aucassin et
Nicolette*, a playfully ironic romantic tale in prose with passages of
song interspersed, all to the same melody (Ex. 137).[93] The application
of the three phrases of melody (here, A.B.C) to the varying number of
short lines of seven syllables, rounded off with one of five syllables, is
not clear. The five-syllabled melody C evidently concludes the *laisse*;

[91] See note 59 above. The melody, which uses mensural symbols ambiguously, is at line 729
(Varty's edn.); see *Words and Music*, p. 224 (Ex. 83).
[92] BL Roy MS 20. A.XVII, f. 177. See *Words and Music*, p. 224 and Ex. 84.
[93] BN fr. 2168, fos. 70–80ᵛ: the melody is written a number of times in non-mensural notation.
See *Words and Music*, p. 226; Mario Roques, ed. *Aucassin et Nicolette*, *Les Classiques français au
moyen âge* (Paris, 1929); Francis W. Bourdillon, *Cest Daucasin et de Nicolete* (Oxford, 1896),
facsimile edn.

Ex. 137

melodies A and B provide for the preceding lines in some manner, but they do not necessarily alternate. The question is whether this model has any authenticity as narrative melody. Is this flexible and extensible pattern a general one? Sufficient material certainly exists in French and in Latin to establish its validity. Johannes de Grocheo's comments on *cantus gestualis* are a warrant for extending the search more widely. He writes:[94]

We call a song a *chanson de geste* in which the deeds of heroes and the achievements of our forefathers are recounted, like the lives and sufferings of the saints and the conflicts and adversities which men of old endured for the faith and for the truth—the Life of St Stephen the first martyr, for example, and the story of Charlemagne.

[94] Ed. Rohloff, p. 130. Another well-known passage linking epic and saint's life is by Thomas de Cobham (d. 1327); see Frederick Broomfield, ed. *Thomae de Chobham Summa Confessorum, Analecta Mediaevalia Namurcensia*, 25 (Louvain, 1968), 291–2.

To take *cantus gestualis* simply as meaning *chanson de geste* in modern usage is clearly not broad enough. Grocheo refers to a wide repertory of narrative including Saints' Lives and perhaps historical chronicles (*antiquorum patrum opera*). A variety of sources transmit melodic material which not only meets Grocheo's basic demand for stichic repetition (*idem etiam cantus debet in omnibus versibus* [lines] *reiterari*), but also fits the tripartite pattern of *Aucassin et Nicolette*. These include certain types of chanson such as the *pastourelle*; *lais* in Latin and French; troped epistles (especially those with vernacular 'farsing'); narrative drama in Latin. The richest sources of potential narrative melody are the troped epistles; and in view of Grocheo's remarks quoted above, it is especially interesting to find so many vernacular tropes associated with the feast of St Stephen (26 December). It has evidently part of the liturgical jollity of the Christmas season to trope, or 'farse' (literally, 'stuff') Latin 'lessons' with vernacular interpolations telling the saint's *vita* in fresher and more affective detail. Texts survive in French and Provençal for this *Epistola* (Northern French *vita*) *beati Stephani prothomartiris*. The last *laisse* in Provençal version (the only text to have music notated) is given in Ex. 138.[95] This epistle has three melodic units, which can appear in various combinations according to the length of the *laisse*.

Ex. 138

A   A

Cant ac par-lat le sang mar-tir, lo ter-mes fon quel dec mo - rir.

A   A

Li an-gel ven-gron al fe - nir per la su-a ar-ma re - que-rir.

B   C

No fes san-glot ni fes so - spir; ans lo fes dieus si ben trans-ir

A

co s'il se de-gues a - dor - mir.

[95] Montpellier, Bibl. Mun. 120; facsimiles in Léon Gaudin, 'Epitres farcies inédites de la Saint-Etienne', *Revue des langues romanes*, 2 (1871) 133. Further examples in *Words and Music*, pp. 239–49.

In this particular *laisse*-type melody, phrase A always ends the section as well as having begun it. It is important to note that in none of the narratives that appear as tropes do the melodic units form a closed system as they do in strophic forms found in narrative lyrics such as the crusade chanson, the 'Arthurian *lai*', or the *chanson de toile*.

Finally, there is the evidence of narrative drama. It has sometimes been a surprise and a disappointment to historians of drama to discover that Latin texts which they regard as having 'dramatic potential' from a naturalistic point of view were sung in the Middle Ages to music entirely lacking in emotional commitment, as it were, to the text, the 'characters', or the action. Three plays from the Fleury Playbook are sung strophically, as if they were in fact narrative poems. But they have the further interest that the strophe is, again, not a closed form; it always uses the same melodic material but not always in the same way. The principal narrative melody of *Tres Filie* (Ex. 139)[96] is repeated thirty times for lines 15–168. This melody hovers between a short *laisse*-type (i.e. stichic, based on the line-phrase) and a consistent strophe. The important thing is that it can be

Ex. 139

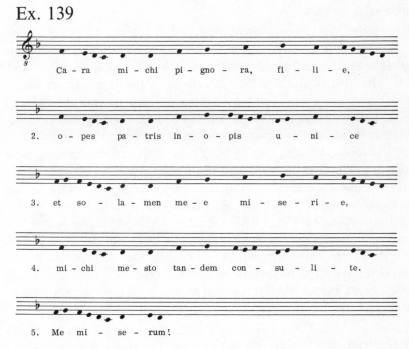

[96] Orleans, Bibl. de la Ville 201 (the so-called Fleury Playbook) contains four 'miracles' of St Nicholas; *Tres Filie* begins on p. 176; non-mensural notation. For the other plays, see *Words and Music*, pp. 257–62.

shortened as required, provided that the music of the final line is always preceded by the music of phrase 4(= 2).

SONG: MIXED FORMS

The *grand chant*, the dance-song, and narrative melody give us three points of vantage from which to survey the lesser song forms. Some of these are 'mixed' forms whose musical language cannot easily be understood from a single point of view.

Most of the song-types to be discussed seem to fall under the heading of what Grocheo calls *cantus versualis*; by this he meant, evidently, a type of chanson lighter than the *cantus coronatus* which he appears to equate with *grand chant*.[97] The *cantus versualis*, 'which some call *cantilena*', is inferior in verbal style (*dictamen*) and in harmoniousness (*concordantia*). Such songs are especially appropriate to young people (*juvenibus*), and keep them out of idleness. Some other song types in this 'mixed' category, however, are still *grand chant*, even if with a difference. In discussing the mixed forms, I shall generally refer to them simply by their northern French names, while taking Provençal and Latin songs into consideration.

CRUSADE SONGS

The *chansons de croisade* form a small but interesting group. Their distinctive feature, when they have one, is the blending of small-scale narrative structures into the chanson style. The song 'Parti de mal' (R401) has a structure A A¹ A A¹ A² B B¹; all the lines cadence with a similar figure, as if in 'musical assonance'.[98] It can be seen as a reduced *laisse*. The poet says 'I wish my song to be heard widely, for God has called us to his need and no honourable man ought to fail him'. Could it be that this otherwise courtly song is modelled on earlier songs of a more popular, overtly recruiting character? Another Crusade chanson, 'S'onques nuls hom' (R1126) (Ex. 140),[99] has in each of its stanzas a smaller strophic structure. Melodically, the song falls into two quatrains: ABCD E (?Ax) BCD (the relationship between A and E is apparent). The rhyme-scheme abba:ccaa does not bring this out; nevertheless the musical experience of hearing the song must be one of a series of repeated quatrains. Still other crusade songs are simply *grand chants* in melodic style and structure, with texts appropriate to the special theme.

---

[97] Ed. Rohloff, pp. 130 ff.

[98] BL MS Harl. 1717, fo. 251. Other Crusade songs are collected by Joseph Bédier and Pierre Aubry, eds. *Les Chansons de croisade* (Paris, 1909).

[99] BL Harl 3775, fo. 14 (facsimile, see *Words and Music*, frontispiece).

Ex. 140

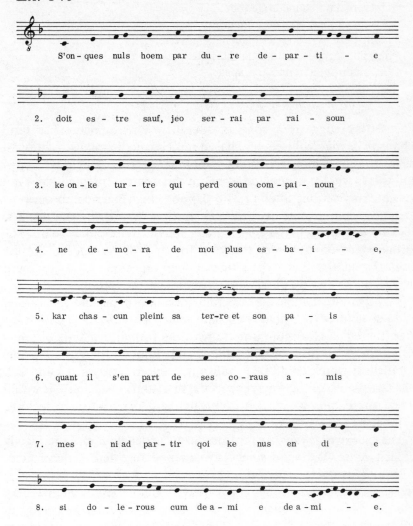

1. S'on - ques nuls hoem par du - re de - par - ti - e
2. doit es - tre sauf, jeo ser - rai par rai - soun
3. ke on - ke tur - tre qui perd soun com - pai - noun
4. ne de - mo - ra de moi plus es - ba - i - e,
5. kar chas - cun pleint sa ter-re et son pa - is
6. quant il s'en part de ses co - raus a - mis
7. mes i ni ad par - tir qoi ke nus en di e
8. si do - le - rous cum de a - mi e de a - mi - e.

CHANSONS DE TOILE, CANTIGAS DE AMIGO

Another type of chanson with some narrative features is the *chanson de toile*. In a passage in the *Lai d'Aristote* (*c.* 1225) by Henri d'Andeli, the young mistress of Alexander the Great, intent on seducing the philosopher Aristotle, comes towards the window:[100]

---

[100] The song (R594) with its melody is amongst the group of *chansons de toile* in the Chansonnier St Germain (BN fr. 20050) at fo. 65ᵛ (non-mensural Messine neumes). The *Lai d'Aristote* is ed. Maurice Delbouille in the Bibliothèque de la Faculté de Philosophie et Lettres de l'Université de Liège, CXXIII (Paris, 1951). See *Words and Music*, p. 230–1, Ex. 91 (the last line of the translation should read, 'Your love takes away all solace and gladness from me').

Vint vers la fenestre chantant
Un vers d'un chancon de toile . . .

'En un vergier, lez une fontenele	A
Dont clere est l'onde et blanche le gravele	A
Siet fille a roi, sa main a sa maissele.	A
En soupirant son doz ami apele:	A'
Hai cuens Guens amis!	B
La vostre amor me tolt solaz et ris'.	C

The setting suggests a song in a courtly environment. The term 'chanson *de toile*' (of weaving) has in this case no literal justification; it seems to refer simply to a song of popular type sung by a woman—and this is what they pretend to be. In this context 'pretend' does not indicate any serious attempt at deception; the singer/composer/poet pretends, as in a game, to a naïveté which is quite disingenuous. The *chanson de toile* is, like the *pastourelle*, a 'courtly-popular' genre. The formal signs of the wider tradition to which it is attached are the monorhyme, the *laisse*-type structure with repeated melody followed by variations and by phrases of closure, and the refrain.

Slightly more complex, but again with monorhyme and elements of *laisse*-structure, is 'Oriolanz en haut solier' (Ex. 141).[101] Here, how-ever, there is a clear compromise with the formal demands of *grand chant*: the AAB form modifies the *laisse*, although there is a melodic parallelism which could be significant between phrases 1/3 and 2/4. The last phrase of the song repeats the first, and closer analysis would reveal the details which contribute to the general effect of melodic economy.

The *chansons de toile* are far from being a particular and specifically French genre. Women's songs, so under-represented in the trouba-dour and trouvère repertories, are found as *kharjas*, in Mozarabic areas; as *winileodas* ('songs for a friend') among Germanic peoples; and as *cantigas de amigo*, in the Iberian peninsula, especially in thirteenth-century Portugal.[102] From this huge treasury of melody only six songs survive: they are ascribed to Martin Codax, a Galician poet-composer of the early thirteenth century.[103] 'Ondas do mar de Vigo' (Ex. 142) is typical of the little group in the economy of its

---

[101] Chansonnier St Germain, fo. 65.

[102] Dronke, *Medieval Lyric*, ch. 3, 'Cantigas de amigo', gives the literary context with abundant illustration.

[103] Facsimiles and transcriptions: Pedro Vindel, ed., *Martin Codax. Las siete canciones de amor: poema musical del siglo xii* (Madrid, 1915). See also the extended discussion and transcription by Higini Anglès, *La musica de las Cantigas de Santa Maria del Roy Alfonso el Sabio* (Barcelona, 1943–64), iii(2), pp. 447–53, and appendix of songs pp. 53–5. The notation of the Codax songs uses mensural symbols apparently without consistent meaning. The most recent study is by Manuel P. Ferreira, *The Sound of Martin Codax* (Lisbon, 1986), with facsimiles.

Ex. 141

O – ri – o – lanz en haut so – lier

2. sos – pi – rant prist a ler – moi – er

3. et re – gra – te son dru He – lier:

4. 'A – mis, trop vos font es – loi – gnier

5. de moi fe – lon et lo – sen – gier.'

REFR: Deus, tant par vient sa joi – e len – te

7. a ce – lui cui e – le a ta – len – te.

Ex. 142

On – das do mar de Vi – go

2. se vis – tes meu a – mi – go?

3. *E ai Deus, se ver – ra ce – do!*

melodic material. The style is closely conjunct within a narrow range (a fifth excepting one note); there is one melodic idea (A), ornamentally varied as A_1, followed by a refrain which is the same again except for the incipit 'E ai Deus'. The song which follows it, 'Mandid' ei comigo', could be described in almost identical terms except that A_1 has an apparently open cadence on the F below the fifth. The melismatic flourish at the line ending in 'Ondas do mar de vigo' is not precisely repeated in this little group of six melodies. The sample is too small for safe generalization, but the likeness in general between the *cantigas de amigo* and the *chansons de toile* is striking; they both have the features of narrative melody on a miniature scale. Whether their melodies are in any way related to folk-music must remain an open question.

DAWN-SONGS: *AUBE, ALBA*

Like the *chanson de toile*, the *alba* (French *aube*, dawn-song) is very widespread. Poems about lovers parting after a night in one another's arms embody a perennial situation.[104] There are many extant texts but few melodies. One of the best known in its own time and today is Guiraut de Borneill's 'Reis glorios' (P-C 242,64).[105] The five-line strophe has the melodic structure AABCD (D, a short line, has initial musical 'rhyme' with C); this structure with its repeated first phrase, recalls some of the *chansons de toile*. 'Reis glorios', also, is a woman's song; she warns her lover of the dangers the dawn brings. The only other extant troubadour *alba* is by Cadenet, 'S'anc fuy bela ni prezada' (P-C 106,14)[106] and is an extended imitation of Borneill's, which supplies much of the musical material for it. There are contrafacta for both of these *albas* (Ex. 143).

There is an earlier *alba*, the macaronic Latin-Provençal 'Phebi claro non dum orto jubare' (When Phoebus's bright beam has not yet risen); the subject, Dronke has argued, is not a lovers' parting but a warning of military ambush with suggestions also of spiritual meanings.[107] The melody cannot be satisfactorily transcribed, since the neumes are only roughly heighted and are, of course, non-mensural.[108]

[104] See Dronke, *Medieval Lyric*, ch. 5; Arthur T. Hatto, *Eos: An Enquiry into the Theme of Lovers' Meetings and Partings at Dawn in Poetry* (The Hague, 1965).

[105] Van der Werf and Bond, *The Extant Troubadour Melodies*, pp. 163*–64*, from BN fr. 22543, fo. 8ᵛ. Often reprinted: see Gustave Reese, *Music in the Middle Ages*, p. 215.

[106] Van der Werf and Bond, *The Extant Troubadour Melodies*, p. 76*, from BN fr. 22543 fo. 52; they also print the fourteenth-century contrafact 'Virgen, madre groriosa' (Ex. 160 below).

[107] Dronke, *Medieval Lyric*, p. 170.

[108] Rome, Vat. Reg. 1462 (late tenth century) fo. 50ᵛ (Walther, *Carmina*, 14086.) Attempted transcriptions by Giuseppe Vecchi, ed. *Poesia Latina Medievale* (Parma, 1958), tav. x; and by Jammers, *Melodien*, no. 11 (p. 146).

Ex. 143

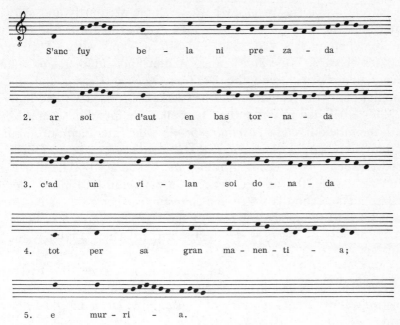

Editors agree, however, that the first three musical phrases are the same. So once more we seem to have a reduced *laisse*-structure—AAA in long lines, followed by four (?) non-repeating shorter, vernacular lines, forming the Provençal refrain.

In the trouvère repertory the *aube* is sparsely represented, and only one has a melody with it, 'Gaite de la tor' (R2015) in which two watchmen and the lover take part.[109] It is in chanson-form, AAB; but the whole of the *cauda* forms a refrain—most unlike the chanson.

The dawn-song was especially popular in medieval Germany, to judge from the number surviving with music, but most of them are of late date.[110] Wizlaw's *Tagelied* 'Der ritter hort den wechter' is the only one extant in a comparatively early source (Jena MS). Unfortunately the melody is given only for the *Abgesang* (*cauda*); but as Jammers observed this could be because the melodic material for the *Stollen* (*frons*) can be inferred from what there is, assuming the form AABA—a contracted *laisse* structure. The cadences are unusually melismatic.

[109] The melody (*unicum*) is in Chansonnier St Germain, fo. 83, along with the oldest *chansons de toile*.

[110] Dronke, *Medieval Lyric*, pp. 177 ff., Jammers, *Melodien*, pp. 110, 231, and No. 88, from the Jena MS, fo. 77 (see n. 48 above).

SUNG DEBATE: THE *JEU-PARTI*

Debate in one form or another was a staple of courtly and clerical entertainment during the Middle Ages.[111] The rhetorical tradition of Latin debate-poems was long and strong—and witty. There are debates between Wine and Water, Winter and Summer, and many love-dialogues, including the *De Ganymede et Helena* and, most popular of all, the Knight *versus* the Clerk, as lovers. Two well-known debates attributed to Philip the Chancellor are found in several MSS with their melodies. His *Disputatio membrorum* 'Inter membra singula' and his even better known *altercatio* between heart and eye, 'Quisquis cordis et oculi' both occur in four musical sources.[112] The first is in sequence form (the double versicles are obviously appropriate to debate). The second is a strophic chanson; furthermore (as has long been known) the melody is that of the famous 'Can vei la lauzeta' (P.-C. 70, 43) by Bernart de Ventadorn, to which Philip wrote a contrafact—as did several other poets in different languages.[113]

There are debate-poems in all European languages: in Provençal they are called *joc-partit*, *partimen*, and *tenso*; in German, *Wechsel*. The only substantial repertory of music, however, is in Old French. Some two hundred *jeux-partis* (or *partures*) survive in the chansonniers, often occupying a section to themselves.[114] Their almost invariable subject is love, which is treated with varying degrees of witty dialectic, intellectual absurdity, and playful irreverence. As verse they are unmemorable. In the *jeu-parti* a named poet poses a *question d'amour* to another, who replies in the following stanza, and so on alternately until the debate concludes. A characteristic opening gambit is:[115]

> If your lady has at long last agreed to see you
> and you wish to please her, which should you do
> first—kiss her mouth or her feet?

In this case Thibaut is for reverence and restraint; the protagonist 'Baudoyn' thinks this would be wasting time and opportunity.

Other similar debates refer to the city of Arras. Thirteenth-century Arras seems to have been the spiritual home of the *jeu-parti*, which

---

[111] See Hans Walther, *Das Streitgedicht in der lateinischen Literatur des Mittelalters* (Munich, 1920) and Frederick J. E. Raby, *Secular Latin Poetry in the Middle Ages*, 2nd edn, (Oxford, 1957), ch. 14.

[112] For details of MSS and edition, see Anderson L21 and K52.

[113] Van der Werf and Bond, *The Extant Troubadour Melodies*, p. 62*.

[114] See Michelle F. Stewart, 'The Melodic Structure in thirteenth-century *jeux-partis*', *AcM*, 51 (1979) 86–107.

[115] 'Une chose, Baudoyn, vous demant' (R 332) by Thibaut, *roi de Navarre*; Goldin, *Lyrics*, p. 470.

Ex. 144

1. Si - re, ne me che - lez mi - e

2. li ques vous ert mieus a gré:

3. sil a - vient ke vo - stre a - mi - e

4. vous ait par - le - ment man - dé,

5. nu a nu les son cos - té

6. par nuit ke nen ve - rez mi - e,

7. u par jour vous baist et ri - e

8. en un bel pré

9. et en bras, mais ne dis mi - e

10. kil i ait de plus par - lé?

was doubtless central to the activities of the largely high-bourgeois *puy*—a society which held meetings and feasts and encouraged the practice of song-writing by festival contests at which songs were 'crowned' and a 'prince' elected.[116]

The music of the *jeu-parti* is in chanson form and style, but is deficient in melodic interest, which seems subordinate to that of verbal play. It is not a closed repertory: there is much borrowing and exchanging of melodies. The melody given in Ex. 144 for 'Sire, ne me chelez mie' (R1185) is only one of several presented for this text.[117]

THE LIGHT CHANSON AND REFRAIN-SONG

A frequent, and characteristic, feature of the *cantus versualis* (Grocheo's term, see above, for the lighter type of chanson) is the use of a refrain, in the normal sense of a line or lines of text and music that recur in each stanza. This is not characteristic of *grand chant*. It is common, as in Thibaut's 'De ma dame souvenir' (R1467), for the refrain to be linked melodically with the rest of the song; in this case line 8 'rhymes' with line 2 (= 4), line 9 (more questionably) with line 7. The refrain may or may not be a *refrain* in the specialized medieval sense described above; the status of 'Nus ne puet' in Thibaut's chanson (Ex. 145) is dubious.[118]

There are many light chansons without refrains. A deservedly popular example is 'Ce fu en mai' by Moniot d'Arras; the melodic structure is ABC ABC' DEF DEF".[119] Other examples, by Colin Muset, are 'Sire cuens, j'ai viele' (R476) and 'En mai, quant li rossignolez' (R967), which, typically of the lighter chanson, blurs the AAB form (Ex. 146).[120] But Colin Muset (mid-thirteenth century) was exceptional in many ways among the trouvères. He was perhaps the only true *jongleur-trouvère*, and one who consistently disregarded the hallowed rules of syllable count.[121]

Further characteristics of the lighter chanson include a tendency to short lines producing a more obvious sense of balanced phrase; unusual structures, sometimes very long (e.g. Moniot de Paris 'Quant je oi aloete', R969), sometime the opposite (e.g. Thibaut's 'Pour

---

[116] On Arras and the constitution of the *puy*, see Marie Ungureanu, *La bourgeoisie naissante: Société et littérature bourgeoises d'Arras* (Arras, 1955). There were *puys* also in London, Toulouse, Amiens, Beauvais, and elsewhere.

[117] Arras, Bibl. Mun. 657, f. 137. Facsimile edn. Alfred Jeanroy, *Le Chansonnier d'Arras: Reproduction en phototype* (Paris, 1925). Rosenberg and Tischler, eds., *Chanter m'estuet: Songs of the Trouvères* (London, 1981), No. 134, give a different melody, from the Chansonnier Cangé (BN fr. 846).

[118] Ed. Van der Werf, *Trouvères-Melodien* II, p. 199.

[119] R94 as 'L'autrier en mai'; see Van der Werf, *Trouvères-Melodien* II, p. 312.

[120] Ed. Van der Werf, *Trouvères-Melodien* II, p. 443.

[121] See *Words and Music*, pp. 43–5 and Ex. 4.

Ex. 145

conforter ma pesance', R237); more stability of tonal plan; and a mainly syllabic style. These refrain-songs are to be distinguished from the *chanson-avec-des-refrains* to be discussed next.

CHANSON-AVEC-DES-REFRAINS

Refrain-songs in the sense just described are common in the extended

Ex. 146

En mai, quant li ros - sig - no - lez

2. Chan - te cler ou vert bois - so - net,

3. Lors m'es - tuet faire un fla - jo - let,

4. Si le fe - rai d'un sau - ce - let,

5. Qu'il m'es - tuet d'a - mors fla - jo - ler

6. Et cha - pe - let de flor por - ter

7. Por moi de - duire et de - por - ter,

8. Qu'a - des ne doit on pas mu - ser.

chanson repertory; indeed, the Latin *cantiones*, even in the grandest style, often have refrains. The *chanson-avec-des-refrains*, on the other hand, appears to be a speciality of the trouvères. In these curious pieces, 'chansons-with-multiple refrains' (van der Werf), each stanza has a different *refrain* and—most baffling of all—the *refrains* vary in length, metrical shape, and melody. Guillaume le Vinier's *pastourelle* 'En mi mai' (R1192) has five *refrains* (Ex. 147).[122] The puzzle with this

---

[122] Chansonnier de Noailles (BN fr. 12615) fo. 29. The strange phenomenon is further discussed by Théodore Gérold, *La Musique au moyen âge* (Paris, 1932), 139–46, and in *Words and Music*, pp. 466–8. In this MS two *refrains* have blank staves.

Ex. 147

En mi mai quant s'est la sai - sons par - ti - e,

2. mal est en - ga - nes cil qui n'ai me mi - e.

3. En - tre beau liu et la noe - ve a - be - i - e

4. tra - ver - sai;

5. da - les la fo - rest tro - vai

6. u - ne da - me em - buis - si - e

7. et chante a vois se - ri - e

8. ne sai des - cort ou lai

9. mais il ot el re - frai:

REFR: Je ne sai dont li maus vient que j'ai,

as with other multiple-*refrain* songs is to know what effect the poet/
composer wanted to achieve. It can hardly be of the highest serious-
ness; and when, as in this song, the concluding *refrains* end on
different finals, then the musical effect is disorientating. The element
of deliberate play—verbal, musical, and perhaps social—must have
been a determining factor. The genre presupposes a sophisticated
audience.

PASTOURELLE

The defining theme of the *pastourelle* is the encounter between a
knight and a country maiden: 'Where are you going, my pretty maid?'
He tries to lead her astray—sometimes successfully, sometimes not.
The courtly fun resides more in the dalliance, than in the action. And
it is all delightfully disingenuous.[123]

There are some 109 surviving *pastourelles* with French texts; 58

---

[123] See, further, *Words and Music*, pp. 471–6, and Exx. 186–8, with bibliography.

Ex. 148

Quant   pert   la   froi - du - re

2. et   re - vient   l'ar - du - re

3. dou   tans   qui   m'a - gre - e,

4. che - val - chant   ma   mu - re

5. to - te   m'am - ble - u - re,

6. vi   par   a - ven - tu - re

7. lez   u - ne   ra - me - e

8. u - ne   cri - a - tu - re

9. soule   et   es - ga - re - e

10. qui   n'ert   pas   se - gu - re

11. por   ceu   qu'ele   ot   a - di - re - e

12. sa   cha - pe - te   bu - re.

13. Fa - ce or   cle - re et   pu - re

14. et   gen - te   fai - tu - re;

15. to - te es - che - ve - le - e

16. se   mau - dit   et   ju - re

17. et   dit   'Trop   fu   du - re

18. l'o - re   que   fu   nei - e'.

have melodies extant, and of those 33 use refrains or *refrains*.[124]
Further literary features of the genre include elegant contrivance in
the making of the verse; the use of short lines and economically
patterned rhymes, with varied weak and strong endings; precisely
numbered syllables as in the *grande chanson*. The *pastourelle* is full of
artifice. This extends in various ways to the melodies. 'Quant pert la
froidure' (R2103) from the Chansonnier St Germain may be one of
the earliest; it is also one of the most complicated (Ex. 148).[125] The

[124] Michelangelo Pascale, 'Le musiche nelle *pastourelles* francesi del XII e XIII secolo', *Annali
della Facolta di lettere e filosofia, Universita degli studi di Perugia*, 13 (1976), 575–631, at p. 585.
[125] Chansonnier St Germain (BN fr. 20050) fo. 46ᵛ; see also transcription by Solange Corbin in
Michel Zink, *La Pastourelle, poésie et folklore au moyen âge* (Paris, 1972), 125.

musical syntax is almost as continuous and unpatterned as the verbal. But the song is unified to some degree by an intricate mesh of melodic 'rhymes', 'half-rhymes', and echoes. For instance, phrase 2 transposes 1 up a fourth; phrases 3, 5, 7, 10, and 11 bear an evident relation to each other; phrase 8 is linked with them, but also presages 12 and the ending 15–18. Almost all of the phrases are of very small range, lying within a 3rd, 4th, or 5th. The tonal plan appears to hinge on a wide variety of open cadences with a general sense of C as the centre. But of the subtleties and ambiguities involved this gives only the sketchiest notion.

A much simpler and more typical *pastourelle* is 'L'autrier en une praele' (R608) (Ex. 149).[126] The varied seven- and five-syllable lines are neatly balanced. The chanson-form (AAB) is reasonably common in *pastourelles*. In the *frons* the disjunct opening combined with the half-close E (1/3) and full-close C (2/4) gives us a false security. The

Ex. 149

1. L'au-trier en u - ne pra-e-le 2. trou-vai pa - sto - re chan-tant;
3. mult fu a - ve - nant et be-le 4. et cor-toise et bien par-lant.

5. Tres tout main-te-nant 6. de-scen-di jus de ma se-le

7. et li dis: "Ma da - moi - se-le,

8. m'a-mor vous pre - sent 9. jo - li - ve - te - ment."

apparently established C is not necessarily contradicted by the phrases cadencing on G; but it is by D final.

Of a different type again is the *pastourelle* 'L'autrier chevauchoie' (R1583) from the same chansonnier.[127] It consists of three melodies, of

---

[126] Chansonnier de l'Arsenal (Paris, Bibl. de l'Arsenal, MS 5198) 414–15; the measured transcription is from Samuel N. Rosenberg and Hans Tischler, *Chanter m'estuet*, p. 47, No. 23.

[127] Fo.170: in *Words and Music*, p. 474, Ex. 187; Pascale, 'Pastourelles', pp. 601–2, five facs. of this source.

which the second is closely related to the first. The first eight lines are verbally monorhymed and have a six-syllable musical 'rhyme' in addition. The general effect is of a narrative *laisse* of the type described earlier. It happens to have multiple *refrains* as well. One might say in general that the *pastourelle* is the meeting place of the three melodic traditions—the chanson, the dance-song, and narrative melody. Rhythmic interpretation should surely take this into account. The *pastourelle*, unlike the *chanson-avec-des-refrains*, was an international species. Indeed, literary genealogists have traced it back far and wide: *pastourelles* appear in Latin and in the European vernaculars.[128]

LAI AND *PLANCTUS*

The *lai* has been called the 'show-piece' of medieval song. It differs from chanson and dance-song in the magnificence of its scope, and from narrative melody in the intricacy of its internal responsions. The repertory of the northern French *lai* is preserved for us mainly in the late thirteenth-century trouvère chansonnier T, which includes some 17 *lais*. Two *lais* only survive with Provençal texts; they are in the same MS. But there is a corpus of Latin *lais* in miscellaneous sources extending over a long period (*c.* 900–1350).[129]

The metrical and melodic procedures of the *lai* have often been referred to the Latin liturgical sequence. This is not surprising since the two genres have one exclusive formal property in common, that of 'progressive repetition'. In its 'classical' form the sequence runs AA BB CC etc.; the analogous procedure in the *lai* can be, and commonly is, much freer (see, for example, 'Samson, dux fortissime').[130]

However, recent research on the sequence itself has tended to show that the particular sequences with similarities to the *lai* are in those same respects dissimilar from the typical sequence, sometimes showing a closer connection to the Latin *versus* of the tenth and eleventh centuries.[131] The Aquitanian sequence repertory of the tenth and eleventh centuries included melodies with titles such as *planctus sterilis*, *planctus pueri captivati*, *planctus Bertane*, and *planctus cigni*,

---

[128] Only one Latin *pastourelle* has associated music, 'Exiit diluculo' (*Carmina Burana*, No. 90); the same is true for Provençal, Marcabru's 'L'autrier iost' una sebissa' (van der Werf and Bond, *The Extant Troubadour Melodies*, p. 226*).

[129] See David Fallows, 'Lai', *New Grove*, x. 364–76 for an account of the French *lai* and a check-list of French and German *lais*. The category of Latin *lais* is harder to establish; but see Hans Spanke, *Beziehungen zwischen romanischer und mittellateinischer Lyrik mit besonderer Berücksichtigung der Metrik and Musik* (Berlin, 1936), 88–9; and Bruno Stäblein, *Schriftbild der einstimmigen Musik, Musikgeschichte in Bildern*, ed. W. Bachmann, iii 4 (Leipzig, 1975).

[130] BL Harley 978, fos. 2–4ᵛ (Anderson, L42); see also the further sources listed in *Words and Music*, p. 455.

[131] See Peter Dronke, 'The Beginnings of the Sequence', *Beiträge zur Geschichte der deutschen Sprache und Literatur*, 87 (1965), 43–73.

which in themselves suggest a background different from that of the liturgical sequence. The melody for the *planctus cigni* (whose text is a moving plaint of the swan who has left the land with its flowers to be caught by winds and storms over the sea), while having the external form of sequence couplets, is most remarkable for its intricate meshing of short motifs and phrases in the style of the *lai*.[132] In any case, in the twelfth and thirteenth centuries we should be clear 'as to the fundamental separateness of the two forms [sequence and *lai*]. The classic sequence has a compactness and clarity of design that are entirely different from either the rambling motivic dialectic of the 13th-century lai or the closely defined stanza and repetition patterns of the form in the fourteenth century.'[133]

The *planctus* of Peter Abelard (1079–1142) are all in *lai* form. These six laments are Biblical and not identified by association with any individual historical personages; yet beneath the fictional skin there pulses in the texts the audible beat of personal emotion. These planctus are extant in a Vatican MS, but only in staffless neumes. The *Planctus virginum Israel*, however, was the model for the French *Lai des Pucelles* (R1012)—or the other way around; and the *Planctus David* is known in staff notation in an English MS of the thirteenth century.[134]

One of the important traditions embodied in the *lai* (and responsible for its individuality relative to the courtly chanson) is that of narrative melody. The *lai* is narrative music. This is not to say that it always tells a story; some do (*Lai des Pucelles, Lai de l'Ancien et du Nouveau Testament, Samson, Canticum diluvii*); others are poems of courtly sentiment or religious praise.[135] But the basic musical procedures of the *lai* are similar to those of sung narrative. A single short phrase may be repeated many times with perhaps slight variants before being changed, or rounded off with a complementary phrase or two. The *lai* has an abundance of open and closed cadences; it is formulaic, using a number of immediately recognizable phrases and

[132] See Bruno Stäblein, 'Die Schwanenklage. Zum Problem Lai-Planctus-Sequenz', in Heinrich Hüschen, ed., *Festschrift Karl Gustav Fellerer zum sechzigsten Geburtstag* (Regensburg, 1962), 491–502; Stablein's transcription of the *planctus cigni* (p. 494), ('Clangam, filii, ploratione una') is reproduced in *Words and Music*, pp. 111–12, Ex. 38.

[133] Fallows, 'Lai', pp. 366–7.

[134] For the music associated with Abelard, see L. Weinrich, 'Peter Abelard as Musician', *MQ*, 55 (1969), 295 ff., 464 ff., and his study of *Planctus David* in *Mittellateinisches Jahrbuch*, 5 (1968), 59. Further transcriptions, see Ian Bent in Peter Dronke, *Poetic Individuality in the Middle Ages* (Oxford, 1970); and *Words and Music*, pp. 121–5, Ex. 39.

[135] The French *lais* are ed. Alfred Jeanroy, L. Brandin, and P. Aubry, *Lais et descorts français du xiiiᵉ siecle; Texte et musique* (Paris, 1901); the melodies are drastically regularized, unmeasured. For *Samson*, see above n. 130. The *Canticum diluvii*, 'Omnis caro peccaverat', occurs in four English sources (see *Words and Music*, pp. 144–55, and Ex. 55a).

cadence figures taken, apparently, from a common stock. The narrative melody, mostly syllabic, is what keeps a *lai* moving, fluent, dynamic. By comparison, the movement of a high courtly chanson, with its mixture of single notes and small melismas, its conjunct melody and more elusive tonality, is leisurely, even clogged. And whereas pattern in the *grand chant* has to be listened for, in the *lai* it obtrudes on the ear. The relationship between the words and the music, though completely non-expressive and non-mimetic, is more physical and direct.

In spite of the strong connection with narrative melody, the *lai* is not, either in Latin or French, a 'mixed' form. Whatever may be the reasons for the use (especially in Provençal) of the term *descort* (Latin *discordia*) in connection with the *lai*, it cannot refer to a mixture of styles such as we find in the *pastourelle* or the *chanson-avec-des-refrains*. It is, indeed, a striking feature of the *lai* that it apparently never incorporates elements of the dance-song (such as the *refrain*), despite occasional similarities of idiom.

The *Lai des Pucelles*, 'Coraigeux/sui des gens' (R1012) exemplifies difficulties of analysis and interpretation as well as the fast-moving melodic style. The opening is given in Ex. 150.[136] The proper formal analysis of this *lai* is perplexing. The French text was edited by Jeanroy in 222 short lines, each one making or completing a rhyme. Jeanroy analysed these as comprising eleven strophes; but Spanke found sixteen, showing that even the textual form is not clear.[137] What makes the determination of strophe, and of phrases within the strophe, difficult is that the short lines of three to eight syllables are set each to a short melodic unit—a 'tag', as it were—and these may be repeated without obvious signification at any stage during the *lai*. Further short melodic units used elsewhere in the *Lai des Pucelles* are shown in Ex. 151. Of these, (a) represents the principal pitch set, with final on G and making prominent use of the F below; (b) and (c) represent other important pitch sets that resolve to d a fifth above, playing with c, e, and sometimes g. The ranges are small—(d) is exceptional—and placed in various high and low configurations within the overall design. The mercurial nature of the motivic procedure of the melody has its counterpart in the verse; the abundance of short lines produces a sprightly verbal 'music', an *armonia* new in the sheer extent of its virtuosity.

The number of contrafacta in the *lai* repertory is large. The *Lai de la*

[136] Chansonnier de Noailles (BN fr. 12615), fo. 71.
[137] Jeanroy, *et al.*, *Lais et descorts*, No. 23; Hans Spanke, 'Sequenz und Lai' (1938) repr. in *Studien zu Sequenz, Lai und Leich* (Darmstadt, 1977), 192.

Ex. 150

1. Co - rai - geus   sui des geus   k'A-mors viaut;

no - tes truis   ou je   pruis   kank' es-piaut

li grans feus   a - mo - reus   ke re-kiaut

li pi - teus   an-gois-seus   ki s'en diaut.

2a. En mes bel-les a - mo - rel-les   lais i - chi

des an-cel-les et de cel-les ad ma-ri,

des pu-cel-les par no-vel-les no-tes di,

qu'autre a-mors n'a nul cors   ki tant ait   de va-lors,

car a - mors   vient et vait   al se-cors as do-lors c'om en trait.

2b. J'ai a - mi - e   sans fo- li - e: pu - celle est.

Vi - lo - ni - e   n'i a - mi - e,   tot a   net.

Cor-toi- si - e   par bai - li - e   s'en -tre - met

de nos deus, ke li gieus   ne fo-loit   quant li   leus.

[The words of the remainder of this versicle (2b) and of the whole of (2c) are written without their music.]

Ex. 151

(a)

(b)

(c)

(d)

Pastourelle is modelled on the widely known Latin song 'Ave gloriosa virginum regina,' attributed to Philip the Chancellor—and leads us back into a nexus of material that lies at the centre of twelfth- and thirteenth-century music (Ex. 152).[138] About twelve monophonic versions of this melody are known; it appears in the Dublin Troper with other Marian sequences, and, non-liturgically, in the MS Harley 978, among the *cantiones* of the Florence MS, and elsewhere. The melody is used for three *lais* with French texts—two secular and one religious ('Virge glorieuse').

RELIGIOUS SONG

Much of the religious song of the early Middle Ages is either contrafact or imitation or adaptation. Just as there was a *chanson d'amour* so there was a *chanson pieuse*. Blondel's 'Bien doit chanter' (R482) was rewritten as a song to the Virgin in a little English collection,[139] 'Bien deust chanter ky eust leale amie' (R1102b). His 'amie' is, of course, 'la douce Marie'. Two of the MSS of the Miracles of Gautier de Coinci provide a quite different contrafact to Blondel's chanson 'Qui que face rotrouenge novele / Pastorele ne sonez ne chancon / Je chanterai de la sainte Pucele ...' (4482).[140] Two other melodies are provided for the new text in other MSS of the *Miracles*. There are 22 manuscripts with music of this enormously popular work, and nearly 60 more without. It was written in the years *c.* 1214–33 and contains, beside eight *grands chants*, examples of *chanson-avec-des-refrains*, *lai*, *pastourelle*, and *conductus*.

LAUDE SPIRITUALI

The earliest corpus of non-liturgical religious songs of which we have knowledge comprises the Latin *versus* of the tenth to twelfth centuries in the repertories of St Martial and St Gall, described in Ch. VII. In the late twelfth and thirteenth centuries there are three main repertories of religious song distinct in themselves and mainly independent of the major song-types which formed the basis for religious contrafacts such as those of Gautier de Coinci. The three repertories are (1) the *conductus* in the strict sense; (2) the Italian *laude spirituali*; and (3) the Spanish *cantiga*.

The conductus has already been discussed; to distinguish it from

---

[138] See Anderson K75 for a substantial list of sources; also Ulysse Chevalier, *Repertorium hymnologicum*, 6 vols. (Louvain, 1892–1920), No. 1828; and Hans Walther, *Initia carminum ac versuum medii aevi posterioris latinorum*, 2 vols. (Göttingen, 1959, 1969), No. 20961. Ex. 152 is from BL Harl. 978, fos. 7–8ᵛ (*Words and Music*, pp. 106–9: Ex. 36).

[139] BL Arundel 248, fo. 155.

[140] See Jacques Chailley, *Les Chansons à la vierge de Gautier de Coinci*, (Paris, 1959), No. 2 (pp. 50, 99, 165) for details and transcriptions.

Ex. 152

1a. A - ve glo - ri - o - sa,   vir - gi - num re - gi - na,

vi - tis ge - ne - ro - sa,   vi - te me - di - ci - na,

cle - men - ci - e   re - si - na.

1b. A - ve co - pi - o - sa   gra - ci - e pis - ci - na,

car - nis ma - cu - lo - sa   mun - da nos sen - ti - na

mun - di - ci - e   cor - ti - na.

2a. Cla - ri - ta - te ra - di - o - sa,   stel - la   ma - tu - ti - na,

bre - vi - ta - te le - gis glo - sa   per te lex di - vi - na

ir - ra - di - at   do - ctri - na.

2b. Ve - nus - ta - te ver - nans ro - sa,   si - ne   cul - pe spi - na,

ca - ri - ta - te vi - sce - ro - sa   au - rem huc in - cli - na,

nos ser - ves a   ru - i - na.

lauda and *cantiga* it is only necessary to recall here that it is loosely associated with the ecclesiastical ceremonies and celebrations of New Year (Feast of the Circumcision) in Northern French cathedrals such as Beauvais; that it is generally a simple, singable, memorable strophic song constructed out of single notes in the syllabic style; and that in contrast to *lauda* and *cantiga* it may inhabit a variety of forms.

In the middle of the thirteenth century, at the same time as the Beauvais Office of the Circumcision was being copied, a different kind of religious song appeared in Italy. The penitential mania which swept many cities in northern Italy (and spread to Provence, Germany, and elsewhere) had nothing in common with Christmas festivities at Beauvais, Sens, Laon. A hermit at Perugia, for instance, was told in a vision that God had wanted to destroy the whole world but that Christ, moved by the Virgin's prayers, granted a respite to repentant Christians: 'He wants the scourge you have used in private to be used by the whole community'. The *lauda* is associated with this extraordinary phenomenon. But mass hysteria does not lend itself to elaborate composition in music or poetry. The flagellants in their processions took over 'lauds' and praises which were already current. Fraternities of *laudesi* (singers of *laude*) had existed in Italy previously (e.g. the *Laudesi della Beata Vergine* in Florence, 1233). *Laude* of some kind or other are associated with the missionary activities of the earliest Franciscans, the *joculatores Dei*. The famous *Cantico del Sole* by St Francis himself (1182–1226), 'Altissimu, onnipotente, bon Signore/ tue so le laude, la gloria e l'onore', survives in an Assisi MS with empty staves.[141] And after the frenzy died down, as it quickly did, it was the fraternities of laymen who kept the *lauda* alive. Their members were often called *disciplinati* (referring to the scourge of penance), or *battuti* (the whipped) or *flagellanti* (whippers); but the *laude* they preserved, in huge numbers (200 MSS survive) are predominantly *reddendo laude con amore*, 'rendering praises with love'.

Of these 200 MSS only two preserve music—one at Cortona contains 46 notated *laude*; the other in Florence contains 89.[142] Most *laude* are anonymous, like the early fifteenth-century English carols which they so much resemble; but the well-known name of Jacopone da Todi, poet and mystic, can be attached to a few.

Typical of the simpler *laude*, which predominate in the Cortona

[141] Assisi, S. Francesco, MS 338. Text in Gianfranco Contini, ed., *Poeti del duecento*, 2 vols. (Milan, 1960), i. 33. The standard work on the *laude* is by Fernando Liuzzi, *La lauda e i primordi della melodia italiana*, 2 vols. (Rome, 1934), which also contains facsimiles of the *laude* in the two principal musical sources mentioned below. See also Luigi Lucchi, ed., *Il laudario di Cortona* (Vicenza, 1987).

[142] Cortona, Biblioteca del Comune, MS 91; Florence, Bibl. Naz. MS Magliabecchi II, 1.122.

Ex. 153

Al – ta   tri – ni – tà   be – a – ta

2. da   noi   sem – pre   si'a – do – ra – ta.

3. Tri – ni – tà   de   glo – ri – o – sa,

4. u – ni – tà   ma – ra – vil – lio – sa,

5. tu   se'   man – na   sa – vo – ro – sa

6. a   tut – or   de – si – de – ra – ta.

laudario, is 'Alta Trinita beata' (Ex. 153).[143] The idea behind the form, which is by no means fixed in a stereotype, is that of the Italian *ballata*, the French *virelai*, and the English carol. The song opens with a *ripresa* (an external refrain) which is repeated after each stanza. The rhyme of the two-line *ripresa* (aa) is picked up at the end of the four-line stanza (bbba); the song is, like all *laude*, strophic, and has in this case thirteen stanzas. There is musical rhyme between stanza and *ripresa*; the musical structure is, then, AB:CCDB. On a more detailed level we may note the resemblance between D (5.1–5) and A (1.2–5). The tonal plan is unambiguously based on C with G as principal structural note (also as open cadence, lines 3 and 4, and varied by F in 5). The verse, however, tends to start at the octave, or at least the fifth above (see 'Altissima luce').[144] The dynamic movement of the melody is carried by the simple structure and tonal balance.

[143] Cortona, fos. 70–72; Liuzzi, *Lauda*, i. 390–3; Contini, *Poeti del duecento*, ii. 39 (without music).
[144] Cortona, fos. 17–18; see Stevens, 'Lauda', *New Grove*, x. 538–43, Ex. 1. Liuzzi, *Lauda*, i. 285 (the verse starts at the sixth above).

It is interesting to compare this with a similar melody in the
Florence *laudario* to the same text (Ex. 154).[145] It is slightly more
melismatic than the first: fewer syllables have only one note, and many
have two. Melodically the form is slightly more inventive; perhaps one
may see in the analogous movement and identical finals of the last
lines of the *ripresa* and stanza a suggestion of musical rhyme rounding
off the song.

Ex. 154

Al - ta   tri - ni - tà be - a - ta

2.   da   nu - i   şi - a   sem — pre   a - do - ra - ta

3.   Tri - ni - tà [de]   glo - ri - o - sa,

4.   U - ni - tà   ma - ra - vil - lio - sa,

5.   tu se' man - na   sa - vo - ro - sa,

6.   a   tutt' or   de - si - de - ra - ta.

Two general questions are raised by this *lauda*. The first concerns
tonal plan. The Florence manuscript provides no B flat in the
signatures; the editors do not hesitate to supply one, yet most of the
melody, especially in the verse, runs more strongly without the flat.
The second query is a metrical one. Both versions are basically
octosyllabic throughout. The *lauda spirituale* displays clear syllabic
melody, for the most part, so there are the expected eight notes or note

---

[145] Florence, fos. 5ᵛ–6; cf. transcription by Higini Anglès, *Cantigas*, vol. iii(2), 'Parte musical',
p. 69. Anglès transcribes thirteen *laude* in a somewhat free rhythmical style. Liuzzi, *Lauda*, ii. 19
(accommodating the melody to 4/4 metre).

groups to each phrase. But in the second phrase of the *ripresa* Cortona appears to have one extra syllable, and Florence may have three (making 10 or 11 instead of 7 or 8) with the necessary notes to fit them. In an otherwise regular song, this must present a problem. In the Provençal and French repertory hypermetrical syllables are infrequent; these Italian songs take a licence otherwise only common in the stressed Teutonic languages (German and English). It seems best to accommodate the extra or missing syllable(s) without upsetting the balance of lines as established in this or subsequent stanzas.

The affinities of these earlier, simpler *laude* appear to be more with the dance-songs (especially the Latin *rondelli*) than with the other genres we have considered. They have repetitive structures of a tightly balanced kind, varied uses of refrain, tonalities which can be clearly defined (even if not confidently interpreted), a preference for syllabic melody, and an energy of movement to which the words contribute. This does not mean that the surviving *laude* were popular dance-songs; but they do have the characteristics that associate song with physical movement, whether dance or procession (the border between the two is frequently blurred), and with a division between leader and group, cantor and choir. They are perhaps the italian civic equivalent of the *rondelli*, the Parisian 'clerical dances'. 'De la crudel morte de Cristo' has all the strength of a sombre march (Ex. 155).[146]

The occasions on which the early *laude spirituali* were sung can be inferred from their texts: their favourite subjects point to celebrations. They praise and honour the Blessed Virgin; the Birth, Passion, and Resurrection of Christ; the goodness of the Saints (St Francis, St George, St Luke, St Laurence, and many others). They also lament the sufferings of Christ, the hardness of man's heart, the imminence of death. The laude are not liturgical, though later they were sung by the guilds in quasi-liturgical rituals, but popular religious songs, glad and sad. Some of the *laudari* without music have songs for the whole year—for saints and for dead members of the fraternity.

The *lauda* did not remain consistently within the realm of ordinary untutored sensibilities, unlettered minds, untrained voices. Two lines of development may be singled out: one leads in the direction of musical professionalism, the other towards literary sophistication. This latter, associated with the philosophical courtliness of Jacopone

---

[146] Cortona, fo. 51^{r-v}; cf. Anglès, *Cantigas* iii(2) 'Parte musical' pp. 67–8; Liuzzi, *Lauda*, i. 354–7. There is no clef in the MS from the beginning of the verse onwards (Liuzzi transcribes the melody a fifth higher than Anglès and in a free recitative-like style). The notes of the last line are not filled in.

Ex. 155

De la cru - del mor - te de Cris - to

2. on' hom pia - nga a - ma - ra - men - te.

3. Quan - do' Ju - de - ri Chris - to pil - lia - ro,

4. d'o - gne par - te lo cir - cun - da - ro;

5. le sue ma - ne stre - cto le - ga - ro

6. co - mo la - dro vi - la - na - men - te.

da Todi, cannot engage us here. The former, musical professionalism, is much in evidence in the later, larger *laudario* from Florence. As the fraternities became more settled and more comfortable, they were evidently able to commission elaborate songbooks and elaborate songs to go in them.

The new note of professionalism is prominent in such songs as 'Nat'e in questo mondo', 'Lo'ntellecto divino', 'Allegro canto popol cristiano'. (Ex. 156).[147] These show a much freer use of melisma, especially though not exclusively in the verse. When, as in 'Gaudiamo tucti quanti', the ornaments or flourishes are at the beginnings or ends of phrases, the basically syllabic movement is not disturbed; nor is it when, as in 'Sancto Lorenco', the melismas, though continuous, are kept short.

[147] 'Nat'e in questo mondo': Florence, fos. 39–40; 'Lauda', Ex. 2; Liuzzi, *Lauda*, ii. 108–12. 'Lo'ntellecto divino': Florence, fos. 122ᵛ–123ᵛ; W. Thomas Marrocco and Nicholas Sandon, eds., *Medieval Music, The Oxford Anthology of Music* (Oxford, 1977), 76–7, No. 27; Liuzzi, *Lauda*, ii. 361–7. 'Allegro canto': Florence, fos. 117–119 cf. Anglès, *Cantigas* iii(2) 'Parte musical', pp. 74–5. Liuzzi, *Lauda*, ii. 348–52.

Ex. 156

Al - le - gro can - to po - pol cri - sti - a - no,

2. del gran - de san Do - me - ni - co,

3. di tan - ti va - lo - ro - so ca - pi - ta - no.

4. Ca - pi - ta - no di mol - ti ca - va - lie - ri

5. fu san - cto pre - ti - o - so,

6. che do - po Cri - sto l'an - no se - gui - ta - to

7. e fu de li mi - glior gon - fa - lo - nie - ri,
8. quel fiu - me gra - ti - o - so,
9. che do - po Cri - sto si - a sta - to tro - va - to
10. per lu - i è su - to sper - to et ri - pro - va - to
11. o - gni per - ver - so he - re - ti - co
12. que nel - la fe - de tro - va - se lon - ta - no.

But in 'Allegro canto popol christiano' the melismas seem to suggest a change of style. It is not at all easy to decide what the change of style means, or how deep it goes. There is no new concept of form: the phrase plan ABC:DEF-GEF-ABC:ABC is simply an expansion of a standard arrangement (phrase G is a variation of D). True, the lines are longer than in most of the Cortona songs; the voice-range is considerably more extended (C–g). But this does not amount to more than inflation of the musical currency. The tonal plan has a traditional stability (the addition of an editorial B flat does not seem justified). The temporal progression of the melody includes a light admixture of smaller melismas (some passing-notes at 3.3; 6.4; 11.1, more ornamental turns at 1.9,11; 2.3; 2.8; 6.9; 9.7, etc.); but single notes still predominate in the song as a whole. What, in this context, are we to make of the larger melismas, some of them ten notes in length and notated as a succession of ligatures? Many (1.3; 5.1; 6.1, etc.) seem to be ornamental—elaborate flourishes, delighting the singer and the audience. Even when they cover a wide range and start with a disjunction (6.8) they do not disrupt the main flow and can be seen as amplifications of a single note or two-note neume. The only problem arises at the cadence 2.8 (repeated 11.8), where the melisma modulates an open ending on C to the recurrent F, and could not be replaced by any simple neume. The longer melismas also have a motivic function in the melody: for example, the descending cbaG(F) constantly recurs.

In these analyses I have assumed a rhythmic interpretation of the *laude spirituali* based on the simplest syllabic metrical patterns. The earliest, least complicated songs can thus be understood in duple meter (modern 2/4) or—by doubling the length of alternate syllables—in triple meter (modern 3/4). In any case, the metrical patterns seem characteristic of a popular (religious or secular) dance-song, of which the *virelai* dance-form is a constant reminder. For the more elaborate *laude* of the Florence *laudario*, sophisticated at least superficially by the art of the *grand chant* (and perhaps by the lost music of the Italian courtly *canzona*), a less metrically committed, freer isosyllabic style is perhaps appropriate.

CANTIGAS DE SANTA MARIA

The other major repertory of religious song to be considered is neither clerical, like the *conductus*, nor civic-bourgeois, like the *lauda*. The Spanish *cantigas*, in their surviving form, are the product of a court. The term *cantiga* (i.e. song, chanson) will be used here to refer to the corpus of some 450 religious *cantigas* extant with their melodies. It is, however, a salutary reminder of how distorted our picture of medieval song may be, that other MSS contain about 1,700 non-religious *cantigas de amigo*, *cantigas de escarnio* (satirical), *cantigas de maldizer* with staves ruled for music but not filled in.[148]

Cantigas were doubtless written throughout the thirteenth century and earlier, but it was during the reign of Alfonso el Sabio (1252–84), King of Castile, that the great collection of *cantigas de santa Maria* was compiled. By his own account, the King himself took the initiative and wrote some of the songs. The historian and music theorist Egidius of Zamora, retained by Alfonso at his court, compared his patron to King David:[149]

In the manner of David and to the honour of the glorious Virgin, he composed many very beautiful songs (*cantilenas*) made harmonious (*modulatas*) by apt melodies and musical proportions.

This statement is confirmed by the prologue to the *cantigas* and many passing remarks in the texts themselves. There seems little reason to doubt that the King did himself compose some of the songs. At the same time, there were many ways in which a king (or anyone else) could compose a song, including the process of making contrafacts.

The cantigas survive in three musical manuscripts.[150] Two Escorial MSS are of the late thirteenth century. The third, from Toledo, originally thought to be the earliest, must be later, since the longs and breves of the Escorial MSS are replaced by breves and semibreves. The Escorial MSS are remarkable. The most complete musical source (E1) contains forty detailed miniatures of musicians, mostly instrumentalists; they decorate every tenth song, the *cantigas de loor* (songs of praise). The other (E2) has the famed collection of 1,262 illuminations, some page-size. Whatever the precise relevance of these to the performance of the *cantigas*, they constitute the most impressive testimony to the rich cultural milieu of Spain in which Moors and Christians alike shared.

The language of the *cantigas* is Galician-Portuguese, which was regarded as a proper language for poetry (it should not be thought of as a dialect). Galicia formed part of Alfonso's kingdom. It would obviously have been proper for the King to have chosen Provençal, the supreme courtly poetic language of the south of Europe (including the north of Italy and Spain) or indeed Castilian Spanish. What were

[148] The rich musical culture of medieval Spain which formed the context for the *cantigas* is described at length in Anglès *Cantigas*, iii(1); vol. i of the same work contains a facsimile edn. of MS Escorial j.b.2, and the *cantigas* are edited in vol. ii.

[149] Latin text cit. Anglès, 'Cantigas de Santa Maria', in *MGG*, ii (1952), col. 774, from Martin Gerbert, ed., *Scriptores ecclesiastici de musica sacra* (St Blasien, 1784) ii. 369 ff.

[150] Madrid, Escorial MS b.I.2 (also known as j.b.2) (E1) contains over 400 songs; Escorial MS T.j.1 (E2) contains 193. The Toledo Cathedral MS is now Madrid, BN 10069, with 104 *cantigas*.

the full implications of this actual choice? It could perhaps point to some kind of rejection of courtly traditions.

The repertory is presented with unusual consistency in the three MSS, even to the order of the songs, but only E1 is complete. Every tenth song is a *cantiga de loor*, addressed to the Virgin, and the rest are *cantigas de miragres* (songs of miracles). The strong narrative content of the great majority of the *cantigas* is one of the factors which most clearly sets them off from the songs previously discussed. There are elements of narrative in *pastourelles* and in *laude spirituali*.[151] But only the *cantigas* set out to sing individual stories in all their particularity: they are accounts in ballad style. Such presentation of the *miracula* in song is, among vernacular survivals, unique.

A number of the *cantigas* display the expected characteristics of narrative melody and may have been influenced by the *chanson de geste*. 'En todo logar á poder' (CSM 168) uses only two melodies, the first having both an open and a closed ending; in a complete performance the two melodies would be heard thirty-one times in succession (Ex. 157).[152]

The most striking single factor distinguishing the *cantigas* from the known (or reconstructed) narrative songs in French and Latin is that they are almost all in *virelai* form (AB:CCAB:AB). There are thirty-six *cantigas* in this most basic of virelai patterns. In 'Sempre seja beeita et loada' (CSM 17), only the first line of the *estribillo* (the external refrain, or burden) is given in MS E1; even this is unnecessary since the *estribillo*, which begins the piece, is always sung complete between each stanza, to which it is commonly linked by verbal rhyme as well as by melodic repetition.

The parallels between the Spanish *cantiga* and the Italian *lauda* are obvious. They are both popular religious songs in a dance-song form, the *virelai*. Neither type shows any signs, in words or in music, of that witty, playful, disingenuous manipulation we encountered in the 'mixed' courtly chansons of the trouvères. The essential parallel is rather with the clerical *rondellus*. The *cantigas* show no *courtois* condescension, however dispassionate, to the *vilain*. They have the unmistakable ring of a genuine (if limited, sentimental, and sensational) piety. They are courtly, however, by patronage and immediate

---

[151] Gautier de Coinci's *Miracles* (cf. n. 140), another comprehensive testimony to the thirteenth century's fascination with 'miracles' of the Virgin, is a *prose* narrative with pious songs interspersed.

[152] CSM = 'Cantigas de Santa Maria'; 'En todo logar' is No. 168 in the manuscript series established by both E1 and E2. Transcribed by Anglès, *Cantigas*, ii. 184, in his characteristic 'mixed'-measured style (here 3/4 and 4/4) from E1, fo. 160ᵛ, and E2, fo. 224ᵛ.

Ex. 157

En to - do lo - gar á po - der

2. a Vir - gen a quen quer va - ler.

3. Seu fi - llo, Deus et om' e rey,

4. po - der lle deu, qual vos di - rey,

5. de fa - zer sem - pre ben, et sei

6. que non lle fal end' o que - rer.

7. En to - do lo - gar á po - der

8. a Vir - gen a quen quer va - ler.

provenance; and they seem—this is somewhat stranger—to have been destined for a courtly audience.

Scholars have stressed the indebtedness of Alfonso and his 'school' of *cantiga* writers to the musical and poetic art of the troubadours and trouvères, pointing to such songs as 'Rosa das rosas' (CSM 10) in which the poet says

Esta dona que tenno por Sennor
e de que quero seer trobador
se an per ren poss' aver seu amor,
dou ao demo os outros amores.

Ex. 158

Ro - sa das ro - sas et Fror das fro - res,

2. Do - na das do - nas, Se - nnor das se - nno - res.

3. Ro - sa de bel - dad' e de pa - re - cer

4. et Fror d'a - le - gri - a et de pra - zer;

5. Do - na en mui pi - a - do - sa se er,

6. Se - nnor en to - ller coi - tas et do - o - res.

The text appears to be a blend of the commonplace of Marian devotional poetry with the expression of unexceptional courtly sentiments. But the style and shape of the song remain entirely that of the dance-song tradition, as the *estribillo* will show. 'Rosa das rosas' (Ex. 158) is one of the *cantigas de loor*, designed evidently to set off the narrative *cantigas* in some way.[153]

It is all the more striking, then, that Alfonso did not choose to strengthen this contrast by interlarding *chansons pieuses* in the high style. Virtually all the *cantigas de loor* are *virelai* types like the *miragres*. One, and one only, of the *cantigas de loor* is in canzone form, without refrain—'Pero cantigas de loor' (CSM 400 (Ex. 159).[154] It is not unlike *grand chant* in its temporal progression of single notes mixed with groups, in its far from obvious tonality and in its self-generated dynamic shape (moving to a perceptible climax in phrase 7 and falling away in the low-pitched last line)—'self-generated' because not imposed by the external demands of a repetitive form such as *virelai* or *rondeau*. But there is one important respect in which even this song distances itself from the high courtly style: despite the absence of a refrain structure it exhibits a high degree of repetition. While a formal scheme would run ABAB:CCDC'E, there are really only three phrases of melody, since B is, with a slight initial difference, a *clos* version of A, and D is in effect C (5.1–4) plus B (2.4–7).

Some of the non-narrative *cantigas*, then, are in a more elevated style, apparent in such a *loor* as 'Virgen, madre groriosa' (CSM 340) (Ex. 160).[155] The following example gives the *estribillo* only; it is a brief *grand chant* in itself and indeed is evidently based on one (Ex. 143 below). The verse (*estropha*) is largely made up of new phrases.

When in 1284 Alfonso the Wise was giving instructions for his eventual interment, he stipulated that 'all books of the *Cantares de loor de Santa Maria* are to be kept in the church where our body will be buried and that on the feast-days of holy Mary there shall be songs taken from them'.[156] This seems to indicate a paraliturgical ceremony, and that the *cantigas de loor* were the most appropriate and honourable. There is, in fact, a small group of songs, mostly more complex and sophisticated, at the beginning of MS E1 headed *Cantigas das cinco festas de Santa Maria*. 'Virgen madre groriosa' appears among

---

[153] E1, fo. 39ᵛ.
[154] E1, fo. 359. The (unique) MS uses mensural symbols and Anglès (ii. 432) transcribes in 3/4. See further below.
[155] E1, fo. 304ᵛ.
[156] Cit. Anglès, 'Die Cantigas de Santa Maria', in Wulf Arlt, *et al.*, eds., *Gattungen der Musik in Einzeldarstellungen: Gedenkschrift Leo Schrade*, (Berne, 1973), 357.

Ex. 159

1. Pe - ro can - ti - gas de lo - or
2. fiz de mui - tas ma - nie - ras
3. a - ven - do de lo - ar sa - bor
4. a que nos dá car - rei - ras
5. co - mo De - us a - ja - mos ben
6. sol non ten - no que di - xe - ren;
7. can a - tant' é com - pri - de
8. a lo - or da que nos man- ten,
9. que nun - ca á fi - i - da.

Ex. 160

them; but others (e.g. 'Como Deus e comprida') are simple *virelai* types.[157]

Because of the known spread of troubadour art into Spain, the attested presence of Giraut Riquier (the 'last of the troubadours') at Alfonso's court from 1269–79, and the suggestive parallel between Alfonso and other royal masters of song from Guillaume IX to 'le roi Thibaut' of Navarre and Charles of Anjou, an assumption has grown up that 'we find a style similar to that of the troubadours in the *Cantigas de Santa Maria*'.[158] This generalization, we see, cannot stand without drastic revision. It is significant—indeed, it has a symbolic propriety—that another of the few convincing contrafacts is between the *cantiga de loor* 'Maldito seja guen non loara' (CSM 290) and the Latin *rondellus* 'Fidelium sonet vox sobria'.[159] The 'sober voice of the faithful' sounds in both to a dance-like and joyful melody.

The rhythmic interpretation of the *cantigas* has special interest and is a matter for dispute. The interest arises from the fact that it is the only one of the repertories under discussion to be notated in mensural symbols throughout in all the sources (three in this case).

This should be a matter for rejoicing. However, the use of mensural

[157] 'Virgen madre', see Anglès, *Cantigas*, ii. 439; 'Como deus', ibid. 441.
[158] Gustave Reese, *Music in the Middle Ages*, p. 245.
[159] E1, fo. 260; Florence MS, fo. 465 (Anderson, M17).

Ex. 161

(i)

Nas men – tes sen – pre tẽ – er

2. De – ve – mo-las sas fei – tu – ras

3. Da Vir – gen, pois re – ce – ber

4. As fo – ron as pe – dras du – ras.

5. Per quant' eu di – zer o – y

6. A – o – mẽes que fo – ron y,

7. Na san – ta Ges – se – ma – ni

8. Fo – ron a – cha – das fi – gu – ras

9. Da Ma – dre de Deus, as – si

10. Que non fo – ron de pin – tu – ras.

Per quant' eu di - zer o - y,

a o - mes que fó - ron y,

symbols does not—even in the late thirteenth century—always imply firm, unambiguous, mensural intention or lead to regularly measured transcriptions. Given that the *cantigas* are popular religious songs in a basic dance-song form, we would expect balanced, symmetrical phrases and equal metrical units within the phrase. Such a transcription is offered by Marrocco and Sandon (Ex. 161(i))[160] of 'Nas mentes sempre tenor' (CSM 29). The transcription of Higini Anglès agrees in every detail for the *estribillo* but differs in the *estropha* (Ex. 161(ii)).[161] The differences represent an attempt to make sense of the mensural symbols of three MSS, which agree quite closely with one another. Here two seven-syllable lines, which in expectation would produce 4 + 4 regular bars, are transcribed as 5 + 4, one of the latter being a 5/4 bar. Anglès, whose life-long study of the *cantigas* deserves respect and attention, wrote:[162]

The notation of the manuscripts from the Escorial (E1, E2) is mensural throughout; it was entered in by a professional notator of the period. ... In the cantigas occur not only the six modes but also their combination. In addition there are duple rhythms, indeed occasionally in the same melody duple- and triple-time patterns.

Anglès was perhaps unnecessarily hampered by the necessity he felt to use the terminology of the rhythmic modes. Nevertheless, the problem of reconciling the notation (self-evidently mensural in some respects) with the claims of genre (evidently dance-song at some stage in its development) and the evidence of analogous forms (*rondellus* and *rondeau*) remains unsolved.

[160] Marrocco and Sandon, *Anthology*, p. 77, No. 28.
[161] Anglès, *Cantigas*, ii. 37, from E1, E2, and the Toledo MS.
[162] Anglès in Arlt, *et al.*, eds., *Gattungen*, p. 354 (translation).

IV

Medieval Polyphony in Western Europe

X

INSTRUMENTS AND INSTRUMENTAL
MUSIC BEFORE 1300

By CHRISTOPHER PAGE

The story of Western instruments from the Fall of Rome to the fourteenth century reaches from the lyres that were played in 'the primeval German forests' to the lutes of the Ars Nova, their sound-holes decorated with grilles as elaborate as any in the mosques of Spain whence they were exported northwards. Since few medieval instruments survive[1] our knowledge of them is based upon representations in the visual arts, supplemented by the testimony of contemporary writers and an archaeological record that is exceptionally rich for the earlier centuries (roughly AD 450–850). The musical record is very meagre (as far as music written specifically for instruments is concerned) and does not begin until the later thirteenth century.

The history that can be written with this evidence divides along familiar lines. There is an early phase (before 1000) which is relatively obscure and a later phase (1000–1300) initiated by the dissemination of the bow throughout the West. The prestige chordophones of the early phase had been the lyre and (towards the end of the period) the pillar-harp, but by the eleventh century both had been eclipsed by the instrument that dominates our view of the years between 1000 and 1300—the bowed *viella*, or fiddle. Changes like this emerge most clearly from a chronological approach, for any attempt to treat families of instruments together carries us ceaselessly back and forth across the centuries. Accordingly, we begin on the threshold of the

---

[1] For a catalogue of the extant instruments see F. Crane, *Extant Medieval Musical Instruments: A Provisional Catalogue by Types* (Iowa, 1972) and G. Lawson, 'Stringed Musical Instruments: Artefacts in the Archaeology of Western Europe 500 BC–AD 1200' (Ph.D. Thesis, University of Cambridge, 1980). Lawson's study is a magnificent guide to the archaeological finds in Western Europe between 500 BC and AD 1200. There can be no doubt that a great deal of material is still waiting to be discovered; see Lawson's report on the lyre fragments recovered from the excavations at Bergh Apton, Norfolk, in B. Green and A. Rogerson, eds., 'The Anglo-Saxon Cemetery at Bergh Apton, Norfolk', *East Anglian Archaeology*, 7 (1978), 87–97.

Middle Ages, and with Boethius, the author who, more than any other, provides a yardstick to measure what is medieval about the instrument-culture of the Middle Ages.

BOETHIUS: THE VIEW FROM THE VILLA

Of all the channels which guided the music theory of the Ancients towards the Middle Ages none was more important than the *De Institutione Musica* of Anicius Manlius Torquatus Severinus Boethius (d. 524). Like a monumental aqueduct, this treatise carried the musical learning of the Ancients across the ruins of Rome to the monasteries of the Dark Age West and in comparison with it every other channel was but a narrow conduit.

Boethius, father of consuls and a member of an ancient senatorial family, held a very low opinion of instrumentalists. In his eyes the *citharoedi* and *tibicines* who played for public games and private feasts were bound in ignorance:[2]

Those musicians dedicated to instruments, and who spend all their efforts upon them such as players of the *cithara*, and those who show their skill on the organ and other musical instruments, are exiled from the true understanding of musical science and are of servile condition, nor do they bear anything of reason, as has been said, for they are wholly destitute of interest in scientific enquiry.

The ancient, lettered tradition of music theory, which the Greeks had bequeathed to Rome, meant little to these lyrists and organists, and because they were 'exiled from the true understanding of musical science' they were bound not only in ignorance but also in 'servile condition', like slaves. The true musician (*musicus*) in Boethius's scheme of things is the gentleman-connoisseur who uses his freedom from public office to master the theory of music; he only enters the clamorous bazaar of practical music to act as a kind of aedile, judging performances and ruling what is good and bad.[3]

Yet although Boethius looked down upon instrumentalists and their practical music, it is an open-stringed instrument, the *cithara*, which provides the abacus for many of his demonstrations in the *De Institutione Musica*. He shows that the music theory of the ancients had been elaborated around the tunings of the *cithara* and that all serious study of the subject therefore began with the names of its strings: *nete*, *paranete*, and the rest. 'If we bring these matters to attention early on it will be easier to understand what is to come',[4] says Boethius, so there was no mistaking the fundamental importance

---

[2] *De Inst. Mus.* 1:34.   [3] Ibid.   [4] Ibid. 1:19.

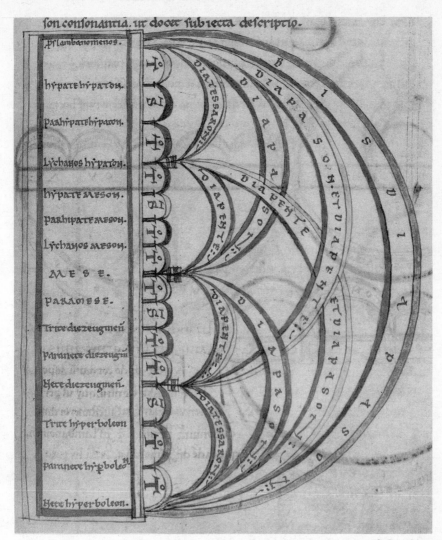

FIG. 1. Schematic diagram of the *cithara* from the *De Musica* of Boethius. Cambridge University Library MS Ii.3.12, fo. 74. Twelfth century.

of learning about the *cithara* and its tuning. It was embodied in some basic terminology of the treatise, duly adopted by medieval theorists, whereby the words *nervus* and *chorda* ('a string') are often used with the generalized sense 'a note'. With the aid of diagrams Boethius illustrates the expansion of the Ancient *cithara* to the point where it came to rest with fifteen strings (Fig. 1), and during the Middle Ages, when men sensed something cabbalistic in all technical figures, these diagrams cast a powerful spell. As early as *c.* 880 we find Hucbald of

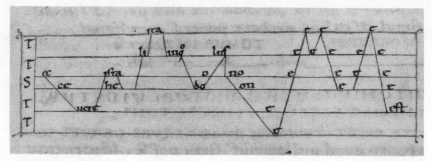

FIG. 2. Schematic diagram of a six-stringed *cithara* from Hucbald's *De Harmonica Institutione*. Cambridge University Library MS Gg.5.35, fo. 266ᵛ. Eleventh century.

St Amand adapting one of them to record a tuning for an instrument of his day, the six-stringed lyre (Fig. 2).

We shall return to Hucbald and his lyre. For the moment it is the contrast between the diagrams offered by Hucbald and by Boethius which is most arresting. They are fundamentally different, and the difference is what stamps Hucbald as a medieval writer working in a new barbarian kingdom long after the Fall of Rome. Both offer schematic representations of *citharae*, yet Boethius's instrument has no more reality (and no more music) that the constellation of Lyra; Boethius is only interested in the *cithara* because the names of its strings (on the left of the figure) serve him in the way that the seven letters ABCDEFG serve the modern musician. Behind Hucbald's diagram, however, we glimpse a Dark Age instrument of the kind which lay among the grave goods of an Anglo-Saxon king at Sutton Hoo. A little learning from the famous Roman theorist has converged with an esteem for string-playing that reaches back into the prehistory of the barbarian peoples of the North.

ROMANS AND BARBARIANS: THE HARPA

In the early seventh century an Anglo-Saxon king was buried with a wealth of luxurious goods at Sutton Hoo near Woodbridge in Suffolk. Among them was a large lyre.[5] Lyres have also been recovered from seventh- and eighth-century graves in Frankish territory; taken together, the fragments indicate a coherent tradition of lyre-design and manufacture. The instruments appear to have been cut from shallow planks with the yoke made separately and then morticed into

[5] For an exhaustive treatment of the Sutton Hoo lyre see R.Bruce–Mitford, *The Sutton Hoo Ship Burial*, 3 vols. in 4 (London, 1975, 1978, and 1983), iii. 611–731, and Lawson, 'Stringed Musical Instruments', *passim*. The reconstruction of the fragments as a lyre has definitively replaced the previous reconstruction, a harp (shown in *NOHM* iii, plate V).

the arms. A soundbox was gouged into the surface of the plank and then covered with a soundboard fastened into place with nails. The yoke generally carried five or six sagittal pegs tuned, like modern piano-pins, with a key; to judge by the condition of the surviving pegs, the strings were of gut, or possibly of horsehair.[6]

The Modern English word 'harp' is a descendant of the only name for a stringed instrument that can be traced back to Common Germanic. We find *harpha* in Old High German, *hearpe* in Old English and *harpa* in both Old Saxon and Old Norse. None of these languages is recorded before c. 700, but long before this Venantius Fortunatus (d. c. 609) had heard a form of the word in Gaul. As he travelled amongst the Franks his ears were assaulted by songs and instrumental music that were unlike anything he had heard in Rome or Ravenna; the noise appalled him, and in the preface to his poems he throws up his hands:[7]

It were as well for me to groan hoarsely as to declaim my verses amongst those who cannot distinguish the screech of a goose from the song of a swan, and where only the buzzing *harpa* strikes out outlandish songs . . .

All the evidence suggests that some antecedent of *harpa* was present in

[6] For the chronology of medieval string-materials, in so far as it may be reconstructed from literary references, see C. Page, *Voices and Instruments of the Middle Ages*, (London, 1987), Appendix 4.

[7] F. Leo, *Venanti . . . Fortunati . . . Opera Poetica, Monumenta Germaniae Historica, Auctorum Antiquissimorum*, IV:1 (Berlin, 1881), 2: '. . . ubi mihi tantundem valebat raucum gemere quod cantare apud quos nihil disparat aut stridor anseris aut canor oloris, sola saepe bombicans barbaros leudos arpa relidens . . .'.

Another—and much more famous—instance of the word *harpa* in Fortunatus's works deserves to be included here in its full context. The message of these lines is that all people praise the addressee of the poem, Lupus, in their own way (the italics are mine):

Sed pro me reliqui laudes tibi reddere certent,
  et qua quisque valet te prece voce sonet,
Romanusque lyra, plaudat tibi barbarus harpa,
  Graecus Achilliaca, crotta Britanna canat.
Illi te fortem referant, hi iure potentem,
  ille armis agilem praedicet, iste libris.
et quia rite regis quod pax et bella requirunt,
  iudicis ille decus concinat, iste ducis.
nos tibi versiculos, dent barbara carmina leudos:
  sic variante tropo laus sonet una viro.
hi celebrem memorent, illi te lege sagacem:
  ast ego te dulcem semper habebo, Lupe.

But let others perform my task for me, vying amongst themselves to praise you; let each, in whatever way he may, praise you in tones of eulogy, the Roman with the *lyra*, the barbarian with the *harpa*, the Greek with the lyre of Achilles, the Briton with the *crotta*. Some proclaim that you are mighty, others that you are firm in justice; one celebrates your alacrity in arms, another in studies. And because you justly ordain all things which are required by peace and war, one sings of your glory as a judge, another as a war-leader. We proclaim it in Latin verslets, let the barbarian give out his foreign songs: thus let one voice of praise be made from diverse poetry. Some proclaim your glory, others your wisdom in law; and I will always hold you dear, O Lupus!

the Primitive Germanic of the first centuries AD. The shallow kind of lyre found at Sutton Hoo and in Frankish lands may be this ancient *harpa*.

The presence of a stringed instrument amongst the grave-goods of a king at Sutton Hoo is most suggestive. There had been a tradition of high-class 'amateur' string-playing in Rome, (grossly, and perhaps unwittingly, parodied by Nero), yet this musicianship had a precious quality; as an attempt to revive a supposed Golden Age of Homeric bards and ancient rhapsodes it was sickly, and by the time of Boethius and Fortunatus it was probably dead. Things appear to have been different amongst the Germanic-speaking barbarians of the seventh and eighth centuries; whatever associations the *harpa* may have had in the lower levels of society, amongst princes and rulers it must have possessed a 'regal' mystique and emblematic force to warrant inclusion amongst the grave-goods at Sutton Hoo and elsewhere.

Literary sources of the first millennium suggest that the *harpa* gained its charisma from its association with the power of the past. Until the eighth century most of the Germanic-speaking peoples were illiterate and relied upon songs and poems for their sense of their own past and their knowledge of it. The Roman historian Tacitus (d. ?120) mentions these songs in his *Germania*, adding that they were 'ancient' and 'the only kind of history amongst them'.[8] These ancient songs included eulogies of dead kings, songs connected with great victories in war, and royal genealogies carrying the reigning kings back to the ancient Gods of the North. There are signs that they were accompanied by the *harpa*, at least amongst the Goths of the sixth century, possibly earlier. Our witness here is a Goth named Jordanes who, around the year 550, summarized a lost history of his nation composed by Cassiodorus, senator and friend of Boethius. According to one of the traditions recorded in this abridgement, the *Getica*:[9]

[The Goths in ancient times] . . . sang of the deeds of their ancestors in strains of song accompanied by *citharas*; chanting of Eterpemara, Hanala, Fritigern, Vidigoia and others whose fame amongst them is great . . .

Jordanes is ostensibly referring to a period at least a thousand years before his own time (whence the past tense in the first line) yet the customs of his own day may lie just below the surface of these words.

---

[8] *Germania*, 2: 'Celebrant carminibus antiquis, quod unum apud illos memoriae et annalium genus est.' The eulogistic songs of the Germanic tribes in Late Antiquity are discussed in J. Opland, *Anglo-Saxon Oral Poetry: A Study of the Traditions* (New Haven, 1980), 28 ff.

[9] Th. Mommsen, *Jordanis Romana et Getica, Monumenta Germaniae Historica, Auctorum Antiquissimorum*, V:1, 65: 'ante quos [*sic*: for 'antiquitus'?] etiam cantu maiorum facta modulationibus citharisque canebant, Eterpamara, Hanale, Fridigerni, Vidigoiae et aliorum, quorum in hac gente magna opinio est . . .'.

'Fritigern' may be the fourth-century Visigothic leader of that name, while the fame of the other heroes named in the passage seems to have been bright in Jordanes' day, to judge by the present tense that closes the extract.

There is a much later (and better-known) reference to what may be instrumentally-accompanied narrative in a letter written by Alcuin of York to Hygbald, bishop of Lindisfarne, in 797. In the letter Alcuin exhorts Hygbald to care for the poor and to be an example of sobriety and continence. As for conduct in the monastery:[10]

Let the word of God be read where monks are eating. There a reader should be heard, not a string-player (*citharistam*); the discourses of the Fathers, not the songs of heathens. What has Ingeld to do with Christ?

This reveals the kind of repertory which Alcuin wished to condemn in the same breath as string-players: 'songs of heathens' about Ingeld, the sixth-century prince of the Heatho-Bards who makes a significant appearance in the Old English heroic poem of *Beowulf*.[11] The syntax of the passage is such that there can be no firm conclusions about the relationship between the *citharista* and the songs of Ingeld, but the possibility seems strong that Alcuin is attacking the monks of Lindisfarne for listening to lays about an ancient hero performed to the lyre.

If the lyre was often used to accompany narrative songs, genealogies, and eulogies, then it becomes possible to understand why the instrument was included amongst the royal grave-goods at Sutton Hoo. It is always the most powerful who have most need to control the past and to be identified with it. A song in praise of a chieftain's forefathers strengthens his claim to power and authority; a genealogy proclaims his right to rule. As J. H. Plumb has written:[12]

This use of the past for social purposes occurs in all early civilisations for which we have written records. In them the past legitimizes authority and status. This is the reason for the primitive king-lists which are some of the earliest historical records of human society ... the overwhelming authority of the past ... enhance[s] the status of those who possess the genealogy.

Perhaps, in aristocratic society, a lyre could serve as an emblem of a chieftain's special relationship with the past. In addition to explaining

---

[10] E. Dümmler, *Alcuini Epistolae*, in *Monumenta Germanicae Historica, Epistolae Karolini Aevi*, 2 (Berlin, 1895), 183: 'Verba Dei legantur in sacerdotali convivio. Ibi decet lectorem audiri, non citharistam; sermones patrum, non carmina gentilium. Quid Hinieldus cum Christo?'

[11] *Beowulf* 2064b.

[12] J. H. Plumb, *The Death of the Past* (London, 1969), 32 f.

the presence of a lyre at Sutton Hoo, this would explain why the lyre is intimately associated with recollection of the past in the Old English heroic poem of *Beowulf*:[13]

There was the sound of the lyre (*hearpe*), the clear song of the minstrel. He who could tell of the beginnings of Mankind from far back spoke; he told how the Almighty wrought the earth ...

And again, where the musician may be the Danish king, Hrothgar:[14]

There was song and rejoicing; the aged king of the Danes, the wise one, told of long ago; at times the battle-bold man, taking pleasure in the lyre, touches the joy-wood; now and again he recites a song, true and sad; sometimes the large-hearted king rightly told true things in a tale of marvels; sometimes, fettered with years, the old warrior began to speak to the young men of battle strength; his heart surged within him as he, wise in winters, remembered many things.

In the eighth and ninth centuries when the monasteries drew many of their members from aristocratic families this special (but not exclusive) association between lyre-playing and high rank could have been a potent one for monks whose Christian faith lay like gold leaf on the barbarian pattern of their minds.

A story recorded by Ekkehard IV, the eleventh-century chronicler of St Gall, reveals how easily this ancient prestige of string-playing could find a home in a great monastic house around the year 900, and how it could extend to other instruments beyond the ancient lyre, or *harpa*. According to Ekkehard, the monk Tuotilo (d. 915) and his fellows, including the poet Notker Balbulus,[15] received an education with a special emphasis on music. 'Their master Iso', Ekkehard relates, 'wise in both sacred and wordly learning, educated them in the Liberal Arts, but especially in the musical arts'. Tuotilo developed into an expert instrumentalist—so gifted, indeed, that he was permitted to teach his art to the sons of noblemen in a place specially set aside for the purpose. He also used one of his instruments, the *rotta*, to compose melodies:[16]

---

[13] *Beowulf* 89b–92b.

[14] Ibid. 2105a–2114b.

[15] On Notker see p. 263.

[16] G. H. Pertz, *Casus Sancti Galli, Monumenta Germaniae Historica, Scriptorum*, 2 (Hannover, 1829), 94 and 101: 'At Tuotilo ... bonus erat et utilis ... erat eloquens, voce clarus, celaturae elegans et picturae artifex, musicus sicut et socii eius; sed in omnium genere fidium et fistularum prae omnibus. Nam et filios nobilium in loco ab abbate destinato fidibus edocuit ... Quae autem Tuotilo dictaverat, singularis et agnoscibilis melodie sunt, quia per psalterium seu per rothtam, qua potentior ipse erat, neumata inventa dulciora sunt...'.

The regal associations of string-playing were reinforced by the iconography of King David as a string-player. For examples of King David as a lyre-player in Dark Age manuscript painting

Tuotilo was a fine and gifted man . . . he was eloquent, with a ringing voice, and was a subtle maker of pictures and engravings. He was a musician (*musicus*) like his fellows, but he surpassed everyone in playing upon every kind of string- and pipe-instrument. He taught string-playing to the sons of noblemen in a place set aside for the purpose by the Abbot . . . As for the pieces he composed, they are matchless melodies and easily recognised; they have an extra sweetness, having been composed upon the *psalterium* or *rotta*, which increased his powers as a composer.

This passage introduces another major instrument of early medieval Europe, the rotta, which remained in use until the fourteenth century. It comprised a peg-arm and base-board, arranged as two sides of a triangle, with a soundbox placed between them. By the twelfth century at least, and probably much earlier, there were two bands of gut strings, one on each side of the soundbox.[17] This extract also introduces the first appearance of the term *musicus* that we have encountered since Boethius—but how its meaning has changed! Ekkehard's *musicus* is not a patrician connoisseur who summons the musicians he disdains to perform for his delight, but a string-playing monk.

So it was an important moment when Boethius's *De Institutione Musica* became available to Frankish scholars after three centuries of oblivion. When it was discovered by monastic readers with an interest in instruments, or at least a respect for their traditions, something was bound to happen.

HUCBALD AND NOTKER: THE VIEW FROM THE DARK AGE CLOISTER

It happened in the *De Harmonica Institutione* (*c.* 880) of Hucbald, a monk of St Amand in North-East France. The very title of this work echoes Boethius, whose treatise had shown Hucbald that the music-theory of the ancients could be used to fence the open pasture of plainchant and turn it into a field of study, a *disciplina*. Boethius has also given Hucbald the terminology to describe the tunings of open-stringed instruments, and Hucbald's references to them make the *De Harmonica Institutione* the earliest known source of information

---

see Hortense Panum, trans. J. Pulver, *The Stringed Instruments of the Middle Ages* (London, 1940), figure 82; H. Steger, *David Rex et Propheta*, (Nuremberg, 1961), plates 3, 24, 28, 35 and 53, and idem. *Philologia Musica*, (Munich, 1971), plates 1–3.

For another learned and clerical instrumentalist of the tenth century see the narratives of the life of St Dunstan in W. Stubbs, *Memorials of St. Dunstan*, Rolls Series (63, 1874), *passim*.

[17] On the rotta see Steger, 'Die Rotte', and, on the identification of the term, Page, *Voices and Instruments of the Middle Ages*, p. 148.

about the musical properties of stringed instruments in the West after the Fall of Rome.

Hucbald begins by presenting a sequence of tones and semitones which corresponds to the Roman theorist's tuning for a fifteen-stringed lyre arranged according to the diatonic genus:

T S T T S T T T S T T S T T
A B C D E F G a ♮ c d e f g a'

(For the sake of clarity the T[one] and S[emitone] signs used by Hucbald are accompanied here by pitch-letters to make the intervallic sequence plain; they imply nothing about absolute pitch).

As we saw above, much of Boethius' musical treatise is anchored by reference to a notional *cithara*. Hucbald knew it well enough, but he also knew that the instruments of his own day did not produce the intervallic series shown above with complete exactitude. As he patiently explains, they began differently, starting from the third rung of the ladder (C) rather than the first (A), and continuing through the interval series T T S T T T S:[18]

Let it cause you no misgiving if perchance when inspecting an organ or any other kind of musical instrument you find that its notes are not arranged in this pattern [i.e. that of the Boethian system given above] or that they clearly exceed this number of strings. For this arrangement is based on the plan of that most sagacious man, Boethius, who weighs all this with careful judgement in the light of the harmony of commensurable numbers. But such musical instruments should not be thought at variance with understanding, since during long ages they have been handled by so many intelligent men that they now stand tested and approved by the greatest intellects, and since,

---

[18] A very faulty text of Hucbald's treatise is available in Gerbert, *Scriptores*, 1, 104–47. All the passages cited here have been checked with the Brussels manuscript of the text. For notes on this manuscript, with facsimiles, see R. Weakland, 'Hucbald as Musician and Theorist', *MQ*, 42 (1956), 66–84. There is a translation of the treatise by Warren Babb, *Hucbald, Guido and John on Music* (New Haven, 1978). For the passage translated here see Gerbert, *Scriptores*, 1, 110; Babb, *Hucbald*, 24:

[N]ec tamen aliquid afferat scrupuli si forte ydraulia vel aliud quodlibet musici generis considerans instrumentum non ibi voces tali repperias scemate deductas, quodque numerum cordarum videantur excedere. Hec enim distribucio secundum viri disertissimi Boecii disposicionem, qui commensurabili concordia numerorum hec omnia diligenti examinat ratione, est instituta. Ceterum non ideo eadem instrumenta intellectualitatis alicuius putanda sunt aliena, cum et ex ipso longevitatis usu sub tot hucusque pertracta prudentibus maximis utique constent exquisita ingeniis et probata. Sed et exemplar disposicionis prefixe eis advertatur omnino inesse. Per easdem namque geminas qualitates rite per omnia diriguntur nihilque aliud distare creduntur nisi quod initia non tali ordine metiuntur. Incipiunt enim quasi a tertio disposicionis illius. Porro numerositas nervorum vel fistularum, ut puta .xxi. aut plurium, non idcirco apponitur quod soni ultra .xv. aut forte .xvi. protendantur, sed ipsi idem qui sunt inferius repetuntur, et hoc pro varietate modorum qui toni nunc appellantur, ut est autentus protus et ceteri, ut qui scilicet non omnes ab imis eisdemque locis possunt ordiri a quocunque ceptum fuerit sufficienter progrediendi repperiat facultatem.

too, one observes that the pattern of the above arrangement of the notes [the Boethian system] appertains fully to these musical instruments. For they are planned in all respects duly according to those same two kinds [of interval, tone, and semitone,] and one may rest assured that they differ in no other respect than that their starting points are not calculated in the way here set forth, for they begin with the third note of the above arrangement. Moreover the large number of strings and pipes (as, for instance, twenty-one or more) is not produced by adding to the fifteen or perhaps sixteen notes [in Boethius's arrangement] but by repeating the same ones as below [in a higher octave]. This large number derives from the variety of modes, which are nowadays called 'tones', such as the authentic protus [i.e. Dorian] and the others. Since, obviously, they cannot all begin with the same bottom notes, the [larger number of notes permits] a mode sufficient scope for its range, whatever note it starts from.

Hucbald's tone is informal, almost genial, and there is light here to dispel some of the shadows that surround Dark Age instruments. All those known to Hucbald, it seems, used a diatonic scale starting on C, and when the number of strings or pipes exceeded fifteen or sixteen these 'extra' components only duplicated lower notes an octave higher. Sometimes, the number of strings and pipes could be extended to twenty-one, and occasionally even more, so that performers could encompass any mode.

Hucbald has read his Boethius with care, but the Roman theorist's disdain for the ignorant *citharoedus*, 'exiled from the true understanding of musical science', finds no echo in the treatise of this, his first true disciple in the Middle Ages. Hucbald feels himself to be looking back upon an ancient tradition in which instruments have been cultivated 'by so many intelligent men' that 'they now stand tested and approved by the greatest intellects'.

These claims would be almost unintelligible if we did not have the Sutton Hoo lyre, *Beowulf*, and Ekkehard's story of Tuotilo. Indeed Hucbald has much to say about the kind of six-stringed lyre placed amidst the royal regalia at Sutton Hoo. We have already encountered his schematic diagram of its six strings (Fig. 2) which gives their tuning as T T S T T. Since Hucbald's purpose in the diagram is to exemplify a system of notation that specifies pitch precisely, he places the syllables of an antiphon, *Ecce vere Israhelita*, upon the strings that must be plucked to produce the chant melody. This turns what is already a remarkable diagram into an astonishing one, since Hucbald's lyre-notation is essentially a form of tablature that has hatched six hundred years before its time.

Other important stringed instruments may be glimpsed behind Hucbald's words. Those with twenty-one (or more) strings, for example, are unlikely to have been lyres, usually equipped with about half a dozen strings at this date; they may well be rottas, and possibly pillar-harps. Caution must be exercised here, for until c. 1000, when harps with pillars begin to be clearly represented in English and continental manuscripts, the history of this instrument in the medieval West is obscure. Sources of the eleventh century show instruments that are instantly recognizable as harps today; small enough to be played on the knees, they often have a straight arm to hold the tuning pins and a gracefully curving pillar. The strings were probably made of gut, the material that was almost universally employed by medieval musicians, although horsehair is another possibility, and so (at least from the twelfth century, and in the Celtic realms of Britain), is some metallic substance.[19]

After Hucbald, silence falls for a century. It is eventually broken in the monastery of St Gall where Tuotilo had taught musical instruments to the sons of noblemen in Hucbald's time. Around the year 1000 a monk—another Notker, called Labeo—compiled a brief *De Musica* for the use of his pupils. In this little treatise he maintains his custom of writing in Old High German rather than Latin, and in the same spirit, so that every point should be clear, he refers to the rotta and the *lira* (?pillar-harp) in order to illustrate certain points of theory. The image of Notker entering his classroom at St Gall weighed down with codices, wax-tablets, and a rotta may seem a fanciful one, but using the rotta in this way would scarcely have troubled a scholar who had taken the revolutionary step of writing school-texts in the vernacular. Indeed it might have come naturally to a man who could write like this:[20]

Know also that in the chant there are only seven different notes which Virgil calls the 'seven distinctions of pitch', and the eighth is the same as the first. Therefore there are always seven notes on the *lira* and *rota*, and seven similarly tuned [on each instrument], and similarly the alphabet of the organ does not go further than the first seven letters: A B C D E F G [that is: T T S T T T].

Notker confirms Hucbald's testimony that open-stringed instruments were tuned diatonically starting on C, each one therefore having seven

---

[19] On the chronology and distribution of metallic strings in the medieval West see Page, *Voices and Instruments of the Middle Ages*, Appendix 4.

[20] P. Piper, *Die Schriften Notkers und seiner Schule*, 3 vols., (Freiburg and Tübingen, 1882–3), 853: 'Uuizîn dârmíte . dáz an démo sánge dero stímmo . échert síben uuéhsela sínt , dî uirgilius héizet septem discrimina uocum únde díu áhtoda in qualitate díu sélba íst . sô diu êrista . Fóne díu sínt án dero lîrûn . únde án dero rótûn îo síben séiten . únde síbene gelîcho geuuerbet . Pe díu negât óuh án dero órganûn . daz alphabetum nîeht fûrder . âne ze síben buóhstaben dien êristen . A B C D E F G'.

different notes. When the number of strings was large (both Hucbald and Notker mention twenty-one as a possibility) then the sequence T T S T T T was simply repeated at different octaves, allowing the musician to perform all melodies complete, without resorting to octave transposition.

THE ORGAN

Mentioned by both Hucbald and Notker, the organ appears to have been the only 'serious' wind instrument known in Dark Age Europe (apart from the horns and trumpets used for signalling and cere-monial purposes). We may suspect that Tuotilo was an organist when Ekkehard relates that he was skilled 'on every kind of ... pipe-instrument'. There are shadowy references to the organ in several Latin poems by Aldhelm of Sherborne (d. 709) and perhaps in an Anglo-Saxon riddle (of uncertain date but before c. 1000).[21] But these count for little beside the firm evidence in Frankish chronicles that the organ first came into Frankish lands in the year 756–7 as a gift to Charlemagne from the Byzantine emperor Constantine Copronymus. In Byzantium the organ was closely associated with Imperial ceremo-nial—indeed with emperor worship—and this charisma, keenly sensed in Francia, may explain why the instrument was adopted in many Frankish monasteries as a means of embellishing the liturgy on certain occasions.[22] In all probability the monastic organs known to Hucbald and Notker Labeo were used to make a clangour, like the bells rung during the performance of sequences, rather than to accompany singers by doubling or harmonizing a chant. As they appear in pictorial sources before the twelfth century, organs are generally equipped with sliders, not with keys, and in order to sound a pipe the player pulled the appropriate slider out and then pushed it home while drawing the next.[23] Brisk passages must have been impossible to accomplish using this mechanism, but the instrument could provide a festive clamour on special feast-days as the organist improvised or played some appropriate chant at whatever speed he could manage.

It is almost impossible to form an accurate impression of the early

[21] For details (and a translation of the riddle) see C. Page, 'The Earliest English Keyboard', *Early Music*, 7 (1979), 313. On the early history of the organ see J. Perrot, *The Organ* (Oxford, 1970); J. McKinnon, 'The Tenth Century Organ at Winchester', *The Organ Yearbook*, 5 (1974), 4–19, and K. Körte, 'Die Orgel von Winchester', *Kirchenmusikalisches Jahrbuch*, 57 (1973), 1–24.

[22] See E. Bowles, 'The Symbolism of the Organ in the Middle Ages: A study in the History of Ideas', in J. LaRue, ed., *Aspects of Medieval and Renaissance Music* (London, 1967), 27–39, and, on the spread of the organ in Francia, Perrot, *The Organ*, 205 ff.

[23] For illustrations of these sliders see Page, 'The Earliest English Keyboard', plates 3 and 4.

medieval organ. About a dozen depictions of the instrument survive from before *c.* 1100, but some are so crudely executed, or so obviously dependent upon Antique models, that almost nothing can be learned from them. Several understate their material; the organ in a well-known illustration of the eleventh century, for example, is too small for the bellows which two men are treading below it.[24]

Firm ground is reached with the detailed account of organ-making in the treatise *De Diversis Artibus* (*c.* 1100) by a German monk known by the pseudonym of Theophilus. This tells how to build an organ and then set it up in a monastery (*infra monasterium*) and the technology involved is both laborious and rudimentary. The curved pipe for the bellows unit, for example, must be made from a curved bough, cut from an oak tree, and then hollowed with a metal implement glowing red-hot at one end. For the pipes Theophilus recommends 'pure and quite flawless copper', so thin that 'when you press your fingernail into it the impression appears on either side', and since there are seven (or eight) sliders controlling a rank of three octaves there must have been about 22 pipes in all.[25] When the sliders were drawn, the fundamental, octave, and double octave must have all sounded together for there is no mechanism to separate them on Theophilus's instrument; an octave-ambiguity would have been manifest in whichever octave the organ played, for while three octaves were required 'so that the performer, mounting up with both hands laid on [the instrument] may perform any piece' (to quote Notker Labeo once more), in performance the organ played its seven or eight notes in three octaves at once.

INSTRUMENTALISTS' REPERTORY *c.* 1000

Scattered references in literary sources suggest that stringed instruments were often used to accompany the voice. Narrative songs (or narrative poems declaimed in some stylized fashion) were an important part of at least professional repertory. As we have already seen, a passage in Jordanes' *Getica* suggests that the Ostrogoths of the sixth century celebrated their national heroes 'in strains of song accompanied by *citharae*', and Alcuin of York may be referring to a similar practice when he rebukes the monks of Lindisfarne for listening to a *citharista* and songs of Ingeld (see above, p. 461).

There was more to this narrative repertory, however, than these survivals of ancient traditions from the North. Around 1050 a

---

[24] Cambridge, St. John's College MS B.18, fo. 1. Reproduced as the frontispiece to *NOHM* ii.

[25] For the text of Theophilus's chapter, with translation, see C. R. Dodwell, *Theophilus: the Various Arts* (London, 1961), 142–50. There are translations with commentary and useful explicative diagrams in Perrot, *The Organ*, 232 ff.

German satirist calling himself Sextus Amarcius describes an entertainment provided by a *citharista* for a wealthy prelate, and as the
string-player 'harmonizes the tuneful strings in fifths' he works
through a programme of narrative songs, including the story of David
and Goliath, a tale of the 'snow-child' (which shows how a little
Swabian plays a macabre trick upon the wife who has deceived him),
and several others. It is unfortunate that nothing is known of the
music of these pieces.[26]

The earliest verse romance of the Middle Ages brings us closer to
the repertory of eleventh-century string-players. The *Ruodlieb*, probably written in southern Germany *c.* 1050, tells of a young warrior
(*miles*) who is forced to leave his homeland. He is a gifted player upon
the *harpa*, and when he is entertained by *harpatores* in a castle where
he is a guest he is far from satisfied with what he hears. Taking a *harpa*
which has been brought for him he plucks the strings expertly, 'now
with two fingers of the left hand, and now with the right, rendering
very sweet melodies ... and producing many flourishes (*uariamina*)
with great distinctness'.[27] This seems to be instrumental music of a
kind used for dancing: 'anyone entirely unversed in moving his feet in
a dance, or in beating time with his hands', enthuses the poet, 'might
learn both of those things quickly [as Ruodlieb played]'. When
Ruodlieb has performed three pieces the lady of the castle asks him to
play another so that his nephew may dance with her daughter:[28]

Quem per sistema siue diastema dando responsa
Dum mirabiliter operetur ue decenter...

He carries this out in a wondrous and decorous
way, playing the *responsa* with *sistema* or *diastema*...

These *responsa* ('replies') are presumably musical reprises of some
kind, while the forbidding terms *sistema* and *diastema* are explained
by the music-theorist Johannes, probably writing in southern Germany, *c.* 1100,[29] and therefore well placed to interpret the musical

---

[26] For the text see K. Manitius, *Sextus Amarcius Sermones, Monumenta Germaniae Historica,
Quellen zur Geistesgeschichte des Mittelalters,* 6 (Weimar, 1969), 74 ff. It is possible that the
content of some of these pieces is preserved, in Latin, in the celebrated 'Cambridge Songs'
collection. See P. Dronke, *The Medieval Lyric* (rev. edn., London, 1978), 28–9.

[27] E. H. Zeydel, *Ruodlieb* (Chapel Hill, 1959), 110, lines 38–40:
Pulsans mox laeua digitis geminis, modo dextra
Tangendo chordas dulces reddit nimis odas,
Multum distincte faciens uariamina quaeque...

[28] Ibid., lines 48–9.

[29] This is the theorist generally known, since van Waesberghe's edition of his treatise, as John
'of Affligem', but the grounds for this toponym are extremely weak. For a useful summary of the
debate concerning the area in which Johannes worked see Babb, *Hucbald,* 91, and M. Huglo,
'L'auteur du traité de Musique dédié à Fulgence d'Afflighem', *Revue Belge de Musicologie,* 31
(1977), 5–19.

terminology of the *Ruodlieb*. According to Johannes 'diastema occurs when the chant makes a suitable pause, not on the final, but elsewhere', while sistema occurs 'whenever a suitable pause in the melody comes upon the final'.[30] Ruodlieb's musical reprises (*responsa*) now begin to sound like repeats with open (*diastema*) and closed (*sistema*) endings, and since he is playing for dancers his rhythm is presumably measured or regular in some way. In short, Ruodlieb seems to be playing something similar to the instrumental genre known as the *estampie*, not recorded until the fourteenth century (Ex. 162).[31]

Ex. 162

JOHANNES DE GROCHEIO AND JEROME OF MORAVIA: THE VIEW FROM THE CITY

For the monk of the ninth and tenth centuries, words like *cithara* and *psalterium* were luminous with the splendour of Christian history and

---

[30] J. Smits van Waesberghe, *Johannis Affligemensis De Musica cum Tonario*, American Institute of Musicology, *Corpus Scriptorum de Musica*, 50 (Rome, 1950), 80.

[31] Extract from *La septime estampie real*, Paris Bibliothèque Nationale, MS fr. 844, fo. 177. Transcribed from P. Aubry, *Estampies et danses royales* (Paris, 1907). This is one of the textless pieces added in a fourteenth-century hand to the Manuscrit du Roi; Aubry gives excellent facsimiles of them all.

prophecy. *Psalterium* evoked Mankind's long journey towards the Incarnation, foretold by David as he sang *in psalterio*; *cithara* spanned the history of Man, from Tubal in the first generation after the Flood, to the Revelation of St John where heavenly *citharae* are heard amidst the marvels that will signal the end of all earthly music.

During the twelfth and thirteenth centuries these Latin terms continued to be used, their aura undimmed, but at the same time new instrument names, not to be found in the Bible nor in any other revered source, began to make an appearance. These new words had no charisma; they were based on the usages of current vernacular speech and were directly tied to instruments in daily use, such as *viella*, *quitarra sarracenica*, *rubeba*, *guiterna*, *liuto*, *cistolla*, *naccara*, and many more. Through the small aperture of this change in vocabulary we may glimpse much of what is new about the position of musical instruments in the twelfth and thirteenth centuries.

Above all, instruments had become involved in that widening of the range of human experience deemed to be consequential which is perhaps the greatest achievement of the twelfth and thirteenth centuries. For monks like Hucbald and Notker, everything in music worthy of reflection and written record was part of monastic life and the defence against Satan's siege. When these two monks refer to musical traditions existing outside the monastery (as they do in their allusions to instruments) it is because they felt at ease with the traditions of a secular aristocracy which had produced so many distinguished founders of monasteries and so many monks.

With the improvement of agricultural techniques in the eleventh and twelfth centuries the population of Europe rose dramatically; many existing towns doubled in size and a large number of new ones were founded. In consequence, a literate cleric of the twelfth and thirteenth centuries was often an urbanized creature whose awareness of music extended beyond the monastery walls to the townscapes he knew or had encountered on his travels. The idea of the city as a complex community of men performing tasks that secured a common good—an idea that took wings with the recovery of Aristotle's philosophy in the twelfth century—revolutionized the way reflective men looked at the world; anything that was good for the *civitas* (they reasoned) was good, and since secular music helped citizens to rest, strengthening them for their work, then secular music must be good. This simple syllogism, brought into existence by the complexity of urban experience, had the power to drive a thousand years of

Christian polemic against secular music and musicians into the dust.[32]

This urban background is powerfully evoked in two Parisian treatises of the late thirteenth century, Jerome of Moravia's *Tractatus de Musica* and Johannes de Grocheio's *De Musica*. Between them they contain virtually all the surviving technical and musical information about Gothic instruments before 1300.

Jerome of Moravia was a Dominican friar and thus a member of a quintessentially urban order founded in the thirteenth century when the growth of towns and cities created a need for itinerant preachers and confessors. His *Tractatus de Musica*, a compilation of Latin music-treatises for 'the brothers of our order or of another', closes with a remarkable chapter on the tunings and techniques of two bowed instruments, the *rubeba* and the *viella*.

Johannes de Grocheio's *De Musica* is almost a manual of the new urban morality for music. In contrast to every other medieval writer on music, Grocheio inventories the musical genres of one city (Paris) and underlines the ways in which the various musical forms cultivated by Parisians help to maintain the health of the *civitas*; narrative songs, or *chansons de geste*, help to reconcile 'working citizens' to their labour by reminding them of the great trials undergone by the heroes of the past; the best trouvère songs encourage great men to magnanimity, and so on.[33] As he works through the musical forms known in Paris, Grocheio has much to say about the leading instrument of the twelfth and thirteenth centuries (and the principal subject of Jerome of Moravia's chapter): the bowed *viella*.

The circumstances surrounding the rise of bowed instruments in Europe are obscure, although it has been established that the bow cannot be traced earlier than *c.* 900 when it was known in the territories of the Islamic and Byzantine Empires.[34] By *c.* 1000 bowing seems to have spread all over Europe and musicians applied the technique to many plucked instruments already in use. The Stuttgart

---

[32] On the intellectual and spiritual consequences of urbanization and population growth during the twelfth and thirteenth centuries see L. K. Little, *Religious Poverty and the Profit Economy in Medieval Europe* (London, 1978), and A. Murray, *Reason and Society in the Middle Ages* (Oxford, 1978). For the forces affecting the relationship between minstrel and cleric in this period, see J. Le Goff, *Pour un autre Moyen Age: Temps, travail et culture on Occident* (Editions Gallimard, 1977), and C. Casagrande and S. Vecchio, 'Clercs et jongleurs dans la société médiévale (XIIᵉ et XIIIᵉ siècles)', *Annales, economies, sociétés, civilisations*, 34 (1979), 913–28.

[33] E. Rohloff, *Die Quellenhandschriften zum Musiktraktat des Johannes de Grocheio* (Leipzig, 1972), 130. Grocheio states that the *chanson de geste* 'is good for preserving the whole city' (iste cantus valet ad conservationem totius civitatis) while the *cantus coronatus* incites great men to virtues which 'help to secure good government' (bonum regimen).

[34] W. Bachmann, *The Origins of Bowing*, trans. N. Deane (Oxford, 1969). For further illustrations of medieval bowed instruments see M. Remnant, *English Bowed Instruments from Anglo-Saxon to Tudor Times* (Oxford, 1986).

psalter, for example, produced in north-east France in the third quarter of the ninth century, shows some very large fingerboard instruments (some more than half the size of a man) which are shaped like elongated spades and played with large plectra; the earliest known depictions of bowing in the West show large instruments which may be directly related to those shown in the Stuttgart psalter.[35]

By the twelfth century various bowed instruments had risen in Southern France and Spain to become courtly instruments *par excellence*. The process may have begun in Provence and Catalonia, home of the troubadours. By *c.* 1200 these territories had produced a count who chose to be represented on his personal seal playing a fiddle, and at least three troubadours who could play the *viola*.[36] Like the ancient lyre of the North, bowed instruments had a noble charisma in Provence according to the status of those who played them, but it was the charisma of courtliness, the new force in aristocratic society during the twelfth century. In the homeland of the troubadours, bowed instruments had found a secure place in the imagery of *cortezia*: insouciant youthfulness, physical beauty, and a nonchalant display of talent. Here is the Catalan troubadour Guiraut de Cabrera (*fl. c.* 1150) playing in the hall of the palace at Arles:[37]

... There was a knight in Catalonia ... of very high birth, dashing in warfare and gracious in manners, whose name was Guiraut de Cabrera. This knight was in the flush of youth, charming, lively, highly skilled on musical instruments, and madly desired by the ladies. In the palace [of Arles] and in the presence of Alfonso of pious memory, the late renowned king of Aragon ... and in the sight of many princes, too, the knight ... used to play the *viola*; the ladies led the dance ...

This kind of sophistication impressed many, and it is no surprise to find Johannes de Grocheio in Paris voicing the opinion that 'of all the instruments of the string family ... the *viella* holds pride of place'.[38] Amongst the literate men and scholars of the thirteenth century, especially the younger ones, there existed a 'Latin quarter' within secular courtliness. In the thirteenth century, for example, we find Henri Bate, a student at Paris around 1266–70, recalling his youth when he knew 'how to play the *viella*, bringing together, in harmonious fashion, a melodious touching of the strings and drawing of

---

[35] Ibid. plates 1 and 16.

[36] For the seal and the original texts pertaining to the troubadours see Page, *Voices and Instruments of the Middle Ages*, figure 1 and 175–9.

[37] Ibid. 177–9 gives the original text (from Gervase of Tilbury's *Otia Imperialia*, *c.* 1211). This account may well derive from the eye-witness testimony of Gervase's mother-in-law.

[38] Rohloff, *Quellenhandschriften* 134: 'Et adhuc, inter omnia instrumenta chordosa, visa a nobis, viella videtur praevalere'.

the bow'.[39] No doubt many young students like Henri Bate, in Paris and elsewhere, were also attracted by the new, savant ethos that fiddling was beginning to acquire in the wake of Aristotle and his Islamic commentators. Here is the Dominican Albertus Magnus:[40]

Aristotle relates in the second book of his *Topics* that in any science there are many facets of two ends: one is the aim, the other is what is directed to that aim. Avicenna gives this example of this principle: there are two sciences in fiddling; one which is the arranging of the strings and another which is the stirring or touching of the strings. The science of arranging strings teaches how to adjust and stop the strings into low, middle and high according to the rudiments and principles of the process.

'The *scientia* of arranging strings' that teaches how to 'adjust and stop the strings into low middle and high'—this is what Albertus's fellow Dominican, Jerome of Moravia, attempts to impart in the chapter on the *viella* in his *Tractatus de Musica*.

The word *viella* is simply a Latinized form of Old French *vïele* and three major forms of bowed instrument were given this name. The first has been called the 'medieval viol' since it was played in the lap with an underhand bow grip. The body, excavated from a solid block and then covered with a soundboard (as was the general medieval practice), took the form of a figure-of-eight, often with a small scallop at the junction of the two circles and with separate soundholes in each section. There were three strings, probably either of gut or horsehair. This kind of instrument appears to have become obsolete during the first quarter of the fourteenth century.

The second variety is the one to which the named 'rebec' has generally been applied in recent years (the term did not pass into general usage until the sixteenth century). The body narrowed into the

[39] Henri's reminiscences, from his *Nativitas magistri Henrici Mechliniensis*, are of the first interest here and worth quoting in full: 'This servant of God gladly heard music performed upon reed-instruments, pipes, and every kind of musical instrument, and meanwhile he delighted in them as keenly as if he wished to become skilled in every aspect of those arts; for truly, he knew how to rule himself when blowing wind into flutes and reed-pipes and instruments of that kind with varied artistry; he also knew how to elicit melody from organs and *choros* [?] by striking the keys. Afterwards he entered the regions of philosophy and became a pupil, cultivating his mind and disciplining his understanding; thus he did not wish to pursue wind instruments further, in line with what Aristotle reports in the *Politics*: Athene, having invented wind instruments, is said to have cast them away. This boy knew how to play the *viella*, bringing together, in harmonious fashion, a melodious touching of the strings and drawing of the bow . . . Further, he was familiar with (and willingly sang) all kinds of monophonic songs in diverse languages; he was a trouvère [*inventor*] of poems and melodies, and a merry and amorous leader of ring-dances and master of dances in wooded places, arranging parties and games, and introducing others to the sport of dancing. These and such things are not inimical to the student life, especially amongst the young.' Latin text in N. Goldine, 'Henri Bate, chanoine et chantre de la cathédrale Saint Lambert à Liège et théoricien de la musique (1246–après 1310)', *Revue Belge de Musicologie*, 18 (1964), 14–15 n. 6.

[40] A. Borgnet, *Beati Alberti Magni . . . Opera Omnia*, 38 vols., (Paris, 1890–9), vii. 4b.

neck, giving the instrument a roughly pear-shaped outline. Sound-holes, often semi-circular, were placed on either side of the bridge. This rebec was generally played upon the shoulder (there are many exceptions to this rule in Spanish sources) and there were usually three strings, although there might be as many as five. Sometimes there was a lateral string running to the side of the fingerboard which was plucked with the thumb—presumably to produce a percussive 'drone' effect—or brushed with the bow.

The third variety, not always easy to separate from the one just described, often had an oval-shaped body clearly distinguished from the neck. There were almost invariably five strings, one of which was often a lateral bourdon that could not be stopped by the fingers.

Jerome of Moravia's *viella* is an instrument of the second or third variety for it has five strings and sometimes uses a lateral bourdon string. According to Jerome's account there were three tunings for it:[41]

1	D	$\ulcorner$	G	d	d
2	D	$\ulcorner$	G	d	g
3	$\ulcorner$	$\ulcorner$	D	c	c

That is, in modern letter-notation (relative pitch):

1	*d*	*G*	*g*	*d'*	*d'*
2	*d*	*G*	*g*	*d'*	*g'*
3	*G*	*G*	*d*	*c'*	*c'*

In tuning 1 the d-course, which Jerome calls the *bordunus*, runs to the side of the fingerboard and cannot be stopped by the fingers.

In all probability the two d' courses in tuning 1 should be represented as one double course, and the same may be said for the G and g strings. Here again we encounter the kind of octave ambiguity that we last met in Theophilus's organ, for when a fiddler ran through the compass of tuning 1, for example, crossing from Gg to d'd' and back again, his melody would comprise a series of parallel octaves one moment and a chain of reinforced unisons the next. The mixture of harmonics in the tune would be constantly—and abruptly—changing. In addition to these octave sounds, springing up suddenly and just as suddenly dropping away, there was the staccato sound of the plucked bourdon string running beside the fingerboard. This tuning highlights the great differences between the medieval *viellator* and his modern counterpart, the violinist: whereas the violinist generally plays a single line the *viellator* thinks in terms of simultaneously sounding strings,

---

[41] See Page, 'Jerome of Moravia on the *rubeba* and *viella*', *Galpin Society Journal*, 32 (1979), 77–98.

whence the double coursing and the choice of tunings so ideal for drone accompaniment. The violinist also seeks evenness of tone from top to bottom, but the *viellator* imposes three different devices of tone-colour (plucked bourdon, octave pair and unison pair) upon just five strings.

This first tuning, according to Jerome, 'encompasses all the modes', while the second is good 'for secular and all other types of song, especially irregular ones' which wish to run through the whole musical compass acknowledged in Jerome's day—two octaves and a sixth.[42] These two remarks, although somewhat vague, balance one another, the first referring to music which obeys the church modes and the second to secular music which flouts them (since this is probably what Jerome means when he says it is 'irregular').[43]

The identity of the 'modal' music is not clear, but it may encompass para-liturgical chants like hymns and sequences so close in form to the trouvère *chanson* and to the lai respectively. As for the secular part of *viella* repertory, Jerome's *laycos ... cantus*, it seems to have been enormous; according to Jerome's Parisian contemporary, Johannes de Grocheio, a good fiddler played every musical form, although in the best circles ('before the wealthy in feasts and festivities') only three: the *cantus coronatus*, the *ductia*, and the *stantipes*.[44] *Cantus coronatus* is Grocheio's term for the finest trouvère songs, and in an arresting passage he reveals that fiddlers usually finished a performance of a *cantus coronatus* with a postlude called a 'mode'.[45] Unfortunately it is not clear whether Grocheio's remarks about the *viella* and the *cantus coronatus* are meant to imply that players accompanied these songs when they were sung, or whether he is referring to purely instrumental performances. Recent research suggests, however, that if Grocheio is referring to accompanied vocal love-songs in the High Style then he may be describing a distinctively Parisian (or at least a distinctively late) performing tradition; the evidence, such as it is, suggests that the troubadours and earlier trouvères associated instrumental accompaniment with the lower styles of their lyric art, as manifested in narrative songs like the *pastourelle* or in dance-songs such as the Old Provençal *dansa* and the Old French *rondet de carole*.[46]

[42] Ibid. 90: 'Alius necessarius est propter laycos et omnes alios cantus, maxime irregulares, qui frequenter per totam manum discurrere volunt'.

[43] Cf. e.g., a fourteenth-century *Tractatulus*: 'Irregular music is called rustic or layman's music ... in that it observes neither modes nor rules'. F. A. Gallo, *Tractatulus de cantu mensurali seu figuratio musicae artis*, American Institute of Musicology, *Corpus Scriptorum de Musica*, 16 (1971), 12.

[44] Rohloff, *Quellenhandschriften*, 136–8.

[45] Ibid. 160.

[46] See Page, *Voices and Instruments of the Middle Ages*, *passim*.

The two remaining forms which Johannes de Grocheio specifically associates with the *viella* are both instrumental ones. The *ductia*, a form of dance music which can 'excite the soul of man to moving in an ornate fashion according to the art called dancing', is a textless melody consisting of three (sometimes four) musical sections, each of which is performed twice, first with an open ending and then with a closed one.[47] Ex. 162, probably written down in Grocheio's lifetime, shows what amounts to a *ductia* according to this description. The third form which Grocheio associates with the *viella*, the *stantipes*, is constructed in the same way as the *ductia*, save that the number of musical sections may be as high as seven and the musical execution is less rhythmic and dance-like.[48]

There is another musical form which Grocheio does not specifically associate with the *viella* but which formed a significant part of the repertory of professional *viellatores*: the epic narrative, or *chanson de geste*.[49] These were poems composed of laisses, of variable length, in which the lines were bound together by assonance. According to Grocheio's description of the form, every line in an epic was sung to the same melody (perhaps the only musical solution possible, since the number of lines in a laisse could vary dramatically).[50] One *chanson de geste* melody survives and it spans only a fourth;[51] since the *viella* seems to have been one of the principal instruments used to accompany these epics it may be that Jerome of Moravia's third *viella* tuning, providing only a compass of a fifth over a drone block, was used for the performance of *chansons de geste*.

Two kinds of playing technique are suggested by the *viella* tunings which Jerome of Moravia gives in the *Tractatus de Musica*. In the first and second arrangements the open strings merely compound a chord of prime, fifth, and octave—ideal for a drone-based technique in which the fiddler plays a melody framed in the tuning of the instrument while bowing one or two strings in addition to the one carrying the tune; at any given moment a string not in use to make the melody would fall back into the drone.

Towards the end of his account Jerome describes an advanced

---

[47] Rohloff, *Quellenhandschriften*, 136–8.

[48] Ibid.

[49] For some of the evidence linking the *viella* with narrative songs including the *chanson de geste* see Page, *Voices and Instruments of the Middle Ages*, ch. 2 n. 9.

[50] For Grocheio's description of the *chanson de geste* see Rohloff, *Quellenhandschriften*, 130 and 132.

[51] This snatch of melody, preserved in Adam de la Halle's *Le Jeu de Robin et Marion*, has been published many times. For a transcription, accompanied by a facsimile from the Aix-en-Provence manuscript of Adam's play, see J. Chailley, 'Du *Tu autem* de Horn à la Musique des Chansons de Geste', in *Mélanges René Louis* (Saint-Père-Sous-Vézelay, 1982), i. 21–32.

manner of playing which involves literacy-based notions about consonance and dissonance that are foreign to the drone-technique described above. In order to accomplish it the fiddler must be able to produce the octave or fifth of any note in a piece; this sounds like an instrumental equivalent of the well-documented vocal practice of fifthing.[52] This device for producing rudimentary polyphony in two-parts requires the singer who is doing the fifthing to double a chant at the fifth above (except at the beginning and ends of phrases where octaves were usually required); Jerome's 'advanced' *viella* technique may have proceeded in a similar fashion. As such it is a landmark in the history of instrumental technique; it shows that *c.* 1300 notions of instrumental artistry were just beginning to come under the influence of vocal polyphony—indeed, of written polyphony, for the effect of fifthing is to turn any monophonic piece into a kind of rudimentary two-part conductus.

It is quite exceptional to have this much information about any medieval instrument other than the organ; our understanding of how other Gothic instruments were tuned and played must be based, for the most part, upon what we know of the *viella*. Amongst the plucked fingerboard instruments, close relatives of the *viella*, three types stand out. The *citole* was characterised by its body, often shaped like a holly leaf, and by a remarkable arrangement whereby the instrumentalist placed the thumb of his stopping-hand through a hole provided in the bulky neck. There were usually frets and four gut strings, played with a large plectrum.[53]

The *gittern* was essentially a small lute. The vaulted back was carved from solid wood, and the fretted neck ended in a sickle pegbox that often terminated in a decorative head. The four strings (or eight, in double courses) were plucked with a plectrum.

The *lute* of the thirteenth century possessed a deep vaulted back (built from staves, following the technology used amongst the Arabs)[54] and a narrow neck, usually fretless, ending in an abruptly turned-back pegbox. In addition to the central rose medieval lutes often possessed two or three 'satellite' roses, and the soundboard was

---

[52] For the technique of fifthing see S. Fuller, 'Discant and the Theory of Fifthing', *AcM*, 50 (1978), 241–75. This interpretation of Jerome's advanced fiddle technique is elaborated in Page, *Voices and Instruments of the Middle Ages*, 69–75.

[53] For the gittern and citole I follow the terminology established by L. Wright, 'The Medieval Gittern and Citole: A Case of Mistaken Identity', *Galpin Society Journal*, 30 (1977), 8–42.

[54] See H. G. Farmer, 'The Structure of the Arabian and Persian Lute in the Middle Ages', *Journal of the Royal Asiatic Society*, (1939), 43–51, and C. Bouterse, 'Reconstructing the Medieval Arabic Lute: A Reconsideration of Farmer's "Structure of the Arabian and Persian Lute"', *Galpin Society Journal*, 32 (1979), 2–9.

also decorated with a wooden panel above the stringholder which served as a plectrum guard.

There is some evidence that these instruments were tuned in ways comparable to those mentioned for the *viella* by Jerome of Moravia. The anonymous author of the *Summa Musicae* (*c*. 1300), for example, records that fingerboard instruments are tuned 'in the consonances of octave, fourth and fifth, and by putting down their fingers the players of these make tones and semitones for themselves ... '.[55] This is reminiscent of Jerome's *viella*, and like the *viellator*, the player of a citole, gittern, or lute could only benefit from an arrangement mixing octaves, fourths, and fifths into an accordatura; with a brush of the plectrum he could turn his instrument into a self-accompanying, heterophonic one.

Relevant here, perhaps, is the evidence of some sixteenth-century lute duets where one lute plays a constant drone to accompany the florid melody of another. These pieces may well be a relic of medieval practice, and so may the special drone tunings which several of them employ. In the light of these a tuning such as d a d' g' (which accords with the evidence of the *Summa Musicae* and of some sixteenth-century lute sources)[56] seems a possibility for Gothic lutes, gitterns, and citoles. By stopping the top course a tone above the nut the player could produce a full accordatura of d a d' a'. The gap of a fourth between the top two courses when open breaks the accordatura but is none the less ideal for drone-playing; it is comfortable for the player to have a finger or two on the fingerboard when the full drone is produced—to hold down the drone, as it were—rather than to find his left hand suddenly redundant every time a sweep of all four strings is required.

The major open-stringed instruments of the thirteenth century, the rotta, pillar-harp, and psaltery, may also have been tuned in ways that allowed the player to perform heterophonically. Of these only the psaltery is a new addition. From the twelfth century (when it first makes a decisive appearance in pictorial sources) until its disappearance during the course of the fifteenth, the psaltery comprised a soundbox mounted with strings that were generally made of some metallic material—in contrast to the stringing of every other instrument of the thirteenth and fourteenth centuries about which evidence

[55] Gerbert, *Scriptores*, III, 214.

[56] See M. Morrow, 'Ayre on the F♯ string', *Lute Society Journal*, 2 (1960), 9–12, and H. M. Brown, *Sixteenth Century Instrumentation: The Music for the Florentine Intermedii*, American Institute of Musicology, Musicological Studies and Documents, (1973), 33.

survives.[57] Usually arranged in double (or even triple and quadruple) courses, they were plucked with quill plectra, one in each hand. At first, trapezoidal instruments seem to have predominated, but with the thirteenth century the classic 'pig-snout' shape became established.

Some suggestion that the harp and psaltery were sometimes tuned for drones and other heterophonic techniques may be found in the terminology of their lowest strings. As early as the thirteenth century the lowest strings of the harp were called in Anglo-Norman *burduns*, which was the prevailing term in Old French for any component of an instrument that produced a fixed and relatively deep note (such as the bagpipe drone). As for the psaltery, no medieval evidence survives, but it is striking that Mersenne, in his *Harmonie Universelle* of 1635, illustrates a form of psaltery (he calls it *psalterion*) in which the lowest string is called the *bourdon* and set a fourth below the next.[58] Mersenne also relates that the strings of the *psalterion* could be tuned in octaves, fifths, and fifteenths 'to augment the harmony'. Might this be a survival of medieval technique?

This leaves what is perhaps the most remarkable of all medieval stringed instruments: the hurdy-gurdy (or, following medieval terminology, the *symfony*).[59] The strings of the symfony were sounded by a rosined wheel and stopped by keys in a keybox. Under the name *organistrum* (a word that appears to have been largely confined to Germany and Austria) the symfony can be traced as early as c. 1100; its origins may lie somewhere in the first millennium. There were essentially two forms. Most remarkable of all was a large instrument, shaped like a modern guitar (or like an Appalachian dulcimer) and handled by two men, one turning the handle while the other operated the keys.[60] There were also smaller instruments for a single player, built in a wide variety of shapes and forms.

Nothing is known for certain about the musical characteristics of these symfonies; the keys which stop the strings are hidden from view in every trustworthy drawing of the instrument which has survived

[57] On metallic stringing in the Middle Ages see Page, *Voices and Instruments of the Middle Ages*, 216–17.

[58] For the diagram and an English translation of the text see R. E. Chapman, *Marin Mersenne: Harmonie Universelle. The Books on Instruments* (The Hague, 1957), 224–6, and on the subject of instrumental heterophony in the Middle Ages see W. Bachmann, 'Die Verbreitung des Quintierens im europäischen Volksgesang des späten Mittelalters', in W. Vetter (ed.), *Festschrift Max Schneider zum achtzigsten Geburstag* (Leipzig, [1955]), 25–9, and idem, *Origins of Bowing*, 87 ff.

[59] The terminology of this instrument is discussed in C. Page, 'The medieval *organistrum* and *symphonia*. 2: Terminology', *Galpin Society Journal*, 36 (1983), 71–87.

[60] For a collection of medieval representations of this type see Bachmann, *Origins of Bowing*, plates 77, 78, 80, and 81.

from the Middle Ages;[61] it is likely, however, that symfonies were often built to play in the same way as their modern descendants in many parts of world, producing a line of melody over a drone. Of their musical function we know little for certain, except that clerical musicians used them to teach poor singers to stay in tune.[62] Outside the choir school the symfony was already a favourite with itinerant blind musicians by the early fourteenth century,[63] and its history in the later Middle Ages is one of rapid decline into the beggar-instruments mentioned by Renaissance writers.

WINDS AND PERCUSSION

By the end of the thirteenth century the organ had shed the old slider system known to Hucbald, Notker, and Theophilus, in favour of keys which allowed the player much more scope for performing melody—and even written polyphony.[64] There were also portative organs which a single player could carry, bellow, and play all at once; these often used buttons rather than keys well into the fifteenth century. A recurrent feature of both portative and positive organs is a long pipe (or it may be several pipes) at one end of the rank, probably used to produce a sustained tone while the organist improvised above on a keyboard which, by c. 1330, was already chromatic for the most part.[65]

Other wind instruments are shrouded in obscurity. The transverse flute appears in the celebrated *Hortus Deliciarum* illustrated c. 1200 for Abbess Herrad of Hohenbourg in Alsace,[66] but the instrument is barely encountered again in pictorial sources until the fourteenth century. Since the *Hortus Deliciarum* owes much to Byzantine models, and transverse flutes are shown in Byzantine manuscripts as early as

[61] The famous drawing reproduced by Martin Gerbert from a lost manuscript of the twelfth or thirteenth century, and purporting to show a symfony with rotating blades that touch all three strings at once, has undoubtedly been tampered with and cannot be trusted. See Page, 'Medieval *organistrum* and *symphonia*', 79 ff.

[62] So says the author of the anonymous *Summa Musicae* (Gerbert, *Scriptores*, III, 216).

[63] The association between the symfony and blind musicians is mentioned by Nicholas de Lyra in his monumental commentary upon the Bible (Page, 'Medieval *organistrum* and *symphonia*', 73, gives text and translation).

[64] The Robertsbridge codex (British Library Additional MS 28550) contains six compositions (two of which are incomplete) which are probably intended for a positive organ. They are all florid and require an almost entirely chromatic keyboard. The pieces are edited in W. Apel, *Keyboard Music of the Fourteenth and Fifteenth Centuries*, American Institute of Musicology, *Corpus of Early Keyboard Music*, 1 (1963), 1–9. Apel (ibid. 4) dates the leaves to c. 1320, but it is conceivable that they date from as much as fifty years later.

[65] Jacques de Liège refers to organ keyboards where the tone is divided 'almost everywhere' (quasi ubique) into two semitones. See R. Bragard, *Jacobi Leodiensis Speculum Musicae*, 7 vols., American Institute of Musicology, *Corpus Scriptorum de Musica*, 3 (1955–73), VI, 146 and 187.

[66] For the illustration see Panum, *Stringed Instruments of the Middle Ages*, figure 135.

the eleventh century, the trustworthiness of Herrad of Hohenbourg's picture as a witness to the currency of the instrument in Europe *c.* 1200 is very uncertain.

The early history of the duct flute (recorder) is even more patchy than that of the transverse flute. Literary references to *fleustes* and *fistulae* reveal little, and most pictorial representations are crude and perfunctory. In all probability the duct flute existed throughout the Middle Ages in popular culture; by the thirteenth century there is firm pictorial evidence for the one-man ensemble of three-holed duct flute and tabor.

Of the reed instruments known in the twelfth and thirteenth centuries only the bagpipe has a history that can be reconstructed with any certainty. Reed instruments fed by a flexible reservoir (so that they may sound continuously without recourse to the technique of circular breathing) were known in Antiquity, although there is no decisive iconographical record of them in the Middle Ages before the twelfth century.[67] In the thirteenth, the pictorial evidence becomes abundant and bagpipes appear both with single and double chanters and with or without drone pipes (predictably, called *bourdons* in Old French). The rustic associations—as well as the obvious sexual symbolism—of the instrument seem to have been very strong.

The brass instruments included the various kinds of trumpets, (in Old French *buisines*, *trompes*, and *gresles*) used in both military and domestic contexts for fanfares and signals. Some of these instruments may have been borrowed from the armies which the Crusaders encountered in the Middle East, for the horrifying sound of the Saracens' martial instruments is often mentioned in Western chronicles and reverberates down the centuries until at least the fifteenth. The Crusaders certainly borrowed the pairs of small kettledrums, or *nakers* (the word is of Arabic origin), that they often combined with trumpets 'to move the souls of men ... in martial games and tournaments' in the words of Johannes de Grocheio. Early information is sparse, but in the fifteenth century the two drums in a pair of nakers were built to produce different pitches. Snares were used as early as the fourteenth century.

INSTRUMENTALISTS' REPERTORY IN THE TWELFTH AND THIRTEENTH CENTURIES

An enormous number of compositions, both monophonic and poly-

[67] The literary record is confused by pseudo-Jerome's epistle to Dardanus; this text, of unknown date, but certainly in existence by the ninth century and possibly of Late Antique origin, mentions an instrument called *chorus* which is either a bag-pipe or bladder pipe. See Page, 'Biblical Instruments in Medieval Manuscript Illustration', *Early Music*, 5 (1977), 299–309.

phonic, have survived from the twelfth and thirteenth centuries, and amongst these are some pieces which may be regarded as instrumental in the sense that they were exclusively or primarily designed for instrumental execution. There are, however, very few such works—scarcely more than the *estampies* added to the Manuscrit du Roi in a fourteenth-century hand (see Ex. 162).[68]

The textless parts in polyphonic compositions, principally the motet, present a more delicate problem. In the days of Jean Beck and Pierre Aubry, for example, it was widely believed that the textless tenors of thirteenth century motets were designed for instrumental execution (see Chap. XIII). This was held to explain why these parts were copied without words (save an incipit indentifying the source of the melody) and why they were notated, in contrast to the texted upper parts, with a preponderance of ligatures.[69] It is difficult to attack this hypothesis or to defend it, since instrumentation simply does not exist as a subject in thirteenth-century writings on music apart from the treatises of Johannes de Grocheio and Jerome of Moravia.

The way Grocheio structures his discussion of the musical forms used in Paris, however, suggests that instruments did not normally perform in learned polyphonic forms such as the motet. Grocheio divides music into three categories.[70] The first comprises monophonic (*simplex*), civil, or laymen's music, and embraces trouvère song, dance-songs, the *chanson de geste*, and the various instrumental forms described in his account of the repertory of the *viella*. The second category comprises composed, measured, or rule-bound music and includes the motet, organum, and conductus. The final classification embraces all liturgical music. This three-fold categorization is clearly articulated and carefully respected in Grocheio's treatise, so it may be significant that he places the discussion of instruments in the first category: monophonic, civil or laymen's music. The implication (and it is no more than that) seems to be that instruments did not normally participate in the category of composed, measured, and rule-bound music in which he discusses motet and conductus.[71]

The threshold of the fourteenth century is an appropriate place to

[68] For an attempt to read a great deal into one of the surviving pieces that seems to be an instrumental composition see W. Arlt, 'The Reconstruction of Instrumental Music: The Interpretation of the Earliest Practical Sources', in S. Boorman, ed., *Studies in the Performance of Late Medieval Music* (Cambridge, 1983), 75–100.

[69] P. Aubry, *Cent Motets du XIIIe siècle*, 3 vols., (Paris, 1908), iii, 147–59.

[70] Rohloff, *Quellenhandschriften*, 124.

[71] See L. Gushee, 'Two Central Places: Paris and the French Court in the Early Fourteenth Century', in H. Kühn and P. Nitsche, eds., *Bericht über den Internationalen Musikwissenschaftlichen Kongress Berlin 1974* (Kassel, etc., 1980), 143.

end—or to begin—a historical survey of musical instruments. The fortunes of the *viella* gradually waned in the later Middle Ages, at least to the extent that by *c.* 1400 the harp had become the leading court-instrument, re-asserting the ancient right of an open-stringed instrument to rule supreme. By the later fourteenth century the psaltery had become, in certain quarters, a toy one gave to children 'to stop them doing harm'; so there is a reason why the Christ child sometimes leans towards an angel with a psaltery in later medieval art.[72] The rotta was regarded as archaic by Petrus de Abano in the early fourteenth century,[73] and among the fingerboard instruments the citole may have been extinct as early as *c.* 1350.[74] We are reminded of a dictum in Johannes de Grocheio's treatise: 'Human art and its practical application can always be improved'; in the later Middle Ages the desire to experiment and develop which is so characteristic of musical culture in the West overwhelmed many of the instruments that Grocheio knew, and transformed others.

[72] The view of the psaltery as a children's instrument is from Nicole Oresme's translation of Aristotle's *Politics* with commentary, undertaken for Charles V of France. For the text see *Transactions of the American Philosophical Society*, 60 (1970), 352.

[73] Petrus de Abano, *Expositio Problematum Aristotelis* (Mantua, 1475), *Particula* 19, problem 39.

[74] Wright, 'Medieval Gittern and Citole', 32.

XI

EARLY POLYPHONY

By Sarah Fuller

The first epoch of Western polyphony may be said to end with the emergence of a distinctive, highly artificial, and influential polyphonic style in the environs of Paris toward the end of the twelfth century. Its inception is less easily fixed in time, for the earliest texts to speak directly and unambiguously of singing in two or more parts treat such singing as familiar practice, while venturing no comment as to its antiquity or origins. These texts stem from approximately the last half of the ninth century—even their dating lacks precision—and establish the recognition of polyphony as a discrete phenomenon during the 800s at the latest.

The nature of *organum* or *diaphonia*, as the singing of two or more specially related lines was called, changed radically over the three centuries of earliest record. In the late ninth century, the *vox organalis* or second voice was a subsidiary line, generated note-by-note from the pitches of a pre-existent melody. Some two hundred years later, by the early twelfth century, this voice was an equal—even dominant— partner in the polyphonic complex, co-ordinated with the principal voice, yet free to pursue its own course melodically and rhythmically, and to adorn single pitches in the principal voice with flourishes of many notes. The story of this transformation is not a continuous one; it must be pieced together from fragments of information which, in so far as they can be placed at all, are distributed unevenly in time and locale, scattered across Western Europe and Britain. Only in exceptional, isolated instances is it possible to ascertain just when and where specific practices held sway. In consequence, the following account must be read rather as a broad outline of general trends than as an exact chronicle of uniform evolution.

Our perspective on early polyphony is inevitably shaped both by accidents of history, which have determined what sources of knowledge have survived, and by the nature of the extant sources, which control the kind of information available to us. The chief sources can be broadly divided into two categories: on the one hand, treatises of didactic intent; on the other, notations of music, both substantial repertories and isolated individual pieces. These two sorts of material are far from equivalent, their relationships far from unproblematic. While the theorists on the whole transmit generalized principles and rationalized accounts of practice, the notations transmit specific compositions in contexts of varying definition. The notated compositions cannot be taken automatically as paradigms merely by virtue of their existence. Factors of aesthetic choice, liturgical function and ritual use, susceptibility to recovery through habits of improvisation, even personal pride may have variously triggered the impulse to notate. Both kinds of information—theorists' accounts and notated pieces—contribute importantly to reconstruction of the historical record, such of it as may be recovered. But the relative contribution of each fluctuates greatly between the 800s and the 1100s. The theorists dominate in the earlier portion of this period. Theirs is the main lens that focuses our image of the earliest polyphony. Even the one large collection of *organa* that survives from the earliest period, that of Winchester, resists interpretation except through the medium of the theorists. During the 1100s, collections of polyphony in decipherable notation proliferate, while the number and contribution of theoretical works decline. The music now becomes the direct medium for our impressions about the nature and style of polyphonic song. This increase in notation of polyphony may be linked in part to a growing appreciation of the distinctive quality of individual compositions. Such a degree of choice now entered into the conception of a polyphonic piece that general rules for extemporization were of little aid in preserving specific musical results. Compositions—deliberately thought-out pieces—had to be fixed in some more durable mode. At the same time, theorists, while recognizing the inadequacy of tradition-al concepts to account for changed musical practices, had yet to frame a new theoretical matrix that would allow them to treat of organum systematically. Uncertainty about the intrinsic nature of organum limits the usefulness of the later theoretical literature as a direct source of knowledge about the polyphony of its time.

The incompleteness and contingency of the historical record is also evidenced by geographical considerations. *Organum* is known to have been practised in various Western rites—Milanese, Hispanic, Urban-Roman, Gregorian. Yet the main sources of information about it (notations and descriptive writings) stem from the Gregorian tradi-tion. Even within that tradition, theorists such as Guido of Arezzo and John of Afflighem scrupulously observe that procedures for making organum differ conspicuously from one locale to another. Their comments may stand corroborated by late traces of an 'archaic' Milanese tradition that reveal a penchant for singing in seconds, quite foreign to the canons of early theorists. Perception of that tradition as peripheral may be justified, but may be due largely to the fact that it left no early records and had no ninth- or tenth-century apologists. The sense of a mainstream of development, inevitable in an account that must rely on concrete, extant documentation, should be tempered by reflection that practices of polyphony were almost surely richer and more varied than the documentation shows.

ORIGINS

The genesis of Western polyphony has never been traced. The earliest unequivocal European references, none demonstrably earlier than the second half of the ninth century, already regard organum as a familiar phenomenon. Indeed, they use it to illustrate a more abstract (and perhaps less widely understood) theoretical concept, that of *symphonia* or *consonantia*. So Hucbald, trying to explain that octave, fifth and fourth belong in a category apart from other intervals writes (*c.* 900):

A *consonantia* [*symphonia*] is then a proportionally determined and concordant mixture of two sounds, which will not come about unless two sounds, produced from different sources, come together in one musical combination, as occurs when a man's voice and a boy's sound at the same time, or indeed in that which they usually call 'making organum'.

(Consonantia siquidem est duorum sonorum rata et concordabilis permixtio, quae non aliter constabit, nisi duo altrinsecus editi soni in unam simul modulationem conveniant, ut fit, cum virilis ac puerilis vox pariter sonuerit; vel etiam in eo, quod consuete organizationem vocant.)

Since the theorists assume organum to be a well-known practice and show no interest in explaining its origins, scholars interested in that question have been forced to look elsewhere for clues. Two primary lines of inquiry have been tried, one ethnomusicological, exploring parallels with polyphony in other cultures, the other etymological, tracking and interpreting Latin texts in which the word *organum* and related compounds such as *vox organica* or *organicum melos* occur.

Study of musical traditions of non-Western cultures has brought to light many varieties of performance in which distinct musical events occur simultaneously.[1] Categorizing them according to conventional Western terminology, the varieties include: heterophony; parallelism

---

[1] See Walter Wiora, 'Zwischen Einstimmigkeit und Mehrstimmigkeit', in Walther Vetter, ed., *Festschrift Max Schneider zum achtzigsten Geburtstag* (Leipzig, [1955]), 319–34, and Marius Schneider, 'Primitive Music', *NOHM*, I (London, 1957), 20–3.

at various intervals (fifths, fourths, thirds, seconds) and with varying degress of adherence to a principal interval; imitative overlap, sometimes fleeting, sometimes an extended round or canon; ostinato or drone accompaniments to a melody; contrapuntal combination of independent melodies. It must be acknowledged from the start that such descriptive terms reflect the bias of Western observers and call attention to aspects of the music that are not necessarily those the culture itself takes as primary. It is, furthermore, a matter of dispute whether all such phenomena should be classed as polyphonic. Heterophony, in which two performers produce the 'same' melody, but with frequent slight deviations from the unison or octave, or a song accompanied by pitched drums, would seem to be of a different order from a canonic round. But is a melody against a drone, or against a free ostinato, more or less polyphonic than any of these? In effect, it proves impossible to draw a rigid dividing line between monophony and polyphony. (The notion that it can or should be done is primarily a convenience of pedagogy.) One of the best lessons ethnomusicology can teach about the 'origins' of Western polyphony is that it is highly suspect and, in the last analysis, arbitrary, to try to pin down an exact point of separation between monophonic and polyphonic music.

Some investigators have thought by study of non-Western musical cultures to uncover a definite phylogeny or sequence of evolutionary development in polyphony that would be universal in scope and would allow any manifestation of polyphony, from the simplest to the most complex, to be located in a specific phase of the process. If such a sequence could be found, then early Western organum could be assigned a definite position along the path of development. If not placed at the very beginning, its prior stages of development would be supplied automatically. No such inevitable sequence of development has been discovered. In fact, observations have led to the opposite conclusion: that the manifold manifestations of polyphony (in its broadest sense) exhibit no co-ordinated, orderly, or sequential pattern of relationships. Societies that cultivate any sort of polyphony generally practise several species, all of which have equal weight as legitimate practices.

The fact that varied practices of simple polyphony do exist in different and widely separated cultures has led some to suppose that early Western polyphony arose in a casual, spontaneous way and became fixed in certain types only as a result of theoretical codification of, and perhaps selection among, informal performance practices. An alternative perspective regards the earliest polyphony of which we have explicit record as simply invented, implying a somewhat deliberate act of conception and subsequent cultivation. There is no sure way to assess the validity of either hypothesis. Both deliberate conception and informal practice may have contributed to the crystallization of the organum described in early European treatises, but the relative contribution of either is imponderable.

Etymological investigation of the term *organum* has contributed to the inquiry into origins through elucidation of the range of meanings of the word and through reinterpretation of the sense of the term as applied to polyphony. A comprehensive study of the term *organum* and associated compounds (*vox organica, organicum melos*) within late antique and medieval texts has shown that the earliest uses of these terms bore no connotation of polyphony.[2] The chief strands of meaning to emerge from careful scrutiny of contexts are:

(1) *organum*: generically a musical instrument, especially one tuned exactly in simple proportions; specifically, the organ (especially as a plural noun).

(2) *organum*: a sacred song of praise, a psalm or even the entire Book of Psalms.

(3) *organicus*: an adjective indicating proportional order, mathematical exactitude, theoretical propriety in musical sounds.

The nuances of any particular instance of *organum/organicus* may be manifold and can only be fully understood within the plenary spectrum of usage. The few passages cited here can but hint at the range and problems of interpretation.

For the sense of *organum* as a musical instrument, one need look no further than the Vulgate, Psalm 150, vv. 1, 4:

Praise the Lord in His holiness	Laudate Dominum in sanctis eius
Praise Him with drum and chorus	Laudate eum in tympano et choro
Praise Him with stringed instruments and organ.	Laudate eum in cordis et organo

The translation of *organo* as 'organ' might appear to be straightforward, even obvious from the context, but St Augustine, for one, equivocates. In his commentary on this psalm in *Enarrationes in Psalmos* (*c.* 414–16), he writes:

Organum, however, is the general name for all musical instruments, although there is already a custom that properly speaking *organa* are those instruments that are inflated with bellows. I do not judge which is meant here.

[2] Fritz Reckow, 'Organum-Begriff und frühe Mehrstimmigkeit', *Forum Musicologicum*, i (*Basler Studien zur Musikgeschichte*, i) (Berne, 1975), 32.

(Organum autem generale nomen est omnium vasorum musicorum; quamvis iam obtinuerit consuetudo, ut organa proprie dicantur ea quae inflantur follibus: quod genus significatum hic esse non arbitror.)

Cassiodorus, writing somewhat later, hesitates not at all but in his *Expositio Psalmorum* reads a direct reference to the organ:

Organum thus is something rather like a tower formed of various pipes, in which, by the breath of bellows, a great abundance of sound is produced.

(*Organum* itaque est quasi turris quaedam diversis fistulis fabricata, quibus flatu follium vox copiosissima destinatur.)

Nearly as widespread and common is a meaning of song or hymn of praise. This early Merovingian hymn juxtaposes *organa* with *carmina* in a context that implies their close affinity.

Exaudi petimus organa carmina
Extendensque manum porrige dexteram.

(Hear, we pray thee, *organa* [and] songs
And, reaching forth, stretch out thy right hand.)

Isidore of Seville frankly equates *organum* with the entire Book of Psalms in his *Etymologies* (seventh century):

The Book of Psalms is called *psalterium* in Greek, *nabla* in Hebrew, and *organum* in Latin.

(Psalmorum liber Graece psalterium, Hebraice nabla, Latine organum dicitur.)

The word *organum* is relatively frequent in texts of the first generation of Aquitanian proses, a fact which has been taken to support polyphonic performance of the proses themselves. The contexts, however, seldom provide sure support for such interpretation and often, indeed, encourage an Isidorian reading, as in this verse from the All Saints prose *Hodierna dies rutilat*:

Casta virginea turma	Let the chaste virginal crowd
albicans super lilia	whiter than the lily
hymnica concinat organa	sing hymns and psalms
voce pudica.	with modest voice.

A similar translation—psalm, song of praise—seems apt to the opening of this Pentecost prose, especially considering the verb in the third line. The plural form argues against interpreting *organa* as polyphony here:

Cantemus organa	Let us sing
pulchra satis atque decora	many beautiful and fitting *organa*

Deo nostro psallentes	psalming to our God
qui pro nobis sumere	who deigned to assume
dignatus est terrena.	mortality for us.

A third sense of *organum* as that which is proportionately measured and exact would appear to flow more from secular currents of culture, to be part of a relatively scientific vocabulary. A glimpse of the theoretical cast of *organicus* may be caught in these lines from the poem 'Aurea personet lira', an entry in the older Cambridge Song-book (eleventh century):

> Philomele demus laudes in voce organica
> Dulce melos decantantes sicut docet musica
> Sine cuius arte vera nulla valent cantica.

> (Let us give praise to the nightingale in *voce organica*
> Sweetly singing melodies, as *musica* teaches
> Without whose art no songs are worth anything.)

Praise *in voce organica* is best construed as being rendered with well-tuned voice, the pitches regulated by exact mathematical proportions as demanded by *musica*, the fundamental principles of music. Such connotations can be traced well back, often in connection with the concept of precise motion among the heavenly bodies. A fable related in the Timaeus commentary of Chalcidius (fourth century) character-izes the motion of the planets as *organicus* in a way that neatly combines the instrumental and theoretical connotations of that word:

cum caelum ascenderet, primitus transeuntum per ea quae in motu planetum ad organicum modum personabant a se inventae lyrae similem miratum quod imago a se inventae operis in caelo quoque reperiretur stellarum collocatione quae causa esset concinentiae recensere.

(while he [Mercury] was ascending through the heavens, first passing through regions which resounded with the motion of the planets *ad organicum modum*, he marvelled at the similitude to the lyre he had invented, because the idea of his invention was also found in heaven in the arrangement of the stars, and in it the reason for [their] harmony might be found.)

'Ad organicum modum' cuts two ways. It conveys not only 'in an instrumental manner', similar to the lyre, but also 'in a proportionally ordered way', by the exact, immutable relationships by which plane-tary motion is governed and lyres are tuned.

It is this last strand of meaning that best conforms with the sense of *organum* projected in the earliest treatises to deal with the musical phenomenon called by that name and that most plausibly accounts for the adoption of this noun as a name for 'singing in fifths and fourths'. Only relatively late, *c.* 1100, when the original premises from which *organum* derived its legitimacy were discredited, did any music theorist seize upon the instrumental sense of *organum* in an attempt to supply a plausible etymology for the current popular name of polyphony. For example, John of Afflighem, in *De Musica*, chapter 23, wrote:

Qui canendi modus vulgariter organum dicitur, eo quod vox humana apte dissonans similitudinem exprimat instrumenti quod organum vocatur.

(This method of singing [*diaphonia*] is commonly called *organum*, because the human voice, aptly differing in sound, resembles the instrument which is called an organ.)

EARLY ORGANUM THEORY

The earliest extant texts definitely to employ organum as the name for a kind of music are at the same time the first treatises to describe the practice of singing organum. These are the *Musica Enchiriadis* and the *Scolica Enchiriadis*,[3] both thought to date *c.* 850–900 and to have originated in the region of Laon. In both these treatises, organum refers not to the multiplicity of voices sung but to the quality of the sounds, all in theory generated from mathematically precise relationships of 2:1, 3:2 and 4:3.[4] Such sounds constituted a privileged group of intervals known as *symphoniae* (octave, fifth, fourth and their compounds up to the double octave). The *Musica Enchiriadis* chapter that initiates the discussion of organum is headed 'De proprietate symphoniarum' (On the Properties of *Symphoniae*), an announcement that squarely emphasizes interval type rather then polyphonic quality. Organum is simply the usual name for singing in *symphoniae*.

Now let us consider the nature and sense of *Symphoniae*, that is, how these pitches [those just defined in the Daseian system] relate to each other when sung together. This is indeed what we call diaphonic song or, customarily, organum.

(Nunc id, quod proprie simphoniae dicuntur et sunt, id est qualiter eadem voces sese in unum canendo habeant, prosequamur. Haec namque est, quam diaphoniam cantilenam vel assuete organum nuncupamus.)

The *Scolica Enchiriadis* concurs with this attitude in proclaiming the

---

[3] *Musica et Scolica Enchiriadis una cum aliquibus tractatulis adjunctis*, ed. Hans Schmid (*Bayerische Akademie der Wissenschaften Veröffentlichungen der Musikhistorischen Kommission*, 3) (Munich, 1981).

[4] A more detailed discussion of the following points may be found in S. Fuller, 'Theoretical Foundations of Early Organum Theory', *AcM*, 53 (1981), 52–84.

essence of an organal voice to be not its 'otherness' but its relationship by *symphonia* to a given chant:

I define the principal voice as the song itself; the organal voice as the one joined to it by the relationship of a *symphonia*.

(Principalem enim vocem absolutam cantionem dico, organalem vero, quae huic subiungitur symphoniae ratione.)

Because in principle the *symphonia* relating the voices remains constant from start to finish of a piece, this earliest kind of organum is often called 'parallel organum' by modern writers. However, as the instructions for realizing organum at the fourth attest, parallelism is not a consistent feature of the music. This early organum might be characterized more aptly as 'symphonic organum', were it not for the eighteenth-century connotations of the modifier.

The *Musica* and the *Scolica Enchiriadis* are not the only treatises to explain the early practice of organum. Table I lists those that are known, seven in number, and summarizes basic data about each.[5] The teaching of organum is by no means the chief subject of the most substantial treatises in this array (Nos. 1, 2, and 7). The *Musica Enchiriadis* and the *Scolica Enchiriadis* focus primarily on a pitch system and the important interrelationships among its elements. As already observed, they treat organum as a concrete embodiment of the properties of *symphoniae*. For Guido, in the *Micrologus*,[6] a pitch system and its articulation in modes and chant is similarly primary. His two chapters on diaphony come as a loose appendage to the main text. Only the terse Cologne treatise can claim to be an independent essay on organum, and even it is sandwiched between the *Musica* and the *Scolica Enchiriadis* in two of four sources and is attached to a treatise on organ-pipe mensuration in a third. As it comes down to us, then, early writing on organum is typically embedded within a larger theoretical framework, presented virtually as a branch of plainsong lore. This fact is significant on two counts. First, it deepens the ambiguity of a categorical distinction between monophony and polyphony and forces careful scrutiny of whether the writers conceive singing in fourths, fifths, and octaves to be in essence a combination of

[5] For Nos. 3, 4, 5a, and 6 of Table I, see Schmid, *Musica et Scolica Enchiriadis*; for No. 5b (and also the organum sections of Nos. 1–2) in German translation, see Ernst Waeltner, *Die Lehre vom Organum bis zur Mitte des 11. Jahrhunderts*, i, *Münchener Veröffentlichungen zur Musikgeschichte*, 13 (Tutzing, 1975). For No. 8, see Albert Seay, 'Guglielmo Roffredi's Summa Musicae Artis', *Musica disciplina*, 24 (1970), 69; Michel Huglo, 'A Propos de la *Summa Artis Musicae* attribué a Guglielmo Roffredi', *Revue de musicologie*, 58 (1972), 90.

[6] Ed. Joseph Smits van Waesberghe, *Corpus Scriptorum de Musica*, 4 (1955). It appears in English, trans. Warren Babb, *Hucbald, Guido and John On Music* (New Haven, 1978).

TABLE 1 Early Organum Treatises

Treatise	Date/Sources	Nature	Categories of Organum	Theoretical Principles
1. *Musica Enchiriadis* (*ME*)	mid-late 9th cent. numerous sources	Independent treatise dealing with many aspects of music. Organum considered in section headed 'On the property of *symphoniae*'.	Organum at the 4th with 8ve doubling (variable intervals). Strict organum at the 5th with 8ve doubling.	Daseian tetrachord structure. Avoidance of inconsonance in organum at the 4th
2. *Scolica Enchiriadis* (*SE*)	mid/late 9th cent. usually paired with *ME*; numerous sources	Independent treatise in dialogue form. Covers many aspects of music. Section on organum headed 'On the *symphoniae*'.	Strict singing at the 8ve, and at the 5th with 8ve doubling. Singing at the 4th with 8ve doubling (variable intervals).	Daseian tetrachord structure. Modal integrity in strict singing
3. Bamberg Dialogues I and II	copied 10th cent. possible origin in 9th; unique source	Insertions in a copy of *ME* but dialogue format as in *SE*. Organum the sole topic. Heading: 'Again concerning the 4th, 5th, and 8ve and the *symphoniae*'.	Singing at the 4th (variable intervals). (Dialogue I refers in passing to strict singing at the 8ve and at the 5th.)	Daseian tetrachord structure. Modal integrity (as in *SE*)
4. Paris Treatise	5 sources, earliest 11th cent.	Appears in a distinct version of *ME*, replacing its usual organum chapters. Heading: 'On organum'.	Organum at the 4th (variable intervals). Doubling at the 8ve mentioned but not emphasized.	Modal final

5a. Cologne Treatise	?late 9th cent. 4 sources, between *ME* and *SE* in 2	Brief independent treatise. Content closely related to Paris treatise, but more condensed in presentation.	Organum at the 4th (variable intervals).	Modal final Unison at phrase endings
5b. Sélestat Treatise	late 10th cent. unique source	Two brief insertions in a treatise on organ-pipe mensuration, reconstructred as a separate 'treatise' by Waeltner. Continues as Cologne treatise.	Organum at the 4th and 5th.	Unison phrase endings (implied).
6. Prague Treatise	10th cent. unique source	Independent treatise on many aspects of music, much of it derived from *ME*.	Organum at the 4th (variable intervals). Strict organum at the 5th. 8ve doubling.	Daseian tetrachord structure
7. *Micrologus* of Guido of Arezzo	c. 1025 numerous sources	Independent treatise on many aspects of music. Organum discussed in a late chapter headed 'On diaphony, that is, the precepts of organum'.	Organum at the 4th (variable intervals). Strict organum at the 4th with 8ve doubling mentioned.	Affinity of pitches *Occursus* Hierarchy of intervals
8. 'Musica est motus vocum'	c. 1142	Section on *diaphonia* derived from Guido's *Micrologus*.	Diaphonia (variable intervals, unison to 4th).	*Occursus* Hierarchy of intervals

Nos. 1–5a and 6 are edited in H. Schmid, *Musica et Scolica Enchiriadis una cum aliquibus tractatulis adiunctis, Bayerische Akademie der Wissenschaften Veröffentlichungen der Musikhistorischen Kommission*, vol. 3 (Munich, 1981). Numbers 3–5b and the organum sections of 1 and 2 are printed with German translation in E. L. Waeltner, *Die Lehre vom Organum bis zur Mitte des 11. Jahrhunderts, Münchener Veröffentlichungen zur Musikgeschichte*, vol. 13 (Tutzing; 1975). No. 7 is edited by Joseph Smits van Waesberghe, *Corpus Scriptorum de Musica* (American Institute of Musicology, 1955). An English translation by Warren Babb appears in *Hucbald, Guido and John On Music* (New Haven, 1978).

distinct elements (hence polyphonic) or a duplication of one (hence essentially monophonic). Second, it helps explain differences in teaching methods manifest even among treatises allied with the *Musica Enchiriadis*, for these differences are largely grounded in disparate theoretical systems.

While early organum theory describes singing at the fourth, the fifth and the octave, it qualifies only the fourth and the fifth as organal intervals. The octave merely duplicates. Fourth and fifth are organal, and also diaphonic, precisely because they break from 'uniform' singing. As the *Musica Enchiriadis* writes:

This [singing in *symphoniae*] then is what we usually call diaphonic song, or customarily organum. But it is called diaphony because it does not consist in singing uniformly but in the concordant agreement of separate sounds. While this name is common to all *symphoniae*, it particularly applies to the fourth and the fifth.

(Haec namque est, quam diaphoniam cantilenam vel assuete organum nuncupamus. Dicta autem diaphonia, quod non uniformi canore constet, sed concentu concorditer dissono. Quod licet omnium simphoniarum est commune, in diatessaron tamen ac diapente hoc nomen optinuit.)

This opinion is echoed in the Paris treatise and in the *Micrologus*, although with respect only to the fourth. Both the exclusion of the octave from the ranks of truly organal intervals and the notion of not singing uniformly—or, as Guido puts it, when 'discrete pitches both diverge concordantly in sound and concord in diverging' ('disiunctae ab invicem voces et concorditer dissonant et dissonanter concordant')—point toward consciousness of what we understand intuitively to be the essence of polyphony: at least two distinct musical elements sounding simultaneously.

The various early descriptions of organum agree in associating it with one or more of the *symphoniae* and in always locating the main organal voice below the principal one. They attest an overall consistency of practice: organum at the fifth is strictly parallel, that at the fourth deviates from parallelism in a regulated way that frequently produces reiterated boundary tones in the organal voice. Here, however, the agreement ends. The various writers concur neither on the procedures for making correct organum nor on the principles underlying these procedures. Instead, the extant treatises present us with three separate strands of teaching. The oldest is represented by the *Musica Enchiriadis*, the *Scolica*, and the Bamberg Dialogues. These texts teach two kinds of organum: (1) an organum at the fifth in which the organal voice (*vox organalis*) strictly follows below the principal line (*vox principalis*) and in which either voice or both may be doubled at the octave (Ex. 163), and (2) an organum at the fourth which is parallel in principle but not in fact, and in which octave doublings are also freely permitted (Ex. 164).[7] Organum at the fourth has its own 'natural law' which forbids the organal voice to descend more than one pitch below the tetrachord in which the chant phrase begins and ends. The organal voice in this kind of organum is characterized by 'boundary tones', which it sustains when the chant is in the lower region of any tetrachord.

Ex. 163

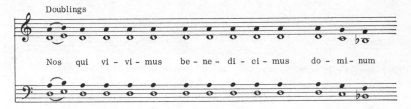

Nos qui vi - vi - mus be - ne - di - ci - mus do - mi - num

ex hoc nunc et us - que in se - cu - lum

● = principal voice
○ = organal voice

The instructions for producing these two types of organum depend on the particular concept of musical order taught in the *Musica* and the *Scolica Enchiriadis*, the Daseian system in which four immutable tetrachords of identical tone-semitone-tone structure succeed each other by the disjunction of a tone. This background system is the basis for two contrasting explanations advanced for the 'natural law' of organum at the fourth. According to the *Musica Enchiriadis*, this law arises from the necessity of avoiding the non-consonant sound (a tritone, although not identified as such) that inevitably results when

[7] For the original notation of Ex. 164, see Heinrich Besseler and Peter Gülke, *Schriftbild der mehrstimmigen Musik (Musikgeschichte in Bildern*, iii/5) (Leipzig, 1973), plate 3, p. 29.

Ex. 164

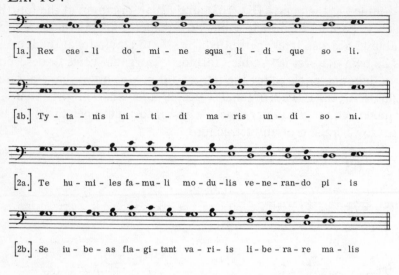

[1a.] Rex cae - li   do - mi - ne squa - li - di - que   so - li.

[1b.] Ty - ta - nis   ni - ti - di   ma - ris   un - di - so - ni.

[2a.] Te   hu - mi - les fa - mu - li   mo - du - lis ve - ne - ran - do pi - is

[2b.] Se   iu - be - as fla - gi - tant va - ri - is   li - be - ra - re   ma - lis

● = principal voice
○ = organal voice

the second pitch (*deuterus*) in any tetrachord sounds simultaneously with the fourth pitch below it, the third member (*tritus*) of the adjacent lower tetrachord. According to the *Scolica*, organum at the fourth deviates from strict parallelism and hence requires special rules because modal integrity—as manifested in equivalent Daseian symbols—cannot be preserved when a melody is duplicated at the fourth below (*protus* will be answered by *deuterus*, *deuterus* by *tritus*, etc.). Conversely, organum at the fifth can maintain strict parallelism because the Daseian system ensures that pitches a fifth apart preserve the same modal quality (*protus* is always answered by *protus*, *deuterus* by *deuterus*, etc.).

At the *symphonia* of the fourth, the organal voice cannot accompany the principal voice as simply and absolutely as at the fifth ... While at the fifth and the octave there is always a recurrence of the modes or tones ... on the contrary, at the fourth the lower voice does not respond to the higher one with the same mode. Hence, of necessity, each must be duplicated at the octave with its own individual mode.

(In diatessaron symphonia non ita simpliciter et absolute sicut in diapente vocem principalem organalis vox comitatur ... Siquidem dum quintis et octavis locis semper sit troporum vel tonorum reversio ... E contrario vero in diatessaron dum vox inferior a superiorem vocem quartis locis non eodem respondeat tropo, necesse est, ut principali et organali voci non eodem, sed singulis a sua octava suo tropo respondeatur.)

A second strand of teaching appears in the Paris and Cologne treatises. These works concern themselves only with organum at the fourth and fashion the organal voice according to the modal final of the given chant, rather than with reference to the Daseian tetrachord system. The procedure for producing this organum is stated succinctly in the Cologne treatise as a series of three rules:

(1) One pitch/voice responds to another at the fourth.

(2) At the end of most phrases (defined as a verbal unit punctuated by a colon or comma) the voices join together either on the modal final or on one of the notes adjacent to it.

(3) When a phrase descends to end on the final or on either pitch directly adjacent to it, the organal voice may descend no lower than the note immediately below the final.

Because the second and third rules take precedence over the first, the organal voice stands stationary in response to the plainchant at least as often as it parallels the chant. (The single extended example from the Paris treatise, Table I, No. 4, also has much unison coupling of the voices, a feature not predicted in the rules.) This pedagogical system includes categories of high, middle, and low organum to accommodate phrase endings that stand outside the region of the main final. The fragment from the sequence 'Benedicta sit beata' reproduced as Ex. 165(i) shows a succession of middle, low, and middle organum segments, ending respectively on G (final), E (adjacent to the 'lower associate' of the final), and G (marked by arrows in the example). A later phrase, Ex. 165(ii), ascends dramatically to high organum and there undergoes a change in *tonus* (G is still the final but changes function from *tetrardus finalis* to *protus finalis*), which remains in effect to the end.

The organum produced by the Paris/Cologne rules superficially resembles that taught in the *Musica Enchiriadis* but differs considerably in detail. Boundary pitches are not restricted to a specific tetrachord position (the *tetrardus*) but fall variously depending on the final and the local phrase ending (they are F, D, and c in Ex. 165). *Deuterus* and *tritus* (in *Musica Enchiriadis* terms) do sound simultaneously (marked * in Ex. 165(i)), causing a conflict between fidelity to the *symphoniae* and the familiar chant melody or fidelity to the Daseian notational symbols. The substantive difference, though, lies not in the musical style but in the pedagogical approach, and it is in this respect that the advantages of the Paris/Cologne doctrine are most plain. Unlike that of the *Musica* and the *Scolica Enchiriadis*, the

Ex. 165

(i)

Al - le - lu - ia

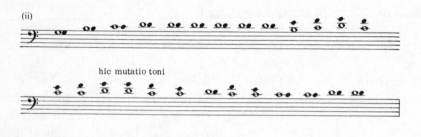

(ii)

hic mutatio toni

● = principal voice

○ = organal voice

Paris/Cologne doctrine does not require allegiance to the Daseian tetrachord system. It only presupposes modal categories based on the final note of the chant, which were the common stock of chant theory. It is inviting to speculate that the Paris and Cologne discourses on organum were attached to the *Enchiriadis* treatises (the former actually substituted for portions of the *Musica Enchiriadis*) because the method of teaching according to the modes enjoyed wider currency. Beyond this, the coexistence of these two quite different ways of teaching about organum at the fourth suggests that the theorists were not dealing with music that was by nature orderly and rule-bound but were attempting in their various ways to contain an intuitive pre-existent practice within the confines of a rational system. This conjecture is the more probable as yet a third way of dealing with organum at the fourth has also come down to us, transmitted by Guido of Arezzo.

Guido turns his attention to organum in the closing chapters of his *Micrologus* (*c*. 1026–8). Unlike any of the other theorists whose works have survived, Guido mentions and illustrates strictly parallel organum at the fourth, but only as a preamble to discussion of the pliant (*molle*) organum at the fourth practised 'according to our custom'.

Three elements are prominent in Guido's explanation of organum. One is *occursus*, the joining of the voices in unison at the end of a phrase or phrase segment. Another is the notion of boundary tones, in this case *tritus* pitches, C and F, which the organal voice holds so as to be ready to proceed properly to *occursus*. Third is a preferential ranking of intervals according to their utility in organum at the fourth. This ranking is simply asserted without reference to any broad supporting theoretical doctrines. Guido admits four intervals—tone, major third, minor third and fourth—to organum while explicitly excluding semitone and fifth. Of the accepted intervals, the fourth holds the principal rank. The others gain status from their value in *occursus*: the tone is the favoured interval of *occursus*, the major third is allowed, but the minor third is categorically excluded from it. Guido's first four examples, consecutive phrases of a short antiphon, illustrate three types of phrase ending (Ex. 166); an *occursus* on the *tritus* C, where the organal voice is locked on that pitch throughout the descent of the principal voice to it; two closes on the *tritus* F, in which the organal voice, remaining a fourth below the principal, does not attempt an *occursus*; and an *occursus* on *protus* D, the final of the antiphon, which occurs in the most favoured way, by a tone.

Ex. 166

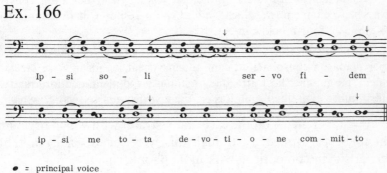

● = principal voice
○ = organal voice

Guido's organum instruction has connections with the two other main strands of teaching about organum at the fourth. It shares with the *Musica Enchiriadis* explanation the concept of fixed boundary tones that remain the same no matter what the mode of the given chant, and with the Cologne/Paris approach the idea of *occursus* as a guiding rule of the organal voice. (Although *occursus* in fact takes place in the *Musica* and *Scolica Enchiriadis* examples of organum at the fourth, it is not openly stated as a principle in the text.) Otherwise, Guido's teaching differs decisively from the others in its assertion of a hierarchic ranking of intervals. The uniqueness of this ranking, as well as the informality with which it is advanced, underline the absence of any systematic doctrine concerning consonance and dissonance within this stage of organum theory as a whole. Doctrine within the *Enchiriadis* group holds only *symphoniae*, the fourth and the fifth, to be legitimately organal in nature. The Cologne treatise characterizes places where the organal voice stands a second or a third from the principal one as *abusivum organum*, not because such sounds are wrong (the teaching specifically demands them), but because they are non-*symphoniae*. The Paris treatise similarly emphasizes the lack of a *legitimate* organal response when, because of mandated boundary tones, the organal voice cannot answer the principal at the fourth.

Although oriented toward technical details of how to produce correct organum, these early treatises do give some hints concerning the performance of organum. Repeated references to the singing of men and boys indicate that both combined in singing organum, the boys duplicating organal and principal voices at the octave. As the *Musica Enchiriadis* puts it:

If one makes organum [at the fourth] with a man's voice together with a boy's, these two voices are consonant at the octave, but the higher one, the boy's, stands a fifth above the [principal] voice which they both contain midway between them, to which, indeed, both respond in organum. The man's stands a fourth below it.

(Si voce virili organizetur simul cum voce puerili, sunt quidem hae duae voces sibi per diapason consonae; ad eam autem vocem, quam inter se mediam continent, ad quam scilicet utraeque organum respondent, acutior, quae est puerilis, quinto extat loco superior, ea, quae virilis, quarto loco gravior.)

Several writers remark on the care and restraint with which organum ought to be performed, as though this were an especially notable characteristic in comparison with monophonic chant.

Thus with two or more singing together with at least moderate and harmonious care, which is proper to this music, you will see that a sweet harmony is born from this mixture of sounds.

(Sic enim duobus aut pluribus in unum canendo modesta dumtaxat et concordi morositate, quod suum est huius meli, videbis suavem nasci ex hac sonorum commixtione concentum.) (*Musica Enchiriadis*)

Organum must always be made accurately and with restrained care, and it is employed most properly with sacred songs.

(Poscit autem semper organum diligenti et modesta morositate fieri, et honestissime sacris canticis adhibetur.) (Cologne Treatise)

The Paris Treatise observes, moreover, that rhythmic differences normally denoted by *puncta* and *virgae* are virtually obliterated in organum because of its slow tempo and weighty character.

Except for fragments of a poem by Martianus Capella set to music in the Bamberg Dialogue I, liturgical plainsong is the foundation of the organum examples presented in these treatises. Antiphons, hymns, and other music from the Offices predominate. Mass items are limited to more recent, medieval chants—a few prose phrases and an entire sequence. Pragmatic factors involving the notational system used for two-part music may account for the absence of melismatic chant examples from theoretical expositions of organum.[8] While the theorists' choice of examples promotes the impression that polyphony chiefly adorned the Offices, such a bias is not at all apparent in the earliest repertory of polyphony we possess, that preserved in one of the Winchester Tropers.

THE WINCHESTER TROPERS

The Winchester Tropers are two manuscripts (Oxford, Bodley 775 (Bo) and Cambridge, Corpus Christi College, 473 (CC)) that transmit a repertory of Winchester Cathedral from around 1000. Both are *cantatoria*, chant books destined for use by soloists. Although invariably mentioned in tandem, the two manuscripts were not conceived as a pair. Only the Corpus Christi manuscript contains organum, a substantial corpus of 12 Kyries (troped and untroped), 7 Gloria tropes, 19 Tracts, 7 Sequences, 53 Alleluias, 53 Responsories, 3 Processional Antiphons, and 3 Invitatories (excluding later additions). Recent research suggests that this manuscript was copied *c*. 996–1006 and that the famous Winchester cantor Wulfstan was composer and scribe of the organa.[9] By this dating, the organa are roughly contemporary with the early Continental descriptions of how to produce organum.

The notation of the Winchester organa poses grave interpretative problems. First of all, the organal voices are notated singly in liturgical groupings marked by the scribe 'Organa super Tractus', 'Organa ad Alleluia', etc. They are not paired with their principal voices in the manuscript (although a few foundation chants happen to occur in early fascicles of the Corpus Christi manuscript). The reason for this isolation of the organa is not difficult to surmise, for the

---

[8] See Reckow, 'Organum, 5', *New Grove*, xiii. 803.

[9] Andreas Holschneider, *Die Organa von Winchester: Studien zum ältesten Repertoire polyphoner Musik* (Hildesheim, 1968), 76–81.

liturgical chants to which they belong were surely well known to the
cathedral singers and had already been inscribed in other service
books. This circumstance poses one obstacle to modern realizations,
for principal voices have to be supplied by an editor on the basis of
neumes from extant Winchester service books, interpreted through
later diastematic notations. This already introduces a major factor of
uncertainty into the reconstruction, for the modern editor cannot
hope to duplicate the exact details of the chants upon which the
organa were framed. Indeed, whenever a foundation chant exists in
both the Bodley and the Corpus Christi manuscripts, the neumes
differ slightly but significantly. A second pervasive source of uncertainty lies in the essentially adiastematic (unheightened) notation of
the organa themselves.[10] What neume heightening there is is uneven,
local in impact, and more indicative of general direction than precise
interval size. Sequences of *puncta* and *virgae* in combination with
litterae significativae somewhat define the course of the organal voice,
but its reconstruction inevitably depends in large measure on the
application of principles from Continental theory and is considerably
affected by choices made in constituting the 'principal voice'. The
variety of precepts encountered in the surviving theoretical documents
naturally complicates the task of reconstruction.

Although we have no direct evidence confirming a connection
between Winchester organum and that practised on the Continent, we
do know of significant musical ties between Winchester and Continental establishments. St Aethelwold (Bishop of Winchester 963–84) sent
monks to Corbie to learn about chant and to Fleury to perfect
themselves in the Benedictine Rule. The Winchester trope repertory
includes a substantial proportion of Continental pieces, most of which
reflect Northern French traditions. These connections, together with
the notation of the organa themselves, attest the probability of a
family relationship between Continental organum theory and the
Winchester corpus of organum, a probability that is strengthened by
the results obtained from bringing the two together.

The organum notation in the Corpus Christi manuscript is informative enough to persuade that organum at the fourth prevailed at
Winchester. Sequences of similar neume forms in both organal voices
and those principal voices recorded in Bo or CC indicate some
inclination toward parallelism. Frequent reiterated pitches in the
organal voices, depicted by series of *virgae* or *puncta* (see pl. 1) can be
construed as the boundary tones featured in all descriptions of flexible

---

[10] Ibid., plates 1–8, 10–13, 16–19; Besseler and Gülke, *Schriftbild*, plates 4a, b, p. 31.

organum at the fourth. These naturally suggest the fourth as the interval of parallelism. The figure   . ∿ /   regularly placed at the ends of sections and melismas, and periodically within lines, suggests a stereotyped manner of closure. When principal and organal voices are combined according to the general precepts of organum at the fourth, this figure coincides with the *occursus* predicted by the theory.

A reconstruction of the Winchester version of 'Alleluia Dies sanctificatus' (Christmas Mass of the Day),[11] carried out according to contemporary theory of organum at the fourth, is shown in Ex. 167. The setting takes in the entire melody, not just those portions which in monophonic performance belonged to the soloist. (The *x* in the organal part indicates an alternative solution; the original neumes are shown in parallel with the modern notation.) Reading of the organal voice is facilitated by a number of *litterae significativae* (*e* = remain on the same pitch; *s* or *l* = ascend; *io* = descend; *t* = hold), which are unnecessary for the familiar liturgical tune (found in both CC and Bo, here represented according to CC).

That Winchester organa do not conform exactly to any one set of rules in the extant organum treatises should not occasion surprise. Whereas the theory states a standard technique for realizing an organum on any chant, the notated organa are to some extent composed music. Their individual features cannot be regimented under set rules and procedures. Nevertheless, they adhere to fairly restricted limits, for organa fashioned to concordant chants tend to be largely the same. On the whole, the modal final teaching articulated in the Paris and Cologne treatises seems to agree best with the Winchester repertory. Neither in this branch of theory nor in the Winchester compositions are boundary tones restricted to any fixed pair of pitches. In the D mode 'Alleluia Dies sanctificatus', for example, not only C and F (those mandated by Guido) but also D serve as boundary tones. Except for a passage on 've-(nite)' where the letters *io* explicitly command a descent below C, the note below the final is the plausible lower boundary of the organum. Both 'higher' and 'lower' organum—singled out in the Paris and Cologne treatises as passages where *occursus* takes place on an upper or lower associate of the final—occur in the Winchester repertory. In the 'Alleuia Dies sanctificatus', the arrival on G midway through the initial phrase (marked with an asterisk in Ex. 167) temporarily produces 'higher' organum.

Some practices in the Winchester organa find no support in written theory. Occasionally the notation indicates an *upper* boundary tone at

---

[11] Cambridge, Corpus Christi 473, fo. 163 (organum), fo. 2ᵛ (principal voice).

Ex. 167

des - cen - dit lux ma -

- gna su - per ter - ram

𝄎 quilisma

+ liquescent

x alternate reading of organum

the beginning of a piece, as in Ex. 168(i).[12] Here the redundant instructions 'l' and 's' urge a higher position on the organum, while the *occursus* immediately following limits the choice of boundary tone. The theory, by contrast, uniformly starts the organum below or with the chant, and only allows it to remain above if the chant momentarily sweeps down below the cadential pitch toward the end of the phrase. The one hint of an exception to this comes in the Paris treatise where in a phrase of the sequence 'Benedicta sit' the organal voice begins in unison with the cantus and remains above as the cantus immediately plunges down a fifth. The Winchester organa would also seem occasionally to admit fifths—Ex. 168(ii) and first interval of (i)—an interval implicitly or explicitly (by Guido) excluded from organum at the fourth in Continental theory. This is to say that attempts at reconstruction sometimes confront situations where fifths are unavoidable. (If fifths were common in the repertory this trait escapes us, since the postulated 'rules' of reconstructing organum at the fourth require avoidance of this interval whenever possible.) Another eventuality not foreseen in the theory is an unequal number of notes between the two voices, typically an excess in the organal line (see Ex. 167, 'venite gentes'). A difference of one note is particularly frequent with the stereotyped closing formula . 𝄎 𝅗 , so frequent

---

[12] Ibid., (i) fo. 164 (organum), fo. 3 (principal voice) (ii) fo. 166 (organum), fo. 4 (principal voice). Reconstruction after Holschneider, *Organa*, pp. 97, 101.

Ex. 168

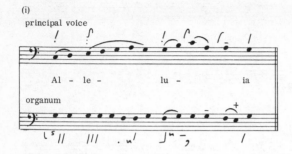

indeed that the discrepancy cannot reasonably be attributed to faults in reconstructing the principal voices. Co-ordination of the two parts in such cases is a matter of modern controversy. Some opt for the piquancy of a second to unison, while others prefer an extension of the penultimate chant note, which generally results in a sustained third. Guido's preference for *occursus* by a whole tone lends weight to the former solution in some contexts. Contemporary Continental theory offers no basis for preferring the third, as by its tenets neither second nor third is legitimate organum.

It must be frankly acknowledged that the details of any particular realization of Winchester organum result in large degree from deliberate editorial choices and are thus conditioned by the editor's own concept of 'the style'. Yet despite this fact, notation and theory agree closely enough to cast a fair image of the repertory as a whole, and to permit plausible, if far from definitive, reconstructions of the music.

NEW ORGANUM TEACHING

A new phase in organum teaching manifested itself in a small cluster of treatises which are conventionally grouped around a work called *Ad organum faciendum* (On the making of organum). These treatises teach a kind of organum that is not based on parallelism at a single interval and is not magnified by octave doubling of either voice, but instead freely intermixes octaves, fifths, fourths and unisons between two voices. They advance new theoretical doctrine to justify and support the practice they teach. The absence of firm data on date or provenance of the sources makes it impossible to estimate just when or where the new organum and its theory emerged or became dominant. The attack on Guido by the author of *Ad organum faciendum* does put this treatise after the *Micrologus*, but at what point in the eleventh century (or even later) is indeterminate. Since the other treatises in the group appear to be no earlier than the *Ad organum faciendum*, this stage of teaching may well be called post-Guidonian.

The four works belonging to this stage of theory are listed in Table 2.[13] These disparate works are not so much united by common precepts as they are set apart by their common isolation from prior or subsequent writing about organum. They possess neither the single-interval focus of the earlier organum treatises nor the commitment to contrary motion characteristic of the discant treatises. The polyphony they describe is not—and cannot be—tightly circumscribed by rules.

Teaching precepts are not all that differentiates these post-Guidonian texts from the earlier body of organum treatises. Their nature and transmission are also strikingly different. These more recent treatises do not belong to comprehensive works on music theory but are independent writings devoted solely to organum. The 'Milan verse treatise' is the only one to expound general music theory to any degree, but what is said (largely derived from Guido) seems selected principally for its relevance to the subject of organum. The circulation of these writings seems to have been very limited indeed. None survives in more than two manuscripts, nor does any belong to a widely disseminated group of treatises. Compared with the earliest writings on organum, these indicate a shift in the place of organum teaching, and of organum itself, within the general scheme of musical thought. A new sense of the identity of organum as a kind of music distinct from plainsong is intimated by the emergence of treatises devoted solely to the subject. At the same time, the confined transmission of those writings we possess, their brevity, and the diversity of their teachings, argue that specific ways of making polyphony were quite localized. The general agreement on style evident among the earliest writers on organum is a condition of the past. Not until the thirteenth century, with the spread and influence of Parisian poly-

[13] All these treatises have been ed. Hans Heinrich Eggebrecht and Frieder Zaminer with German translation, *Ad Organum Faciendum: Lehrschriften der Mehrstimmigkeit in nachguidonischer Zeit*, Neue Studien zur Musikwissenschaft, 3 (Mainz, 1970).

TABLE 2 Later Organum Treatises

Treatise	Date/Sources	Teaching	Theoretical Concepts
1. *Ad organum faciendum* 'Milan prose treatise'	MS copied *c.*1100 unique source, Milan, Biblioteca Ambrosiana M. 17. sup., fo. 56–58'	5 *modi organizandi* Recommended intervals: unison, 4th, 5th, 8ve.	*Copula* Affinity between pitches. 4th and 5th proper to organum.
1a. Berlin A variant version of 1, followed by 'Milan verse treatise'	MS copied *c.*1300 Berlin, Staatsbibliothek, Preussischer Kulturbesitz, Ms. theol. lat. quart. 261, fo. 48–48'		
1b. Bruges Treatise work combining passages from 1 and the 'Milan verse treatise'	MS copied 13th/ early 14th cent. Bruges, Stadsbibliotheek, Ms. 528, fo. 54' (marginalia)		
2. Berlin B	MS copied *c.*1300 unique source, Berlin, Staatsbibliothek, Preussischer Kulturbesitz. Ms. theol. lat. quart. 261, fo. 50'–51'	3 *modi organizandi* Recommended intervals: unison, major and minor 3rd, 4th, 5th, 8ve. Both contrary and parallel motion between voices permitted.	*Copula* Affinity between pitches.
3. 'Milan verse treatise' Follows after 1	MS copied *c.*1100 Milan, Biblioteca Ambrosiana, M. 17. sup., fo. 58'–61	No general rules.	*Copula* Affinity between pitches. 4th and 5th proper to organum.
4. Montpellier Treatise	MS copied *c.*1100 unique source, Montpellier, Bibliothèque de l'Université, Section de Médecine, Ms. H. 384, fo. 122–123	Proceed by choice of end, beginning, and middle. Limit of phrase, 8 cantus notes. Recommended intervals: unison, 3rd, 4th, 5th, 6th, 8ve. Organum may begin above or below the cantus.	*Copula* by contrary motion. 4th and 5th proper to organum.

phony, is it possible to document broad diffusion of a characteristic polyphonic style.

The energetic attack on Guido's organum teaching in *Ad organum faciendum* proclaims a definite break from earlier organum style and theory. But the break is not total. The new theory retains two significant elements: the definition of polyphony as pitches (or voices) which 'concorditer dissonant et dissonanter concordant', and the notion of *occursus*, now called *copula*. The first element is now qualified by stipulating that the organal voice should follow the principal not on the basis of a single interval but with a mixture of fourths and fifths; the second is qualified by the admission of the octave along with the unison as an interval of *copula*. This latter development is highly significant, for it both expands the range of the organal voice (in earlier organum at the fourth, boundary tones frequently confine it to a three-to-four-note range), and paves the way for introduction of the sixth as a preparatory interval for *copula* at the octave. The new idea of *copula* differs from *occursus* in yet another important way. *Occursus* in earlier theory coincides with the primary verbal units of the given text, grammatically defined by colon and comma punctuation. *Copula* is not so co-ordinated. The segments that it punctuates are determined by no criteria, grammatical or musical. (The Montpellier treatise alone of the four arbitrarily decrees eight notes as the maximum limit of a segment.)

In all but the 'Milan verse treatise', the new pedagogy bases the operation of making organum on position within a phrase segment: beginning, middle, or end. Implicitly or explicitly (Montpellier), the methods emphasize motion from an initial point to an arrival (*copula*), a place of repose where the voices join together on the same pitch, either in unison or octave. *Ad organum faciendum* limits the choice of beginning and middle intervals more severely than the others, allowing only unison, octave, fourth or fifth. Other sounds may occur only as part of *copula*, which may be effected via 'any appropriate interval' ('aliqua decenti consonantia'). This anonymous theorist casts his instruction in terms of five *modus organizandi*, or ways of making organum, each of which pertains to a particular aspect of an organum phrase. Conjunct inception (organum starting at unison or octave with the principal voice) is labelled first *modus organizandi*; the alternative, disjunct inception (organum starting a fourth or a fifth from the principal), is second *modus organizandi*. Participation of fourths and fifths only *within* a phrase constitutes the third *modus organizandi*, while intermixture of all four acceptable intervals (unison, fourth, fifth, and octave) between inception and *copula* is a fourth *modus organizandi*. A fifth category designates elaboration in the organal voice such that several pitches sound against one in the cantus. This fifth *modus organizandi* not only introduces textural variety but also widens the sound spectrum to include intervals other than unison and *symphoniae*, judging from the sole concrete illustration (Ex. 169 phrase 1).

The precepts of the *Ad organum faciendum* theorist are exemplified not only by brief phrases within the treatise but also by four complete pieces written in alphabetic notation (six if the multiple organa for the 'Benedicamus Domino' are counted separately). Only one of these, the 'Alleluia Justus ut palma', is unquestionably integral to the treatise. The other three precede the formal title, but may be understood as a special kind of preface if the text of the third, 'Hoc sit vobis iter' (Let this be your way), is taken as introductory to the treatise following. The polyphony for the Alleluia, which extends only to those portions of the chant sung by a soloist, closely reflects the teaching of the theorist (Ex. 169).[14] The main segments, expressly marked by the scribe with vertical lines, close with *copula* to unison or octave (number 5 only excepted). Within segments, fourths and fifths intermingle, joined occasionally by octave or unison as in the fourth *modus organizandi*. *Copula* takes place either from a fourth or a fifth (segments 2, 3, 7, and 8) or from one of the undefined appropriate intervals: once a third (segment 6), twice a sixth (segments 4 and 9). These other intervals are chiefly restricted to a role in *copula*, although one occasionally appears elsewhere. The succession of three before the final cadence may be emphatic in intent (see asterisks in segment 9).

Other features of the 'Alleluia Justus ut palma' organum not explicitly mentioned by the theorist do appear from the other examples to be normal to the style. In contrast with earlier practice in which the organum lies below the chant, the organal voice here holds the higher position, only occasionally descending below the chant. The total range of the organal voice considerably exceeds that of its companion, suggesting increased versatility and skill on the part of those singers who supplied the organal part. Both the expanded range and the elevated position of the organal voice help to explain the disappearance of octave doubling of the voices from this stage of practice. *Copula* invariably occurs by contrary motion. This usually seems to happen quite naturally, but the abrupt descent of the organal voice at the end of segment 6 suggests deliberate purpose. In addition, the voices usually move out of any unison or octave in opposite

---

[14] Milan, Biblioteca Ambrosiana, M. 17, sup., fo. 58 (organal voice); Berlin Staatsbibliothek Preussischer Kulturbesitz, MS theol. lat. quart. 261, fo. 48ᵛ (principal voice).

Ex. 169

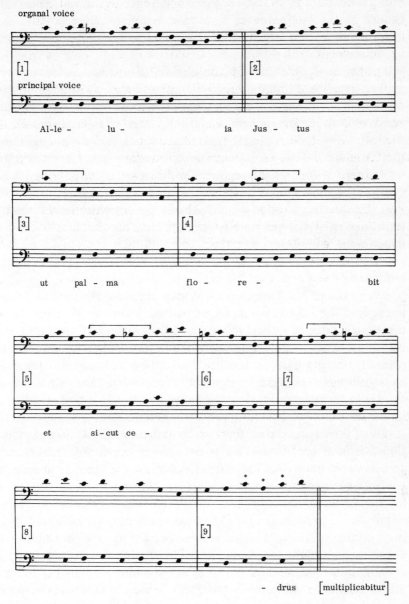

directions. Hence *copula* is more than a blended union of the voices, it is a regulated way of creating opposite melodic movement between the parts. Contrary motion is also integral to the stereotyped octave-fourth-unison progression which occurs four times, once in reverse, and once with a third intermediate to the fourth and unison (see brackets in Ex. 169). The prevalence in the organal voice of the three-note group a-c-d gives some sense of coherence to the line. This figure occurs at the beginning of a phrase (segment 2, repeated), as a cadential motive (segments 4, 7, and 9) and within phrases (segment 1 twice, segment 5).

The five *modi organizandi* postulated in *Ad organum faciendum* seem artificially devised to mould recalcitrant practice into some semblance of system. Although these categories appear more than a little contrived, they nevertheless underline some vital concerns of the organum singer. The choice between conjunct and disjunct beginnings (first and second *modus organizandi*), for example, controls whether subsequent motion of the organum will be parallel or contrary to the cantus. Proliferation of notes in the organal voice (the fifth *modus organizandi*) bears upon the rhythmic co-ordination and relative prominence of the parts. Historically, it gives the first inkling of experiment with florid organum, even though the single example supplied (Ex. 169, phrase 1) has but one short flourish, situated just before the *copula*.

Berlin B and the Montpellier treatise respectively modify or dispense with the five *modi organizandi* without, however, departing from the central idea that beginnings, middles, and ends are functional positions. They differ principally from *Ad organum faciendum* in formally accepting intervals other than unison and simple *symphoniae* at beginnings and middles: Berlin B allows major thirds and minor thirds, Montpellier admits sixths as well as thirds (unqualified as to larger or smaller). In the absence of independent evidence on the status of thirds and sixths, this circumstance cannot be taken to show that Berlin B or Montpellier is necessarily later than *Ad organum faciendum*. What it does indicate is the demise of a theoretical basis for legitimate organum.

The *Ad organum faciendum* and the 'Milan verse treatise', which admit only *symphoniae* and the unison as regular intervals of organum, preserve the old *Musica* and *Scolica Enchiriadis* notion of organum as 'singing in *symphoniae*'. They justify the limited choice of organal notes by the doctrine of affinity or *modus vocum*, a doctrine advanced in the *Micrologus* (chapters 7–9), which asserts a special kinship among pitches separated by octave, fifth, or fourth. Thirds and sixths have no claim to privilege as organal tones under the principle of affinity. Those writers who regularly permit thirds and sixths in organum do so in recognition of practice, but in contravention of theoretical propriety. The organum they teach lacks theoretical legitimacy. It is not 'singing in *symphoniae*', nor does it rest on any other formal criterion determining a hierarchy among intervals. The author of the Montpellier treatise comes closest to rationalizing practice by informally observing that seconds and sevenths cannot be initial sounds because they sound bad; but a developed concept of consonance and dissonance is no more in evidence in this stage of organum theory than it was earlier. The formulation of such theory in the first half of the thirteenth century responded to the need to account for the complete spectrum of diatonic intervals within polyphony and so to formulate a firm theoretical foundation for music in two or more parts.

Despite its outward guise of simplistic didactic verse, the 'Milan verse treatise' appears in retrospect to be the most 'progressive' work of the post-Guidonian group, simply because its teaching method foreshadows that of the thirteenth-century discant treatises. The anonymous author does not explain organum in terms of phrase segments with beginning, middle, and end, but illustrates it with individual series of interval progressions.

When the cantus holds D, the organum will be on a
If the cantus ascends to F, let there be a *copula* there.
Afterwards sounding C in descending to the first A
[with] G accompanying the C, a then joins as one [the cantus A].
The cantus immediately ascending, let there be a *copula* on D.
C and E were looking toward [this], just as a sweet [organ] pipe.
and let D, the fourth note [of the scale], render the sound
in sweet friendship
for those who kiss should be close.

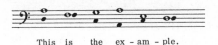

This is   the   ex - am - ple.

⎡line⎤
⎣ 79 ⎦

Si cantus tenebit .D. organum erit in .a.
Si ascendat in .F. cantus ibi fiat copula.
Postea sonando .C. descendendo primam .A.
G. vero sequendo .C. a. coniungit sic una.
Cantus confestim ascendens in .D. fiat copula.
C. et E. erunt spectantes quasi dulcis fistula.
Et .D. quarta reddat sonum dulci amicitia.
Quia prope debent esse illa que dant oscula.

D   FCA   C   D   a   F Ga   E   D
Hoc est e- xemplum   Hoc est e- xemplum

This is a laborious way of teaching, one which awaits, and ultimately receives, a more generalized formulation independent of individual cases. Its limitations apart, this approach manifests a decided conceptual change. The singer of the organum, is directed to think not in terms of an entire phrase or phrase segment, a coherent musical unit, but in terms of one discrete moment to the next. The reason for this novel approach is unclear, but a growing concern for contrary motion between the voices might have been a contributing factor. An inclination toward contrary motion is mildly apparent in the examples of this treatise, but the text demands contrary motion only before *copula*.

Although the two Milan treatises differ sharply in approach, the organum style they illustrate is not dissimilar. Any of the examples in the 'verse treatise' could equally well appear within *Ad organum faciendum*. That shown as Ex. 170(i) shows unison *copula* with intermediate sounds of fourth, fifth, and octave (the one third belongs to the first *copula*). The terminal octave-fourth-unison progression is familiar from the 'Alleluia Justus ut palma' in *Ad organum faciendum* (Ex. 169). A version of this progression, mediated by a third, also begins the example. The last example of the 'verse treatise', Ex. 170(ii), centres on this progression, which is the framework of a voice-exchange.

Ex. 170

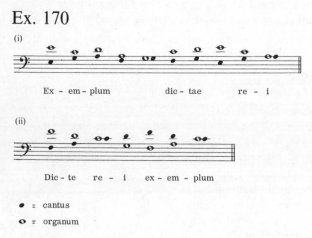

(i)

Ex - em - plum   dic - tae   re - i

(ii)

Dic - te   re - i   ex - em - plum

● = cantus
○ = organum

Besides pointing forward to a new pedagogical technique, the 'Milan verse treatise' also heralds a radically new concept of the organal voice. In the other treatises of this group, the organal voice is called the follower and is plainly regarded as an accompanying part, subsidiary to the original chant. In the 'verse treatise', the organal voice is regarded as dominant. It is characterized vividly as the strongest of soldiers, a prince and lord who masters musical sounds. It ranges over upper and lower registers and possesses greater power than the cantus, a point demonstrated by appeal to no less an authority than Boethius. This elevation in status of the organal voice conforms with the emergence of a new style in the twelfth century (a style not fully represented in the 'verse treatise' examples) in which the organal voice commands attention both by its position above the principal voice and by its more active melodic movement.

THE NEW ORGANUM STYLE

The five examples within the body of the *Ad organum faciendum* treatise illustrate a variety of ways to add a second voice to a twelve-note Alleluia. Variety is the key word: whereas earlier theory held to a one-to-one correspondence between any specific principal pitch in a given context and the organal tone appropriate to it, the new practice allows considerable choice in couplings. Factors contributing to the larger range of choice are the wider interval permitted between the organal and chant lines (expanded from a fifth to a full octave) and the freedom of the organal voice to intermix intervals of different kinds and to range above and below the principal voice. (In the examples of *Ad organum faciendum* it invariably starts above the chant and remains there most of the time.)

Given the multiple possibilities for fashioning organa set forth in the pedagogical texts, it is disconcerting to confront the void of notated music from this post-Guidonian period. No major collection of polyphony datable to the middle or the latter half of the eleventh century, or corresponding stylistically with the theorists' dicta, is known to exist. Only some dozen manuscripts preserve polyphony that might fall into the gap between the Winchester repertory (*c*. 1000) and the earliest Aquitanian collection (*c*. 1100), and none of these is primarily a musical source. Such remnants of polyphony from this time as we possess are seldom found in chant books for services or special collections of music but appear typically on odd leaves in text manuscripts. Some may once have belonged to a music manuscript, but many appear as isolated additions, copied singly or in small groups. The largest project is a series of nine polyphonic Office responsories of which only three ultimately were given neumes. In all, there come down to us less than two dozen pieces that might conceivably illustrate later eleventh-century practice, few of them in notation that can be readily transcribed.

Manuscript and liturgical evidence tends to place the majority of these polyphonic jottings in the north of France, at such places as

Chartres, St Maur-des-Fossés (near Paris), and Fleury. A few can be assigned to northern Italy. Because of the repute of these northern monasteries and cathedral schools as centres of learning and religious observance, one is tempted to claim the scraps of polyphony that remain from them as traces of a flourishing polyphonic tradition. Scholarly prudence, however, commands restraint in the absence of concrete contemporary documentation on musical culture in these areas. Some documentary evidence does exist for Chartres. In one poem about illustrious Chartres students, Adelman (a disciple of Fulbert of Chartres) praises the cantor Sigo (d. c. 1040) for his peerless excellence in organal music.

In so far as the scant remnants of polyphony can—and must, by default—be considered representative of their time, they testify to an emphasis on liturgical pieces, as in the Winchester repertory. Alleluias, Graduals, Office or processional Responsories, and the *Benedicamus Domino* are the main chants set polyphonically. Only one piece, a single entry in an Italian manuscript at Lucca, has rhymed, poetic text, an incidence that hardly foreshadows the prevalence of polyphonic verse songs in the Aquitanian repertory of the early twelfth century. The manuscripts from Chartres, because they can be fixed to one locale, make the most appropriate group for study. In all, the three manuscripts of which we still have record transmit sixteen compositions: ten Alleluias, four Responds, and two processional verses. The repertory is by no means uniform in style but exhibits a shift away from an organum characterized by boundary tones and parallelism toward one that moves more freely against the given chant, a shift congruent with that voiced by the theorists. In the sources, this stylistic change is closely allied with new notational practices, virtually a new technology of notation. (Slow development of an appropriate notation could be one reason why so little polyphony from the mid-to-late eleventh century has been preserved.) In the oldest Chartres source (MS 4), the organal voice is notated alone in adiastematic neumes. The notation reveals a boundary-tone style akin to that of the Winchester repertory. In the two other sources (Chartres 130 and 109), the two voices are notated in score.[15] The music in one of these (Chartres 130) cannot be reliably transcribed because of indefinite neume heightening, but the neume patterns indicate a melodically active organal voice and a considerable degree of contrary motion with the chant. The notation of the other (109) can be read and leaves no doubt about the range of the organal voice and its inclination to contrary motion with the chant.

[15] The Chartres manuscripts were destroyed in 1944, but facsimiles are published in *Fragments des manuscrits de Chartres*, ed. Yves Delaporte, *Paléographie musicale*, 17 (1958).

The five pieces preserved in Chartres 109 are closely related to the teaching of the Berlin B and Montpellier treatises. The freedom with which they mix parallel and contrary motion and employ intervals other than *symphoniae* and unisons patently dissociates them from the strict conventions of *Ad organum faciendum*. In the 'Alleluia Angelus domini descendit', (Ex. 171)[16] the voices move in tandem both with fourths and with thirds, at 'An-(gelus)' and '(de-)scend-(it)'. Alternative treatments of the recurring C–G ascent in the principal voice show either parallel or contrary motion to be valid choices, although the latter is the more frequent. This ascent is three times countered by descent in the organal voice from octave to unison (8–5–3–U), a move plainly related to the octave-fourth-unison formula observed in the 'Alleluia Justus ut palma' and in examples in the 'Milan verse treatise'. Once, however, at the beginning of the verse, the organal voice parallels the chant ascent in fourths before turning down to make a *copula* on the G.

Ex. 171

[1]
Al – le – lu – ia

[2]
An – ge – lus do – mi– ni

[3]
des–cen –

[4]
dit de ce – lo

[5]
et ac – ce – dens

[6]
re – vol –

[7]
vit la – pi – dem

[et sedebat super eum]

---

[16] Chartres, Bibliothèque de la ville 109, fo. 75.

Judging empirically, considerations of range and position of the final would seem central to the conception of this piece. The two lines are balanced around the final, G. If the chant is below G, the organum tends to be above. If the chant rises above G('descendit'), the organum seeks the lower range. This accounts in part for the degree of contrary motion between the voices. The chant dictates that most cadences fall on the final, and the voices consistently unite in unison at these points. This highlights the sense of final as centre. The inclination toward seconds before the unison cadences, marked with an asterisk in Ex. 171, may be a vestige of earlier organum practice. Guido, in any event, counsels that manner of *occursus*.

A remarkable feature of this 'Alleluia' is the melodic design of the organal voice. This design is partly co-ordinate with, partly independent of, the clear phrase pattern of the chant, as Figure 1 shows. While the chant has essentially three distinct phrase types (grouped by threes after the initial single), the organum has but two. That designated x in Figure 1 starts in various ways (hence the subscripts) but on sounding a oscillates on G and F, leaps to b flat and falls by step to cadence on G. That designated y starts on low D and rises to the c above, making an octave *copula* with the chant. The odd fifth phrase, which starts the second large phrase group, commences as x_1 but echoes the beginning of x_3 at its end. To some extent, cadential concerns doubtless operate in the organal voice: the y phrase accompanies the two chant segments that cadence on low C, and the x phrase accounts for four of five chant cadences on G. However, x sets in too far before phrase closure to be considered simply a cadential figure. The coupling of x with quite different chant phrases (*a* and *b*) and the combination of two previously-heard initial figures in phrase 5 argue that melodic factors, along with contrapuntal and cadential ones, influenced the conception of this organal voice. The organum here is not just a foil to the chant but manifests its own integrity of design.

Organum	x_1	x_2	x_3	y	x_1/x_3	y'	x_1
Chant	a	a	b	c	a	c'	a
Phrase order	1	2	3	4	5	6	7

FIG. 1. Melodic design in the 'Alleluia, Angelus domini descendit'.

Only two of the pieces that can be reliably transcribed from other dispersed sources adhere very closely to specific teaching advocated in treatises of the *Ad organum faciendum* group. The 'Alleluia O quam 'pulchra', a single entry in alphabetic notation in a manuscript now at Autun,[17] could serve as an example in the Montpellier treatise. 'Regi regum glorioso', a two-part 'Benedicamus Domino' versus inserted in an antiphoner from the convent of St Maria di Pontetto, near Lucca,[18] matches the teaching of *Ad organum faciendum*, although the voices parallel each other far less than in the treatise examples. This versus (Ex. 172) might be classified as the fourth *modus organizandi* in which 'beginnings' (unisons and octaves) and 'middles' (fourths and fifths) mingle within the phrase. The only intervals other than these are elements of *copula*, the one position where *Ad organum faciendum*

Ex. 172

----

[17] Autun, Bibliothèque municipale 46 (olim 40B), fo. 63.

[18] Lucca, Biblioteca capitolare Feliniana 603, fo. 256. Facsimile in *I più antichi Monumenti sacri italiani*, ed. F. Alberto Gallo and Giuseppe Vecchi, *Monumenta lyrica medii aevi italica*, ser. 3, *Mensurabilia*, i (Bologna, 1968), plate XCVII.

admits 'any interval'. The exceptional degree of contrary motion
arises both from the choice of conjunct phrase beginnings and from
frequent unisons within phrases, features that are entirely compatible
with the teaching of *Ad organum faciendum*. By chance, the opening of
the first phrase even parallels the opening of the *Ad organum
faciendum* example for the fourth *modus organizandi* (Ex. 173): a
similarity reinforced by the identity of the first four chant pitches. As
in the Chartres 'Alleluia Angelus domini descendit', registral balance
and modal design guide the course of the organal voice. In those
phrases where the lower voice centres and ends on the final, D (text
lines 1, 2, 5), the organum starts at the octave and descends in
controlled fashion to the final. In the medial phrases, where the lower
voice dwells and ends on the upper fifth, a, the organum starts on the
unison, expands to an octave on the lowest note of the phrase, and
rejoins its companion for a unison *copula*. The rhymed, accentual text
and the repetitive design of the lower voice accentuate the balanced
interaction of the voices.

Ex. 173

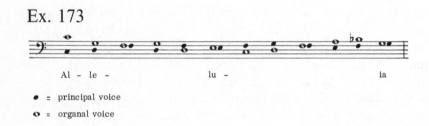

Al - le -   lu -   ia

● = principal voice
○ = organal voice

Taken *en masse*, the examples within the treatises of the *Ad
organum faciendum* group and the compositions that are plausibly
contemporary with them show no clear dividing line between 'parallel
motion' organum and 'contrary motion' organum. As already
observed, both *copula/occursus* and conjunct phrase beginnings incorporate contrary motion. As these become more densely intermixed,
the degree of intermediate parallelism diminishes. When theorists
proclaim contrary rather than parallel motion to be a prime rule of
polyphony they are not advocating a radical break with past practice.
The musical style had already evolved to a point where contrary
motion could be commonplace without departing from the basic
precepts of post-Guidonian theory. The theorists are, rather, responding to a conflict between concept and practice which forces them to
replace the outmoded insistence on coupling by fourths and fifths with
some new principle of organum. Their solution to this problem
initiates a new phase of theory in which independent directional

motion, not the sounding quality of *symphoniae*, is taken to be the guiding principle of interaction between the voices.

TWELFTH-CENTURY POLYPHONY

John of Afflighem was the first theorist to promote contrary motion between voices as a feature of organum, but he qualifies his stance with the laconic observation that 'different persons practise it [organum] differently' ('Ea diversi diverse utuntur', *De Musica, c.* 1100). Not a rigid prescription, it is simply the easiest practice for the organum to descend when the original melody ascends and the reverse.

The easiest practice of all is to consider carefully melodic movement so that when the principal melody rises, then the organum descends, and vice versa.

(Caeterum hic facillimus eius usus est, si motuum varietas diligenter consideretur; ut ubi in recta modulatione est elevatio, ibi in organica fiat depositio et e converso.) (*De Musica*, Chapter 23)

John's chapter on organum, (which, like Guido's is attached to a plainsong treatise) gives little concrete instruction on how to make organum, perhaps because of his sensitivity to diverse practices, perhaps because codification of custom into a coherent set of precepts had yet to be worked out. (In this respect he is at the same stage as the author of the 'Milan verse treatise'.) Only two general policies are commended to the singer of organum. One is attention to melodic progressions in the chant and consequent response to ascending intervals with descending motion, to falling intervals with rising motion. The other is attention to chant range, answering extremes of high and low register in the chant with the octave below or above (respectively), and seeking unisons in the middle range. John also notes the possibility of countering single intervals in the cantus with groups of notes in the organal voice. His chief concerns are not incompatible with those inferrable from pieces in Chartres MS 109 and from the Lucca 'Regi regum'.

John of Afflighem's manner of dealing with organum—not giving fixed rules but merely offering guidance on appropriate concerns—is symptomatic of a crisis in the very concept of organum. John seems even to be aware of this crisis, and cleverly responds to it by appropriating Guido's theory of melodic motion in a single line ('motus vocum') to control his own discussion of relationship between two lines. The practice of organum as presented in the *De Musica* no longer rests on solid theoretical concepts that determine why certain pitches or intervals are appropriate to a specified chant pitch or location in a phrase, but rather fluctuates with mutable, diverse custom. This situation led ultimately to a new teaching about the interaction of two voices that stressed discrete voice-leading pairs rather than the syntax of whole phrase units. It led also to a new theory of polyphony whose chief tenets were a systematic classification of consonance and dissonance and a regulated system of rhythm.

Though the sparseness and uncertain dating of the documents preclude precise charting of developments in organum teaching during the twelfth century, the outcome is plain: by the late twelfth or early thirteenth century, a form of teaching voice-leading had emerged which was to remain standard through the fourteenth century. Emergence of the new teaching method coincides with the adoption of a new term for the matter taught—*discantus*, a Latinization of *diaphonia*, the term John of Afflighem prefers to *organum*. Instead of dealing with substantial segments of a cantus, with phrase units closed off by cadential formulas as earlier methods did, the new teaching concerns itself abstractly with the single intervals that characteristically occur in chant, without reference to any aspect of surrounding context or phrase position. Given two parameters (the magnitude of the interval between two adjacent cantus notes and a starting position), the organal voice is instructed to respond in a particular way:

If the cantus ascends a second and the organum begins at the octave, let the organum descend a third and it will be at the fifth.
If the cantus descends a second and the organum begins with it [i.e. in unison], let the organum ascend a fourth and it will be at the fifth.
(Si cantus ascenderit duas voces. et organum incipiat in dupla. descendat organum .3. voces et erit in quinta.
Si cantus descenderit duas voces et organum incipiat cum cantu, ascendat organum 4 voces et erit in quinta.) (*Ars organi*, 'Vatican organum treatise', rules 1 and 5[19])

The writers of such instructions no longer teach how to generate entire phrases or pieces. Instead they enumerate a collection of stock formulas which appear *in vacuo*, with no guidance on how they might appropriately be fitted together in composition.

The transition from the earlier manner of teaching to the new formalism is best observed in an anonymous treatise found in London, Brit. Lib., Egerton 2888, and in Naples.[20] Sometimes called

[19] Facsimile and edition, ed. Frieder Zaminer, *Der Vatikanische Organum-Traktat (Ottob. lat. 3025)*, *Münchener Veröffentlichungen zur Musikgeschichte*, 2 (Tutzing, 1959), 175–208.
[20] Editions by Marius Schneider, *Geschichte der Mehrstimmigkeit*, ii (Berlin, 1935), 106–20 (London MS.), and by Guido Pannain, 'Liber musicae. Un teorico anonimo del XIV secolo', *Rivista musicale italiana*, 27 (1920), 407 (Naples MS).

the 'Schneider anonymous' (after one of its earlier editors), it will be referred to here as the 'London/Naples' treatise. This is a work in the tradition of Guido's *Micrologus* and John's *De Musica*, a lineage apparent both in its content and in its pervasive quotation from both of those books. The anonymous author repeats Guido's and John's definitions of diaphony, and follows John in bringing Guido's notion of 'motus vocum' (linear melodic motion) to bear on the relationship between two voices. He also harks back to the pedagogy of *Ad organum faciendum* and the Montpellier treatise in framing his precepts in terms of beginnings, middles, and ends of phrase. But these distinctions no longer function in a very useful way, for beginnings and middles share the same sounds, and ends (now called *distinctio* rather than *copula*) may fall on fourths and fifths as well as octaves and unisons. Really characteristic sound quality is only vouchsafed to some beginnings, where fifths and octaves may be approached through the next smaller interval.

In composition, one ought to consider whether one wishes the discant to start with the cantus, or at the fifth, or at the octave. If at the fifth or octave, once in a while the phrase starts on the fourth or the seventh and from there proceeds to the fifth or the octave [respectively]. For example, if the cantus is on D, the course of the discant voice may thus be fashioned from fourth to fifth: G G a.

(Item componenti considerandum est quod si libet discantus cum cantu incipi licet vel in quinta vel in octava. Sed in quinta vel in octava hoc modo ut aliquantulus tenor sit in quarta vel in septima, unde progrediatur ad quintam et ad octavam. Verbi gratia; sit cantus in D, tenor discantus taliter formetur a quarta ad quinta g g a.)

Despite the author's reliance on prior authorities, the London/ Naples discussion of polyphony does look forward in several ways beyond John of Afflighem's chapter on diaphony. It is, in fact, the most original section of the treatise. One new aspect is a formulaic list of two-part progressions appropriate to common cantus intervals, both ascending and descending. Such lists became the stock-in-trade of thirteenth and fourteenth-century pedagogues, as evidenced by their proliferation as separate 'discant treatises'. The voice-leading progressions itemized in the London/Naples treatise constitute the student's guide to movement in the *cursus* or middle of the phrase.

Now let us turn to the course [of a phrase]. If the discant is with the cantus and the cantus descends a whole tone, let the discant rise a minor third and it will be at the fourth, and the reverse, or it will rise a minor third and a whole tone and will be at the fifth, and the reverse.

(Item de cursu animadvertendum est. Si discantus fuerit cum cantu et cantus

remittatur tono, discantus intendatur semiditono et erunt in quarta et e
contrario, vel intendatur semiditono et tono et erunt in quinta et e contrario.)

The catalogue continues with many similar progressions, confining
itself to movement to and from unison, fourth, fifth, and octave.
Although other sonorities are not explicitly excluded, they do not, by
implication, have structural status. The focus on *symphoniae* and
unisons recalls traditions bypassed by John of Afflighem, but it is here
cast in the modern frame of voice-leading progressions.

The London/Naples treatise also articulates a new attitude toward
contrary motion between the voices. John of Afflighem presents
contrary motion as an 'easy' convention but does not insist upon
observance. The London/Naples treatise makes it a rule and requires
discanting partners to proceed in opposite directions melodically.

Variety of cantus and discant motion must be carefully considered so that
when the cantus rises, the discant voice makes an appropriate descent, and
the reverse.

(Cantuum et discantuum motuum varietas diligenter consideranda est ut ubi
cantus sit intensio ibi discantus congrua fit remissio et contra.)

This stress on contrary motion coincides with formalization of
standard voice-leading progressions, which are founded upon the
premise of opposite movement between the partners.

A third feature of the London/Naples treatise, one that relates it to
a style of music later than that described by John of Afflighem, is the
distinction drawn between two species of polyphony—discant and
organum. John mentions compound melodic movement in the discant
voice without in the least suggesting it to be a sub-category of style.
The later author explicitly differentiates between discant and organum
texture, in vague language that nevertheless conforms with subsequent understanding of the distinction.

Now the difference between discant and organum should be considered.
Discant proceeds in simple notes or neumes, organum in diverse ones.

(Item consideranda est differentia inter discantum et organum. Discantus
namque tamen in simplicibus notis vel neumis discurrit, organum vero tum in
diversis.)

That 'diverse notes and neumes' refers to florid motion in one of the
parts is implied in a later statement:

Again, from Guido we understand that, if you like, the cantus can be
expanded with diverse neumes with respect to the organum, or the organum
with respect to the cantus.

(Item a Guidone habemus quod cantus cum organo et organum cum cantu potest diversis neumis multiplicari si placuerit.)

The mustering of prior authority is typical of this author, but the way in which is it done here (by twisting a comment of Guido's about octave doubling) suggests that the distinction between florid and note-against-note texture was relatively new, and shows that in any event the writer knew of no legitimate predecessor to cite.

Neither the London/Naples treatise nor the voice-leading progression manuals are at all informative about the relation of organum and discant textures to sounded music. The voice-leading manuals, indeed, are largely indifferent to the very notion of contrasting textures, although the anomalous Vatican organum treatise does offer over 250 melismatic elaborations of two-interval progressions (Ex. 174).[21] In comparison with earlier treatises on polyphony (which tend to have the aspect of practical manuals even when rooted in solid theoretical ground) such works as John of Afflighem's *De Musica*, the London/Naples treatise, and the discant treatises seem remote from the actual creation of polyphony. Their value is not in instructions for generating pieces, but in their recognition of contrapuntal propriety. For an idea of how standard interval progressions, distinctions between discant and organum, and voice-leading by contrary motion are applied in actual composition, the repertories themselves must be consulted.

Ex. 174

[21] Rome, Bibl. Apost. Vat. Ottob. lat. 3025, fo. 46.

From the early twelfth century on, sources of polyphony become relatively numerous and informative. Not only do they preserve a significant quantity of pieces, but they preserve them in a decipherable notation that is fairly explicit about pitch and elementary co-ordination between the voices. Theoretical comments remain helpful, but are no longer absolutely requisite to recovery of the music. The surviving sources preserve three principal twelfth-century repertories of polyphony: one from Aquitania, whose sources span a century from about 1100 to the early 1200s; another of Cluniac affiliation associated with the great pilgrimage centre of Santiago de Compostela and copied about mid-century; and one from Paris whose beginnings are traditionally put in the 1160s, the decade in which a new Cathedral of Notre-Dame began to take shape on the Île Saint-Louis in Paris. Only the first two will be considered here, for the Parisian repertory initiates a new stage of development which goes beyond two-part writing and decisively shapes the course of thirteenth-century music. Both the Aquitanian and the Compostelan repertories comprise monophonic as well as polyphonic music. The restriction to their polyphony in the present chapter derives not from the sources but from the modern convention that sharply distinguishes between single and multi-voiced setting.

AQUITANIAN POLYPHONY

The Aquitanian repertory of polyphony comprises some seventy pieces largely preserved in nine different sources, several of which were early (thirteenth century) bound together in single volumes. Three of the resulting four codices were preserved in the monastery library of Saint Martial at Limoges, a circumstance which gave rise to the designation 'Saint-Martial' polyphony for their contents.[22] As the original sources are quite diverse in nature and in content—only one-sixth of the pieces, monophony and polyphony, appear in more than one collection—it seems wise to discard this misleading label and to designate the repertory as Aquitanian after the primary element, Aquitanian notation, that all the sources have in common.

In comparison with earlier known polyphonic traditions, Aquitanian polyphony impresses in two respects: in choice of texts and in range of possible rhythmic relationships between the voices. The composers bypassed the liturgical chants of Mass and Office, and chose rather to set contemporary Latin religious poetry, rhymed, strophic, accentual texts called *versus* by the scribes. Although some

---

[22] The three codices from the St Martial library are Paris, Bibl. Nat. lat. 1139, 3549, and 3719; the fourth, related manuscript is London, Brit. Lib. Add. 36881.

of the poems terminate with the versicle 'Benedicamus Domino' or its response, 'Deo Gratias', thus manifesting a function within the Offices, these in no way differ in musical or textual manner from the other versus. The twelve polyphonic proses are eclipsed in quantity by the fifty-nine versus and 'Benedicamus Domino' versus that constitute the bulk of the collections. While the proses appear in no orderly liturgical series, the versus focus topically on the birth of Christ and on Mary, His virgin mother. As proper to the Christmas season, they doubtless contributed to the festivity of its celebrations. Several of these versus texts and melodies are transmitted in thirteenth-century Circumcision Offices, a valuable clue to their earlier usage.

Besides linking polyphony with rhythmic poetry, the Aquitanian composers also emancipated the organal voice rhythmically, often allowing it clusters of many notes against single pitches or two-to-three-note neumes in the principal voice. Although, to judge from theoretical testimony, multiplication of notes in the organal voice had been known in the eleventh century, the Aquitanian repertory is the first in which it is a commonplace of style. This rhythmic independence of the organal voice substantially extends the range of textural possibilities, and the texture of Aquitanian polyphony indeed spans a wide range: from strict note-against-note conduct of the parts to neume-against-neume writing (with the upper, organal voice generally more active than the lower, principal one), to a florid manner in which the organal voice sings melismatically against sustained notes in the lower voice. The highly florid manner is particularly conspicuous in the proses and in the few anomalous compositions on older chant, but occurs also in some versus settings. Changes of texture are a compositional resource, used within pieces to differentiate phrases or sections, or to articulate cadential points. A typical plan, seen in the versus 'Viderunt emmanuel' (see Ex. 176 below), has the upper voice beginning with a relatively ornamental line and later joining the principal melody in co-ordinated note-against-note movement. In thirteenth-century Parisian terminology, these contrasts of texture would be distinguished as 'organum' and 'discant'. These terms seem inappropriate to the Aquitanian repertory, however, not only because 'organum' tends to misrepresent the upper-voice melismata (which are typically far shorter and less ambitious than those in Parisian 'organum purum') but also because, positing two polar extremes, they mask the subtle gradations of texture characteristic of Aquitanian polyphony. While John of Afflighem's word 'discant' may aptly denote passages in which the voices are relatively equal in motion, passages in which one voice is consistently more active than the other may be characterized as more or less florid.

The first strophe of 'Primus homo corruit', Ex. 175(i),[23] illustrates a moderately florid texture and exemplifies some of the problems encountered in transcribing it from the original notation. While the scribe of the version represented here indicates the general alignment of parts with vertical lines (retained in the transcription), the co-

Ex. 175

(i)

[23] Brit. Lib. Add. 36881, fo. 7ᵛ.

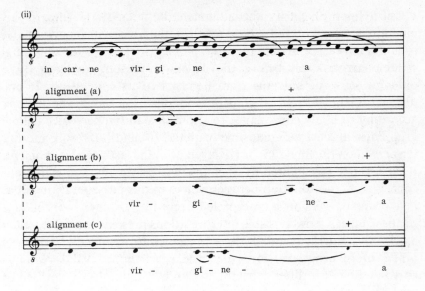

ordination of the voices is by no means clear within lines when the voices have neumes of unequal length—note especially '(*cor*)-ru-(*it*)' and '(*femi*)-ne-(*a*)'. The notation gives no clue concerning the relative duration of individual notes or note groups, or the presence of a metric pulse. Numerous aspects of the notation and transmission of Aquitanian polyphony suggest that such ambiguities are deliberate, that there was indeed no prevailing pulse or single correct way to co-ordinate the voices in this music. Some idea of freedom (or, better, indeterminacy) in execution may be gleaned from concordant versions preserved in other sources. Ex. 175(ii)[24] shows the final phrase of the first strophe of 'Primus homo' in another source whose notation shows it to have been written earlier than the version in Ex. 175(i). To start with, the organal voice in this earlier version is slightly more elaborate than that of the later one. Its timing will therefore be somewhat different—whether of equivalent or of longer duration than the first version cannot be determined. The variation in the figural detail gives some inkling of the malleability of the florid voice. Although its essential motion is the same in both versions—a circling around D and rising to a, followed by descent to C, a rise and cadential descent to D—the melodic details agree only partially, disagreeing particularly on the final cadence figure.

Contrapuntal aspects of the two versions pose problems that concern not only freedom in performance but also basic issues of editing and transcription. The scribe of the earlier version uses no

[24] Bibl. Nat. lat. 3549, fo. 152.

division lines to clarify the alignment between the voices. If his
alignment is read literally, Ex. 175(ii)(*a*), the lower voice neumes and
syllables fall earlier than in the later, plainly marked version. The final
syllable arrives well before the cadential unison, giving a quite
different sense of how the phrase comes to its conclusion. If one
disregards the written alignment and disposes the lower melody
according to likely consonance relationships and upper-voice neume
groupings, at least two plausible readings, (*b*) and (*c*), result, more if
the arrival on the final D is not delayed until the last possible moment.
If each source is read literally, then the two scribes offer quite different
concepts of co-ordination between voices in this passage. If the more
indeterminate version is interpreted according to likely consonance
relationships, several possible interpretations present themselves, each
apparently equally valid. If it is pressed into conformity with the
other, more exact, version, then the spectrum of valid readings
narrows. Scholars differ substantially in their opinions over which of
the above courses is preferable for editor or performer. No matter
how the problem of aligning the voices is resolved, questions about
durations of individual notes and the rhythmic character of the
passage remain to be confronted. Performance choices and uncertainties of the sort briefly sketched for this short phrase are endemic to the
Aquitanian repertory. They constitute an aspect of the 'style' that
traditional Western notation is quite unsuited to convey. The lapse of
a performance tradition, which must have animated the original
notations, means that the constraints controlling plausible realizations of these compositions can now only be surmised, especially in
cases (the majority) where but one version survives. The transcriptions offered here, beyond showing what seems clear in the source
chosen for presentation, suggest appropriate alignment between the
voices and rhythmic interpretation *ex contingenti* (to borrow a phrase
from a much later observer, John of Garland).

Although rhythmic details remain uncertain, higher levels of rhythmic structure—those resulting from phrases and phrase groups and
from manner of setting text (syllabically, neumatically or melismatically)—are readily apparent from the notation. Here the interplay of
text and music is of critical importance, for the clear shape of the
rhymed, strophic versus texts carries over into the musical settings.
Indeed, the structure of the poetic text can be viewed as a matrix
within which virtually all important large-scale features of the musical
setting originate. Formal design, tonal plan, phrasing, placement and
weighting of cadences all relate intimately to poetic structure in the
majority of pieces. Such interaction between text and music may

readily be seen in the first strophe of 'Primus homo', Ex. 175(i). The 'odd' opening syllable, 'O', is set apart by an introductory vocalization that cadences on the first syllable of the regular seven-syllable line. The four even seven-syllable lines of the strophe (alternately proparoxytonic and paroxytonic) are reflected in four musical phrases, each articulated at the end by a particularly prominent flourish leading to a unison arrival. The first bi-hemistich, rhymed *ab* ('corruit ... -nea') is reflected in a repeated phrase, *x x'*. The answering couplet receives a loosely related pair of phrases in the lower voice, each of which begins on G and descends to D. The melodic interval of a third beginning phrase three, 'sed secundus', links it with the first phrase, audibly associating the 'first' and the 'second man' of the text. The syntactical relation within each couplet is realized through alternation of cadences a tone apart: a/G for the first pair, E/D for the second. The strophic unit is defined by a sequence of cadence tones (a–G–E–D) that outlines a directed descent toward the final, D, established in the opening vocalization. The remaining six strophes of 'Primus homo' continue the close interaction between poetic and musical structure begun in the first strophe.

The versus 'Viderunt Emmanuel' (Ex. 176) illustrates well the complex relationships that may be created through interaction of texture, text settings, and poetic structure.[25] The text is two strophes of parallel construction, containing four seven-syllable lines grouped in pairs by the rhyme scheme *abab cded*. The music emphasizes the paired lines of each strophe by its phrase repetitions, *xy xy' vz vz'*, but does not observe the poetic balance of the two strophes. The setting of the first strophe is longer than that of the second, so masking the equivalent length of their texts. The second strophe contrasts with the first in its severely note-against-note texture and uniformly syllabic text setting (up to the penultimate syllable). While this strophe is conceived as a unit, the first is partitioned through subtle variations in texture. In the initial strophe, the first seven-syllable line of each pair is moderately florid in texture. The second is strictly discantal and blossoms into a long melisma on the penultimate syllable. These two melismata both sharply articulate the end of each text couplet and break the melodic parallelism between the two rhymed units. Viewing 'Viderunt Emmanuel' as a whole, the terminal melismata create a musical division of three (not two) main sections, through their

---

[25] This is not a trope to the Christmas Gradual in origin, as has sometimes been represented. There are two Aquitanian sources. That shown here is from Paris, Bibl. Nat. lat. 3719, fo. 68ᵛ. In the other reading, Paris, Bibl. Nat. lat. 3549, fo. 151ᵛ, the third and fourth text lines are written without neumes as text for a repetition of the first two musical phrases.

Ex. 176

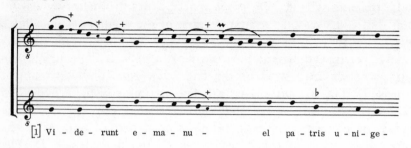

[1] Vi - de - runt e - ma - nu - el pa - tris u - ni - ge -

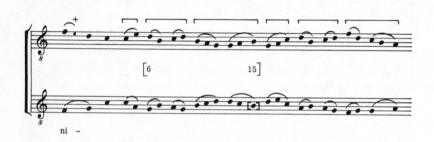

[6   15]

ni -

tum In ru - i - nam Is - ra - el

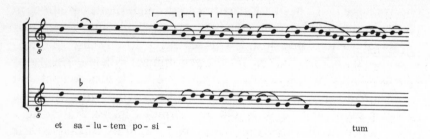

et sa - lu - tem po - si - tum

[2] Ho - mi - nem in tem - po - re   ver - bum in   prin - ci - pi - o

Ur - bis quam fun - da - ve - rat   na - tum in pa - la - ci -

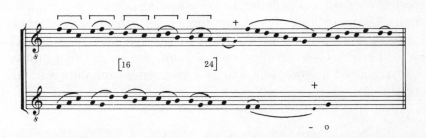

[16   24]

- o

+
• = liquescent note

placement at the end of both couplets in the first strophe, but of the last only in the second strophe. Instead of two equal sections, expected from the two matching poetic strophes, the listener perceives three main musical units, each closed by an extended vocalization.

Prominent terminal melismas of the sort seen in 'Viderunt Emmanuel' are common in the versus (and bring to mind the *caudae* of Parisian conductus). They normally fall on the penultimate syllable of a text line or strophic unit, and have a strong articulatory effect. A striking feature of these melismas—so pervasive as to constitute a central stylistic feature of the repertory as a whole—is their construction in short motives that converge and diverge symmetrically about poles of unison, fourth, fifth, and octave. The melismas are virtual mosaics of two- and three-note figures diverging outward from unison to fourth or fifth or converging inward from octave to fifth, or from

fifth/fourth to unison (see the brackets in Ex. 176). Sometimes these
brief motives cohere into larger units, as in the first melisma
('unigeni-' notes 6–15), where consecutive figures contract and expand
from G–d to b natural, or in the last ('palaci-' notes 16–24), where a
unison-fourth-unison figure drops by step down toward the final
cadence on G. Sometimes the motives seem to be juxtaposed almost at
random. The potential metric effects of these figural units are apparent in the last melisma, which maintains three-note units, most
converging on unisons, until the organal voice breaks away into a last
flourish. The second melisma ('positum') maintains two-note units
until the cadential ornament. Assuming uniform duration of equal
motivic units, these sequences of two- or three-note figures will tend to
generate a sense of metre through the regular groupings they create.
Such regularity of motivic units is not, however, a consistent feature
of the terminal melismas, most of which freely intermix figures of two,
three, and four notes.

Although they find their most cogent expression in discantal
melismas, symmetrical converging and diverging figures anchored on
perfect consonances underlie the voice-leading in many longer phrase
units. The first phrase of 'Viderunt Emmanuel' can be understood as a
series of symmetrical figures, the first a cross-over from the octave G–
g to the fifth G–d, pivoting on a unison, the second two motives
converging on unisons, followed by a divergence from unison to fifth
(Figure 2).

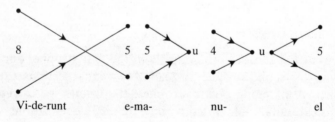

FIG. 2.

The second strophe begins similarly, but with the voices reversed and
the unison pivot extended to three notes. Indeed, the short, symmetrical motives characteristic of the terminal melismas embody the
cardinal principle of voice-leading in this repertory—contrary motion
to and from simple *symphoniae* and unisons. Such voice-leading may
be carried out over diverse temporal spans varying from two notes to
an entire phrase. Although the two voices sometimes do move in the

same direction or in parallel (Ex. 176, 'unige-', '-nem in tem-'), they proceed contrary to each other far more frequently.

The integration between voices evident in discantal melismas like those of 'Viderunt Emmanuel' suggests that in these passages the voices were conceived together as a pair. The usual assumption (grounded in discant expositions and in a comment of Franco of Cologne) is that the voices in medieval polyphony were created successively; that the composer started with a given cantus, usually a known chant or monophonic song, and added another voice to it. While this seems a reasonable assumption for polyphony on older chant, it is not so obvious for the versus. Only eleven of the polyphonic versus are known in monophonic versions (one of them, 'Prima mundi', a fragment of a prose); hence it is not unlikely that some of the polyphonic versus were conceived from the start in two voices. Broadly speaking, stylistic features of the lower voices, such as their tonal clarity and formal coherence, urge their priority over the more loosely defined upper voices. But interrelationships between the voices in some passages do strongly imply simultaneous conception of both lines. So, for example, in 'Noster cetus psallat letus',[26] (Ex. 177), the voice-exchange in the opening phrase and, at the motivic level, within the terminal melisma of the initial couplet, makes it appear that the two voices took shape concurrently. Similar voice-exchange between phrases occurs in '[D]eus quam brevis est' and in 'Par partum virginis', but is not a regular feature of the style. Simultaneous conception of the voices in terminal melismata often appears plausible because of interlocking motivic figures in which the voices function as a unit, as in Ex. 176. It is sometimes broached by differences of opinion between scribes over which of a pair of lines belongs to the principal voice, which to the organal one. Priority of the two-voiced

Ex. 177

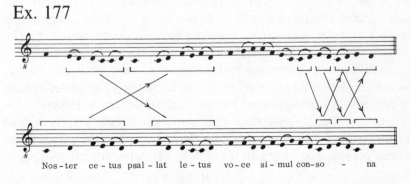

Nos-ter   ce-tus psal-lat   le-tus   vo-ce si-mul con-so   -   na

[26] Bibl. Nat. lat. 1139, fo. 61.

complex is suggested in still another way in the first two melismata of
'Viderunt Emmanuel' (Ex. 176, 'unigeni-', 'posi-'), for the melodic
parallelism of the main voice yields to a tightly woven interplay
between the voices just as the melismata begin.

In versus discant passages, the principal sonorities between the
voices are octave, fifth, and unison. Fourths and thirds occur less
frequently, the latter often within a voice-leading pattern between
perfect consonances. This stress on the *symphoniae* and the unison
may also be construed in most florid passages. In 'Primus homo',
Ex. 175(i), the upper-voice figure on '(pri-)mus' essentially decorates a
fifth-to-unison, as does that on '(ho-)mo'; the figure on '(pro-)fu-'
clearly ornaments the octave and fifth of the C in the lower voice. The
extent to which florid lines are governed by underlying progressions
between perfect concords is particularly noticeable in the proses. The
intricate organal voice above the first phrase of 'Alma chorus
domini',[27] (Ex. 178(i)), can, for instance, be reduced to a bald succession of octaves, fifths, and unisons with the cantus (Ex. 178(ii)).
Generally the main concord sounds on the last note of the upper-voice
figure, giving each neumatic group an end-directed quality. The initial
figure decorates a single pitch, g, in a manner possibly akin to the
longa florata mentioned by thirteenth-century commentators on Parisian 'organum purum'. Some groups move from one stable interval to
another, as on '(do-)mi-'. Phrases 2*a*, *b* illustrate the variety of
organum possible even when the vocabulary of basic sonorities is
extremely limited: the upper voices start quite differently and only
gradually become similar over the last third of the chant phrase.

The discant reduction for the first phrase, Ex. 178(ii), possesses a
remarkable degree of parallel motion in fifths. For the most part, the
elaborate and varied detail in the upper voices masks the parallelism,
but the contrary motion to cadential octaves and unisons (placed in
this phrase at the end and at the internal caesura) still stands out. The
discant reduction poses *musica ficta* problems in a particularly harsh
way, for in so far as *symphoniae* are, by convention, preferred choices,
both occurrences of b natural in the cantus are accompanied by the
note a fifth above. Lowering both b's is unsatisfactory, for it changes
the mode of the chant from *tetrardus* to *protus*. The first f can be
raised—a solution supported by the Vatican organum treatise (Bibl.
Vat. Ottob. 3025)—but raising the second causes an unpleasant
melodic tritone if carried back from the reduction to the actual piece.
In this second case, both notes should probably be left natural in

---

[27] Bibl. Nat. lat. 3719, fo. 49. Lines 3*b* and 4*b* occur in the manuscript with only the chant
sketched in above. Three more verse pairs follow in monophonic sources.

Ex. 178

(i)

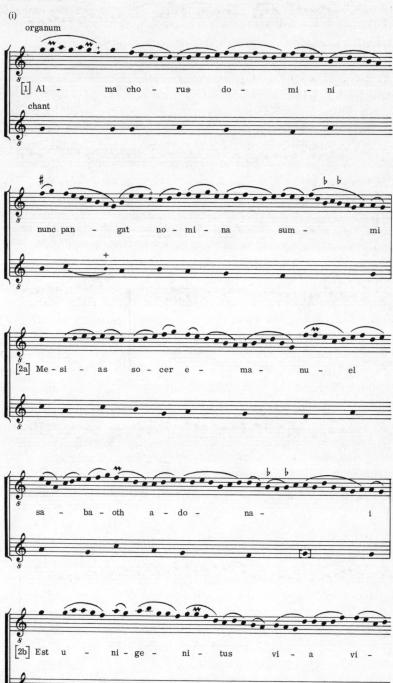

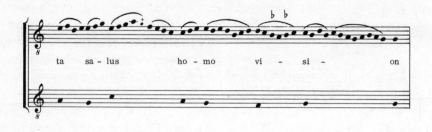

ta sa - lus ho - mo vi - si - on

[3a] Prin-ci - pi - um pri-mo - ge - ni - tus
[3b] Al - pha ca - put fi - nis - que si - mul

sa - pi - en - ci - a vir - tus [4a] Fons et
vo - ci - ta - tus et est O [4b] Ag - nus

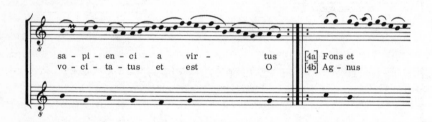

o - ri - go bo - ni pa - ra - cli - tus
o - vis vi - tu - lus ser - pens a - ri -

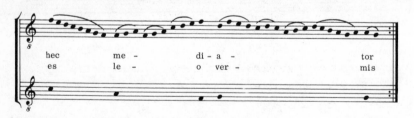

hec me - di - a - tor
es le - o ver - mis

[3 more verse pairs follow in monophonic sources]

(ii)

performance, although abstractly the interval should surely be construed as a fifth, in the sense of f being the fifth note from b. Discant
reductions of florid textures are, in any event, artificial. It should not
be supposed that the composer started with such a note-against-note
scaffolding and then ornamented it; the degree of parallelism and the
absence of common contrary-motion figures in the discant reductions
dispute such a notion. In inventing a florid upper-voice line, however,
the composer or singers seem to have been very much aware of
primary relationships of *symphonia* and unison between it and the
syllabic cantus, for these are not only pervasive but remain stable even
when variant readings reveal fluctuations in specific upper-voice
figures.

THE CODEX CALIXTINUS

One copy of the Codex Calixtinus,[28] a remarkable work incorporating
liturgy, 'history', and a pilgrim's guide for the great shrine of Saint
James of Compostela, includes a supplement of twenty polyphonic
pieces. Judging from the notation as well as from what can be
surmised about the history of the whole book, the polyphonic
supplement probably stems from north-central France and was
perhaps assembled at Cluny in the middle of the twelfth century. Little
credence can be given to the attributions assiduously provided by the
compiler but the predominance of Northern dignitaries among them
further supports the theory of a Northern origin. The pieces, all for
two voices, are quite varied in kind, and include four conductus (to
adopt the rubric used in the Codex Calixtinus for what in Aquitanian
circles were known as versus), four 'Benedicamus Domino' conductus, four Office Responsories, one *prosa* to a Responsory, a Gradual
and an Alleluia for a Mass for Saint James, two Latin Kyries and
three plain 'Benedicamus Domino' versicles. As all four Responsories,
the Gradual and the Alleluia occur monophonically within the
liturgies for Saint James copied in Book I, the polyphonic supplement
would appear to have been expressly compiled for this Codex.
Strengthening this connection, principal melodies of three other
polyphonic works (two conductus and a Latin Kyrie) also occur in

[28] Ed. Walter Whitehill and Germain Prado, *Liber Sancti Jacobi Codex Calixtinus*, 3 vols.
(Santiago de Compostela, 1944).

Book I. In addition, a subsequent hand, perhaps the copyist of the supplement, added a second voice to two monophonic conductus in Book I, one of which duplicates a two-part piece in the supplement.

The total constitution of the Calixtine repertory, with both sacred poems and the chief melismatic chants of Mass and Office represented, duplicates in miniature the constitution of Parisian polyphony in its initial stages. The number and kind of liturgical pieces within the Calixtine repertory also recall the liturgical cast of the early polyphonic fragments from Chartres.

The conductus and the 'Benedicamus' conductus are of two kinds. About half are primarily discantal, the other half fairly florid in texture. All those whose lower voice is found in Book I belong to the latter category. The discantal group has ties with the Aquitanian repertory, including a *contrafactum* of one piece ('Noster cetus' has become 'Ad superni regis decus'), and a partial concordance with another ('Gratulantes celebremus' shares its lower voice—transposed—and part of its upper line with 'Ad honorem sempiternum regis' from Brit. Lib. Add. 36881). These relationships suggest possible differences in provenance between the two groups, with the florid conductus, like the liturgical pieces, more directly within the (Cluniac) orbit of the Saint James Offices. One piece, 'Congaudeant catholici', bestrides the two groups, possessing both a florid upper voice written on a separate staff above the principal tune, and a starkly discantal counterpoint added in red ink on the staff of the lower voice. Although some scholars believe 'Congaudeant catholici' to be the earliest known example of three-part polyphony, its exceptional manner of notation and the graceless relationship between the two organal lines indicate rather that the two upper voices are alternatives. The simple discant, a model of conventional voice-leading, might have been provided for less experienced singers or for processional use.

Although only two of the conductus in discant style possess direct connections with the Aquitanian repertory, those not so allied still display marked affinities with Aquitanian style. Symmetrical figures of the sort familiar in Aquitanian versus generate both the first and third phrases of 'Nostra phalans' (Ex. 179).[29] Contrapuntal patterns in the second phrase—an ornamented succession of fifths to unisons, voice-crossing to an octave arrival—also agree with Aquitanian practice.

The florid conductus, of which the first strophe of 'Jacobe sanctum

²⁹ Santiago de Compostela, Biblioteca de la Catedral (no shelfmark), fo. 185.

Ex. 179

No - stra pha - lans | plau - dat le - ta | hac in di - e

qua ath - le - ta | Chri - sti gau - det si - ne me - ta

[Refrain]

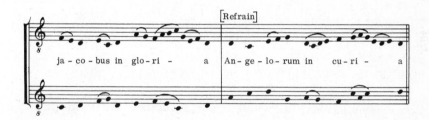

ja - co - bus in glo - ri - a | An - ge - lo - rum in cu - ri - a

tuum'[30] is characteristic (Ex. 180), do not directly incorporate symmetrical figures, but the preference for contrary motion and for primary poles of unison, fifth and octave does produce underlying patterns akin to those in the discantal conductus. The florid settings differ primarily from their Aquitanian counterparts in characteristic, recurrent motives which shape the upper line and contribute to overall formal design. In 'Jacobe sanctum tuum', a common cadential motive articulates the two halves of the strophe ('tuum', 'festum'). The caesura of the second half shares its cadential motive with the refrain ('repetito', 'colentes'). The same initial motivic succession allies both segments of the second half of the strophe ('re-petito', 'tem-pore'). The three-note ascending motive e–f–g initiates closure in the first three phrase divisions marked by the scribe. To the extent that these motivic repetitions clarify text structure and associate particular phrases, they fulfil a formal role. But, in addition, they are clearly

[30] Ibid., fo. 186ᵛ.

Ex. 180

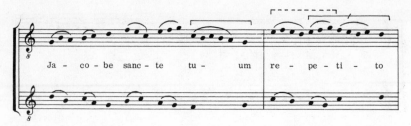

Ja - co - be sanc - te tu - um   re - pe - ti - to

tem - po - re fes - tum │ Fac pre-clu - es ce -lo co -len - tes

related to recurrent situations in the principal voice, and hence are also integral to discant structure. The two distinct cadential motives correspond respectively to cadences on G and d, and, save for one instance, the ascending three-note motive coincides with a lower G or a–G.

Recurrent figures are even more conspicuous in the florid liturgical compositions. Indeed, so many motives are common among the eleven pieces of this group as to give the impression of familiar formulas employed in a single locale or even by a specific singer. (The attribution of all the responsories and the Gradual to a single person (Hatto, Bishop of Troyes) might truthfully indicate a single cantor.) A number of these formulas are bracketed on the score of 'Huic Jacobo'[31] the ninth responsory in the Office of St James (Ex. 181). Others, unmarked, are embedded between neumes or are more distant cousins of labelled motives. A three-note motive spanning a third (marked m_a and m_d for ascending and descending versions respectively) is ubiquitous, appearing both alone and in configurations that occur so frequently as to take on individual identity. The ascending form of m regularly appears at cadences to the octave. Motive a ornaments the fifth over a cantus D. It links the beginnings of Respond and Verse. Motive b is more varied in context. It may begin on the fifth and move to a unison when the cantus ascends a step (segments 5, 9, and perhaps 10), or begin on an octave and move to a

---

[31] Ibid., fo. 188.

Ex. 181

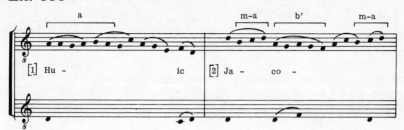

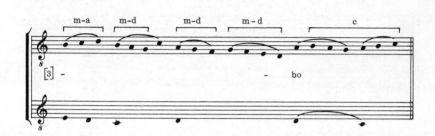

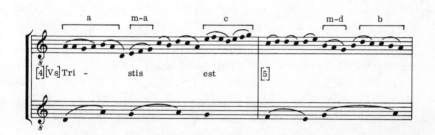

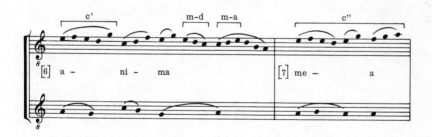

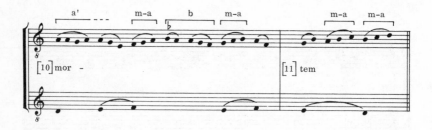

fifth (segment 9, beginning). It may appear anywhere within a phrase. Motive c, a compound of m_a and m_d, always terminates on an octave, starting either on the fifth or sixth.

Comparison among the liturgical compositions shows certain figures to be typically encountered in particular contexts or even over specific pitch successions in the principal voice. Motive b in Ex. 181 frequently occurs elsewhere above a cantus ascent of a second, and is a conventional way of moving to a unison (Ex. 182(i)). The progression from octave to unison over a cantus C–D, the gist of segment 9 in 'Huic Jacobo', happens several times elsewhere, often with some form of motive b at the end (Ex. 182(ii)). (When the final D is anticipated in the preceding neume, its co-ordination with the upper voice is a matter of conjecture.)

Conventions of the florid style extend beyond individual motives. Virtually all segments, as marked by the scribe, end on octave or unison, with the choice strictly determined by the approach in the cantus: unison if the last note is approached from below (Ex. 181, segments 1, 5, 6, 9, 10), octave if it is approached from above. Upper-voice neumes normally move toward a stable sound (octave, fifth, or unison) on their last note. Initial notes of neumes are somewhat less stable, except at the beginning of segments where the relationship between parts is normally established by a clear fifth or octave (less often a unison). The high degree of uniformity in the florid works of the Calixtine repertory distinguishes them from the florid Aquitanian

Ex. 182

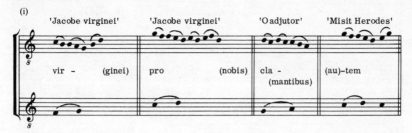

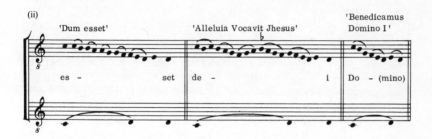

proses. Such uniformity could spring from established conventions of extemporization or from habits of a single creator, or could result from some combination of both.

Recurrent patterns of neumes in particular intervallic contexts, which permeate the Calixtine liturgical settings, have led some to argue for performance of this repertory in the measured modal rhythms characteristic of a substantial segment of Parisian music. The density and position of perfect consonances facilitates such reading, as a possible modal version of the opening of 'Huic Jacobo' shows (Ex. 183). It does seem highly likely that the stereotyped melodic figures of the Calixtine repertory (illustrated in Exx. 181 and 182) would have been performed in somewhat consistent rhythmic patterns, but it does not necessarily follow that the rhythms adopted by the singers or composers of this music would have been modal in nature. Each figure could simply have had a conventional manner of performance, partly dependent on (and inferable from) consonance relationships, not inevitably geared to rhythmic feet of set length. The characteristic irregularity of consecutive neume and pitch patterns within these florid pieces indeed suggests an irregular intermixture of durations not controlled by a prevailing sequence of long and short values.[32] In any event, there is no firm evidence to link rhythmic

---

[32] See e.g. the facsimile of a florid versus and a Respond in Besseler and Gülke, *Schriftbild*, plate 6, p. 35.

Ex. 183

theories promulgated for discant in thirteenth-century Parisian circles with this music in florid style copied *c*. 1170 at the latest. As in the Aquitanian repertory, rhythmic interpretation of the Calixtine pieces remains conjectural in its detail. Any performance or transcription necessarily involves individual decisions on co-ordination between the parts, on choice of measured or unmeasured rhythm, on the degree to which factors such as consonance, neume patterns, the melodic thrust of a phrase, will be taken into account in working out rhythms.

THE CAMBRIDGE SONGBOOK: THREE-PART POLYPHONY

A compact manuscript of only eight leaves, now in the Cambridge University Library (Ff. i. 17) but probably copied in Northern France in the late twelfth or very early thirteenth century, provides another summary glimpse of the context within which Parisian polyphony developed. This manuscript, sometimes referred to as the 'Cambridge songbook', preserves a collection of monophonic song (sacred and secular) and polyphony, a dozen two-voice compositions and one for three voices. In both nature and subject matter, the content shows close kinship with the Aquitanian repertory. The compositions are predominantly conductus (versus) and 'Benedicamus Domino' conductus; their texts concentrate on Nativity or pertain to feasts near that season: St Nicholas, St Stephen, St Thomas of Canterbury. 'Cantu miro', a two-voice 'Benedicamus Domino' conductus, links the two repertories, for it appears in the Cambridge collection as well as in two of the Aquitanian sources (once *a 1*, once *a 2*). The three-voiced piece, 'Verbum patris humanatur', shares text and principal melody with a polyphonic addition (*a 2*) to another Aquitanian collection.

In musical style also, the Cambridge settings as a group closely

Ex. 184

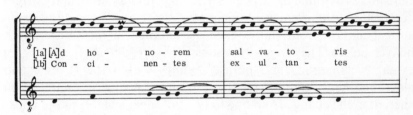

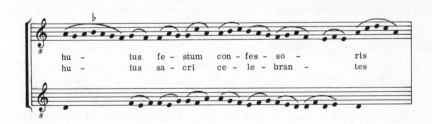

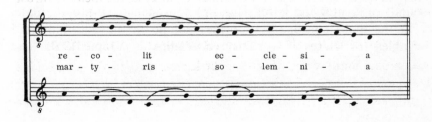

resemble Aquitanian polyphony, so much so as to suggest wide diffusion of musical traditions now chiefly associated with the one major cluster of sources to survive. 'Ad honorem salvatoris' (Ex. 184)[33] would not appear out of place in an Aquitanian *versarium* with its mixture of florid and discantal texture, the reflection of poetic structure in its musical phrasing (the two balanced eight-syllable text lines matched by parallel arches of a fifth, D–a, a–D, in the principal melody), its deployment of symmetrical motivic figures.

Unlike any among the Aquitanian sources, the Cambridge collection gives evidence for the cultivation of polyphony in three parts. Its single three-part setting, a Christmas song, 'Verbum patris humanatur',[34] is strikingly simple in both text setting and texture (Ex. 185). The music is strictly discantal in all parts until the refrain when the two upper voices venture two notes each to one in the cantus on the exclamation 'Hei'. Whether problems of synchronizing three parts imposed a rigid pairing of single notes with single syllables in all voices seems likely but cannot be proven. The result, in any event, is that the primary word and syllable groups of the text assume controlling rhythmic influence. The regular four-syllable units within the poem ('verbum patris', 'humanatur', 'salutatur') encourage even musical units of four pulses each, as adopted in the transcription (quaver pulse). The longer durations in this reading both emphasize textual exclamations and phrase endings within the strophe and underline the beginning of the refrain, realizing an implication inherent in the change from one to two notes per syllable in the upper voices.

The three-voice texture of 'Verbum patris' is not only more sonorous in effect than a two-voice texture, but also richer in harmonic sound. In both, octaves and fifths prevail at beginnings and ends of phrases, but the three-part writing includes medial sounds of greater complexity and more dissonant quality than are usual in two-voice discant (in line 1, for example, a second plus fourth on '(pa)-tris', a fifth plus seventh and a third coincident with fourth on middle syllables of '(hu-)mana-'). Similar conjunctions occur in subsequent phrases with a frequency that quells any impulse to dismiss them as fortuitous clashes. Indeed within the first, second, and fourth phrases, sounds of greater and lesser degree of consonance tend to alternate, with the more consonant sonorities falling on the odd-numbered syllables (or pulses if a measured reading is adopted), the less

---

[33] Cambridge, Univ. Libr. Ff.i.17, fo. 299ᵛ.
[34] Ibid., fo. 4.

Ex. 185

Ver - bum pa - tris hu - ma - na - tur o o dum pu - el - la

sa - lu - ta - tur o o sa - lu - ta - ta fe - cun - da - tur

[a?]

vi - ri ne - sci - a he - i he - i no - va gau - di - a

consonant ones on even-numbered syllables.[35] The patently unstable
sounds in these phrases on the penultimate odd syllable, the seventh,
give extra impetus toward the stable arrival on the last odd syllable of
each line.

The Cambridge 'Verbum patris' may or may not have been a
singular work in its day. In any event, it provides some sense of how a
practice based on the interaction of two voices might be adapted to
three. This composition surely was conceived from the start in three
voices, for, judged by the norms of two-voice discant, neither upper
voice alone makes a really satisfactory counterpoint with the principal
melody. Each of the upper parts seems to take its cue from the
principal melody, commonly moving contrary to it. The resulting high
concentration of parallel and similar motion between the upper voices
is especially apparent in the last two phrases. The two upper parts
together keep to the normal locus of a single organal line, the space of
an octave. For each, the main territory is fairly well defined. The
middle voice moves from the fifth above the final down to the final,
countering the principal melody which rises from the tone below the
final to the fifth above. The highest voice is concentrated in the
tetrachord from the octave above the final down to the fifth (Ex. 186).
The prominent role of c as a lower neighbour to d in this line mirrors
that of F to the final G in the principal line. Prevailing intervals
between voices conform with characteristic ranges. Fifth, third, and
unison (in that order) are most frequent between the middle voice and
the melody, fifth and octave between the highest part and the melody.
The fourth is by far the most common interval between the two upper
voices. Hence, despite the variety of sonorities when all parts sound
together, *symphoniae* and unisons still control the relationship
between the principal, given, melody and each of the other voices.

Ex. 186

---

[35] This situation recalls a dictum of the *Discantus positio vulgaris*: 'Those odd-numbered
notes/sounds that are consonant are more consonant than even-numbered ones; those that are
dissonant are less dissonant than even-numbered notes.' (*Omnes notae impares, hae quae
consonant, melius consonant, quae vero dissonant, minus dissonant quam pares.*)

The three-part writing of 'Verbum patris' does not depart radically from two-part writing, though it markedly extends the resources of sonority and counterpoint. At the same time, composition in three parts poses the acute problem of co-ordination among the lines, solving it in this case by strictly syllabic text setting. As far as we know, a more flexible solution to this problem was only attained within Parisian circles, with the adoption of a rhythmic convention that could stand independently of a text.

TRADITIONS AND INFLUENCE IN TWELFTH-CENTURY POLYPHONY

Traditionally, the first phase of medieval polyphony has been seen to culminate in the Parisian repertory of the late twelfth and the thirteenth centuries. Various factors have contributed to this view: the number and scope of the Parisian sources, the dispersal of the style on the Continent and in Britain, the emergence of the motet—the dominant genre of the later thirteenth century—from Parisian circles, the existence of a significant theoretical literature pertaining to the repertory, and, not least, the stature of Paris itself as the principal cultural and intellectual centre of the time. This view of history has naturally prompted historians to seek the background for Parisian polyphony in other twelfth-century repertories and to interpret these repertories largely as preparatory stages to the Parisian achievement. The historical evidence, however, poses difficulties for such a bias, beginning with uncertainties of chronology. The dates for the Calixtine supplement, the later Aquitanian sources, and the earliest stages of the Parisian repertory are partly conjectural. For all we really know at present, these musical cultures may have been concurrent and independent or even mutually influential.

Other polyphonic traditions, now lost to us, may also have had significant bearing on stylistic trends. Scholars can hardly be confident of mastering fully the world of twelfth-century polyphony when so few sources survive, and these of uncertain provenance and date. Very little is known about the circulation of polyphonic repertory, the spread of performance traditions, the cultivation of part-music in major monasteries and cathedrals during the twelfth century. Contemporary observers are remarkably quiet about musical impressions. The scattered comments filtering down to us tend to be diatribes against presumptuous vocal display, not descriptions of music itself (cf. John of Salisbury, *Policraticus* I, 6). Even the copious jottings of Bernard Itier (subcantor, then cantor at Saint Martial of Limoges,

1195–1225), a person ideally situated to comment on local musical culture, contain no reference to the singing of polyphony, although they sometimes record performance of a particularly beautiful antiphon on a certain feast. The account of polyphonic singing in Wales and Yorkshire given by Giraldus Cambrensis in his *Descriptio Cambriae* (*c.* 1194) constitutes a singular case, a circumstance that contributes in no small measure to difficulties in interpreting it. Giraldus observes, in the course of a general exposition of the character and customs of the Welsh, that the people 'sing songs not uniformly as elsewhere but compositely, with many modes and melodic lines' ('In musico modulamine non uniformiter ut alibi, sed multipliciter multisque modis et modulis cantilenas emittunt'), a custom shared by the people of Yorkshire who, however, practise a different style with only two parts. Even if this report were to be corroborated, we should still have no idea what connection might exist between church polyphony of the time and this popular practice (which, Giraldus claims, is so ingrained culturally as to be learned from the cradle). It is unclear, moreover, whether in describing this music through such phrases as 'organic melody' ('organicam melodiam') and 'symphonic harmony' ('symphonica harmonia') he demonstrates anything more than his familiarity with erudite musical terms. Quite possibly his purpose was more to proclaim the cultural distinctiveness of the Welsh than to provide a factual account of a musical practice. The possibility of interchange between ecclesiastical polyphony and informal partsinging by the people of certain cultures should not be ruled out, but evidence for such interchange has yet to be produced.

Because of uncertainties and gaps in information even about ecclesiastical polyphony in the twelfth century, general explanations of stylistic evolution in twelfth-century polyphony necessarily involve a fair degree of speculation. The available evidence permits little more than some modest observations on relationships between Parisian polyphony and remnants of other notated twelfth-century repertories, uncoloured by a priori judgements of priority or influence.

The versus/conductus constitutes the most direct link between Aquitanian and Parisian repertories. The connections range from the poetic (rhymed, strophic, accentual verse, choice of Nativity subjects) to the musical—discantal and florid textures, long melismata on single syllables (dubbed *caudae* by Parisian theorists). Relationships in musical style tend to be more generic than specific in nature, however. For instance, the melismas of Aquitanian versus fall chiefly at the end of strophes or main poetic lines, whereas the *caudae* of Parisian conductus often also begin or break out in the middle of a text line.

Additionally, Parisian *caudae* tend to considerable length and are commonly far more expansive than even the longest terminal melismas in Aquitanian versus. Changes between florid and discantal textures are more a compositional resource in Aquitanian versus than in Parisian conductus. In fact, florid organal voices are relatively infrequent in Parisian conductus compared with versus/conductus of non-Parisian collections.

The Codex Calixtinus supplement and the Chartres fragments (variously assigned to the eleventh and twelfth centuries) are the only collections to provide direct parallels with the responsorial chant settings of Paris. In them, the chants chosen for polyphonic adornment are the Gradual and the Alleluia at Mass, and the Great Responsories of the Office. A shared tradition limits the polyphony to those portions sung by the soloist—the beginning of the Respond and the greater part of the Verse. Within this common framework, however, musical style differs considerably. Even the most complex of the extant Chartres settings remain essentially note-against-note in texture. The florid organal voices of the Calixtine liturgical polyphony are nowhere near as elaborate and grand in scale as their Parisian counterparts. Nor do the Calixtine compositions incorporate the sharp contrast between discantal and organal textures indigenous to the Parisian manner. Musically speaking, basic contrapuntal structure is the closest link between the liturgical polyphony of the Compostela ritual and that of Paris. In both styles, intervals of octave, fifth and unison define the beginnings and ends of phrases and control the counterpoint.

In retrospect, the decisive distinction between early stages of Parisian polyphony and other traditions of twelfth-century polyphony is not so much one of style (although significant stylistic differences do exist) but of future development. The other polyphonic traditions seem to have remained within the confines of two-part texture; musicians in Parisian circles explore the complexities of three and even four-part writing. The Aquitanian and Calixtine repertories exhibit relatively stable, direct rhythmic co-ordination between the voices which is not basically altered by choice of ametric or metric performance. Parisian polyphony manifests considerable rhythmic inventiveness, exemplified in manipulation of tenor patterns in discant clausulas, in the use of pauses to create complex voice interlockings, in codification of diverse modal rhythm patterns. Behind this is an even more fundamental difference, one ratified in the thirteenth century when John of Garland christened polyphony *musica mensurabilis*. Parisian polyphony is, as it were, a new genre—measured music; its subsequent tradition becomes literate and learned, requiring considerable training for mastery. This new classification, *musica mensurabilis*, effectively divided practices of unmeasured part-singing from true polyphony. They were not thereby extinguished, however. The principles of unmeasured polyphony survive in a modest, but apparently widespread, tradition of simple (mostly two-part) church polyphony, traces of which appear in miscellaneous notations through the Renaissance.[36] Some scholars have called this 'retrospective' polyphony, but a more fitting term would be 'vernacular polyphony'. Although its roots (norms of voice-leading, preferred intervals) are to be found in twelfth-century practice, there is nothing demonstrably backward-looking about its genesis. Arguably, the tradition is continuous, a performance practice transmitted by word of mouth from one generation to the next and cultivated in locales where taste, resources, or other factors militated against *musica mensurabilis*. It is possible, then, to trace two distinct but coexistent currents of polyphony from the twelfth century: one a vernacular practice, simple and unassuming in nature, passed along by example and spoken precept (with perhaps some help from discant manuals), a branch of *musica plana*; the other, *musica mensurabilis*, complex and artificial in nature, typically committed to writing, informed by a spirit of experiment, exploration, and change.

---

[36] A curious corroboration of the persistence of such vernacular polyphony in the late fifteenth century is furnished by some exceptional Greek polyphony produced in imitation of 'the Latins', see Dimitri Conomos, 'Experimental Polyphony "according to the ... Latins", in late Byzantine Psalmody', *Early Music History*, 2 (1982), 1.

XII

POLYPHONY AT NOTRE DAME OF PARIS

By JANET KNAPP

The first book of the *Policraticus* by John of Salisbury is devoted to a discussion of courtly frivolities, which include, among others, gaming, music, miming, and magic. There is no intent to slander music by placing it in this company, we are told. It is, after all, a liberal art; its use in the divine service is sanctioned by the Scriptures and by the Church Fathers; and it is shown by Plato, the prince of all philosophers, to be governed by the very ratios which govern the harmony of the soul. But music has been corrupted:

... before the face of the Lord, in the very recesses of the sanctuary, showing off in a riot of wanton sound they (the singers) strive through effeminate mannerisms to astound and to weaken simple souls. Were you to hear these caressing melodies, starting, chiming in, resounding, falling away, intertwining, and twittering, you would think it to be the harmony not of men but of sirens. You would marvel at the facility of their voices, unrivalled by that of the nightingale or the parrot or any other more melodious. This facility is displayed in long ascents and descents, in the dividing or doubling of notes, in the repetition of phrases, and the piling of all these together. The high or even the highest notes are so tempered by the lower and the lowest that the ear loses its power to distinguish, and the mind, soothed by such sweetness, is unable to judge of that which it has heard'.[1]

For all his disapproval, John described in vivid and suggestive language a vocal polyphony of some sophistication. There is good reason to believe that he had made its acquaintance in Paris. The *Policraticus* was provided with a dedicatory prologue and presented to Thomas Becket in 1159, but the book as such was written in the

---

[1] For the original Latin see Joannis Sarisburiensis Episcopi Carnotensis, *Policratici sive de nugis curialium et philosophorum* Libri VIII, ed. Clement C. J. Webb (Oxford, 1909), i. 41. The translation is greatly dependent upon that of H. E. Wooldridge, *Oxford History of Music*, i (London, 1901, 290), 290, n. 1.

period immediately following John's return to England from Paris after what has now been established as a sojourn of no less than ten years (1137–47[2]). If indeed Parisian polyphony was the object of John's reproach—and the appropriateness of his description to the surviving repertory leaves little doubt about this—then it is safe to say that by 1140 the French capital had become the centre of a lively musical culture. We do not know at what time or in what manner that culture took root. Was it a spontaneous local growth? Was it a transplant, or was it a hybrid, produced by grafting foreign material onto native stock? Some day, perhaps, we shall be able to answer these questions. This much we now know: it marks the beginning of a polyphonic tradition of heretofore unparalleled brilliance and scope, one destined to exert widespread and enduring influence.

A little over a century after the completion of the *Policraticus* by John, another Englishman was to report in a more particular, albeit less colourful, manner on the music and musicians of Paris. In an essay on measured rhythm and discant composition, the so-called Anonymous 4[3] leaves off for a time the discussion of theoretical matters to relate what he knows about the development of the repertory that is his immediate concern. Most significant, in his view, were the contributions of two men—Master Leonin, reputed to be ('secundum quod dicebatur') the finest composer of organum, and Master Perotin, the finest composer of discant. Although his formulation seems to suggest that he himself was not acquainted with the music of Leonin, the theorist attributes to him the composition of a large book of organum on the Graduale and the Antiphonale. This book was in use until the time of Perotin, who shortened it and made more and better clausulas or periods ('clausulas sive puncta'). Anonymous 4 then mentions some of Perotin's compositions by name: 'Viderunt' and 'Sederunt', which he describes as the best four-voiced organa (quadrupla); the noble three-voiced organa Alleluia 'Posui adjutorium' and 'Nativitas'; a conductus for three voices, 'Salvatoris hodie', and one for two, 'Dum sigillum'. Perotin's books were in use in the choir of Notre-Dame ('ecclesie beate marie parisiensis') until the time of Robert of Sabilone (of whom nothing further is known save that he was a singer), and from his time to the present.[4]

Elsewhere in his treatise the author observes that the polyphonic

---

[2] R. W. Southern, 'Humanism and the School of Chartres', *Medieval Humanism and Other Studies* (Oxford, 1970), 61.

[3] His is the fourth in a group of Anonymous treatises ed. Edmond de Coussemaker, *Scriptorum de musica medii aevi nova series*, i (Paris, 1864). Also ed. Fritz Reckow, *Der Musiktraktat des Anonymous 4*, 2 vols. (Wiesbaden, 1967).

[4] Coussemaker, *Scriptorum*, p. 342; Reckow, *Musiktraktat*, p. 46.

repertory from Notre Dame is contained in a series of books, each devoted to a particular category of composition. One contains four-voiced organa as, for example, the 'Viderunt' and 'Sederunt' already mentioned; a second has three-voiced organa such as 'Alleluia Dies sanctificatus', etc.; a third has two-voiced organa exemplified by 'Judea et Jerusalem' and 'Constantes'. Three other volumes have conductus of various kinds: those for three voices with melismata (*caudis*, literally 'tails'), as 'Salvatoris hodie' and 'Relegentur ab area'; those for two voices with melismata, as 'Ave Maria', 'Pater noster commiserans', and 'Hac in die rege nato', in which are contained the names of several conductus; and those for two, three, and four voices without melismata. His failure to cite any examples of the last-named along with the observation that such pieces were popular with less accomplished singers ('cantores minores') suggests that the simple conductus were not greatly esteemed by the theorist.[5]

MANUSCRIPT SOURCES

Anonymous 4's brief historical digressions are interesting in their own right, but their great significance lies in the fact that they make it possible for us to identify the chief sources of Notre-Dame poly-phony. The most comprehensive of these is the manuscript Florence, Biblioteca Laurenziana, Pluteus 29.1 (F).[6] Recently shown, on the basis of its handsome illuminations, to have originated in Paris in the atelier of Johannes Grusch, painter between *c*. 1245 and 1255,[7] this manuscript not only contains all of the genres listed by Anonymous 4 in essentially the same order, it has all of the pieces cited as examples. The four-voiced compositions, both organa and conductus, appear in the first fascicle, three-voiced organa for Office and Mass in the second, two-voiced organa for the Office ('de Antiphonario') in the third, and two-voiced organa for the Mass ('de Gradali') in the fourth. The fifth fascicle is devoted to clausulas, the sixth and seventh to three- and two-voiced conductus respectively. Separate fascicles are not provided for melismatic and syllabic conductus, but the composi-tions are loosely arranged in groups or blocks, primacy of place granted in each case to those with melismata.

A smaller, though still very substantial collection is contained in the manuscript Wolfenbüttel, Herzog-August Bibliothek 677, formerly Helmstedt 628 (W₁).[8] The ordering of the materials is less rigorous

[5] Coussemaker, *Scriptorum*, p. 360; Reckow, *Musiktraktat*, p. 82.

[6] Facs. edn. Luther Dittmer (Brooklyn, NY, 1960).

[7] Rebecca Baltzer, 'Thirteenth-Century Illuminated Miniatures and the Date of the Florence Manuscript', *JAMS*, 25 (1972), 1.

[8] Facs. edn. J. H. Baxter, *An Old St. Andrews Music Book* (London, 1931).

than in F, but the overall design is much the same. The surviving portion of the initial fascicle contains organal compositions for four voices. If at one time there were also some four-voiced conductus, these are now missing along with the two outer leaves of the original quaternion. From here on, all of Anonymous 4's genres are represented and (with the exception of Alleluia 'Posui adjutorium', *a3* and the conductus 'Dum sigillum') all of the examples cited are present.

Both the date and the provenance of W_1 are subject to debate. The core of the repertory is clearly Parisian, but there can be little doubt that the manuscript was copied in Great Britain.[9] In the middle of the sixteenth century it was acquired in Scotland by an agent of the Protestant church historian Flacius Illyricus and ultimately found its way into the ducal library at Wolfenbüttel. An inscription on fo. 64 of the manuscript indicates that at one time it had belonged to the priory of St Andrews—'liber monasterii S. andree apostoli in Scocia'. This does not prove that the monastery was the original owner, of course, but the inclusion of two unique responsories for St Andrew in the cycle of two-voiced organa suggest that from an early date, if not, indeed, from the beginning, the manuscript was in the possession of an institution or community which held that saint in special veneration. The evidence at hand does not suffice to prove or disprove the long-held view that W_1 is truly a St Andrew's Music Book.

We are hardly better off where the date of the manuscript is concerned. Paleographical considerations led Baxter to place it in the early fourteenth century. Roesner favours this date, but others— among them Jacques Handschin,[10] Willi Apel,[11] and most recently Brown, Patterson, and Hiley[12]—have proposed the middle of the thirteenth century. This earlier date is more attractive, for it narrows the chronological gap between the composition of the music and its disposition in the manuscript. Whether it will stand in the light of more decisive evidence than has yet been brought to bear remains to be seen.

If the date of the manuscript itself remains in dispute, there is nearly universal agreement first, that the repertory as a whole is somewhat older than that of F,[13] and second, that embedded in the collection of

[9] Jacques Handschin, 'A Monument of English Polyphony: Wolfenbüttel 677', *MT*, 73 (1932), 510; and 74 (1933), 679; Heinrich Husmann, 'Zur Frage der Herkunft der Notre-Dame Handschrift W_1', in Heinz Wegener, ed., *Musa-mens-musici: Im Gedenken Walther Vetter* (Leipzig, 1969), 33; Edward Roesner, 'The Origins of W_1', *JAMS*, 29 (1976), 337.

[10] 'The Summer Canon and its Background', *Musica disciplina*, 5 (1951), 113.

[11] *The Notation of Polyphonic Music: 900–1600*, (4th edn., Cambridge, Mass., 1953), 200 n. 1.

[12] Julian Brown, Sonia Patterson, and David Hiley, 'Further Observations on W_1, *Journal of the Plainsong & Mediæval Music Society*, 5 (1981), 53.

[13] See also below, p. 563.

two-voiced organa is the oldest surviving version of Leonin's *Magnus liber organi*.

Two further manuscripts transmit limited portions of the repertory described by Anonymous 4. Wolfenbüttel, Herzog August Bibliothek 1206, formerly Helmstedt 1099 (W_2),[14] without doubt of Parisian origin, appears to be approximately twenty years younger than F.[15] The organum is still generously represented but the number of conductus has fallen off from just under 200 to a mere 29.

The origins in time and place of the manuscript Madrid, Biblioteca Nacional 20486, formerly 167 (Ma),[16] are even more obscure than those of W_1. The repertory, again, is Parisian, but with a heavy preponderance of sacred conductus. More limited in this sense than the repertory of conductus in F, the collection in Ma is, nevertheless, closely allied to it. In addition to the fact that virtually all of the pieces in Ma are also present in F, they are grouped in much the same way and the readings show remarkably few variants. There is no particular reason to think that Ma was copied from F, only that the redactors must have had access to some of the same models.

CHRONOLOGY OF THE NOTRE-DAME SCHOOL

Anonymous 4 gives us to understand that although Perotin was a respecter and continuator of the tradition established by Leonin, he was considerably younger than his predecessor—his time was not Leonin's time. As to exactly when these masters were at work, however, he says nothing. Documents issued by the Bishop of Paris in 1198 and 1199 not only shed some light on this question, they confirm the serious involvement of the cathedral in the polyphonic movement.[17] The first document concerns the conduct of services in the cathedral on the Feast of the Circumcision (1 January). In Paris, as in many other cities, the merry-making which attended the climax of the Christmas season and which, in some instances, ended in ugly violence, spilled over into the celebration of the Divine Office, making of the Lord's feast a feast of fools. Bishop Eudes de Sully's letter 'contra facientes festum fatuorum', presumably from the very end of 1198, enumerates the abuses which are to be eliminated, among others the inordinate ringing of bells, the presence of mimes and maskers, and the song-filled processions which accompany the ruler of the feast

[14] Facs. edn. Dittmer (Brooklyn, NY, 1960).
[15] So Baltzer, 'Thirteenth-Century Illuminated Miniatures', p. 17.
[16] Facs. edn. Dittmer (Brooklyn, NY, 1975).
[17] The relevant excerpts from both letters, which appear in their entirety in J. P. Migne, *Patrologia latina*, ccxii, col. 70 ff., are printed by Handschin, 'Zur Geschichte von Notre Dame', *AcM*, 4 (1932), 6 f.

(on this occasion a subdeacon) from his house to the church and back. The letter continues, in more positive vein, with suggestions for the appropriately dignified conduct of the services. During Vespers, for example, the responsory and the 'Benedicamus domino' may be sung ('poterunt decantari') 'in triplo, vel quadruplo, vel organo'. In addition, the third and sixth responsories of Matins and the responsory, that is the gradual, and the Alleluia of the Mass, are to be sung ('cantabuntur') in organum *a2*, *a3*, or *a4*. The edict of 1199, relative to the feast of St Stephen (26 December), renews the admonitions of the earlier one toward sobriety and decorum and further states that payments will be made 'to all of the clerics who, during the Mass, sing the gradual or the Alleluia in organum *a2*, *a3*, or *a4*'.

It so happens that the graduals for the Masses of Circumcision and St Stephen are, respectively, 'Viderunt omnes' and 'Sederunt principes', the very liturgical items, according to Anonymous 4, for which Perotin composed organal settings *a4*. The assumption must be that Eudes had heard some four-voiced polyphony and considered it suitable for the services. Whether the pieces in question already existed or were composed in response to the Bishop's letters, they can with reasonable safety be assigned a date between *c.* 1195 and 1199. There is no reason to doubt Perotin's authorship of these grand compositions, the only responsories *a4* to have survived.[18] It is not clear just what stage of his composition they represent, but the weight of the evidence (most of it the admittedly slippery stylistic sort) is on the side of an early stage. We may not be far from the mark in setting the date of his birth around 1165,[19] just about the time Leonin was embarking on the composition of his organum cycle.

It is true that no firm date of any kind can be associated with Leonin. It is possible, however, that one Leonellus, who is named in a handful of notices from the cathedral and from the nearby Abbey of St Victor between 1163/4 and 1192, is to be identified with the composer.[20] If so, a birthdate around 1140 is suggested, one that accords well enough with Anonymous 4's implication that Leonin was

[18] The third of the liturgical pieces *a4*, preserved like 'Viderunt' and 'Sederunt' in all the Notre-Dame sources, is the clausula 'Mors'.

[19] This is the date proposed by Ernest Sanders, 'The Question of Perotin's Oeuvre and Dates', *Festschrift für Walther Wiora zum 30. Dezember 1966* (Kassel, 1967), 241. Yvonne Rokseth, *Polyphonies du XIIIe siècle*, 4 vols. (Paris, 1936–9), iv. 42 f., prefers 'circa 1170'. Hans Tischler's arguments for *c.* 1155–60 (*Speculum*, 15 (1950), 21 and *passim*) are not persuasive.

[20] See G. Birkner, 'Notre-Dame Cantoren und Succentorum', in Higini Anglès, *et al.*, eds., *In Memorian Jacques Handschin* (Strasburg, 1962), 123. The notice of 1192 refers to the anniversary of Leonellus's death without, however, mentioning the date. It must have occurred sometime after 1187, as a notice from that year shows him still alive. Craig Wright, 'Leoninus, Poet and Musician,' *JAMS*, 39 (1986), 1–35, identified the composer with a poet of the same name who was a canon at the Cathedral.

a full generation older that Perotin. It accords well, too, with what we are able to infer from John of Salisbury's testy remarks about the music. We do not know who Leonin's artistic predecessors or mentors were, but it would not be surprising to discover that they were the very musicians against whom John railed and that the centre of their activity was the old cathedral of Notre Dame. If they did not equal Leonin in stature, they laid the foundations of an art which attracted and nurtured him and which he, in turn, would lift to its first lofty eminence.

It may appear that one arrives at a chronology of the Notre-Dame school by a highly speculative route, and to some extent this is so. We can, however, rely on what Anonymous 4 tells us, namely that Leonin was older than Perotin, and that he was the finest organista, while Perotin was the finest composer of discant. We can also proceed—at least as a working hypothesis—on the idea that W_1, F, and W_2 represent successive states of the repertory, with W_1 showing less discant than F (and next to no motets), while W_2 shows no interest in independent clausulas but devotes much space to motets.

There are, furthermore, within the repertory a number of compositions which support the suggested timetable. These are the historical or topical conductus, including laments on the deaths of secular and ecclesiastical princes, coronation pieces, celebrations of victory. One of the oldest of these is the monophonic conductus 'In Rama sonat gemitus', a bitter complaint against Thomas Becket's enforced sojourn on the Continent from November 1164 to December 1170. A polyphonic song, 'Novus miles sequitur', mourns the death of the Archbishop, slain but a few weeks after his return to England. Thomas was canonized within two years, and was honoured almost at once with an altar in the new cathedral. Any one of these events—his death, his canonization, or the dedication of the altar—might have occasioned the composition of the lament. Further examples of the historical conductus are identified with the coronation of Philippe Auguste of France in 1179 ('Ver pacis aperit') and of Richard Plantagenet in 1189 ('Redit etas aurea'), and with the death of Barbarossa in 1190 ('Pange melos lacrimosum'), and of Henry, Count of Champagne, in 1198 ('Jherusalem, Jherusalem'). These pieces, like most of the others in the repertory, are anonymous, but they are clearly in the mainstream of Notre-Dame composition and their dates dovetail nicely with those projected for this history of the Parisian school in the twelfth century.

Conductus of this sort continue to appear with some frequency in the first four decades of the thirteenth century. To name but a few,

'Anni favor jubilei', a highly sophisticated composition for two voices, is an exhortation to join the crusade against the Albigenses, undertaken by Innocent III in 1209. The victory of Louis VIII over the English at LaRochelle in 1224 is celebrated in 'De rupta Rupecula'; and the loss in 1233 of one of St Denis' most precious relics, a nail from the true Cross, prompted the composition of 'Clavus clavo retunditur'. The youngest of the historical compositions to have been identified is 'Aurelianis civitas', inspired by the massacre of a number of university students at Orleans in 1236.

Again the dates so obtained buttress the more generalized chronology deducible from other sources. Evidence from style suggests that the revisions of the *Magnus liber* along with a large number of the organa *a3* originated over a period of some twenty years after the turn of the century. Many of these compositions are associated with Perotin, directly or by stylistic analogy, and may be taken as works of his maturity. On the strength of Anonymous 4's attribution of 'Beata viscera' to Perotin we may place the composer's death after 1217.[21] The text of the monophonic conductus is one of several written by Philip, Chancellor of Notre Dame from 1217/18 to 1236.

A post-Perotinian layer of composition may extend the period of serious interest in the organum-clausula to 1230 or even 1240, but repertorial investigation leaves little doubt that the appeal of the genre was dissipating rapidly. It may have left its last faint trace in a new, but scarcely progressive composition of the mid-1250s.[22]

The decline of the organum was paralleled by that of the conductus, both genres displaced at last by a new—and for the thirteenth century, endlessly fascinating one—known as the motet. Its origin initiates the second broad phase of Notre-Dame composition, to be pursued in the following chapter.

ORGANUM

The collection of organa *a2* in the manuscript W_1 contains settings of 46 liturgical items—13 responsories for the Office, 13 Graduals, 19 Alleluias, and the dismissal formula 'Benedicamus domino'. Four compositions are unique to this manuscript: the two responsories in honour of St Andrew, one of two settings of the Marian Gradual 'Propter veritatem' (a late addition to the manuscript), and one of four settings of 'Benedicamus domino I'.[23] All of the others are

[21] See above, n. 19.

[22] Kenneth Levy, 'A Dominican Organum Duplum', *JAMS*, 27 (1974), 183.

[23] The numbers used for the 'Benedicamus domino' melodies are those of Friedrich Ludwig, *Repertorium organorum recentioris et motetorum vetustissimi stili*, I, 1 (Halle, 1910).

preserved, in varying states of revision, in F, or in F and W_2. The number of items in F (a handful of which appear in more than one setting) is more than double that in W_1, with the greatest increase in Office responsories (thirty-four) and Alleluias (forty).

The increase in the number of organa in F is accompanied by an extension in the amount of polyphony applied to at least some of the liturgical melodies in question. The responsorial chants of the Mass are three-part structures, each consisting of a respond, a verse, and the repetition of the respond. Those of the Office further include the *Gloria Patri*, sung to the same formulaic melody as the verse. The performance of these chants is traditionally divided between soloists and the chorus. These divisions are accentuated in the organa of the *Magnus liber*, almost all of which contain polyphony only for the soloistic portions of the chant. The choral parts, not copied anew in the polyphonic sources even though essential from both a liturgical and a musical point of view, are left to monophonic performances. The outlines of the earliest extant settings can be shown as follows:

R̥. Alleluia, Alleluia   V. Pascha nostrum immola-
                                           tus est   Christus.
(soloists *a2*) (chorus *a1*) (soloists *a2*)   (chorus *a1*)

Save for the second of the Andrew responsories, which includes the *Gloria Patri*, all of the organa in W_1, including those for the Office, are arranged in this manner. By contrast, twenty-one Mass organa in F have new polyphonic settings for the repetition of the respond after the verse (using the same chant melody, of course), while twenty-two Office responsories include settings of the *Gloria Patri*. Much of the same tendency toward an expanded use of polyphony may be observed in W_2, the youngest of the sources for the *Magnus liber*. The collection here (which is almost exactly the same size as that in W_1) contains no wholly original material, only revisions—or in some instances quite literal copies—of earlier compositions.

All three of the central manuscripts present the organa in much the same way: the Office responsories come first, in proper liturgical order, followed in separate fascicles by the Mass pieces. In both cases feasts of saints (from the Sanctorale) are inserted into the calendar of the Temporale. A small number of compositions for the Common of saints (Apostles, Several Martyrs, Confessor Bishops, Confessors not Bishops, Virgins) similarly inserted into the larger series in W_1 and F, forms a separate concluding group in W_2. The settings of the 'Benedicamus domino' are copied in F directly after the Office responsories, in W_2 after those for the Mass. W_1 has them at some distance from the responsories in a fascicle otherwise devoted largely to conductus.

In recent years a number of scholars have undertaken to test the inference from Anonymous 4 that the *Magnus liber*, not only in its original form, but also in its revised and enlarged versions, was indeed composed at and for the Cathedral of Notre Dame. Heinrich Husmann[24] came to the conclusion that while a central core of material common either to all three manuscripts or to F and W_2 was properly associated with the Cathedral, organa common to F and W_1 or unique to F were written for other Parisian churches—St Geneviève, perhaps, or St Victor or St Germain l'Auxerrois. Craig Wright, however, was able to show that with two possible exceptions, all of the organa in F had a place in cathedral liturgies.[25] Through an investigation of service books appropriate to the Cathedral and closely related in time to the development of the *Magnus liber* he determined that the polyphony has been applied to the liturgy 'in a rigidly hierarchical manner'. Thus the four great annual feasts of Christmas, Easter, Pentecost, and Assumption (the Virgin of the Assumption was the patroness of the Cathedral) were provided with the largest number of organa, including five to seven for use in Vespers, Matins, Mass, and in some instances for processions inside or outside the church. Two or three organa were typically available for feasts of duplex rank, only one or two for those of semiduplex rank.

Parisian organum is characterized by a combination of two contrasting styles of polyphony. The oldest compositions, which presumably reflect a tradition of long standing, are dominated by what Anonymous 4 refers to as 'organum purum', that is two-voiced composition based on a chant melody, whose successive notes are sustained to accommodate the ornamental *figurae* of a second, newly created voice. At least once in the course of such a setting, however, at a point where a melisma occurs in the chant, the organum purum is interrupted by a passage or 'clausula' of discant, in which the chant voice moves more quickly to approximate the motion of the new one. Subsequent versions of these organa, along with new compositions, show a shift in emphasis, the number and often the dimensions of the discant clausulas having been greatly increased. Neither one of these polyphonic textures is original with the Parisians; what is new—apart

[24] 'The Origin and Destination of the Magnus Liber Organi', *MQ*, 49 (1963), 311; 'The Enlargement of the Magnus Liber Organi and the Paris Churches of St. Germain l'Auxerrois and Ste. Geneviève du Mont', *JAMS*, 16 (1963), 176.

[25] In a paper read before the national meeting of the American Musicological Society, Boston, Mass., Fall, 1981.

from the monumental proportions of the works—is the early association of the discant with measured rhythm.

MODAL RHYTHM

For the Notre-Dame composer, rhythm was of the very essence of the
discant, and his steadily increasing preoccupation with so-called note-
against-note writing is inseparably linked with the expansion and
refinement of rhythmic practice. The details of the practice are
described in five theoretical treatises ranging in date from *c.* 1240 to
1279. The earliest, known simply as the *Discantus positio vulgaris,* is a
brief statement included by Jerome of Moravia in his comprehensive
Tractus de musica.[26] It is the first of four 'positions' on polyphony and
'because the nations [that is, of the University of Paris] commonly use
it, and because it is older than all the others, we have called it
vulgarem. Because it is defective, however, we have added the position
of Johannes de Garlandia.' The second of two treatises assignable to
Johannes (the first deals with chant), the *De Mensurabili musica* from
shortly after 1250, is of central importance.[27] Tersely formulated and,
for the most part, rigorously organized, it presents a fully formed
theory of what had come to be known as modal rhythm. A short essay
by Coussemaker's Anonymous 7[28] stands in time between the *Discantus positio vulgaris* and Johannes' treatise. Two theorists of somewhat
later date, Anonymous 4 (whom we have already met) and the St
Emmeram Anonymous,[29] whose work is explicitly dated 1279,
modelled their expansive treatises closely on that of Johannes.

The system of modal writing formulated by the theorists involves
six characteristic patterns or feet, roughly analogous to poetic metres,
but identified only by number.

1. Long-breve   3. Long-breve-breve   5. Long-long
2. Breve-long   4. Breve-breve-long   6. Breve-breve-breve

The short note or breve is said to contain one pulse or time unit
(*tempus*), the long two units. Accordingly modes 1, 2, and 6 add up to
ternary groups, which may be indicated in modern notation as in
Ex. 187(i). Were the same values to be used for the remaining three
modes the result would be a series of binary groups compatible only

---

[26] Coussemaker, *Scriptorum,* pp. 1–154. Simon Cserba, *Hieronymus de Moravia O.P. Tractatus de Musica* (Regensburg, 1935). *Discantus positio vulgaris,* trans. Janet Knapp, 'Two
Thirteenth-Century Treatises on the Discant', *Journal of Music Theory,* 6 (1962), 201.

[27] Coussemaker, *Scriptorum,* pp. 97–117 and 175–82. See also Eric Reimer, *Johannes de
Garlandia: De mensurabili musica,* 2 vols. (Wiesbaden, 1967).

[28] Coussemaker, *Scriptorum,* pp. 378–83. Trans. Knapp, 'Two Thirteenth-Century Treatises'.

[29] Ed. Ernst Rohloff, *Ein Anonymer Glossierter Mensuraltraktat: 1279* (Kassel, 1930).

Ex. 187

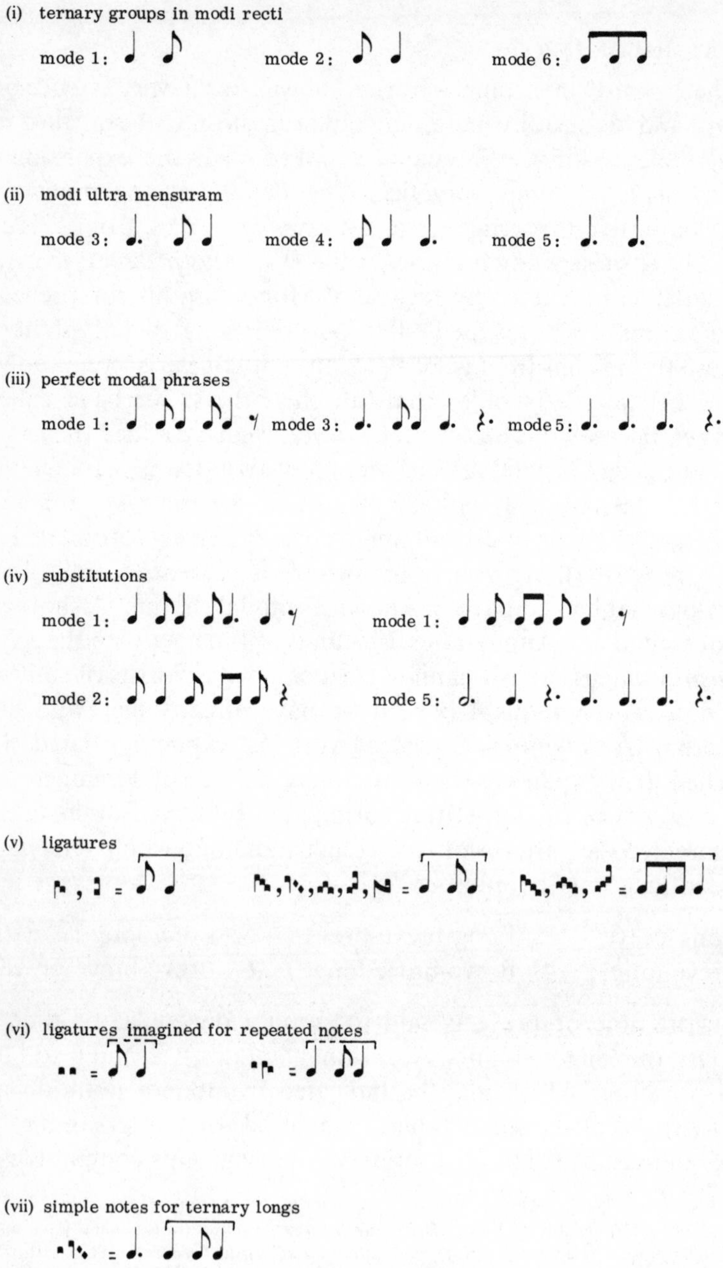

(i) ternary groups in modi recti

    mode 1:   mode 2:   mode 6:

(ii) modi ultra mensuram

    mode 3:   mode 4:   mode 5:

(iii) perfect modal phrases

    mode 1:   mode 3:   mode 5:

(iv) substitutions

    mode 1:   mode 1:

    mode 2:   mode 5:

(v) ligatures

(vi) ligatures imagined for repeated notes

(vii) simple notes for ternary longs

(viii) syllabic setting

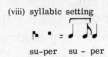

su-per   su - per

(ix) plica

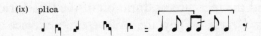

(x) ligatures in modal patterns

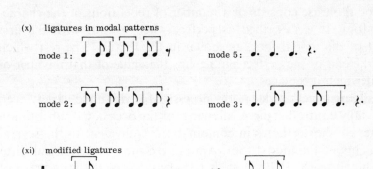

(xi) modified ligatures

(xii) alternate mode 3

(xiii) notations for mode 6

with each other. As the theorists well knew, such binary patterns did not exist in the discant and it was necessary for them to adust their theory to fit the facts. The long notes in the second set of modes are assigned three units of time, and the breves in modes 3 and 4 prove to be of unequal value: the first of one unit, the second of two. All three of the modes represented by these feet are characterized as *ultra mensuram*, that is, beyond the measure or duration of the three prior ones, which are called *modi recti*.[30] They are, in fact, exactly twice as long, as shown in Ex. 187(ii), and so can be combined not only with each other, but with the modi recti as well.

A modal phrase consists of a number of repetitions of the characteristic foot. It is described as perfect when it ends with the first element of the modal foot, as shown in Ex. 187(iii). The rest which marks the end of the perfect phrase has the value of that member of the foot which it replaces.

The theorists acknowledge the necessity for rhythmic variety even in a modally controlled piece, allowing for the occasional substitution of longer or shorter notes in combinations equivalent to the several constituents of the modal foot. Among the most common substitutions (shown in Ex. 187(iv)) are a ternary long for the long-breve of the first mode, two breves for the long of the first or second mode, and a duplex long for two ternary longs of the fifth mode. Less frequent is the substitution of two semibreves for a breve.

After explaining what the modes are, the theorists describe the way in which they are notated. As practical musicians are wont to do, the Notre-Dame composer and scribe made use of materials already at hand. To the several members of the ligatures or 'bound' forms traditionally associated with chant, symbols whose function had long been purely melodic (at least as far as the general tradition was concerned), they assigned more-or-less specific temporal values. The theorists are in general agreement as to the new rhythmic interpretation of these figures—so much so that we can argue backwards from the theorists' formulations of these points to assume that they represent practices generally followed by the musicians in the development of the repertory. The first specific rule is that the last note of a ligature is a long, the penultimate is a breve, and everything ahead of that is equal to a long. Thus the ligature of two notes (*binaria*, see Ex. 187(v)) is to be construed as breve-long; that of three (*ternaria*) as long-breve-long; and that of four (*quaternaria*) as a breve-breve-breve-long. Although the author of the *Discantus positio vulgaris*

---

[30] So Johannes de Garlandia, Coussemaker, *Scriptorum*, pp. 175 f.; Reimer, *Johannes de Garlandia*, pp. 37 f.

asserts that there is no prescribed way of reading ligatures of more than four notes, the later theorists apply the foregoing rule to ligatures of five and six notes, which most often appear as descending scalar figures.

The specific rule is regularly followed in the treatise by the more general one: never write as a simple note anything that can be written in ligature. This rule has the effect—which, given the circumstances, we can imagine to be its cause—that notes in a ligature can have durational meaning relative to each other by virtue of their positions in the ligature; thus the 'penultimate note of the ligature' is unambiguously identified, and the specific rule says it is a breve. In any case, it is to ligatures, not to individual 'simple' note forms that rhythmic values were first assigned.

There are a few circumstances under which simple notes cannot be avoided. Two notes of the same pitch, for example, cannot be written in ligature. The usual procedure is to write the repeated notes in such a way as to suggest a ligature, by placing a square punctum close to the following punctum or ligature. Such a configuration is to be construed by the singer or the reader as a ligature of two or three notes, and interpreted accordingly (Ex. 187(vi)).

It is also necessary to use simple, non-ligated forms to start a phrase with a long note of three units (*tempora*), or to indicate a series of such ternary longs. The theorists have another rule for this case, and this one, too, enjoys such general acceptance as to indicate its prior status in practice. The rule is, a long before a long is a ternary long—that is, where no ligature pattern allowing for an alternation of longs and breves appears, the longs must be made ternary to fill out the time equivalent to a long-breve alternation (Ex. 187(vii)).

Finally, a ligature may be interrupted or broken by the entrance of a new syllable of text, simply because, by the nature of a ligature, the notes in it cannot be distributed between two syllables without some kind of division (Ex. 187(viii)). Comparatively rare in the organum, such interruption of ligatures becomes the norm in the wordier categories of conductus and motet.

Along with the ligatures, two other symbols are widely used: the tractus and the plica. The tractus, a vertical stroke drawn through the middle of the staff, indicates an interruption of one sort or another in the sound; this may be a measured rest marking the end of a phrase, or an unmeasured pause for breath, or the enunciation of a new syllable of text. The plica ('fold') appears as a line, ascending or descending from the end of a simple note or a ligature (Ex. 187(ix)). Subject to a variety of rhythmic interpretations depending on its context

(Johannes de Garlandia says simply, ' ... plica nihil aliud est quam signum dividens sonum in sono diverso ... '), the plica frequently effects the division of a long note into two breves, as shown in Ex. 187(ix)). It is indicated here as elsewhere by a horizontal stroke through the note stem. The pitch of the plica, like the duration, is variable. Most often implied is the interval of a second, but the third is not uncommon, and there are places where as much as a fifth is called for.

The theorists, whose approach is largely systematic as opposed to historical, show little if any interest in the evolution of the rhythmic modes. Having placed the overwhelmingly popular trochaic mode at the head of the list, they assign to the others numbers which have a logical rather than a chronological significance. The order is made to depend on the content of the several modal feet: modes 1 and 2 each contain one long and one breve; modes 3 and 4 have one long and two breves; modes 5 and 6 have only like elements, either longs or breves, as the case may be.

Does this mean that we are to be denied any knowledge of the historical development of the rhythmic modes? I think not. There are many clues to the progress of events, some of the most significant of which reside in the notation itself—specifically in its most basic rules, which (I have argued) represent musicians' practice from the time of the development of the repertory. The theorists point out that a mode is recognizable through the sequence of figures in a given phrase or ordo. An initial ternaria followed by an indeterminate number of two-note ligatures indicates the first rhythmic mode (see Ex. 187(x)). Each of the ligatures is read according to the first rule (the penultimate is a breve, the last note a long), and a tractus stands for the rest which replaces the breve at the end of each phrase. A series of simple notes arranged in odd-numbered groups add up to the fifth mode. Here the second rule is observed: a long before a long is a ternary long. The sequence of figures for the second mode, on the other hand, involves a severe erosion of these rules. According to the theorists this mode proceeds by an indeterminate number of binarias with an ultimate ternaria. The smaller ligatures are read normally, but the first note now falls at the beginning of the foot rather than at the end; there is, however, no law against this. It is the reading of the ternaria which gives pause, for as breve-long-breve it violates every provision of the rule. The situation is scarcely better where the third mode is concerned. Here a phrase consists of a simple note followed by any number of ternarias (Ex. 187(x)). There would seem to be no reason to read the initial note as a ternary long inasmuch as it is followed by a breve. We could rationalize this by saying that the two breves at the beginning of the ligature together constitute a long, hence making the simple note a long of three tempora. This leaves us, however, with a ternaria standing for two breves and a long. The distortion is less violent than in the second mode, for the last note is a long and while the penultimate has two tempora, it is—in theory—identified as a breve. On the other hand, there is no satisfactory way to explain the first breve.

The theorists, at least from Johannes de Garlandia on, did not have to deal with all of these irregularities, thanks to a number of lately developed refinements in the musical notation. Among those with special relevance to the matter at hand were the introduction of tractus of fixed length (a line drawn through one space of the staff equals a rest of one tempus, one through two spaces a rest of two tempora, etc.[31]) and the alteration of the beginning of a ligature to indicate a reversal of the normal succession of values, as shown in Ex. 187(xi)). While these changes had little effect on the third mode other than to make clear the duration of the rest, they did eliminate the equivocation associated with the second mode. These refinements are largely absent from the Notre-Dame manuscripts, however, with the result observed, namely that some figures—above all the ternaria—are subject to more than one reading depending on their context. Anonymous 4 was aware of the ambiguity of the earlier notation and wrote sympathetically of the hours that must have been consumed in deciphering it. Like his predecessors, we, too, are obliged to engage in a certain amount of trial and error in resolving the equivocal symbols. The situation is not without its positive side, however, for it is from the very confusion of the notational symbols that some sense of historical order can be inferred.

Working from the premise that the greater the distortion of the rules, the later the mode, we are able to establish at least a relative chronology. Modes 1 and 5, which are read strictly according to rule[32] and which appear to have originated more or less simultaneously, are without any doubt the oldest. The formulation of mode 3 seems to have involved two stages. In the first of these the normal sequence of forms is employed, but the notes between the ternary longs are long-breve pairs (Ex. 187(xii)). The chronological priority of this alternate form of the mode, said by Anonymous 4 to be especially popular

---

[31] See, among others, Johannes de Garlandia, Coussemaker, *Scriptorum*, p. 182; Reimer, *Johannes de Garlandia*, p. 66.

[32] The use of a three-note ligature for the first perfect ordo of the fifth mode in discant tenors was a convention of which the theorists disapproved.

among the English,[33] is suggested by its kinship with the first mode and by the strictness with which it adheres to the rules of notation. In the second stage, characterized by a reversal of the values between the ternary longs, the same succession of figures is maintained in spite of the fact that the interpretation of the ternaria is distorted. Mode 2, a series of breve-long patterns allied in sound if not in name to those of mode 3, involves even greater distortion. In all probability it is one of the last to have been formulated.

Two modes have been omitted from the chronology—the fourth, which (so far as I can determine) is purely hypothetical, and the sixth. It is my guess that the breves which characterize the latter, though widely used in all periods of Notre-Dame composition, were not organized into modal patterns as such until a comparatively late date. Johannes and Anonymous 4 both suggest two ways of notating the mode: one way has a quaternaria with a plica followed by a series of two-note ligatures, also with plicas; the other way uses a quaternaria followed by a series of ternarias (Ex. 187(xiii)). Although the first of these ways can be explained in terms of the rules, the second cannot, and it is of some interest that the theorists do not attempt to rationalize it. They simply cite as their authority for including it an example found in the organum *a3* Alleluia 'Posui adjutorium'.[34] When the sixth mode is finally established, it is used in conjunction now with the first mode, now with the second.

The chronology suggested by the notation of the modes coincides with that arrived at through examination of the repertory as transmitted by the three major sources. The oldest materials in W_1 contain passages representing inchoate stages of modes 1 and 5, while some pieces of demonstrably later date show a marked tendency toward the alternate (that is, prior) form of mode 3. In addition to the first and fifth modes, now in the 'classic' form, F contains some examples of the regular third mode. The third mode occurs in a goodly number of the organa *a3* attributed to Perotin, for example, and in a limited number of compositions copied in the youngest of the clausula fasicles which follow the organa *a2* in W_1 and F. Modes 2 and 6 have only a small place in the discant clausula, and assume greater importance in the Latin and French motets of W_2.

ORGANUM PURUM

The theoretical notice given to the organum purum is scant by

[33] Coussemaker, *Scriptorum*, p. 346; Reckow, *Musiktraktat*, p. 54.

[34] Coussemaker, *Scriptorum*, pp. 101, 347; Reimer, *Johannes de Garlandia*, p. 56; Reckow, *Musiktraktat*, p. 56.

comparison with that accorded the discant. Johannes de Garlandia devotes a mere twenty lines to this style of two-voiced composition— and he is more expansive than most. Furthermore, while the doctrine of the rhythmic modes and their application to discant is fairly consistent from one author to the next, the interpretation of the organum is not. The explanation for the imbalance as well as for the inconsistency is doubtless to be found in the historical position of the authors in question. All of them wrote at a time when interest in the composition of organum had declined, and when the measurement of polyphonic music in whatever style was taken for granted. They knew that there had once been a rhythmic distinction between organum and discant; but that distinction had become blurred, and they would seem to have retained a vague or partial notion, at best, as to the temporal order of earlier, pre-modal organum.

The *Discantus positio vulgaris*, oldest of the surviving treatises, contains the following observations: 'There are two kinds of discant; one is pure discant, the other is organum. The latter, in turn, is of two kinds, namely organum duplex and what is called pure organum . . . Organum duplex is the same in words but not in notes because long notes are formed in the tenor while in the discanting voice there is a second melody, consonant with, but different from the chant'.[35] The author does not bring up the subject of rhythmic measurement in this context, saving it rather for the discussion of discant—which he calls 'pure organum'.[36]

Johannes de Garlandia turns to organum as a species of measured music only in the final chapter of the *De Mensurabili musica*. He notes that organum may be described in two ways, as *per se* or *cum alio*. Although these terms refer to organum *a2* and *a3* respectively, they do so by indirection. As Edward Roesner has pointed out, they are used by Johannes not for the totality of a given polyphonic complex, but for the newly composed voice or voices of such a complex.

This use of the word, while not original with Johannes, is remark-ably apt, for what is at once distinctive and problematical—above all in organum *a2*—is the rhythmic motion of the organizing voice. 'Organum per se', writes Johannes, 'is the name for that which is performed according to a modus non rectus, not a modus rectus. The

---

[35] Coussemaker, *Scriptorum*, p. 96; Cserba, *Hieronymous*, pp. 192 f.

[36] Discrepancies in the terms applied to polyphony and its several species are as old as the art itself. This particular author uses 'discant' generically, for all polyphony, and specifically for the improvised ornamentation of the plainchant, reserving 'organum' for composed or written polyphony, some of which has the tenor in long notes ('organum duplex'), some of which has the voices moving together ('pure organum').

latter is here understood as that in which discant is performed'.[37] He continues with the observation that while in modus rectus breves and longs are first and foremost taken in the proper way, in modus non rectus they are understood *ex contingenti*, that is, from the context or (to put a finer point on it) coincidentally. Long notes can, in fact, be distinguished in modus non rectus in one of three ways: by consonance, by graphic symbol, and by way of the penult. Harmonic consonances have earlier been defined by Johannes as aurally compatible combinations of sounds which are ranked according to how closely they proceed from equality—in other words, by the simplicity of the ratios which govern them. Thus the unison and the octave are perfect consonances, thirds are imperfect, and fourths and fifths are of medium consonance. We may guess that the rule applies to simultaneously articulated intervals; whether it refers to all concords or only some of them—the perfect and the medium ones, for instance—is not clear. Johannes does not describe the symbol or *figura* which signifies a long, but he apparently has in mind the note which is not bound with others in a ligature, a form encountered even less frequently in the organum purum than in the discant. The third suggestion is more fully explained in the rule, 'whatever is recognized as preceding a long pause or preceding a perfect consonance is said to be a long'.[38] It seems clear from his remarks that Johannes understood the overall movement of the duplum to have been short, relatively fast notes, interrupted from time to time by longer notes, chiefly at points of structural importance. He did not imagine longs and breves to have been arranged in predictable sequence or as elements of fixed patterns of rhythm.

The St Emmeram Anonymous follows Johannes closely in his discussion of organum speciale or duplex, quoting almost verbatim the description of the organizing voice as one which proceeds in modus non rectus, etc. He rephrases Johannes' statement in subsequent remarks on the harmonic aspect of the organum: ' ... it [organum *per se*] wishes to spurn regular measure, reaching after another which is called not regular'.[39]

Anonymous 4's brief comments on organum purum[40] lead to similar conclusions about the movement of the second voice: notes are short except when otherwise indicated by the figure, the position in the phrase, or the harmonic context. The figure is here identified as the

[37] Coussemaker, *Scriptorum*, p. 114; Reimer, *Johannes de Garlandia*, pp. 88 ff.
[38] Coussemaker, loc. cit.; Reimer, *Johannes de Garlandia*, pp. 88 ff.
[39] Rohloff, *Anonymer Glossierter Mensuraltraktat*, p. 129.
[40] Coussemaker, *Scriptorum*, pp. 358 f.; Reckow, *Musiktraktat*, pp. 78 ff.

longa florificatio, which automatically lengthens the note, first by repeating it, then by ornamenting it with the upper or lower neighbour. (Whether this or a simpler form was what Johannes de Garlandia had in mind is almost impossible to say.) The rule of the penult is introduced with the observation that, in the interest of greater subtlety, certain good composers of organum ('boni organistae') use discords in place of concords. The rule is that every penultimate note before a rest which marks the end of the phrase is long. 'And if the penultimate is a second in the duplum above the tenor, as in organum purum, it will concord splendidly, even though the second is not a concord'. Anonymous 4 then spells out a short passage of organum to illustrate. Over a single note, G, in the tenor (which he likens to the pedal note of an organ), he calls for some twenty-one notes in the duplum. In the position of the penult are two notes on *a*; these, of necessity, take up more time than any of the individual notes preceding. Curiously the author advises that the note of resolution, unison G, may or need not be lengthened.

COPULA

What the theorists call organum (variously modified as duplex, speciale, and purum) corresponds, in all probability, to the earliest sustained-tenor composition associated with Paris. A variant of this style of writing, almost certainly developed under the influence of discant, is first mentioned by Johannes de Garlandia, who identifies it as *copula*.[41] He devotes to the technique but a single paragraph, the main points of which may be summarized as follows: (1) *copula* stands between organum and discant, for it is performed in modus rectus; (2) *copula* has a multitudo punctorum, punctus being here understood as something with a multitudo tractuum; (3) the *copula* has two equal parts, standing in the relationship of antecedent and consequent, and each of these has several tractus; (4) a tractus occurs wherever there are many intervals such as unisons and seconds, uniformly arranged in proper modal order.

It is apparent at once that the presentation of this material lacks the orderliness and the integrity characteristic of Johannes, and indeed Eric Reimer holds that only the first half of the description is his.[42] Whether this is so or whether (as Fritz Reckow[43] and Jeremy Yudkin[44] believe), Johannes was responsible for the entire passage, the descrip-

[41] Coussemaker, *Scriptorum*, p. 114; Reimer, *Johannes de Garlandia*, p. 88.

[42] Reimer, *Johannes de Garlandia*, ii, pp. 35 ff.

[43] *Die Copula: Über einige Zusammenhänge zwischen Setzweise, Formbildung, Rhythmus und Vortragsstil in der Mehrstimmigkeit von Notre-Dame* (Wiesbaden, 1972).

[44] 'The *Copula* According to Johannes de Garlandia', *Musica disciplina*, 34 (1980), 67.

tion does have the appearance of a composite. For all its brevity it is somewhat repetitive (compare the references to modal rhythm in items (1) and (4) and the comments on a plurality of phrases in items (2) and (3): furthermore, while the structural and melodic features described in items (3) and (4) may be characteristic of one and the same musical segment, they are by no means interdependent.

The conclusion to be drawn from this initially puzzling compilation is, I think, twofold. First, the rhythm of the *copula* is modal, and second, the *copula* consists of at least two phrases, marked off by tractus. As investigation of the repertory shows, the melodic content of the *copula* is variable. Many examples are sequential ('many intervals ... uniformly arranged ... '), but there are those in which the parallelism of the constituent phrases is at most partially dependent on melodic repetition.

Although Johannes describes *copula* as something between organum *per se* and discant, it is surely to be subsumed under the former, for the measurement of the duplum does not alter the essential relationship of the voices: the chant continues to move at a deliberate pace against the florid embellishments of the newly composed line. A *copula* as here defined is not a separate entity, but a passage of organum momentarily subject to rhythmic organization. The silence of the earlier theorists, Anonymous 7 and the author of the *Discantus positio vulgaris* (neither of whom so much as mentions the word 'copula') serves to buttress the idea that passages of *copula* did not appear in the oldest of the Parisian organa.

The St Emmeram Anonymous follows Johannes closely at first, placing *copula* between organum and discant and calling attention to the presence of multiple phrases set off by tractus. He goes on to say, however, that ligatures are disposed 'in the form of the first mode and with a regular series of notes, as in the Alleluia *Posui [adjutorium]* in the third as well as the second voice, and in the duplum of *Judea et Jerusalem*'.[45] *Copula*, in other words, has the outward appearance of the first mode, but (as the author continues) it is more subtle, more delicate than the discant. This no longer sounds like Johannes, but like the author's contemporaries, Anonymous 4 and Franco of Cologne,[46] both of whom indicate explicitly or by implication that, despite its notation, *copula* is modally irregular. The framework of the first mode is preserved, but the individual notes are distorted, the longs made extra long, the breves uncommonly short. The relationship between organum *per se* and *copula* is, in a sense, unchanged, the

[45] Rohloff, *Anonymer Glossierter Mensuraltraktat*, p. 125.
[46] Franco's is the third of the treatises on polyphony handed down by Jerome of Moravia.

latter representing now as before the more refined rhythmic practice. It is the point of reference which is different. The earlier *copula* formed a contrast with essentially unmeasured organum, the later one with organum governed by modal rhythm. In its earlier form *copula* was distinguishable from organum by its notation and melodic shape; but when organum (sustained-tenor style) became governed by modal rhythm in its duplum, the basis for the distinction of *copula* vanished. At that point the decision to treat certain passages 'in the form of the first mode' as *copula* was presumably left to the performer.

With the possible exception of this later form of *copula*, all of the procedures described by the theorists in relation to organum *a2* are represented in the musical sources. Like the treatises, these were compiled well after interest in this particular category of composition had subsided; the tradition they preserve is none the less of long standing.

ORGANA OF THE *MAGNUS LIBER*

Although it is safe to say that the manuscript W_1 contains the oldest extant repertory of Parisian organum *a2*, this is not to be interpreted to mean that all of the compositions are of the same age. With the chronological succession of Leonin and Perotin in mind, and also our assumptions about the succession of states represented by the sources W_1, F, and W_2, we can attempt a more detailed reconstruction of the development of style. While there is little reason to believe that any of Leonin's works survives intact, a substantial number of compositions appear to be in the tradition initiated by him. These consist of extended passages of organum interrupted occasionally by discant. The organum *per se* has, however, in many instances given way to copula, and for their part the clausulas represent not one but several stages of rhythmic order and design. Other compositions in W_1 are dominated by discant of a different type—very particular and consistent: these appear to have been conceived in a wholly new manner from the outset. That two distinct (though not necessarily unrelated) traditions are illustrated here is confirmed by comparing pieces of each type with their counterparts in the later repertory. Those of the first type, presumed to be in Leonin's style, may already be in various states of revision in W_1; in any case they reappear in radically altered form in F (or F and W_2). Compositions of the second type reappear in F (or F and W_2) essentially unchanged—suggesting that this is very nearly their original form. These two types will be illustrated in two compositions transmitted in all of the major sources: the Easter Alleluia 'Pascha nostrum' will represent the first type; the responsory for First Vespers of the feast of the Purification, 'Gaude Maria', V. 'Gabrielem archangelum' will represent the second.

The Alleluia respond for 'Pascha nostrum' (W₁ fo. 31v) represents one of those passages that seem to survive intact from an early stage, while adjoining passages in this composite work show later stages. This Alleluia is in organum purum throughout. Although there is nothing new about the technique as such, the limits to which it is pushed are unprecedented. What in its chant form is but a fleeting melody (Ex. 188) has become the basis of an imposing polyphonic structure (Ex. 189(i), W₁ fo. 31v). The notes of the chant are all present in the first or given voice, but they have lost their melodic integrity, serving now as structural supports—or better perhaps, points of reference for the expansive melody of the second voice. Others have transcribed this passage in measured rhythm,[47] but it is transcribed here as one of the few remaining examples of the early

Ex. 188

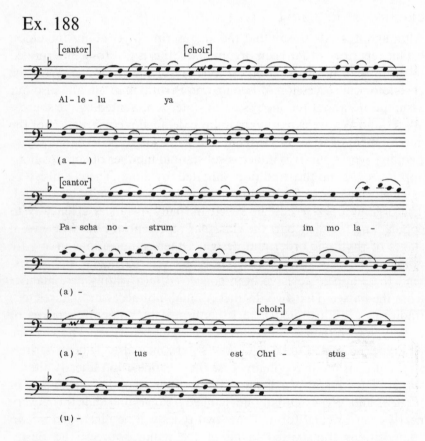

[cantor] [choir]

Al- le - lu - ya

(a ___)

[cantor]

Pa - scha no - strum im mo la -

(a) -

(a) - tus est Chri - stus [choir]

(u) -

[47] See, among others, William G. Waite, *The Rhythm of Twelfth-Century Polyphony* (New Haven, Conn., 1954), 126 f.

Ex. 189

(i)

(1)   (1)   (1)

Al –   le –   lu –

(1)

(1)

ya.

(ii)

Pas -   cha

no -

strum

im –   mo –   la –

tus

est.

Parisian organum purum. The sequence of ligatures is not that of a modus rectus, but accords well with the modus non rectus of the theorists, whose suggestions for reading this particular type of organum are here observed as closely as possible. The initial note in the duplum, which serves at once as tuning note and as a signal for attention, may presumably be sustained more or less at will. Taking into account the fact that a specific ratio between long and breve is never indicated for the organum *per se*, I have introduced editorial dashes over certain notes to suggest a moderate increase in length over simultaneously enunciated and penultimate consonances, and still longer values of penultimate dissonances and final notes of phrases. Anonymous 4's *longa florificatio* (marked here with '1') is generously represented. The grouping of notes in the duplum by twos, threes, and so on, is that of the manuscript and may serve as a guide to the articulation of what I believe was intended as a rhythmically flexible melodic line.

Is this respond the work of Leonin? We are hardly in a position to develop a clear picture of his style, but there is a piece of external evidence that favours an affirmative answer to this question. Although the verse 'Pascha nostrum' is drastically altered in F and W_2, the Alleluia respond is maintained intact, making this the strongest polyphonic link between the extant settings. It is tempting to believe that it is a link between these and the original composition as well.

The verse (Ex. 189(ii)) continues in much the same manner as the respond. Long-spun phrases in the duplum move in what most often appears to be a free rhythm over and around sustained notes in the tenor. There are, however, two brief passages, one directly following the cadence with the enunciation of the syllable 'no(strum)', the other toward the very end of the verse, in which the newly composed voice assumes a different rhythmic-melodic shape. The succession of ligatures approximates that of the first mode and the melody is disposed in antecedent-consequent pairs of phrases. These are examples of *copula* which, as argued earlier, had no place in the work of the first generation of Notre-Dame composers. It seems likely that they represent a type of revision introduced after the time of Leonin but before that of Perotin. Another kind of interruption in the organum purum of the verse occurs with the syllable '-la' of 'immolatus', where the given voice picks up speed, moving with the newly composed counterpoint in measured discant. The two simple notes at the beginning of the duplum are, like those of the tenor, beyond measure, but the third must be understood as part of a three-note ligature which cannot be written because of the repeated pitch. The last note of the second phrase, and again of the fourth, could also be construed as a ternary long, followed by a ternary rest. The tractus in W_1 are of essentially the same length regardless of the duration of the rests for which they stand. The fracture of the long note into two breves in the ninth and tenth phrases, commonly indicated by means of a plica, is here effected by the compression or telescoping of two ligatures.[48]

While both voices of the discant are measured, neither one can be said to be genuinely modal. A large majority of phrases in the tenor consist of even numbers of long notes, rather than the odd numbers characteristic of the fifth mode; and the variety of rhythmic units in the duplum is not in keeping with the modal principle of repetition. This particular style of discant writing is described in the *Discantus positio vulgaris*: 'Discant [the author's term, as we saw, is pure organum] is that in which every note, ultra mensuram, of the plain chant is matched in the discanting voice by a long and a breve or by the equivalent of these'.[49] It is significant that there is no mention of the modes in this early description of discant. The materials for the

---

[48] Compare the alternative method of notating the sixth mode.
[49] Coussemaker, *Scriptorum*, p. 96; Cserba, *Hieronymous*, p. 193.

first and the fifth modes may be present, but they have not yet been arranged in the regular, repetitive patterns by which the modes are identified. Clausulas of this type (hereafter identified as type D.p.v.) outnumber all others in W_1, accounting for no fewer than 71 out of a total of approximately 118.[50]

There is no gainsaying the rhythmic ambiguity of the organum purum in the version of Alleluia 'Pascha nostrum' handed down by W_1. One day, perhaps, it will be resolved. In the meantime there are other matters which merit attention. One of the most interesting of these has to do with the fine distinctions between organum purum and discant. The notes in the given voice of the organum purum are sustained and enveloped in the richly ornamental phrases of the duplum, phrases which commonly circumscribe a fourth or a fifth, but which may span as such as a tenth. The abundant dissonances, tempered much of the time when they fall against the pedal-like tones of the tenor, become strident and full of tension when prolonged or articulated. In the discant, the freedom of the organum purum is checked by a series of interlocking restraints on the several musical elements involved. The chant melisma which is the source of the tenor is broken down into short phrases that cut across and obscure the divisions of the original (Ex. 190). The reordering of the melodic material is carried out in such a way as to limit severely the range of the individual phrases. Five phrases cover only the range of a second, and four only a third, while two extend as far as a fourth; all of this in contrast to the phrases in the chant itself, which range from a fifth to a seventh or an octave. Other clausulas of this type in W_1 show a preference for phrases covering a third or a fourth; next most popular

Ex. 190

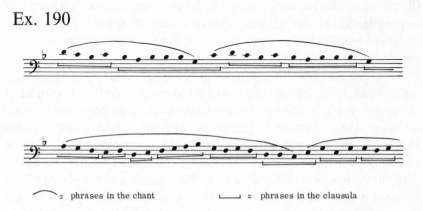

⌒ = phrases in the chant   ∟—⌐ = phrases in the clausula

[50] The count may vary slightly depending on the more or less arbitrary decision as to the minimum number of tenor longs required to form a clausula.

are those limited to a second, followed by those which extend to a fifth. Wider-ranging phrases are rare.

The duplum, which is less restricted in range than the tenor (though more restrained then elsewhere in the composition), matches each of the tenor phrases with one of its own. Moreover, it is subject to the harmonic control of the tenor: save for one, every note in the duplum which is sounded simultaneously with a note in the tenor is concordant with it. The exception is the discordant second (b–c) in the fourth phrase approached obliquely from a unison with the tenor and directly abandoned for the same unison. The handful of dissonances formed by short notes in the duplum are similarly approached and even more quickly resolved.

The voices of the discant most often proceed from one concord to another by contrary motion, although neither oblique nor parallel motion is excluded. Voice leading by step or at least by small intervals is preferred—and doubtless it is this, combined with the limited number of consonances admitted to discant composition, that accounts for the narrowly circumscribed range of the tenor phrases. The interaction of all these preferences or restrictions produces a relatively small number of stereotypical progressions that govern the D.p.v. clausulas as a group. The following examples of the progressions, many of which can be found in the clausula illustrated, are the most common. In every case the progression is reversible (Ex. 191).

The version of Alleluia 'Pascha nostrum' transmitted by the manuscript F (fol. 109) is not a copy of the earlier organum but a substantive revision, effected, we may suppose, by a composer of Perotin's generation (Ex. 192). The most obvious changes are in the inclusion of polyphony for the second Alleluia, and the use of two discant clausulas in the verse, one with 'nostrum' and one with the last two syllables of 'immolatus'. More subtle distinctions are to be observed chiefly, though not solely, in the rhythmic organization of the discant.

As indicated earlier, the music for the initial Alleluia is essentially unchanged. It is as if the reviser wished to make clear his obligation to the earlier work before proceeding along lines more nearly of his own devising. These lines begin to emerge with great clarity in the verse. First of all the five-note group in the duplum with the syllable 'Pa-' is expanded, starting now an octave above the tenor and arriving at the original fifth a few notes ahead of the syllable change (Ex. 192(i)). From this point to the cadence at 'no-' the old material is left intact. At precisely the place where the older version changes from organum purum to *copula*, however, a clausula is introduced (Ex. 192(ii)), one

Ex. 191

third to unison third to fifth

fourth to unison

fourth to fifth

fifth to unison

octave to fifth

octave to fourth

which differs markedly from the discant passage illustrated in Ex. 189. In the new clausula the rhythm of both voices is modally organized. The tenor, in the fifth mode, is further governed almost throughout by a fixed pattern consisting of two equal parts. A group of three ternary longs followed by a ternary rest—the first, most characteristic ordo of the mode—alternates with one in which the first two ternary longs are replaced by a duplex long. A little more than halfway through the clausula (tenth bar) there is an interruption in the pattern by an ostensible omission of one set of ternary longs. This is not an oversight, however, but a signal of sorts that the chant melisma is about to be repeated. The pattern is re-established at once, continuing to within four notes of the cadence, where the two halves of the pattern are merged into a single phrase made up entirely of duplex longs.

Ex. 192

Pas -   cha

no -   strum

etc.

Such repetition of a portion of the chant in the tenor of the clausula is first encountered in the revision of the *Magnus liber* in F.[51] The procedure became a commonplace in this and subsequent layers of clausula composition. Two types of tenor repetition have been noted. The first (presumably older) one results from the combination of two or more separate clausulas. The second, illustrated here, controls the large design of a continuous, unified whole.[52]

The duplum of the 'Nostrum' clausula is organized in the first rhythmic mode. The trochaic pattern characteristic of the mode clearly dominates, seldom giving place to substitutions of any kind. The strictness of the rhythm is offset by the flexibility of the phrase structure. Over the rigidly-patterned tenor the second voice imposes its own compatible but independent symmetries. All of the phrases are multiples of four ternary longs: those with the first tenor statement are equal to 8 (7 plus a rest), 16, 4, 4, and 4, respectively; those with the second, avoiding both extremes, are all of 8. Although the tenor pattern also contains 8 (4 plus 4) ternary longs, the relationship is frequently blurred by the continuation of the duplum through part of the tenor rest.

Composers of clausulas based on double statements of the chant had two options where the duplum was concerned. They could, and often did, cause it to overlap the tenor at the point where the repetition commenced, leaving no doubt that the piece had been

---

[51] The repetition is not called for here by the chant; and while chant books sometimes show such repetition in responsory melismata—in varying ways—other details of the polyphonic manuscripts suggest that in some cases tenor repetition was seen as peculiar to polyphony.

[52] Norman E. Smith, 'Tenor Repetition in the Notre-Dame Organum', *JAMS*, 19 (1966), 229.

conceived from the outset as a single entity. They could also empha-size the articulation of the clausula into two distinct sections by having the duplum cadence simultaneously with the tenor at the end of the initial statement. The composer of 'Nostrum' chose the latter way. What ensures the integrity of his clausula is the uniform character of the melodic style, something indissolubly linked with the new rhythmic procedures.[53] Examined closely the duplum proves to be made up of a limited number of tiny, constantly recurring melodic-rhythmic cells. The same melodic shapes not only appear again and again as incipits and cadential formulas, they comprise the principal building material of entire phrases. When these shapes are reinforced by association with the same rhythmic patterns the resulting structure is one of the utmost coherence. A reduction of the duplum to its constituent elements may help to clarify the way in which this works (Ex. 193). The cadential figure is measured in ternary longs; all other groups are arranged in the sequence long-breve-long. What is remark-able in the face of these stringent limitations is the freshness and vitality of the duplum. Through the use of the multiple pitch levels, the ingenious grouping and regrouping of the cells, and subtle changes in the ways of approaching or joining them, the composer has produced a line which, for all its consistency, is astonishingly unpre-dictable.

Ex. 193

At the close of the discant clausula the redactor of Alleluia 'Pascha nostrum' returns to the original organum purum by way of *copula* (Ex. 192(iii)). The passage is not subdivided into the antecedent-consequent phrases described by Johannes de Garlandia but consists instead of a long, descending sequence. The symmetry and the

---

[53] The interaction between melody and rhythm in Notre-Dame polyphony is noted by Rudolf Flotzinger, *Der Discantussatz im Magnus Liber und seiner Nachfolge* (Vienna, 1969), 198.

Ex. 194

la -

tus

repetitive quality of the melody leave little room for doubt as to its identification as a *copula*. A last trace of the old composition occurs in a passage of organum purum which connects the *copula* with a new setting of 'Latus' (F fo. 109^{r-v}) (Ex.194). In this new 'Latus' clausula, the tenor rhythm is organized as in 'Nostrum', except that the constituent elements of the rhythmic pattern occur in reverse order; and the chant is stated only once. The reason for this is not hard to find: the melisma is twice as long as that with 'Nostrum' (fifty-five notes as opposed to twenty-two) and it already contains a certain amount of internal repetition. The duplum, governed by the first rhythmic mode, forms an interesting contrast to that of 'Nostrum'. Where the duplum of 'Nostrum' shows a flexibility of phrase structure balanced by the most rigorous interpretation of the mode, the newly composed voice of 'Latus' shows just the opposite. The phrases regularly coincide with complete statements of the tenor pattern; and the rhythmic values of the modal pattern are frequently subdivided. In bars 9 and 13, for example, there is a breve rest separating the two halves of the phrase, while in bars 1 and 17 the *longa florificata*, used as a cadential ornament in discant composition, calls attention to the rest in the tenor even as it forms a link between the parts of the duplum phrase. Once that same ornament fills in the rest between two of the longer phrases (bar 4). The regularity of the phrasing is countered by a certain relaxation in the treatment of the rhythm. Never sufficient to obscure the identity of the mode, substitutions for the long-breve of the first-mode foot do occur with some frequency. These substitutions are not made at random, but are carefully calculated to point up melodic sequences (bars 5–6, 15), to expand the melodic sweep (bars 3, 18, 19), and to relieve the singsong quality into which the first mode so readily lapses (Bars 1, 5).

The polyphony for the second Alleluia is little more than an extended passage of discant (F fo. 109ᵛ) (Ex. 195). The first note of the chant forms the basis for a short introduction in organum purum; the remaining nine notes are organized into the fifth mode pattern employed for the melismatic portions of the verse. The composer did not stop here, but continued the clausula with a threefold restatement of the whole of the soloistic chant fragment, less one of the repeated C's. The brief organal phrase at the conclusion is again limited to a single note of the chant. What distinguishes this particular clausula is not so much the insistent reiteration of the tenor, fully understandable given the brevity of the chant, but the way in which the grouping of the notes changes from statement to statement. Each time the melody starts over it falls with a different note in the rhythmic ordo, taking on a new shape with every appearance.

The organization of the three clausulas immediately at hand (Ex. 192(ii), 194, 195) sets them apart from the simple D.p.v. type clausula in the earlier version of Alleluia 'Pascha nostrum' (Ex. 189). Other aspects of style establish a certain continuity in the structure of the discant. The segments of the tenor in each of these more modern passages are characterized by the same restricted range as before, and the leading of the voices from one simultaneously articulated consonance to another is essentially unchanged, although the extension of the time values in the tenor now allows for a larger number of passing dissonances between concords.

I intimated earlier that more than one composer had had a hand in the revision of Alleluia 'Pascha nostrum', something which shows up clearly in the clausulas. 'Nostrum' and 'Latus' are expertly made and despite their differences could have been the work of one and the same person. By contrast, the second Alleluia appears as a less than successful imitation of 'Latus'. The similarities between the two passages are obvious, and include the coincidence of duplum and tenor phrases at the outset, the characteristic substitution of the ternary long for the long-breve of the first mode foot, and the shift from short, sharply-profiled phrases to a long, uninterrupted progress to the climax. For all the superficial resemblance, however, the Alleluia is no match for 'Latus', and could hardly have been written by the same composer. It is not well made—the second half, in particular, is marred by a certain technical ineptness—and it does not show the same originality of invention.

Except for the omission of the second Alleluia, the W₂ version of

Ex. 195

Al - le -

lu - 2

3

4

ya.

the Alleluia 'Pascha nostrum' is virtually identical to that in F. The one noteworthy deviation occurs at the beginning of the verse, where the first syllable retains its earlier, more compact setting.

The responsory 'Gaude Maria', V. 'Gabrielem archangelum' is a very different sort of composition; it represents the second type mentioned, one which remains stable throughout the sources, and has a distinctive style of discant (W_1 fo. 18^v) (Ex. 196). The intonation of the respond (Ex. 196(i)) has the duplum first sounding alone,[54] then moving up to the simpler form illustrated in Alleluia 'Pascha nostrum'. It is possible that the entire intonation was meant to be construed as *copula*. In any case, there can be no question about the word 'Maria', where the ligatures fall into more or less regular patterns and where the components of the first phrase, three sub–phrases which explore the 3rd d–f, are repeated a step lower in the second.

The verse 'Gabrielem archangelum', just over half of which is reproduced in Ex. 196(ii), opens with an extended *copula* passage, switching at 'scimus divinitus' to a species of discant that stands, stylistically and chronologically, between that of the type D.p.v. clausulas and the Perotinian substitutes. The tenor proceeds in simple notes that look like those of the earlier discant but which, in fact, are twice as long. The phrases all contain odd numbers of notes and so have some affinity with the fifth mode. Despite what proves to be the enormous popularity of this particular manner of organizing discant tenors, however, it is never mentioned by the theorists. The duration of the tenor notes, which is contingent on the rhythm of the duplum, is unambiguous, but because there is not a consistent pattern of notes, one cannot really speak of a mode. The duplum, on the other hand, does make use of repetitive patterns, most often those of the so-called alternate third mode. In 'scimus divinitus te esse affatum' the mode is strictly maintained, fractures of the initial ternary long occurring in just two of the twenty-two feet. A second, very much longer clausula (only the concluding portion of which, 'natum' is given in Ex. 196(iii)) shows a little more variety, but there is no doubt as to the dominant pattern. This style of discant writing was to be used more often than any other in organal settings of the Office responsories. The reason is probably to be found in the nature of the chant itself, which is largely neumatic rather than melismatic. The syllables of the text come in comparatively rapid succession, interrupting the normal sequence of ligatures by which a given mode is identified. Of all the rhythmic

[54] This type of intonation is discussed by Roesner, 'The Performance of Parisian Organum', *Early Music*, 7 (1979), 178.

Ex. 196

(i)

Gau -   de

Ma -

ri -

a

(ii)

Ga -

bri -   e -

lem

ar -   chan -

ge -

lum sci - mus

di - vi - ni - tus te es -

se af - fa - tum

etc.

na - tum

modes, the one most easily adapted to a plethora of syllables is the third, whether in its trochaic or its iambic form. The first member of the foot is a simple note and that remains unchanged in music *cum littera*. The ternarias which follow are replaced, when new syllables are introduced, by an 'imperfect' binaria plus a simple note or by the second half of a *longa florificata* and a simple note. Both of these imaginary ligatures are illustrated with the word 'affatum'.

'Gaude Maria' is a grandiose work, and it is plain that the composer made some effort to link the larger sections by means of a limited, but telling, amount of literal repetition. The second member of the sequence with '-chan-' (Ex. 196(ii) at '5') returns in the *copula* following the discant clausula, while the first four bars of '-fatum' are repeated with the similarly sounding 'natum' toward the very end of the piece. Smaller melodic fragments are subject to repetition as well: for example, the twice-stated cadential figure (Ex. 196(i) at '2') in the respond is echoed at the close of the second *copula* passage, and the five-note group with '-lem' (Ex. 196(ii) at '3') is heard again at the close of '-tum'.

The revisions of the responsory in F and W_2 are minimal and give no sign of the generation gap which separates the versions of Alleluia 'Pascha nostrum'. Next to nothing from the model is discarded, and such changes as have been made reinforce the initial impulse toward consistency of texture and design. Two small but noteworthy adjustments are made in the respond. First, the figure leading to the cadence on 'Ma-' (Ex. 196(i) at '1') is expanded by ten notes in such a way as to bring it into close conformity with the organal fragment with which the verse concludes, a fragment unaccountably omitted from F, though maintained in W_2. Second, the rhythm of the sequence on 'Mari-' is regularized so that the penultimate unit or subphrase of each member is the same as the final one (Ex. 196(i) at '2'). The verse remains intact apart from the omission of the final organ point in F. The *'Gloria Patri'*, which appears in both F and W_2, is closely related to the verse. This is not surprising, for it is based on the opening (seventeen notes) and closing (twelve notes) portions of the same chant melody.[55] The polyphony is not transferred bodily from verse to doxology; rather, selected fragments are woven together with new material.

Only three other organa in W_1 are written in the manner of 'Gaude Maria'—'Vir perfecte' and 'Vir iste', in honour of St Andrew, and 'Concede', for the common of several martyrs. The pieces for Andrew are unique, but 'Concede,' preserved as well in F and W_2 is (like the Marian responsory) all but unchanged from one source to another. The relatively small role of works of this type in W_1 is not augmented in F; while F contains more examples than W_1, the increase is barely proportionate to the increase in the total repertory.

This leaves a very large number of pieces of the first type, related, however loosely, to the tradition represented by Alleluia 'Pascha nostrum'. The task of sorting these out chronologically and stylistically is formidable. In the case of the W_1 repertory we can only speculate as to which pieces are in their original form and which are in one of several states of revision. Adaptations of these pieces in one or both of the other principal manuscripts are easily detected, but what of the stages of composition reflected by the new pieces, especially numerous in F? Two complemetary approaches to the problem of classification would seem to be required. One of these, which is concerned with changes in both the relative weight and the style of the discant used, has already been thoroughly investigated. The other, which focuses on the sustained tenor portions of the organa, has scarcely been alluded to in the scholarly literature.

One of the most striking phenomena to be observed throughout the repertory is the proliferation of what may be described as stock figures—stereotyped melodic-rythmic combinations which recur in one composition after another. Some are characteristically identified

---

[55] The formulas for the responsory verses are adjustable to accommodate verses of differing lengths. For a less complex relationship between verse and *Gloria Patri*, see the responsory for St Andrew, 'Vir perfecte', in Waite, *Twelfth-Century Polyphony*, pp. 51 ff. The reading of the clausulas should surely be changed from genuine to alternate third mode, the form favoured by the English.

with cadences and some with incipits,[56] while others appear seemingly at random. Certain figures which occur fragmentarily in one composition or in one version of a composition are expanded and regularized in others. The *copula* sequence common to the F/W_2 settings of the Alleluia 'Pascha nostrum' (Ex. 192(iii)) and the conclusion of the W_1/W_2 copies of 'Gaude Maria' (Ex. 196) are examples of the stock figure. Of a host of others which might be cited, the four given in Ex. 197 are among the most popular. An exhaustive study of these figures would help to define with greater precision the technique of composition used by the Parisians and to identify more specifically the several stylistic layers within the large repertory of liturgical organa *a2*. Until such a study is forthcoming, a number of questions will have to remain unanswered. When did these figures come into use and in what order? At what point did a given melodic shape first carry with it the implication of a fixed rhythmic progression? Is rigid stereotyping characteristic of the latest phase of Notre-Dame composition or is there yet a subsequent phase in which the use of stock figures begins to decline? No doubt there are other questions.

The use of figures is not wholly unrelated to another practice of considerable importance in organum composition, namely contrafac-

Ex. 197

[56] Smith, 'Interrelationships among the Graduals of the Magnus Liber Organi', *AcM*, 45 (1973), 73 *N*. 97, has called attention to the frequency with which organal settings of certain mode 5 Graduals share opening and concluding formulas.

ture. By no means excluded from the Mass pieces,[57] this is especially prominent in settings of Office responsories.

The verse 'Adjuvent nos' (W_1 fo. 16) from 'Concede', is sung to the first responsorial tone. The polyphony with 'scelera', a combination of copula and discant, is not only repeated in the lesser doxology to the same organum (F fo. 81) with 'filio', it is used as well in four other responsories with verses in the first tone—'Descendit de celis', V. 'Tamquam' (F fo. 65^v) with 'procedens'; 'Et valde', V. 'Et respicientes' (F fo. 69) with 'lapidem'; 'Inter natos', V. 'Fuit homo' (F fo. 73) with 'Deo' and with 'filio'; and 'Ex ejus tumba', V. 'Catervatim' (F fo. 81 and W_2 fo. 55) with 'populi' and 'filio'.

Occasionally there is an unexpected sharing of materials between the respond of one piece and the verse of another. Immediately following 'scelera' in 'Adjuvent nos' is a longer passage with text 'excuset inter(cessio)', the duplum of which corresponds, note-for-note, with that which extends from the beginning through the penultimate phrase with 'Mari(a)' in the respond 'Gaude Maria' discussed above. The latter is not built on a formula, strictly speaking, but it does happen that five of the tenor notes involved are identical to those from the verse; a sixth appears in one melody as a B flat, in the other as an F. (It is not unusual for notes at the remove of a fifth to support the same polyphonic line.)

DISCANT CLAUSULA

Following directly upon the cycle of organa *a2* in the manuscripts W_1 and F are collections of discant clausulas, the overwhelming majority of which are based on fragments of liturgical melodies used for polyphonic elaboration in the *Magnus liber*.[58] W_1 has two groups of clausulas for Office and Mass, arranged for the most part in the order of the church year. The first contains 34 pieces, the second, entered by a different hand, 68. The total of 102 is modest compared with that in F, which preserves no fewer than 462 compositions. These are disposed in four liturgically ordered groups, with the newer clausulas at the beginning, the older ones at the end.

The vastness of the independent clausula repertory testifies to the ultimate preference of the Parisians for discant composition; it also raises a number of questions, some of which have not yet been fully answered. First of all, what purpose did these pieces serve? Friedrich

---

[57] Smith, 'Interrelationships among the Graduals'; also 'Interrelationships among the Alleluias of the Magnus Liber Organi', *JAMS*, 25 (1972), 175.

[58] Smith, 'The Clausulae of the Notre-Dame School: A Repertorial Study' (Diss., Yale University, (1964); Baltzer, 'Notation, Rhythm, and Style in the Two-Voice Notre-Dame Clausula' (Diss., Boston University, 1974).

Ludwig did not hesitate to identify them as substitutes for sections of existing organa. Support for this view can be found in the sources themselves, which show revision by replacement to have been a commonplace. What was fixed in the page of an organum fascicle could, in fact, be altered on performance by the substitution of an item from one of the clausula sets—either for an older piece of discant or for a passage of organum purum. If, for example, the user of W_1 wished to update Alleluia 'Pascha nostrum', he had only to turn to the independent clausulas to find the setting of 'nostrum' actually incorporated into the F and W_2 revisions of this work.[59]

A second question has to do with the frequency with which certain chant melismas were singled out for discant setting. The favourite is 'Regnat', or simply 'Reg' (Alleluia 'Hodie Maria'), for which twenty different clausulas exist; 'Dominus' (Gradual 'Viderunt omnes') survives in fifteen versions; 'Tamquam' (Responsory 'Descendit'), 'In seculum' and 'Domino quoniam' (Gradual 'Haec dies'), and 'Latus est' each in twelve versions; 'Ta' (Alleluia 'Ascendens') and 'Go' (Gradual 'Benedicta') in eleven versions; and 'Omnes' and 'Et confitebor' (Alleluia 'Adorabo') in ten. I think it would be a mistake to overlook the possibility that the repeated use of these melodies was dependent in part on artistic considerations, on the inherent musical qualities which make them particularly suitable for polyphonic treatment. At the same time, there seems little reason to suggest, as some have done, that these multiple settings were liturgically redundant. Eight of the ten chant melismata in question are associated with the annual feasts of the Cathedral, one is for a Marian feast other than Assumption, and one is for Ascension, a feast of duplex rank. Alleluia 'Hodie Maria' was performed, at the very least, twice a year—at Second Vespers on the patronal feast of the Cathedral and on Sunday within the Octave. Given the span of the Notre-Dame era, twenty 'Regnat' clausulas for this Alleluia would not seem excessive.

The most puzzling question of all arises from the fact that in many instances displaced clausulas were not discarded, but preserved in the very collection under discussion. So it is that the W_1 clausula for 'Latus', set aside in the revision of Alleluia 'Pascha nostrum', reappears in the supplement to the fourth group of pieces in F; similarly, 'Ex semine' from the organum Alleluia 'Nativitas' in W_1, though removed from the version in F, is preserved in the second group; and

---

[59] Frank Ll. Harrison's objection to the substitution theory (*Music in Medieval Britain* (London, 1958), 123), which he bases on the difficulty of fitting the clausulas into the organa, cannot in most instances be sustained, and while the independent instrumental performance he proposes is possible, there is no indication from contemporary sources that it actually took place.

so in other cases. What prompted the redactor, above all of F, to save clausulas which by his time must have been regarded as outmoded? I cannot answer the question with certainty, but suggest that it may have had less to do with aesthetic considerations than with the purpose for which the repertory in F was assembled. In contrast to W_1, this sumptuous manuscript shows no sign of having been used for performance. Indeed, in the case of many of the motets in the eighth and ninth fascicles, this would have been precluded by the arrangement of the music on the page. It would seem that F was intended as a repository, a complete and permanent record of Notre-Dame polyphony. Only this would account for the virtual duplication of some of the organa a2, on the one hand, and the inclusion, on the other, of a goodly number of clausulas and conductus which are, at best, inept and which, significantly, appear in no other source. While the artistic level of the repertory as a whole is high, it seems clear that for the compiler of F the criterion of completeness or comprehensiveness took precedence over that of quality.

As in the several versions of the *Magnus liber* itself, so in the independent clausula fascicles do three broad types of discant writing predominate. These three types are distinguished by the arrangement of the cantus firmus in ternary longs, in duplex longs, and in patterns of the fifth rhythmic mode, respectively. The first type, with the tenor in simple ternary longs, seems to be the oldest and the most enduring; it is represented by approximately 150 of the pieces in the several groups of clausulas in W_1 and F. While many of these clausulas duplicate discant passages contained in the complete organa, close to 100 appear only as independent clausulas. Within this group there are three distinct chronological layers. The earliest layer consists of the 'abbreviation clausulas', so called because, being shorter discant versions of sustained-tenor passages of the *Magnus liber*, they have appeared to scholars to be the means by which Perotin would have 'abbreviated' the organa, as Anonymous 4 reports in passing (see page 558). Sometimes built on melismata and sometimes not, these are minuscule pieces commonly involving fewer than six or seven notes of the chant. Occasional examples of such fragmentary discant remain in the organa of the *Magnus liber* but the great majority—twenty-five each for the Office and Mass—are relegated to the third and fourth groups of clausulas in F. The treatment of 'Adjutori' from the verse of the Gradual for Holy Innocents, 'Laqueus contritus est', (F fo. 180^v), is characteristic (Ex. 198). A subsequent layer of this very numerous first type consists of longer pieces generally comparable to the D.p.v. clausula illustrated previously (Ex. 189). The youngest layer is made

Ex. 198

Ad - ju - to - ri.

up of clausulas which combine the simple ternary longs of the tenor with rigorously organized modal dupla. One of the numerous settings of 'Reg' (F fo. 166) matches tenor phrases of first four and then eight ternary longs to a first mode duplum, the melodic features of which are akin to those so often encountered in *copula* (Ex. 199).

Although clausulas in which ternary longs are countered by the breves of the sixth mode seldom show any such regularity of phrasing, they may be quite as tightly knit. Consider, for example, the handling of 'Ejus' (F fo. 166) from the Responsory 'Styrps Yesse' (Ex. 200). The concluding organ point is characteristic of many of the newer discant passages recorded in F.

Like the clausulas just described, those of the second type, with duplex longs in the tenor, have an important place in the organa of the *Magnus liber*. Of the 150-odd that occur as independent clausulas, over 100 are contained in the third and fourth groups in F. These, again, are abbreviation clausulas, with pre-modal dupla. The remaining pieces, from W_1 and from the more modern groups in F (the first and second), are marked by a tendency toward modal organization of the dupla. They proceed either in the third mode—most often the alternate form thereof—or in something approaching the first. Although the writing in these clausulas may be skilful and imaginative, it is often marred by a certain unrelenting sameness. It is as if the duplex longs in the tenor acted as a constraint upon the organizing voice, forcing it into repetitive, predictable phrases. Only when composers began to cast the chant in the patterns of the fifth mode was it possible, apparently, to realize increasingly sophisticated, original designs.

The third type of clausula, built on fifth mode tenors, includes roughly 130 pieces in W_1, and in F; the vast majority of these are melismata drawn from the responsories of the Mass. The pattern most often used to organize the chant melodies consists of groups of three ternary longs separated by ternary rests. It is illustrated in a setting of

Ex. 199

Reg -

the fragment 'Hec dies' (W_1 fo. 54ᵛ) from the Easter Gradual
(Ex. 201).

Far behind this in popularity is the pattern (seen earlier) that has
the three-note unit alternating with paired simple notes. A few tenors
use only a single note alternating with the characteristic ternaria.
Multiple tenor statements are common in the clausulas of this type,
and while a single pattern may govern an entire piece, a change to
another in the same mode is sometimes introduced at the start of a
new cursus of the melody.

Ex. 200

E -

jus

More often than not, the dupla of these clausulas proceed in a highly regular form of the first mode. There are, to be sure, those in which the long-breve of the modal foot is often replaced by a ternary long, especially when the cadence in the duplum coincides with that in the tenor. Persistent ternary longs in the duplum can make it appear to be in the fifth mode, as in a very long clausula for 'Domino quoniam' (F fo. 155^v)—in which the tenor for each word is stated twice. The opening is given in Ex. 202. What follows shows even fewer

Ex. 201

Hec

di -

es.

fractures of the ternary long—just one in fifteen. Combination of the third and fifth modes, though possible, is rare; in the cases where it does occur, the distinction between the trochaic and iambic versions of the third mode is almost impossible to establish.

In addition to the three main types of clausula, a restricted number of clausulas use modes other than the fifth for their tenors; use of the first, second, and third modes together accounts for approximately ninety pieces. With the rarest of exceptions clausulas using these

Ex. 202

Do -   mi -

no

2   etc.

modes in the tenor are copied into F at the beginning of series—that
is, as the most modern of the independent groups. Some clausulas of
this kind also appear (in one version or another) in the *Magnus liber*
itself.

Clausulas with third mode tenors number just fourteen. Of several
organizing patterns, the most characteristic consists of a simple note
followed by a ternaria, that is, the first perfect ordo of the mode, as in
this setting of 'Tamquam' (W$_1$ fo. 55) (Ex. 203). Double statements of
the tenor are the rule, although two clausulas have three statements of
the melody while one even has four. The dupla of the clausulas are
also in the third mode, and if they are somewhat more flexible than the
tenors, they nevertheless admit relatively little substitution of values.
Such deviations from the modal pattern as do occur may affect either
part of the foot. Thus the initial ternary long may be subdivided into
two or three breves, while the brevis and brevis altera may also be
replaced by three notes. It is not clear from the modal sources just

Ex. 203

Tam -

how these three were distributed, but it seems likely that at least some of the time they effected the fracture of the first rather than the second, longer breve. The earliest of the more readily decipherable sources to continue the modal tradition give evidence of exactly this procedure. Characteristic of melismatic discant in the third mode is the seamless texture created by the overlapping of tenor and duplum.

Clausulas with tenors in first or second mode, preserved in about equal numbers, have many features in common, including a prefer-

Ex. 204

(i) mode 1:

(ii) mode 2:

(iii) mode 2:

(iv) mode 1:

ence for two-part patterns that alternate two rhythmic elements (Ex. 204). In the second mode longer patterns are often used (Ex. 204(iii)). In the first mode the figure at Ex. 204(iv) is used, but less frequently. Tenor repetition occurs in nearly all of the first-mode pieces; it is present in a good majority of those governed by the second mode. There is every reason to believe that the first mode pieces as a group predate those in the second mode. At the same time, both groups show a chronological stratification into earlier and later subgroups. The earlier, illustrated by the first mode and second mode settings of 'Nobis' (W₁ fo. 55ᵛ, fo. 49ᵛ) from Alleluia 'Dies sanctificatus', contains pieces whose dupla are rhythmically consistent and notationally unproblematical (see Ex. 205 and 206). The pieces of the later group show an increase in rhythmic complexity accompanied by a considerable amount of notational irregularity. William Waite was of the opinion that these pieces were, in fact, motets from which the texts had been removed—without, however, any corresponding adjustment of the notation.[60] Gordon Anderson was one of the first to call Waite's position into question, suggesting that these clausulas were not created out of motets but rather written *in the manner of* the motet, which in the meantime had become increasingly difficult to account for in strictly modal terms.[61] If details of Anderson's argu-

---

[60] *Twelfth-Century Polyphony*, pp. 100 f.

[61] 'Clausulae or Transcribed Motets in the Florence Manuscript?', *AcM*, 42 (1970), 109. For a summary of the dispute and some useful conclusions, see Baltzer, 'Notation, Rhythm, and Style', pp. 33 ff. and *passim*.

Ex. 205

[N]o -

2

bis

ment are often open to criticism, his central thesis is undoubtedly sound. A setting of the 'In seculum' melisma, copied in the first clausula set of F (fo. 157) and in the organum *a2* in W_2, may serve to illustrate the strain placed on the first rhythmic mode by the urge toward greater variety and complexity (Ex. 207).

TRIPLA

Although the repertory of Parisian liturgical polyphony is dominated by the two-voiced organum, there is a significant body of material for three voices—the so-called tripla—and even, as noted earlier, a small group of quadrupla or four-voiced pieces.

The tripla are represented by approximately thirty complete compositions, and half that number of clausulas and other partial settings. The collection in F, the core of which is copied in the second fascicle, is the largest and the most comprehensive, embracing all of the pieces handed down by W_2 (contrafacts excepted) and all but one of those in W_1.

Ex. 206

No -

bis

In contrast to the organa, which are seldom, if ever, encountered outside of the Notre-Dame manuscripts, fully a quarter of the tripla are preserved in sources of varying provenance—an indication, surely, of the great esteem in which these compositions were held. Polyphonic supplements to the Circumcision Ordo from Beauvais, copied in the MS London, B.L., Egerton 2615 (LoA), contain three complete tripla: 'Descendit de celis', known from all three of the principal sources; 'Gaude Maria', known from none of them, but closely linked to the two-voiced setting examined above;[62] and 'Christus manens', which despite the fact that it had no place in Parisian cathedral liturgies is present in F. As a verse to the prose 'Letemur gaudis', 'Christus manens' did have a place at Beauvais, where it was sung during First Vespers on the Feast of the Circumcision. Not only liturgical, but also stylistic aspects of the composition suggest that 'a

[62] Wulf Arlt, *Ein Festoffizium des Mittelalters aus Beauvais in seiner liturgischen und musikalischen Bedeutung*, ii (Cologne, 1970), 174 ff., bars 54–76, 93–153, 172–6.

Ex. 207

In   se -

cu – lum

2

local musician trained in the Parisian technique supplied music for a text belonging to a local use'.[63] The inclusion of that music in an otherwise Parisian repertory of tripla was obviously part of the programme to make the collection in F as complete as possible.

The introductory fascicle of the late thirteenth-century MS. Montpellier, Faculté de Médicine, H 196 (Mo) contains five tripla, four of which appear in one or more of the Notre-Dame sources. The fifth, 'Abiecto' (unique to Mo) may for reasons of style be related to the Parisian repertory, but thus far its liturgical position has not been established. One chant-based 'Benedicamus domino' along with a freely-composed rondellus on that text survives in the Spanish MS. Las Huelgas; and the Christmas Alleluia 'Dies sanctificatus' is all but complete in the fragmentary MS. Cambridge, Univ. Lib., Ff II 29. From a liturgical point of view the tripla are directly related to the organa of the *Magnus liber*. Nearly all of them have two-voiced counterparts, and of those that do not, at least one, 'Virgo', V. 'Sponsus amat sponsam', for the Feast of St Catherine, would have been appropriate for Paris.

From a musical point of view the relationship between the tripla and the organa is more complex. The tenors of the liturgical items common to both repertories are, with two exceptions,[64] the same, and the same amount of chant is subject to polyphonic elaboration. Moreover, the tripla, like the organa, are commonly composed of alternating passages of organum purum and discant which may or may not be linked by *copula*.

The measurement of the tenor in the discant clausulas brings nothing new. Movement in ternary longs is most characteristic, followed, above all in the Office responsories, by that in duplex longs. The only patterned rhythms to appear with any frequency are those of the fifth mode.

The traditional *copula*, described by the St Emmeram Anonymous as having the appearance of the first mode ('sub specie primi modi') but sounding subtler and more delicate, may well be represented in the tripla. The problem is to identify it. The theorists refers to a passage in the Alleluia 'Posui adiutorium', calling attention to the multiple phrases and to the fact that *copula* is present in both the second and third voices. It is difficult to say whether all first mode periods consisting of antecedent-consequent phrases in each of the newly-

[63] David Hughes, 'Liturgical Polyphony at Beauvais in the Thirteenth Century', *Speculum*, 34 (1959), 192; 'The Sources of Christus Manens', *Aspects of Medieval and Renaissance Music: A Birthday Offering to Gustave Reese* (New York, 1966), 423; Arlt, *Festoffizium*, i, pp. 66 ff.

[64] Alleluia 'Judicabunt sancti' (see below); and the verse 'Cumque evigilasset Jacob' for the responsory 'Terribilis est'.

composed voices—and there is a substantial number of these—were rhythmically altered in performance.

Franco of Cologne, writing just a few years after the St Emmeram Anonymous, but concerned, by and large, with later musical procedures, identifies not one but two types of *copula*—bound, that is, written in ligature, and unbound.[65] The former, which after the first long note looks like the second mode,[66] differs from it in sound by virtue of its faster rhythm. Examples of this are not readily discernable in the polyphony under discussion. The unbound *copula*, on the other hand, is fairly common and again it would seem that there was a discrepancy between appearance and sound. Franco advises that the simple notes should be sung a little faster than the breves of the sixth mode, and there is little reason to doubt that this was the practice in his time, for the unbound *copula* translated into later notation in which longs and breves are clearly differentiated (as in the MS. Mo, for example) invariably appears as strings of breves. In the Notre-Dame sources, however, successions of simple notes normally represent ternary longs. We may guess that in the context of this particular *copula*, which most often appears at or near the end of a self-contained musical passage, they did not change their value as such but were subject, in performance, to a certain climactic hastening.

What distinguishes the tripla most clearly from the compositions *a2* is the style of the sustained-tenor passages, which, in the settings *a3*, actually involve a twofold relationship between voices. On the one hand, the duplum and the triplum work as a unit in opposition to the slower moving tenor, commonly 'composing out' as Helmut Schmidt puts it,[67] the intervals introduced with the enunciation of a new note of the chant as in this passage from 'Diffusa est gratia' by Perotin (F fo. 12) (Ex. 208). At the same time the newly composed voices are in discant with each other and hence subject to many of the same restraints observed in the clausulas *a2*. The freedom of the organum *per se* is inevitably sacrificed when a second organizing voice is introduced. Given this, it is not surprising that there are few literal ties between the two- and three-voiced pieces and that the majority of these occur in clausulas. Moreover, where there is shared material, the

---

[65] Cserba, *Hieronymous*, pp. 255 f.

[66] 'Copula non ligata ad similitudinem quinti modi fit'. Cserba, *Hieronymous*, p. 256. Franco understood the old first and fifth modes to have been one—a succession of ternary longs subdivided into longs and breves; hence, his fifth mode corresponds to what earlier writers named the sixth. If this is less tidy in a scholastic sense, it undoubtedly reflects more precisely the historical process.

[67] *Die drei- und vierstimmige Organa* (Kassel, 1933), 11 and *passim*.

Ex. 208

passages for two voices most often appear as reductions of those for three.[68]

Within the repertory, compositions are frequently related by means of contrafacture. The most striking example of this involves Perotin's music for Alleluia 'Nativitas', which is also used with four other texts—'Optimam partem', 'Diffusa est gratia', 'Sanctissimi Jacobe', and 'Judicabunt sancti'. The first of these is copied in W_1 as an alternate text under the original one, 'Nativitas', being sung to the same three-voiced setting (the same text is also copied under 'Nativitas' for the two-voiced setting, which is different music). Such practice merely reflects the multiple texting common in Alleluia verses in the chant repertory. The last two texts cited, however, are entered with their music written out in full in W_2.

There are other, less extended examples of contrafacture. The music for 'Tamquam sponsus', from the Christmas responsory 'Descendit',

---

[68] Ludwig, *Repertorium*, p. 64 and *passim*. Cf. Schmidt, *Die drei- und vierstimmige Organa*, p. 23, who assumed the reverse of this process.

is used again on Easter with 'Et respicientes', only the incipit of which was written out by the scribe of F. Polyphony for the Epiphany Alleluia, omitted from F, was presumably borrowed from another triplum with the same chant tenor, in this case, the Alleluia for Christmas. Shared fragments which consist of a few phrases and which cut across liturgical or functional lines are a commonplace.

The origins and the continuing history of the tripla are obscure. The limited amount of external evidence available suggests that three-voiced liturgical composition was probably first undertaken *c.* 1190, and Yvonne Rokseth proposed as an approximate terminal date for the cultivation of the category the year 1230.[69] She did so on the ground that nobody after Perotin is mentioned in the theoretical sources as a composer of tripla, and while the argument loses some of its force by reason of the fact that nobody before him is mentioned either, there may be some justification for thinking that triplum composition was largely the work of Perotin and his contemporaries.

Evidence from the manuscripts points to the existence of two or perhaps even three chronological layers within the repertory. The tripla in W_1, for example, do not form a self-contained, liturgically ordered cycle, but are scattered over three separate fascicles—the second, the seventh, and the eighth. The four tripla in the second fascicle (including Perotin's Alleluia 'Nativitas') are all found in F and W_2 as well. By contrast, none of the five tripla in the seventh fascicle (which seems not to have been a part of the manuscript as originally planned) occurs in W_2, the source with the youngest repertory. This suggests an earlier phase of composition, something substantiated if not confirmed by considerations of style, for tenor repetition plays no role here and one piece, 'Crucifixum in carne', is in organum purum throughout. The last group in W_1, a supplement to the eighth fascicle, contains two tripla which may represent the work of younger contempories of Perotin—'Hec dies', not only a late addition to the manuscript, but unique to it, and the clausula 'In odorem'. 'Hec dies' (W_1 fo. 90) proceeds in almost uninterrupted discant. The alternation between duplex longs and fifth mode patterns in the tenor, started in the respond, continues in the much longer verse where, again, patterns and repetition in the tenor go hand in hand (Ex. 209).

In F, the triplum 'Judea et Jerusalem' appears out of sequence toward the very end of the fascicle, after settings of the 'Benedicamus domino' and a group of clausulas. This may indicate that, like 'Hec dies', it is one of the later pieces and again there is some stylistic evidence for that view. Organum purum alternates with discant, but

[69] *Polyphonies du xiiie siècle*, iv, p. 8.

Ex. 209

Hec

1
di -

2

es

there is a certain schematic quality to the writing that is not character-istic of the works that have been attributed to Perotin. Whereas the 'abundant colors' associated by Anonymous 4 with the Perotinian tripla serve to ornament and enrich those pieces, here they become of the essence of the composition. It is of some interest that the collection or collections of tripla known to Anonymous 4 did not have the piece in question, for the theorist says quite specifically that 'Judea et Jerusalem was never made into a triplum ... '.[70]

Unlike the organa of the *Magnus liber* the tripla are characterized by a high degree of stability. Sixteen of the tripla are preserved in their entirety in from two to four manuscripts and not one is subject to the radical revisions so often encountered among the organa *a2*. It is true that their rhythmic notation is not always consistent, which may indicate that the tripla were occasionally updated by means of transmutation from the first mode, for example, to the more modern second. But the substitution of one clausula for another simply does

[70] 'Est et sextum volumen de organo in duplo ut *Iudea et Ierusalem* et *Constantes*, quod quidem numquam fit in triplo ...', Reckow, *Musiktraktat*, p. 82.

not occur.[71] For whatever reason, evidence which is so helpful in arriving at a chronology of the older category is altogether absent here.

There can be little doubt that the independent clausulas *a3*, nine in number, represent a late, perhaps even the latest stage in triplum composition. Tenors with double statement are, with one exception,[72] modally organized, and while the fifth mode still dominates, the first appears in three pieces, each time in a different form, while the second mode seems to govern one. The second and third voices of the clausulas with faster moving tenors are heavily fractured, which may suggest (as in the case of some of the clausulas *a2*) influence from the motet. Finally, three of the independent pieces are based on chants for which no complete tripla have survived. One of these, 'Et gaudebit', is a rare example of a composition *a3* built on or expanded from one *a2*; for the other two, 'Et illuminare' and 'Domine', both model and context are wanting.

QUADRUPLA

There are but three extant quadrupla: the Graduals 'Viderunt' and 'Sederunt', assigned by Anonymous 4 to Perotin, and the clausula 'Mors', for the Alleluia 'Christus resurgens'. They are preserved in all of the principal manuscripts, including Madrid, from which we may conclude that they are neither the oldest nor the youngest of the extant liturgical compositions from Paris, but rather, as it were, of middle age. 'Viderunt', suitable to both Christmas and its Octave, is further recorded in LoA.

These compositions, which are even more consistent from one source to another than the tripla, show a remarkable degree of internal, stylistic unity as well. In contrast to the tripla, which are characterized by frequent shifts of mode, the quadrupla are governed almost exclusively by the longs and breves of the first. 'Sederunt' is exceptional in having a short introductory passage in the third mode, and longer passages in the verse; the second respond (unique to F) is in the sixth mode. The discant tenors in the graduals proceed in unpatterned longs, either ternary or duplex, while that of 'Mors', (F fo. 7ᵛ), stated twice, makes use of two comparatively rare 5th mode formulas (Ex. 210). Not only the treatment of the tenor, but the

---

[71] The closest thing to the latter is the inclusion in F of two clausulas each for 'Yesse' and 'Eius' in the triplum *Styrps Yesse*. The original ones, which correspond to those in W₁, are not eliminated but relegated to second place. In neither case are there stylistic distinctions of any real significance.

[72] The initial statement of 'Domine', from the Gradual 'Gloriosus', has unpatterned ternary longs.

Ex. 210

Mors

2

staggering of the phrases in 'Mors' (which has simultaneous rests in all voices only four times before the final cadence) may be an indication of the comparative youth of this piece. At any rate, it is less typical of the Graduals, which move, for the most part, in clearly defined blocks of sound. The texture is remarkably dense: the four voices are effectively restricted to a range of a ninth or a tenth and seldom exceed at any given time the span of an octave. This, together with the restrained rhythm and staggered phrases, imparts to the music a grandeur which, shared only with 'Viderunt' and 'Sederunt', stands out unprecedented in medieval polyphony.

CONDUCTUS

The Parisian repertory of the twelfth and thirteenth centuries is not limited to liturgical music. Quite as important as the chant-based responsories for Mass and Office are the freely-composed Latin songs known as conductus. Indeed, the polyphonic examples of the genre— for two, three, and four voices—take up almost as much space in the manuscript F as the organa and the independent clausulas combined.

Older pieces with which these songs show some kinship seem to have originated well to the south of Paris, where they were sometimes called 'conductus' (in Madrid, B.N. MS. 289 and the Codex Calixtinus), more often 'versus' (in the Aquitanian manuscript Paris B.N. lat. 1139). A direct link between the Notre-Dame repertory and any that may pre-date it is lacking. The same is true of the liturgical Notre-Dame compositions, which appear to be unrelated to those of prior repertories from Winchester or Chartres, for example.

The subject matter of the Notre-Dame conductus is varied. The chief preoccupation of the poets is with the most fundamental of Christian mysteries, the Incarnation, and its corollary, the Atonement. Hardly less important is the attention to Mary, channel of the Incarnation and gentle mediatrix between God and his errant creatures. A sizeable number of poems do homage to other saints, ancient and modern: John, Apostle and Evangelist, Stephen, Nicholas, Germanus of Paris, Thomas Becket, and William of Bourges. Of the songs which allude to contemporary events (see above, p. 563, a handful are sacred and may have had some ritual function; others belong to the large group of admonitory satirical pieces which decry the abuse of clerical or political privilege and responsibility. Despite the presence of a few love songs and some witty, thinly-disguised requests for money, the conductus repertory as a whole is characterized by a serious tone far removed from that of the Goliardic verse of the same period.

Most of the poems are anonymous although a few are attributed (in other sources) to Philip the Chancellor (four), Walter of Chatillon (two), and John of Howden (one). Whoever the authors were, their poetry is highly sophisticated. The syntax is complex, the language rich in allegory and allusion. The learned writers turned constantly to earlier sources for material, drawing not only on the Bible and the Christian Fathers, but on pagan authors as well: Ovid, Horace, Juvenal, and others. A single strophe (the second of 'Rose nodum reserat', F fo. 315; W₁ fo. 62) from a commentary on the Incarnation will illustrate the universal love of symbol, the delight in paradox, and the respect for both canonic and pagan literature.

> The rod of Jesse comes to bud
> And a new graft is made.
> The scion is implanted
> But no incision is made.
> When Christ is conceived
> Chastity is not harmed.
> A marvellous thing:
> A maiden gives birth,
> And the firmament
> Is embraced by a star!

The biblical figure of the rod of Jesse is a commonplace as is the identification of Mary with a star; the allegory of grafting, on the other hand, expressed in a technical vocabulary current at least from the time of Virgil, is singular.

The uses to which this and other compositions were put is by no means clear. The sacred songs can nearly all be linked with one festival or another, but Parisian service books give no hint as to what their place in any given liturgy might have been. The original processional function of the genre (as indicated by the name 'conductus') may well have been preserved in Paris, but there is no reason to assume that it excluded all others. The Beauvais manuscript of the liturgies for the Feast of the Circumcision (see above, p. 561) shows some of the grandiose pieces to have been used in the cathedral there at the musical high point of the Mass, immediately following the Gradual and the Alleluia with its verse.

Even more problematical than the sacred pieces are the critical or admonitory ones. It is difficult to imagine when or where these trenchant lines from the third strophe of 'Deduc Sion uberrimas', preserved in no fewer than four manuscripts, (F fo. 336; W₁ fo. 159'; Ma fo. 83; W₂ fo. 93) might have been sung:

Behold, God of vengeance,
Behold, seeing all things,
How the Church is become
A den of stealers of grave cloths;
How the Prince of Babylon
Has come and set up his throne
In the temple of Solomon.
Now, with drawn sword,
Avenge this crime.
Come, Judge of the nations,
Overturn the stalls
Of those selling doves.

Musically speaking, the conductus is distinguished from the other categories of Notre-Dame polyphony by its original tenor. There are, to be sure, a few contrafacts of vernacular songs as well as occasional brief quotations from pre-existent melodies, but the overwhelming majority of the tenors are newly composed. Even settings of liturgical texts—'Pater noster qui es in celis', 'Ave Maria', and 'Alma redemptoris mater'—are based on freely composed melodies.

As Anonymous 4 observes, there are two broad types of conductus: those with melismata and those without. The latter, which constitute about a third of the repertory, allow the design of the poetry to shine through with great clarity. Their strophic melodies are characterized by balanced, sharply profiled phrases and by a substantial amount of text-related repetition. Normally found at the beginning of the piece, such repetition may, in stanzas of the lai or sequence type, continue to the end.

In contrast to the syllabic conductus, the melismatic ones show almost no text-related repetition. Although many of the poems in question consist of a number of similar strophes, the music is through-composed. Within the strophe, furthermore, corresponding lines of poetry are set to different, albeit stylistically consistent melodies. Repetition does play a significant role in the melismata, which appear most typically at the end of the conductus, but which may also introduce or conclude strophes within the composition.

The final melisma of 'Legem dedit olim Deus' (F fo. 312), *a2*, embodies a number of characteristic procedures (Ex. 211). The passage consists of essentially two phrases, each of which is repeated. Phrase 1*b*, which at first glance appears to be new, is a literal restatement of *1*a in which the melodic material is exchanged by the two voices ('voice exchange', German *Stimmtausch*). This exceedingly popular device is used not only in two-voiced but also in three-voiced

Ex. 211

conductus, where the exchange normally occurs between duplum and triplum. Phrase 2*b* repeats 2*a* with an adjustment which brings it to close on the final, D, and the melisma ends with a quasi-organal passage. Anonymous 4 takes note of such passages, as does the author of the so-called St Martial treatise, who points out that their excessive use in discant composition will so alter the texture that it will no longer be distinguished as discant.

Not all melismata are as heavily dependent on literal repetition as the one cited and not all show the same symmetry or the same regular phrase breaks. Neither are all melismata as heavily dependent, melodically or harmonically, on the interval of the third, sometimes taken to be suggestive of English influence (see below, p. 689). As in all Notre-Dame polyphony *a2*, the voices occupy the same range. A third voice not uncommonly extends the total range upward by a fourth.

The theorists are consistent in describing the conductus as a species of discant or precisely measured polyphony. They include it with the organum, the motet, and the hocket among the genres governed by the rhythmic modes. The notation of the melismatic portions of the conductus, like that of the discant clausula, is largely unproblematical. A given sequence of material *figurae*, most of which are ligatures, suggest a particular mode. Predictably, the first mode is by far the most popular. The third mode is sparingly used as are the fifth and the sixth, both of which are oriented toward the first. Appearances of the second mode are rare.

The notation of the syllabic pieces, and even of the syllabic portions of the more elaborate works, is by contrast fraught with difficulties. The ligatures which provide the clue to the mode are decomposed by successive syllables of text into a series of undifferentiated simple notes. These must be recast in the mind ('in intellectu') into patterns with rhythmic significance. The theorists sketch out a few guidelines for this procedure, and some help is to be had from a handful of pieces that survive in both texted and melismatic form. Combining the information from theoretical and musical sources with a careful analysis of poetic rhythm, scholars have been able to solve at least some of the problems related to the proper delivery of the text.

A great deal of the poetry is governed by a perfectly regular trochaic rhythm. (The word 'trochaic' is used, after the manner of the medieval poetic theorists, by analogy to the classical metre and carries with it no quantitative implications.) The alternation of stressed and non-stressed syllables evidently corresponded, in the mind of the Notre-Dame composer, to the alternation of longs and breves in the first rhythmic mode and the two were often wedded as Ex. 212 shows.

The seven-syllable verse with an antepenultimate or proparoxytonic accent (7pp) outnumbers all others, appearing now alone, now as part of a fifteen (8 + 7)- or thirteen (7 + 6)-syllable couplet. The former is typically set to a continuous phrase consisting of eight first mode feet. The latter, which is not only shorter, but which cadences with a paroxytonic accent (6p), is brought into conformity with the foregoing through the substitution of a ternary long for the long-breve ahead of the close (Ex. 212(ii)).

Ex. 212

(i) Mí - nor ná - tu fí - li - ùs

(ii) Fás et né - fas am - bu - lant / fé - re pás - su pá - ri

(iii) Sál - va - tó - ris hó - di - è / sán - guis pre - gu - stá - tur

(iv) Ín quo Sý - on fí - li - è

(v) Vel ín fis - cél - la scír - pe - à

(vi) Ní - tor et lé - tor ág - gre - dì

(vii) Mé - mor ún - de ce - cí - de - rìs

(viii) De món - te lá - pis scín - di - tùr

(ix) Pro - cú - rans ó - di - ùm

(x) Néx - us est cór - di - ùm

(xi) Vé - ri fló - ris súb fi - gú - ra

(xii) Fló - rem fé - cit mí - sti - cùm

(xiii) Fló - ris á na - tú - ra

Not infrequently, above all in the large melismatic compositions, the declamatory rhythm of the trochaic verse is augmented to produce phrases in the fifth rhythmic mode (Ex. 212(iii)). Fractures of the declamatory long in any or all of the voices superimpose on the fifth mode a secondary level of rhythmic activity most often oriented toward the first (Ex. 212(iv)).

Apart from the trochaic verses, there are none which are rhythmically consistent. An eight-syllable proparoxytone line (8pp), 'De monte lapis scinditur', for example, may proceed in iambs from beginning to end, but there is not so much as a single complete strophe composed exclusively of such lines. Only in the latter half of the verse is the succession of accents fixed. Ahead of this, any one of these three patterns may occur: x ´ x ´ (as above); ´ x x ´ or ´ x ´ x. There is no mode which can, in its pure form, accommodate all of these, but the first is frequently adjusted in such a way as to bring the stressed syllables into alignment with the long notes. A substitution in the first foot accomplishes this for verses starting with either of the first two patterns (Ex. 212(v) and (vi)). The replacement of a long-breve pair with a ternary long later in the line works best for the last one (Ex. 212(vii)). No two pieces are exactly the same and evidence from the context of the music and its notation must be brought to bear on the decision as to where the substitution is to be introduced and whether or not a consistent pattern of substitutions is to be sought. The declamation of the syllabic pieces tends to be more varied than that of the melismatic ones, which are most often characterized by stable declamatory rhythm. All of 'De monte lapis scinditur', to name one such case, is delivered in augmentation of the first of the two patterns just cited (Ex. 212(viii)).

Polyphonic settings of six-syllable proparoxytones (6pp), whether melismatic or syllabic (the latter are more common by far) are regularly declaimed in the ternary longs of the fifth mode. Because a perfect phrase in that mode consists of an odd number of longs, a substitution of values is always required. The notation leaves no doubt whatever that this takes place with the third syllable, which is declaimed as a duplex long or its equivalent, a ternary long and a ternary rest (Ex. 212(ix) and (x)). In the latter case, one voice of the harmonic complex may give continuity to the musical line by singing through the rest in the tenor.

The use of mid-line extensions, essential to the irregular six-syllable lines, is not limited to these. One of the most popular of all syllabic conductus a3, 'Veri floris sub figura', is a setting of a perfectly regular trochaic poem. Lines of eight and seven syllables declaimed in the fifth mode are subdivided into two parts by internal extensions (Ex. 212(xi) and (xii)). Only the unique six-syllable verse at the close of the strophe moves in uninterrupted ternary longs as far as the penultimate accent (Ex. 212(xiii)).[73]

Jacques Handschin proposed on more than one occasion that the earliest conductus were to be declaimed in equal notes of relatively long value, and there would seem to be at least indirect support for that view in the existing repertory. A significant number of the syllabic conductus declaimed in the fifth mode can be placed, by virtue of their association with contemporary events, among the oldest songs in the Notre-Dame repertory. While these pieces are genuinely modal, it is easy to imagine a still older layer of compositions in which the long notes had not yet been rhythmically organized, a situation which has its parallel in the history of the discant clausula.

The first and fifth rhythmic modes, although early to develop, retained their popularity in both clausula and conductus. The increasing complexity in the treatment of the first and second modes from perhaps the second decade of the thirteenth century was eventually to destroy the modes, and the conductus did not survive the old style. The new was to find its most striking example in the motet, a genre which has its roots in the manuscripts F and W_2.

MOTET

The last two of the polyphonic fascicles in the Florence manuscript are devoted to the oldest surviving motets or 'troped'—more properly 'prosulaic'—clausulas (see p. 682), or what some scholars prefer to call 'texted clausulas'.[74] The new genre did indeed come about through the introduction of words into the newly composed voice or voices of the discant. Of sixty-nine such compositions in F, fifty-nine are texted versions of discant passages appearing earlier in the manuscript.[75] Compare, for example, Ex. 213, a texted version of the 'Regnat' clausula (F fo. 403), with the melismatic original given in Ex. 199. Both Johannes de Garlandia and Anonymous 4, however, used the term *motellus*, at least in passing. That they were aware of the relationship between clausula and motet is made especially clear by the reference in Anonymous 4 to the 'tenor discantum sive motellorum', that is, the tenor of discant or motets.[76]

[73] Knapp, 'Musical Declamation and Poetic Rhythm in an Early Layer of Notre Dame Conductus', *JAMS*, 32 (1979), 383.

[74] Sanders, 'The Medieval Motet', in Wulf Arlt, *et al.*, eds., *Gattungen der Musik in Einzeldarstellungen: Gedenkschrift Leo Schrade*, i (Berne, 1973), 497; 'Motet, I, 1: Medieval', *New Grove*, xii, 617.

[75] Two more can be traced to the repertories of St Victor and Beauvais, respectively. The second of these, 'Veni doctor previe', is derived not from discant, however, but from organum.

[76] Reckow, *Musiktraktat*, i, p. 55.

Ex. 213

In - fi - de - lem po - pu - lum   Ha - man ad pa - ti - bu - lum

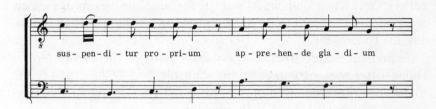

sus - pen - di - tur pro - pri - um   ap - pre - hen - de gla - di - um

fran - ge ma - nus hos - ti - um   ve - ni in au - xi - li - um

nau - fra - gan - ti se - cu - lo et po - pu - lo fi - de - li - um

Je - bu - se - os e - i - ce, nos re - spi - ce per fi - li - um.

In a sense the texting of the clausula draws togther what had hitherto been two distinct lines of composition, one liturgical and melismatic, the other free and full of words. In every case of texted discant, the music of the clausula remains intact, but the texting, contrived to match each note of the duplum with a syllable, transforms that voice into something resembling the conductus. The verses taken individually are remarkably similar to those used in the older Latin songs, but they do not add up to the large structural groups or strophes characteristic of both Latin and vernacular poetry of the period. Only when Wilhelm Meyer[77] recognized the genesis of the new composition in the clausula did the reasons for the irregular combinations become clear.

Setting the texted discant apart from both of the earlier Notre-Dame categories of composition—clausula and conductus—is the simultaneous presentation of two texts, one syllabic, the other melismatic. Although the tenor might one day be played on an instrument, the textual underlay in F and also in W_2 leaves little doubt that at the outset the words of the chant were still being sung in the tenor.

The eighth fascicle of F contains twenty-six compositions *a3*, only two of which have not been traced to melismatic models. It comes as something of a surprise, however, that with a single exception (and that from Beauvais rather than Paris) all of the models are for two voices. We cannot be entirely sure of the sequence of events, but it seems clear that the two additions to the clausula, one verbal, the other musical, were introduced at much the same time. The texting added to the orginal duplum was shared with a newly-composed third voice. The relationship between these two voices, in strict discant marked off by simultaneous cadences, is at odds with that of the corresponding voices in the three-voiced melismatic clausulas, which are typically articulated by staggered cadences.

These motets *a3* with one text shared by duplum and triplum are sometimes called 'conductus motets', and, indeed, their appearance on the page emphasizes their relationship to the conductus. The texted voices, notated primarily in simple note forms, are copied in score, while the melismatic tenor, which is still notated in ligature, is more economically placed at the end. Small wonder that three other texted clausulas, two for four voices, and one for three, were copied with the conductus *a3* in F. The same four-voiced pieces further appear with

---

[77] 'Der Ursprung des Motetts', *Nachrichten von der Wissenschaften zu Göttingen, Philosophisch-historische Klasse II* (Göttingen, 1898). Reprinted in Meyer's *Gesammelte Abhandlungen zur mittellateinischen Rhythmik*, ii (Berlin, 1905), p. 303.

conductus in W_1, where, whether by accident or by design, the tenors are omitted.

Eleven of the pieces from the eighth fascicle of F reappear in W_2 with the same Latin texts, and four of these, together with one enlarged from a Latin trope *a2*, appear yet again in the younger manuscript as French contrafacts. Hereafter the conductus motet was abandoned—a failed experiment, so it would seem.

The ninth fascicle of F contains what prove to be more durable types of composition—the Latin motet *a2*, and the Latin double motet, that is, a three-voiced composition with two different texts in duplum and triplum. The Latin motet *a2* dominates with forty pieces, thirty of which are derived from two-voiced clausulas and four of which are reduced from clausulas *a3*.

If the dependence of these motets on the clausula repertory marks them as conservative, their arrangement in the fascicle adumbrates the eventual independence of the genre from their liturgical matrix. Whereas the texted clausulas in fascicle 8 follow quite strictly the order of the Church year, those in fascicle 9 are presented without reference to the calendar.

There are just three Latin double motets in F,[78] clearly not enough to merit a fascicle of their own. It is of some interest that, although the number of Latin motets *a2* in W_2 is nearly double that of F, the polytextual pieces *a3* do not increase. It is only in the French repertory of W_2, to be explored in the following chapter, that the double motet begins to flourish.

---

[78] Ludwig, *Repertorium*, pp. 111–16.

XIII

FRENCH POLYPHONY OF THE THIRTEENTH CENTURY

By RICHARD CROCKER

Up to the stage at which the discant clausula was provided with a Latin text in the duplum, the development of polyphony at Notre Dame in Paris could be traced in relative isolation from other music of the twelfth and early thirteenth centuries. Chapter XII describes the features that set Notre-Dame organa style apart—consistent use of a cantus firmus from the Gregorian repertory of the archetype, very extended melismatic writing for two, three, or four voices, modal rhythm, and eventually overlapping phrases between tenor and upper parts. All of that development seemed to have a logic and momentum of its own, and the kind of music it produced in the organa and independent clausulas in Perotin's style were distinctly different from any other music we know of that time. Then, with the Latin texting of the clausula duplum, more similarities with other kinds of music appear; and from then on, in fact, the Notre-Dame style merged with other music, eventually losing its individuality.

The manuscript sources of thirteenth-century polyphony present us with many subtle variations in style and repertory. Study of these began source by source, and tended to group these sources by location; the result is the traditional distinction of French or continental polyphony from English polyphony, reflected in this chapter and the next. As study continued, however, more purely musical groupings and tendencies emerged, and it is now difficult to carry out the traditional ones. On one hand, polyphony with French texts remained more or less restricted to France and French sources, while developing certain styles of its own; on the other, polyphony with Latin texts appears not only together with the French but especially in English sources, and there exemplified some of the most important features of Latin polyphony on the Continent as well. To complicate the study of

Latin polyphony still further, the line of research on Notre-Dame polyphony founded by Friedrich Ludwig and so brilliantly carried out in his *Repertorium*[1] had the effect of emphasizing the 'central repertory' of Notre Dame and its role in the broader development. Against this notion of 'central', Jacques Handschin kept directing attention to what was going on before, around, and in spite of the Notre-Dame style.[2] The dialogue continues to affect the ways we see thirteenth-century polyphony.[3]

This chapter will focus primarily on polyphony with French texts, while keeping in view the repertories of continental Latin polyphony that appears alongside the French in the sources. French polyphony emerged early in the century, close to the Notre-Dame repertory but soon moving in its own direction; it developed rapidly, and dominated continental polyphony throughout the century. A piece of French texted discant came generally to be called a 'motet', but the term is not without ambiguity. Later in the century the term 'motet' more usually referred to a stich from a *roman*.[4] Its application to French texted discant might be related to the frequent quotation of such stichs in these French texts. Sometimes the term 'motet' seems to be used to refer specifically to the duplum with its French text; and modern scholars regularly use the Latin form 'motetus' (coined in the thirteenth century) in this way. The motet repertory eventually included hundreds of items, which in the latter half of the century were collected in several large anthologies. Writing shortly after 1300, Jacques de Liège[5] complained that whereas the old composers cultivated several different kinds of music—organum, discant, hocket, conductus—the moderns wrote 'almost nothing but motets and chansons', and that seems to some degree at least to characterize polyphony on the Continent from the mid-thirteenth century on.[6]

The interplay between the early Latin and French motet was intense and exceedingly complex. When we compare the French texted

---

[1] *Repertorium organorum recentioris et motetorum vetustissimi stili* (2nd edn. ed. Luther Dittmer, *Musicological Studies*, 7, 26, Institute of Medieval Music, 1964, 1978).

[2] In numerous studies from 1923 onward; see the bibliography in *MGG*, v (1956), cols. 1441–3.

[3] Ernest Sanders, 'Peripheral Polyphony of the 13th Century', *JAMS*, 17 (1964), 261.

[4] Klaus Hofmann, 'Zur Entstehungs- und Frühgeschichte des Terminus Motette', *AcM*, 42 (1970), 138.

[5] *Speculum musicae*, vii, ed. Roger Bragard, *Corpus scriptorum de musica*, 3 (American Institute of Musicology, 1973), 89.

[6] A comprehensive account of the motet in the thirteenth century by Yvonne Rokseth, *Polyphonies de xiiie siécle*, 4 vols. (Paris, 1935–9), in particular iv, 'Études et Commentaires'. See also Sanders, 'The Medieval Motet', in Wulf Arlt, *et al.*, eds., *Gattungen der Musik in Einzeldarstellungen: Gedenkschrift Leo Schrade*, i (Berne, 1973); 'Motet. I. Medieval', *New Grove*, xii. 617.

discant—the French motet—to the repertory of early Latin texted discant as a whole, we find that a great many pieces exist with both a Latin text and a French one, as alternative settings. This situation persists far into the thirteenth century. If we know in any given case which text came first, we call the other a 'contrafact'. In some cases this priority can be determined with reasonable assurance; but in many cases one can only guess, or draw believable conclusions from purely circumstantial evidence. Among early French motets are many contrafacts; but it is also true that many Latin motets throughout the century are contrafacts of French versions. While the earliest texting of Notre-Dame discant seems to have been with Latin texts,[7] the French texts started soon after 1200, and the repertory of French motets seems to have established itself almost as fast as the Latin—in some respects faster.

We can discern some general tendencies (to be discussed) that distinguish the French motet from the Latin one. The question still to be answered is, to what factor or factors are those different tendencies due? The French texts themselves raise a series of questions concerning who made these texts and their music, who performed them, who heard them. Many (but not all) aspects of the French texts are related to the trouvère repertory, and that brings with it some musical factors different from those of Notre-Dame polyphony.

In social terms, Notre-Dame polyphony was a function of the urban cathedral, more specifically of the cathedral in its new Gothic form (and like that form, the new music first appeared in the Ile de France). The cathedral was the locus of the new style, and as such we need to compare its musical role to that of the other, more traditional loci, the monastery and the court. Medieval society being as complex as any other, only generalities can be offered here. Out in the countryside was the monastery with its musical performers, the cantor and choir, with the whole community participating in psalmody and hymns of the Office. Also often in the country, in some ways parallel to the monastery, in other ways opposed, was the manorial court; here the performer was the noble singer, supported and eventually supplanted by the professional musician—certainly in the case of instrumental performance, and perhaps for singing too. The monastery maintained the Gregorian repertory, and developed new repertories, up to and including the most recent one of the versus, representing modern music of the twelfth century. The court developed the repertory of trouvère songs during the same century. This repertory was taken to town, recorded in anthologies and performed there by

[7] See Ch. XII.

professional musicians for the *haute bourgeoisie* in the thirteenth century. There was, however, another kind of patron, even creator, of vernacular song in town in the person of a high-ranking cathedral cleric; such persons, with cathedral-school education and frequently secular tastes, were to play an important if not decisive role in the development of the French motet.

The monastic life in its way also approached the town, through the medium of communities of secular clergy living under a rule—'canons regular' such as the Augustinians. These played an important role in the development of the twelfth-century sequence, among other things. The locus of twelfth-century polyphony is hard to specify: the new polyphonic experiments seem to turn up in a wide variety of places; yet all lay on the continuum between the monastery and the cathedral. The musical establishment at the cathedral was manned by a professional musician of clerical rank, at the head of one or more choirs. We can imagine a schema in which music from the monastery converges on the cathedral, hence on the town, from one side; and music from the court converges on the town, hence on the cathedral, from the other. They meet at the residences of the cathedral nobility.

A trouvère song, as preserved in the great anthologies, had typically between three and eight strophes; all strophes of a poem were of course on the same structure, except for a concluding *envoi*, consisting of between six and ten lines.[8] Lines were typically of between six and eleven syllables long, with normally two rhymes in various patterns of alternation. A typical strophe began with a couplet (with lines three and four sung to the same melody as lines one and two). The lines following, usually with different melody, were of approximately the same length, with occasionally a single shorter line.

This large repertory of song texts was but a part of a much larger body of literature centred on the *roman*—a literature that was well known to the manorial aristocracy, and became well known to the bourgeois classes that now adopted the aristocratic culture. The favourite stichs that Friedrich Gennrich identified as refrains of rondeaux were only some of a vast repertory of stichs that he and others have identified simply as 'refrains'—apparently quoted in a wide variety of contexts as current allusions to familiar themes, characters, situations, and stories.[9] When refrains are quoted, their

[8] See Ch. IX.

[9] Friedrich Gennrich, 'Rondeau', *MGG*, xi (1963), cols. 867–72; *Rondeaux, Virelais und Balladen aus dem Ende des XII., dem XIII. und der ersten Drittel des XIV. Jahrhunderts, mit den überlieferten Melodien, Gesellschaft für romanische Literatur*, 43, i, Texts (1921); 47, ii, Commentary (1927). Nico H. J. Van den Boogaard, *Rondeaux et Refrains du XIIe siècle au début du XIVe, Bibliothèque française et Romane, Série D: Initiation, Textes et documents*, 3 (Strasburg, Paris, 1969). See also Ch. IX.

text seems to be the more stable element, the melody less so; and in fact there seems to be relatively little quotation of secular melody. (Similarly in sacred chant, it is sometimes only the text of a chant that is quoted in a play or a farsed Office, without reference to the original melody; in the case of chant from the archetype of Mass or Office, however, the quotation usually seems to include the chant.) This use of the vernacular literature under the general heading of refrains is important for the text of the French motet. In this context the term does not imply a repetitive structure, only the use of a favourite stich.

Alongside the professional trouvère singers and composers, there were also professional instrumentalists; it is easier to document their purely instrumental performances than their participation in vocal performance. Some scholars believe that the monophonic trouvère songs were accompanied by instruments in a non-written tradition, but the evidence for this is under debate.[10] In any case, we have but little specific idea of what an instrumental accompaniment would have been, and whether it would have resembled the tenor of a French motet. The assumption is that the tenors of French motets were performed on instruments, which might suggest that the instrumentalists exerted an influence on the French motet, contributing to its distinctive qualities as compared to the Latin motet.

Against all of these possibilities is the fact that the French motet is a motet like the Latin one, embodying essential and distinctive features of the discant clausula; and these could have been drawn only from Notre Dame. In general, the early French motet makes much less use of ready-made discant clausulas than does the Latin: enough early French motets do this to demonstrate the close connection with Notre Dame, but a greater number do not, and their proportion rises rapidly as the repertory develops. Much more important to the composer of French motets was the fund of modal rhythms, and the contrapuntal experience of the kind of clausula associated with Perotin's style, in which the duplum's phrases can be staggered relative to the repetitive tenor. As shown in chapter XII, this style was a decisive development within the clausula repertory. Most important of all was the Notre-Dame tenor itself—the chant melisma cast into a repeating rhythmic pattern for use in a discant clausula. While the early French motet made relatively little use of Notre-Dame discant clausulas as such, it made heavy use of tenors from clausulas. Thus to the composer of the French motet the essential feature of the discant was the tenor, and best way to assure success was to build upon the tenor in adapting the new Notre-Dame style for use with French texts and new dupla.

---

[10] See Ch. X.

The use of Notre-Dame tenors in clausula and motet shows a pattern of distribution familiar to us from the development of the Kyrie repertory, among others. There is alternatively (sometimes simultaneously) a concentration on a few favourite tenors, and a broadening of the selection to include a large number of tenors, even if only once or twice each. Scholars have often expressed the wish to know why a few tenors were favoured; several kinds of explanations have been advanced, with varying satisfaction.[11] For the French motet, at least, the 'liturgical' explanation seems the least useful. A more sophisticated structural analysis seems called for, but awaits the development of reliable ideas about melodic and contrapuntal structure in thirteenth-century polyphony (which in turn await the clear understanding of musical structure in twelfth-century chant as well as polyphony). In the mean time we can observe *ad hoc* that each tenor by nature embodies a very particular—unique, even—solution to musical form, one which we can consider appropriately case by case; and that repeated use of one tenor can be registered as fact, even when we cannot yet see the reason, which might be as pragmatic as, say, the more a tenor was observed to succeed, the more often it was used. One thing is clear: a tenor, typically an excerpt from chant, often does not end on the final of the chant, and the relationship of the tenor final to its structure is to be evaluated anew—and, in any case, not in terms of mode, which as a method of classification had little to do with melodic structure, as we have seen. About rhythmic structure, and especially about rhythmic mode, we can generalize a little further. All rhythmic possibilities of the clausula seem to be used in one motet or another. None the less, there is a distinct shift within the early and middle French motet sources from tenor rhythms on mode 5 based on groups of three perfect longs—the mainstay of the discant clausula—to tenor rhythms in modes 1 or 2, that is, in the same mode as the duplum.

We can approach this shift in tenor rhythms through the central matter of phrase structure—as important in the French motet as in the discant clausula with or without Latin text or as in the trouvère song, the versus, or any kind of medieval chant. The phrase structure of the French motet is usually of a different kind from the phrase structure on a trouvère song, and in order to grasp the difference we need to go a long way round. The long-short rhythm ('pre-modal trochaic', eventually first mode) of Notre Dame was probably developed within melismatic discant apart from syllabic considerations; phrases of discant were generated out of the long-short module apart

---

[11] See, for instance, Kurt Hofmann, *Untersuchungen zur Kompositionstechnik der Motette im 13. Jahrhundert, Tübinger Beiträge zur Musikwissenschaft*, 2 (Neuhausen-Stuttgart, 1972).

from considerations of any kind of verse. Yet when Latin text was laid under these rhythms and phrase shapes the result was very close to the twelfth-century Latin versus, with its immediate succession of multiple rhymes forming very short phrases. From this point of view, it is possible to understand the Latin motet as the direct result of the Latin versus, the whole of the Notre-Dame organa then being an irrelevant parenthesis; perhaps that is the way Handschin wanted us to understand it. From other points of view, however, Notre-Dame polyphony—discant in particular—was an essential step in the development of the motet. In the case of the French motet, anyway, a direct line of succession from the monophonic antecedent cannot be imagined, for the trouvère song did not show the short, irregular, but intensely rhyming lines of the Latin versus, and when these appear in the French motet it has to have had something to do with the Latin texted discant, or with the melismatic clausula, or just with the fact of its being a motet. It must be acknowledged that not all French motets have such a phrase structure; some have a phrase structure as regular or almost as regular as a trouvère song. In most realistic terms, the maker of a French motet was between the poles of a trouvère song and a discant clausula, so it is no wonder if at some time or other he tried all the possibilities within that range. Of these possibilities, however, that of irregular length verses is the one that cannot be easily explained by trouvère art.

Whether the short lines of irregular length (in Latin or French) came from the twelfth-century versus or were developed afresh out of the discant, the decisive, distinctive element in their polyphonic implementation was modal rhythm and ordo structure in the tenor. The modal rhythms in the texted duplum—the motetus—are of course important, and make possible the close integration of the duplum with the tenor. By themselves, however, (that is, without a tenor), the modal rhythms of the duplum would only inflect the phrase rhythms with additional intensity. It is the repeated pattern in the tenor (which as we saw is a modal pattern of a set length, that is, of a certain ordo) that adds the distinctively new dimension to the phrase structure. The tenor rhythmic pattern is typically shorter than all but the shortest phrases of the duplum. Thus many phrases of the duplum can be integral multiples of the tenor pattern in length, containing two, three, four, or more tenor ordines. This provides a powerful momentum to the longer phrases, and furthermore sets out a common denominator by which phrases of different length can be related: we hear such phrases as not simply different, but as consisting of various numbers of a common unit, whose incessant repetition provides continuity and momentum. That is only the simplest possibility. Instead of consisting of an integral number of tenor ordines, a phrase can end in the middle of a tenor ordo, creating overlap or staggering of phrases. There is a whole range of possibilities between complete coincidence and noncoincidence of phrasing between tenor and motetus, as well as a complete range between regular and irregular phrasing in the motetus. The identity of any given motet is largely a function of its phrasing and patterns of coincidence. These relationships are made more intensive by the preference in French motet tenors for modes 1 and 2 over mode 5, since it is in these modes that the tenor tends to get even more involved in the rhythmic activity of the motetus. Staggered phrasing under these conditions has an especially intimate effect.

MOTET MANUSCRIPTS

The fact that the French motet is related on the one hand to the trouvère chanson and on the other to cathedral polyphony is reflected in the manuscript sources in which it is preserved. These are of several distinct types; and since modern scholarly editions of motets have so far been made according to the manuscript sources, we need to be aware of their nature.[12] Alongside—perhaps even before—the Notre-Dame source W_2 with its important collection of motets stands another 'central' source, Munich, Cod.gall.42,[13] often referred to as Munich A ('MuA'); it may reflect the earliest stage of the French motet. A third, somewhat enigmatic source is Paris, Bibl.Nat. lat.15139, the so-called St Victor melismata.[14]

There are among the many large trouvère chanson anthologies some that include French motets, either as separate sections or scattered throughout. These include the Chansonnier du Roi, Paris, Bibl.Nat. fr. 884 ('R'), the Chansonnier de Noailles, Paris Bibl. Nat.fr.12615 ('N'), and others.[15] These have many interesting features; they may or may not include tenors of the motets, and some have only the texts.

Clearly distinct from the chanson anthologies are the motet anthologies, including the two large ones, Codex Montpellier, Bibl.Univ. H 196 ('Mo'), and Codex Bamberg, Ed. IV 6; and two smaller ones, 'La

---

[12] The entire early repertory of motets is edited by Hans Tischler, *The Earliest Motets (to circa 1270): A Complete Comparative Edition* (3 vols.) (New Haven, 1982), hereafter, Tischler, *EM*.

[13] Luther Dittmer, *A Central Source of Notre Dame Polyphony* (Institute of Medieval Music, Brooklyn, New York, 1959).

[14] Jurgen Stenzl, *Die vierzig Clausulae der Handschrift Paris Bibliothèque nationale latin 15139* (Berne, 1970).

[15] Ludwig, *Repertorium*, pp. 285–305. A facsimile of R ed. Jean Beck, *Le Manuscrit du Roi, Corpus cantilenarum medii aevi*, 1st ser. 2 (Philadelphia, London, 1938).

Clayette' (Paris B.N.n.a.frç. 13521), and Turin, Bibl.reale, vari 42.[16] Finally there are a number of sources that do not fit into any of these categories. Each contains one or a few motets, but although such sources may be very valuable for the transmission of individual motets, they do not tell us much about the repertory in general. The first three kinds of sources, taken in the order suggested by their contents as analysed by Ludwig and others, can give us a good idea of the development of the motet in the thirteenth century.

Concordances, that is, appearances of a given piece in another manuscript, are the most powerful lever we have to pry apart the blocks of material in the large anthologies and uncover the development of the repertory. The basic listing of concordances is Ludwig's *Repertorium*; subsequently scholars have studied in detail the concordances of individual motets in order to reconstruct the history of each of these separately, and on the other hand have scrutinized each manuscript collection in order to reconstruct *its* history—where its individual items have come from, how they came together. Two motets adjacent in two manuscripts might suggest a relationship; analysis of surrounding motets, taking into account direct or indirect concordances, may reveal a larger complex of related pieces. The circle can sometimes be widened still further through motets that have similar stylistic features but are found in other places.

FRENCH MOTETS IN 'MUNICH A'

The fragments that constitute MuA preserve, among other music indigenous to the Notre-Dame repertory, a small portion—about thirty—of what was once apparently an extensive collection of French and Latin motets. Judging from what remains, the motet collection was arranged in the order of the tenors as taken from the *Magnus liber*, that is, from the order of the chants in the Graduale; what is preserved is part of the Christmas cycle, including tenors for chants from Christmas and Epiphany. There are several motets on each of the tenors 'Omnes', 'Dominus', 'Manere', and others. The French motets themselves are not necessarily related in theme to the Latin tenors; hence the liturgical order reflects merely the closeness of this particular manuscript to the cathedral environment. Beyond that, over a third of the preserved motets use not merely tenors but entire

---

[16] Codex Montpellier ed. Yvonne Rokseth, *Polyphonies du xiiie siécle*, 4 vols. (Paris 1935–9; re-ed. Hans Tischler, *The Montpellier Codex*, 3 vols., Madison, 1978). Codex Bamberg re-ed. Gordon A. Anderson, *Compositions of the Bamberg Manuscript, Corpus mensurabilis musicae*, 75 (American Institute of Musicology, 1975). Antoine Auda, ed., *Les 'motets wallons' du manuscrit Turin: Vari 42* (Brussels, 1953). Anderson, *Motets of the Manuscript La Clayette, Corpus mensurabilis musicae*, 68 (American Institute of Musicology, 1975).

clausulas; they are, in effect, texted clausulas—and this is a relatively high proportion of such pieces compared with the other motet collections. Furthermore, and directly related to the use of a discant clausula, a substantial majority of these motets of MuA are close to Notre-Dame discant. This is especially apparent in the first series of motets (Nos. 2–19 of Dittmer's 'Complex A' in his edition of MuA).

MuA also contains, however, other kinds of French motets not so closely related to the Notre-Dame clausula, instead having connections to the trouvères. These motets tend to occur later in the first series (Nos. 22–8) and include two concordances with trouvère anthologies to be mentioned. Three motets, plus a fourth that was copied several times later in the century, all use mode 2 in the motetus, and either mode 5 or mode 2 in the tenor. They are not derived from Notre-Dame clausulas. Still another motet in this group, No. 26, uses mode 1 in the tenor. These rhythmic features were to be most characteristic of the French motet. No. 25 of this series, 'Dame vostre doz regart', T. 'Manere', (the one with several later concordances[17]) is a very attractive representative of this kind of piece, with mode 2 in both motetus and tenor (Ex. 214). The tenor, using a melisma on 'Manere', has the minimum ordo for mode 2, brevis-longa-brevis. The motet has mode 2 with almost continuous division of the longa into two breves, or of the breves into two semibreves, giving a lilting flow to the upper part. The phrase structure of the upper part seems to start a couplet:

> Dame vostre doz regart   (7)
> M'oci-ent qant de vos part   (7)
> Ne je certes cele part   (7)
> Ne me puis torner   (5)

with regular seven-syllabled lines, rhyming; the melody of the third line is the same as that of the first line, and each of these first three lines includes two tenor ordines. This regularity is then broken by the short fourth line, which brings about the very characteristic 'head-to-tail' phrasing between motetus and tenor, used here only briefly but in many motets extensively. The phrasing continues now regular, now irregular, coinciding or not with the tenor ordines, and in particular bridging over the place where the tenor starts to repeat its melody. A special interplay occurs on 'aler, parler', where the head-and-tail phrasing combines with a habit of using unisons between the voices at their juncture.

[17] Facs. in Dittmer, *A Central Source*, pp. 21–2; cf. Tischler, *EM* No. 142 (ii, p. 957), Mo 5, 90.

Ex. 214

The last pair of lines,

Li maus d'amer me debrise   (8)
Et la dolor qe je sent   (7)

is one of the refrains identified by Gennrich.[18]

The tenor moves in a locus around c, with excursions to the g above and the G below, but with a clear centre on c. Yet, since the chant melisma ends on a, with one of those seemingly off-hand descents at its phrase ending, the motet tenor comes to its final on a (which is not the final of the original Gradual) rather than the central note c. (The a is probably heard as *re* in spite of some b flats in the motetus in MuA.)

The net effect of these various procedures is to create a special and apparently new kind of accompaniment to the song. The motet tenor has something of the quality of an ostinato—a repeated figure, as if an animated drone. It is only the rhythmic pattern of the tenor that is literally repeated, for the pitches do not repeat with the ordo. The repetitive ordo helps give the tenor on the one hand its drone-like, subsidiary status, but on the other hand its independence from the rhythms, or at least from the phrasing, of the song. Similarly the

[18] *Rondeaux, Virelais und Balladen*, No. 1421.

fragment of chant in the tenor makes it melodically subordinate to the lyric melody of the song, while simultaneously giving it independence. This accompaniment can move either in synchronized contrary motion with the song, thus very strictly 'accompanying' it through a series of dichords (as at the beginning of 'Dame de vostre doz regart'); or it can alternate with the song, filling in the song's phrases while continuing the song's rhythmic motion and often its very line; or it can enter into a variety of relationships between these two extremes. A range of possibilities exists for this subordinate yet independent kind of accompaniment. The intimacy and flexibility of its relationships with the song must have been a strong attraction for chanson singer and professional instrumentalist alike. The particular kinds of relationship evident in the mid-century repertory seem more suited to these two performers at court or in the house of a high cathedral official than to cathedral singers in a cavernous Gothic choir. At any rate the techniques of the new discant, adapted in the ways described, gave impetus to a French motet repertory that proliferated much more vigorously than the Latin one.

FRENCH MOTETS IN THE CHANSONNIERS

The two chanson anthologies 'Roi' (R) and 'Noailles' (N) share a motet repertory that stands close to the begining of the French motet; but R and N show the other side of the beginning, the trouvère song. These two chansonniers are among the dozen or so that preserve the trouvère repertory from the thirteenth century; after their chanson collections, R and N each includes a collection of motets—a small one in R and a larger one (that includes all of R) in N.[19]

Several features of these sources show how the motet appeared from the point of view of the chanson repertory. While chansons are usually attributed to a specific composer—meaning thereby, in the first place, the composer of the text—the motets in R and N are all anonymous. This can be taken to reflect on the one hand the pride the trouvère took in his chanson texts; and on the other hand the extensive use in motet texts of common material, popular stichs or refrains, along with a less individual and elevated style. Anonymity of motet texts continues the anonymity characteristic of the stichic tradition in general, and the anonymity affects specifically the text; as motets became attributed to composers (increasingly towards 1300), it seems to be the style of the music that prompts the attribution.

To the collector of chansons, then, motets seemed to be a less distinctive genre, at least as texts. And to this collector, whose primary

---

[19] Ludwig *Repertorium*, pp. 285–305.

concern was the chanson and especially its texts, the motet appears as a song that included some other, not very well understood element— an accompaniment, in the form of a tenor. While the compiler of MuA used the tenor as the basis of the whole collection, the compiler of the chansonnier sometimes omitted the tenor altogether, or provided space but failed to enter it, or frequently notated the tenor in erroneous or incomprehensible ways. The scribes of the chansonnier met in the motet—in particular in its tenor—an unfamiliar kind of music.

The motet repertory of R and N includes about a hundred motets, mostly *a2*; the repertory is arranged in no particular order, but does fall into dimly perceptible groupings of different kinds and origins. The series N1–N24 includes motets well known in other later sources, representing the core of the early French motet repertory. The tenors are, with a few very interesting exceptions, standard Notre-Dame tenors. Only one is made of a Notre-Dame clausula, however. In other words, this series shows the distinctive features of the French motet as opposed to the Latin one. The rhythms of the tenors are frequently in modes 1 or 2, not so often in the mode 5 patterns so prevalent in the clausula repertory. The motets of the first series in R and N include one with very regular phrasing, 'Qui loiaument sert s'amie', T. 'Laetabitur' (Ex. 215).[20] The verses are 8 + 7, bi-hemistichs, rhyming consistently *a b*; there are five bi-hemistichs, the last being by exception 8 + 8—but this last hemistich is the conclusion of the refrain quoted in line 1:

> Qui loiaument sert s'amie
>
> . . .
>
> Bien li doit sa joie doubler

which makes this motet a *motet enté* (see below, p. 653). Each hemistich fits exactly over a statement of the tenor rhythmic pattern; furthermore, the melody of the second bi-hemistich almost exactly repeats that of the first, forming a couplet, with open and closed endings. This motet represents a maximum accommodation of Notre-Dame technique to the ideal of trouvère song. Another example quotes the begining text and melody of a well-known song, 'Molt m'abellist' ('Mout m'abelist') by the troubadour Folquet de Marseille.[21] This is one of the few points of contact between motets and troubadours, and—perhaps not by coincidence—one of the few

---

[20] Facs. in Beck, *Le manuscrit de Roi*, fo. 197; cf. Tischler, EM No. 155 (ii, p. 1012); Mo 6, 209.

[21] N 12; cf. Tischler, *EM* No. 212 (ii, p. 1182); Mo 5, 109; facs. of the song in Beck, *Le manuscrit du Roi*, p. 178b.

Ex. 215

Qui loi - au - ment sert s'a - mi - e, Ne li set que

Letabitur

de - man - der. J'ai bien la moi - e ser - vi - e,

Et loi - au - ment sans faus - ser. Et qui en - si

ne sert mi - e, pe - tit i doit con - quest - er,

Mais qui dei tot s'u - me - li - e Sans or - gueil et

sans van - ter, Je di bien que que nus di - e

Bien li doit sa joi - e dou - bler.

French motets using rhythmic mode 3 in motetus and tenor. Phrasing is regular up to the end with one verse of text set to two tenor patterns.

Other less regular, more typical examples predominate in this first series.[22] Initial regularity of phrasing is typically dislocated later in the piece by a short verse standing by itself or tacked on to the preceding verse. As a corollary the coincidence with tenor pattern usually gives way to the typical staggered phrasing. The mode 2 rhythms of the motets often show division of the modal values, sometimes heavy, as in 'Aucun m'ont par leur envie', T. 'Angelus', where very few measures are left as simple short-long.[23]

The repertory of R and N shows manifold contacts with the chanson repertory in the various manifestations of refrain and rondeau. A number of motets throughout R and N include refrains—stichic texts reminiscent of idioms from the vernacular literature. More specific, in some ways unique, to R and N, is the appearance of motets that either consist entirely of one refrain in the duplum (and hence are very short pieces even for motets) or that have a repetitive structure similar to what we know as a rondeau. The first kind of motet—'refrain motet'—appears at the end of R (Nos. 35–41; and N Nos. 66–72). The second kind—'rondeau motet'—appears in the middle of N (Nos. 25–9). Additional isolated instances occur at N 73, 'Aimmi aimmi' and N 89, 'C'est la jus'. Furthermore N 91, 'Cele m'a

[22] N 4: Tischler, *EM* No. 133 (ii, p. 890); Mo 5, 89. N 6: Tischler, *EM* No. 152 (ii, p. 1001); Mo 6, 216. N 9: Tischler, *EM* No. 275 (ii, p. 1451); Mo 6, 213. N 10: Tischler, *EM* No. 276 (ii, p. 1454); Mo 6, 231. N 14: Tischler, *EM* No. 139 (ii, p. 936); Mo 5, 110. N 15: Tischler, *EM* No. 240 (ii, p. 1335); Mo 5, 128. N 22: Tischler, *EM* No. 136 (ii, p. 908); Bamberg No. 64.
[23] N 15; cf. Tischler, *EM* No. 240 (ii, p. 1334); Mo 5, 128.

s'amour', is made entirely of twelve refrains; it falls somewhere between the refrain motet and the use of only one or two refrains in a motet text. This type, of which there are a few other examples, is called a 'refrain-cento'.

These materials are as important as they are difficult to handle. Both R and N, especially R, have *lacunae* and often lack tenor notation; when present, the notation is often difficult if not impossible to interpret rhythmically without a concordance, and concordances— for these motets in particular—are often lacking, for they tend to be unica, as is a large portion of R and N. Those are the purely technical difficulties; there are other difficulties of interpretation both for refrains and rondeaux. As we have seen, refrains represent a perfectly believable stichic practice; but they are more often than not identified by their intrinsic verbal style rather than by actual documentation. A closing verse of a motet 'looks like a refrain', and is so identified, even if it appears in no other source. Even though the evidence supports the idea that motet texts frequently include quotations of favourite stichs, the identification of particular stichs is often provisional. While there are some instances of a refrain appearing in two different motets with the same melody, there are other instances where the same text has different melodies. Ludwig's attention was especially drawn to cases where the melody used for a motet refrain could be traced to the Notre-Dame clausula used for that motet; an important instance is in R 12–13, N 35–6, 'Quant revient'—'L'autrier jouer', T. 'Flos filius ejus'.[24] Such instances suggest that while the quotation of text depended upon the vernacular literature, that of the melodies depended upon the Notre-Dame repertory.

What concerns us here in R and N is that the entry of rondeau procedures into polyphonic music apparently took place through the motet—a relatively sophisticated musical form—rather than through simple discant settings, which occurred only later in the century in the works of Adam de la Hale and Jehan de Lescurel.[25] While many later rondeaux reflect this simplicity, examples can be found throughout the fourteenth and fifteenth centuries that echo the paradoxical combination of simple folklike procedure and sophisticated counterpoint of the motet. And, as described in Chap. IX, the thirteenth-century rondeau is not yet the 'fixed form' of the fourteenth.

Early steps in the development of polyphony *en rondeau* can be

---

[24] Ludwig, *Repertorium*, p. 291; Tischler, *EM* No. 65 (i, p. 461).

[25] Ed. Nigel Wilkins, *The Lyric Works of Adam de la Hale, Corpus mensurabilis musicae*, 44 (American Institute of Musicology, 1967); *The Works of Jehan de Lescurel, Corpus mensurabilis musicae*, 30 (American Institute of Musicology, 1966).

traced in R and N.[26] Since only a very little music is involved in singing *en rondeau* (merely the music of the refrain), we can imagine the very short refrain motets of R and N being used in a manner exactly parallel to that of monophonic refrains, that is, with a leader supplying new verses. The only difference would be the presence of an accompanying tenor—and that we can imagine to be characteristic of the way the whole motet repertory appeared to those who cultivated secular song: it was a new way of performing a familiar kind of song.

A second step would be represented by the rondeau motet, in which the verses were written out in the motetus voice. When this happens in the early motet repertory (that is, in N 73 and N 89) it may not conform exactly to rondeau form, and therefore represents the variable procedure *en rondeau*. The relationship of the tenor to this procedure is the crux of the problem. We should note, first, that it is entirely characteristic of the motet as a genre that the tenor with its patterns does not simply coincide with the repetitions of the refrain melody in the motetus, for in general tenors do not systematically coincide with the phrasing of their dupla—indeed, their most characteristic use is in staggered phrasing relative to the dupla. Here we can see the essence of the tenor as an accompaniment: it is an independent accompaniment, something that is even more true and important for the secular musician than it is for the sacred one. Secondly, if and when the tenor is brought into some kind of synchronization with the repeats in the motetus, this is accomplished through the tenor ordines, and depends on their being short enough to be modular parts of the motetus phrasing—again, as throughout the motet repertory.

Relevant to this discussion, even if not so named in R and N, is the 'graft motet', *motet enté*.[27] This term appears in manuscripts of the same type, in particular Paris, Bibl.Nat.fr. 845, a chansonnier of the thirteenth century, and Oxford, Bodleian, Douce 308 ('D'), a large text manuscript containing the lyrics of seven categories of songs. Paris 845, at the end of a large collection of chansons, has 'Ci commencent li motets ente', and then follow fifteen (originally more) motetus voices (no tenors). Typically the motetus text consists of a refrain that has been separated into two sections with new verses added in between; the refrain then forms first and last verses of a moderately long text. This recalls the use of a refrain *en rondeau*, but with several differences, including the fact that the refrain appears only at the beginning and end, and there may be no internal

---

[26] N 73; cf. Tischler, *EM* No. 315 (ii, p. 1511). N 89; cf. Tischler *EM* No. 324 (ii, p. 1521). Cf. Mo 6, 248.

[27] Ludwig, *Repertorium*, pp. 305–13; *EM* No. 324 (ii, p. 1521). Cf. Mo 6, 248.

repetitions of refrain melodies for verses. We should understand the *motet enté* as one of a cluster of stichic procedures, along with simple refrains and *en rondeau*, which were brought to the motet.

A much larger collection of *motets enté* appears as the seventh section of Douce 308, after 'Grans chans, estampies, jeus partis, pastourelles, ballettes, sottes chansons contre amours'. There are 101 texts in this seventh section, of which 64 are motet texts, almost all *motets enté*, with concordances in Paris 845. Although definitely motet texts, these have neither music nor tenors in this manuscript. The rest of the 101 texts are rondeaux; this mixture of motets and rondeaux in a fourteenth-century collection carries out the pattern set by R and N in the thirteenth, and is explicit in other similar sources. The large collection Rome, Vatican, Reginensis 1490 ('V') contains, after its 'chancons' and 'pastoureles', a section 'motet et rondel', followed by 'chansons de Nostre Dame', and 'partures'.[28]

This mixture is characteristic, then, of chanson collections that include polyphony. It also occurs in the large fourteenth-century polyphonic anthology 'La Tremoille', of which only the index is preserved. There the mixture is problematic, for by that time motets and rondeaux are set in very different musical styles. But the earlier sources show us that the mixture is indigenous: it depends upon the fact that, to the chanson compiler, motet texts and texts *en rondeau* both involve stichs and refrains in a less individual and elegant style, hence both were treated as anonymous and grouped together, apart from the more elegant and elevated chansons. Interesting exceptions to this are provided by four cases in R and N of motetus voices entered in the chanson part of the manuscript (without any indication of tenor) and there all ascribed to composers. Hence for at least these motets we have a composer's name: 'Jehan Erars', [Er]nous li [V]ielle', and 'Li moines de St. Denis'.[29]

The instance in which the independent use of melody as well as text of a refrain is clear is provided by the rondeau motet N 89, 'C'est la jus en la roi pree', T. 'Pro patribus'. There was a Notre-Dame clausula on tenor 'Ne', used for two Latin motets and for the French motet 'En mai quant nest la rosee', which appears already in MuA.[30] The last bi-hemistich of this motet,

> Cele m'a s'amours dounee
> ki mon cuer a mon cors a

[28] Ludwig, *Repertorium*, Part 2 (Institute of Medieval Music, 1978), 569–90.

[29] Ludwig, *Repertorium*, p. 336.

[30] Ludwig, *Repertorium*, pp. 296 f.; Gennrich, *Rondeaux, Virelais und Balladen*, ii, p. 268; Tischler, *EM* No. 67 (i, p. 474), No. 324 (ii, p. 1521), and No. 1168 (ii, p. 1059).

with its melody as found in the motetus (and in the duplum of the clausula) provides the refrain of the rondeau motet 'C'est la jus en la roi pree' in N. The same refrain appears as the first of six refrains in the refrain-cento motet N 91, that is, as a stich quoted in a different function; the melody is the same as before. The same text and melody are also quoted in the middle of a triplum of the motet Mo 5,138, 'J'ai les biens d'amours', T. 'In seculum'; the motetus, 'Que ferai', is itself a rondeau in text and melody—one of the few in the older portion of Codex Montpellier that continues the experiments of R and N. Here the refrain 'Cele m'a s'amour dounee' has still a different function. Finally this refrain, for one, appears outside the motet repertory: it is used by Pierre de Corbeil as the concluding bi-hemistich—the 'refrain'—of the first strophe of his pastourelle, 'Pensis com fuis amourous', which appears in the main chanson section of R and N with the same melody. This is perhaps an exceptionally extensive use of a refrain, from which we should conclude only that it *could* happen in this way, not that it frequently did.

In two latter portions of the repertory of R and N (the two portions are separated by the group of refrain motets) there is a high proportion of motets not represented in any other manuscript, and—among the same pieces—a high proportion of concordances with the puzzling source Paris Bibl.Nat.lat. 15139, known as the 'St Victor clausulae', or 'St Victor melismata'.[31] This is a section of a manuscript containing forty pieces of melismatic discant (two *a3*, thirty-eight *a2*), some over Notre-Dame tenors. Most have the incipits of French motets entered in the margin; indeed these pieces represent melismatic notation of motets found elsewhere with French texts, especially in R and N. While most observers agree, however, that the melismatic notations of discant pieces in F (discussed in the previous chapter) represent melismatic performance of clausulas in the course of a Gradual or Alleluia (or Office Responsory) and hence probably an existence prior to the texted form we call motet, there is no such agreement about the St Victor melismata. It is possible that the St Victor melismata are simply a melismatic notation of pieces composed as motets, an alternate form of recording such pieces, much as sequences had been notated in two forms, one syllabic the other melismatic. A possible reason for such recording in two forms is that melismatic notation can give more specific information, especially in the case of discant and modal rhythms, for the ligatures of the melismatic notation are at this stage the only means of notating the rhythm. While St Victor melismata turn up as motets frequently in other manuscripts as well

---

[31] Stenzl, *Die vierzig Clausulae*.

(but sporadically—only once, for instance, in the first series in MuA) the connection with R and N seems especially close, all the more because many of the pieces involved appear nowhere else as motets. It seems reasonable that this early collection of secular motets, standing outside the Notre-Dame sphere and reflecting the approach of the secular musician, should have as counterpart a melismatic source that also stands outside the Notre-Dame sphere.

Alongside its various manifestations of secular song, the repertory of R and N also contains some of the earliest examples of the motet *a3* with two different French texts, the 'double motet'. This type, consisting of two voices (triplum and motetus) each with its own text, over a tenor, became the dominant one after the mid-century, and since it was preceded by the very impressive repertory of Notre-Dame organa *a3* of Perotin, there is a tendency to take the three-voiced double motet for granted. In this moment of its emergence, however, we should not take it for granted, and in particular the designation 'double motet' should make us pause. If there is a 'double motet', what is a 'single' one? A motet, then, in the most specific sense, is a voice, the motetus, with a French text, accompanied by a tenor. This is the phenomenon we have been tracing in MuA, and in R and N. While a few examples come from melismatic clausulas *a2*, most are newly composed over Notre-Dame tenors. A double motet must then be two such voices over an instrumental tenor. The five cases of double motets in R and N witness the wide variety of approaches to development of this new form:[32]

1. N 7–8 'Hare hare hie Goudalier'—
   'Balaan Goudalier', T. 'Balaam'
2. N 16– 'Le premier jour'—'Par un matin'—
   18   'Je n'i puis plus', T. 'Justus germinabit' (Mo 2,32)
3. R 12– N 35–6 'Quant revient'—
   13   'L'autrier jouer', T. 'Flos filius' (F fo. 11, *a3*; Mo 2,21)
4. R 17– N 40–41 'De la ville'—
   18   'A la ville', T. 'Manere' (St V *a3*, Mo 4,61)
5. N 79– 'Se valors'—
   80   'Bien me sui', T. 'Hic factus est' (Mo 5,149)

These five vary tremendously in almost every respect, showing clearly a developmental stage. Three appear only in N, not R. Only No. 3 uses a three-voiced clausula as source. Only No. 4 has a St Victor concordance. The Notre-Dame tenors vary from much used to little

---

[32] N 7–8: Tischler, *EM* No. 131 (ii, p. 876); N 16–18: Tischler, *EM* No. 143 (ii, p. 962); N 35–6: Tischler, *EM* No. 65 (i, p. 461); N 40–1: Tischler, *EN* No. 144 (ii, p. 973); N 79–80: Tischler, *EM* No. 135 (ii, p. 904); W2, fo. 201ᵛ; Mo 5, 149.

used. Taken together, these four double motets and one triple motet represent the spectrum of possibilities found in the motet repertory at large. No. 2 has mode 2 in tenor and motetus (and quadruplum), mode 6 in the triplum—an important instance of this use of mode 6, found also in certain other early double motets. Phrasing is staggered and occasionally irregular. The motetus is a *motet enté*. No. 3, a double motet that appears in Montpellier with a quadruplum, is the one that uses a famous clausula *a3*, 'Flos filius eius', which with Latin texts was one of the three double motets in F. It uses mode 1 throughout, with staggered and irregular phrasing. No. 4 is a relatively isolated piece (appearing with fragmentary Latin texts in Mo 4,61), with regular song-like phrasing in motetus, phrasing at first synchronized then staggered; mode 1 is used throughout. It is a short, simple piece. No. 5 has mode 2 throughout, with heavy divisions in motetus and triplum, very irregular phrasing, densely staggered. Of the five it perhaps best represents the style the double motet took around the mid-century (Ex. 216).

Thus the chansonniers R and N give us a picture of the first stages of the French motet, a picture different in important ways from that of the large anthologies later in the century, which have to some extent been cleansed of earlier peculiarities. The basic posture of the motet collections R and N is embodied in their first motet, 'Onques n'amia tant com', T. 'Sancte Germane'. We should note that the first item in a series of medieval motets, or other pieces in anthologies, is often selected with some care, although the rationale varies from case to case and needs to be determined by inspection. The text of the motetus is the first strophe of a chanson by Richard de Fournival (*c.* 1190–1260, from at least 1240 canon at Amiens). Taken together with the motetus melody, it appears as a perfect example of trouvère art, in its form, with an opening couplet and freer continuation, in its elevated text, and in its flowing, independent melody. The tenor, for its part, is not a Notre-Dame tenor, and Ludwig had not even identified its liturgical use, even though it seems to be from a Latin chant (possibly a melisma for an Office responsory for St Germain). It is not notated in a repetitive pattern. There is only one concordance (W$_2$). As an emblem, then, of their new motet collections, the compilers of R and N selected what for all intents and purposes is a fine trouvère song, with an accompaniment in the guise of a melisma taken from some convenient or appropriate source, and treated casually like a tenor in the new style of cathedral polyphony.

FRENCH MOTETS IN W$_2$

With the French motet collections contained in W$_2$, we encounter a

Ex. 216

Se va - lors vient d'estre a - mo - rous et gay,

Bien me sui a - per - ce - us Qe de vi - vre

Hic factus

A tout jors se deu plest la main ten - drai

en joie m'est grans bien ve - nus. Mes ge men sui

Si je sai c'est bien drois qu'en voi - sie soi - e

trop te - nus, Ce poi - se moi d'a - ler ou ma

Qant ce - le s'a - mor m'o - troi e qe pru-miere a -

da - me voi - e Qar ne doi jo - ir se par

mai. Ne ja ne m'en par - ti - rai Por mal ne

li n'en joi. Dieus tant m'es tart que je soi - e

por dou - lor mes de cuer verai.

Tant en ai grant fain! Trop

A mes pru - mier - es a - mors me ten - drai.

me poi - se qe ne la voi ce - le qui j'aim.

more stable state of the repertory, and simultaneously seem to be closer to the Notre-Dame orbit. W$_2$ is the third great Notre-Dame source, containing conductus (now decreasing in number), organa *a3* and *a4*, the *Magnus liber organi*, Latin motets (increasing) and French motets—these for the first time in Notre-Dame sources, except for those in MuA.[33]

The very first collection of motets in W$_2$ includes motets *a3* with the same text in duplum and triplum, encountered in F as the first type of Latin motet *a3*, the so-called 'conductus motet'. This first collection in W$_2$ includes five French motets of the same type, a very interesting phenomenon, but apparently with no further results. It presumably reflects the same early stage of development, and in case of the French motet another failed experiment. All five go back to well-known antecedents in clausulas or Latin motets, and none of the five remained important in the later repertory.

After the large collection of eighty Latin motets *a2*, arranged in three alphabetical series (plus additions), come the collections of French motets. First is a small series of one motet *a4* and twenty-two double motets *a3*, in no discernible order. This is the oldest *collection* of its type (the five in R and N are not a collection), and one of the most central, with numerous concordances to all sectors of the repertory at large. Next comes a large collection of eighty-eight French motets *a2*, arranged in two alphabets with the beginning of a third, and a short supplement. Each alphabet tends to have its own characteristics, but the full description of these (started by Ludwig), the relationship with other manuscripts, and the stylistic implications have yet to be fully worked out. For instance, in the first alphabet, with nineteen French motets *a2*, about half go back to a clausula of

---

[33] French motets in W2 are listed in Ludwig, *Repertorium*, pp. 178–80, 198–222, and edited in Tischler, *EM*. Many are also edited and discussed in Anderson, *The Latin Compositions of Fascicles 7 and 8 of W2*, and many appear also in Codex Montpellier.

Latin motet, and half do not, appearing here as original French motets. Several have concordances in R and N, one in MuA, none in the St Victor melismata. In the sixty motets of the second alphabet, ten appear in St Victor melismata, yet there are relatively fewer concordance with R and N; even so, Ludwig emphasizes the relationship to the chansonniers and the use of refrains in this second alphabet. The first alphabet shows frequent use of mode 2 in both motetus and tenor, and overall heavy use of mode 1 and 2 in tenors, with little use of mode 5. The first alphabet begins with the justly famous French version 'A la clarté', of a clausula and Latin motet in mode 6.[34] The much larger second alphabet shows more use of mode 5 tenors, but still with modes 1 and 2 prevailing, in the custom of French motets.

The twenty-three double motets *a3* (and one *a4*) that begin the French collection in W₂ are well connected with the repertory at large, including Notre-Dame clausulas, St Victor melismata, Latin motets in W₂, the collection in R and N; and many items were taken up in Montpellier and Bamberg, attesting to their continued popularity. A few motets use tenors in mode 5, but the large majority, again, are in modes 1 or 2. The tenors are mostly Notre-Dame tenors—but not completely, and the collection even includes French tenors of the kind that became important much later in the century.

Each motet continues to have its own subtle individuality. In general we can see two ways in which the voices (in particular motetus and triplum) can be related. Either these two voices can be synchronized, both phrasing together, with verses of the same number of syllables in triplum as in motetus, or the phrasing may be staggered by using phrases of different lengths, in triplum and motetus. The early conductus motet with the same text in both voices of course had synchronized phrasing, and we might hence conclude that the type of motet with two texts in synchronized phrasing might logically be the earlier. On the other hand, the examples in R and N more often showed irregular and staggered phrasing. By the time of W₂, in any case, all the alternatives are current, and materials can be so easily adapted that we probably cannot reconstruct such a chronology reliably. Furthermore, motets *a3* are frequently formed by adding a triplum to an existing motetus and tenor, or even—according to an old hypothesis of Ludwig's—by discarding an old triplum, and replacing it with a new one.

It needs to be emphasized that this series of twenty-three motets in

---

[34] Tischler, *EM* No. 149 (ii, p. 332); Mo 6, 189.

W$_2$ is not only the earliest documented collection of French double motets; it is the earliest such of any kind of double motet. Not counting the conductus motets in F, that important source includes only three Latin double motets, all important but isolated ('Mors', the 'Flos filius' motet mentioned earlier, and the very famous 'Hypocrite'—'Velut stellam', T. 'Et gaudebit'.[35]) As far as the sources go, we have to deal with the French double motet as an established repertory before the Latin double motet. This becomes an especially important consideration in view of the extensive re-texting of motet voices to make French texts into Latin and vice versa. Definite priorities can be assigned only in individual cases, if there. The process as a whole cannot be said to go one way or the other, and without urging that it does so, it can be emphasized that what the sources show us is the role played by the French motet in the development of the mid-century motet repertory in general.

Considered as a collection, the twenty-three double motets in W$_2$ are a fascinating cross-section. The first, 'Encontre le tans', 'Quant feuillant', T. 'in odorem', is emblematic and important, although not necessarily typical: it goes back to a clausula *a3*, one of three or four that do so here. The upper voices are in mode 1. There is a strong tendency for the voices to phrase together, with a phrasing that seems indigenous to versus and hence Latin discant texting. (The motet appears earlier in W$_2$, *a2*, with Latin text.) The work is long and impressive, recalling to some observers the style of Perotin himself. The second piece of the collection is a French contrafactum of 'Hypocrite'. Next come, in grotesque contrast, a curious unicum and 'Hare, hare' from N. All the five double motets from R and N are included here, scattered throughout the series. The next five, all found later in Montpellier fascicle 5, are more typical. A pair of motets, reappearing as a pair in Montpellier, represent both regular and irregular phrasing.[37] 'Lonc tans', 'Au commencement', T. 'Hec dies' appears *a2* in R and N. It is hard to say which version came first. The phrasing of the motetus is song-like but irregular and complex. The triplum consistently overlaps, except at two important internal cadences. 'Se j'ai servi', 'Trop longuement', T. 'Pro patribus' is also *a2* in R and N. The double motet has a triplum whose phrasing almost exactly coincides with the very lyric motetus and tenor in mode 2.

The picture of the French double motet that emerges from this

---

[35] Tischler, *EM* No. 71 (i, p. 493).
[36] Tischler, *EM* No. 129 (ii, p. 849).
[37] Tischler, *EM* No. 132 (ii, p. 881); for 'Se j'ai servi' see ibid., No. 133 (ii, p. 890).

collection is one of a work with either rhythmic mode 1 or mode 2 in all three voices, with occasionally heavy division of longa or brevis in up to three semibreves (almost always neumatic, however, with only one syllable to the modal long or brevis). The tenor may have longer notes in addition to its modal values, and a moderately long ordo. The phrasing of the motetus is often more regular than that of the triplum, and often includes an integral number of tenor ordinates. It is the triplum that often provides the overlapped phrasing by being itself irregular. Both upper voices may, however, contribute to the irregularity, and either or both may be regular and coincide—but this is less and less characteristic.

In all this we can see the tremendous importance of the tenor ordo—the truly seminal innovation of Perotin. It is the repetitive rhythmic pattern in the tenor that makes it possible to co-ordinate the relatively regular phrases of motetus with relatively irregular ones of the triplum (or, on occasion, vice versa), hence to bring these intensely individual parts together into a whole. Regular or irregular, an upper voice may do nothing not already known from the monophonic versus or the trouvère chanson, although (to take up an earlier point) there is no vernacular model for such irregular phrasing as appears in the French motet. But it is the Notre-Dame tenor that combines them and opens up possibilities for new kinds of combinations. It seems, however, that the maker of French motets was more sensitive to these possibilities than cathedral singers. At any rate, he contributed a great deal of new music to the motet repertory.

MOTETS IN THE CODEX MONTPELLIER

The most extensive, most important collection of motets of the whole century is the Codex Montpellier, as important for its wide concordances as for its large number of unica. So massive is the whole (also in its modern editions[38]) that it is difficult to think of it not as one series of 345 pieces, but rather as eight separate collections (fascicles) each with its own individuality and each, considered by itself, far more characteristic of other thirteenth-century collections than is the whole.

These other collections need to be briefly recapitulated here as context for the Codex Montpellier. The collection in R and N includes roughly a hundred French motets, mostly *a2*, but with five *a3* and one *a4*. The collections in W$_2$ include twelve Latin motets *a3* (one text), four Latin double motets, and eighty Latin motets *a2*; five French motets *a3* (one text), twenty-three French double motets (including

---

[38] Rokseth, *Polyphonies du xiiie siècle*; Tischler, *EM*.

one triple motet) and eighty-eight French motets *a2*.[39] The collection La Clayette has fifty-five motets, mostly with at least one of the texts in French, and largely French double motets; there are a dozen motets *a4*, and a few Latin double motets.[40] The lost collection Besançon had presumably fifty-seven motets, about half French double motets, about half French-Latin double motets, and a few French triple motets *a3*.[41] Codex Bamberg, from later in the century, has a hundred motets, of which fifty are French double motets, forty-one are Latin double motets, and nine French-Latin double motets.[42] Turin has thirty-one motets.[43]

Each of the fascicles of Montpellier (after the first, which contains a 'Benedicamus', a conductus, three hockets, and five organa—two by Perotin), can be compared to one or the other of the collections just reviewed, as follows (taking the Montpellier fascicles in an order that presumably represents a chronological development):

(fascicle 6): a collection of seventy-five French motets *a2*, comparable to the eighty-eight French motets *a2* in the tenth fascicle of W_2, or to the roughly one hundred French motets in the motet fascicle of the chansonnier N;

(fascicle 5): a collection, central to the Codex, of one hundred French double motets, comparable to the fifty-five motets of La Clayette, or the fifty-seven motets of the lost codex Besançon, or the later collections of one hundred motets in Bamberg or the thirty-one in Turin; only those of La Clayette, or the twenty-three motets of the ninth fascicle of W_2 would be earlier;

(fascicle 2): a unique collection of seventeen triple motets *a4*—all French but one; a number of these appear also *a3* in the earlier stages;

(fascicle 4); a collection of twenty-two Latin double motets, the earliest such collection, analogous in size to the twenty-three French double motets in W_2, but similar only to the Latin component of Bamberg;

(fascicle 3): a small group of eleven double motets, each with one French and one Latin text, comparable, again, only to Bamberg; with several curious features, this group provides a transition to the two later fascicles of the codex;

(fascicle 7): a collection of thirty-nine double motets, mostly French, some Latin, a few mixed, from near the end of the century, with an appendix of

---

[39] These and all numbers following are to be taken as approximate; they are drawn from Ludwig's enumeration in the *Repertorium*, but subsequent research occasionally proposes changes in the enumeration by, for instance, showing that two separately numbered items constitute really one motet, or by showing that a motet should be counted *a3* instead of *a2* (or vice versa). There is also the problem of how to reckon the texted voices that had tenors added or taken away.

[40] Anderson, *Motets of the Manuscript LaClayette*.

[41] Ludwig, *Repertorium*, pp. 505–13.

[42] Anderson, *Compositions of the Bamberg Manuscript*.

[43] Auda, *Les 'motets wallons'*.

eleven more; comparable in size with La Clayette and Besançon, this one reveals a period of development rather than of stabilization in the repertory;

(fascicle 8): a collection of forty-two double motets, largely French but with an important group of Latin motets; as a collection this comes from the first decade of the fourteenth century.

Up to (but not including) fascicle 7, the Notre-Dame tenors continue to function as guidelines of the contrapuntal web; and during these stages of development, the multiple uses of 'In seculum', 'Omnes', 'Portare', 'Veritatem' accumulate. This raises the question of the tonal structure of motets, a question that can best be approached through the repertories contained in Montpellier and Bamberg, for these extensive collections, being preserved more or less intact (unlike, for instance, MuA), offer a broad base for generalities and one that we can assume to be representative.[44] Fascicle 5 of Montpellier, containing one hundred motets *a3*, or the hundred motets *a3* in Bamberg, would be the best place to study tonal procedures in the mid-century motet. We can hear in the motets *a2* of Montpellier fascicle 6 the wealth of lyric melody as well as the intricacy between motetus and tenor—between song and contrapuntal accompaniment; but because the texture *a2* is more transparent, we are more sensitive to the linear qualities and less struck by the overall tonal design. In the motets *a3* we experience these same linear qualities rather as intensity of texture; and by the same token we are confronted by a steady stream of three-note sonorities, whose overall organization requires attention.

In this organization the tenor is the starting point of the tonal organization. Each of its pitches, taken by itself, helps to determine (through choice of concord) the coincident pitches of motetus and triplum; and the *succession* of pitches in the tenor helps to determine the succession of three-note sonorities in the piece as a whole. Typically motetus and triplum are at the fifth and the octave above the tenor. If this were consistent, of course, the piece would consist of nothing but a tenor melody doubled at the fifth and the octave. While this concept of consonance is essential to discant, just as essential is that of contrary motion, and motet counterpoint is an endless series of compromises between these two principles. So the tenor's succession of pitches is only the starting point of the tonal organization.

Several procedures characteristic of the mid-century motet can be observed in the fifth fascicle of Montpellier. In the typical tenor in mode 1 or 2, some tenor notes have clear consonances above them, others do not. The composer's choices in this regard reflect his

---

[44] See the tables in Rokseth, *Polyphonies du xiiie siécle*, iv, pp. 143–98.

conception of the tonal plan implied by the tenor—what its central pitch is, for instance. We should note that these tenors from Gregorian melismata embody the kind of melodic motion characteristic of that ancient repertory (and not of more recent medieval chant) with much decorative, seemingly random, back and forth motion within a locus, with occasional, but equally unpredictable, strong moves outside the locus, up or down, within the melisma or sometimes at its conclusion. One option open to the motet composer is to reinforce the note at the centre of the locus with fifth-octave consonance. Another means of reinforcement is the way the tenor rhythmic pattern is superimposed on the pitches of the melisma, which sometimes has the effect of, say, making a central pitch consistently fall on a long duration. No rule is observable, but the composer's concern for interesting and fruitful arrangements is abundantly evident—as is the complex interdependence of the factors of pitch and duration in the relationship of tenor and upper voices. The net effect of this possible confluence of factors can be to present one particular pitch with persistent fifth-octave consonance at the tonal centre of the piece. We can observe that when this happens, it is usually on *fa–ut* or *re*, less often on *sol–ut*, seldom on *mi* or *la*.[45]

Out of this confluence can emerge an overall tonal organization, sometimes remarkably stable. Just as the tenor melody moves *through* this organization, without every one of its pitches basic to it (especially in the French motet tenors in modes 1 and 2), so upper voices sometimes follow a characteristic procedure of moving through a stable sonority with animated melodic motion. In a C-G-c sonority, for instance, the triplum may supply the upper c, then descend by step to supply the G in the next bar, while the motetus, in contrary motion, supplies the G in the first bar, the c in the second. This very simple model is followed again and again in endlessly complex ways, and there are many other procedures for maintaining a relatively slow, stable succession of sonorities with rapid contrary motion in animated rhythms. This leads to the phenomenon of 'motivic repetition' in the upper voices of motets, but we must bear in mind that the upper voices in general move in restricted pitch sets, and that the rhythmic motion consists of modal longs and breves, or conventionalized divisions of them, so that 'motivic' repetition is almost unavoidable.

The whole complex also leads to the idea that the French motet is 'contrapuntal' in the sense of having several simultaneous, independently active voices, which in turn suggests to some observers an

---

[45] Identification of a *mi* final, usually on a, is sometimes indeterminate because of an optional b flat; but there may be a dozen cases of *mi* final in Codex Montpellier.

opposition to tonal structure in the sense of overall organization of sonorities into 'harmonies' or 'keys'. But if we take 'tonal organization' in the broader sense of planned relationships among tones or pitches, including simultaneously sounding intervals, and succession of intervals, a very clear concern for tonal organization is apparent in all but some inept or corrupt motets. And anyway, 'counterpoint' always meant a balance between independently active voices and overall organization, especially in medieval polyphony. The balance may sometimes seem to be a compromise, at other times a mutual reinforcement, but is almost always present. Medieval research still needs to discover the appropriate terms in which to conceive and describe this balance.

The relationship of tonal locus (as embodied most obviously in a central pitch, if there is one) to the final of a motet tenor is often a problem for us, and was perhaps for the medieval musician too; at least we can observe a variety of solutions. In general we can say that, like clear central pitches, finals are most often *fa/ut* or *re*, sometimes *sol/ut*, seldom *mi*. In any given motet, however, the final may be different from the central note or lie outside the locus. The most frequent reason for this is an abrupt terminal descent at the end of the melisma: the classic case is 'In seculum', which drops from a central c–*fa/ut* to an F–*fa/ut* in its last tenor ordo. In the chant, of course, this fall is no cadence, but rather the truncation of a penultimate descent that soon returns to a for its cadence. It is the fate of motets, however, to inherit a non-final chant tone for their final. But before concluding that this and similar endings show how motet counterpoint exemplifies purely linear considerations without regard for overall tonal plan, we need to observe that the motet composer can and does change a tenor to suit his purposes; that he can and does supply his own final by dropping the motetus below the tenor's final; and that he did not have to use 'In seculum' instead of, say, 'Omnes', with its close on the same *fa/ut* that is central throughout. However, he did use 'In seculum', and even more frequently than 'Omnes'. We can more profitably imagine reasons why he did so, and some of these might be that 'In seculum' allows both a concentration on a tonal centre and a fresh, distinctive ending, approached through a fall. (A fruitful subject of study is the treatment of the drop to F in 'In seculum' in the middle of motets that repeat the melody in the tenor.) The fall to the F is through G; and the progression G–F in the tenor is accompanied by b natural and e over the G, c and f over the F. Not only is this the cadence that became standard in the fourteenth century, it occurs in the relationship expressed by the 'split signature' of b flat in tenor, b natural in upper voices, which is frequent in that century. Clearly the encounters with 'In seculum' were one of the sources for these seminal constructions.

More generally, the Notre-Dame tenor guided the motet composer to successful plans and stimulated him to create others. The composer of medieval chant, of course, had long since carried out very stable tonal plans on his own; so had the composer of polyphonic conductus, without benefit of a cantus firmus. The long-range effect of the curious intrusion of these Notre-Dame tenors, with their old fashioned Gregorian contours, was to generate tonal plans more intricate, more complex than those inherited from medieval chant and used in common discant. These will provide an important term of comparison when we survey thirteenth-century English polyphony, which shared many of the techniques of Notre-Dame polyphony but made less use of a tenor cantus firmus. In English polyphony we can watch the composer constructing his own tenor to suit an independently conceived tonal plan and we may wonder how often the French composer actually did likewise.

From its beginning, the Latin double motet, as we have seen, tended to develop in complex ways, producing multiple versions of a given motet, and much exchange of individual voices among versions. On the one hand, there was much contact with the clausula repertory (clausulas *a2* as well as *a3* were involved); on the other hand, there was contact with the French motet, in contrafacts made from both directions, and in the very particular form of new tripla added to a Latin tenor-duplum pair, perhaps after an original Latin triplum had been discarded. Following Ludwig's lead, much attention has been paid to various stages of motet construction, and various prior or intermediate stages, no longer represented by extant works, have been hypothesized for individual motets or groups of motets.[46]

Because of the process of adding a triplum to a tenor-duplum pair, or of replacing one triplum with another, and because of the importance of cantus firmus construction specifically within the Notre-Dame school, it has often been thought that medieval polyphony by nature consisted of laying one independent voice upon another—a duplum on a tenor, a triplum on top of that. This idea has tended to obscure the fact that what the medieval composer is composing is a two-part framework, complete in itself in a piece *a2*, and basic to a piece *a3* or *a4*. This is the significance of using clausulas *a2* for motets: the borrowed clausula represents a particular successful solution to a contrapuntal problem posed by the tenor. On the other hand, when

---

[46] Anderson, *The Latin Compositions in Fascicles 7 and 8 of W2*, i, pp. 115–17, 294–6, 311–13, 331, etc.

the French motet composer uses only a tenor (which is the more frequent case), he feels free to reshape it rhythmically—even melodically—to create a new two-voice framework as the basis for further motet composition.

The fifth fascicle of Codex Montpellier, containing a hundred French double motets (of which about half are unica) shows relative stylistic solidity and stability compared to the fourth fascicle with its twenty-two Latin double motets—which represent, as we have seen, the first substantial collection of such works. This fourth fascicle has been studied at length in an effort to untangle the web of stylistic factors represented in its heterogenous contents.[47] The most cautious assessment sees a broad spread of combinations, stylistic features, and possible provenance (but all continental) in the first part of the fascicle (Nos. 51–61), with more specifically English sources, or at least pieces, represented towards the end of the fascicle. There are relatively few unica, and some motets have broad concordances. Some stand close to the rhythms and textures of the French motets, while a relatively high proportion of the others are mode 3 (seldom used for French motets), possibly representing the older 'alternate third mode' of Perotin's time. Some stand close to the Latin discant *a3* with one text in the duplum and triplum. At the other extreme, a few show a style that is to become more important as the century goes on. Precisely these pieces also show a very strong tenor-duplum pair, one that seems to have a life of its own.[48] 'O Maria maris stella', T. 'Veritatem', with a complex history in motet repertories, appears here (as Mo 4,52) with its triplum, 'O Maria virgo davitica', a classic case of mode 6, with breaking of the initial breves of certain ordines into two syllabic semibreves. The next motet (Mo 4,53) has the ubiquitous 'Ave gloriosa mater' with tenor 'Domino'—another classic case of fashioning a strong two-voice framework without too much regard for antecedents. The triplum here is 'Ave virgo regia', also in mode 6 with semibreves. Similar rhythms appeared in the fifth fascicle too: there, however, in three unica, and seemingly more at home among French motets.[49] Two more important cases occur in the third fascicle of Montpellier. This, the smallest and most problematic of all the motet fascicles in Montpellier, contains eleven motets with Latin dupla over mostly Notre-Dame tenors, and French tripla. Once these were taken by modern observers to reveal bizzare medieval combinations of sacred and secular elements; more recently, they are regarded rather in

[47] See Sanders, 'Peripheral Polyphony'.
[48] Anderson, *Latin Compositions*, i, pp. 18–29.
[49] Mo 5: 102, 103, 143; Mo 5, 77 = Bamberg, No. 70.

terms of a stylistic revision of older works with tripla in a newer style. Whatever the provenance or rationale of these combinations, they certainly have to be dealt with case by case, allowing no generally valid conclusions; and it is a small group, after all, not representative of any broad moment in the history of the motet. Included are two motets with faster tripla. The tenor-duplum pair 'Mellis stilla', T. 'Domino', very solid is its rhythmic-tonal shape, has the charming triplum 'Par une matinee' with an animated interjection by 'Marot' (Marie) in the middle (Mo 3,40). Similarly, 'Flos de spina', T, 'Regnat' (a very important tenor-duplum pair) has the triplum 'Quant repaire', which begins with normal long-short rhythms but becomes more animated later (Mo 3,44).

These and similar motets constitute a mid-century group of perhaps a dozen or so; they turn up also in the La Clayette collection and (becoming more numerous) in the later Bamberg collection. This is contemporaneous with the seventh fascicle of Montpellier, and here the faster style of triplum is the link to the remarkable group of motets associated with Pierre de la Croix. This 'Petronian' style of motet is the most prominent and one of the most advanced of Montpellier; but there are other important types as well.

Two of Pierre's motets lead off the seventh fascicle.[50] Both have very firm tenor-duplum pairs, combining mode 5 with mode 1; the first is on G-*sol/ut*, the second on F-*fa/ut* (with b natural) (Ex. 217). The breve is subdivided as far down as seven 'semibreves', although usually only to two or three 'semibreves'. More important seem the new style of melody and the new ways of matching melodic phrases with text lines and rhymes. These tripla do not resemble trouvère chanson in melodic style; rather, their style is born of the polyphonic motet. Yet we should not think of it, on the one hand, as simply declamatory or 'parlando'—the melodic movement is far too carefully fashioned for that—nor on the other hand as completely a product of its contrapuntal environment. Rather, this seems indeed to be a new style of melody, one that depends on the firm foundation of traditional tenor-duplum pair. It has often been noticed that the texture is really one of melody and accompaniment; this texture, always latent in the French motet, here comes out in the open. All that would be required to turn this into the polyphonic song style of the fourteenth century would to play the duplum rather than sing it (a matter of performance option), and release the tenor from a modal or ordinal

---

[50] Mo 7,253, triplum 'S'amours eust point de poet'—'Au renouveler', T. 'Ecce'; 7,254, triplum 'Aucun ont trouve'—'Lonc temps', T. 'Annuntiantes'. Similar works in Mo 7: 255, 264, 289, 297, 299; Mo 8: 316, 317, 330, 332. Ex. 217 = Mo 7,254, fo. 273ʳ.

Ex. 217

Au-cun ont trou-ve chant par u-sa-ge, Mes a moi en donne o-choi-

Lonc tans me sui

Annun[tiantes]

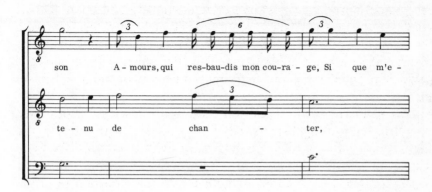

son A-mours,qui res-bau-dis mon cou-ra-ge, Si que m'e-

te-nu de chan - ter,

stuet fai - re chan - çon, Car a - mer me

Mes or ai rai - son

fait da - me bele et sage Et de bon re - non.

de joi - e me - ner,

Et je qui li ai fait hou - ma - ge, Pour li ser - vir tout mon

Car bonne

a - a - ge De loi - al cuer sans pen ser tra - hi -

a - mour me fait de - si -

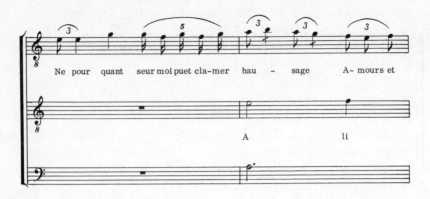

Ne pour quant seur moi puet cla-mer hau - sage A- mours et

A li

moi tout mon vi-vant te - nir en sa pri - son

ne doit on nule au - tre com -

Ne ja pour ce ne pen - se-rai vers li me - pri - son;

pa - rer. Et

II (etc.)

pattern, which happens more and more frequently elsewhere in the seventh and eighth fascicles of Montpellier. (In actual fact, however, the fourteenth-century song texture was not generated in this way, but rather directly out of the tenor-duplum pair, now as cantus-tenor, provided with a 'triplum', i.e. upper instrumental part, or 'contra-tenor', i.e. lower instrumental part, or both.)

The seventh and eighth fascicles of Codex Montpellier contain essentially the same kind of repertory; both include a small number of independent works in the individual style of Pierre de la Croix; both contain a larger number (in relation to the older repertory, a *much* larger proportion) of French motets with song tenors, sometimes rondeaux, but other kinds as well; and both fascicles include well-defined groups of Latin, characteristically Marian, double motets. In addition, or among the types listed, numerous special forms or techniques are represented in both fascicles, showing end of the century experimentation along a broad front. The seventh fascicle tends to have concordances with either Bamberg or Turin, or scat-tered, isolated concordances, or none, for a substantial number of its motets are unica. In the eighth fascicle almost all are unica, the main exception being the English ones at the end (339, 340–1). One never knows, of course, in the case of an unica fascicle, whether that reflects lack of extant sources or a truly unique repertory—a collection assembled, or even written, by one composer, or works known only in his circle. If so, it would go well with the frequently experimental quality of these works. They are, however, important for the future, which means either that they were part of a larger repertory not preserved, or that the circle from which they came was extremely important, even if small.

The motets in the style of Pierre de la Croix involve two very different rhythmic levels (a slow one in the tenor—and to some extent in the duplum—and a fast one in the triplum). This difference became a basic feature of the fourteenth-century motet, and the gradual appearance of this difference in the thirteenth-century motet can be taken as a moment of great significance, especially since it ran counter to the basic trend of all but the oldest thirteenth-century motets to place the tenor in mode 1 or 2 as an accompaniment. The motets on song tenors, for their part, have little rhythmic differentiation.[51] These tenors, being songs, however, show no tendency to become accompa-niments, and the result can be three more or less equal voices, a kind of simultaneous polymelody often attributed to thirteenth-century

[51] Mo 7: 256, 260, 271, 272, 280, 295, etc. Mo 8: 319, 321, etc.

discant but not really there until this moment. The emphasis is on density, linearity, continuity: small wonder that the song forms (sometimes *en rondeau* but more often individually structured) are hardly supported at all by the other voices. Song forms, whether already 'forms' in the fixed fourteenth-century sense, or still only procedures, as *en rondeau*, are to be sought rather in the monophonic medium, or in the simple discant settings *a3* of Adam de la Hale or Jehan de Lescurel.[52] Motets, in contrast, are by nature continuous and use song forms only as ingredients. Adam de la Hale, incidentally, has two motets in the seventh fascicle,[53] and these, along with several tenors presumably by professional instrumentalists,[54] testify to the primary secular and vernacular nature of these collections. The two series of Latin motets are relatively conservative in spite of certain idiosyncrasies;[55] they can hardly be liturgical music for the cathedral itself, but devotional music in the households of cathedral hierarchy.

It has long been obvious that between the use of the brevis in Perotin as a relatively fast—indeed, 'short'—note and the use of the same shape in 1600 as a relatively long note in common time, there extended an historical continuum characterized by a gradual slowing-down of tempo relative to notation; the slowing-down was persistent, even though often interrupted or deflected in complex ways. Within the thirteenth and fourteenth century there is some direct evidence concerning the slowing-down, such as the remark by Jacques de Liège that semibrevis and brevis now go approximately as fast as the former brevis and longa. Heinrich Besseler once proposed an interpretation of what such evidence might mean in terms of actual tempos.[56]

Perhaps more important than absolute tempo is the clear existence, at the end of the century, of several different tempi associated with different kinds of notation and different styles of music. At least, it is clear from internal evidence as well as from theorists' comments that such different tempi were used, even though it is not yet clear exactly which were which. Some pieces, such as certain of the hockets at the end of the Bamberg collections, the textless, presumably instrumental, pieces in Brit. Lib., Harley 978,[57] certain pieces of English polyphony of *c.* 1300, and certain of the motets—especially Latin ones—in

---

[52] See n. 25.

[53] Mo 7,258,279.

[54] 'Tassin'—Mo 7,292,294; 'Loyset'—Mo 7,297.

[55] Mo 7, 282–7, 300–2; Mo 8, 326–31, 339–41, 343–4.

[56] 'Studien zur Musik des Mittelalters II: Die Motette von Franko von Köln bis Philippe von Vitry', *AMw*, 8 (1926), particularly p. 214. See also the tempi and discussion in Willi Apel, *The Notation of Polyphonic Music, 900–1600* (5th ed., Cambridge, Mass., 1953) 342–3; further, pp. 320–4, 340–1.

[57] See chap. XIV.

Montpellier fascicles 7 and 8, continue to use longa and brevis as primary rhythmic values, with relatively little breaking of the brevis into semibreves; these, when they do occur, are ornamental and seem to be very quick. Clearly such pieces were intended to be performed at a tempo much faster than the motets of Pierre de la Croix, if we use the duration of the brevis as the basis of comparison. It is in this context that the theorists' comments can be taken, in the most general sense, to refer to a slow, medium, and fast performance of the brevis, based largely on the extent to which the brevis is subdivided into semibreves.

Franco of Cologne is credited with one of the first attempts to rationalize and stabilize the subdivision of the brevis, and this along with his other rationalizations of notation constitutes what scholars refer to as 'Franconian notation', which is taken to mark a new epoch in thirteenth-century music.[58] Franco's teaching about semibreves can be interpreted to mean that the brevis is subdivided into three equal parts, no more; and that if three semibreves replace a breve they are equal in duration, but if only two, then the second is twice as long as the first. The important point is that until after 1300 semibreves are all written alike in French notation, with diamond-shaped notes; but they could be performed with various relative durations, shorter or longer. The performer could follow the manner of semibreve perform-ance of some leading musician such as Franco or Pierre de la Croix. Some of these manners of performance are described in treatises; they differ among themselves, and obviously represent personal styles.[59] Thus when we read in the *Speculum musicae* of Jacques de Liège that composers sudivided the brevis into as many as seven (or nine) semibreves, we should not take this as a merely theoretical subdivi-sion; but as a style of performing semibreves. Unfortunately the account is not precise enough to tell us the relative durations of these semibreves (at least, scholars do not agree about its interpretation), but perhaps no amount of durational precision would inform us about the actual style of performance, which is the most important aspect. This level of rhythm was called *prolatio*, which means 'bring-ing forward' or 'delivery'. When this level, in turn, became rational-ized in the fourteenth century, *prolatio* then acquired a specific meaning analogous to the terms for the upper rhythmic levels, *tempus* and *modus*. Within the thirteenth century, however, we can think of the semibreves as subject to the performer's ideas about 'delivery', and we need to determine for each piece which set of ideas might govern its

---

[58] See Apel, *Notation of Polyphonic Music*, pp. 310–18.
[59] See Apel, *Notation of Polyphonic Music*, p. 320.

performance. This may in some cases be indeterminable; the closely related question of the proper tempo may be easier to determine, once the various comments by theorists have been sorted out and connected to various styles of notation.[60]

---

[60] The most penetrating recent study is Ernest Sanders, 'Duple Rhythm and Alternate Third Mode in the 13th Century', *JAMS*, 15 (1962), 249–91.

XIV

POLYPHONY IN ENGLAND IN THE THIRTEENTH CENTURY

By RICHARD CROCKER

Students of English polyphony of the thirteenth century have argued persuasively that it belongs to the mainstream of polyphonic development, that it is not peripheral. Ernest Sanders pointed out[1] that many of the features previously taken to be peculiarly English and, when found in continental sources, to indicate English influence or provenance, were better considered to be widespread in polyphonic practice on the Continent as well as in England, even if not characteristic of Notre-Dame polyphony. Sanders went on to try to identify those other features which could be described as specifically English; they will concern us in due course. Our first concern, however, is to see that English polyphony combines the novelties of Notre-Dame style with more traditional features of polyphony as practised by cathedral musicians. From this we can gain a valuable perspective on the continental Latin motet; for just as it is instructive to see the new French texted discant—the French motet—through the eyes of the trouvère and professional instrumentalist, so it helps to see the Latin texted discant through the eyes of the cathedral musician, taking into account his response to the peculiarities of Notre-Dame style.

COMMON DISCANT

For an understanding of the position of English polyphony in the thirteenth century and its relationship to the Notre-Dame repertory, it seems fruitful as well as justified to posit a 'common discant' practice, as described at the end of chapter XI (see above p. 556); this would have been in use by cathedral musicians at numerous places on the Continent and in England. The matrix of this common discant

---

[1] 'Peripheral Polyphony of the 13th Century', *JAMS*, 17 (1964), 261. For the views of Jacques Handschin, see 'The *Sumer* Canon and its Background', *Musica disciplina*, 3 (1949), 55; and 5 (1951), 65.

(beyond the 'new organum teaching' of the eleventh and twelfth centuries) was the composition of chant in the forms and styles current in the same period. These included the traditional forms of antiphons, hymns, and responsories for the Office; Alleluias and sequences for the Mass; settings of Kyrie, Sanctus, and Agnus dei, with their tropes.[2] The texts of any of these items could involve the techniques of rhyme and scansion, and the structures of couplet and strophe, that had become popular in the new styles of chant since the eleventh century. This flow of new chant composition was in close contact with discant composition, shaping and being shaped by discant.

Common discant lacks the strong, distinctive features of the Notre-Dame style. Paradoxically, that style, in all its individuality, became known as 'universal', while the common discant practice around it was ubiquitous even if nondescript. It is represented by the polyphonic pieces in Cambridge Univ.Lib. Ff i 17;[3] in the collection of special pieces in honour of the Blessed Virgin in the eleventh fascicle of W_1 (attributed to the English repertory[4]); and in part of the collection in Codex Las Huelgas.[5] (For examples of this common discant see above, Exx. 172, 185, and below, Ex. 218.)

Before the impact of the Notre-Dame style, this common discant is mostly *a2*, with the same text in both voices, simultaneously. The relationship of the voices ranges from note-against-note to several or even many notes in the upper voices against one in the lower (but never approaching the extension of the dupla in Notre-Dame organa). The relationship with the text may range from syllabic to melismatic (the same in both voices), but melismata tend to be localized at obvious points such as beginning and ending, in Frankish fashion, rather than distributed unpredictably throughout as in the Gregorian Graduals and Alleluias which were set in Notre-Dame polyphony. The lower voice is often not pre-existent; that is, discant can be and often is composed anew in two voices. In their text and function the new compositions tend to be 'paraliturgical', so that even if pre-existent melodies are used they tend to be those of recent chant styles rather than those fixed in the Gregorian repertory. Throughout the

---

[2] See Ch. VII.

[3] See Ch. XI.

[4] See Rudolf Flotzinger, *Der Discantussatz im Magnus Liber und seiner Nachfolge*, Wiener Musikwissenschaftliche Beiträge, vii (Vienna, 1969), 232; Edward Roesner, 'The Origins of W_1', *JAMS*, 29 (1976), 337; Julian Brown, Sonia Patterson, and David Hiley, 'Further Observations on W_1', *Journal of the Plainsong & Mediæval Music Society*, 4 (1981), 53.

[5] Ed. Higini Anglès, *El Codex musical de Las Huelgas* (*Musica a veus des segles xii–xiv*), 3 vols (Barcelona, 1931), and Gordon Anderson, *The Las Huelgas Manuscript: Burgos, Monasterio de Las Huelgas*, Corpus mensurabilis musicae, 79, 2 vols (American Institute of Musicology, 1982).

common discant practice there is a relaxed approach to the use of pre-existent chant. We should note that the bulk of the Notre-Dame repertory contained in W_1 consists actually of conductus, not organa; and in so far as the Notre-Dame conductus shares the features of common discant, the early Notre-Dame repertory reflects common practice in this respect. As we saw, however, the Notre-Dame conductus is distinguished by the rhythmic innovations as well as certain other features that apparently originated at Notre Dame; and beyond that it was with the organa, not the conductus, that the Notre-Dame school made its special impression.

The more Notre-Dame polyphony expanded in development of florid dupla, and of the organa tripla and quadrupla in Perotin's style, the further from common procedures of twelfth-century chant and discant it seemed to be. With the syllabic texting of the dupla of clausulas, however, Notre-Dame polyphony re-entered the orbit of common procedures—at least as far as certain outward features were concerned. (Other basic differences had developed, some obvious, some latent—so that their implications would not be worked out for decades.) We have seen how syllabic texting of the clausula duplum produced music that seemed to the trouvère or his instrumentalist to be accompanied song. We need now to ask how this same music appeared to the cathedral musician looking at it from the point of view of common chant and discant procedures.

For him, the syllabic texting was in some respects identical with the procedure we call 'prosula'. We have encountered prosulae in the ninth century, when a text was added syllabically to, say, an Alleluia in such a way as to incorporate the original chant text while supplying enough additional syllables for every note in the chant.[6] This procedure could be applied to a whole chant (as in 'Psalle modulamina') or to only a portion, often a melisma, as when the melisma on 'permanebit' (of the Gloria trope 'Regnum tuum') was given a syllabic text. Prosulae were provided with increasing frequency in the tenth and eleventh centuries, and in fact remained popular both in repertory and procedure during the time the polyphonic repertories were being developed in the thirteenth. By nature, prosulae for melismata begin and end with the syllables of the original text, and they often reflect, in their internal assonance, the sound of the vowel on which the melisma is sung. The syllabic texting of the Notre-Dame clausulas follows these procedures so frequently and so closely that these clausulas can be described as prosulaic; and, apart from the term, the procedure and result must have not only seemed familiar to musicians outside the

---

[6] See Ch. VII.

Notre-Dame school, but even paralleled procedures and results that they themselves cultivated.

A prosulaic clausula had some significant differences from a chant prosula, however. For one thing, it kept the prosula text more distinct from the original text and chant, since it was in the duplum. In Smits van Waesberghe's proposed mode of performance, a chant prosula would have been sung by a soloist simultaneously with the choir singing the chant in melismatic form, and only timbre would have separated the two.[7] More important, since the duplum in a clausula had up to three notes per tenor note, a prosulaic text added to the duplum would be roughly twice as long as a prosulaic text added to the tenor as chant. The immediate effect of this was that the prosulaic duplum text no longer resembled the style of the typical chant prosula (which tended to have a continuous, unphrased, largely unstructured text), but instead resembled the versus, with clear, often regular phrases, marked off by rhyme, and with regular accentuation. This by itself made the prosulaic clausula look suddenly familiar in a way that clausulas without prosulae—even though with the same musical phrasing—could not have been. Just as the clausula with a French text looked like an accompanied song, so the prosulaic clausula looked like an accompanied versus, that is, a polyphonic versus in which only one voice was sung with the versus text (unlike the common polyphonic versus or conductus in which both voices sang the text simultaneously); the other voice would then appear to a casual or uninitiated observer as simply an untexted, unidentified, subordinate melodic line. Here again, in the prosulaic clausula, Notre-Dame polyphony seemed suddenly to rejoin common practice, centred on the twelfth-century versus.

The context became especially close in the case of discant *a3* in which the same prosulaic text was sung simultaneously in duplum and triplum. Here the two upper voices, considered apart from the tenor, were indistinguishable from a polyphonic versus or conductus—and were in some cases not distinguished, but included, without their tenors, in conductus collections (along with dupla without *their* tenors, treated as monophonic conductus). In other words, if a prosulaic clausula appeared to be a versus with accompaniment added, the accompaniment could logically be taken away; or replaced by another; or supplied if not present; or composed for a new piece. While the Notre-Dame clausula with its archetypal Gregorian Gradual or Alleluia may have seemed remote and unapproachable, a

<hr>

[7] 'Zur ursprünglichen Vortragsweise der Prosulen, Sequenzen, und Organa', *Bericht über den siebenten internationalen musikwissenschaftlichen Kongress, Köln 1958* (Kassel, 1959), 251–4.

prosula or versus with accompaniment stood close to the common practice of the cathedral musician, a practice in which he habitually composed or adapted the lower voice along with the upper one. This was not the way the Notre-Dame composer worked; but outside the Notre-Dame school, it was the way their results appeared to other musicians, who worked with these results in their own way. Around this point of contact, cathedral musicians in France, the Rhineland, Spain, and especially England, generated free-and-easy procedures involving versus and accompanying parts. The prime example of this process is the famous work—better, group of works—associated with 'Ave gloriosa mater'.[8] If we endorse Heinrich Husmann's generally accepted opinion,[9] there was first a versus, 'Ave gloriosa mater', to which various other voices were added to produce several polyphonic works, some of which resembled the conductus, some of the motet. In whichever version it appears, the tenor, although marked 'Domino' in Codex Montpellier, as if it came from a 'Benedicamus Domino', varies significantly in melody. Sometimes the tenor is apparently to sing the text along with the duplum; elsewhere apparently to be played on an instrument (perhaps to accompany 'Duce creature', the French contrafactum); or simply as standard Latin motet tenor. (Ex. 218).

SOURCES

Gilbert Reaney has observed[10] that, judging from the number of remnants (often pitifully fragmented) of polyphonic music in the thirteenth and fourteenth centuries, England can be said to have had more documentary sources than any Continental repertory. From this it may be surmised that the repertory of thirteenth-century English polyphony was relatively large, although it is difficult to determine how much was produced in this century—that is, within the chronological limits of this volume—and how much in the next.[11]

Because of the nature of the sources, the thirteenth-century repertory is elusive, and a survey of it difficult. First, there are the so-called

---

[8] Ed. Ernest Sanders, *English Music of the Thirteenth and Early Fourteenth Centuries, Polyphonic Music of the Fourteenth Century*, 14 (Monaco, 1979), 223; also ed. Gordon Anderson, *The Latin Compositions in Fascicules 7 and 8 of the Notre-Dame Manuscript Wolfenbüttel Helmstadt. 1099 (1206)* (Institute of Medieval Music, 1976), ii, pp. 32, 235; facs. edn. Carl Parrish, *The Notation of Medieval Music* (New York, 1957), plate XXXII–XXXIII; discussion by Friedrich Ludwig, *Repertorium organorum recentioris et motetorum vetustissimi stili*, 2nd edn. Dittmer, *Musicological Studies*, 7 (Institute of Medieval Music, 1964), 180; Sanders, 'Peripheral Polyphony', pp. 278 ff; Anderson, *The Latin Compositions*, i, pp. 68–77.

[9] 'Bamberger Handschrift', *MGG*, i (1949–51), col. 1205.

[10] 'Some Little-known Sources of Medieval Polyphony in England', *Musica disciplina*, 15 (1961), 15.

[11] On fourteenth-century English polyphony, see *NOHM* iii, chs. III (Church Music) and IV (Popular and Secular Music).

Ex. 218

A - ve glo - ri - o - sa   ma - ter sal - va - to - ris,

A - ve glo - ri - o - sa   ma - ter sal - va - to - ris,

(etc.)

a - ve spe - ci - o - sa   vir - go flos pu - do - ris,

a - ve spe - ci - o - sa   vir - go flos pu - do - ris,

a - ve lux io - co - sa   tha - la - mus splen - do - ris,

a - ve lux io - co - sa   tha - la - mus splen - do - ris,

a - ve pre - ci - o - sa   sa - lus pec - ca - to - ris,

a - ve pre - ci - o - sa   sa - lus pec - ca - to - ris,

a - ve vi - te vi - a   ca - sta mun - da pu - ra,

a - ve vi - te vi - a   ca - sta mun - da pu - ra,

dul - cis mi - tis pi - a   fe - lix cre - a - tu - ra,

dul - cis mi - tis pi - a   fe - lix cre - a - tu - ra,

pa - rens mo - do mi - ro   no - va par - i - tu - ra,

pa - rens mo - do mi - ro   no - va pa - ri - tu - ra,

vi - rum si - ne vi - ro   con - tra le - gis iu - ra.

vi - rum si - ne vi - ro   con - tra le - gis iu - ra.

Vir - go vir - gi - num   ex - pers cri - mi - num,

Vir - go vir - gi - num   ex - pers cri - mi - num,

et ad gau - di - a   nos per-hen - ni - a

et ad gau - di - a   nos per-hen - ni - a

duc pre- ce pi - a,   vir - go Ma - ri - a.

duc pre- ce pi - a,   vir - go Ma - ri - a.

Worcester fragments, Worc. Chapter Lib.Add.68, known to some extent already to W. H. Frere and Friedrich Ludwig. They were assembled and edited first in 1928 by Dom Anselm Hughes, then by Luther Dittmer, and finally those pieces preserved complete have been re-edited by Ernest Sanders.[12] This is the central corpus for study of the repertory as such, extending over the whole of the thirteenth century and including all important types of English polyphony. Relationships among the parts of this corpus, however, are complex and still not well understood; and only some of its items are complete pieces, the rest posing problems of reconstruction whose solutions await agreement. One particular smaller set of fragments may be singled out for mention from Oxford, Bodleian Library, Rawl. c. 400. These fragments, containing English Alleluia settings, have been edited by Dittmer, who understood them to represent a large collection of liturgical polyphony comparable to the *Magnus liber organi*.[13]

Still another representation of a lost collection is provided by a list in Brit.Lib. Harl. 978. Like similar lists in Continental music, this one provides fascinating material for study, revealing as it does an extensive repertory of English polyphony, liturgical and otherwise. The list has been much discussed; it is headed by the name of 'W. de Winton', presumably William of Winchester. This omnibus manu-

[12] Dittmer, *The Worcester Fragments* (*Musicological Studies and Documents*, 11, American Institute of Musicology, 1957); facs. edn. *Worcester add.68, Westminster Abbey 33327, Madrid, Bibl.nac.192* (*Medieval Musical Manuscripts*, v, Institute of Medieval Music, Brooklyn, 1959); Sanders, *English Music of the Thirteenth and Early Fourteenth Centuries*.

[13] 'An English Discantuum Volumen', *Musica disciplina*, 8 (1954), 19; transcription and facs., p. 46.

script to which the list was added contains other material in the form of actual compositions. The most famous are the versions of 'Ave gloriosa mater'/'Douce creature' already mentioned, and the celebrated rota, 'Sumer is icumen in'/'Perspice Christicolae'.

Part of the Harleian manuscript has been shown to come from Reading; together with the location of the Worcester Cathedral Chapter Library, this has inspired a network of supposition connecting them with the observations made around 1200 by Giraldus Cambrensis, and with a remark by Anonymous IV, the English observer of the Notre-Dame school, towards 1270, about cantors in the 'Westcuntre' and their preference for thirds. (In a review of this material, Christopher Hohler has queried all these suppositions, and offered an alternative suggestion: that the Harleian collection was assembled by a music master at Oxford, with connections in London, and that the Worcester fragments actually represent a repertory associated with the court chapel in London.[14]) The problems that concern us here, in a peculiarly complex English version, are that of monastery versus cathedral and of the contact with Notre-Dame polyphony.

ENGLISH POLYPHONIC STYLE

The specifically English repertory, parts of which are indicated in the Harleian list and exemplified in the Worcester fragments, was naturally based upon the flow of new chant composition and common discant. But the English repertory, like that of Notre Dame, developed its own characteristic features.[15] Some English features are simply those of twelfth-century cathedral music in general; thus English polyphony tends to involve Kyries, Alleluias, sequences, Sanctus, Agnus dei, certain tropes, and versus. And English polyphony often treated existing chants, when used as lower voices of discant, with the freedom characteristic of common discant of the twelfth century, in which it is often hard to decide whether a lower voice is borrowed or newly-composed in the style of recent chant.

Two of the most distinctive features of thirteenth-century English polyphony are voice-exchange and a relatively heavy use of imperfect consonances, primarily thirds. It has long been observed that both these features are abundant in Notre-Dame organum and discant at

---

[14] 'Reflections on Some Manuscripts Containing 13th-Century Polyphony', *Journal of the Plainsong & Mediæval Music Society*, 1 (1978), 2; particularly pp. 12 ff.

[15] Sanders, 'Peripheral Polyphony'; 'Tonal Aspects of 13th-Century English Polyphony', *AcM*, 37 (1965), 19; 'Die Rolle der englischen Mehrstimmigkeit des Mittelalters in der Entwicklung von Cantus-firmus-Satz und Tonalitätsstruktur, *AMw*, 24 (1967), 24; 'Duple Rhythm and Alternate Third Mode in the 13th Century', *JAMS*, 15 (1962), 249.

the time of Perotin (1190–1220); and before that, in the Notre-Dame conductus repertory, including—but by no means limited to—works datable to around 1170 and connected to England, largely through association with Thomas à Becket. Were these features indigenous to English twelfth-century polyphony and incorporated thence into Notre-Dame style? Or were they developed within the Notre-Dame repertory, subsequently to become characteristic of English polyphony? Or were they derived from earlier practice, in ways and from sources yet to be discerned clearly? It is certainly true (as Sanders emphasizes) that Perotin included and assimilated a broad variety of materials from many sources. It is also true that in the intense creation of a new style, these ingredients were transfigured, in meaning as well as form, and that new configurations emerged—including aspects of musical style that were not there before but became important.

Instances of 'hidden polyphony' suggest that voice exchange might be another feature of traditional discant: instances of 'hidden polyphony' can involve 'successive notation' in which what looks like two lines of text, each with its own melody, occur in succession on the page, but can be shown (by concordance and other evidence) to represent performance *a2*, the two melodic phrases being sung simultaneously twice, using the first line of text, then the second.[16] It is easy to imagine a performance of a sequence (or other piece with couplets) set *a2*, in which the two performers exchange parts for the second line of the couplet. We shall see how the various manifestations of English voice exchange could follow from this possibility.

The predilection for imperfect consonances, especially thirds, in English polyphony of the thirteenth century has often been thought to be indigenous to English musicality, owing to mis-understanding of a passage in the *Descriptio Cambriae* of Gerald de Barri (Giraldus Cambrensis) (*c.* 1147–1220). H. E. Wooldridge long ago discussed the passage with exemplary clarity and discretion, and came to the conclusion that 'no known documents exist which can with any show of probability associate the use of thirds and sixths with the popular practice, or which represent it as at any time exclusively English'. Christopher Hohler came to a similar conclusion.[17] Direct evidence of English predilection for thirds before contact with Notre Dame is completely wanting.

With nothing to start from except the broad spectrum of twelfth-

---

[16] Sarah Fuller, 'Hidden Polyphony—a Reappraisal', *JAMS*, 24 (1971), 169; Frank Ll. Harrison, *Music in Medieval Britain* (London, 1958), 129 and 141 ff. See also Sanders, *English Music*, No. 6 and commentary p. 239.

[17] 'The Polyphonic Period, Part I. *Oxford History of Music*, i (London, 1901), 16–33; Hohler, 'Reflections', p. 17.

century chant and discant on one hand, and the Notre-Dame repertory on the other, we can most easily observe the development of the
English repertory in the Worcester fragments by following the grouping and chronology supplied by Sanders.[18]

CONDUCTUS STYLE

Three early pieces a2, c. 1200, among the Worcester fragments,
represent the common discant practice. WF 100 (the extant text
begins 'Mundi pressuram', identified with Alleluia 'Virga florem', in
W_1, fasc. 11) shares cadential ornamentation with St Martial versus,
but shows many more parallel thirds. WF 106, 'Paranymphus salutat',
is even more like a St Martial versus. The text (which also appears in
W_1, fasc. 11) is actually a sequence in later style: its couplets are
governed by rhyme and regular accent. The text is sung by the voices
simultaneously, with frequent two-note ligatures for syllables in the
lower voice, and occasionally three notes in the upper voice for one in
the lower. WF 101, 'O Maria virgo pia',[19] is similar in style. In both
works, the lower voice repeats its melody for the second line of the
couplet, and uses the idioms of the twelfth-century chant sequence;
indeed, these lower voices might have begun as chants. They could
just as well, however, have been newly composed as lower voices for
the works as we find them. In any case, the upper voices also repeat
for the second lines of couplets—and here we can see possible
examples of the presumed first stage of voice exchange, in which the
two performers could exchange parts for the second lines of couplets.
While the score notation of the original permits this, it does not
specify it, and voice exchange would here be a matter of performance
practice only; but performance practice was to be an important factor
in the subsequent tradition of voice exchange.

The versus set in common discant a3, in conductus style with the
text in all voices simultaneously, could presumably occur anywhere in
France or England towards 1200. Examples are WF 97, 'Singularis et
insignis', WF 98, 'Sponsa rectoris omnium', WF 99, 'O sponsa dei
electa'.[20] Like the pieces a2, these are all from the earliest Worcester
layer, dating from around 1200. WF 98, 'Sponsa rectoris', uses the
hymn melody traditionally associated with the ninth-century text
'Veni Creator Spiritus', but is not otherwise distinguished in style

---

[18] 'Duple Rhythm and Alternate Third Mode in the 13th Century', pp. 277 ff. In the following
discussion, WF refers to Dittmer's edition in The Worcester Fragments, EMu to Sanders's
edition in English Music.

[19] EMu Appendix, No. 1.

[20] Ibid., No. 14; EMu, No. 64; EMu, No. 21.

from the other two. 'O sponsa dei electa' has initial and final caudae in the manner of Notre-Dame conductus.

A work such as 'De supernis sedibus',[21] (Ex. 219) *a3* with text in all voices simultaneously, also corresponds to a Notre-Dame conductus in its larger shape, and may represent a 'second generation' of English thirteenth-century polyphony. There is a good-sized cauda at the beginning, then a texted section, (four lines of seven syllables each, rhyming *abab*); a middle cauda; another texted section (six lines of seven syllables each, rhyming *cdcdcd*); and a short concluding cauda. In stature, rhythm (with long-short pattern and tending towards twos, fours, and eights at higher levels), sonorities, and melodic style, the piece stands close to the Notre-Dame conductus repertory.

VOICE EXCHANGE AND RONDELLUS

Also in common with Notre Dame is the use of voice exchange. But at Notre Dame this appears sporadically in the caudae of conductus and also in organum *a3* in the style of Perotin, between the two upper parts moving in long-short patterns over a long-note tenor. What is distinctively thirteenth-century English is the systematic use of voice exchange in conductus and motets. Voice exchange between two voices is represented in Figure 1(a). This involves the immediate repetition of a phrase of discant with performers exchanging melodies (not necessarily texts). This is primarily a matter for the performers; what reaches the listener is a phrase of two-part counterpoint immediately repeated, with a slight change in timbre as the result of voice exchange.

Voice exchange can also occur among three voices, and in more than one way. The most complete way involves three phrases of melody, all three sung (but in different orders) by all three voices; the result, shown in Figure 1(b) is a three-fold statement of the one phrase of three-voice counterpoint. It is this three-part arrangement that is most distinctive of English practice; it is associated with the term 'rondellus', and some specialists restrict the term to voice exchange *a3* of this type.[22] By this definition, the rondellus is in the thirteenth century an almost exclusively English phenomenon.

Rondellus appears most characteristically as a self-contained section in a larger piece. In 'De supernis sedibus', a rondellus section appears in the initial cauda, starting at bar 11. The section comes three times, followed by a three-bar close, just before the start of the texted

[21] *EMu*, No. 31.

[22] Harrison, *Music in Medieval Britain*, p. 134; Robert Falck, 'Rondellus, Canon, and Related Types before 1300', *JAMS*, 25 (1972), 38; Fritz Reckow, 'Rondeau/rota', in Hans-Heinrich Eggebrecht, ed., *Das Handwörterbuch der musikalischen Terminologie* (1980).

Ex. 219

De su – per – nis se – di – bus for – ti –

De su – per – nis se – di – bus for – ti –

De su – per – nis se – di – bus for – ti –

tu – do mit – ti – tur ad sa – lu – tem

tu – do mit – ti – tur ad sa – lu – tem

tu – do mit – ti – tur ad sa – lu – tem

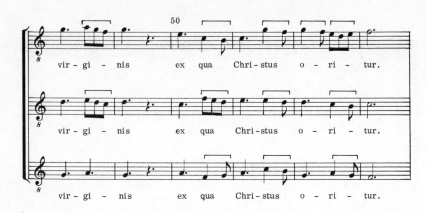

vir – gi – nis   ex   qua   Chri – stus   o – ri – tur.

vir – gi – nis   ex   qua   Chri – stus   o – ri – tur.

vir – gi – nis   ex   qua   Chri – stus   o – ri – tur.

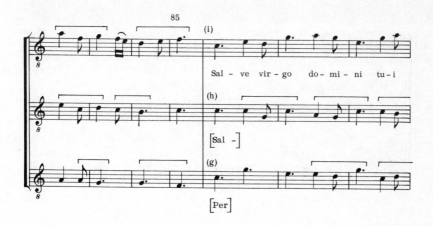

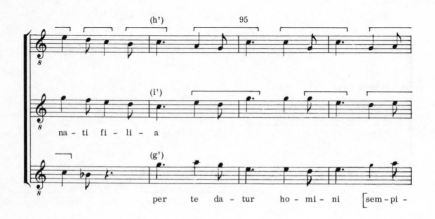

ter - na glo - ri - a

Na - ti cu - ius no - mi - ni fit ma -

g[ni - fi - cen - ci - a.]

Na - ti cu - ius no - mi - ni fit [ma -

gni] - fi - cen - ci - a.

(*a*)   voice exchange a2

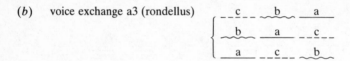

(*b*)   voice exchange a3 (rondellus)

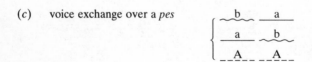

(*c*)   voice exchange over a *pes*

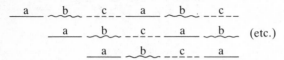

(*d*)   voice exchange in successive entries

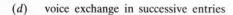

(*e*)   voice exchange a3 with 6 phrases, in successive entries

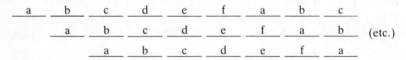

FIG. 1. Schematic representation of several kinds of voice exchange.

section. Another rondellus section, with new melodic material, starts directly after the texted section. This one come six times, the last slightly altered for a close, followed by four bars of another close. A third rondellus section begins immediately with the rest of the text. This time the three-voiced phrase is stated twice only. After these two statements come another two of almost the same melodic and contrapuntal arrangement, and then yet another two. In other words, this section is like the preceding one, with six statements, except that successive pairs of statements are varied instead of repeated literally. The form of the whole may be represented as in Figure 2.

The salient feature is the insistent, immediate repetition in the rondellus sections—whether texted or not. Compared with Notre-Dame practice, the repetition is more literal, more pervasive; some repetition of discant phrases is indeed characteristic of some Notre-

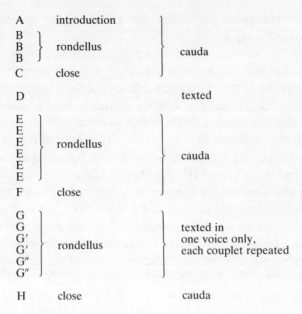

A	introduction	}	
B		}	
B	} rondellus	} cauda	
B		}	
C	close	}	
D		texted	
E		}	
E		}	
E	} rondellus	}	
E		} cauda	
E		}	
E		}	
F	close	}	
G		} texted in	
G		} one voice only,	
G'	} rondellus	} each couplet repeated	
G'		}	
G"		}	
G"		}	
H	close	cauda	

FIG. 2. Schematic representation of sections in 'De supernis sedibus', Ex. 219.

Dame conductus and of Perotinian organum, but in less schematic ways. (It is certainly uncharacteristic of discant clausula and motet.) What Perotin accomplished by maintaining the same length of phrases with varying content is realized in rondellus through exact repetition of discant units.

Arguing from the way the text is entered in 'Flos regalis' (a similar piece in another fragment[23]), Sanders proposes that rondellus sections appeared first in the caudae, and then some of them were partially texted, leading eventually to more extensively texted independent rondellus sections. (The passage in 'Flos regalis', however, is stylistically closer to a texted section of a conductus than to a cauda.) In any case, it is not at all unusual—indeed, it is typical—for only one or two voices of a rondellus to carry text, as in 'Flos regalis'. The effect is on one hand that of accompanied song, on the other hand, that of responsorial performance, as one singer states a verse and another repeats it. In *WF* 69, 'Quem trina pollent',[24] a conductus especially rich in rondellus sections, one source provides two lines of text in the second and third texted sections, implying repetition of each. This repetition of sections, on top of the repetition already produced by the voice exchange, results in dizzying redundancy that dominates the

[23] *EMu*, No. 28.   [24] Ibid., No. 34.

interior of the piece—recalling the effect of the eleventh-century monophonic versus.

Among the several different ways rondellus can be used, one, represented in *WF* 21, 'Munda Maria', (Ex. 220)[25] is important not so much for its use in the thirteenth century—it was apparently not used much then—as for its later history. 'Munda Maria' consists exclusively of one rondellus *a3*. The three phrases of melody are written consecutively, marked 'I ... II ... III'. According to Sanders's interpretation, this means that voice I starts, followed at the indicated intervals by voices II and III. This beginning with successive entries is not at all characteristic of thirteenth-century polyphony, nor would it make much sense for rondellus sections within a conductus to start in this way. It seems to be a special arrangement, a special way of beginning a piece that consists of only one rondellus—unless it was a performer's option to be used elsewhere too. This kind of beginning does not affect the contrapuntal structure of the piece; it merely provides a simplified lead-in: we hear the melodic material gradually, rather than all at once (see Figure 1(d)). As the third voice enters, the piece becomes identical with what it would have been had all singers started simultaneously. Sanders believes that because of this beginning, 'Munda Maria' should be called a 'rota' ('wheel-song' or 'round-song'), but there may be another aspect of rota, not present here, that better corresponds to the idea of 'rotation'.

In 'Munda Maria', only phrases II and III are texted; but the first syllable, 'Mun-', appears at the start of phrase I, in the manner of the initial cauda of a conductus. When all three voices are singing, then, only two are texted, with different texts (that is, with successive verses of text sung simultaneously), while the third voice sounds like textless accompaniment; and this textless voice is also the lowest sounding and slowest moving of the three. The net result is structurally indistinguishable from what we shall see as voice exchange *a2* over a *Pes*.

ENGLISH CHANT SETTINGS

The contact with Notre-Dame organum is fortunately documented in one work, *WF* 81, Alleluia 'Nativitas gloriosae',[26] which dates from 1230–40; its presence in the Worcester fragments is almost as curious as its almost complete uniqueness there. The work has the outward

---

[25] Ibid., No. 35.
[26] *EMu* Appendix, No. 16. See also Codex Montpellier, ed. Yvonne Rokseth, *Polyphonies du xiiie siècle*, i–iv (Paris 1935–9), re-ed. Hans Tischler, *The Montpellier Codex*, 3 vols. (Madison, 1978), Nos. 9, 10, and 62.

Ex. 220

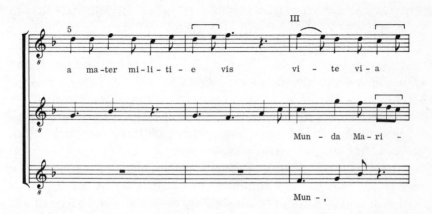

features of a work by Perotin: certain of the notes of the Alleluia in the tenor are immensely prolonged under extended passages in modal rhythm in the duplum and triplum. In the verse, after 'Ex semine', there is a prosulaic versus to be sung by duplum and triplum together. The music of this discant section is the same as in the organum *a3*, Alleluia 'Nativitas' by Perotin (as in Codex Montpellier, Nos. 9–10); in other words, the Worcester organum includes a prosulaic clausula by Perotin inserted in the appropriate place. The Worcester organum itself, however, was apparently written in England by an Englishman.

This is the only piece of organum in Perotin style—or indeed in Notre-Dame style—in the Worcester fragments. When English composers made polyphonic settings of chant, they proceeded differently. Handschin used the term *Choralbearbeitung* to emphasize this different English procedure; Dittmer translated it as 'English organum' and Sanders suggests 'chant setting', which is preferable. We need to apply to the idea of chant setting, however, our hard-won distinctions among various kinds of chant, and note that here, too, is a basic difference between Notre-Dame choice of chant on one hand, and common practice on the other. For there are virtually no English settings of chants from the Gregorian archetype, as the *Magnus liber* has them, with the exception of the important group of English Alleluia settings, which require special qualification. In general it can be said that English chant settings involve either medieval chants (often recent if not *ad hoc*), or genuine tropes, or prosulaic texts in the manner of motets, or a combination of all these elements. Of the complete 'chant settings' published by Sanders,[27] No. 62 is an old Alleluia ('Dies sanctificatus') with a new text; No. 63 is a recent Alleluia; No. 64 is the hymn setting 'Sponsa rectoris'; No. 65 is a Sanctus trope (the Sanctus melody itself being sung in chant); No. 66 is a straight setting of a Sanctus chant from the tenth or eleventh century—and this one, interestingly, is from close to 1300, when such settings seem to have become much more frequent than earlier in the century. Among pieces published as 'troped chant settings', No. 73 involves a trope only; No. 68 a chant prosula only; Nos. 67 and 74 (also very late in the century) the special Introit antiphon, 'Salve sancta parens', a pair of hexameters set to the melody of 'Ecce advenit'; and four more Alleluia settings. All this represents straightforward use of medieval chant materials from which only Notre-Dame held aloof. In general, the category 'chant setting' does not help us much outside the Notre-Dame repertory; much more useful are various aspects of texture and musical form, in particular kinds and

[27] All in *EMu*.

application of texts, rhythmic organization of lower part and upper ones, and use of voice exchange.

MOTET STYLE

The factor that seems most important in distinguishing at least part of the 'second generation' of Worcester fragments from the first is the differentiation of the lower voice from the upper voice or voices. This can be due to one of several things: the lower voice may have a different text from the upper voices, or less text, or no text at all; it may have a repeating rhythmic or melodic pattern, or simply move slower. Now in considering Notre Dame, we had, for various reasons, to understand the presence of a prosulaic versus in the upper voice of a piece of discant as an added element; but in the wider world we have to remember that prosulaic versus were indigenous to common-practice discant, and what was new was a differentiated *lower* voice, one that often appeared to observers outside Notre Dame to be an accompaniment. Such differentiated lower voices appear in English music at the same time as contact with the Notre-Dame repertory; and in the absence of stronger evidence to the contrary, we must regard the appearance of such voices, in whatever local variation, as some kind of response to Notre-Dame style.

Seen from this point of view, the varieties of English polyphony are simpler to understand. From around mid-century, we find among the Worcester fragments a relatively large number of items with differen-tiated lower voices, and with prosulaic versus in the upper voices. These are edited as 'Latin motets on a cantus firmus' and 'Latin motets on a *pes*', and the difference between these subclasses may in certain cases be only that a lower voice has or has not been identified as a pre-existing chant. The Worcester fragments usually mark lower voices in these works as *pes* (foot), rarely as 'tenor'; other English sources may mark them differently; in neither case is a chant origin of a voice specifically implied. Thus *WF* 72,[28] 'Virginis Marie—Salve gemma—*Pes*' (=Veritatem, a Notre-Dame tenor); but *WF* 76,[29] 'Puellare—Purissima—*Pes*', while different in certain structural ways, is not to be distinguished simply on the basis of source of lower voice. Indeed, the spectrum extends from *WF* 2,[30] 'Lux polis—Lux et gloria—Kyrie lux et origo', with two sets of Kyrie verses over a well known Kyrie melody sung straight through in Notre-Dame tenor modal rhythms, to pieces with no perceptible relation to the Notre-Dame tenor repertory. It is sometimes thought that English com-posers did not find the motet a congenial form. Indeed, they did not

[28] Ibid., No. 77.　　　[29] Ibid., No. 49.　　　[30] *EMu* Appendix, No. 21.

cultivate French motets and seldom composed motets in their native tongue. But if we are willing to consider only Latin motets—and understand thereby a piece of discant with syllabic versus over a differentiated lower voice—then we find that motets constitute at least a third of the English repertory, exceeded in bulk only by versus without differentiated lower voices, which we usually call 'conductus': Even restricting the term 'motet' to a piece in which the lower voice incorporates a pre-existent chant, there still remain a respectable number. It is, by the way, possible to make relatively clear distinctions of a purely structural or stylistic kind between motets from mid-century and later ones, and perhaps between typically English ones and those reflecting Continental practice.

WF 15,[31] 'Eterne virgo memorie—Eterna virgo mater', places two versus over a *pes* as in a Latin double motet. The two texts begin alike in the manner of a prosulaic motet, but have different length lines and phrases to bring about the staggering characteristic of motet texture. The *pes* is mostly on *ut-re-mi* (F-G-a) with occasional *re* (D) below, used also for a final, reached by a terminal descent through *mi*. The *pes* melody is long, and stated twice. In movement and locus it resembles, say, the Notre-Dame 'Omnes', except for the final. *WF* 71,[32] 'Te Domine laudat—Te Dominum clamat', is similar, except that the *pes* is on *ut-re-mi-fa* (F-G-a-b flat) and is stated five times. Within the statement, this and other *pedes* move in regular rhythms similar to, but not identical with, the favourite Notre-Dame mode 5 patterns.

WF 11,[33] 'Senator regis curie', has a *primus pes* that ranges more widely in melody through an octave from D, final on G-*ut*, and moves in a simple mode 1 pattern; it has four statements of this pattern. There is a *secundus pes*, not patterned like a tenor, but rather behaving like an untexted triplum in range and phrasing. *WF* 10,[34] 'O quam glorifica—O quam beata—O quam felix' has three texted voices and a *pes*, like a triple Latin motet *a4*. The *pes* is very clearly structured: it has two very similar phrases, the first ending open (on G-*re*), the second closed (on F-*ut*); these two phrases are stated as a pair nine times. Also similar is the *pes* of 'Prolis eterne—Psallat mater', stated eleven times. Its final is G-*sol/ut*, in a locus from the F-*fa* below to the c-*fa/ut* above.

WF 76,[35] 'Puellare gremium—Purissima mater', (Ex. 221) has a *pes* that moves largely in long-short patterns like the texted parts; but the *pes* occupies a position in mid-range, acting like a duplum. It has two

[31] *EMu* No. 52.   [33] Ibid., No. 50.   [35] Ibid., No. 49.
[32] Ibid., No. 47.   [34] Ibid., No. 58.

Ex. 221

Tr. Pu – ci – la – re gre – mi – um

Du. Pu – ris – si – ma ma – ter do – mi – ni Ma –

(A)
T. I
Pes super puellare et purissima

mun – do fu – dit gau – di – um et ce – lo le –

ri – a fit Ga – bri – e – lis

(A)

ti – ci – am dum fi – li – um sum – mi re – gis

nun – ci – i fi – de – lis pre – mis – si de ce – lis

(B)

ge – nu –it et   te – nu – it   pu –di –ci – ti – am.   O

pi – a per col – lo – qui – a.   O   gre –mi – um

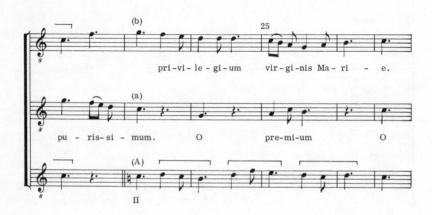

pri –vi – le –gi –um   vir – gi –nis Ma – ri – e.

pu – ris –si – mum.   O   pre –mi –um   O

Ven –

pri – vi – le –gi – um   vir –gi –nis Ma – ri – e.

est tri-cli-ni-um tri-ni-ta-tis di - vi - ne.

(c)

(d)

Ven - ter

(B)

I - stud pu - er -

est tri-cli-ni-um tri-ni-ta-tis di - vi - ne dum

(B)

pe - ri-um ma-gnum ha-bet mi - ste-ri-um dum du-um a-ni-ma-li -

vir-go fi-li-um re-gem o-mni-um la-cte fo-vet

(A)

III

patterns different in melody and slightly different in rhythm; they are repeated in the order AA BB, all that being stated three times. Over the second statement, the texted voices have voice exchange (a/b b/a, c/d d/c)—and this is a characteristic way of combining the two English techniques of *pes* and voice exchange. In one sense it is indistinguishable from a rondellus (*a3*) in that the melody in each of three voices is repeated. In another sense it is different, in that only two voices actually exchange, and hence there are only two statements of the section. The middle of the piece is dominated by the repetition; but by placement of text, and rests, the starting points of these repetitions are obscured, making the procedure less like that of a simple succession of rondellus sections and more like the continuous overlapping of voices in a typical French motet.

In *WF* 41,[36] 'Dulciflua—Precipua' the *pes* has five distinct melodies, even though all move in similar rhythms; each is stated twice—AA BB CC DD EE. Over each pair of statements comes a voice-exchange pattern (over AA comes a/b b/a, etc.). The first voice-exchange section (*pes* AA) is textless like the initial cauda of a conductus. The texting is staggered in each voice, alternating with textless phrases, so that for the most part only one text is heard at a time; but again, the texting overlaps to create the impression of overlapping phrases, and consequently the voice-exchange pattern is artfully obscured.

WF 12,[37] 'Virgo regalis', has a *pes* six bars long, on *ut-re-mi*; it is exactly repeated nine times. Over it is placed a series of voice-exchange sections *a2*; each of these melodies is also six bars long. Only one voice carries the text, so each line of text is clearly heard twice in succession. After two statements, however, the upper voices proceed to new melodies, still in voice exchange, and still over the repeating *pes*. This continues to the end of the piece. Since all these voice-exchange sections are over the same *pes*, all fit with each other more or less: the piece could be performed with eighteen simultaneous counterpoints over the same *pes*. Since it was not so intended, there would be much doubling and clogging of texture, and much dissonance, due to alternate choices of consonance over certain notes of the *pes*; still, by and large, the counterpoint is compatible. It is easy to see how, after making such a piece, English composers could go on to construct an elaborate many-voiced piece, on similar lines, with more care for contrapuntal detail.

All these English pieces have the outward appearance of motets. Their specific difference from continental motets is in the treatment of the untexted voice. Even if it was a pre-existing chant melody, it was

---

[36] Ibid., No. 55.   [37] Ibid., No. 51.

selected from a broader range of sources than at Notre Dame; or it might be treated in freer rhythmic or melodic ways. More often it was not a pre-existent melody, but simply a convenient succession of pitches resembling a continental tenor but, again, treated in a more relaxed manner. The English composers knew, but did not favour, the mode 5 pattern carried out with such rigour in the continental motet. Coming from a tradition of common discant with versus texts, English composers seem to have regarded the continental motet with interest but also freedom born of objectivity and detachment. They adopted such of its manners as suited them. It was not, however, a matter of being free and casual in all aspects of composition, for while English composers were less schematic in the use of mode 5 ordines, they made much more use of repetition within one motet of the whole melody selected for the *pes*—not just two, three, or four statements, as could happen in continental motets, but up to nine or eleven statements. Also they made more use of repetition of sections of the *pes*, in particular in connection with voice exchange. We need to remember that voice exchange in the English motet is *a2*, not *a3* (as in rondellus)—even if the result is the same because of the repeat of the *pes* under the voice exchange. This repeat is necessary of course, and represents an interesting adaptation of continental tenor technique for the sake of voice exchange and its repetitive structure. Precisely this kind of exact, immediate repetition is not much used in continental tenors because it is not wanted in the contrapuntal web of the motet as a whole. When such repetition appears, for one reason or another, in one voice, it is characteristically obscured by varying counterpoint in another. The most extreme example is the placement of a voice in rondeau form over a tenor constructed on quite other principles. Although rare, this type of piece is a vivid illustration of procedures used throughout the Continental repertory less intensively but more pervasively.[38]

In any case, the interior of an English motet is sometimes repetitive in a manner a continental composer would not want. The continental, keeping rigorously to a Gregorian melisma rhythmicized in an arbitrarily regular ordo, was forced through an ever-changing set of contrapuntal conditions. Some English composers showed a desire to make their characteristic repetition of voice-exchange sections less obvious—more like the continuity of the Continental motet—by

---

[38] The fact that two distinct musical phenomena were called by virtually the same name—'rondellus/rondel', 'rondeau'—has repeatedly tempted both medieval and modern observers to identify or at least connect the two phenomena; see Reckow, 'Rondeau/rota', Falck, 'Rondellus, Canon, and Related Types', and Sanders's reply to Falck in *JAMS*, 31 (1978), 170. A connection is possible, but a clear concept should be formed of each separately.

arranging the details of texting and phrasing to give the impression of overlap among the voice exchange elements. These various ways of structuring the interior of a motet lead to some of the basic points of contrast between English and French styles in the thirteenth century.

TONAL ORGANIZATION

The salient features of the English style, whether in the 'conductus' (common discant *a3*) or 'motet' (*a3* with differentiated lower voice), seem to depend essentially upon the frequent use of voice exchange, of a kind that entails much contrary contrapuntal motion within a well-defined, stable octave space (very often F–f). The stability is evident not merely in the fact that pieces regularly begin and end on the same pitch, but also in similar placement of internal cadences; there is heavy use of the sonorities on the *re* and *mi* as well as on the *ut* that is final. The sound is made rich through the frequency of thirds generated out of the voices being led through the voice-exchange patterns. There is a strong tendency to group the low-level rhythms (which are usually long-short) into four-bar groups (eight longae); longer phrases tend to be built out of these in duple. As we have seen, this complex of features was characteristic of Notre-Dame style in the time of Perotin. The important point here is that English composers kept composing in this style with remarkable consistency of method, and uniformity of result, ringing the changes on solutions that seemed to them pleasing and workable. They did not, for the most part, open themselves to the variety of structures associated with cantus firmus construction in the continental motet, but concentrated on the F-final and the smooth solutions it could provide. (At this same time there was a strong preference in chant composition for the F-final with b flat, in contrast to preferences in early medieval chant.) It was, of course, a matter of degree: English composers also used a D-*re* final frequently, and less often a G-*sol/ut* final, while continental composers showed a preference—even if less strongly marked—for F-*ut* final, along with much use of D-final and some of G-final. The point is the greater spread of the continental choice, the greater frequency of endings outside the central locus through a terminal descent (most often in motets on 'In seculum').[39]

It is sometimes said that English polyphony is more 'harmonic' and French polyphony more 'contrapuntal'; such comparisons often refer to the greater use of thirds in English polyphony as against the avoidance of thirds in the mid-century French motet.[40] It is, however, arbitrary to contrast 'harmonic' and 'contrapuntal' in this way; for we

[39] See above, p. 667.   [40] See above, pp. 688–9.

should also have to observe that the voice-leading procedures of the French motet led to the accompanied song textures of the fourteenth century, while the English procedures, with their concentration on voice exchange, led to the wealth of technique later ages called 'canonic', and deserve the description 'contrapuntal' as well as anything the French did.

THE 'SUMER' ROTA

The most famous instance of thirteenth-century English harmonious counterpoint is 'Sumer is icumen in', in Brit.Lib. Harley 978, and designated 'rota'.[41] After much discussion there now seems to be agreement that it can be dated 1240–60; indeed, there is no *stylistic* reason requiring a date later than, say, 1220. There is no agreement, however, about what the piece represents in terms of polyphony, English or French, cultivated or ingenuous, and about its specific provenance. The 'Sumer' rota is distinguished by having two *pedes* sung simultaneously in close-fitting voice exchange (which is unusual in a *pes*), according to directions provided in a rubric, with further directions that the one notated upper voice is to be sung by four singers in turn, each entering at the mark provided (at two-bar intervals). The *pes* produces an F-*ut* at the beginning of every bar and a G-*re* in the middle of every bar; the F is always set with fifth (c) and octave (f), the G-*re* with fifth (d) and facilitative sixth (e) to return to the octave. The counterpoint produces the interval of a third over almost every F or G of the *pes*. Every two-bar unit of the melody fits with the *pes*, and hence with every other two-bar unit. Rhythm at the lower level is long-short, and at higher levels is regular in two or four bars. The only point of rhythmic intricacy is that the phrases in the melody are four bars long (against the *pes* in two-bar units), except for 'Sing cuccu', which has the motet-like effect of setting four-bar units out of place with each other. ('Cuccu, cuccu' eventually restores the regularity.)

Six-voiced texture is found nowhere else in the thirteenth century, neither in England nor on the Continent. Voice exchange (or rondellus) *a4* is not found either, while discant *a4* is well represented in the seventeen motets in Montpellier, fascicle 2. The use of two tenors is not unknown on the Continent (appearing in the Bamberg Codex) but very rare. It is true that a number of English pieces have more than one *pes*, but we would often have to say either that *pes* was used for any untexted voice (which might behave like tenor, duplum, or triplum), or that the combination of two tenor-like voices in voice

[41] *EMu* No. 4, and the critical note on p. 239.

exchange was rare even in England. We have seen a pattern in a *pes* repeated many times, with and without a voice exchange over it, and we have to understand the pair of *pedes* in the 'Sumer' rota as an extrapolation from that.

The really distinctive feature of the 'Sumer' rota is the provision of many more phrases of melody (twelve—all forming counterpoint with the *pes*) than voices to sing them (four). It is true that 'Sumer' could be sung by twelve voices (plus the *pes*), in which case, after all twelve had entered, the result would be simply a continuing repetition of a two-bar phrase of counterpoint—a rondellus *a12* (or *a14*).[42] That may have been the intent or, more appropriately, an option in perform-ance, for the complex of procedures generated from voice exchange seems always to have left the performers with options. Sung *a12*, however, this rota would be not so different from a rondellus, and the distinctive name 'rota' would then have to apply simply to the voices entering one at a time in succession. (A rondellus could be sung as a rota in this sense optionally, the performers deciding how and when to enter in succession, instead of starting simultaneously, but this would not make much sense for the usual rondellus section in the middle of a piece.) Most authorities have imagined a performance of 'Sumer is icumen in' with only four voices. In singing any rondellus-type section of counterpoint with fewer voices than the number of phrases, not all the counterpoint is revealed at once, and listeners (as well as the singers) have a sense of progressing through the available material more in the manner of a melody than a simultaneous counterpoint. After all four voices have entered, we hear in successive voice-exchange sections first phrases 1, 2, 3, 4, then 2, 3, 4, 5, then 3, 4, 5, 6, and so forth, eventually (assuming continuation) 10, 11, 12, 1, then 11, 12, 1, 2, until all possible combinations are reached (see Figure 1(e)). Can we speak of a sense of *rotation* through the contrapuntal material? It depends on a smaller number of singers than phrases; and that is indeterminate in the nature of the piece—or better, of the procedure. On one hand we should have to say that, six voices being unique in the thirteenth century, we can hardly imagine twelve; on the other hand, if so many as six, why not more? In any case, even with only four plus two singers, not only is the repetitive harmony perfectly clear (chord on F, chord on G, in every bar) but also every two-bar unit has an upper profile either f/d/f ('Sing cuccu' four times in succession), or f-e-d-e-f ('Murie sing cuccu' four times in succession),

---

[42] See the score notation in Harrison, *Music in Medieval Britain*, p. 143, which gives the alternative Latin text, 'Perspice Christicolae', written in red ink under the English words. See also Wolfgang Obst, '"Svmer is icumen in"—a contrafactum?' *ML*, 64 (1983), 151.

or f-e-d-e-f-f-e-d-c ('Sumer is icumen in' four times in succession), so that the variation in inner voices is of minimal effect. If it is true that the 'Sumer' rota is quintessential of English thirteenth-century polyphony, that in itself may be sufficient explanation for why it is the only one of its kind.

It is often pointed out that, besides voice exchange and *pes*, many of the ingredients of 'Sumer is icumen in', namely melody, rhythm, and harmony, are present (in some cases abundantly) in the Notre-Dame style from 1200 on. It needs to be added that the impressive increase in size, complexity, and consistency manifest in the English rota are also characteristic of its time: the logical extrapolation from clear foundation to previously unexplored dimensions is characteristic of Gothic art, as apparent in Perotin's organa as in the new Gothic cathedrals in which that music was sung.

Yet 'Sumer' is often linked not to cathedral polyphony but to the form of ingenuous group singing unclearly suggested by Giraldus Cambrensis.[43] Ethnomusicological evidence suggests that an ingenuous part-singing using 'round-song' could appear anywhere at any time, and Giraldus's account may refer to something of the kind in Wales around 1200. It can be imagined as a form of call-and-response in which the leader sang a phrase, then, while the chorus repeated it, sang a different but compatible phrase—compatible at least in having the same short, clear rhythmic shape.[44]

We do not, however, need to choose between ingenuous 'song-canon' and cathedral polyphony as background for the 'Sumer' rota, nor to confuse the two. The cultivated techniques of voice exchange could have developed in Notre-Dame polyphony out of the inner momentum of that style, and then could have found readiness and reinforcement in ingenuous song-canon wherever the two came into contact, as in England. As with the rondeau, where the eventual complex fixation could have had antecedents in both Latin monastic chant and a vernacular call-and-response procedure, several traditions can be imagined to flow together to produce a new form such as the 'Sumer' rota. But we should not project the specific features of the new form backwards, for readiness is not identity. Ingenuous procedures are by nature not recorded; we should not assume we can know what they were like from the cultivated, recorded procedure we assume they resembled.

---

[43] See again Wooldridge, loc. cit., and Hohler, loc. cit.

[44] Walter Wiora, 'Der mittelalterliche Liedkanon', *Kongressbericht der Gesellschaft für Musikforschung, Lüneburg 1950*, p. 71. See also Shai Burstyn, 'Gerald of Wales and the *Sumer* Canon', *Journal of Musicology*, 2 (1983), 135.

ALLELUIA SETTINGS

To return to well-documented forms of English polyphony, and to one much more frequently documented than rota, the English Alleluia settings are the most numerous of English chant settings. In these Alleluia settings, many of the stylistic features encountered so far are combined to produce a kind of piece as charming as 'Sumer is icumen in'. Chant Alleluia production, as we have seen, had continued apace through the eleventh and twelfth centuries into the thirteenth, especially for Marian occasions; Alleluia production may be considered a bridge between that of other Mass Propers, largely completed in the archetype, and the composition of Kyrie, Gloria in excelsis, Sanctus, and Agnus dei, which continued into the thirteenth and fourteenth centuries.

Like most English thirteenth-century polyphony, the Alleluia settings come to us in pitifully fragmented state, and since these Alleluia settings consist of several distinct sections, we cannot always be sure whether a particular instance is complete—or indeed, whether there was a norm for completion. The solo portions were generally set polyphonically:[45] this included the first Alleluia, then the greater part of the verse, the remaining chorus parts being sung in chant. The solo parts were set in discant *a3*, in simplest form using only the text of the chant, and setting one-to-several notes against each note of the melody. (Only Alleluia 'Nativitas' shows the extended organal style of Notre Dame.) Frequently, however, these settings of the Alleluia solo parts were provided with prosulaic text or texts in the upper voices in the Alleluia, or in verse, or in both, as in 'Alme jam ad gaudia—Alme matris dei—Alleluia', verse 'Per te genitrix—Per te O beata—Per te Dei genitrix'.[46] This very distinctive texting makes such pieces look like motets—very different from Notre-Dame Alleluia settings. An equally distinctive feature is a set of tropes (usually a rhyming, scanning distich or polystich with its own independent music) used as introductory polystich to the Alleluia, and sometimes another to the verse.[47] These were set *a3* as a series of voice-exchange sections, over a repeating *pes*, with two refinements, seemingly introduced especially for this kind of piece. Each line of text was sung twice in succession, as usual in voice exchange (the other voice being textless or melismatic), only in this case instead of literal repetition there could be slight

[45] Dittmer, 'An English Discantuum Volumen', pp. 30 ff.
[46] *EMu*, No. 72.
[47] *EMu* Appendix No. 18a; *EMu* No. 70 is the only four-section Alleluia setting it was possible to restore completely.

changes; sometimes the changes were substantial, only the syllable count and the word-form remaining constant.

Ave magnifica Maria
Ave mirifica Maria

Salve salvifica deigera Maria
Ave mundifica puerpera Maria

Ave gratifica mundoque salutifera Maria
Ave glorifica luce corusca supera Maria

Ave Maria

From one section to the next the line-form becomes progressively longer, and this is reflected in the progressively longer phrases in the *pes* (Ex. 222). Here the refinement is that the second phrase is lengthened by motivic expansion of the interior of the first phrase; the third phrase is similarly an expansion of the second. The published examples of this very successful kind of piece are almost all on D-*re* (or G-*re*), not on F-*ut*, and show a very strong sense of locus and concentration on the final. The predominance of D-*re* finals in these Alleluia settings should caution us against overemphasizing the importance of the F-final for English polyphony. Seemingly unique English products, such pieces made an impression abroad so that a version of 'Ave magnifica' was included (as 'Alle psallite') at the end of Montpellier fascicle 8[48]—one of the two English pieces to find their way there.

THE MOTET AROUND 1300

Two motets in the Worcester fragments from the very end of the thirteenth century bring the special features of English polyphony to bear upon the larger design of motets. Both are *a4*, and both relatively long; in length and texture they behave in ways not characteristic of the contemporary continental motet. *WF* 53,[49] 'Candens crescit lilium—Candens lilium columbina—Quartus cantus—Primus pes' has two texted voices, triplum and motetus. The *pes* has numerous rests—more than a usual tenor—and for the most part the *Quartus cantus* simply fills in these rests, so that these two parts together produce one continuous supporting voice (presumably instrumental). Thus the texture mostly sounds *a3*, like a conventional motet. None the less, the combination of two lower untexted voices is characteristic of thirteenth-century English rather than French practice.

WF 53 is built of modules each of four longae. The form created by

---

[48] Codex Montpellier, No. 339.

[49] *EMu* No. 60; sections are labelled as in Dittmer, *Worcester Fragments*, No. 53.

Ex. 222

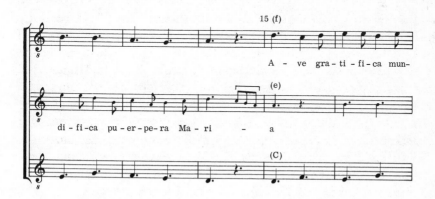

the periodic return of certain of these modules has been variously described, and may be represented as follows, each letter representing a four-bar module with its own rhythmic and contrapuntal content:

$$
\begin{array}{ccc}
 & a & b \\
 & a & c \\
d & e & b \\
d & e & c \\
 & a & b \\
 & a & c \\
f & e & b \\
f & e & c \\
 & a & b \\
 & a & c \\
\end{array}
$$

At the beginning, a b and a c can be construed as a couplet with open and closed endings; but we have to understand these endings as falling in the third bar of their modules, the fourth bar being in each case a link from the cadence to the start of the next module. The whole piece is on D-*re*, the open and closed endings coming on C-*ut* and D-*re*.

Then follows another couplet, d e b and d e c; d e is of course twice as long as a, expanding the length of the first couplet, but preserving the same endings, b and c. The beginning of d is characterized by a move to F-*fa*, and e ends on a-e-*mi*, so the locus of d e as a whole is fresh compared to the first couplet. After this, the music a b a c is repeated en bloc, with different text; this is not the immediate repeat characteristic of rondellus, but is none the less English, not French. As the couplet structure continues in f e b, f e c, the amount of new material is limited to f, and the use of e increases the amount of rounding that links this couplet to the others. Module f begins with the high a, peak of the melodic structure of the piece. It is concluded by another statement of a b a c.

Another large motet from around 1300, *WF* 67,[50] 'Thomas gemma Cantuarie—Thomas cesus in Doveria—*Primus tenor—Secundus tenor*', similarly shows English features in the motet form. The two supporting instrumental parts have many interlocking rests, but sound together more than in 'Candens' to produce a four-voiced texture. The 'Thomas' motet is similarly cast in isometric modules, here of four bars. Each of the thirty modules has roughly the same tonal shape—as if each had been built on or around the same tenor or *pes*; this tenor is never exactly present, but is expressed in ever-varying counterpoint. It can be imagined as /*ut*—/*mi re*/*re*—/*re ut* (on F), with

[50] *EMu* No. 61.

the greatest amount of variation coming in the first of the four bars, which is sometimes *ut re*, sometimes based on *mi* or *sol* consonant with the *ut*. The basic tonal movement is from *ut* to *re*, open at the end of bar 2, then *re* to *ut*, closed at the end of bar 4. (The very first module is anomalous, being all on *ut*; the last is extended one bar.) The cadential movement in bar 4 of the module is very strong, and furthermore very little attempt is made to bridge it over to produce the continuous flow characteristic of the continental motet. Instead, the periodicity of the module is allowed to be very prominent, and emphasis is placed on the variety of melodic, contrapuntal, and textural expression from one statement to the next—or often from one pair of statements to the next, for the statements are sometimes paired in their melodic configurations. At irregular intervals a module is given a hocket-like texture; and other recurring similarities suggest a large-scale design, which, however, is never made definite. This particular lack of definition is perhaps the most motet-like feature of the piece. In other words, it stands somewhere between the rondellus-like repetition of the 'Sumer' rota, with its much more regular *pes* (*ut re*/ *re ut*), and a motet in continental style, in which the repeats of a tenor melody (when present) are typically obscured by ever-changing counterpoint.

The relationships between English polyphony and Notre-Dame style on one hand, and the French motet of the fourteenth-century on the other, are complex. In four-voiced texture and regularity of bar groups these English motets may be said to anticipate the fourteenth-century isorhythmic motet in ways that those by Pierre de la Croix do not. And it can also be said that these are among a complex of factors (including long-short rhythms, use of thirds, voice exchange, tonal locus on *ut*) that show a clear, close connection of English polyphony with the grand style of Perotin. Before Perotin, we have not enough information to assign origins to these stylistic features of his work. After Perotin we see them developing differently in French and English polyphony, but we should not be surprised to see them developing in analogous ways or producing similar results.

BIBLIOGRAPHY

Introductory Note

The following Bibliography consists mainly of items cited in the individual chapters. A handful of standard works have also been included, and, because of the unfamiliarity of the literature, the early chapters have been treated more generously. For more comprehensive bibliographies the following publications may be consulted:

HUGHES, ANDREW: *Medieval Music: The Sixth Liberal Art, Toronto Medieval Bibliographies*, 4 (Toronto, 1974; rev. 2nd edn. 1980).

LEVY, KENNETH, and EMERSON, JOHN: 'Plainchant', *New Grove*, xiv (London, 1980), 800–44 [bibliography 832–44, with cross-references to other articles].

SMITH, NORMAN E.: 'Organum and Discant: Bibliography', *New Grove*, xiii (London, 1980), 808–819.

CHAPTER I   CHRISTIAN CHANT IN SYRIA, ARMENIA, EGYPT AND ETHIOPIA

SYRIAN CHANT

(i) *Sources*

HUSMANN, HEINRICH, ed.: *Die melkitische Handschrift Sinai Syr. 261, Göttinger Orientforschungen*, ix/1–2 (Wiesbaden, 1975–6).

Transcriptions of Syrian chants are included in the following studies:

ASHKAR, P. P.: *Mélodies liturgiques syro-maronites* (Jounieh, Lebanon, 1939).

HUSMANN, HEINRICH, ed.: *Die Melodien des chaldäischen Breviers: Commune nach den Traditionen Vorderasiens und der Malabarküste, Orientalia Christiana Analecta*, 178 (Rome, 1967).

—— *Die Melodien der jakobitischen Kirche, I: Die Melodien des Wochenbreviers (Shūmtā), Sitzungsberichte der Österreichische Akademie der Wissenschaft*, Phil.-hist. K1., 262 (1969); *II. Die Qāle gaoānāie des Beit gazā*, Ibid., 273/pt. 4 (1971).

JEANNIN, J. C., PUYADE, J., and CHIBAS-LASSALE, A.: *Mélodies syriennes* (Paris, 1924–8).

PARISOT, JEAN: 'Rapport sur une mission scientifique en Turquie d'Asie', *Nouvelles archives des missions scientifiques et littéraires*, ix (1899), 265–511.

(ii) *Books and Articles*

BAUMSTARK, ANTON: *Festbrevier und Kirchenjahr der syrischen Jakobiten. Studien zur Geschichte und Kultur des Altertums*, iii/3–5 (Paderborn, 1910).

—— *Geschichte der syrischen Literatur* (Bonn, 1922).

CODY, AELRED: 'The Early History of the Octoechos in Syria', *East of Byzantium: Syria and Armenia in the Formative Period* (Washington, DC, Dumbarton Oaks, 1982), 89–113.

DALMAIS, I. H.: 'L'Apport des églises syriennes à l'hymnographie chrétienne', *L'Orient syrien*, 2 (1957), 243–60.

HAGE, LOUIS: 'Le Chant maronite', *Encyclopédie des musiques sacrées*, ii (1969), 218–22.

HANNICK, THEODOSE: 'Syriens occidentaux et Syriens orientaux', J. Porte, ed, *Encyclopédie des musiques sacrées*, ii (1969), 214–17.

HEIMING, ODILO: *Syrische Eniane und griechische Kanones*, (Munich, 1922).

HUSMANN, HEINRICH: 'Syrische (assyrische) Kirchenmusik', *MGG*, xiii (1966), cols. 1–10.

—— 'Die Tonarten der chaldäischen Breviergesänge', *Orientalia Christiana Periodica*, 35 (1969), 215–48.

—— 'Arabische Maqamen in ostsyrischer Kirchenmusik', *Musik als Gestalt und Erlebnis: Festschrift Walter Graf* (*Wiener Musikwissenschaftliche Beiträge*, 9) (Vienna, 1970), 102–8.

—— 'Hymnus und Troparion', *Jahrbuch des Staatlichen Instituts für Musikforschung, Preussischer Kulturbesitz* (Berlin, 1971), 7–86.

—— 'Die antiphonale Chorpraxis der syrischen Hymnen nach den Berliner und Pariser Handschriften', *Ostkirchliche Studien*, 21 (1972), 281–97.

—— 'Die Gesänge der melkitischen Liturgie', 'Die Gesänge der syrischen Liturgien', 'Die ostkirchlichen Liturgien und ihre Kultmusik', in K. G. Fellerer, ed., *Geschichte der katholischen Kirchenmusik*, i (Kassel, 1972), 160, 69–98, 57–68.

—— 'Die syrischen Auferstehungskanones und ihre griechischen Vorlagen', *Orientalia Christiana Periodica*, 38 (1972), 209–42.

—— 'Eine Konkordanztabelle syrischer Kirchentöne und arabischer Maqamen in einem syrischen Musiknotizbuch', *Orientalia Christiana Analecta* (*Symposium syriacum 1972*), 197 (Rome, 1974), 371–85.

—— 'Ein syrisches Sticherarion mit paläobyzantinischer Notation (Sinai, Syr. 261)', *Hamburger Jahrbuch für Musikwissenschaft*, i (1974), 9–57.

—— 'Die melkitische Liturgie als Quelle der syrischen Qanune iaonaie', *Orientalia Christiana Periodica*, 41 (1975), 5–56.

—— 'Die syrischen Handschriften des Sinai-Klosters, Herkunft und Schreiber', *Ostkirchliche Studien*, 24 (1975), 281–308.

—— 'Eine alte orientalische christliche Liturgie: altsyrisch-melkitisch', *Orientalia Christiana Periodica*, 42 (1976), 156–96.

—— 'Madrase und Seblata: Repertoire-Untersuchungen zu den Hymnen Ephraems des Syrers', *AcM*, 48 (1976), 113–50.

—— 'Syrischer und byzantinischer Oktoechos, Kanones und Qanune', *Orientalia Christiana Periodica*, 44 (1978), 65–73.

—— 'Zur syrischer Neumenschrift', *Erkenntnisse und Meinungen*, ii = *Göttinger Orientforschungen*, i. Reihe: *Syriaca*, 17 (1978), 191–222.

—— 'Syrian Church Music', *New Grove*, xviii. 472–81.

IDELSOHN, A. Z.: 'Der Kirchengesang der Jakobiten', *AMw*, 4 (1922), 364–89.

JEANNIN, DOM. J.: 'Le Chant liturgique syrien', *Journal asiatique* (Sept.–Oct. 1912), 295–363; (Nov.–Dec. 1912), 299–448.

—— and PUYADE, J.: 'L'Octoechos syrien: 'Étude historique, étude musicale', *Oriens Christianus*, NS, 3 (1913), 82–103, 227–98.

LERCHUNDI, G.: 'Notation musicale syrienne', *L'Orient syrien*, 4 (1959), 114–18.

MACOMBER, WILLIAM F., SJ: 'A Theory on the Origins of the Syrian, Maronite and Chaldean Rites', *Orientalia Christiana Periodica*, 39 (1973), 235–42.

MATEOS, JUAN: *Lelya-Sapra: Essai d'interprétation des matines chaldéennes*, *Orientalia Christiana Analecta*, 166 (Rome, 1959).

PUYADE, J.: 'Composition interne de l'office divin syrien', *L'Orient Syrien*, 2 (1957), 77–92 and 3 (1958), 25–62.

RAASTED, JØRGEN: *'Musical Notation and Quasi Notation in Syro-Melkite Liturgical Manuscripts*, *Cahiers de l'Institut du moyen âge grec et latin*, 31 (University of Copenhagen, 1979), 11–37, 53–77.

VÖOBUS, ARTHUR: *History of the School of Nisibis, Corpus Scriptorum Christianorum Orientalium*, 266 [= Subsidia, 26] (Louvain, 1965).

—— *Handschriftliche Überlieferung der Memre-Dichtung des Ja'qob von Serug, Corpus Scriptorum Christianorum Orientalium*, 344 [= Subsidia, 39] (Louvain, 1973).

ARMENIAN CHANT

(i) *Sources*

The most important of recent editions of Armenian chant is that by Léonce Dayan (1864–1962), *Les Hymnes de l'eglise arménienne*, published by the Mekhitarist congregation in Venice (a series of now more than ten vols., starting after 1950).

(ii) *Books and Articles*

ABEGHIAN, MANUK: *Istoriya drevnearmyanskoi literatury* (2nd rev. edn., Yerevan, 1975). [In Russian.]

ATAJAN, ROBERT ARSHAKOVICH: *Armenian khaz notation* (Yerevan, 1959). [In Armenian.]

—— 'Armenische Chazen', *Beiträge zur Musikwissenschaft*, 10 (1968), 65–82.

—— 'O systemach ormiańskiej notacji', *Muzyka* (Warsaw), 13 (1968), 49–62.

—— 'Les chants des maîtres arméniens du Moyen Âge', *Musica Antiqua* ii (Bydgoszcz, 1969), 321–41.

—— 'Die armenische professionelle Liederkunst des Mittelalters', *Revue des études arméniennes*, 7 (1970), 241–66.

—— 'Armyanskaya muzyka', 'Armyanskaya notopis', Yu. V. Keldysh, ed., *Muzykalnaya entsiklopediya*, i (Moscow, 1973), cols. 209–18, 218–20.

—— 'Nerses Shnorhali i nekotorye voprosy ego muzykalnogo tvorchestva', *Musica Antiqua*, iv (Bydgoszcz, 1975), 421–37.

—— 'Ambartsum Limondzhian i ego notopis', *Musica Antiqua*, v (Bydgoszcz, 1978), 493–511.

—— 'Ob izuchenii mugamov v Armenii', *Makomy, Mugamy i sovremennoe kompozitorskoe tvorchestvo, konferentsiya, Tashkent, 1975* (Tashkent, 1978), 20–32.

—— 'The "tagh" as the Bearer of Humane Principles in 10–12th Century Armenian Monodic Music', *II. International Symposium on Armenian Art* (Erevan, 1978).

BOYADJIAN, GERARD: 'Le Chant arménien', *Encyclopédie des musiques sacrées*, ii (1969), 223–8.

CONYBEARE, F. C.: *Rituale Armenorum* (Oxford, 1905).

DAYAN, LÉONCE: 'Armenische Kirchenmusik', *Lexikon für Theologie und Kirche*, 2nd edn., i (1957), cols. 873–4.

DER NERSESSIAN, SIRARPIE: *The Armenians* (New York, 1970); vol. 68 in the series 'Ancient Peoples and Places'.

EMIN, N.: *Sharakan, bogosluzhebnye kanony i piesni armyanskoi vostochnoi tserkvi* (2nd edn., Moscow, 1914).

HANNICK, CHRISTIAN: 'Armenian rite, music of the', *New Grove*, i. 596–9.

HAUSHERR, I.: 'Arménienne (spiritualité)', *Dictionnaire du spiritualité*, 1 (1937), cols. 862–6.

HICKMAN, HANS: 'Armenische Musik', *MGG*, i (1949–51) cols. 653–5.

HUSMANN, HEINRICH: 'Die Gesänge der armenischen Liturgie', K. G. Fellerer, ed., *Geschichte der katholischen Kirchenmusik*, i (Kassel, 1972), 99–108.

KUSHNAREV, KH.: *Voprosi istorii i teorii armyanskoi monodicheskoi muzyki* (Leningrad, 1958).

ORMANIAN, MALACHIA: *The Church of Armenia* (London, 1912).

OUTTIER, BERNARD: 'Recherches sur la genèse de l'octoëchos arménien', *Eg*, 14 (1973), 127–211.

SARAFIAN, KRIKOR, A.: *The Armenian Apostolic Church: Her Ceremonies, Sacraments, Main Feasts and Prominent Saints* (Fresno, California, 1959). [Textbook for Sunday schools of the California Diocese of the Armenian churches.]

T'AHMIZYAN, NIKOGOS KIRAKOSOVICH: 'Les Anciens Manuscrits musicaux arméniens et les questions rélatives à leur déchiffrement', *Revue des études arméniennes*, NS, (1970), 267–80.

—— 'Monodische Denkmäler Alt-Armeniens, Die Tradition der armenischen Psalmodie', *Beiträge zur Musikwissenschaft*, 12 (1970), 29–59.

—— *Teoriya muzyki v drevnei Armenii* (Erevan, 1977). [With full bibliography.]

—— 'Zwiazki muzyki ormianskiej i bizantyjskiej we wczesnym sredniowieczu', *Muzyka* (Warsaw), 22 (1977), 3–12. [p. 13 has an English summary!]

—— 'Ob izuchenii metodov improvizatsii v professionalnom muzykalnom iskusstve ustnoi traditsii Vostoka', in *Makomy, Mugamy i sovremennoe kompozitorskoe tvorchestvo, konferentsiya, Tashkent, 1975* (Tashkent, 1978), 71–86.

COPTIC CHANT

(i) Source

O'LEARY, DE L.: *The Difnar (Antiphonarium) of the Coptic Church* (London, 1926–30).

(ii) Books and Articles

BORSAI, ILONA: 'À la recherche de l'ancienne musique pharaonique', *Cahiers d'histoire égyptienne*, 11 (1969), 25–42.

—— 'Caractéristiques générales du chant de la messe copte', *Studia Orientalia Christiana Collectanea*, 14 (1970–1), 415–42.

—— 'Un Type mélodique particulier des hymnes coptes du mois de Kiahk', *Studia musicologica*, 13 (1971), 73–85.

—— 'Le Tropaire byzantin "O Monogenes" dans la pratique du chant copte', *Studia musicologica*, 14 (1972), 329–54.

—— 'Y a-t-il un "octoechos" dans le système du chant copte?', *Studia Aegyptiaca*, i (= *Festschrift V. Wessetzky*), (Budapest, 1974), 39–53.

—— 'Deux chants caractéristiques de la Semaine Sainte copte', *Studies in Eastern Chant*, 4 (1979), 5–27.

—— 'Coptic rite, music of the', *New Grove*, iv. 730–4.

—— and TOTH, M.: 'Variations ornementales dans l'interprétation d'un hymne copte', *Studia musicologica*, 11 (1969), 91–105.

BROGI, MARCO, OFM, *La santa salmodia annuale della chiesa copta* (Cairo, 1962).

BURMESTER, OSWALD, H. E.: *The Egyptian or Coptic Church: A Detailed Description of her Liturgical Services and the Rites and Ceremonies Observed in the Administration of her Sacraments* (Cairo, 1967).

CRAMER, MARIA: 'Zum Aufbau der koptischen Theotokie und des Difnars. Bemerkungen zur Hymnologie', Peter Nagel, ed., *Probleme der koptischen Literatur*, i (Wissenschaftliche Beiträge d. Martin-Luther Universität, Halle-Wittenberg, 1968), 197–223.

GILLESPIE, JOHN: 'The Egyptian Copts and Their Music', *Church Music*, 1 (1971), 18–28.

GRAF, GEORG, ed. and trans.: 'Der kirchliche Gesang nach Abu Ishaq Al-Mu'Taman Ibn Al-'Assal', *Bulletin de la société d'archéologie copte*, 13 (1948–9), 161–78.

GUILLAUMONT, ANTOINE: 'Copte /littérature spirituelle', *Dictionnaire du spiritualité*, ii (1952/53), cols. 2266–78.

HAMMERSCHMIDT, ERNST: 'Some Remarks on the History of, and Present State of Investigation into the Coptic Liturgy', *Bulletin de la société d'archéologie copte*, 19 (1967–8), 89–113.

HICKMANN, HANS: 'Observations sur les survivances de la chironomie égyptienne dans le chant liturgique copte', *Annales du Service des antiquités de l'Égypte*, 49 (1949), 417–27.

—— 'Koptische Musik', *Koptische Kunst: Ausstellungkatalog Villa Hügel* (Essen, 1963), 116–21.

MALAK, HANNA: 'Les Livres liturgiques de l'église copte', *Mélanges Eugène Tisserant*, iii (= Studi e Testi, 223, Vatican City, 1964), 1–35.

MENARD, RENÉ: 'La Musique copte, problème insoluble?' *Les cahiers coptes*, 1 (1952), 35–40.

—— 'Notation et transcription de la musique copte', *Les cahiers coptes*, 3 (1953), 34–44.

—— 'Notes sur la mémorization et l'improvisation dans le chant copte', *Eg*, 3 (1959), 135–43.

—— 'Die Gesänge der ägyptischen Liturgien', in K. G. Fellerer, ed., *Geschichte der katholischen Kirchenmusik* (Kassel, 1972), 109–27.

MOFTAH, RAGHEB: 'The Coptic Music', *Bulletin de l'Institut des études coptes* (1958), 42–53.

NABIL, KAMAL BUTROS: 'Coptic Music and its Relation to Pharaonic Music' (summary of a MA thesis), *Enchoria*, 8 (1978), 67*(113)–69*(115).

NEWLAND SMITH, E.: *The Ancient Music of the Coptic Church* (London, 1931).

QUECKE, H.: *Untersuchungen zum koptischen Stundengebet* (Louvain, 1970).

REMONDON, ROGER: 'Égypte chrétienne', *Dictionnaire de spiritualité*, iv (1960), cols. 532–48.

VIAUD, GÉRARD: *La Liturgie des coptes d'égypte* (Paris, 1978).

VILLOTEAU, G. A.: *Description de l'Égypte: état moderne; De l'état actuel de l'art musical en Égypte* (Paris, 1812), 134–77.

YASSA, 'ABD AL-MAS&H: 'Remarks on the Psalis of the Coptic Church', *Bulletin de l'Institut des études coptes* (1958), 85–100.

—— and RONCAGLIA, MARTINIAN: 'Introduction to the Faith and Practices of the Coptic Church', *Klio*, 49 (1967), 359–78.

ETHIOPIAN CHANT

(i) *Sources*

No collection of transcriptions for the Ethiopian tradition is available. See, however, the publications of Bernard Velat under 'Books and Articles'.

(ii) *Books and Articles*

COHEN, MARCEL: 'Sur la notation éthiopienne', *Studi orientalistici in onore di Giorgio Levi della Vida*, i (Rome, 1956), 199–206.

CONTI ROSSINI, C., ed.: *Vitae Sanctorum Antiquiorum: I. Acta Yared et Pantalewon. Corpus Scriptorum Christianorum Orientalium, Scriptores Aethiopici*, 2nd Ser., xvii (Paris, 1904).

DERAY, A.: 'Le Chant liturgique en Éthiopie', *Revue du chant grégorien*, 40 (1936), 134–7, 182–5.

FÉTIS, F.-J.: *Histoire générale de la musique*, iv (Paris, 1874), 101–16.

GUIDI, I.: 'La chiesa di Etiopia', *Enciclopedia Italiana*, xiv (1932), 480–5.

HANNICK, CHRISTIAN: 'Ethiopian rite, music of the', *New Grove*, vi. 272–5.

HERSCHER-CLEMENT, J.: 'Chants d'Abyssinie', *Zeitschrift für vergleichende Musikwissenschaft*, 2 (1934), 51–7 & 24*–38* [examples].

HEYER, FRIEDRICH: *Die Kirche Äthiopiens* (Berlin and New York, 1971).

HICKMAN, HANS: 'Äthiopische Musik', *MGG*, i (1949–51), cols. 105–12.

KEBEDE, ASHENAFI: *Éthiopie, musique de l'église copte* (Publication de l'institut international d'études comparative de la musique; Berlin, 1969).

—— 'The Music of Ethiopia: Its Development and Cultural Setting', (Ph.D. diss., Wesleyan University, 1971; University Microfilms, 71–27, 875).

LEPISA, ABBA TITO: 'The Three Modes and the Signs of the Songs in the Ethiopian Liturgy', *Proceedings of the Third International Conference of Ethiopian Studies*, ii (Addis Ababa, 1970), 162–87.

LITTMANN, E.: 'Geschichte der äthiopischen Literatur', C. Brockelmann, ed., *Geschichte der christlichen Literaturen des Orients* (2nd edn., Leipzig, 1909).

—— *Semitistik*, Handbuch der Orientalistik, Abteilung 1: Der Nahe und der Mittlere Osten, Bd. III (Leiden/Cologne, 1964), 375 ff.

—— Äthiopien' in *Religion in Geschichte und Gegenwart*, i (3rd edn., 1957), cols. 137–44.

MONDON-VIDAILHET, M.: 'La Musique éthiopienne', A. Lavignac and A. de la Laurencie, eds., *Encyclopédie de la musique*, pt. 1, vol. v (1922), cols. 3179–6.

PICKEN, L.: 'A Note on Ethiopian Church Music', *AcM*, 29 (1957), 41–2.

POWNE, MICHAEL: *Ethiopian Music: An Introduction* (London, 1968).

SAROSI, BALINT: 'The Music of Ethiopian Peoples', *Studia musicologica*, 9 (1967), 9–20.

—— 'Melodic Patterns in the Folk Music of the Ethiopian Peoples', *Proceedings of the Third International Conference of Ethiopian Studies*, ii (Addis Ababa, 1970), 280–7.

SHELEMAY, KAY K.: 'The Liturgical Music of the Falasha in Ethiopia' (Ph.D. diss., University of Michigan, 1977; University Microfilms, 77–20, 539).

ULLENDORFF, EDWARD: *Ethiopia and the Bible* (London, 1968).

VELAT, BERNARD: 'Hymnes eucharistiques éthiopiennes', *Rythmes du Monde*, 27ᵉ année (1953) [NS vol. 1], 26–36.

—— 'Les Dabtara éthiopiens', *Les cahiers coptes*, 5 (1954), 21–9.

—— 'Éthiopie', *Dictionnaire du spiritualité*, iv (1961), cols. 1453–77.

—— 'Le Mawāšè' et et les livres de chant liturgiques éthiopiens', *Mémorial du cinquantenaire de l'école des langues orientales de l'institut catholique de Paris, 1914–1964*, Travaux de l'institut catholique de Paris, 10 (Paris, 1965), 159–70.

—— *Études sur le Me'eraf, Commun de l'office divin éthiopien* [Introduction, French translation, with liturgical and musical commentary, *Patrologia Orientalis*, 33 (Paris, 1966)].

—— ed.: *Me'eraf, Commun de l'office divin éthiopien pour toute l'année*, (Paris, 1966). [Ethiopian text.]

—— Ṣoma deggū̄a, *antiphonaire du Carême, Quatre premières semaines* [Ethiopian text and translation with commentaries *Patrologia Orientalis*, 32 (1966 and 1969)].

—— 'Musique liturgiques d'Éthiopie', J. Porte, ed., *Encyclopédie des musiques sacrées*, ii (Paris, 1969), 234–8.

VILLOTEAU, M.: 'De la musique éthiopienne', C. L. F. Pancoucke, *Description de l'Égypte*, xiv (2nd edn., Paris, 1836), 270–99.

WELLESZ, EGON, 'Studien zur äthiopischen kirchenmusik', *Oriens Christianus*, NS, 9 (1920), 74–107; see also addendum by S. Euringer, ibid., 10–11 (1923), 151–4.

—— 'Die Kirchenmusik der Kopten und Äthioper', Guido Adler, ed., *Handbuch der Musikgeschichte* (2nd edn., Berlin, 1930), 138–9.

CHAPTER II BYZANTINE CHANT

(i) *Sources*

CONOMOS, DIMITRI: *The Late Byzantine and Slavonic Communion Cycle: Liturgy and Music*, Dumbarton Oaks Studies, 21 (1985).

TOULIATOS-BANKER, DIANE: *The Byzantine Amomos Chant of the Fourteenth and Fifteenth Centuries*, Analecta Vlatadon, 46 (Thessaloniki, 1984).

WELLESZ, EGON: *Trésor de musique byzantine* (Paris, 1934).

—— *Die Musik der byzantinischen Kirche, Das Musikwerk*, 15 (Cologne, 1959).

Monumenta musicae byzantinae, ed. Carsten Høeg, H. J. W. Tillyard, Egon Wellesz (Copenhagen, Levin, and Munksgaard, 1935–).

1. *Sticherarium: codex vindobonensis theol. graec. 181*, ed. Carsten Høeg, H. J. W. Tillyard, Egon Wellesz (1935).

2. *Hirmologium Athoum: codex Monasterii Hiberorum 470*, ed. Carsten Høeg (1938).

3. *Hirmologium Cryptense: Codex cryptensis E.g.II*, ed. Laurentius Tardo (1951).

4. *Contacarium Ashburnhamense: Codex Bibl. Laurentianae Ashburnhamensis 64*, ed. Carsten Høeg (1956).

5. *Fragmenta Chiliandarica Palaeoslavica*, ed. Roman Jakobson (1957).

6. *Contacarium Palaeoslavicum Mosquense*, ed. Arne Bugge (1960).

7. *Specimina notationum antiquiorum*, ed. Oliver Strunk (1966).

8. *Hirmologicum Sabbaiticum: codex Monasterii S. Sabbae 83*, ed. Jørgen Raasted (1968–70).

9. *Triodium Athoum: codex Monasterii Vatopedii 1488*, ed. Enrica Follieri and Oliver Strunk (1975).

Lectionaria

1. *Prophetologium*, ed. Carsten Høeg and Gunther Zuntz (1939).

Subsidia

1. (i) TILLYARD, H. J. W.: *Handbook of the Middle Byzantine Musical Notation* (1935).
   (ii) HØEG, CARSTEN: *La Notation ekphonétique* (1935).
3. PALIKAROVA VERDEIL, R.: *La Musique byzantine chez les Bulgares et les Russes (du IXe au XIVe siècles)* (1953).
4. VELIMIROVIĆ, MILOŠ: *Byzantine Elements in Early Slavic Chant: The Hirmologion* (1960).
6. HANNICK, CHRISTIAN, ed.: *Fundamental Problems of Early Slavic Music and Poetry* (1978).
7. RAASTED, JØRGEN: *Intonation Formulas and Modal Signatures in Byzantine Musical Manuscripts* (1966).
8. THODBERG, CHRISTIAN: *Der byzantinische Alleluiarionzyklus: Studien im kurzen psaltikonstil* (1966).

Transcripta

1.   *Die Hymnen des Sticherarium für September*, ed. Egon Wellesz (1936).
2.   *The Hymns of the Sticherarium for November*, ed. H. J. W. Tillyard (1938).
3., 5. *The Hymns of the Octoechus*, ed. H. J. W. Tillyard (1940 and 1949).
4.   *Twenty Canons from the Trinity Hirmologium*, ed. H. J. W. Tillyard (1952).
6., 8. *The Hymns of the Hirmologium*, ed. Aglaia Ayoutanti and Maria Stohr (1952 and 1956).
7.   *The Hymns of the Pentecostarium*, ed. H. J. W. Tillyard (1960).
9.   *The Akathistos Hymn*, ed. Egon Wellesz (1957).

(ii) *Books and Articles*

There is an extremely large bibliography on Byzantine music. A useful survey of most significant studies is available in *New Grove*, iii. 563–6. Only a selective listing of seminal works and basic literature, with more recent publications, is presented here.

AMARGIANAKIS, GEORGE: *An Analysis of Stichera in the Deuteros Modes,* in *Cahiers de l'Institut du moyen âge grec et latin*, 22–3 (University of Copenhagen, 1977).
BAUMSTARK, A.: *Comparative Liturgy* (rev. edn. by B. Botte; Eng. edn. by F. L. Cross, Westminster, Maryland, 1958).

BECK, H. G.: *Kirche und theologische Literatur im byzantinischen Reich* (Munich, 1959).

CONOMOS, DIMITRI: *Byzantine Trisagia and Cheroubika in the Fourteenth and Fifteenth Centuries* (Thessaloniki, 1974).

—— 'Communion Chants in Magna Graecia', *JAMS*, 38 (1980), 241–63.

FLOROS, C.: *Universale Neumenkunde* (Kassel, 1970).

FOLLIERI, E.: *Initia Hymnorum ecclesiae graecae* (Rome, 1960–6).

GROSDIDIER DE MATONS, JOSÉ: *Romanos le Mélode et les origines de la poésie réligieuse à Byzance* (Paris, 1977).

HAAS, MAX: 'Byzantinische und slavische Notationen', Wulf Arlt, ed., *Palaeographie der Musik*, I/2 (Cologne, 1973).

HANNICK, CHRISTIAN: 'Die Lehrschriften der klassisch-byzantinischen Musik', 'Die Lehrschriften zur byzantinischen Kirchenmusik', *Die hochsprachliche profane Literatur der Byzantiner*, ii (= *Byzantinisches Handbuch*, V/2, ed. H. Hunger, Munich, 1978), 183–218.

HUSMANN, HEINRICH: 'Die oktomodalen Stichera und die Entwicklung des byzantinischen Oktoechos', *AMw*, 27 (1970), 304–25.

—— 'Modulation and Transposition in den bi- und trimodalen Stichera', *AMw*, 27 (1970), 1–22.

—— 'Hymnus und Troparion. Studien zur Geschichte der musikalischen Gattungen von Horologion und Tropologion', *Jahrbuch des Staatlichen Instituts für Musikforschung, Preussischer Kulturbesitz* (Berlin, 1971), 7–86.

—— 'Modalitätsprobleme des psaltischen Stils', *AMw*, 28 (1971), 44–72.

—— 'Strophenbau und Kontrafakturtechnik der Stichera', *AMw*, 29 (1972), 150–61, 213–33.

—— 'Der Aufbau der byzantinischen Liturgie nach der Erzählung von der Reise des Äbte Johannes und Sophronios zum Einsiedler Nilos auf dem Berge Sinai', Heinrich Hüschen, ed., *Musicae Scientiae Collectanea: Festschrift Karl Gustav Fellerer* (Cologne, 1973), 243–9.

—— 'Kolorierung in byzantinischer und orientalischer Musik', Heinrich Hüschen and Dietz-Rüdiger Maser, eds., *Convivium Musicorum: Festschrift Wolfgang Boetticher* (Berlin, 1974), 141–50.

—— 'Syrischer und byzantinischer Oktoechos, Kanones und Qanune', *Orientalia Christiana Periodica*, 44 (1978), 65–73.

JAMMERS, EWALD: 'Byzanz und die abendländische Musik', *Reallexikon der Byzantinistik*. ser. A, vol. i, bk. 3 (Amsterdam, 1969), cols. 169–227.

LEVY, KENNETH: 'The Byzantine Sanctus and its Modal Tradition in East and West', *Annales musicologiques*, 6 (1958–63), 7–67.

—— 'A Hymn for Thursday in Holy Week', *JAMS*, 16 (1963), 127–75.

—— 'Byzantine rite, music of the', *New Grove*, iii. 553–66.

MOTHER MARY and WARE, ARCHIMANDRITE KALLISTOS: *The Festal Menaion* (London, 1969).

MATEOS, JUAN: *Le Typicon de la grande église. Orientalia Christiana Analecta*, 165/166 (Rome, 1962).

MORAN, NEIL K.: *Singers in Late Byzantine and Slavonic Painting, Byzantina Neerlandica*, 9 (1986).

RAASTED, JORGEN: *Intonation Formulas and Modal Signatures in Byzantine Musical Manuscripts, Monumenta musicae byzantinae*, Subsidia, 7 (1966).

RICHTER, LUKAS: 'Antike Überlieferungen in der byzantinischen Musiktheorie', *Deutsches Jahrbuch der Musikwissenschaft*, 6 (1961), 75–115.

SCHMIDT, HANS: *Zum formelhaften Aufbau byzantinischer Kanones* (Wiesbaden, 1979).

STRUNK, OLIVER: *Essays on Music in the Byzantine world* (New York, 1977). [= republication of 22 studies on Byzantine Chant published 1942–72].

SZÖVERFFY, JOSEPH: *A Guide to Byzantine Hymnography: A Classified Bibliography of Texts and Studies*, i (Brookline, Mass., and Leiden, 1978).

TAFT, ROBERT, SJ: *The Great Entrance, Orientalia Christiana Analecta* 200 (Rome, 1975).

THODBERG, CHRISTIAN: *Der byzantinische Alleluiarionzyklus: Studien im kurzen psaltikonstil, Monumenta musicae byzantinae*, Subsidia, 8 (Copenhagen, 1966).

TILLYARD, H. J. W.: *Byzantine Music and Hymnography* (London, 1923).

VELIMIROVIĆ, MILOŠ: 'The Byzantine Heirmos and Heirmologion', Wulf Arlt, *et al.*, eds., *Gattungen der Musik in Einzeldarstellungen: Gedenkschrift Leo Schrade* i (Berne, 1973), 192–242.

WELLESZ, EGON: *A History of Byzantine Music and Hymnography* (3rd edn., Oxford, 1963).

WILLIAMS, EDWARD V.: 'John Koukouzeles' Reform of Byzantine Chanting for Great Vespers in the Fourteenth Century' (Ph.D. diss., Yale University, 1968).

RUSSIAN CHANT

(i) *Sources*

BUGGE, ANNE, ed.: *Contacarium Palaeoslavicum Mosquense, Monumenta musicae byzantinae*, 6 (Copenhagen, 1960).

DOSTAL, A., ROTHE H., with TRAPP, E., eds.: *Der altrussische Kondakar'— Blagověšč enskij Kondakar'*, *Facsimileausgabe, Bausteine zur Geschichte der Literatur bei den Slawen*, edn. 3, bk. 8,2 (Giessen, 1976).

JAKOBSON, ROMAN, ed.: *Fragmenta Chiliandarica Palaeoslavica, Monumenta musicae byzantinae*, 5a 'Sticherarium', 5b 'Hirmologium' (Copenhagen, 1957).

METALLOV, V. M.: *Russkaia simiografiya* (Moscow, 1912). [A paleographical atlas with 115 plates of which more than 80 are illustrations from medieval musical manuscripts.]

SMOLENSKIJ, S. V.: *Paläographischer Atlas der altrussischen linienlosen Gesangsnotationen*; ed. J. v. Gardner, Bayerische Akademie der Wissenschaften, Phil.-Hist. Kl., Abhandlungen, N.F., vol. 80 (Munich,

1976). [Although originally prepared and lithographed in 1885, this volume was actually never published; a copy passed on through several hands, and it is finally available for general public. As an 'atlas' it contains samples of notation, traced through tracing paper, with rather limited number of medieval sources, most of which are of somewhat later date.]

(ii) *Books and Articles*

BELAYEV, V.: *Drevnerusskaya muzykalnaya pismennost* (Moscow, 1962).

BELONENKO, A. S., ed.: *Problemy istorii i teorii drevnerusskoi muzyki* (Leningrad, 1979/1980). [Memorial volume dedicated to the late M. V. Brazhnikov, with posthumous publication of a study by Brazhnikov and studies by the editor and S. V. Frolov, B. A. Shindin, A. N. Kruchinina, A. V. Konotop, and N. S. Seregina.]

BRAZHNIKOV, N. V.: *Puti razvitiya i zadachi rasshifrovki znamennogo rospeva XII–XVIII vekov: primeneniye nekotorikh statisticheskikh metodov k issledovaniyu muzykalnikh yavlenii* (Leningrad, 1949).

—— 'Russkoe tserkovnoe penie XII–XVIII vekov,' *Musica antiqua Europae orientalis, i, Bydgoszcz, 1966* (Warsaw, 1966), 455–69.

—— *Drevnerusskaya teoriya muzyki* (Leningrad, 1972).

—— *Staty o drevnerusskoi muzyke* (Leningrad, 1975). [Posthumous reprint of seven articles.]

FLOROS, C.: 'Die Entzifferung der Kondakarien-Notation', *Musik des Ostens*, 3 (1965), 7–71; 4 (1967), 12–44.

—— *Universale Neumenkunde*, 3 vols. (Kassel, 1970).

GARDNER, J. v.: *Das Problem des altrussischen demestischen Kirchengesanges und seiner linienlosen Notation, Slavistische Beiträge*, 25 (Munich, 1967).

—— *System und Wesen des russischen Kirchengesanges* (Wiesbaden, 1976); rearranged Eng. trans., V. Morosan: *Russian Church Singing: I Orthodox Worship and Hymnography* (Crestwood, NY, St Vladimir's Seminary Press, 1980).

HANNICK, CHRISTIAN, ed.: *Fundamental Problems of Early Slavic Music and Poetry, Monumenta musicae byzantinae*, Subsidia, 6 (1978). [Articles by C. Hannick, F. Mareš, A. Bugge, Dj. Sp. Radojičić, M. Velimirović, K. Levy, and A. Gove.]

HØEG, CARSTEN: 'The Oldest Slavonic Tradition of Byzantine Music', *Proceedings of the British Academy*, 39 (1953), 37–66.

KARASTOYANOV, B. P.: 'K voprosu rasshifrovki kryukovykh pevcheskikh rukopisei znamennogo raspeva', *Musica Antiqua*, 4 (Bydgoszcz, 1975), 487–503.

KOSCHMIEDER, E.: *Die ältesten Novgoroder Hirmologien-Fragmente, Abhandlungen der Bayerischen Akademie der Wissenschaften, Phil.-Hist. Kl.*, N.F., 35, 37, 45 (Munich, 1952, 1955, 1958).

LEVY, KENNETH: 'The Slavic Kontakia and their Byzantine Originals', *Queens College Twenty-Fifth Anniversary Festschrift* (New York, 1964), 79–87.

METALLOV, V. M.: *Ocherk istorii pravoslavnogo tserkovnogo peniya v Rossii* (Saratov, 1893; 4th edn. Moscow, 1915).

—— *Bogosluzhebnoe peniye russkoy tserkvi: period domongolskii* (Moscow, 1906; 2nd edn. 1912).

PALIKAROVA VERDEIL, R.: *La Musique byzantine chez les Bulgares et les Russes (du IXe au XIVe siècles)*, Monumenta musicae byzantinae, Subsidia, 3 (1953).

PREOBRAZHENSKII, A. V.: *Kultovaya muzyka v Rossii* (Leningrad, 1924).

RAZUMOVSKY, D. C.: *Tserkovnoe peniye v Rossii*, i–iii (Moscow, 1867–9).

ROGOV, A. I., ed.: *Muzykalnaya estetika Rossii XI–XVIII vekov* (Moscow, 1973).

SEREGINA, N.: 'Muzykalnaya estetika drevnei Rusi (po pamyatnikam filosofskoi mysli)', *Voprosy teorii i estetiki muzyki*, 13 (1974), 58–78.

—— 'O nekotorykh printsipakh organizatsii znamennogo raspeva', *Problemy muzykalnoi nauki*, 4 (Moscow, 1979), 164–86.

STEFANOVIĆ, D.: 'Services for Slavonic Saints in Early Russian Music Manuscripts', *Musica antiqua Europae orientalis,* iv (Bydgoszcz, 1975), 211–17.

USPENSKY, N. D.: *Drevnerusskoye pevcheskoe iskusstvo* (Moscow, 1965; 2nd edn., 1971).

—— *Obraztsi drevnerusskogo pevcheskogo iskusstva* (Leningrad, 1968; 2nd expanded edn., 1971).

VELIMIROVIĆ, MILOS : *Byzantine Elements in Early Slavic Chant: The Hirmologion, Monumenta musicae byzantinae*, Subsidia, 4 (1960).

—— 'Struktura staroslovenskih muzičkih irmologa', *Hilandarski zbornik*, i (Belgrade, 1966), 139–61.

—— 'Russian and Slavonic Church Music', *New Grove*, xvi. 337–46.

VLADYSHEVSKAYA, T.: 'Tipografsky Ustav kak istochnik dlya izucheniya drevneishikh form russkogo pevcheskogo iskusstva', *Musica Antiqua*, 4 (Bydgoszcz, 1975), 607–20.

—— 'K voprosu ob izuchenii traditsii drevnerusskogo pevcheskogo iskusstva', *Iz istorii russkoi i sovetskoi muzyki*, ii (Moscow, 1976), 40–61.

—— 'K voprosu o svyazi narodnogo i professionalnogo drevnerusskogo pevcheskogo iskusstva', *Muzykalnaya folkloristika*, ii (Moscow, 1978).

CHAPTER III   LATIN CHANT OUTSIDE THE ROMAN TRADITION

BENEVENTAN CHANT

(i) *Sources*

AVERY, M.: *The Exultet Rolls of South Italy* (Princeton, 1966).

GAMBER, K.: *Codices liturgici latini antiquiores* (2nd edn., Freiburg Schweiz, 1968), 238–58.

HUGLO, MICHEL: 'Liste complémentaire de manuscrits bénéventains', *Scriptorium*, 18 (1964), 89–91.

LOEW, E. A.: *The Beneventan Script* (Oxford, 1914).

—— 'A New List of Beneventan Manuscripts', *Collectanea vaticana* ... *Albareda*, ii (*Studi e testi*, 220), (Rome, 1962), 211–44.

Paléographie musicale, vol. 14: *Le codex 10673 de la Bibliothèque vaticane fonds latin (XIᵉ siècle): graduel bénéventain* (1931).

—— vol. 15: *Le codex VI.34 de la Bibliothèque capitulaire de Bénévent (XIe–XIIe siècle): graduel de Bénévent avec prosaire et tropaire* (1937).

REHLE, S.: *Missale Beneventanum von Canosa*, in K. Gamber, ed., *Textus patristici et liturgici*, 9 (Ratisbon, 1972).

(ii) *Books and Articles*

ANDOYER, RAPHAEL: 'L'Ancienne Liturgie de Bénévent', *Revue du chant grégorien*, 20–4 (1911–21) [articles spread over 21 issues].

BAILEY, TERENCE: 'Ambrosian Chant in Southern Italy', *Journal of the Plainsong & Mediæval Music Society*, 6 (1983), 1–7.

BAROFFIO, B.: 'Liturgie im beneventanischen Raum', K. G. Fellerer, ed., *Geschichte der katholischen Kirchenmusik*, i (Kassel, 1972), 204–8.

—— 'Benevent', *MGG*, xv (1973), cols. 653–6.

—— 'Le origini del canto liturgico nella chiesa latina e la formazione dei repertori italici', *Renovatio*, 1 (1978), 26–52.

BOE, J.: 'A New Source for Old Beneventan Chant: The Santa Sophia Maundy in MS Ottoboni lat. 145', *AcM*, 52 (1980), 122–8.

BRUNNER, L.: 'A Perspective of the Southern Italian Sequence: The Second Tonary of the Ms. Monte Cassino 318', *Early Music History*, 1 (1981), 117–64.

HESBERT, RENÉ-JEAN: 'Les Dimanches du Carême dans les manuscrits romano-bénéventains', *Ephemerides liturgicae*, 48 (1934), 198–222.

—— 'L'Antiphonale missarum de l'ancien rit bénéventain', *Ephemerides liturgicae*, 52–3 (1938–9), 28–66, 141–58, 168–90, and vols. 59–61 (1945–7), 69–95, 103–41, 153–210.

—— 'Un Antique Offertoire de la Pentecôte', *Organicae voces: Festschrift J. Smits van Waesberghe* (Amsterdam, 1963), 59–69.

HUGLO, MICHEL: 'Relations musicales entre Byzance et l'Occident', *Proceedings of the Thirteenth International Congress of Byzantine Studies, Oxford, 1966*, 266–80.

KELLY, THOMAS F.: 'Montecassino and the Old Beneventan Chant', *Early Music History*, 5 (1985), 53–83.

KING, A. A.: *Liturgies of the Past* (Milwaukee, 1958), 52–76.

LEVY, KENNETH: 'Lux de luce: The Origin of an Italian Sequence', *MQ*, 57 (1971), 40–61.

SCHLAGER, K.: *Thematischer Katalog der ältesten Alleluia-Melodien* (Munich, 1965).

—— *Alleluia-Melodien I, bis 1100, Monumenta monodica medii aevi*, 7 (Kassel, 1968).

—— 'Beneventan rite, music of the', *New Grove*, ii. 482–4.

STÄBLEIN, BRUNO: *Schriftbild der einstimmigen Musik, Musikgeschichte in Bildern*, iii/4 (Leipzig, 1975), 20–1, 142–5.

CENTRAL AND NORTHEAST ITALY

(i) *Sources*

CASARSA, M., *et al.*: *Mostra di codici liturgici aquileisi* (Udine, 1968).

GAMBER, K.: *Codices liturgici latini antiquiores* (2nd edn.; Freiburg Schweiz, 1968), 73–93, 287–91, 311–18.

GOI, E.: *Catalogo dei codici liturgici aquileisi ancora esistenti, Quaderni di cultura*, iv (Udine, 1966–7), Nos. 19–20.

GULLOTTA, G.: *Gli antichi cataloghi e i codici della Abbazia di Nonantola, Studi e testi*, 182 (Vatican City, 1955).

HUGLO, MICHEL, *et al.*: *Fonti e paleografia del canto ambrosiano, Archivio ambrosiano*, 7 (Milan, 1956).

Paléographie musicale, Vol. 18: *Le codex 123 de la Bibliothèque Angelica de Rome (XIe siècle): graduel et tropaire de Bologne* (1969).

RUYSSCHAERT, J.: *Les Manuscrits de l'abbaye de Nonantola, Studi e testi*, 182 (Vatican City, 1955).

SCALON, C.: *La biblioteca arcivescovile di Udine* (Padua, 1979).

VECCHI, G.: *Troparium sequentiarium nonantulanum, Monumenta lyrica medii aevi italica, Ser. 1, Latina*, 1/1 (Modena, 1955). [Rome, Bibl. Casanatense MS 1741.]

(ii) *Books and Articles*

ALBAROSA, N.: 'La notazione neumatica di Nonantola', *Rivista italiana di musicologia*, 14 (1979), 225–310.

BANNISTER, H. M.: 'Gli inni di S. Pietro Damiano', *Rassegna gregoriana*, 8 (1908), 262–4.

BAROFFIO, B.: 'Liturgie im beneventanischen Raum', K. G. Fellerer, ed., *Geschichte der katholischen Kirchenmusik*, (Kassel, 1972), 204–8.

—— 'Le origini del canto liturgico nella chiesa latina e la formazione dei repertori italici', *Renovatio*, 1 (1978), 26–52.

DAMILANO, P.: 'Sequenze bobbiese', *Rivista italiana de musicologia*, 2 (1967), 3–35.

GHERARDI, L.: 'Il codice Angelica 123', *Quadrivium*, 3 (1959), 5–115.

HUGLO, MICHEL: 'Notes historiques à propos du second Decret sur la Vigile pascale', *Revue grégorienne*, 31 (1952), 121–36.

—— 'Antifone antiche per la Fractio panis', *Ambrosius*, 31 (1955), 85–95.

—— 'Liturgia e musica sacra aquileiese', *Storia della cultura veneta dalle origini al Trecento (Storia della cultura veneta*, 1) (Vicenza, 1976), 312–25.

KING, A. A.: *Liturgies of the Past* (Milwaukee, 1958), 1–52.

LEVY, KENNETH: 'The Italian Neophytes' Chants', *JAMS*, 23 (1970), 181–227.

—— 'Lux de luce: The Origin of an Italian Sequence', *MQ*, 57 (1971), 40–61.

—— 'Ravenna rite, music of the', *New Grove* xv. 621–2.

MODERINI, A.: *La notazione neumatica di Nonantola*, 2 vols. (Cremona, 1970).

ROPA, G.: 'Liturgia, cultura, e tradizione in Padania nei secoli XI e XII: I manoscritti liturgico-musicali', in *Contributi e studi di liturgia e musica nella regione padana (Festschrift ad honorem Joseph Vecchi: Antiquae Musicae Italicae Studiosi: Miscellanee, Saggi, Convegni*, vi (Bologna, 1972), 17–175.

STÄBLEIN, BRUNO: 'Von der Sequenz zum Strophenlied', *Die Musikforschung*, 7 (1954), 257–68.

—— *Schriftbild der einstimmigen Musik, Musikgeschichte in Bildern*, iii/4 (Leipzig, 1975), 34–7, 122–31, 134–41.

VALE, G.: 'La Liturgia nella Chiesa Patriarcale di Aquileia', *La Basilica di Aquileia* (Bologna, 1933), 367–81.

—— Bibliography of publications on Aquileia, *Ephemerides liturgicae*, 65 (1951), 113–14.

VECCHI, G.: 'Lirica liturgica ravennate', *Studi Romagnoli* (1952), 243–8.

WILMART, A.: 'Le recueil des poèmes et des prières de Saint-Pierre Damien', *Revue Bénédictine*, 41 (1929), 342–57.

MILANESE OR 'AMBROSIAN' CHANT

(i) *Sources*

BAROFFIO, B.: 'Die Offertorien der ambrosianischen Kirche (diss., Cologne, 1964).

GAMBER, K.: *Codices liturgici latini antiquiores* (2nd edn., Freiburg Schweiz, 1968), 259–86.

HUGLO, MICHEL, *et al.*: *Fonti e paleografia del canto ambrosiano, Archivio ambrosiano*, 7 (Milan, 1956).

MAGISTRETTI, M., ed.: *Beroldus, sive ecclesiae ambrosianae mediolanensis kalendarium et ordines saec. XII* (Milan, 1894).

Paléographie musicale, vols. 5–6: *Antiphonarium ambrosianum du Musée britannique (XIIe siècle): Codex Add. 34209* (1896 and 1900).

SUÑOL, GREGORY, ed.: *Antiphonale missarum . . . mediolanensis* (Rome, 1935).

—— *Liber vesperalis . . . mediolanensis* (Rome, 1939).

(ii) *Books and Articles*

BAILEY, TERENCE: 'Ambrosian Psalmody: An Introduction', *Rivista italiana di musica sacra*, 1 (1980), 82–99.

—— *The Ambrosian Alleluias* (Englefield Green, 1983).

—— *The Ambrosian Cantus* (Ottawa, 1987).

BAROFFIO, B.: 'Die mailändische Überlieferung des Offertoriums Sanctifica-vit', Martin Ruhnke, ed., *Festschrift Bruno Stäblein* (Kassel, 1967), 1–8.

—— 'Ambrosianische Liturgie', G. Fellerer, ed., *Geschichte der katholischen Kirchenmusik*, i (Kassel, 1972), 191–204.

—— 'Osservazioni sui versetti degli offertori ambrosiani', *Ricerche storiche sulla chiesa ambrosiana*, 3 (1972), 54–8.

—— 'Verso una storia dell'antica euchologia ambrosiana', *Archivio ambrosiano*, 33 (1977), 5–25.

—— 'Le origini del canto liturgico nella chiesa latina e la formazione dei repertori italici', *Renovatio*, 1 (1978), 26–52.

—— 'Ambrosian rite, music of the', *New Grove*, i. 314–20.

BORELLA, P.: *Il rito ambrosiano* (Brescia, 1964). [With exhaustive bibliography, 475–92.]

—— 'Il responsorio Tenebrae', *Miscellanea liturgica in honore di sua eminenza il Cardinale Giacomo Lercaro*, i (Rome, 1966), 597–607.

CATTANEO, E.: *Il breviario ambrosiano* (Milano, 1943).

—— 'I canti della frazione e comunione nella liturgia ambrosiana', *Miscellanea liturgica in honorem L. Cuniberti Mohlberg*, ii (Rome, 1949), 147–74.

CLAIRE, J.: 'La Psalmodie responsoriale antique', *Revue grégorienne*, 41 (1963), 8–29, 49–62, 77–102, 127–51.

HOURLIER, J.: 'Notes sur l'antiphonie', Wulf Arlt, *et al.*, eds., *Gattungen der Musik in Einzeldarstellungen: Gedenkschrift Leo Schrade*, i (Berne, 1973), 116–43.

HUCKE, H.: 'Die gregorianische Gradualweise des 2. Tons und ihre ambrosianischen Parallelen', *AMw*, 13 (1956), 284–314.

HUGLO, MICHEL: 'A proposito di una nuova enciclopedia musicale; le melodie ambrosiane', *Ambrosius: bollettino liturgico ambrosiano*, 27 (1951), 114–19.

—— 'L'invito alla pace nelle antiche liturgie beneventana e ambrosiana', *Ambrosius: bollettino liturgico ambrosiano*, 30 (1954), 158–61.

—— 'Antifone antiche per la Fractio panis', *Ambrosius: bollettino liturgico ambrosiano*, 31 (1955), 85–95.

—— 'L'annuncio pasquale della liturgia ambrosiana', *Ambrosius: bollettino liturgico ambrosiano*, 33 (1957), 88–91.

—— 'Relations musicales entre Byzance et l'Occident', *Proceedings of the Thirteenth International Congress of Byzantine Studies, Oxford, 1966*, (London, 1967), 266–80.

—— 'Altgallikanische Liturgie', K. G. Fellerer, ed., *Geschichte der katholischen Kirchenmusik*, i (Kassel, 1972), 219–33.

HUSMANN, HEINRICH: 'Zum Grossaufbau des ambrosianischen Alleluia,' *Anuario musical*, 12 (1957), 17–33.

JESSON, ROY: 'Ambrosian Chant', Willi Apel, *Gregorian Chant* (Bloomington, 1958), 465–83.

KING, A. A.: *Liturgies of the Primatial Sees* (Milwaukee, 1957), 286–456.

LEVY, KENNETH: 'A Hymn for Thursday in Holy Week', *JAMS*, 16 (1963), 127–75.

MONETA CAGLIO, E. T.: 'I responsori cum infantibus nella liturgia ambrosiana', *Studi in onore di Mons. C. Castiglioni* (Milan, 1957), 481–578.

—— 'Stato attuale delle ricerche concernenti il canto ambrosiano', *Actes du
Troisième Congrès International de Musique Sacrée, Paris, 1957*,
pp. 218–21.

—— 'Alle origini dello jubilus', *Musica sacra*, 3rd ser., 94 (Bergamo, 1970),
5–14.

STÄBLEIN, BRUNO: *Schriftbild der einstimmigen Musik, Musikgeschichte in
Bildern*, iii/4 (Leipzig, 1975), 18–20, 34–7, 132–4, 174–5.

WEAKLAND, REMBERT: 'Milanese Rite, Chants of', *New Catholic Encyclopedia*, 9 (San Francisco, Toronto, London, Sydney, 1967), 842–3.

—— 'The Performance of Ambrosian Chant in the Twelfth Century',
*Aspects of Medieval and Renaissance Music: A Birthday Offering to
Gustave Reese* (New York, 1966), 856–66.

CELTIC AND ANGLO-SAXON CHANT

(i) *Sources*

GAMBER, K.: *Codices liturgici latini antiquiores* (2nd edn., Freiburg Schweiz,
1968), 130–52, 226–38.

Paléographie musicale, vol. 12: *Antiphonaire monastique (XIIIe siècle): codex
F.160 del Bibliothèque de la Cathédrale de Worcester* (1922).

WARREN, F. E.: *The Antiphonary of Bangor, Henry Bradshaw Society*, 4, 10
(London, 1892 and 5).

(ii) *Books and Articles*

CURRAN, M.: 'The Hymns and Collects of the Antiphonary of Bangor' (diss.
Pont. Athen. Anselmianum, Rome, 1974).

FLEISCHMANN, ALOYS: 'Celtic rite, music of the', *New Grove*, iv. 52–4.

HESBERT, RENÉ-JEAN: *Antiphonale missarum sextuplex* (Bruxelles, 1935),
p. cxxi f.

KENNY, J. F.: *The Sources for the Early History of Ireland: Ecclesiastical* (2nd
edn., ed. L. Bieler, New York, 1966).

KING, A. A.: 'Celtic Rite', 'English Medieval Rites', *Liturgies of the Past*
(Milwaukee, 1958), 186–275, 276–374.

MORIN, G.: 'Fragments inédits ... d'antiphonaire gallican', *Revue bénédictine*, 22 (1905), 329–56.

STÄBLEIN, BRUNO: 'Zwei Melodien der altirischen Liturgie', *Heinrich Hüschen*, ed., *Musicae Scientiae Collectanea: Festschrift Karl Gustav Fellerer
zum siebzigsten Geburtstag* (Cologne, 1973), 590–7.

—— *Schriftbild der einstimmigen Musik, Musikgeschichte in Bildern*, iii/4
(Leipzig, 1975), 17–18.

WOODS, ISOBEL: 'Our Awin Scottis Use', *Journal of the Royal Musical
Association*, 112 (1987), 21–37.

GALLICAN CHANT

(i) *Sources*

DEKKERS, E. and GAAR, E.: *Clavis patrum latinorum*, 2nd edn. (*Sacris erudiri*, 3, 1961), 434–8.

GAMBER, K.: *Ordo antiquus gallicanus, Textus patristici et liturgici*, Fasc. 3 (Regensburg, 1965).

—— *Codices liturgici latini antiquiores* (2nd edn., Freiburg Schweiz, 1968), 57–66, 152–93.

MIGNE, J.-P.: *Patrologiae cursus completus ... Series latina ...*, 72 (Paris, 1849). [Material on Gallican liturgy.]

MOHLBERG, L. C., ed.: *Rerum ecclesiasticarum documenta* (Rome, 1954–).

QUASTEN, J.: *Expositio antiquae liturgiae gallicanae, Opuscula et textus. Series liturgica*, 3 (Munster, 1934).

RATCLIFF, E. C.: *Expositio antiquae liturgiae gallicanae, Henry Bradshaw Society*, 98 (London, 1971).

SALMON, P.: *Le lectionnaire de Luxeuil, Collectanea biblica latina*, 7, 9 (Rome, 1944, 1953).

(ii) *Books and Articles*

ANGLÈS, HIGINI: 'St. Césaire d'Arles et le chant des hymnes', *La Maison-Dieu*, 92 (1967), 73–8.

BROU, LOUIS: 'Le Sancta sanctis en occident', *Journal of Theological Studies*, 46, 47 (1945 and 1946), 160–78, 11–29.

—— 'Le Trisagion de la messe d'après les sources manuscrites', *Ephemerides liturgicae*, 61 (1947), 309–34.

COMBE, P.: 'Notes sur la vigile pascale au rit Lyonnais', *Revue grégorienne*, 31 (1952), 162–8.

DOLD, A.: *Das älteste Liturgiebuch der lateinischen Kirche, Texte und Arbeiten*, sect. I, Nos. 36–8 (Beuron, 1936).

GASTOUÉ, A.: *Le Chant gallican* (Grenoble, 1939).

GRIFFE, E.: 'Aux origines de la liturgie gallicane', *Bulletin de littérature ecclésiastique*, 52 (Lyons, 1951), 17–43.

HESBERT, RENÉ-JEAN: 'Le chant de la bénédiction épiscopale', *Mélanges ... M. Andrieu* (Strasburg, 1956), 201–18.

HUGLO MICHEL: 'Les preces des graduels aquitains empruntées à la liturgie hispanique', *Hispania sacra*, 8 (1955), 361–83.

—— 'Altgallikanische Liturgie', K. G. Fellerer, ed., *Geschichte der katholischen Kirchenmusik*, i (Kassel, 1972), 219–33.

—— 'Gallican rite, music of the', *New Grove*, vii. 113–24.

—— AGUSTONI, LUIGI, CARDINE, EUGÈNE, AND MONETA-CAGLO, ERNESTO: *Fonti e paleografia del canto ambrosiano* (Milan, 1956).

KING, A. A.: 'Rite of Lyons', *Liturgies of the Primatial Sees* (Milwaukee, 1957), 1–154.

—— 'Gallican Rite', *Liturgies of the Past* (Milwaukee, 1958), 77–185.

KLAUSER, T.: 'Die liturgischen Austauschbeziehungen zwischen der römischen und der fränkisch-deutschen Kirche vom 8. bis 11. Jh.', *Historisches Jahrbuch der Görresgesellschaft*, 53 (1933), 169–89.

LEVY, KENNETH: 'The Byzantine Sanctus and its Modal Tradition in East and West', *Annales musicologiques*, 6 (1958–63), 7–67.

—— 'Toledo, Rome, and the Legacy of Gaul', *Early Music History*, 4 (1984), 49–99.

—— 'Trisagion', *New Grove*, xix. 153.

MORIN, G.: 'Fragments inédits ... d'antiphonaire gallican', *Revue bénédictine*, 22 (1905), 329–56.

NEALE, J. M., and FORBES, G. H., eds.: *The Ancient Liturgies of the Gallican Church* (Burntisland, 1855–7).

OURY, G.: 'Les Messes de St. Martin', *Eg*, 5 (1962), 73–97.

—— 'Psalmum dicere cum alleluia', *Ephemerides liturgicae*, 79 (1965), 97–108.

PORTER, W. S.: *The Gallican Rite* (London, 1958).

QUASTEN, J.: 'Oriental Influence in the Gallican Liturgy', *Traditio*, 1 (1943), 55.

STÄBLEIN, BRUNO: 'Gallikanische Liturgie', *MGG*, iv (1955), cols. 1299–325.

—— *Schriftbild der einstimmigen Musik, Musikgeschichte in Bildern*, iii/4 (Leipzig, 1975), 13–17.

SZÖVERFFY, J.: *Die Annalen der lateinischen Hymnendichtung*, i (Berlin, 1964), 110–66.

VOGEL, C.: 'Les échanges liturgiques entre Rome et les pays francs jusqu'à l'époque de Charlemagne', *Le chiese nei regni del Europa occidentale*, VII/1 (Spoleto, 1960), 185–295.

—— 'La Réforme cultuelle sous Pépin le Bref et sous Charlemagne', in Erna Patzelt, ed., *Die Karolingische Renaissance* (Graz, 1965), 171–290.

HISPANIC, OLD-SPANISH, OR 'MOZARABIC' CHANT

(i) *Sources*

Antifonario visigotico mozárabe de la catedral de León, Monumenta hispaniae sacra, serie litúrgica, V, 2 (Madrid, 1953).

AYUSO MARAZUELA, T.: *Biblia polyglotta matritensia. Series VII. Vetus latina, L. 21: Psalterium visigothicum-mozarabicum* (Madrid, 1957).

BLUME, C.: *Die mozarabischen Hymnen des alt-spanischen Ritus, Analecta hymnica medii aevi*, 27 (Leipzig, 1897).

BROU, LOUIS, and VIVES, J.: *Antifonario visigótico mozárabe de la catedral de León, edicion facsimil*, (Madrid, 1953); edn. of the text, *Monumenta hispaniae sacra, serie liturgica*, V, 1 (Barcelona and Madrid, 1959).

FEROTIN, M.: *Le liber ordinum en usage dans l'Église ... d'Espagne du cinquième au onzième siècle* (Paris, 1904).

—— *Le liber mozarabicus sacramentorum* (Paris, 1912).

GAMBER, K.: *Codices liturgici latini antiquiores* (2nd edn., Freiburg Schweiz, 1968), 67–72, 194–225.

MIGNE, J.-P.: *Patrologiae cursus completus . . . Series latina . . .* 85–6: *Liturgia mozarabica* (Paris, 1850).

Monumenta hispaniae sacra, Serie liturgica (Barcelona, Madrid, Leon, 1946–).

RANDEL, D. M.: *An Index to the Chant of the Mozarabic Rite* (Princeton, 1973).

RIVERA RECIO, J. F., ed.: *Estudios sobre la liturgía mozárabe, Publicaciones del Instituto Provinçial de Investigaciones y Estudios Toledanos*, series III, vol. 1 (Toledo, 1965). [With exhaustive bibliography.]

URBEL, J. P. DE and RUIZ-ZORRILLA, GONZALEZ Y: *Liber commicus, edicion critica*, 2 vols. (Madrid, 1950–5).

VIVES, J., and CLAVERAS, J.: *Oracional visigótico* (Barcelona, 1946).

(ii) *Books and Articles*

ANGLÈS, HIGINI: 'La música medieval en Toledo hasta el siglo XI', *Spanische Forschungen der Görresgesellschaft*, series I, 7 (1938), 1–68.

—— 'Hispanic Musical Cultures from the 6th to the 14th Century', *MQ*, 26 (1940), 494–528.

—— 'Spanisch-mozarabische Liturgie', K. G. Fellerer, ed., *Geschichte der katholischen Kirchenmusik*, i (Kassel, 1972), 208–17.

BAROFFIO, B.: 'Le origini del canto liturgico nella chiesa latina', *Renovatio*, 1 (1978), 26–52.

BISHOP, W. C.: *The Mozarabic and Ambrosian Rites: Four Essays in Comparative Liturgiology*, ed. from his papers by C. L. Feltoe (London, 1924).

BROCKETT, C. W.: 'Antiphons, Responsories, and Other Chants of the Mozarabic Rite', (Brooklyn, 1968).

BROU, LOUIS: 'Le Psallendum de la Messe et les chants connexes', *Ephemerides liturgicae*, 61 (1947), 13–54.

—— 'Le Trisagion de la Messe d'après les sources manuscrites', *Ephemerides liturgicae*, 61 (1947), 309–34.

—— 'Les "Benedictiones" ou cantique des trois enfants dans l'ancienne Messe espagnole', *Hispania sacra*, 1 (1948), 21–33.

—— 'Les Chants en langue grecque dans les liturgies latines', *Sacris erudiri*, 1 (1948), 165–80; 4, (1952), 226–38.

—— 'L'antiphonaire visigothique et l'antiphonaire grégorien au debut du VIII siècle', *Anuario musical*, 5 (1950), 3–10.

—— 'L'Alleluia dans la liturgie mozarabe', *Anuario musical*, 6 (1951), 3–90.

—— 'Séquences et tropes dans la liturgie mozarabe', *Hispania sacra*, 4 (1951), 27–41.

—— 'Notes de paléographie musicale mozarabe', *Anuario musical*, 7 (1952), 51–76; 10 (1955), 23–44.

—— 'Encore les "Spanish Symptoms" et leur contrepartie', *Hispania sacra*, 7 (1954), 467–85.

—— 'Le joyau des antiphonaires latins', *Archivos leoneses*, 8 (1954), 7–114.

HUGLO, MICHEL: 'Mélodie hispanique pour une ancienne hymne à la Croix', *Revue grégorienne*, 28 (1949), 191–6.

—— 'Source hagiopolite d'une antienne hispanique pour le Dimanche des Rameaux', *Hispania sacra*, 5 (1952), 367–74.

—— 'Les "Preces" des graduels aquitains empruntées à la liturgie hispanique', *Hispania sacra*, 8 (1955), 361–83.

—— 'Le Chant des Béatitudes dans la liturgie hispanique', *Miscelanea en memoria de Dom Mario Ferotin* (*Hispania sacra*, vols. 17–18; 1964–5), 135–40.

HUSMANN, HEINRICH: 'Alleluia, Sequenz und Prosa im altspanischen Choral', *Miscelanea en homenaje a Monseñor Higinio Angles*, i (Barcelona, 1958–61), 407–15.

KING, A. A.: 'Rite of Toledo', *Liturgies of the Primatial Sees* (Milwaukee, 1957), 457–631.

LEVY, KENNETH: 'Lux de luce', *MQ*, 57 (1971), 40–61.

—— 'The Trisagion in Byzantium and the West', *Report of the Eleventh Congress of the International Musicological Society*, ii (Copenhagen, 1972) 761–5.

MEYER, W.: *Die preces der mozarabischen Liturgie, Abhandlungen der königlichen Gesellschaft der Wissenschaften zu Göttingen, Philologisch-histor. Klasse*, NS, XV/3 (Berlin, 1914).

MUNDÓ, A.: 'La datación de los códices litúrgicos visigóticos toledanos', *Miscelanea en memoria de Dom Mario Ferotin* (*Hispania sacra*, vols. 17–18; 1964–5), 529–53.

PINELL, J.: 'Las "missae", grupos de cantos y oraciones en el oficio de la antiqua liturgia hispana', *Archivos leoneses*, 8 (1954), 145–85.

PRADO, G.: 'Estado actual de los estudios sobre la música mozárabe', J. F. Rivera Recio, ed., *Estudios sobre la liturgía mozárabe* (Toledo, 1965), 89–106.

RANDEL, D. M.: 'Responsorial Psalmody in the Mozarabic Rite', *Eg*, 10 (1969), 87–116.

—— *The Responsorial Psalm Tones for the Mozarabic Office, Princeton Studies in Music*, 3 (Princeton, 1969).

—— 'Antiphonal Psalmody in the Mozarabic Rite', *Twelfth Congress of the International Musicological Society, Berkeley, 1977* (Kassel, 1981).

—— 'Mozarabic rite, music of the', *New Grove*, xii. 667–75.

ROJO, C., and PRADO, G.: *El canto mozárabe* (Madrid, 1929).

STÄBLEIN, BRUNO: *Schriftbild der einstimmigen Musik, Musikgeschichte in Bildern*, iii/4 (Leipzig, 1975), 9–13, 33–4, 214–17.

SZÖVERFFY, J.: *Iberian Hymnody: Survey and Problems, Medieval Classics, Texts and Studies* (Albany, New York, 1971).

WAGNER, P.: 'Der mozarabische Kirchengesang und seine Überlieferung', *Spanische Forschungen der Görresgesellschaft*, 1st ser., I (1928), 102–41.

—— 'Untersuchungen zu den Gesangstexten und zur responsorialen Psalmodie der altspanischen Liturgie', *Spanische Forschungen der Gör-resgesellschaft*, 1st ser., II (1930), 67–113.

CHAPTERS IV–VI LITURGICAL MATERIALS OF ROMAN CHANT, CHANTS OF THE ROMAN OFFICE, CHANTS OF THE ROMAN MASS

(i) *Sources*

FRERE, WALTER HOWARD, ed.: *Graduale Sarisburiense* (Plainsong & Mediæval Music Society, London, 1894).

—— *Antiphonale Sarisburiense* (Plainsong & Mediæval Music Society, London, 1901–25).

HANSEN, F. E.: *H 159 Montpellier: Tonary of St. Bénigne of Dijon* (Copenhagen, 1974).

HESBERT, RENÉ-JEAN: *Antiphonale missarum sextuplex* (Brussels, 1935).

—— *Corpus Antiphonalium Officii. Rerum Ecclesiasticarum Documenta*. Series maior. Fontes VII–IX. I 'Cursus romanus; II 'Cursus monasticus'; III 'Invitatoria et Antiphona'; IV 'Responsoria'; V (analysis); VI (analysis) (Rome, 1963–79).

SCHLAGER, K.: *Alleluia-Melodien I (bis 1100), Monumenta monodica medii aevi*, (1968).

STÄBLEIN, BRUNO, and LANDWEHR-MELNICKI, MARGARETA: *Die Gesänge des altrömischen Graduale Vat.lat. 5319, Monumenta monodica medii aevi*, 2 (1968).

Paléographie musicale. Les principaux manuscrits de chant grégorien, ambrosien, mozarabe, gallican, publiés en facsimiles phototypiques (Société de Saint Jean l'Evangeliste, 1889–).

First series

1. *Codex 339 de la Bibliothéque de Saint-Gall (Xe siècle): antiphonale missarum Sancti Gregorii* (1889).
2.–3. *Le répons-graduel Justus ut palma, reproduit en fac-simile d'après plus de deux cents antiphonaires manuscrits du IXe au XVIIe siècle* (1891–2).
4. *Le codex 121 de la Bibliothèque d'Einsiedeln (Xe–XIe siècle): antiphonale missarum Sancti Gregorii* (1894).
5.–6. *Antiphonarium ambrosianum du Musée britannique (XIIe siècle): codex Add. 34209* (1896 and 1900).
7.–8. *Antiphonarium tonale missarum (XIe siècle): codex H.159 de la Bibliothèque de l'Ecole de médecine de Montpellier* (1901).
9. *Antiphonaire monastique (XIIe siècle): codex 601 de la Bibliothèque capitulaire de Lucques* (1906).
10. *Antiphonale missarum Sancti Gregorii (IXe–Xe siècle): codex 239 de la Bibliothèque de Laon* (1909).

11. *Antiphonale missarum Sancti Gregorii (Xe siècle): codex 47 de la Bibliothèque de Chartres* (1912).
12. *Antiphonaire monastique (XIIIe siècle): codex F.160 de la Bibliothèque de la Cathédrale de Worcester* (1922).
13. *Le codex 903 de la Bibliothèque nationale de Paris (XIe siècle): graduel de Saint-Yrieix* (1925).
14. *Le codex 10673 de la Bibliothèque vaticane fonds latin (XIe siècle): graduel bénéventain* (1931).
15. *Le codex VI.34 de la Bibliothèque capitulaire de Bénévent (XIe–XIIe siècle): graduel de Bénévent avec prosaire et tropaire* (1937).
16. *Le manuscrit de Mont-Renaud (Xe siècle): graduel et antiphonaire de Noyon* (1955).
17. *Fragments des manuscrits de Chartres* (1958).
18. *Le codex 123 de la Bibliothèque Angelica de Rome (XIe siècle): graduel et tropaire de Bologne* (1969).
19. *Le manuscrit 807 Universitätsbibliothek Graz (XIIe siècle): graduel de Klosterneuburg* (1974).
20. *Le manuscrit VI-33 Archivio Arcivescovile Benevento: missel de Bénévent (début du XIe siècle)* (1983).

Second series

1. *Antiphonaire de l'office monastique transcrit par Hartker: MSS. Saint-Gall 390–391 (980–1011)* (2nd edn., 1970).
2. *Cantatorium (IXe siècle): No. 359 de la Bibliothèque de Saint-Gall* (1924).

Roman chant books:

Antiphonale monasticum pro diurnis horis ... ordinis sancti Benedicti a Solesmensibus monachis restitutum (Desclée, 1934).
Antiphonale sacrosanctae romanae ecclesiae pro diurnis horis a Pio Papa X restitutum et editum ... (Rome, 1919).
Graduale sacrosanctae romanae ecclesiae de tempore et de sanctis, SS.D.N.Pii X. Pontificis Maximi jussu restitutum et editum (Rome, 1908). (Or, with the same title, Editio altera Ratisbonensis juxta Vaticanam. Ratisbon, 1911.)
Graduale sacrosanctae romanae ecclesiae de tempore et de sanctis, SS.D.N.Pii X. Pontificis Maximi jussu restitutum et editum, ad exemplar editionis typicae concinnatum et rhythmicis signis a Solesmensibus monachis diligenter ornatum (Desclée, 1945).
Graduale Triplex, seu Graduale Romanum Pauli PP.VI cara recognitum et rhythmicis signis a Solesmensibus monachis ornatum, Neumis Laudunensibus (Cod. 239) et Sangallensibus (Codicum San Gallensis 359 et Einsidlensis 121) nunc auctum (Solesmes, 1979).
Liber responsorialis pro Festis I. Classis et communi sanctorum juxta ritum monasticum (Solesmes, 1895).

Liber usualis, with introduction and rubrics in English, ed. Benedictines of Solesmes (Tournai: Desclée, 1934).

Offertoires neumés avec leurs versets, ed. R. Fischer (Solesmes 1978). [Re-edition of Ott, Carolus: *Offertoriale sive Versus offertorium*, Tournai, 1935. New edn. as *Offertoriale Triplex cum Versiculis*, Solesmes, 1985.]

Processionale monasticum ad usum congregationis Gallicae ordinis sancti Benedicti (Solesmes, 1893).

(ii) *Books and Articles*

APEL, WILLI: *Gregorian Chant* (Bloomington, 1958).

BABB, WARREN, trans., and PALISCA, CLAUDE V., ed.: *Hucbald, Guido and John on Music* (New Haven, 1978).

BAILEY, TERENCE: *The Intonation Formulas of Western Chant* (Toronto: Pontifical Institute of Medieval Studies, 1974).

—— 'Accented and Cursive Cadences in Gregorian Psalmody', *JAMS*, 29 (1976), 463–71.

BAROFFIO, BONIFACIO, and STEINER, RUTH: 'Offertory', *New Grove*, xiii. 513–17.

BOMM, U.: *Der Wechsel der Modalitätsbestimmungen in der Tradition der Messgesänge im IX.–XIII. Jahrhundert* (Einsiedeln, 1929).

CLAIRE, JEAN: 'L'Evolution modale dans les répertoires liturgiques occiden-taux', *Revue grégorienne*, 40 (1962), 196–211, 229–36, 237–45.

—— 'La psalmodie responsoriale antique', *Revue grégorienne*, 41 (1963), 8–29, 49–62, 77–102, 127–51.

—— 'Les Répertoires liturgiques latins avant l'octoéchos. L'Office férial Romano-Franc', *Eg*, 15 (1975), 5–192.

CONNOLLY, T.: 'Introits and Archetypes: Some Archaisms of the Old Roman Chant', *JAMS*, 25 (1972), 157–74.

—— 'The Graduale of S. Cecilia in Trastevere and the Old Roman Tradi-tion', *JAMS*, 28 (1975) 413–58.

—— 'Psalm II. Latin monophonic Psalmody', *New Grove*, xv. 322–32.

CROCKER, RICHARD L.: 'Hermann's Major Sixth', *JAMS*, 25 (1972), 19–37.

CUTTER, PAUL F.: 'Die altrömischen und gregorianischen Responsorien im zweitem Modus', *Kirchenmusicalischer Jahrbuch* (1970), 33–40.

—— *Musical Sources of the Old-Roman Mass*, Musicological Studies and Documents, 36 (American Institute of Musicology, 1979).

DYER, J.: 'The Offertory Chant of the Roman Liturgy and its Musical Form', *Studi musicali*, 11 (1982), 3–30.

ELLARD, G.: *Master Alcuin, Liturgist* (Chicago, 1956).

EMERSON, J.: 'Sources, MS., II. Western Plainchant', *New Grove*, xvii. 609–34.

FERRETTI, PAOLO: *Esthétique grégorienne*, i, trans. A. Agaësse (Tournai, 1938).

GAJARD, J.: 'Les Récitations modales des 3e et 4e modes et les manuscrits bénéventains et aquitains', *Eg*, 1 (1954), 9–45.

GERBERT, M.: *De cantu et musica sacra a prima ecclesiae aetate usque ad praesens tempus* (St Blasien, 1774).

GEVAERT, FRANÇOIS AUGUSTE: *La Melopée antique dans le chant de l'église latine* (Ghent, 1895–6).

HOURLIER, J.: 'Notes sur l'antiphonie', Wulf Arlt, *et al.*, eds., *Gattungen der Musik in Einzeldarstellungen*: Gedenkschrift Leo Schrade, i (Berne, 1973), 116–43.

HUCKE, HELMUT: 'Die Entwicklung des christlichen Kultgesangs zum gregorianischen Gesang', *Römische Quartalschrift* 48 (1953), 147–94.

—— 'Die Einführung des Gregorianischen Gesangs im Frankenreich', *Römische Quartalschrift*, 49 (1954), 172–87.

—— 'Gregorianischer Gesang in altrömischer und frankischer Uberlieferung', *AMw*, 12 (1955), 74–87.

—— 'Die gregorianische Gradualweise des 2. Tons und ihre ambrosianischen Parallelen', *AMw*, 13 (1956), 285–314.

—— 'Tractusstudien', in Martin Ruhnke, ed., *Festschrift Bruno Stäblein zum 70. Geburtstage* (Kassel, 1967), 116–20.

—— 'Die Texte der Offertorien', H. Becker and R. Gerlach, eds., *Speculum musicae artis: Festgabe für Heinrich Husmann zum 70. Geburtstage* (Munich, 1970) 193–203.

—— 'Das Responsorium', W. Arlt, *et al.*, eds., *Gattungen der Musik in Einzeldarstellungen: Gedenkschrift Leo Schrade*, i, 144–91 (Berne, 1973).

—— 'Karolingische Renaissance und Gregorianischer Gesang', *Die Musikforschung*, 28 (1975), 4–18.

—— 'Gregorian and Old Roman Chant', *New Grove*, vii. 693–7.

—— 'Towards a New Historical View of Gregorian Chant', *JAMS*, 33 (1980), 437–67.

HUGLO, MICHEL: *Les Tonaires, inventaire, analyse, comparison, Publications de la Société française de musicologie*, Troisième série, ii (Paris, 1971).

—— 'Antiphon', *New Grove*, i. 471–81; 'Antiphoners', i. 482–90; 'Communion', iv. 591–4.

JEFFERY, P.: 'The Introduction of Psalmody into the Roman Mass by Pope Celestine I (422–432): Reinterpreting a Passage in the *Liber pontificalis*', *Archiv für Liturgiewissenschaft*, 26 (1984), 147–65.

JUNGMANN, J. A.: *Missarum solemnia* (5th edn., Vienna, 1962).

LEROUX, R.: 'Aux origines de l'office festif. Les antiennes et les psaumes de matines et de laudes pour Noël et le 1er Janvier selon les cursus romain et monastique', *Eg*, 6 (1963), 39–148.

LEVY, KENNETH: 'Charlemagne's Archetype of Gregorian Chant', *JAMS*, 40 (1987), 1–30.

LICHTENHAHN, E., ed.: *Musik und lateinische Ritus, Schweizer Jahrbuch für Musikwissenschaft, Neue Folge*, ii (1982).

LIPPHARDT, WALTHER: *Der karolingische Tonar von Metz, Liturgiewissenschaftliche Quellen und Forschungen*, xliii (Munster, 1965).

MCCANN, J., ed. and trans.: *Regula: The Rule of St. Benedict, in Latin and English* (London, 1963).

NOWACKI, EDWARD: 'The Gregorian Office Antiphons and the Comparative Method', *Journal of Musicology*, 4 (1985), 243–75.

POWERS, HAROLD S.: 'Mode', *New Grove*, xii. 376–84.

SCHLAGER, K.: *Thematischer Katalog der ältesten Alleluia-Melodien aus Handschriften des 10. und 11. Jahrhunderts, Erlanger Arbeiten zur Musikwissenschaft*, ii (Munich, 1965).

—— 'Alleluia I. Latin rite', *New Grove*, i. 269–74.

STÄBLEIN, BRUNO: 'Alleluia', 'Antiphon', 'Choral', 'Graduale', 'Introitus', *MGG*, i, i, ii, v, vi (1949–51, 1952, 1956, 1957), cols. 331–50, 523–45, 1265–303, 632–59, 1375–82.

—— *Schriftbild der einstimmigen Musik, Musikgeschichte in Bildern*, iii/4 (Leipzig, 1975).

STEINER, RUTH: 'Some Questions about the Gregorian Offertories and Their Verses', *JAMS*, 19 (1966), 162–81.

—— 'Introit', 'Invitatory', *New Grove*, ix. 281–4, ix. 286–9.

TREITLER, LEO: 'Homer and Gregory: the Transmission of Epic Poetry and Plainchant', *MQ*, 60 (1974), 333–72.

—— 'Centonate Chant: Übles Flickwerk or E pluribus unus?', *JAMS*, 28 (1975), 1–23.

WAESBERGHE, JOSEPH, SMITS VAN: *Musikerziehung: Lehre und Theorie der Musik im Mittelalter, Musikgeschichte in Bildern*, iii/3 (Leipzig, 1969).

WAGNER, PETER: *Einführung in die gregorianischen Melodien, i, Ursprung und Entwicklung der Liturgischen Gesangsformen bis zum Ausgänge des Mittelalters* (3rd edn., Leipzig, 1911); iii, *Gregorianische Formenlehre, Eine Choralische Stilkunde* (Leipzig, 1921).

WEAKLAND, REMBERT: 'Hucbald as Musician and Theorist', *MQ*, 42 (1956), 66–84.

CHAPTER VII   MEDIEVAL CHANT

(i) *Sources*

ARLT, WULF: *Ein Festoffizium des Mittelalters aus Beauvais* (Cologne, 1970).

BARTH, PUDENTIA, RITSCHER, M. IMMACULATA, and SCHMIDT-GÖRG, JOSEPH: *Hildegard von Bingen: Lieder* (Salzburg, 1969).

BLUME, CLEMENS, ed.: *Die Hymnen des Thesaurus Hymnologicus H. A. Daniels ... I: Die Hymnen des 5.–11. Jahrhunderts, und die Irische-Keltische Hymnodie, Analecta hymnica medii aevi*, 51 (1908).

CROCKER, RICHARD L.: *The Early Medieval Sequence* (Berkeley, 1977).

DEUSEN, NANCY VAN: *Music at Nevers Cathedral: Principal Sources of Medieval Chant*, Musicological Studies, 30/1–2 (Institute of Medieval Music, 1980).

DREVES, GUIDO MARIA, ed.: *Lateinische Hymnendichter des Mittelalters, Analecta hymnica medii aevi*, 50 (1907).

DRINKWELDER, OTTO: *Ein deutsches Sequentiar aus dem Ende des 12. Jahrhunderts* (Graz, 1914).

EVANS, PAUL: *The Early Trope Repertory of Saint Martial de Limoges* (Princeton, 1970).

GOEDE, NICHOLAS DE: *The Utrecht Prosarium, Monumenta musica Neerlandica*, vi (1965).

Graduale sacrosanctae romanae ecclesiae de tempore et de sanctis, SS.D.N.Pii X. Pontificis Maximi jussu restitutum et editum . . . (Rome, 1908).

HESBERT, RENÉ-JEAN, ed.: *Le prosaire de la Sainte-Chapelle, Monumenta musicae sacrae*, 1 (Macon, 1952).

—— *Le prosaire d'Aix-la-Chapelle, Monumenta musicae sacrae*, 3 (Rouen, 1961).

Liber usualis, with Introduction and Rubrics in English, ed. Benedictines of Solesmes (Tournai: Desclée, 1934).

MATHIESEN, THOMAS: 'The Office of the New Feast of Corpus Christi in the *Regimen animarum* at Brigham Young University', *Journal of Musicology*, ii (1982), 13–44.

MOBERG, CARL ALLAN: *Über die schwedischen Sequenzen* (Uppsala, 1927).

STÄBLEIN, BRUNO: *Hymnen I: Die mittelalterlichen Hymnenmelodien des Abendlandes, Monument monodica medii aevi*, 1 (1956).

TREITLER, LEO: *The Aquitanian Repertories of Sacred Monody in the Eleventh and Twelfth Centuries* (Ph.D. diss., Princeton Univ., 1967).

VILLETARD, HENRI: *Office de Pierre de Corbeil* (Paris, 1907).

—— *Office de Saint Savinien et de Saint Potentien* (Paris, 1956).

WEAKLAND, REMBERT: 'The Compositions of Hucbald', *Eg*, 3 (1959), 155–62.

WEISS, GÜNTHER: *Introitus-Tropen, Monumenta musica medii aevi*, 3 (1970).

Corpus Troporum [*Studia Latina Stockholmiensia*], ed. Ritva Jonsson, *et al.* (Stockholm, 1975–).

1. *Tropes du propre de la messe, 1, Cycle de Noël*, ed. Ritva Jonsson, (1975), [*SLS*, 21].
2. *Prosules de la messe, 1, Tropes de l'alleluia*, ed. Olof Marcusson (1976), [*SLS*, 22].
3. *Tropes du propre de la messe, 2, Cycle de Pâques*, ed. Gunilla Björkvall, Gunilla Iversen, and Ritva Jonsson (1982), [*SLS* 25].
4. *Tropes de l'Agnus Dei*, ed. Gunilla Iversen (1980), [*SLS*, 26].
5. *Les deux tropaires d'Apt*, ed. Gunilla Björkvall (1986), [*SLS*, 32].
6. *Prosules de la Messe, 2, Le prosules limousines de Wolfenbüttel*, ed. E. Odelman (1986), [*SLS*, 31].

(ii) *Books and Articles*

ATKINSON, CHARLES: 'The Earliest Agnus Dei Melody and its Trope', *JAMS*, 30 (1977), 1–19.

BABB, WARREN, trans., and PALISCA, CLAUDE V., ed.: *Hucbald, Guido and John on Music* (New Haven, 1978).

BJORK, DAVID: 'Early Settings of the Kyrie eleison and the Problem of Genre Definition', *Journal of the Plainsong & Mediæval Music Society*, 3 (1980), 40–8.

—— 'The Kyrie Trope', *JAMS*, 33 (1980), 1–41.

BJÖRKVALL, G., and STEINER, RUTH: 'Some Prosulas for Offertory Antiphons', *Journal of the Plainsong & Mediæval Music Society*, 5 (1982), 13–35.

BOSSE, DETLEV: *Untersuchungen einstimmiger mittelalterlicher Melodien zum 'Gloria in excelsis'* (Erlangen, 1954).

BROU, LOUIS: 'Séquences et tropes dans la liturgie mozarabe', *Hispania sacra*, 4 (1951), 27–41.

BROWN, JULIAN, PATTERSON, SONIA, and HILEY, DAVID: 'Further Observations on W_1', *Journal of the Plainsong & Mediæval Music Society*, 4 (1981), 53–80.

CHAILLEY, JACQUES: *L'École musicale de St. Martial de Limoges* (Paris, 1960).

—— ed.: *Alia musica* (Paris, 1965).

CROCKER, RICHARD L.: 'The Troping Hypothesis', *MQ*, 52 (1966), 183–203.

—— 'Hermann's Major Sixth', *JAMS*, 25 (1972), 19–37.

—— 'The Sequence', in Wulf Arlt, *et al.*, eds., *Gattungen der Musik in Einzeldarstellungen: Gedenkschrift Leo Schrade*, i (Berne, 1973), 269–322.

—— 'Matins Antiphons at St. Denis', *JAMS*, 39 (1986), 441–90.

ELLINWOOD, LEONARD: *Musica Hermanni Contracti* (Rochester, NY, 1936).

FASSLER, MARGOT: 'Who Was Adam of St. Victor? The Evidence of the Sequence Manuscripts', *JAMS*, 37 (1984), 233–69.

FRERE, WALTER HOWARD: *Hymns Ancient and Modern (Historical Edition)* (London, 1909).

GUSHEE, LAWRENCE; 'Some Questions of Genre in Medieval Treatises on Music', in Wulf, Arlt, *et al.*, eds., *Gattungen der Musik in Einzeldarstellungen: Gedenkschrift Leo Schrade*, i (Berne, 1973), 365–433.

HANDSCHIN, JACQUES: 'Conductus', *MGG*, ii (1952), cols. 1615–26.

HUGHES, ANDREW: 'Rhymed Office', *New Grove*, xv. 804.

—— 'Modal Order and Disorder in the Rhymed Office', *Musica disciplina*, 37 (1983), 29–51.

HUSMANN, HEINRICH: 'Sequenz und Prosa', *Annales musicologiques*, 2 (1954), 61–91.

—— 'Sinn und Wesen der Tropen, veranschaulicht an den Introitustropen des Weihnachtsfestes', *AMw*, 16 (1959), 135–47.

—— *Tropen- und Sequenzenhandschriften, Répertoire Internationale des Sources Musicales*, 1 (Duisburg, 1964).

IVERSEN, GUNILLA ed.: *Research on Tropes: Proceedings of a Symposium Organized by the Royal Academy of Literature, History and Antiquities and the Corpus Troporum, Stockholm, June 1–3, 1981* (Stockholm, 1983).

JONSSON, RITVA: *Historia: Étude sur la genèse des offices versifiés* (Stockholm, 1968).

—— 'Quel sont les rapports entre Amalaire de Metz et les tropes liturgiques?', *Atti des XVIII Convengno di Studi Todi 1977* (Todi, 1979).

KELLY, T. F.: 'Melodic Elaboration in Responsory Melismas', *JAMS*, 27 (1974), 451–74.

—— 'New Music from Old: The Structuring of Responsory Prosas', *JAMS*, 30 (1977), 366–90.

—— 'Introducing the Gloria in Excelsis', *JAMS*, 37 (1984), 479–506.

LANDWEHR-MELNICKI, MARGARETA: *Das einstimmige Kyrie des lateinischen Mittelalters, Forschungsbeiträge zur Musikwissenschaft*, i (Regensburg, 1968).

LEVY, KENNETH: 'The Byzantine Sanctus and its Modal Tradition in East and West', *Annales musicologiques*, 6 (1958–63), 7–67.

OESCH, HANS: *Berno und Hermann von Reichenau als Musiktheoretiker* (Berne, 1961).

OSTHOFF, WOLFGANG: 'Die Conductus des Codex Calixtinus', in Martin Ruhnke, ed., *Festschrift Bruno Stäblein zum 70. Geburtstag* (Kassel, 1967), 178–86.

PHILLIPS, NANCY, and HUGLO, MICHEL: 'The Versus Rex caeli—Another Look at the so-called Archaic Sequence', *Journal of the Plainsong & Mediæval Music Society*, 5 (1982), 36–43.

PLANCHART, ALEJANDRO: *The Repertory of Tropes at Winchester* (2 vols., Princeton, 1977).

RABY, F. J. E.: *A History of Christian-Latin Poetry from the Beginning to the Close of the Middle Ages* (2nd edn., Oxford, 1953).

RÖNNAU, KLAUS: *Die Tropen zum Gloria in excelsis Deo* (Wiesbaden, 1967).

SCHILDBACH, MARTIN: *Das einstimmige Agnus Dei und seine handschriftliche Überlieferung vom 10. bis zum 16. Jahrhundert* (Erlangen, 1967).

SCHMID, HANS, ed.: *Musica et Scolica Enchiriadis una cum aliquibus tractatuli adjunctis, Bayerische Akademie der Wissenschaften, Veröffentlichungen der Musikhistorischen Kommission*, 3 (Munich, 1981).

SILAGI, G., ed.: *Liturgische Tropen: Referate zweier Colloquien des Corpus Troporum in München (1983) und Canterbury (1984), Münchener Beitrage zur Mediävistik und Renaissance-Forschung*, 36 (Munich, 1985).

STÄBLEIN, BRUNO: 'Gloria in excelsis', *MGG*, v (1956), cols. 302–20; 'Kyrie', vii (1958), cols. 1931–46; 'Sequenz', xii (1965), cols. 1262–72; 'St. Martial', xi (1963), cols. 522–49; 'Tropus', xiii (1966), cols. 797–826.

—— 'Die Unterlegung von Texten unter Melismen. Tropus, Sequenz und andere Formen', *Kongress-Bericht New York*, i (New York, 1961), 12–29.

—— 'Zu Frühgeschichte der Sequenz', *AMw*, 18 (1961), 1–33.

—— 'Zum Verständnis des "klassichen" Tropus', *AcM*, 35 (1963), 84–95.

STEINEN, WOLFRAM VON DEN: 'Die Anfänge der Sequenzendichtung', *Zeitschrift für Schweizerische Kirchengeschichte*, 40 (1946), 190–212, 241–68; 41 (1947), 19–48, 122–62.

—— *Notker der Dichter* (2 vols., Berne, 1948).

STEINER, RUTH: 'Some Melismas for Office Responsories', *JAMS*, 26 (1973), 108–31.

—— 'The Gregorian Chant Melismas of Christmas Matins', J. C. Graue, ed., *Essays on Music for Charles Warren Fox* (Rochester, NY, 1979), 241–53.

—— 'Trope(i)', *New Grove*, xix. 172–87.

Szövérffy, Joseph: *Die Annalen der lateinischen Hymnendichtung* (Berlin, 1964–5).

Thannabaur, Peter: *Das einstimmige Sanctus der römischen Messe in der handschriftlichen Überlieferung des 11. bis 16. Jahrhundert, Erlanger Arbeiten zur Musikwissenschaft*, i (Munich, 1962).

—— 'Anmerkung zur Verbreitung und Struktur der Hosanna-Tropen in deutschsprachigen Raum und den Ostländern', Martin Ruhnke, ed., *Festschrift Bruno Stäblein zum 70. Geburtstag* (Kassel, 1967), 250–9.

Waesberghe, Joseph Smits van: 'Zur ursprunglichen Vortragsweise der Prosulen, Sequenzen, und Organa', *Bericht über den siebenten internationalen musikwissenschaftlichen Kongress, Köln 1958* (Kassel, 1959), 251–4.

—— *Musikerziehung: Lehre und Theorie der Musik im Mittelalter, Musikgeschichte in Bildern*, iii/3 (Leipzig, 1969).

Weakland, Rembert: 'Hucbald as Musician and Theorist', *MQ*, 42 (1956), 66–84.

CHAPTER VIII   LITURGICAL DRAMA

(i) *Sources*

Arlt, Wulf: *Ein Festoffizium des Mittelalters aus Beauvais in seiner liturgischen und musikalischen Bedeutung*, 2 vols. (Cologne, 1970).

Avalle, D'Arco Silvio, and Monterosso, Raffaello: *Sponsus: Dramma delle vergini prudenti e delle vergini stolte* (Milan and Naples, 1965).

Bevington, David: *Medieval Drama* (Boston, 1975).

Bischoff, Bernhard, ed.: *Carmina Burana: Faksimile-Ausgabe der Hs. Clm 4660 + Clm 4660a* (Brooklyn, New York, 1967).

Corbin, Solange: 'Un jeu liturgique d'Hérode', *Mittellateinisches Jahrbuch*, 8 (1973), 43–58.

Coussemaker, E. de, ed.: *Drames liturgiques de moyen-âge* (Paris, 1861).

Delamare, René, ed.: *Le De officiis ecclesiasticis de Jean d'Avranches, archevêque de Rouen (1067–79)* (Paris, 1923).

Du Méril, Édelstand, ed.: *Origines latines du théâtre moderne* (Paris, 1849).

Frere, Walter Howard, ed.: *The Winchester Troper, Henry Bradshaw Society* viii (London, 1894).

Gasté, Armand, ed.: *Les Drames liturgiques de la cathédrale de Rouen* (Evreux, 1893).

Hennecke, E.: *New Testament Apocrypha*, ed. W. Schneemelcher (London, 1963).

Hesbert, René-Jean: *Corpus antiphonalium officii*, 6 vols. (Rome, 1963–79).

Jonsson, Ritva, ed.: *Corpus troporum*, 1, *Tropes du propre de la messe, 1, Cycle de Noël* (Stockholm, 1975).

—— Björkvall, Gunilla, and Iversen, Gunilla, eds.: *Corpus troporum, 3, Tropes du propre de la messe, 2, Cycle de Pâques* (Stockholm, 1982).

LANGOSCH, KARL, ed.: *Geistliche Spiele: Lateinische Dramen des Mittelalters mit deutschen Versen* (Berlin, 1957).

LIPPHARDT, WALTHER, ed.: *Lateinische Osterfeiern und Osterspiele*, 6 vols. (Berlin, 1975–81).

LORIQUET, HENRI, POTHIER, JOSEPH, and COLETTE, ARMAND: *Le Graduel de l'église cathédrale de Rouen au xiiie siècle*, 2 vols. (Rouen, 1907).

MIGNE, J.-P.: *Patrologiae cursus completus: Patrologia Latina*, 221 vols. (Paris, 1844–64).

RANKIN, SUSAN: 'A New English Source of the *Visitatio Sepulchri*', *Journal of the Plainsong & Mediæval Music Society*, 4 (1981), 1–11.

SCHUBIGER, ANSELM: *Musikalische Spicilegien* (Berlin, 1876).

SCHUMANN, OTTO, BISCHOFF, BERNHARD, and HILKA, ALFONS, eds.: *Carmina Burana*, 3 vols. (Heidelberg, 1930, 1941, and 1970).

SYMONS, DOM THOMAS: *Regularis Concordia: The Monastic Agreement of the Monks and Nuns of the English Nation* (London, 1953).

TINTORI, GIAMPERO, and MONTEROSSO, RAFFAELLO: *Sacre rappresentazioni nel manoscritti 201 della Bibliothèque municipale di Orléans* (Cremona, 1958).

WAESBERGHE, JOSEPH SMITS VAN: 'A Dutch Easter Play', *Musica disciplina*, 7 (1953), 15–37.

YOUNG, KARL: 'Officium Pastorum: A Study of the Dramatic Developments within the Liturgy of Christmas', *Transactions of the Wisconsin Academy of Sciences, Arts and Letters*, 17 (1912), 299–396.

—— *The Drama of the Medieval Church*, 2 vols. (Oxford, 1933).

Performing Editions

GREENBERG, NOAH, ed.: *The Play of Daniel*, transcribed by Revd Rembert Weakland, narration by W. H. Auden (Oxford, 1959).

—— and SMOLDON, WILLIAM L., eds.: *The Play of Herod* (Oxford, 1965). [From the Fleury Play-book.]

SMOLDON, WILLIAM L., ed.: *The Play of Daniel*, Plainsong & Mediæval Music Society (London, 1960).

—— *Visitatio Sepulchri* (Oxford, 1964). [From the Fleury Play-book.]

—— *Peregrinus* (Oxford, 1965). [From Beauvais.]

—— *Planctus Mariae* (Oxford, 1966). [From Cividale.]

—— *Officium Pastorum* (Oxford, 1967). [From Rouen.]

(ii) *Articles and Books*

ALBRECHT, OTTO E.: *Four Latin Plays of St Nicholas from the 12th Century Fleury Play-book* (Philadelphia, 1935).

ANGLÈS, HIGINI: *La Musica a Catalunya fins al segle XIII* (Barcelona, 1935).

ANZ, HEINRICH: *Die lateinischen Magierspiele* (Leipzig, 1905).

AXTON, RICHARD: *European Drama of the Early Middle Ages* (London, 1974).

BERGER, BLANDINE-DOMINIQUE: *Le Drame liturgique de Pâques du xe au xiiie siècle: Liturgie et théâtre* (Paris, 1976).

BERNARD, MADELEINE: 'L'Officium Stellae Nivernais', *Revue de musicologie*, 51 (1965), 52–65.

BINKLEY, THOMAS: 'The Greater Passion Play from Carmina Burana: An Introduction', Peter Reidemeister and Veronika Gutmann, eds., *Alte Musik, Praxis und Reflexion* (Winterthur, 1983), 144–57.

BJORK, DAVID A.: 'On the Dissemination of *Quem quaeritis* and the *Visitatio Sepulchri* and the Chronology of Their Early Sources', *Comparative Drama*, 14 (1980), 46–69.

BÖHME, MARTIN: *Das lateinische Weihnachtsspiel* (Leipzig, 1917).

BOOR, HELMUT DE: *Die Textgeschichte der lateinische Osterfeiern* (Tübingen, 1967).

BOWLES, EDMUND A.: 'The Role of Musical Instruments in Medieval Sacred Drama', *MQ* 46 (1959), 67–84.

BRANDEL, ROSE: 'Some Unifying Devices in the Religious Music Drama of the Middle Ages', Jan LaRue et al, eds., *Aspects of Medieval and Renaissance Music: A Birthday Offering to Gustave Reese* (London, 1967), 40–55.

BROCKETT, CLYDE W.: 'Easter Monday Antiphons and the *Peregrinus* Play', *Kirchenmusikalisches Jahrbuch*, 61–2 (1977–8), 29–46.

—— 'The Role of the Office Antiphon in Tenth-Century Liturgical Drama', *Musica disciplina*, 34 (1980), 5–27.

BROOKS, NEIL C.: *The Sepulchre of Christ in Art and Liturgy with Special Reference to the Liturgic Drama* (Urbana, 1921).

CAMPBELL, THOMAS P., and DAVIDSON, CLIFFORD, eds.: *The Fleury Playbook: Essays and Studies* (Kalamazoo, 1985). [Includes a complete facsimile of the Play-book.]

CHAILLEY, JACQUES: 'Le drame liturgique médiéval à Saint-Martial de Limoges', *Revue d'Histoire du Théâtre*, 7 (1955), 127–44.

—— *L'École musicale de Saint-Martial-de-Limoges jusqu'à la fin du XIe siècle* (Paris, 1960).

—— 'Du drame liturgique aux prophètes de Notre-Dame-la-Grande', Pierre Gallais and Yves-Jean Riou, eds., *Mélanges offerts à Rene Crozet*, ii (Poitiers, 1966), 835–41.

CHAMBERS, E. K.: *The Mediæval Stage*, 2 vols. (Oxford, 1903).

COLLINS, FLETCHER, JR.: *The Production of Medieval Church Music-Dramas* (Charlottesville, 1972).

CORBIN, SOLANGE: 'Le Manuscrit 201 d'Orléans: drames liturgiques dits de Fleury', *Romania*, 74 (1953), 1–43.

—— *La Déposition liturgique du Christ au vendredi saint: sa place dans l'histoire des rites et du théâtre religieux* (Paris, 1960).

DAVRIL, ANSELME: 'Johann Drumbl and the Origin of the *Quem Quaeritis*: A Review Article', *Comparative Drama*, 20 (1986), 65–75.

DOLAN, DIANE: *Le Drame liturgique de Pâques en Normandie et en Angleterre au moyen-âge* (Paris, 1975).

DONOVAN, RICHARD B.: *The Liturgical Drama in Medieval Spain* (Toronto, 1958).

—— 'Two Celebrated Centers of Medieval Liturgical Drama: Fleury and Ripoll', E. Catherine Dunn, Tatiana Fotitch, and Bernard M. Peebles, eds., *The Medieval Drama and its Claudelian Revival* (Washington, 1970), 41–51.

DRUMBL, JOHANN: 'Ursprung des liturgischen Spiels', *Italia medioevale e umanistica*, 22 (1979), 45–96.

—— *Quem quaeritis: Teatro sacro dell'alto medioevo* (Rome, 1981).

DUMVILLE, D. N.: 'Liturgical Drama and Panegyric Responsory from the Eighth Century? A Re-examination of the Origin and Contents of the Ninth-Century Section of the Book of Cerne', *Journal of Theological Studies*, new ser. 23 (1972), 374–406.

ELDERS, WILLEM: 'Gregorianisches in liturgischen Dramen der Hs. Orléans 201', *AcM*, 36 (1964), 169–77.

FLANIGAN, C. CLIFFORD: 'The Liturgical Context of the *Quem queritis* Trope', *Comparative Drama*, 8 (1974), 45–62.

—— 'The Roman Rite and the Origins of the Liturgical Drama', *University of Toronto Quarterly*, 43 (1974), 263–84.

—— 'The Liturgical Drama and its Tradition: A Review of Scholarship 1965–75', *Research Opportunities in Renaissance Drama*, 18 (1975), 81–102; 19 (1976), 109–36.

—— 'Karl Young and the Drama of the Medieval Church: An Anniversary Appraisal', *Research Opportunities in Renaissance Drama*, 27 (1984), 157–66.

FRANK, GRACE: *The Medieval French Drama* (Oxford, 1954).

FULLER, SARAH: 'The Myth of "Saint Martial" Polyphony', *Musica disciplina*, 33 (1979), 5–26.

HALLINGER, KASSIUS: 'Die Provenienz der Consuetudo Sigiberti: Ein Beitrag zur Osterfeierforschung', Ursula Henning and Herbert Kolb, eds., *Mediev-alia Litteraria: Festschrift für Helmut de Boor zum 80. Geburtstag* (Munich, 1971), 155–76.

HARDISON, O. B., JR.: *Christian Rite and Christian Drama in the Middle Ages*, (Baltimore, 1965).

HEITZ, CAROL: *Recherches sur les rapports entre architecture et liturgie à l'époque carolingienne* (Paris, 1963).

HILEY, DAVID: 'The Norman Chant Traditions: Normandy, Britain, Sicily', *PRMA*, 107 (1980–1), 1–33.

HUGHES, ANDREW: *Medieval Music: The Sixth Liberal Art* (2nd edn., Toronto, 1980).

HUGHES, DAVID G.: 'The First Magdalene Lament of the Tours Easter Play', *JAMS*, 29 (1976), 276–83.

HUGLO, MICHEL: 'Analyse codicologique des drames liturgiques de Fleury', in Jacques Lemaire and Emile van Balberghe, eds., *Calames et Cahiers:*

Mélanges de codicologie et de paléographie offerts à Léon Gilissen (Brussels, 1985), 61–78.

JACOBSEN, PETER CHRISTIAN: 'Zur Entwicklung des lateinischen geistlichen Spiels im 11. Jahrhundert', *Mittellateinisches Jahrbuch*, 12 (1977), 44–68.

JUNGMANN, JOSEF A.: *The Mass of the Roman Rite*, 2 vols. (New York, 1951 and 1955).

KARSAI, GEZA: *Kozepkori vizkereszti jatekok. A gyori 'Tractus Stellae' es rokonai* (Budapest, 1943).

KING, NORBERT: *Mittelalterliche Dreikönigsspiele*, 2 vols. (Freiburg, 1979).

KRETZMANN, PAUL EDWARD: *The Liturgical Element in the Earliest Forms of the Medieval Drama* (Minneapolis, 1916).

KRIEG, EDUARD: *Das lateinische Osterspiel von Tours* (Würzburg, 1956).

LANCASHIRE, IAN: *Dramatic Texts and Records of Britain: A Chronological Topography to 1558* (Cambridge, 1984).

LANGE, CARL: *Die lateinischen Osterfeiern: Untersuchungen über den Ursprung und die Entwickelung der liturgisch-dramatischen Auferstehungsfeier* (Munich, 1887).

LEROQUAIS, ABBÉ VICTOR: *Les Bréviaires manuscrits des bibliothèques publiques de France*, 6 vols. (Paris, 1934).

LIPPHARDT, WALTHER: *Die Weisen der lateinischen Osterspiele des 12. und 13. Jahrhunderts* (Kassel, 1948).

—— 'Liturgische Dramen', *MGG*, viii (1960), cols. 1010–51.

—— 'Das Herodesspiel von Le Mans nach den Handschriften Madrid, Bibl. Nac. 288 und 289 (11. und 12. Jhd)', *Organicae voces: Festschrift Joseph Smits van Waesberghe* (Amsterdam, 1963), 107–22.

—— 'Die Mainzer *Visitatio Sepulchri*', in Ursula Henning and Herbert Kolb, eds., *Mediaevalia litteraria: Festschrift für Helmut de Boor zum 80. Geburtstag* (Munich, 1971), 177–91.

—— 'Studien zur Musikpflege in den mittelalterlichen Augustiner-Chorherrenstiften des deutschen Sprachgebietes', *Jahrbuch des Stiftes Klosterneuburg*, new ser. 7 (1971), 7–102.

LIUZZI, FERNANDO: 'L'Espressione musicale nel dramma liturgico', *Studi Medievali*, new ser. 2 (1929), 74–109.

—— 'Le Vergini savie et le vergine folli', *Studi Medievali*, new ser. 3 (1930), 82–109.

MCGEE, TIMOTHY J.: 'The Liturgical Placements of the *Quem quaeritis* Dialogue', *JAMS*, 29 (1976), 1–29.

MARSHALL, MARY H.: 'Aesthetic Values of the Liturgical Drama', Jerome Taylor and Alan H. Nelson, eds., *Medieval Drama: Essays Critical and Contextual* (Chicago, 1972), 28–43.

MEYER, WILHELM: *Fragmenta Burana: Festschrift zur Feier des Hundertfünfzigjährigen Bestehens der Königlichen Gesellschaft der Wissenschaften zu Göttingen* (Berlin, 1901).

MICHAEL, WOLFGANG F.: *Das deutsche Drama des Mittelalters* (Berlin, 1971).

MILCHSACK, G.: *Die Oster- und Passionsspiele,* i, *Die lateinischen Osterfeiern* (Wolfenbüttel, 1880).

NORTON, MICHAEL L.: 'The Type II Visitatio Sepulchri: A Repertorial Study' (Unpub. Ph.D. Diss., The Ohio State University, 1983).

—— 'The Type II *Visitatio Sepulchri*', unpub. paper, read for the Annual Meeting of the American Musicological Society, Vancouver, 8 Nov. 1985.

—— 'Of "Stages" and "Types" in *Visitatione Sepulchri*', *Comparative Drama*, 21 (1987), 34–61 and 127–44.

RANKIN, SUSAN: 'Shrewsbury School, Manuscript VI: A Medieval Part Book?', *PRMA*, 102 (1975–6), 129–44.

—— 'The Mary Magdalene Scene in the *Visitatio Sepulchri* ceremonies', *Early Music History*, 1 (1981), 227–55.

—— 'The Music of the Medieval Liturgical Drama in France and in England' (Unpub. Ph.D. Diss., University of Cambridge, 1981).

—— 'Musical and Ritual Aspects of *Quem queritis*', Gabriel Silagi, ed., *Liturgische Tropen* (Munich, 1985), 181–92.

ROEDER, ANKE: *Die Gebärde im Drama des Mittelalters: Osterfeiern, Osterspiele* (Munich, 1974).

SCHULER, ERNST AUGUST: *Die Musik der Osterfeiern, Osterspiele und Passionen des Mittelalters* (Kassel, 1951).

SCHÜTTPELZ, OTTO: *Der Wettlauf der Apostel und die Erscheinungen des Peregrinispiels im geistlichen Spiel des Mittelalters* (Breslau, 1930).

SEVESTRE, NICOLE: 'Les Tropes d'introït de Noël et de Pâques à l'origine du drama liturgique: Étude du répèrtoire aquitain des xe et xie siècles' (unpub. doc. diss., École Pratique des Hautes Études, Paris, 1976).

—— 'The Aquitanian Tropes of the Easter Introit', *Journal of the Plainsong & Mediæval Music Society*, 3 (1980), pp. 26–39.

SMOLDON, WILLIAM L.: 'Liturgical Drama', Dom Anselm Hughes, ed., *Early Medieval Music up to 1300, NOHM*, ii (London 1954), 175–219.

—— *The Music of the Medieval Church Dramas* (Oxford, 1980).

SPANKE, HANS: 'St. Martial-Studien: Ein Beitrag zur frühromanischen Metrik', in Ulrich Mölk, ed., *Studien zur lateinischen und romanischen Lyrik des Mittelalters* (Hildesheim, 1983), 1–103.

STÄBLEIN, BRUNO: 'Zur Musik des Ludus de Antichristo', in Christoph-Hellmut Mahling, ed., *Zum 70. Geburtstag von Joseph Müller-Blattau* (Kassel, 1966), 312–27.

STEER, GEORG: ' "Carmina Burana" in Südtirol: Zur Herkunft des clm 4660', *Zeitschrift für deutsches Altertum und deutsche Literatur*, 112 (1983), 1–37.

STEMMLER, THEO: *Liturgische Feiern und geistliche Spiele: Studien zu Erscheinungsformen des Dramatischen im Mittelalter* (Tübingen, 1970).

STEVENS, JOHN: 'Music in Some Early Medieval Plays', Francis Warner, ed., *Studies in the Arts: Proceedings of the St Peter's College Literary Society* (Oxford, 1968), 21–40.

—— 'Medieval Drama', *New Grove*, xii, 21–58.

STICCA, SANDRO: 'The Montecassino Passion and the Origin of the Latin Passion Play', *Italica*, 44 (1967), 209–19.

—— *The Latin Passion Play: Its Origin and Development* (Albany, 1970).

STRATMAN, CARL J.: *Bibliography of Medieval Drama* (2nd edn., rev. and enlarged, 2 vols., Berkeley, 1972).

SYMONS, THOMAS: '*Regularis Concordia*: History and Derivation', David Parsons, ed., *Tenth-Century Studies* (London, 1975), 37–59.

SZÖVERFFY, JOSEF: *Die Annalen der lateinischen Hymnendichtung*, 2 vols. (Berlin, 1964 and 1965).

—— *Religious Lyrics of the Middle Ages* (Berlin, 1983).

WAGENAAR-NOLTHENIUS, HELÈNE: 'Sur la construction musicale du drame liturgique', *Cahiers de civilisation médiévale*, 3 (1960), 449–56.

WALLACE, ROBIN: 'The Role of Music in Liturgical Drama: A Revaluation', *ML*, 45 (1984), 219–28.

WERNER, WILFRIED: *Studien zu den Passions- und Osterspielen des deutschen Mittelalters in ihrem Übergang vom Latein zur Volkssprache* (Berlin, 1963).

WICKHAM, GLYNNE: *The Medieval Theatre* (London, 1974).

WRIGHT, EDITH: *The Dissemination of the Medieval Drama in France* (Bryn Mawr, 1936).

CHAPTER IX   MEDIEVAL SONG

(i) *Sources*

AARBURG, URSULA, ed.: *Singweisen zur Liebeslyrik des deutschen Frühe* (Düsseldorf, 1956).

ALBRECHT, OTTO, E.: *Four Latin Plays of St Nicholas from the 12th-century Fleury Playbook* (Pennsylvania, 1935).

ANDERSON, GORDON, A.: *The Las Huelgas Manuscript: Burgos, Monasterios de las Huelgas, Corpus Mensurabilis Musicae*, 69: II, *Motetti et Conductus* (1973).

—— ed.: *Notre-Dame and related conductus: Opera Omnia*, VI: *1 pt. Conductus—Transmitted in fascicle X of the Florence Manuscript*, Institute of Medieval Music [1978].

—— *Notre-Dame and related conductus: Opera Omnia*, vol. 8: *1 pt. Conductus—The Latin Rondeau Repertoire*, Institute of Medieval Music [1978].

ANGLÈS, HIGINI, ed.: *El Codex musical de Las Huelgas*. (*Musica a Veus dels Segles XIII–XIV*), 3 vols. (Barcelona, 1931 [facs.]).

—— *La musica de las Cantigas de Santa Maria del Rey Alfonso el Sabio*, 3 vols. in 4 (Barcelona, 1943, 1958, 1958, 1964). [Facs.]

—— 'El *Llibre Vermell* de Montserrat y los cantos y la danza sacra de los peregrinos durante el siglo xiv', *Anuario musical*, 10 (1955), 45–78.

APPEL, CARL: *Bernart von Ventadorn, seine Lieder mit Einleitung und Glossar* (Halle, 1915).

—— 'Die Singweisen Bernarts von Ventadorn', *Beihefte zur Zeitschrift für romanische Philologie*, 81 (1934), 1–43.

ARLT, WULF: *Ein Festoffizium des Mittelalters aus Beauvais in seiner liturgischen und musikalischen Bedeutung*, 2 vols. (Cologne, 1970).

BARBI, M., *et al.*, eds.: *Le opere di Dante, Testo critico della Società Dantesca Italiana* (2nd edn., Florence, 1960).

BARTH, PUDENTIA, RITSCHER, M. IMMACULATA, and SCHMIDT-GÖRG, JOSEPH: *Hildegard von Bingen: Lieder* (Salzburg, 1969).

BARTSCH, KARL. ed.: *Altfranzösische Romanzen und Pastourellen* (Leipzig, 1870).

BAXTER, JAMES H., ed.: *An Old St Andrew's Music Book* (Oxford, 1931). [Facs. edn. of W1.]

BECK, JEAN B., ed.: *Le Chansonnier Cangé. Corpus Cantilenarum Medii Aevi*, ser. 1, 2 vols. (Paris, 1927). [Facs.]

—— and BECK, LOUISE, eds.: *Le manuscrit du Roi, fonds français 844 de la Bibliothèque Nationale de Paris, Corpus Cantilenarum Medii Aevi*, ser. II. 2 vols. (London, 1938). [Facs.]

BÉDIER, JOSEPH, ed.: *Les chansons de Colin Muset, avec la transcription des mélodies par Jean Beck, Classiques français du moyen-âge* (Paris, 1912; 2nd edn. enlarged [without music], 1938).

—— and AUBRY, PIERRE: *Les chansons de croisade* (Paris, 1909).

BERGIN, THOMAS G., ed.: *Anthology of the Provençal Troubadours* (2nd edn. rev. and enlarged, New Haven, 1974).

BISCHOFF, BERNHARD, ed.: *Carmina Burana: Faksimile-Ausgabe* (Brooklyn, 1967).

BOURDILLON, FRANCIS W., ed.: *Cest Daucasin et de Nicolete* (Oxford, 1896). [Facs.]

BREUL, KARL H., ed.: *The Cambridge Songs: A Goliard's Song Book of the Eleventh Century* (Cambridge, 1915). [Facs.]

CHAILLEY, JACQUES: *Les Chansons à la vierge de Gautier de Coinci* (Paris, 1959).

CONTINI, GIANFRANCO, ed.: *Poeti del duecento*, 2 vols. (Milan, 1960).

CUESTA, ISMAEL FERNANDEZ DE LA, and LAFONT, ROBERT, eds.: *Las cançons dels trobadors (Institut d'estudis occitans)* (Toulouse, 1979).

DE RIQUER, MARTIN: *Los trovadores: Historia literaria y textos*, 3 vols. (Barcelona, 1975).

DITTMER, LUTHER A., ed.: *Faksimile-Ausgabe der Hs. Firenze, Biblioteca Mediceo-Laurenziana Pluteo 29.1*, Institute of Medieval Music (Brooklyn, n.d. [1966–7]).

DOBSON, ERIC J., and HARRISON, FRANK LL., eds.: *Medieval English Songs* (London, 1979).

FISCHER, CARL, KUHN, H., and BERNT, G.: *Carmina Burana: Die Lieder der Benediktbeurer Handschrift, Zweisprachige Ausgabe* (Munich, 1979).

GATIEN-ARNOULT, ADOLPHE F., ed.: *Las Flors del gay saber, estier dichas Las Leys d'amors*, 4 pts. *Monuments de la littérature romane*, i–iii (Toulouse, 1841–3).

GENNRICH, FRIEDRICH, ed.: *Rondeaux, Virelais und Balladen*, 1 (Dresden, 1921); 2 (Göttingen, 1927); 3 (Langen, 1963).

—— *Der musikalische Nachlass der Troubadours, Summa musicae medii aevi*, 3, 4, 15 (Darmstadt, 1958, 1960, 1965).

—— *Le Jeu de Robin et de Marion. Li Rondel Adam. Studien-Bibliothek*, 20 (Langen, 1962).

—— *Die Colmarer Liederhandschrift: Faksimile-Ausgabe ihrer Melodien, Summa musicae medii aevi*, 17 (1967).

GMELCH, JOSEPH, ed.: *Die Kompositionen der heiligen Hildegard* (Düsseldorf, 1913). [Facs.]

GOLDIN, FREDERICK, trans.: *Lyrics of the Troubadours and Trouvères* (New York, 1973). [With original texts.]

GREENE, RICHARD L. ed.: *The Lyrics of the Red Book of Ossory, Medium Ævum Monographs*, NS, 5 (Oxford, 1974).

HATTO, ARTHUR T., and TAYLOR, RONALD J, eds.: *The Songs of Neidhart von Reuenthal* (Manchester, 1958).

HESBERT, RENÉ-JEAN, ed.: *Le Tropaire-Prosaire de Dublin. MS Add. 710 de l'Université de Cambridge (vers 1360), Monumenta Musicae Sacrae*, 4 (Rouen, 1966).

HILKA, ALFONS, SCHUMANN, O., and BISCHOFF, BERNHARD: *Carmina Burana* (Heidelberg, 1930–70).

HUGHES, ANDREW: 'The *Ludus super Anteclaudianum* of Adam de la Bassée', *JAMS*, 23 (1970), 1–25.

JAMMERS, EWALD: *Ausgewählte Melodien des Minnesangs* (Tübingen, 1963).

JEANROY, ALFRED, ed.: *Le Chansonnier d'Arras: Reproduction en phototype* (Paris, 1925).

—— BRANDIN, L., and AUBRY, P. eds.: *Lais et descorts français du xiiie siècle: Texte et musique* (Paris, 1901; repr. New York, 1969).

LIPPHARDT, WALTHER: 'Unbekannte Weisen zu den *Carmina Burana*', *AMw*, 12 (1955) 122–42 [3 facs.]

—— 'Einige unbekannte Weisen zu den *Carmina Burana* aus der zweiten Hälfte des 12. Jahrhunderts', *Festschrift Heinrich Besseler* (Leipzig, 1961), 101–25. [7 facs.]

LIUZZI, FERNANDO, ed.: *La Lauda e i primordi della melodia italiana*, 2 vols. (Rome, 1934) [Facs.]

MAILLARD, JEAN: *Anthologie de chants de troubadours* (Nice, 1967).

—— with CHAILLEY, J., eds.: *Anthologie de chants des trouvères* (Paris, 1967).

MARROCCO, THOMAS, and SANDON, NICHOLAS, eds.: *Medieval Music, The Oxford Anthology of Music* (Oxford, 1977).

MAURER, FRIEDRICH, ed. and trans.: *Walther von der Vogelweide: Die Lieder* (Munich, 1972).

MEYER, PAUL. and RAYNAUD, G.: *Le Chansonnier de Saint-Germain-des-Prés* (*Bibl. nat. fr. 20050*) (Paris, 1892). [Facs.]

MOSER, HUGO, and MÜLLER-BLATTAU, JOSEPH, eds.: *Deutsche Lieder des Mittelalters, von Walther von der Vogelweide bis zum Lochamer Liederbuch* (Stuttgart, 1968).

NELSON, DEBORAH H., and VAN DER WERF, HENDRIK: *The Lyrics and Melodies of Adam de la Halle* (New York and London, 1985).

PRESS, ALAN R.: *Anthology of Troubadour Lyric Poetry* (Edinburgh, 1971). [Texts and trans.]

RIVIÈRE, JEAN-CLAUDE, ed.: *Pastourelles, Textes littéraires français*, 3 vols. (Geneva, 1974).

ROQUES, MARIO, ed.: *Aucassin et Nicolette, Les classiques français du moyen-âge* (Paris, 1929; rev. 1954).

ROSENBERG, SAMUEL N., and DANON, S., ed. and trans., and VAN DER WERF, HENDRIK, music ed.: *The Lyrics and Melodies of Gace Brulé* (New York and London, 1985).

ROSENBERG, SAMUEL N., and TISCHLER, H., eds.: *Chanter m'estuet: Songs of the Trouvères* (London, 1981).

SCHMIEDER, WOLFGANG: *Lieder von Neidhart (von Reuental), Denkmäler der Tonkunst in Österreich*, xxi (Jg. 37) (Vienna, 1930) [Facs.]

SCHUMANN, OTTO: 'Die jüngere Cambridger Liedersammlung', *Studi Medievali* NS, 16 (1943–50), 48–85.

SESINI, UGO: *Le melodie trobadoriche nel Canzoniere provenzale della Biblioteca Ambrosiana (R. 71 sup.)* (Turin, 1942).

SPAZIANI, MARCELLO: *Il canzoniere francese di Siena—Biblioteca Comunale, H.x.36, Introduzione, testo critico e traduzione* (Florence, 1957).

STEFFENS, GEORG, ed.: 'Die altfranzösische Liederhandschrift von Siena', *Archiv für des Studium der neueren Sprachen und Literaturen*, 88 (1892), 301–60.

——'Die altfranzösische Liederhandschrift der Bodleiana in Oxford, Douce 308', *Archiv für das Studium der neueren Sprachen und Literaturen*, 97, 98, 99, 104 (1896–7; 1900).

STEINER, RUTH: 'La musique des lais', G. Fotitch and Ruth Steiner, eds., *Les lais du roman en prose d'après le manuscrit de Vienne 2542* (Munich, 1974).

STRENG-RENKONEN, WALTER O.: *Les Estampies françaises, Les classiques français de moyen-âge* (Paris, 1931).

SUÑOL, GRÉGOIRE (DOM): 'Els Cants dels Romeus (segle xiveᵉ)', *Analecta Montserratensia*, 1 (1918) pp. 110–92. [*Llibre Vermell.*]

TAYLOR, RONALD J., ed.: *The Art of the Minnesinger*, 2 vols. (Cardiff, 1968).

TINTORI, GIAMPIERO, and MONTEROSSO, RAFFAELLO, eds.: *Sacre rappresentazioni nel manoscritto 201 della Biblioteca Municipale di Orléans* (Cremona, 1958). [Fleury Play-book.]

VARTY, KENNETH, ed.: *Le Jeu de Robin et de Marion par Adam de la Halle* (London, 1960). (Musical transcriptions by Eric Hill.)

VECCHI, GIUSEPPE, ed.: *Pietro Abelardo: i planctus* (Modena, 1951).

—— *Poesia Latina Medievale* (Parma, 1958). [14 plates.]

WEINRICH, LORENZ: 'Dolorum solatium: Text und Musik von Abelards Planctus David', *Mittellateinisches Jahrbuch*, 5 (1968), 59–78.

WERF, HENDRIK VAN DER, ed.: *Trouvères-Melodien I and II, Monumenta monodica medii aevi*, 11 and 12 (1977 and 1975).

—— and BOND, G. A., eds.: *The Extant Troubadour Melodies: Transcriptions and Essays for Performers and Scholars* (Rochester NY, 1984).

(ii) *Books and Articles*

ANDERSON, GORDON A.: 'Notre-Dame and Related Conductus: A Catalogue raisonée', *Miscellanea Musicologica*, 6 (1972) pp. 153–229; 7 (1975), 1–81.

ANGLÈS, HIGINI: *Scripta Musicologica*, ed. I. López-Calo, 3 vols. (Rome, 1975).

BABB, WARREN, trans., and PALISCA, CLAUDE V., ed.: *Hucbald, Guido, and John on Music* (New Haven, 1978).

BAUM, R.: 'Le descort ou l'anti-chanson', I. Cluzel and F. Pirot, eds., *Mélanges de philologie romane, dédiés à la memoire de Jean Boutière*, i (Liège, 1971), 75–98.

BEC, PIERRE: *La Lyrique française au moyen-âge (xiie–xiiie siècles). Contribution à une typologie des genres poétiques médiévaux*, 2 vols. (Paris, 1977 and 1978).

BECK, JOHANN B. [JEAN]: *Die Melodien der Troubadours* (Strasbourg, 1908).

BERTAU, KARL H.: *Sangverslyrik. Über Gestalt und Geschicklichkeit mittelhochdeutscher Lyrik am Beispiel des Leichs* (Göttingen, 1964).

—— 'Epenrezitation im deutschen Mittelalter', *Études germaniques*, 20 (1965), 1–17.

BOOGAARD, NICO H. J. VAN DEN: *Rondeaux et refrains du XIIe au début du XIVe siècle* (Paris, 1969).

BRUNNER, HORST: 'Epenmelodien', Otmar Werner, ed., *Formen mittelalterlichen Literatur* [Festschrift: Siegfried Beyschlag] (Göppingen, 1970), 149–78.

BRUYNE, EDGAR DE: *Etudes d'esthétique médiévale*, 3 pts. (Bruges, 1946).

BUTLER, CHRISTOPHER: *Number Symbolism* (London, 1970).

CATTIN, GIULIO: *Il Medioevo I, Storia della Musica*, i (Turin, 1979; English edn. trans. S. Botterill, Cambridge, 1984).

CHAILLEY, J.: 'Etudes musicales sur la chanson de geste et ses origines', *Revue de Musicologie*, 17 (1948), 1–27.

—— 'La nature musicale du *Jeu de Robin et Marion*', *Mélanges . . . G. Cohen* (Paris, 1950), 111–17.

—— 'Autour de la chanson de geste', *AcM*, 27 (1955), 1–12.

—— 'Les premiers troubadours et les *versus* de l'école d'Aquitaine', *Romania*, 76 (1955), 212–39.

CORBIN, SOLANGE: *Die Neumen*, in Wulf Arlt, ed., *Palaeographie der Musik*, i/3 (Cologne, 1977).

CROCKER, RICHARD L.: 'Musica Rhythmica and Musica Metrica in Antique and Medieval Theory', *Journal of Music Theory*, 2 (1958), 2–23.

—— *A History of Musical Style* (New York, 1966).

DAVENSON, HENRI [pseudonym of Henri Marrou]: *Les Troubadours* (Paris, 1961; rev., 1971).

DRAGONETTI, ROGER: *La technique poétique des trouvères dans la chanson courtoise* (Bruges, 1960).

DRONKE, PETER: 'The Beginnings of the Sequence', *Beiträge zur Geschichte der deutschen Sprache und Literatur*, 87 (1965), 43–73.

—— *Medieval Latin and the Rise of the European Love-Lyric*, 2 vols. (Oxford, 1965; 2nd (corr.) edn., 1968).

—— *The Medieval Lyric* (London, 1968; 2nd edn. 1978). [With extended bibliography.]

FALCK, ROBERT A.: *The Notre Dame Conductus: A Study of the Repertory. Musicological Studies*, 33 (*Institute of Medieval Music*, [1981]).

FALLOWS, DAVID: 'Lai', 'Sources, MS (III)', *New Grove*, x. 364–76, xvii. 634–49.

FARAL, EDMOND: *Les jongleurs en France au moyen-âge* (Paris, 1910).

—— *Les Arts poétiques aux XIIe et XIIIe siècles* (Paris, 1924).

FENLON, IAIN, ed.: *Cambridge Music Manuscripts 900–1700* (Cambridge, 1982).

FOSTER, KENELM, and BOYDE, P.: *Dante's Lyric Poetry*, 2 vols. (Oxford, 1966).

FRANK, ISTVAN: *Répertoire métrique de la poésie des troubadours, Bibliothèque de l'Ecole des Hautes Etudes*, 303, 308 (Paris 1953, 1957).

GALLO, F. ALBERTO: *Il Medioevo II, Storia della Musica*, ii (Turin, 1977; Eng. edn. trans. K. Eales, Cambridge, 1985).

GENNRICH, FRIEDRICH: 'Die altfranzösische Liederhandschrift, London British Museum Egerton 274', *Zeitschrift für romanische Philologie*, 45 (1926), 402–44.

—— *Grundriss einer Formenlehre des mittelalterlichen Liedes als Grundlage einer musikalischen Formenlehre des Liedes* (Halle (Saale), 1932).

GÉROLD, THÉODORE: *La Musique au moyen âge, Les Classiques français du moyen-âge*, 73 (Paris, 1932).

GOUGAUD, LOUIS: 'La Danse dans les églises', *Revue historique écclésiastique*, 15 (1914), 5–22; 229–45.

HANDSCHIN, JACQUES: 'Die Modaltheorie und Carl Appels Ausgabe der Gesänge von Bernart de Ventadorn', *Medium Ævum*, 4 (1935) 69–82.

HOHLER, CHRISTOPHER: 'Reflections on some Manuscripts containing 13th-century Polyphony', *Journal of the Plainsong & Mediæval Music Society*, 1 (1978), 2–38.

HOPPER, VINCENT F.: *Medieval Number Symbolism* (New York, 1938).

HUGHES, ANDREW: 'The *Ludus super Anti-claudianum* of Adam de la Bassée', *JAMS*, 23 (1970), 1–25.

—— *Medieval Music: The Sixth Liberal Art* (Toronto, 1974).

HUSMANN, HEINRICH: 'Das Prinzip der Silbenzählung im Lied des zentralen Mittelalters', *Musikforschung*, 6 (1953), 8–23.

IRTENKAUF, WOLFGANG: 'Zum Stuttgarter Cantionarium HB.1.95', *Codices Manuscripti*, 3 (1977), 22–30.

JAMMERS, EWALD: 'Der musikalische Vortrag des altdeutschen Epos', *Der Deutschunterricht*, 9 (1959), 48–116.

—— *Ausgewählte Melodien des Minnesangs* (Tübingen, 1963).

—— *Schrift Ordnung Gestalt: Gesammelte Aufsätze zur älteren Musikgeschichte* (Berne, 1969).

—— *Aufzeichnungsweisen der einstimmigen ausserliturgischen Musik des Mittelalters, Palaeographie der Musik*, i/4 (Cologne, 1975).

JONSSON, RITVA, and TREITLER, LEO: 'Medieval Music and Language' *Studies in the History of Music I: Music and Language* (New York, 1983).

KEIL, H., ed.: *Bede: De arte metrica, Grammatici latini*, 7 (Leipzig, 1860), 227–60.

KIPPENBERG, BURKHARD: *Der Rhythmus im Minnesang* (Munich, 1962).

LINKER, ROBERT W.: *A Bibliography of Old French Lyrics, Romance Monographs*, 31 (University of Mississippi, 1979).

LIPPHARDT, WALTHER: 'Unbekannte Weisen zu den Carmina Burana', *AMw*, 12 (1955), 122–42.

—— 'Einige unbekannte Weisen zu den *Carmina Burana* aus der zweiten Hälfte des 12. Jahrhunderts', *Festschrift Heinrich Besseler zum 60. Geburtstag* (Leipzig, 1961), 101–25.

LUDWIG, FRIEDRICH: 'Die geistliche nichtliturgische, weltliche, einstimmige und die mehrstimmige Musik des Mittelalters bis zum Anfang des 15. Jahrhunderts', Guido Adler, ed., *Handbuch der Musikgeschichte*, i (2nd edn., Berlin, 1930).

MACHABEY, ARMAND: 'Introduction à la lyrique musicale romane', *Cahiers de Civilisation Médiévale*, 2 (1959), 203–11, 283–93.

MAILLARD, JEAN: *Evolution et esthétique du lai lyrique des origines à la fin du XIVème siècle* (Paris, 1963).

—— ed.: *Lais et chansons d'Ernoul de Gastinois, Musicological Studies and Documents*, 15 (Rome, 1964).

—— *Roi-trouvère du XIIIᵉ siècle: Charles d'Anjou, Musicological Studies and Documents*, 18 (Rome, 1967).

MARI, GIOVANNI, ed.: 'I trattati medievali di ritmica Latina', in *Memorie del Reale Istituto Lombardo di Scienze e Lettere; Classe di lettere*, vol. 20 (Milan, 1899), 373–496.

MÖLK, ULRICH, and WOLFZETTEL, FR.: *Répertoire métrique de la poésie lyrique française des origines à 1350* (Munich, 1972).

MONTEROSSO, RAFFAELLE: *Musica e ritmica dei trovatori* (Milan, 1956).

NORBERG, DAG: *Introduction à l'étude de la versification latine médiévale* (Stockholm, 1958).

OPLAND, JEFF: *Anglo-Saxon Oral Poetry: A Study of the Traditions* (New Haven, 1980).

PASCALE, MICHELANGELO: 'Le musiche nelle *pastourelles* francesi del XII e XIII secolo', *Annali della Facolta di lettere e filosofia, Università degli studi di Perugia*, 13 (1976), 575–631.

PHILLIPS, NANCY, and HUGLO, MICHEL: 'The Versus Rex caeli: Another Look at the so-called Archaic Sequence', *Journal of the Plainsong & Mediæval Music Society*, 5 (1982), 36–43.

PILLET, ALFRED, and CARSTENS, H.: *Bibliographie der Troubadours, Schriften der Königsberger Gelehrten Gesellschaft, Sonderreihe*, iii (Halle, 1933).

RÄKEL, HANS-HERBERT: *Die musikalische Erscheinungsform der Trouvèrepoesie* (Bern, 1977).

REISS, EDMUND: 'Number Symbolism and Medieval Literature', *Medievalia et Humanistica*, NS, 1 (1970), 161–74.

RIGG, ARTHUR GEORGE, and WIELAND, G. R.: 'A Canterbury Classbook of the mid-eleventh century [the Cambridge Songs Manuscript]', P. Clemoes, ed., *Anglo-Saxon England*, iv (Cambridge, 1975).

RIQUER, MARTIN DE: *Los trovadores: Historia literaria y textos*, 3 vols. (Barcelona, 1975).

ROHLOFF, ERNST: *Die Quellenhandschriften zum Musiktraktat des Johannes de Grocheio* (Leipzig, 1972). [Facsimiles; Latin text; German trans.)

SAHLIN, MARGIT: *Etude sur la carole médiévale* (Uppsala, 1940).

SCHALLER, DIETER, and KÖNSGEN, E.: *Initia carminum Latinorum saeculo undecimo antiquiorum: Bibliographisches Repertorium für die lateinische Dichtung der Antike und des früheren Mittelalters* (Göttingen, 1977).

SCHLAGER, KARL-HEINZ: 'Cantiones', K. G. Fellerer, ed., *Geschichte der katholischen Kirchenmusik*, i (Kassel, 1972), 286–93.

SCHUBERT, JOHANN: *Die Handschrift Paris Bibl. Nat. fr. 1591: Kritische Untersuchung der Trouvèrehandschrift R* (Frankfurt, 1963).

SCHWAN, EDUARD: *Die altfranzösischen Liederhandschriften: ihr Verhältnis, ihre Entstehung und ihre Bestimmung* (Berlin, 1886).

SEIDEL, WILHELM: 'Rhythmus/Numerus', Hans-Heinrich Eggebrecht, ed., *Handwörterbuch der musikalischen Terminologie* (1980).

SPANKE, HANS: 'Das lateinische Rondeau', *Zeitschrift für französische Sprache und Literatur*, 53 (1930), 113–48.

—— *Beziehungen zwischen romanischer und mittellateinischer Lyrik mit besonderer Berücksichtigung der Metrik und Musik* (Berlin, 1936).

—— 'Ein lateinisches Liederbuch des 11. Jahrhundert', *Studi Medievali*, NS, 15 (1942), 111–42. [The Cambridge Songs.]

—— ed.: *G. Raynauds Bibliographie des altfranzösischen Liedes* (Leiden, 1955; repr. 1980).

—— *Studien zu Sequenz, Lai und Leich*, selected by Ursula Aarburg (Darmstadt, 1977).

STÄBLEIN, BRUNO: 'Die Schwanenklage. Zum Problem Lai-Planctus-Sequenz', Heinrich Hüschen, ed., *Festschrift Karl Gustav Fellerer zum sechzigsten Geburtstag* (Regensburg, 1962), 491–502.

—— *Schriftbild der einstimmigen Musik, Musikgeschichte in Bildern*, iii/4 (Leipzig, 1975).

STEINER, RUTH: 'Some Monophonic Latin Songs' (Unpub. diss., Catholic University of America, 1964).

STEVENS, JOHN: ' "La Grande Chanson courtoise": the songs of Adam de la Halle', *PRMA*, 101 (1974–5), 11–30.

—— 'The Manuscript Presentation and Notation of Adam de la Halle's Courtly Chansons', Ian Bent, ed., *Source Materials and the Interpretation of Music: A Memorial Volume to Thurston Dart* (London, 1981), 29–84.

—— *Words and Music in the Middle Ages: Song, Narrative, Dance and Drama, 1050–1350* (Cambridge, 1986).

STEWART, MICHELLE F.: 'The Melodic Structure in thirteenth-century *jeux-partis*', *AcM*, 51 (1979), 86–107.

TREITLER, LEO: 'Homer and Gregory: The Transmission of Epic Poetry and Plainchant', *MQ*, 60 (1974), 333–72.

VAN DER VEEN, J.: 'Les Aspects musicaux des chansons de geste', *Neophilologus*, 41 (1957), 82–100.

WAESBERGHE, JOSEPH SMITS VAN, ed.: *Johannes Afflighemensis: De musica cum Tonario, Corpus Scriptorum de Musica*, 1 (Rome, 1950).

WALTHER, HANS: *Initia carminum ac versuum medii aevi posterioris latinorum. Alphabetisches Verzeichnis der Versanfänge*, 2 vols. (Göttingen, 1959, 1969).

WEINRICH, LORENZ: 'Peter Abelard as Musician', *MQ*, 55 (1969), 295–312; 464–86.

WERF, HENDRIK VAN DER: 'Deklamatorischer Rhythmus in den Chansons der Trouvères', *Musikforschung*, 20 (1967), 122–44.

—— *The chansons of the Troubadours and Trouvères: A Study of the Melodies and Their Relation to the Poems* (Utrecht, 1972).

YEARLEY, JANTHIA: 'A Bibliography of Planctus', *Journal of the Plainsong & Mediæval Music Society*, 4 (1981), 12–52.

ZINK, MICHEL: *La Pastourelle, poésie et folklore au moyen âge* (Paris, 1972). [Music ed. S. Corbin.]

CHAPTER X INSTRUMENTS AND INSTRUMENTAL MUSIC BEFORE 1300

(ii) *Books and Articles*

ADKINS, CECIL: 'The Technique of the Monochord', *AcM*, 39 (1967), 34–43.

ANDERSON, E. A.: 'Passing the Harp in Bede's Story of Caedmon: A Twelfth Century Analogue', *English Language Notes*, 15 (1977), 1–4.

ARLT, WULF: 'The "Reconstruction" of Instrumental Music: The Interpretation of the Earliest Practical Sources', S. Boorman, ed., *Studies in the Performance of Late Medieval Music* (Cambridge, 1983), 75–100.

ARTILES, J.: *El 'Libro de Apolonio': Poema espanol del siglo XIII* (Madrid, 1976).

AVENARY-LOWENSTEIN, H.: 'The Mixture Principle in the Medieval Organ: An Early Evidence', *Musica Disciplina*, 4 (1950), 51–7.

BABB, WARREN, trans., and PALISCA, CLAUDE V., ed.: *Hucbald, Guido and John on Music* (New Haven, 1978).

BACHMANN, WERNER: 'Die Verbreitung des Quintierens im europäischen Volksgesang des späten Mittelalters', Walther Vetter, ed., *Festschrift Max Schneider zum achtzigsten Geburtstag* (Leipzig, [1955]), 25–9.

—— *The Origins of Bowing*, trans. N. Deane (Oxford, 1969).

BARASSI, E. F.: *Strumenti musicali e testimonianze teoriche nel medio evo* (Cremona, 1979).

Basler Jahrbuch für Historische Musikpraxis, 8 (1984). [Issue devoted to medieval musical instruments.]

BEDBROOK, G. S.: 'The Problem of Instrumental Combination in the Middle Ages', *Revue Belge de musicologie*, 25 (1971), 53–67.

BINKLEY, THOMAS: 'Zur Aufführungspraxis der einstimmigen Musik des Mittelalters: ein Werkstattbericht', *Basler Jahrbuch für Historische Musikpraxis*, 1 (1977), 19–76.

BOWLES, EDMUND: 'Haut and Bas: the Grouping of Musical Instruments in the Middle Ages', *Musica disciplina*, 8 (1954), 115–40.

BRÖCKER, MARIANNE: *Die Drehleier* (2nd rev. edn., Bonn, 1977).

BUCKLEY, A.: 'What was the *tiompán*? A Problem in Ethnohistorical Organology: Evidence in the Irish Sources', *Jahrbuch für musikalische Volks- und Völkerkunde*, 9 (1978), 53–88.

BULLOCK-DAVIES, C.: 'The Form of the Breton Lay', *Medium Ævum*, 42 (1973), 18–31.

CASAGRANDE, C., and VECCHIO, S.: 'Clercs et jongleurs dans la société médiévale (XIIᵉ et XIIIᵉ siècles)', *Annales, économies, sociétés, civilisations*, 34 (1979), 913–28.

CRANE, FREDERICK: *Extant Medieval Musical Instruments: A Provisional Catalogue by Types* (Iowa, 1972).

—— 'On performing the *Lo estampies*', *Early Music*, 7 (1979), 25–33.

CROCKER, RICHARD: 'Alphabet Notations for Early Medieval Music', M. H. King and W. M. Stevens, eds., *Saints, Scholars and Heroes: Studies in Medieval Culture in Honour of Charles W. Jones*, 2 vols. (Minnesota, 1979), vol. i, pp. 79–104.

DEVOTO, DANIEL: 'La enumeración de instrumentos musicales en la poesía medieval castellana', *Miscelánea en homenaje a Monsenor Higinio Anglés*, 2 vols., (Barcelona, 1958–61), i, 211–22.

DROYSEN, D.: 'Über Darstellung und Benennung von Musikinstrumenten in der mittelalterlichen Buchmalerei', *Studia Instrumentorum Musicae Popularis*, 4 (Stockholm, 1976), 51–5.

FARAL, EDMUND: *Les Jongleurs en France au Moyen Âge* (2nd edn., Paris, 1971).

FOSTER, G.: 'The Iconology of Musical Instruments and Musical Performance in thirteenth century French Manuscript Illuminations' (unpub.
doctoral diss, City University of New York, 1977).

GALPIN, FRANCIS WILLIAM: *Old English Instruments of Music: Their History
and Character* (4th edn., rev. Thurston Dart, London, 1965).

GERSON-KIWI, EDITH: 'Drone and "dyaphonia basilica" ', *Yearbook of the
International Folk Music Council*, 4 (1972), 9–22.

GOLDINE, NICOLE: 'Henri Bate, chanoine et chantre de la cathédrale Saint
Lambert à Liège et théoricien de la musique (1246–après 1310)', *Revue
Belge de musicologie*, 18 (1964), 10–27.

HIBBERD, LLOYD: '*Musica Ficta* and Instrumental Music, *c*.1250–*c*.1350',
MQ, 28 (1942), 216–26.

—— '*Estampie* and *Stantipes*', *Speculum*, 19 (1944), 222–49.

—— 'On "Instrumental Style" in Early Melody', *MQ*, 32 (1946), 107–30.

—— 'Giraldus Cambrensis and English "Organ" Music', *JAMS*, 8 (1955),
208–12.

HICKMANN, ELLEN: *Musica Instrumentalis* (Baden-Baden, 1971).

HOFFMAN-AXTHELM, DAGMAR: 'Instrumentensymbolik und Aufführungspraxis. Zum Verhältnis von Symbolik und Realität in der mittelalterlichen Musikanschauung', *Basler Jahrbuch für Historische Musikpraxis*, 4
(1980), 9–90.

HOLSCHNEIDER, ANDREAS: *Die Organa von Winchester* (Hildesheim, 1968).

—— 'Instrumental Titles to the Sequentiae of the Winchester Tropers', in F.
W. Sternfeld, *et al.*, eds., *Essays on Opera and English Music in Honour
of Sir Jack Westrup* (Oxford, 1975), 8–18.

—— 'Die instrumentalen Tonbuchstaben im Winchester Troper', *Festschrift
Georg van Dadelsen* (Neuhausen-Stuttgart, 1978), 155–66.

HUGHES, ANDREW: 'Viella: Facere non possumus', *International Musicological Society: Report of the Eleventh Congress* (Copenhagen, 1972), ii.
453–6.

HUGLO, MICHEL: 'Les Instruments de musique chez Hucbald', G. Cambier,
ed., *Hommages à André Boutemy* (Brussels, 1976), 178–96.

KÄSTNER, H.: *Harfe und Schwert: Der höfische Spielmann bei Gottfried von
Strassburg* (Tübingen, 1981).

LAWSON, G.: 'Stringed Musical Instruments: Artefacts in the Archaeology of
Western Europe 500 BC–AD 1200' (unpub. doctoral thesis, Cambridge,
1980).

LEMAY, R.: 'A propos de l'origine arabe de l'art des troubadours', *Annales,
économies, sociétés, civilisations*, 140 (1966), 990–1011.

MAILLARD, J.: 'Coutumes musicales au moyen âge d'après le *Tristan* en
prose', *Cahiers de civilisation médiévale*, 2 (1959), 341–53.

MARCUSE, SIBYL: *A Survey of Musical Instruments* (Newton Abbot and
London, 1975).

MCKINNON, JAMES: 'The Church Fathers and Musical Instruments' (unpub.
doctoral thesis, Columbia, 1965).

—— 'The Meaning of the Patristic Polemic against Musical Instruments', *Current Musicology*, 1 (1965), 69–82.

—— 'Musical Instruments in medieval Psalm Commentaries and Psalters', *JAMS*, 21 (1968), 3–20.

MONTAGU, JEREMY: *The World of Medieval and Renaissance Musical Instruments* (Newton Abbot, etc., 1976).

MUNROW, DAVID: *Instruments of the Middle Ages and Renaissance* (Oxford, 1976).

PAGE, CHRISTOPHER: 'Biblical Instruments in medieval Manuscript Illustration', *Early Music*, 5 (1977), 299–309.

—— 'Jerome of Moravia on the *rubeba* and *viella*', *Galpin Society Journal*, 32 (1979), 77–95.

—— 'Anglo-Saxon Hearpan: Their Terminology, Technique, Tuning and Repertory of Verse 850–1066' (unpub. doctoral thesis, York, 1981).

—— 'The medieval *organistrum* and *symphonia*: 1. A Legacy from the East?', *Galpin Society Journal*, 35 (1982), 37–44.

—— 'The medieval *organistrum* and *symphonia*: 2. Terminology', *Galpin Society Journal*, 36 (1983), 71–87.

—— *Voices and Instruments of the Middle Ages* (London, 1987).

PANUM, HORTENSE, trans. J. PULVER: *The Stringed Instruments of the Middle Ages* (London, 1940).

PERKUHN, EVA RUTH: 'Beispiele Arabisch-Spanischer Glossographie in instrumentkundlicher Sicht', *Studia Instrumentorum Musicae Popularis*, 4 (1976), 94–7.

PERROT, JEAN, trans. N. DEANE: *The Organ: From its Invention in Hellenistic Times to the End of the Thirteenth Century* (Oxford, 1970).

PIPER, P., ed.: *Die Schriften Notkers und seiner Schule*, 3 vols. (Freiburg and Tübingen, 1882–3).

POPE, MILDRED, ed.: *The Romance of Horn by Thomas*, 2 vols., Anglo Norman Text Society (Oxford, 1955 and 1964).

REMNANT, MARY: *English Bowed Instruments from Anglo-Saxon to Tudor Times* (Oxford, 1986).

—— 'Rebec, Fiddle and Crowd in England', *PRMA*, 95 (1968–9), pp. 15–28. [See also *PRMA*, 9 (1969–70), 149–50.]

—— and MARKS, R.: 'A Medieval "Gittern"', *Music and Civilisation*, The British Museum Yearbook, 4 (London, 1980), 83–135.

RENSCH, ROSLYN: *The Harp* (London, 1969).

ROHLOFF, ERNST, ed.: *Die Quellenhandschriften zum Musiktraktat des Johannes de Grocheio* (Leipzig, 1972).

SAHLIN, M. *Étude sur la carole médiévale* (Uppsala, 1940).

SEEBASS, TILMAN: *Musikdarstellung und Psalterillustration im Mittelalter*, 2 vols. (Berne, 1973).

SPITZER, L.: 'Debailadas-bailar', *Boletín de la Academia Argentina de letras*, 14 (1945), 729–35.

STEGER, H.: *David Rex et Propheta* (Nuremburg, 1961).

—— *Philologia Musica* (Munich, 1971).

ULLAND, WOLFGANG: '*Jouer d'un instrument*' *und die altfranzösischen Bezeichnungen des Instrumentenspiels* (Bonn, 1970).

CHAPTER XI   EARLY POLYPHONY

Sources, Books, and Articles

ARLT, WULF: 'Peripherie und Zentrum. Vier Studien zur ein- und mehrstimmigen Musik des hohen Mittelalters', *Forum Musicologicum*, i (Berne, 1975), 169–222.

—— 'Analytische Bemerkungen zu "Veri solis radius" ', 'Die mehrstimmigen Sätze der Handschrift Madrid, Biblioteca nacional, Ms. 19421 (MAD)', *Bericht über den internationalen musikwissenschaftlichen Kongress Berlin 1974* (Kassel, 1980), 84–8, 25–47.

BABB, WARREN, trans., and PALISCA, CLAUDE V., ed.: *Hucbald, Guido and John On Music* (New Haven, 1978).

BARCLAY, BARBARA: 'The Medieval Repertory of Polyphonic Untroped Benedicamus Domino Settings' (Ph.D. diss. University of California at Los Angeles; University Microfilms, 1977).

—— 'Organa leticie', *Musica disciplina*, 32 (1978), 5–18.

BONDERUP, JENS: *The Saint Martial Polyphony: Texture and Tonality* (Copenhagen, 1982).

BOWER, CALVIN: 'A Bibliography of Early Organum', *Current Musicology*, 21 (1976), 16–45.

CONOMOS, DIMITRI: 'Experimental Polyphony, "according to the . . . Latins", late Byzantine Psalmody', *Early Music History*, 2 (1982), 1–16.

DELAPORTE, YVES, ed.: *Fragments des manuscrits de Chartres, Paléographie musicale*, 17 (1958).

EGGEBRECHT, HANS HEINRICH: 'Die Mehrstimmigkeitslehre von ihren Anfängen bis zum 12. Jahrhundert', Frieder Zaminer, ed., *Die mittelalterliche Lehre von der Mehrstimmigkeit, Geschichte der Musiktheorie*, 5 (Darmstadt, 1984), 9–87.

EGGEBRECHT, HANS HEINRICH, and ZAMINER, FRIEDER: *Ad Organum Faciendum: Lehrschriften der Mehrstimmigkeit in nachguidonischer Zeit, Neue Studien zur Musikwissenschaft*, 3 (Mainz, 1970).

FULLER, SARAH: 'An Anonymous Treatise *dictus de Sancto Martiale*: A New Source for Cistercian Music Theory', *Musica disciplina*, 31 (1977), 5–28.

—— 'Discant and the Theory of Fifthing', *AcM*, 50 (1978), 241–75.

—— 'The Myth of "Saint Martial" Polyphony: A Study of the Sources', *Musica disciplina*, 33 (1979), 5–26.

—— 'Theoretical Foundations of Early Organum Theory', *AcM*, 53 (1981), 52–84.

GALLO, F. ALBERTO, and VECCHI, GIUSEPPE: *I più antichi Monumenti sacri italiani, Monumenta lyrica medii aevi italica* ser. 3, *Mensurabilia*, i (Bologna, 1968).

GERBERT, MARTIN: *Scriptores Ecclesiastici de Musica* (St Blasien, 1784; repr. Hildesheim, 1963).

GILLINGHAM, BRYAN: 'Saint-Martial Polyphony--A Catalogue Raisonné', *Gordon Athol Anderson (1929–1981) In Memoriam, Musicological Studies* (Basel, 1984), 211–262.

GUSHEE, MARION: 'Romanesque Polyphony: A Study of the Fragmentary Sources', (Ph.D. diss. Yale University, Ann Arbor: University Microfilms, 1965).

HOLSCHNEIDER, ANDREAS: *Die Organa von Winchester: Studien zum ältesten Repertoire polyphoner Musik* (Hildesheim, 1968).

HUGLO, MICHEL: 'Les débuts de la polyphonie à Paris: les premiers *organa* parisiens', *Forum musicologicum*, 3 (Winterthur, 1982), 93–163.

—— 'Note sur l'organum vocal du XIe siècle', *Revue de musicologie*, 71 (1985), 177–9.

LÜTOLF, MAX: *Die mehrstimmigen Ordinarium Missae-Sätze vom ausgehenden 11. bis zur Wende des 13. zum 14. Jahrhundert*, 2 vols. (Berne, 1970).

OSTHOFF, WOLFGANG: 'Die Conductus des Codex Calixtinus', Martin Ruhnke, ed., *Festschrift Bruno Stäblein zum 70. Geburtstag* (Kassel and Basle, 1967), 178–86.

PHILLIPS, NANCY, and HUGLO, MICHEL: 'The versus Rex caeli: Another Look at the so-called Archaic Sequence', *Journal of the Plainsong & Mediæval Music Society*, 5 (1982), 36–43.

RECKOW, FRITZ: 'Organum-Begriff und frühe Mehrstimmigkeit', *Forum Musicologicum* i (*Basler Studien zur Musikgeschichte*, i), (Berne, 1975), 32–167.

SCHMID, HANS, ed.: *Musica et Scolica Enchiriadis una cum aliquibus tractatulis adjunctis, Bayerische Akademie der Wissenschaften, Veröffentlichungen der Musikhistorischen Kommission*, 3 (Munich, 1981).

SCHNEIDER, MARIUS: *Geschichte der Mehrstimmigkeit* (Berlin, 1934–5; repr. Tutzing, 1969).

TREITLER, LEO: 'The Polyphony of St. Martial', *JAMS*, 17 (1964), 29–42.

WAELTNER, ERNST LUDWIG: *Die Lehre vom Organum bis zur Mitte des 11. Jahrhunderts*, i, *Münchner Veröffentlichungen zur Musikgeschichte*, 13 (Tutzing, 1975).

WAESBERGHE, JOSEPH SMITS VAN, ed.: *John of Afflighem: De Musica cum Tonario, Corpus Scriptorum de Musica*, 1 (1950).

—— *Guido of Arezzo: Micrologus, Corpus Scriptorum de Musica*, 4 (1955).

WHITEHILL, WALTER, and PRADO, GERMAIN: *Liber Sancti Jacobi Codex Calixtinus*, 3 vols. (Santiago de Compostela, 1944).

WIORA, WALTER: 'Zwischen Einstimmigkeit und Mehrstimmigkeit', Walther Vetter, ed., *Festschrift Max Schneider zum achtzigsten Geburtstag* (Leipzig, [1955]), 319–34.

WOOLDRIDGE, H. E.: *Early English Harmony from the 10th to the 15th Century* (London, 1897–1913).

CHAPTER XII POLYPHONY AT NOTRE DAME OF PARIS

(i) *Sources*

(a) Musical

ANGLÈS, HIGINI: *El Códex musical de las Huelgas (Musica a veus des segles xii–xiv)*, 3 vols. (Introduction, Facsimile, Transcription), (Barcelona, 1931).

ARLT, WULF: *Ein Festoffizium des Mittelalters aus Beauvais in seiner liturgischen und musikalischen Bedeutung*, 2 vols. (Introduction, Transcription), (Cologne, 1970).

BAXTER, JAMES H.: *An Old St. Andrews Music Book* (London, 1931). [Facs. edn. of MS. Wolfenbüttel 677 (olim Helmstedt 628).]

DITTMER, LUTHER: *Ms. Madrid, Biblioteca nacional 20486* (Facs. edn., Brooklyn, NY, 1957).

—— *Ms. Florence, Biblioteca Medicea-Laurenziana, Pluteus 29.1* (Facs. edn., Brooklyn, NY, 1960).

—— *Ms. Wolfenbüttel, Herzog August Bibliothek, 1206 (olim Helmstedt 1099)* (Facs. edn., Brooklyn, NY, 1960).

HUSMANN, HEINRICH: *Die drei- und vierstimmigen Notre-Dame-Organa* (Leipzig, 1940; repr. Hildesheim, 1967).

KNAPP, JANET: *Thirty-five Conductus for Two and Three Voices* (New Haven, Connecticut, 1965).

ROKSETH, YVONNE: *Polyphonies du xiiie siècle*, 4 vols. (Paris, 1936–9).

(b) Theoretical

COUSSEMAKER, EDMOND DE: *Scriptorum de musica medii aevi nova series*, 4 vols. (Paris, 1864–76).

CSERBA, SIMON: *Hieronymus de Moravia O.P. Tractatus de Musica* (Regensburg, 1935).

KNAPP, JANET: 'Two Thirteenth-Century Treatises on the Discant', *Journal of Music Theory*, 6 (1962), 201–15.

RECKOW, FRITZ: *Der Musiktratat des Anonymus 4*, 2 vols. (Wiesbaden, 1967).

REIMER, ERIC: *Johannes de Garlandia: De mensurabili musica*, 2 vols. (Wiesbaden, 1967).

SOWA, HEINRICH: *Ein anonymer glossierter Mensuraltraktat: 1279* (Kassel, 1930).

(ii) *Books and Articles*

ANDERSON, GORDON: 'Clausulae or Transcribed Motets in the Florence Manuscript?', *AcM*, 42 (1970), 109–28.

APEL, WILLI: *The Notation of Polyphonic Music: 900–1600* (4th edn., Cambridge, Mass., 1953).

BALTZER, REBECCA: 'Thirteenth-Century Illuminated Miniatures and the Date of the Florence Manuscript', *JAMS*, 25 (1972), 1–18.

—— 'Notation, Rhythm, and Style in the Two-Voice Notre-Dame Clausula' (Diss., Boston University, 1974).

BIRKNER, G.: 'Notre-Dame Cantoren und Succentoren', Higini Anglès, *et al.*, eds., *In Memoriam Jacques Handschin* (Strasburg, 1962), 107–26.

BROWN, JULIAN, PATTERSON, SONIA, and HILEY, DAVID: 'Further Observations on W_1', *Journal of the Plainsong & Mediæval Music Society*, 4 (1981), 53–80.

FALCK, ROBERT: *The Notre Dame Conductus: A Study of the Repertory* (Henryville, Pennsylvania, 1981).

FLOTZINGER, RUDOLF: *Der Discantussatz im Magnus Liber und seiner Nachfolge, Wiener Musikwissenschaftliche Beiträge*, viii (Vienna, 1969).

HANDSCHIN, JACQUES: 'A Monument of English Polyphony: Wolfenbüttel 677', *MT*, 73 (1932), 510–13, and 74 (1933), 697–704.

—— 'The Summer Canon and its Background', *Musica disciplina*, 3 (1949), 55–94, and 5 (1951), 65–113.

HARRISON, FRANK LL.: *Music in Medieval Britain* (London, 1958).

HUGHES, DAVID G.: 'Liturgical Polyphony at Beauvais in the Thirteenth Century', *Speculum*, 34 (1959), 184–200.

HUSMANN, HEINRICH: 'The Enlargement of the Magnus Liber Organi and the Paris Churches of St. Germain l'Auxerrois and Ste. Geneviève du Mont', *JAMS*, 16 (1963), 176–203.

—— 'The Origin and Destination of the Magnus Liber Organi', *MQ*, 49 (1963), 311–30.

—— 'Zur Frage der Herkunft der Notre-Dame Handschrift W_1', Heinz Wegener, ed., *Musa-mens-musici: Im Gedenken Walther Vetter* (Leipzig, 1969), 33–5.

KNAPP, JANET: 'Musical Declamation and Poetic Rhythm in an Early Layer of Notre Dame Conductus', *JAMS*, 32 (1979), 383–407.

LEVY, KENNETH: 'A Dominican Organum Duplum', *JAMS*, 27 (1974), 183–211.

LUDWIG, FRIEDRICH: *Repertorium organorum recentioris et motetorum vetustissimi stili*, I/1 *Handschiften in Quadratnotation* (Halle, 1910).

PAYNE, THOMAS: '*Associa tecum in patria*: A Newly Identified Organum Trope by Philip the Chancellor', *JAMS*, 39 (1986), 233–54.

RECKOW, FRITZ: *Die Copula: Über einige Zusammenhänge zwischen Setzweise, Formbildung, Rhythmus und Vortragsstil in der Mehrstimmigkeit von Notre-Dame* (Wiesbaden, 1972).

ROESNER, EDWARD: 'The Origins of W_1', *JAMS*, 29 (1976), 337–80.

—— 'The Performance of Parisian Organum', *Early Music*, 7 (1979), 178–80.

SANDERS, ERNEST: 'The Question of Perotin's Oeuvre and Dates', Ludwig Finscher and Christoph-Hellmut Mahling, eds., *Festschrift für Walther Wiora zum 30. Dezember 1966* (Kassel, 1967), 241–9.

—— 'Conductus and Modal Rhythm', *JAMS*, 38 (1985), 439–69.

SCHMIDT, HELMUT: *Die drei- und vierstimmige Organa* (Kassel, 1936).

SMITH, NORMAN E.: 'The Clausulae of the Notre-Dame School: A Repertorial Study' (Diss., Yale University, 1964).

—— 'Tenor Repetition in the Notre-Dame Organum', *JAMS*, 19 (1966), 229–51.

—— 'Interrelations among the Alleluias of the Magnus Liber Organi', *JAMS*, 25 (1972), 175–202.

—— 'Interrelationships among the Graduals of the Magnus Liber organi', *AcM*, 45 (1973), 73–97.

—— 'From Clausula to Motet: Material for Further Studies in the Origin and Early History of the Motet', *Musica disciplina*, 34 (1980), 29–65.

WAITE, WILLIAM G.: *The Rhythm of Twelfth-Century Polyphony* (New Haven, Conn., 1954).

WRIGHT, CRAIG: 'Leoninus, Poet and Musician', *JAMS*, 39 (1986), 1–35.

YUDKIN, JEREMY: 'The *Copula* According to Johannes de Garlandia', *Musica disciplina*, 34 (1980), 67–84.

CHAPTER XIII   FRENCH POLYPHONY OF THE THIRTEENTH CENTURY

(i) *Sources*

ANDERSON, GORDON, A.: *The Latin Compositions in Fascicules 7 and 8 of the Notre Dame Manuscript Wolfenbüttel Helmstadt 1099 (1206)*, vol. i: Critical commentary, etc., vol. ii: Transcriptions (New York, 1972 and 1976).

—— *Motets of the Manuscript La Clayette, Corpus mensurabilis musicae*, 68 (American Institute of Musicology, 1975).

—— *Compositions of the Bamberg Manuscript, Corpus mensurabilis musicae*, 75 (American Institute of Musicology, 1977).

—— *The Las Huelgas Manuscript: Burgos, Monasterio de Las Huelgas, Corpus mensurabilis musicae*, 79 (2 vols.), American Institute of Musicology, 1982).

ANGLÈS, HIGINI, ed.: *El Codex musicale de Las Huelgas (Musica a veus des segles xii-xiv)*, 3 vols. (Barcelona, 1931).

AUDA, ANTOINE: *Les 'motets wallons' du manuscrit Turin: Vari 42* (Brussels, 1953).

BECK, JEAN: *Le Manuscrit du Roi, Corpus cantilenarum medii aevi*, 1st ser., 2 (1938).

DITTMER, LUTHER: *A Central Source of Notre Dame Polyphony* (Brooklyn, New York, 1959).

GENNRICH, FRIEDRICH: *Rondeaux, Virelais und Balladen aus dem Ende des XII., dem XIII. und dem ersten Drittel des XIV. Jahrhunderts, mit den überlieferten Melodien, Gesellschaft fur romanische Literatur*, 43, i, Texts (1921); 47, ii, Commentary (1927).

ROKSETH, YVONNE: *Polyphonies du xiiie siècle*, 4 vols. (Paris, 1935–9).

STENZL, JÜRG: *Die vierzig Clausulae der Handschrift Paris Bibliothèque nationale latin 15139* (Berne, 1970).

TISCHLER, HANS: *The Earliest Motets (to circa 1270): A Complete, Comparative Edition* (3 vols.) (New Haven, 1982).
—— *The Montpellier Codex* (Madison, 1978).
WILKINS, NIGEL: *The Works of Jehan de Lescurel, Corpus mensurabilis musicae*, 30 (American Institute of Musicology, 1966).
—— *The Lyric Works of Adam de la Hale, Corpus mensurabilis musicae*, 44 (American Institute of Musicology, 1967).

(ii) *Books and Articles*

ANDERSON, GORDON A.: 'A Small Collection of Notre Dame Motets *c.*1215–1235', *JAMS*, 22 (1969), 157–96.
—— 'Notre Dame Latin Double Motets *c.*1215–1250', *Musica disciplina*, 25 (1971), 35–92.
APEL, WILLI: *The Notation of Polyphonic Music 900–1600* (5th edn., Cambridge, Mass., 1953).
BESSELER, HEINRICH: 'Studien zur Musik des Mittelalters II: Die Motette von Franko von Köln bis Philipp von Vitry', *AMw*, 8 (1926), 137–258.
BOOGAARD, NICO H. J. VAN DEN: *Rondeaux et Refrains du XIIe siècle au début du XIVe, Bibliothèque française et Romane, Série D: Initiation, Textes et documents*, 3 (Strasbourg, Paris, 1969).
HOFMANN, KURT: *Untersuchungen zur Kompositionstechnik der Motette im 13. Jahrhundert, Tübinger Beiträge zur Musikwissenschaft*, 2 (Neuhausen-Stuttgart, 1972).
JEFFERY, PETER: 'A Four-part *In Seculum* Hocket and a Mensural Sequence in an Unknown Fragment', *JAMS*, 37 (1984), 1–48.
LUDWIG, FRIEDRICH: *Repertorium organorum recentioris et motetorum vetustissimi stili* (2nd edn., ed. Luther Dittmer, *Musicological Studies*, 7, 26 (Institute of Medieval Music, 1964, 1978).
SANDERS, ERNEST: 'Peripheral Polyphony of the 13th Century', *JAMS*, 17 (1964), 261–87.
—— 'The Medieval Motet', Wulf Arlt, *et al.*, eds., *Gattungen der Musik in Einzeldarstellungen: Gedenkschrift Leo Schrade*, i (Berne, 1973), 497–573.
—— 'The Medieval Hocket in Theory and Practice', *MQ*, 60 (1974), 246–56.
—— 'Motet. I. Medieval. 1. Ars antiqua', *New Grove*, xii. 617–24.

CHAPTER XIV
POLYPHONY IN ENGLAND IN THE THIRTEENTH CENTURY

(i) *Sources*

ANDERSON, GORDON A.: *The Latin Compositions in Fascicules 7 and 8 of the Notre-Dame Manuscript Wolfenbüttel Helmstadt 1099 (1206)*, vol. i: Critical Commentary, etc., vol. ii: Transcriptions (New York, 1972 and 1976).

—— ed.: *The Las Huelgas Manuscript: Burgos, Monasterio de Las Huelgas, Corpus mensurabilis musicae*, 79, 2 vols. (American Institute of Musicology, 1982).

ANGLÈS, HIGINI, ed.: *El Codex musical de Las Huelgas (Musica a veus des segles xii–xiv)*, 3 vols. (Barcelona, 1931).

DITTMER, LUTHER: 'An English Discantuum Volumen', *Musica disciplina*, 8 (1954), 19–58.

—— *The Worcester Fragments* (American Institute of Musicology, 1957).

HUGHES, ANSELM: *Worcester Medieval Harmony* (Burnham, 1928).

SANDERS, ERNEST: *English Music of the Thirteenth and Early Fourteenth Centuries, Polyphonic Music of the Fourteenth Century*, 14 (Monaco, 1979).

(ii) *Books and Articles*

FALCK, R.: 'Rondellus, Canon, and Related Types before 1300', *JAMS* 25 (1972), 38–57.

HANDSCHIN, J.: 'The *Sumer* Canon and its Background', *Musica disciplina*, 3 (1949), 55–94; and 8 (1951), 65–113.

HARRISON, FRANK LL.: *Music in Medieval Britain* (London, 1958).

HOHLER, CHRISTOPHER: 'Reflections on Some Manuscripts Containing 13th-century Polyphony', *Journal of the Plainsong & Mediæval Music Society*, 1 (1978), 2–38.

LEFFERTS, PETER, and BENT, MARGARET: 'New Sources of English thirteenth and fourteenth century polyphony', *Early Music History*, 2 (1982), 273–362.

LUDWIG, FRIEDRICH: *Repertorium organorum recentioris et motetorum vetustissimi stili* (2nd edn., ed. Luther Dittmer, *Musicological Studies*, 7, 26, Institute of Medieval Music, 1964, 1978).

REANEY, GILBERT: 'Some Little-known Sources of Medieval Polyphony in England', *Musica disciplina*, 15 (1961), 15–26.

RECKOW, F.: 'Rondeau/rota', Hans-Heinrich Eggebrecht, ed., *Das Handwörterbuch der musikalischen Terminologie* (1980).

SANDERS, ERNEST: 'Duple Rhythm and Alternate Third Mode in the 13th Century', *JAMS*, 15 (1952), 249–91.

—— 'Peripheral Polyphony of the 13th Century', *JAMS*, 17 (1964), 261–87.

—— 'Tonal Aspects of 13th-Century English Polyphony', *AcM*, 37 (1965), 19–34.

—— 'Die Rolle der englischen Mehrstimmigkeit des Mittelalters in der Entwicklung von Cantus-firmus-Satz und Tonalitätsstruktur', *AMw*, 24 (1967), 24–53.

—— 'Worcester Polyphony', *New Grove*, xx. 524–8.

INDEX

compiled by Frederick Smyth

Page numbers in **bold** type indicate the more important references.

Musical examples are collected respectively under the headings: **Christian chant to 1300, liturgical drama, medieval songs**, and **polyphony**

Aarburg, Ursula 383 nn
abcedary hymn 241
Abeghian, Manuk 10–12 nn
Abelard, Peter 429
acoustic jars 33 & n[10]
acrostic hymn 241
Ad organum faciendum, prose
    treatise **508–23**, 525
Adam de la Bassée, *Ludus super
    Anticlaudianum* 359
Adam de la Halle (Hale) 364, 375–7
    (Ex. 119), 396, 652, 676; *Robin et
    Marion* 396, 407–8, 477 n[51]
Adam of St Victor 308
Adelman of Chartres 518
Aethelwold (Ethelwold), Bishop of
    Winchester 316, 504
Agaësse, A. 138 n[36], 15 n[20], 175 n[1]
'Agnus Dei', medieval **298–9**
Akathistos, Byzantine hymn 37
Akolouthiai, liturgical book 45, 53
alba, dawn-song **416–17** (Ex. 143)
Albertus Magnus q. 474
Alcuin of York 226, q.461, 468
Aldhelm of Sherborne 467
Alexander II, Pope 102
Alexandrinus, Codex 38
Alfonso VIII, King of Castile, *cantio* on his
    death **394–5** (Ex. 130)
Alfonso X ('el Sabio'), King of Castile 443,
    446–7, 449
Alia musica 280
All Saints prose q. 490
Alleluias: Beneventan 75–6 (Ex. 18); English
    (13th C.) **715–18** (Ex. 222);
    medieval **245–6**, 248, 261, 264;
    Milanese 86–7 (Ex. 28); Ravennate 79–80
    (Ex. 23); Roman **214–22** (Ex. 71)
Amalarius of Metz **126–7**, 129, 195, 228,
    244–5, 258
Ambrose, St 30, 82–3, 231; his strophic
    hymns **233–6**, 238–9, 242, 283, 286

Ambrosian chant, *see* Milanese
Ambrosian strophe 304, 307
anagrammatismata, wordless chants 41
Analecta hymnica 264 & n[44]
Anderson, Gordon A.: on medieval
    song 361, 392 n[53], 401 nn, 418 n[112], 428 n[130],
    433 n[138], 449 n[159]; on polyphony 613,
    644 n[16], 660 n[33], 664 nn, 668–9 nn, 683 n[8]
Andrew of Crete 38
Andrieu, Michel 139 n[38], 213 n[85], 229 n[7],
    265 n[45], 272 nn
Angles, Higini 394 n[57], 414 n[103], 437–9 nn,
    443–9 nn, 451, 562 n[20], 680 n[5]
Anglo-Saxon chant **91–2** (Ex. 33)
Anonymous 4 **558–9**, 560–7 *passim*, 573–8
    passim, 585, 622–32 *passim*, 688
Anonymous 7 567
antiphon, the term 128
antiphonal singing: Eastern churches 5, 30;
    Milanese 83; Roman 128–9
Antiphonale monasticum (1934) 117
Antiphonale romanum (1919) 117
Antiphonales: Carolingian 168, 248;
    Chartres 116; Compiègne 91; Laon 116;
    Lucca 117; Mont Blandin 245;
    Montpellier 116; St Gall 116; Sarum 117;
    Senlis 91; Worcester 117
Antiphoners: Bangor 90, 99; Leon 107
antiphons: 'ad pacem' 109; 'ad
    Sanctus' 109–10; Anglo-Saxon 91–2
    (Ex. 33); *ante evangelium* 78, 87;
    Celtic 90–1 (Exx. 31–2); Ferial Office 147
    (Ex. 43), 148, **150–4** (Exx. 44–8), 164–5;
    fraction **98–9** (Ex. 39), 110; Frankish
    classification **165–8**; Gallican 95–6
    (Ex. 36), **98–9** (Ex. 39); Gregorian **129–32**,
    146–73; Hispanic 109–10;
    invitatory 162–4 (Ex. 53); introit 139–40,
    175, 265–9; listed in tonaries **168–9**;
    Marian **300**; medieval **299–301**;
    Milanese 87; pericope 131; *post
    evangelium* 87; Psalter **129–33**, **146–54**